1. *Scratch off security foil (gently).*

2. *Use code to register online.*

STARTED

3. *Start your experience.*

4. *Discover, interact, learn.*

login.cengagebrain.com

Dear Student:

Every day we're bombarded by information, and it's impossible to take it all in. You may have a similar experience when you stare at a textbook page. Do you ever feel confused about what's *essential* to focus on—and perhaps more on your mind, do you wonder what will be on the final exam?

Discovery Series: Introduction to Human Sexuality was created for students who want to do their best in their courses, but sometimes find themselves trying to figure out what's most relevant in their reading material. This book is briefer than many introductory textbooks, without some of the details that can cause information overload. In addition, as you read this text, you'll *always* know what's important because learning objectives throughout each chapter describe exactly what you're expected to learn. As a result, you'll be able to focus your attention on the "must know" topics.

DISCOVER

A NEW WAY OF LEARNING

At the same time, knowing *what* to focus on doesn't mean you'll "get it," or remember it. That's why this textbook is also paired with interactive online resources that reflect methods known to help learners absorb, understand, and retain concepts more effectively. By guiding your active involvement with text discussions, images, videos, animations, and quizzing (sorry, there's no avoiding quizzing), this new approach to learning meets you in your comfort zone—*and* helps you meet the course learning objectives in a way that a textbook alone cannot.

You've invested in this book, so take a minute to check out the next few pages, which introduce you to the learning path you'll follow in every chapter. It's a brief user's guide that will help you take full advantage of your course materials—and do your best in the course.

You're about to discover a new way of learning. Enjoy the journey.

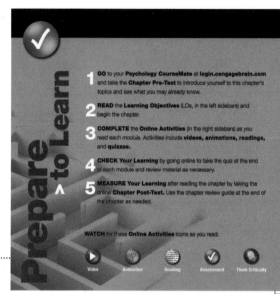

Prepare to Learn lays out the steps you'll complete as you work through each chapter. This page is the same in every chapter, serving as a reminder that keeps you on track as you complete the chapter's lessons.

Online Activities

Activities are essential to mastering this chapter. Go to www.cengagebrain.com.

 os Explore diverse
 ectives on sex as well
 mmon questions:

 o change the size of my

 roblem breastfeeding if I
 es pierced?

ast augmentation, surgery, and cos-
etic surgery

 women who live together really get
ir periods at the same time every
nth?

rst Periods" explores teens' reactions
d thoughts about menarche.

"PMS: Real or Imagined?" young
men and men discuss their thoughts

 Animations Interact with and visualize important processes, timelines, and concepts:

* The External Genital Structures of the Mature Female
* The Female Internal Reproductive System (Side)
* The Female Internal Reproductive System (Front)
* The Female Breast
* The Ovarian and Menstrual Cycles
* Key Terms Exercises

 Readings Delve deeper into key content:

Assessment Measure your mastery:

* Chapter Pre-Test
* Check Your Learning Quizzes
* Chapter Post-Test

Think Critically Challenge your thinking about data and accepted norms:

* Female Genital Mutilation

Watch for these icons as you read. They direct you to go online where videos, animations, additional reading, and quizzes illuminate the text discussion at hand. You'll be quizzed on information covered in these online activities when you take the chapter test, so be sure to complete them.

On the page next to **Prepare to Learn**, check out the resources you'll interact with online. In the chapter shown here, you'll see a video about breast augmentation, interact with animations of the female reproductive system, explore myths about virginity, and more.

o PREPARE

TO LEARN

FIND OUT

QUIZ SUMMARY

CORRECT **7**	INCORRECT **18**	TOTAL ANSWERED **25**	SCORE **28%**

1.	_____ is a condition that destroys cells in the brain, resulting in significant memory loss.	✓	✎
2.	The cause of Alzheimer's disease is:	✓	✎
3.	The result of fertilization of the mother's egg by the father's sperm is a(n) _____ .	✓	✎
4.	What will happen when a recessive gene is paired with a dominant gene?	✓	✎
5.	The theory of evolution was postulated by which author of Origin of Species?	✓	✎
6.	Accidental errors in genetic instructions that produce changes are called	✗	✎

Accidental errors in genetic instructions that produce changes are called _____ .

○ a. genetic misprints
⊗ b. adaptations ⊗
○ c. mutations
○ d. polymorphisms

> Incorrect. Adaptations are common features of a species that provide it with improved function.

7.	Of the 1 trillion cells that make up your brain, approximately 900 billion of them are _____ .	✓	✎
8.	A(n) _____ is a brain cell with two specialized extensions.	✓	✎
9.	The neuron's genetic instructions are contained in the _____ of the cell body.	✗	✎

Screenshots are for illustrative purposes only; content may be from other courses.

Step 1 when you begin a new chapter is to go to Psychology CourseMate at login.cengagebrain.com and take the Chapter Pre-Test to introduce yourself to the chapter's topics. Seeing your correct and incorrect answers will help you identify topics to pay particular attention to in the chapter—and those that may not require as much attention. You may already know more than you think you do!

Each chapter is divided into several brief learning modules. **Learning Objectives (LOs)** appear in the upper left sidebar throughout each module. They keep you focused by highlighting what you are expected to learn in the pages that immediately follow. Study each objective, and then read the accompanying narrative.

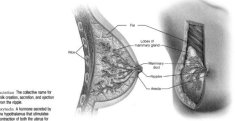

4.3 *The Breasts*

▶ **LO7** Describe how the female breasts can be used for infant nourishment as well as an erogenous zone.

▶ **LO7** Describe how the female breasts can be used for infant nourishment as well as an erogenous zone.

Breasts, or mammary glands, are modified sweat glands that produce milk to nourish a newborn. The breasts contain fatty tissue and milk-producing glands, and are capped by a nipple surrounded by a round, pigmented area called the areola (ah-REE-oh-luh). Each breast contains between 15 and 20 lobes, made up of a number of compartments that contain alveoli, the milk-secreting glands (see Figure 4.4). Alveoli empty into secondary tubules, which, in turn, pass the milk into the mammary ducts, and into the lactiferous sinuses, where the milk is stored until the milk exits from the nipple. When lactation begins, infant suckling signals the pituitary gland to release prolactin, which signals milk synthesis, and oxytocin which allows the milk to be ejected.

Many women use their breasts as an erogenous zone and include stimulation of the breasts during sex. Some women can even experience orgasm from breast and nipple stimulation. Female breasts come in various sizes and shapes.

Labels on figure: Fat; Ribs; Lobes of mammary gland; Mammary duct; Nipples; Areola

lactation The collective name for milk creation, secretion, and ejection from the nipple.

oxytocin A hormone secreted by the hypothalamus that stimulates contraction of both the uterus for

Copyright © Cengage Learning 2012

② # FOCUS ON

THE TEXT

③ INTERACT

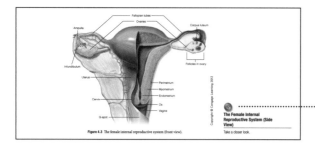

Remember the icons on the **Prepare to Learn** page? They always appear in the lower right sidebars throughout each module, prompting you to go online to enhance your understanding of text discussions through videos, animations, and readings.

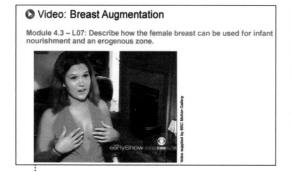

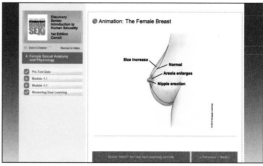

You'll view and interact with online resources many times as you work through each chapter. You may find them so interesting that you won't even know you're studying.

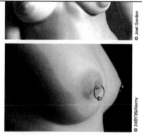

The Female Breast

Explore underlying structures and functions.

On Your Mind

Will I have a problem breastfeeding if I have my nipples pierced?

Breast Augmentation and Cosmetic Surgery

A woman discusses her decision to get breast implants.

Check Your Learning Quiz 4.3

Go to login.cengagebrain.com and take the online quiz.

Nevertheless, because breasts are a constant source of attention in our society and are considered an important part of a woman's attractiveness, women may worry that their breasts are unattractive, too small, or too large. As of 2010, breast augmentation was the most commonly performed cosmetic procedure among American women (Pelosi & Pelosi, 2010).

This **Check Your Learning Quiz** icon signifies that you've reached the end of a module.

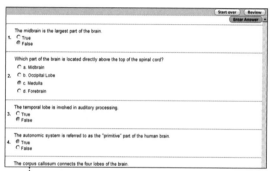

Go online and take this self-study quiz to make sure you "get it" (in other words, that you can demonstrate your understanding of the module's learning objectives).

For the questions you miss, go back and review the text and related online materials before you move on. Reviewing is also a great way to ensure that what you've just learned "sinks in."

④ CHECK

YOUR LEARNING

⑤ MEASURE

After reading each chapter, find out how well you've absorbed the material in all of the modules by taking the online **Chapter Post-Test**. Results go to your instructor's gradebook, so take your time and answer carefully. Your results, tied to **Learning Objectives**, will also help you identify areas that require further review so you can overcome weak areas and prepare more effectively for course exams.

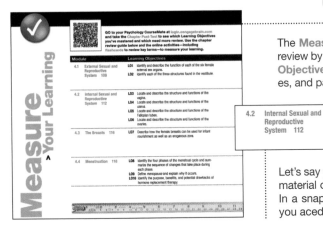

The **Measure Your Learning** chart simplifies study and review by providing an at-a-glance summary of **Learning Objectives**, key terms, important online media resources, and page references to discussions of key topics.

4.2	Internal Sexual and Reproductive System 112	LO3	Locate and describe the structure and functions of the vagina.
		LO4	Locate and describe the structure and functions of the uterus.
		LO5	Locate and describe the structure and functions of the

Let's say your **Post-Test** indicates that should review the material on the internal sexual and reproductive system. In a snap, you can see where the discussion begins. If you aced the **Post-Test**, you're done with the chapter.

GET STARTED FOR REAL

Now that you've got the hang of how *Discovery Series: Introduction to Human Sexuality* works, it's time to get started for real. Use the printed card on the inside front cover of this text to register at **login.cengagebrain.com**. Good luck!

Author Janell Carroll would like to extend her appreciation to the reviewers for their time, opinions, and helpful suggestions.

Lisa Alastuey, *University of Houston*
Katherine Aumer, *Hawai'i Pacific University*
Linda Bajdo, *Macomb Community College*
Kim Coffman, *Florida International University*
Kathy Coiner, *Scott Community College*
Carrie Crandall, *College of DuPage*
Kathy Damm, *Nevada State College*
Terry Dennison, *University of Oklahoma*
Tony Fowler, *Florence-Darlington Technical College*
Eric Has, *Mount San Jacinto Community College*
James Jordan, *Lorain County Community College*
Callista Lee, *Fullerton College*
Corey Miller, *Wright State University*
Jennifer Noble, *Pasadena City College*
Cassandra Sturges, *Washtenaw Community College*

A special thank you goes to Konnie McCaffree of Widener University for her valuable input and advice about pedagogy and learning objectives. Konnie is a wonderful teacher and mentor and the author appreciates all she has done to help make **Discovery Series: Introduction to Human Sexuality** a success.

About the Author

Dr. Janell L. Carroll received her Ph.D. in human sexuality education from the University of Pennsylvania. A certified sexuality educator with the American Association of Sexuality Educators, Counselors, and Therapists, Dr. Carroll is a dynamic educator, speaker, and author, who has published many articles, authored a syndicated sexuality column, and has appeared on numerous television talk shows. Dr. Carroll has traveled throughout the world exploring sexuality—from Japan's love hotels to Egypt's sex clinics—and has been actively involved in the development of several television pilots exploring sexuality. She has lectured extensively; received several teaching awards; appeared on and has been quoted in several national publications, Internet news media outlets, and cyber-press articles; and has hosted sexuality-related radio talk shows. Dr. Carroll's popular website (http://www.drjanellcarroll.com) is a resource for people to learn about sexuality and ask questions.

INTRODUCTION TO
HUMAN SEXUALITY

DISCOVERY SERIES

INTRODUCTION TO HUMAN SEXUALITY

JANELL L. CARROLL
University of Hartford

WADSWORTH
CENGAGE Learning·

Australia • Brazil • Japan • Korea • Mexico • Singapore • Spain • United Kingdom • United States

Discovery Series:
Introduction to Human Sexuality
Janell L. Carroll

Publisher: Jon-David Hague

Executive Editor: Jaime Perkins

Associate Development Editor:
 Nicolas Albert

Freelance Development Editor: Mary Falcon

Assistant Editor: Jessica Alderman

Sr. Media Editor: Lauren Keyes

Marketing Program Manager: Laura Localio

Senior Marketing Manager: Christine Sosa

Sr. Content Project Manager: Pat Waldo

Sr. Art Director: Vernon Boes

Manufacturing Planner: Karen Hunt

Rights Acquisitions Specialist:
 Tom McDonough

Production Service: Kate Mannix,
 Graphic World Inc.

Photo Researcher: Roman Barnes

Text Researcher: Karyn Morrison

Copy Editor: Graphic World Inc.

Illustrators: Argosy and Graphic World Inc.

Text Designer: Gary Hespenheide

Cover Designer: Irene Morris

Compositor: Graphic World Inc.

For product information and technology assistance, contact us at
Cengage Learning Customer & Sales Support, 1-800-354-9706

For permission to use material from this text or product,
submit all requests online at **www.cengage.com/permissions**
Further permissions questions can be e-mailed to
permissionrequest@cengage.com

Library of Congress Control Number: 2012930051

ISBN-13: 978-1-111-84189-8

ISBN-10: 1-111-84189-6

Wadsworth
20 Davis Drive
Belmont, CA 94002-3098
USA

Cengage Learning is a leading provider of customized learning solutions with office locations around the globe, including Singapore, the United Kingdom, Australia, Mexico, Brazil, and Japan. Locate your local office at **www.cengage.com/global**

Cengage Learning products are represented in Canada by Nelson Education, Ltd.

To learn more about Wadsworth, visit **www.cengage.com/wadsworth**

Purchase any of our products at your local college store or at our preferred online store **www.CengageBrain.com**

Printed in the United States of America
1 2 3 4 5 6 7 16 15 14 13 12

CHAPTER 1

Exploring and Understanding Human Sexuality 1

2 *Communication and Sexuality* 29

 Prepare to Learn   30

 Think Critically   50

 Measure Your Learning   52

Gender Development, Gender Roles, and Gender Identity 57

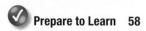

Prepare to Learn   58

Think Critically   88

Measure Your Learning   90

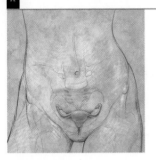

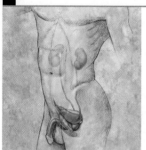

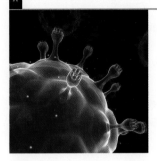

 Prepare to Learn   452

 Think Critically   484

 Measure Your Learning   486

 **Prepare to Learn   492**

14

Power and Sexual Coercion 523

1

Exploring and Understanding Human Sexuality

© Noel Weasley/Alamy

Chapter Outline and Learning Objectives

Prepare ^ to Learn

1 **GO** to your **Psychology CourseMate** at **login.cengagebrain.com** and take the **Chapter Pre-Test** to introduce yourself to this chapter's topics and see what you may already know.

2 **READ** the **Learning Objectives** (LOs, in the left sidebars) and begin the chapter.

3 **COMPLETE** the **Online Activities** (in the right sidebars) *as you read each module.* Activities include **videos, animations, readings, and quizzes.**

4 **CHECK Your Learning** by going online to take the quiz at the end of each module and review material as necessary.

5 **MEASURE Your Learning** after reading the chapter by taking the online **Chapter Post-Test.** Use the chapter review guide at the end of the chapter as needed.

WATCH for these **Online Activities** icons as you read:

Video

Animation

Reading

Assessment

Think Critically

In the late 19th and early 20th centuries, many doctors taught that masturbation was harmful, and so devices such as the two barbed rings and the shock box shown here were created to keep boys from achieving unwanted erections.

The Wellcome Trust, London

Europe in the early 16th century, when reformers Martin Luther and John Calvin challenged papal power and founded the Protestant movement. Instead of valuing celibacy, they saw in the Bible the obligation to reproduce, saw marital love as blessed, and considered sexuality a natural function of marriage. Protestantism broke away from the Catholic Church's forbiddance of divorce; however, it did accept the belief that women are weaker than men and should humble themselves before their fathers and husbands.

The Enlightenment and the Victorian Era (1700–1900)

The Enlightenment, a European intellectual movement of the 18th century, prized rational thought over traditional authority and suggested that human nature was to be understood through a study of human psychology. Sexual pleasure was considered natural and desirable; however, homosexuality was condemned and persecuted.

During Queen Victoria's reign in England, the most important aspect of society was public propriety. Conservative values were preached, if not always practiced. Women were considered virtuous; no respectable Victorian woman would ever admit to a sexual urge. The Victorian era had great influence on sexuality in the United States, as well as in England. Many of the conservative attitudes that still exist today are holdovers from Victorian standards.

Sex in Real Life

The history of vibrators.

Check Your Learning Quiz 1.4

Go to **login.cengagebrain.com** and take the online quiz.

▶ **LO10** Identify and explain the key departures of the Puritans from Protestantism regarding their views of sexuality and morality.

▶ **LO11** Identify the sexuality-related impacts of slavery on Black men and women in 18th- and 19th-century America.

▶ **LO12** Identify and describe the movements of 20th-century America that had lasting effects on the rights of women and gay men.

▶ **LO13** Summarize the impact of sex as a media commodity on American culture today.

The Colonial Era

The Puritans were a religious group that fled England to set up a biblically based society in the New World. They had severe sanctions for sexual transgressions: the death penalty was applied for sodomy, bestiality, adultery, and rape. In Puritan ideology, the entire community was responsible for upholding morality (D'Emilio & Freedman, 1988).

As the New World began to grow, the lack of women offered the women who did come greater independence than they had in Europe. Still, women were generally expected to tend to their homes and children.

The pendulum swung back to the liberal side after the Revolutionary War in the late 1700s. This was mostly due to the diminishing power of the church in the United States, leading to more liberal sexual attitudes. This liberalization, together with the continuing slave influx from Africa, had powerful effects on our culture's developing sexuality.

The 19th Century

A number of controversial social movements focusing on sexuality continued the liberal attitudes about sexuality in the 19th century. The free love movement, which began in the 1820s, preached that love, not marriage, should be the prerequisite to sexual relations. In 1852, the Church of Jesus Christ of Latter Day Saints, or Mormons, announced that many of its members practiced polygamy. As with the free love movement, Americans accused the Mormons of loose morals even though, despite their acceptance of polygamy, they were very sexually conservative (Iverson, 1991).

By the close of the 19th century, the medical model of sexuality began to emerge. Americans became obsessed with sexual health, and physicians and reformers began to advocate self-restraint, abstention from masturbation, and eating bland foods.

The movements for more open sexual relationships were countered by strong voices arguing for a return to a more religious and chaste morality. The Comstock Act of 1873 prohibited the mailing of obscene and indecent writing or advertisements, including articles about contraception or abortion. Thousands of books and contraceptive devices were destroyed (D'Emilio & Freedman, 1988). It wasn't until 1965 that the U.S. Supreme Court struck down the Comstock Laws.

sexual revolution Changes in sexual morality and sexual behavior that occurred throughout the Western world during the 1960s and 1970s.

The 20th Century

Beginning in the early part of the 20th century, the pioneers of sexual research were beginning to make scientific advances into the understanding of sexuality. Rejecting the religious and moral teachings about how people "should" behave, researchers brought sex out into the open as a subject worthy of medical, scientific, and philosophical debate. During this time the values and attitudes about sexuality that were rooted in the Christian tradition slowly began to change as society became more permissive and accepting of sexual freedom. Advertising and other media became more sexualized, and fashion trends changed as the flapper era was ushered in. The trend toward more liberal ideas and values about sexuality continued in the late 1920s, but it wasn't until the early 1960s when many would say the real **sexual revolution** took place.

Two important events helped set the stage for the 1960s sexual revolution—the discovery of antibiotics in the mid-1930s and the development of other media. Television, radio, and other mass media began to broadcast more liberal ideas about sexuality to viewers and listeners. Pornography also became more acceptable, and in 1953, Hugh Hefner began publishing *Playboy* magazine. The introduction of the first contraceptive pill was another important event that liberated female sexuality in the early 1960s.

Sexuality in America Today

Although in many ways the United States is still a sexually "repressed" society, images of sexuality are all around us. In late 20th- and early 21st-century America, sex is a commodity found all over television, the movies, and the Internet. Most movies have sexual scenes that would not have been permitted in movie theaters 50 years ago. Countless websites sell sex toys and pornographic pictures and videos. Today's teens rate the media as one of their leading sources of sex information (Strasburger et al., 2010).

As of 2011, same-sex marriage was legal in six states and in the District of Columbia. Still, gays and lesbians are subject to prejudices in the United States, and some states are passing laws making it illegal for homosexuals to be considered a minority group worthy of special protections.

Archive Photos/Getty Images

Sex and Slavery

Explore settlers' attitudes toward sex and minorities in the colonies.

The Sexual Revolutions

1920s and 1960s.

The Feminist Movement

Beginning in early 1900s.

The Gay Liberation Movement

Beginning in mid 1900s.

Timeline

Television and sex.

Are Reality Shows Realistic?

Two college students discuss the impact of reality shows on college student attitudes about gender and sexuality.

Check Your Learning Quiz 1.5

Go to **login.cengagebrain.com** and take the online quiz.

Theories provide the framework for conceptualizing human behavior and guide the kinds of questions researchers ask about human sexuality.

Psychoanalytic Theory

Sigmund Freud developed psychoanalytic theory during the Victorian era when there was a strong cultural repression of sexuality. He believed the sex drive was one of the most important forces in life. Two of Freud's most controversial concepts included personality formation (the development of the id, ego, and superego) and **psychosexual development** (oral, anal, phallic, latency, and genital stages).

Sigmund Freud

© Hulton-Deutsch Collection/Corbis

Behavioral, Social Learning, and Cognitive Theories

Behaviorists stress that it is necessary to observe and measure behavior to understand it. Thoughts and emotions are not measurable and, therefore, cannot be studied. Sexual behaviors are learned through processes they define as *reinforcement,* or rewards, and *punishment,* or withholding of rewards. Two approaches developed out of behaviorism: social learning theory and cognitive theory. Social learning theorists look at the role of reward and punishment but also consider the effects of internal feelings and external observations on behavior. Cognitive theory holds that our feelings and behaviors, including sexual behavior, are a result of how we perceive and conceptualize what is happening around us.

Biological and Evolutionary Theories

The study of evolution is a specialized area within the broader discipline of biology. However, when it comes to theories about sexual behavior, biological theories consider it primarily from the perspective of individual human biological processes, whereas evolutionary theories are interested in sexual behavior as it relates to the adaptation of the human species throughout its evolutionary history.

psychosexual development The childhood stages of development during which the id's pleasure-seeking energies focus on distinct erogenous zones.

self-actualization Fulfillment of an individual's potentialities, including aptitudes, talents, and the like.

correlations, or relationships, between variables, such as a correlation between sexual abuse and other marital difficulties.

- Internet-based methods—allow researchers to access a wider group of diverse participants online but presents issues with the possibility of multiple submissions.

Whatever techniques they use, researchers must be certain that their experiment passes the following standards:

- Validity—the study actually measures what it is designed to measure.
- Reliability—the questions asked are consistent enough to get similar answers if they are asked again months later.
- Generalizability—the study includes a broad enough sample to have wide applicability to the general population.

Sexuality Research Problems and Issues

Many problems in sexuality research are more difficult to contend with than they are in other types of research. Problems and issues that sexuality researchers must deal with include:

- **Ethical issues**—Ethical standards are necessary for all social science studies and sexuality research in particular. For example, researchers can't study people without first obtaining their **informed consent** and ensuring them of **confidentiality**.
- **Volunteer bias**—Because research participation is voluntary, the findings of a study may not be generalizable to those who chose not to participate. This is especially important in sexuality research where a person's attitudes and values may influence his or her participation in a sexuality study.
- **Sampling problems**—It can be difficult to find subjects for sexuality studies. Because most sexuality researchers work at universities, sexuality studies routinely involve the use of college students as participants. Rather than being a **random sample** of the entire population, these **samples of convenience** do not include those who do not go to college.
- **Reliability issues**—Because societal attitudes vary from decade to decade, participant comfort in discussing sexuality also varies. For a study to be reliable, researchers must take into account the time period when evaluating the results.

On Your Mind

How do researchers know that what people tell them is true?

On Your Mind

How do issues related to race and ethnicity affect sexuality research?

Bikini Sex Project

A student's unique research project.

Check Your Learning Quiz 1.8

Go to **login.cengagebrain.com** and take the online quiz.

Think Critically

Challenge Your Thinking

Consider these questions:

1. Is sexuality research as valid and reliable as other areas of research? Explain.
2. Why is it important to critically analyze information about sexuality even when it is based on research?
3. The relationship between theory and research might best be demonstrated by the differences in the types of questions asked by theorists from different schools of thought. In what basic ways might the types of research questions about human sexuality asked by behaviorists, biologists, and feminists differ? (See also Module 1.6 and online reading Sex in Real Life 1.3)
4. Do you think that people would be more honest about their sex lives if they were filling out an anonymous questionnaire or if they were being interviewed by a researcher? Which method of research do you think yields the highest degree of honesty? With which method would you feel most comfortable? (See also Module 1.8)
5. If you could do a study on sexuality, what area would you choose? What methods of data collection would you use? Why? How would you avoid the problems that many sex researchers face? (See also Modules 1.8 and 1.9)

Research and Skepticism

When you read a story in a magazine or newspaper about a research study, do you believe what you read? For example, if the headline in your daily newspaper claimed that eating an orange a day could decrease your risk for sexual problems, would you believe it? Are research studies accurate? Dr. John Ioannidis, an expert on the credi- bility of research, believes that 90% of the published medical research is flawed (Freedman, 2010). He points out that flaws can be in several areas, such as:

1. The questions asked
2. The methodologies used
3. The participants recruited
4. How the data are analyzed

Although Dr. Ioannidis was referring specifically to medical research, similar issues affect sexuality research. Methodological issues are important, especially because a hurdle in sexuality research is getting participants to respond honestly about very personal and sensitive issues. Embarrassment, social pressures, and/or a lack of an ability to discuss such issues can interfere with honest responses. In an attempt to increase honesty, sexuality researchers have used a variety of data collection methodologies. Do you think that you'd be more honest in answering personal questions about sexuality in the privacy of your own home? Researchers thought so.

In the National Survey of Sexual Health and Behavior, online polling was used in hopes that participants would be more comfortable and honest in their responses. The research supports this idea; one study found that when self-administered questionnaire results were compared with online polling results, significant differences were found (Figure 1.1).

However, even with the best data collection methods, the numbers in sexuality research don't always add up (Bialik, 2010). For example,

- Whereas 14- to 17-year-old male individuals reported using condoms 79% of the time during sex-

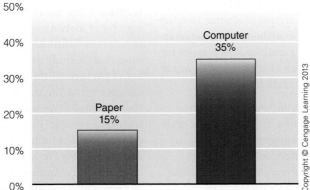

Partner or self was drunk or high at last sex

Teenage males (age 15–19)

Paper 15%

Computer 35%

Figure 1.1 Computer-assisted self-interviews have been found to elicit greater responses on sensitive questions than questionnaire methods. Little difference was found on questions that concerned less sensitive behaviors.

ual intercourse, 14- to 17-year-old female individuals reported their male partners used condoms 58% of the time.

- Whereas 85% of heterosexual men reported their partners having an orgasm at the most recent sexual event, 64% of heterosexual women reported having had an orgasm at their most recent sexual event.

Another example has to do with the reported number of sexual partners. In one study, male individuals reported a median of seven female sexual partners, whereas female individuals reported a median of four male sexual partners (Kolata, 2007). Another study found male individuals had an average of 12.7 lifetime sexual partners, whereas female individuals reported an average of 6.5 (Johnson et al., 2001). Why the differences? It's too simple to assume that the participants are dishonest or exaggerating. There are a multitude of reasons for the differences (Kolata, 2007). Some reasons might include:

- *Sampling differences*—inherent group differences within the male participant group contribute to the differences.
- *Sexual orientation issues*—some of the male responders were engaging in same-sex behavior, which could result in gender dif-

ferences (however, the difference in number of partners is too large to be accounted for simply by this factor; Bialik, 2010).

- *Societal norms and dishonesty*— societal pressures contributed to male overexaggeration and female underexaggeration and/or participants provided false information.
- *Open populations*—because participants can have sex with partners outside the study population, this can lead to a "potential mismatch" between sexual encounters (Bialik, 2010).
- *Greater number of available female partners*—more available female partners would give men more potential partners (Henke, 2010).

Numbers are more likely to add up equally if a study is done on a *closed population*. Think about it this way: If I were to do a study on the average number of partners of the other sex students dance with at the prom, do you think the male and female average would be similar? Probably. Because it is a closed population, they can dance only with each other (Figure 1.2). However, most large sexuality studies have open populations, which means participants have sexual partners outside the study population.

The bottom line is that it is important to critically analyze sexuality research. Although great care is taken to ensure that results are valid and generalizable, the sensitive nature of this area of research brings up many issues that could potentially interfere with the questions that are asked, data collection, participant populations, and the interpretation of the data. Sometimes research can raise more questions than it answers.

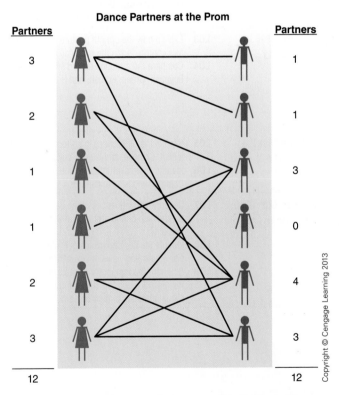

Dance Partners at the Prom

Partners   **Partners**

3   1

2   1

1   3

1   0

2   4

3   3

_____   _____

12   12

Figure 1.2 Let's say we did a study on the average number of partners of the other sex males and females danced with at the prom. Because the prom is a *closed event,* we would expect there to be consistent answers for both groups. In this example, each male and female danced with an average of two partners.

Think Critically

This article and its questions are available in interactive format online.

GO to your Psychology CourseMate at login.cengagebrain.com and take the Chapter Post-Test to see which Learning Objectives you've mastered and which need more review. Use the chapter review guide below and the online activities—including flashcards to review key terms—to measure your learning.

Measure ^ Your Learning

Key Terms	Video	Animation	Reading	Assessment
human sexuality, family of origin, sexologist	Cross-cultural Differences and Sex		How do you decide what type of sex you'll engage in?	Check Your Learning Quiz 1.1
homoerotic, platonic karma, patriarchal, Kama Sutra, yin and yang, polygamy, Koran	Do female primates experience orgasm? Did the Greeks really believe that sex between a man and a boy was a "natural" form of human sexuality?	Timeline: Exploring Human Sexuality: Past and Present		Check Your Learning Quiz 1.2
karma, patriarchal, Kama Sutra, yin and yang, polygamy, Koran	Do honor crimes really happen? Sexuality in the Muslim World		Beauty, status, and Chinese foot binding	Check Your Learning Quiz 1.3
chastity, celibacy, asceticism			The history of vibrators	Check Your Learning Quiz 1.4

Measure ^ **Your Learning**

Online Activities

Key Terms	Video	Animation	Reading	Assessment
Puritans, antimiscegenation laws, free love movement, women's suffrage, sexual revolution	Are Reality Shows Realistic?	Timeline: Television and Sex	Sex and Slavery The Sexual Revolutions The Feminist Movement The Gay Liberation Movement	Check Your Learning Quiz 1.5
theories, repression, id, ego, superego, psychosexual development, oral stage, anal stage, phallic stage, latency, genital stage, behaviorists, cognitive theory, self-actualization, unconditional positive regard	When scientists come up with new theories, how do they know they are true? I've been having some trouble reaching orgasm. Could there be a physical reason for this?		Freud, Sex, and the Unconscious What would they ask?	Check Your Learning Quiz 1.6
		Timeline: History of Sex Research		Check Your Learning Quiz 1.7
case studies, interviewer bias, direct observation, participant observation, correlational studies, correlations, validity, reliability, generalizability, informed consent, confidentiality, volunteer bias, random sample, samples of convenience	How do researchers know that what people tell them is true? How do issues related to race and ethnicity affect sexuality research? Bikini Sex Project			Check Your Learning Quiz 1.8
				Research and Skepticism

Communication and Sexuality

Chapter Outline and Learning Objectives

Prepare to Learn

1 **GO** to your **Psychology CourseMate** at **login.cengagebrain.com** and take the **Chapter Pre-Test** to introduce yourself to this chapter's topics and see what you may already know.

2 **READ** the **Learning Objectives** (LOs, in the left sidebars) and begin the chapter.

3 **COMPLETE** the **Online Activities** (in the right sidebars) *as you read each module.* Activities include **videos, animations, readings, and quizzes.**

4 **CHECK Your Learning** by going online to take the quiz at the end of each module and review material as necessary.

5 **MEASURE Your Learning** after reading the chapter by taking the online **Chapter Post-Test.** Use the chapter review guide at the end of the chapter as needed.

WATCH for these **Online Activities** icons as you read:

Video

Animation

Reading

Assessment

Think Critically

with **tag questions** (e.g., "It's really cold in here, isn't it?" or "That's an interesting idea, isn't it?") to invite discussion and minimize disagreements. Women also use **disclaimers** (e.g., "I may be wrong, but . . ."), **question statements** ("Am I off base here?"; Vanfossen, 1996), and **hedge words** such as "sort of," "kind of," "aren't you," or "would you mind?" All of these tend to decrease the speaker's perceived assertiveness of speech. Although tag questions are fre-

A female model of communication uses more rapport-talk, which establishes relationships and maintains intimacy.

PhotoDisc/Getty Images

quently used in English, they are not used as much in other languages. In fact, the French and Swedish languages lack an equivalent feature (Cheng & Warren, 2001).

Criticisms of Tannen's Findings

There have been criticisms of Tannen's genderlect theory. One of the biggest criticisms has been in her unidimensional approach of studying gender differences in communication. To Tannen, gender is based on biological sex. Therefore, all women communicate one way and all men another way. However, it could be that differences in communication skills, rather than differences in gender, could contribute to communication differences.

▶ **LO8** Explain the influence of same-sex play groups on the differences in the rules and assumptions about communication learned by girls and boys.

Differences Based on Values

Research has found that we value different types of communication skills in our relationships with others. For example, when we need social support or want to "vent," we are more likely to prefer the company of our friends with affectively oriented skills; but if we want to discuss strategies or learn more about a particular topic, we are more likely to prefer the company of our friends with instrumentally oriented skills (Kunkel & Burleson, 1998). Overall, women are more likely than men to value affectively oriented communication skills, whereas men are more likely to value instrumentally oriented skills (Burleson et al., 1996; Samter & Burleson, 2005).

Differences Based on Speech Quantity

Another interesting area of research involves speech quantity. The stereotype is that women talk more than men. This stereotype was supported by the research of neuro-psychiatrist Louann Brizendine, who reported that women used 20,000 words per day, whereas men used only 7,000 (Brizendine, 2006). Brizendine claimed these differences were due to hormones during fetal development (Brizendine & Allen, 2010). However, when a group of researchers tried to replicate Brizendine's study using electronically activated recorders, they found that men and women both used about 16,000 words a day (Mehl et al., 2007). The subjects in this study were college students, which may limit the results, but the researchers point out that if the differences were biologically based, they would have appeared in this sample regardless.

Keep in mind that numerous studies on gender and communication have found that overall differences in many areas of communication are small (Aries, 1996; Dindia & Canary, 2006). Many other factors contribute to our ability to communicate, such as

© weestock Images/Alamy

Purestock/Getty Images

social philosophies, gender roles, dominance, power, and, as we talked about earlier, our family of origin. Many of the studies on gender differences in communication have studied only young, well-educated, middle-class Americans (Mortenson, 2002), and it is not known whether these findings are generalizable to different groups and cultures within and outside of the United States.

Origins of Gender Differences

What contributes to gender differences in communication? Some researchers have suggested that gender communication can often be best understood as a form of cross-cultural communication (A. M. Johnson, 2001; Mulvaney, 1994). If you were suddenly in a conversation with a person from another country who had no experience with your culture, you might find this conversation difficult. You wouldn't know the subtleties of that person's communication style, and he or she wouldn't know yours. It has been hypothesized that even though men and women grow up in similar environments, they learn different ways of communicating, which resembles a form of cross-cultural communication.

According to Maltz and Borker (1982), the influence of gender on learning to communicate begins when children divide into same-sex groups to play. During same-sex conversations, girls and boys learn the rules and assumptions about communication, and these rules follow them through life. As adolescents, they begin to communicate in mixed-sex groups with the rules they learned from same-sex communication, which can cause problems. For example, girls learn to nod their head during conversations with other girls. This lets the talker know that she is being listened to. When a woman nods her head during a conversation with a man, she may simply be showing him that she is listening, but he thinks she agrees with him. When a man doesn't nod his head when a woman is talking to him, she may think he isn't listening to her. All of this can lead to feeling misunderstood and to poor communication.

On Your Mind

Why does my girlfriend get angry when I try to offer solutions to her problems?

Sex in Real Life

Gossiping and complaining.

Check Your Learning Quiz 2.2

Go to **login.cengagebrain.com** and take the online quiz.

Although the majority of research on communication has focused on heterosexual couples in the United States, we do have limited information about communication patterns and strategies in other cultures and in same-sex couples.

Communication and Culture

Cultures differ in many ways, and these differences affect communication patterns. One important dimension that has been extensively studied is the degree to which a culture encourages individual versus group needs (Cai et al., 2000). Individualistic cultures encourage their members to have individual goals and values, and an independent sense of self (Matsumoto, 1996), whereas collectivist cultures encourage members to value group needs over their individual needs. The United States is among the more individualistic countries, along with Canada, Australia, and Great Britain, whereas Asian and Latin cultures tend to be more collectivistic (Adler et al., 2007). This individualistic approach is probably why men and women from the United States are more comfortable disclosing personal information to a variety of people than are members of collectivistic cultures (Gudykunst & Nishida, 1986). Persons from collectivistic cultures, such as Japan or Korea, rarely disclose personal information to those outside of their immediate family because it is thought to be inappropriate to do so (Chen & Danish, 2010; Gudykunst et al., 1987; Seki et al., 2002).

Communication and Sexual Orientation

Like heterosexual couples, conversational styles in gay and lesbian relationships have been found to reflect power differences in the relationship more than the biological sex of the communicator (Steen & Schwartz, 1995).

Differences in same-sex communication may also have to do with gender roles. For example, stereotypically "feminine" men and women have been found to use more submissive speech patterns, whereas stereotypically "masculine" men have been found to use more dominance language than stereotypically "feminine" or androgenous men and women (Ellis & McCallister, 1980). It may be that gay men and lesbian women are more flexible in their gender roles, and their communication patterns could reflect this comfort.

Self-Disclosure and Asking for What You Need

Opening up and talking with your partner and sharing feelings, or self-disclosure, helps deepen intimacy and sexual satisfaction (Moore, 2010; Noland, 2010; Schiffrin et al., 2010). Self-disclosure lets your partner know what is wrong and how you feel about it, and it enables you to ask for specific change (Fowers, 1998). When you open up and share, your partner will be more likely to reciprocate by opening up and sharing as well (Posey et al., 2010).

Too often, we assume that being good in bed also means being a mind reader. Somehow our partner should just know what turns us on. In reality, good lovers are simply willing to listen and communicate with their partners. Doing so helps ensure you are both on the same page when it comes to various sexual activities and behaviors. Without communication, you may think you are doing exactly what your partner wants, but your partner may be wondering why you're doing what you're doing! Eventually, your relationship may end, mainly because you and your partner were unable to open up and talk about what you needed and wanted in the sexual relationship, leaving you both feeling confused and frustrated.

Good lovers are sensitive to their partner's needs and desires, and can communicate their own desires.

Trusting Your Partner

A key factor that is related to the ability to self-disclose in sexual relationships is trust (Ignatius & Kokkonen, 2007). If we trust our partner and feel confident and secure in our relationship, self-disclosure will be much easier.

Building trust takes time, and it is typically a process of *uncertainty reduction* (Holmes & Rempel, 1989). Our prior relationships, especially those we had in our family of origin, influence our ability to trust. Being hurt by someone in a previous relationship, experiencing a loss, or being fearful about rejection can all interfere with the ability to trust an intimate partner, but over time trust can be improved.

Men and women who report being more trusting of their partners also tend to be more optimistic about the relationship and think more positive thoughts about their partner's negative behaviors, for instance, often being late to meet them (Simpson, 2007). However, nontrusting partners would have many doubts and concerns, and might think their partner doesn't love them anymore.

Obstacles to Sexual Communication

Several factors.

On Your Mind

What can I do to make my partner more attracted to me?

On Your Mind

How can I overcome my fear of talking about sex?

Check Your Learning Quiz 2.6

Go to **login.cengagebrain.com** and take the online quiz.

Active Listening

Listening is one of the most important communication skills (Adler et al., 2007). Adults spend nearly 70% of their waking time communicating and 45% of this time listening (Adler et al., 2007; Rankin, 1952). The majority of couples spend too much time criticizing each other and not enough time really listening and making affectionate comments (P. Coleman, 2002). Active listening involves using nonverbal communication to let your partner know that you are attentive and present in the conversation. For example, as your partner talks, you can maintain eye contact, nod, or say "um-hum" (Fowers, 1998) to let him or her know you are actively listening.

Nondefensive Listening

Another important skill is **nondefensive listening,** which involves focusing your attention on what your partner is saying without being defensive (Gottman, 1994). Nondefensive listening relies on self-restraint, which is often absent in distressed couples, who have a difficult time hearing and listening to each other. It can be very difficult to listen fully, but this skill reduces your inclination to interrupt or to defend yourself.

Poor listeners often think that they understand what their partner is trying to say, but they rarely do. Instead, they try to find a way to circumvent the discussion and talk about something else. It is difficult to really listen to someone when you are angry or defensive. Good listening allows you to understand and retain information while building and maintaining your relationships (Adler et al., 2007).

Effective Listening

Many things interfere with our ability to be an effective listener (Golen, 1990; Hulbert, 1989):

1. *Information overload:* It is easy to reach information overload today. We hear so much during the course of our day that it can be difficult to listen carefully to everything we hear. As a result, we must choose what information we will listen and pay attention to.

2. *Preoccupation with personal concerns:* A preoccupation with personal concerns may also interfere with our ability to listen. If we are wrapped up in our own thoughts and issues, it is difficult to listen to someone else.

3. *Rapid thoughts:* Listening is also affected by our brains actively processing information around us—other conversations, music, traffic, and noise. Consider this: we are capable of understanding speech at rates of up to 600 words per minute

nondefensive listening Listening strategy in which the listener focuses attention on what his or her partner is saying without being defensive.

(Versfeld & Dreschler, 2002); however, the average person speaks between 100 and 140 words per minute. This gives your brain time to think about other things.

Showing That You Are Listening

We don't ever realize how important it is to have others listen to us until someone we really care about doesn't listen to us (P. Coleman, 2002). Being listened to can make your partner feel worthy, protected, and cared about. Encouraging your partner through active listening shows your partner that you are "tuned in" and that you believe he or she has something worthwhile to say.

Summarizing and Validating

When your partner is finished talking, it is important to summarize what your partner has told you as accurately as possible and allow your partner the opportunity to correct any misunderstandings. Finally, regardless of whether you agree with your partner, it is important to validate your partner's statement. Saying "I can understand why you might feel that way" or "I know what you mean" shows that you accept your partner's point of view.

Interpreting the Message

When walking across campus one day, you trip and fall. Your partner sees you and says, "Be careful!" How do you interpret that? Does it mean you need to slow down? Or that your partner is genuinely worried you might hurt yourself? In all conversations, the recipient of the message must interpret the intended meaning of the message (R. Edwards, 1998), which is dependent on several factors, such as the nature of the relationship with the person and your mood at the time.

If you are angry or upset, you may perceive more hostility in ambiguous or benign comments than someone who is not angry or upset (Epps & Kendall, 1995). If you are worried about something or preoccupied with an issue, this can also bias how you interpret a message. In one study, women who were preoccupied with their weight were more likely than women who were not preoccupied with their weight to interpret ambiguous sentences with negative or "fat" meanings (Jackman et al., 1995). For example, if a woman who was preoccupied with her weight heard someone say, "You look good today!" she might interpret this to mean that she didn't look good yesterday. However, couldn't she also interpret the message in other ways? Perhaps she looked tired yesterday or even stressed out.

Are You Listening?

Match the description with the listening pattern.

Check Your Learning Quiz 2.7

Go to **login.cengagebrain.com** and take the online quiz.

John Gottman, a relationship expert, found that happy couples experienced 20 positive interactions for every negative one (Nelson, 2005). Couples who were in conflict experienced only five positive interactions for every negative one, and those couples soon to split up experienced only 0.8 positive interactions for every negative one. This research suggests that positive and negative interactions can shine light on a couple's relationship happiness.

Constructive Contributions to Communication

Two of the most positive contributions to effective communication in a relationship are for each partner to control his or her temper and accept criticism graciously.

Controlling Our Temper

We all get angry sometimes, and we know that not all conversations have happy, peaceful endings. However, the key is in managing the tension. When we disagree with our partner, the opening minutes of a disagreement can indicate whether the conversation will turn angry or simply be a quiet discussion (P. Coleman, 2002). If harsh words are used, chances are the disagreement will build, and the tension will escalate. However, if softer words are used, there is a better chance the disagreement can be resolved.

Accepting Criticism

Accepting criticism isn't an easy thing to do—we are all defensive at times. Although it would be impossible to eliminate all defensiveness, it's important to reduce defensiveness to resolve disagreements. If you are defensive while listening to your partner's criticism, chances are good that you will not be able to hear his or her message. Common defensive techniques are to deny the criticism (e.g., "That is just NOT TRUE!"), make excuses without taking any responsibility (e.g., "I was just exhausted!"), deflecting responsibility (e.g., "Me? What about your behavior?"), and righteous indignation (e.g., "How could you possibly say such a hurtful thing?"; P. Coleman, 2002). All of these techniques interfere with our ability to really understand what our partner is trying to tell us.

Mistaken Communication Patterns

Couples often make many mistakes in their communication patterns that can lead to arguments, misunderstandings, and conflicts.

overgeneralization Making statements that tend to exaggerate a particular issue.

overkill A common mistake that couples make during arguments, in which one person threatens the worst but does not mean what he or she says.

name-calling Using negative or stereotyping words when in disagreement.

Exaggerating

Three forms of exaggeration inhibit healthy communication:

1. **Overgeneralization:** Overgeneralizations, such as "Why do you always . . . ?" or "You never . . . ," lead to defensiveness and arguing. Try to be specific about your complaints. For example, say, "I would like us to spend more time together," rather than "You always want to be with your friends!"
2. **Overkill:** Another form of exaggeration is overkill, or making threats you don't intend to carry out (e.g., "If you even *speak* to another woman tonight, I will leave you.").
3. **Name-Calling:** Try to stay away from name-calling or stereotyping words, such as calling your partner a "selfish bastard" or a "nag." These derogatory terms will only help to escalate anger and frustration and will not lead to healthy communication.

Widening the Discussion

Broadening the scope of the discussion, for example, by bringing up past arguments or other current issues, is another nonconstructive communication pattern that accomplishes nothing. Stay away from old arguments and accusations. The past is just that—the past. So try to leave it there and move forward. Try not to throw too many issues into the conversation at once (e.g., the fact that your partner came home late or ignored you when he or she was with friends). This approach makes it difficult to focus on resolving any one issue because there is just too much happening.

Yelling and Screaming

Yelling or screaming can cause your partner to be defensive and angry and less likely to be rational and understand what you are saying. Even though it's not easy, it's important to stay calm during conversation.

Fighting

Verbal disagreements are a common part of intimate relationships and are much more likely during times of stress (Bodenmann et al., 2010). Couples may disagree about public issues, concerns outside of their relationship, or concerns related to their relationship (Johnson, 2009).

Regardless of the type of argument, couples who disagree are usually happier than those who say, "We never, ever fight!" (P. Coleman, 2002). It's important to point out, however, that verbal disagreements are different from physical disagreements. (We discuss domestic violence in Chapter 14.)

Healthy and Unhealthy Approaches to Disagreements

Happy and unhappy couples.

Key Terms Exercise

Match the key terms with their definitions.

Check Your Learning Quiz 2.8

Go to **login.cengagebrain.com** and take the online quiz.

Think Critically

Challenge Your Thinking

Consider this scenario: As you and your date are watching the film *Limitless*, your date whispers in your ear, "I love Bradley Cooper." Later, on the way home from the movie theater, your date holds your hands, looks into your eyes, and says, "I love you."

1. What would the author's German student say about these two statements?
2. How would an American see these two statements?
3. Do you see any difference in the two statements? Why or why not?
4. What role did body language play in your interpretation of the two statements?
5. What role did context and other situational cues play in your interpretation?

I Love Peanut Butter!

The story that follows was written by an international student of mine. We had many interesting discussions about the cultural differences in communication. If you have ever traveled to or lived in a different country, you've probably experienced some cultural differences in communication. Not all cultures communicate in the same way, and our cultural background affects our communication strategies and patterns.

I was born in Regensburg, Germany, and I have lived there all of my life. For the past year, I have been living in the United States, and during this time, I have learned a lot about cross-cultural

differences in communication. Americans have a very emotional way of using language. They "love" peanut butter—what does this mean? When someone says, "I love you," does this mean that a person loves you as much as peanut butter? Or is it a different kind of love? This was really confusing for me.

I think that special expressions or words lose their real meaning when you use them all the time. This is especially true when it comes to relationships. Americans say, "I love you," but I'm not sure what that really means. A little boy tells his mother he loves her, good friends say it, you hear it being said in advertise-

ments, and everyone loves everyone! But how can you express real deep feelings if you are using the phrase "I love you" all the time? Does it still mean the same thing? How do you know if Americans really love you, if they also love peanut butter? What does "I love you" really mean?

In Germany, we say something that is between "I love you" and "I like you"; maybe it means more, "You are in my heart." You would use the phrase, "Ich hab' dich lieb" to tell your mother and father, your friends, or your new boyfriend how you feel about them. But when someone says, "Ich liebe Dich"—the German "I love you"—then your relationship is really serious. This phrase is reserved only for relationships in which you know your partner really well. Saying "Ich liebe Dich" is very hard for some people, because it can make you more vulnerable. When a man would say "Ich liebe Dich" after three months of dating, it would make me wonder whether he could be taken seriously. Germans only use these words when they really mean it, and this gives the phrase much more respect.

I like how Americans are so open about letting someone know that they care about them, but it's hard to tell when it's really serious. Why is there no phrase in the English language that means something between liking and loving someone? Every culture and every country has its own ways of communicating and expressing ideas. What is most important is learning how to accept and learn from the differences. (Author's files)

Think Critically

This article and its questions are available in interactive format online.

Measure
Your Learning

GO to your Psychology CourseMate at login.cengagebrain.com and take the Chapter Post-Test to see which Learning Objectives you've mastered and which need more review. Use the chapter review guide below and the online activities—including flashcards to review key terms—to measure your learning.

Module	Learning Objectives
2.1 The Importance of Communication 32	**LO1** Identify two ways that communication has changed over the last few years.
	LO2 Explain the onion theory of communication.
	LO3 Describe three positive results of good communication in relationships.
	LO4 Identify three goals that people have when communicating with others.
	LO5 Identify two or three positive and negative communication strategies that children may learn from their families of origin.
2.2 Gender Differences in Communication Styles 34	**LO6** Identify the difference between male and female styles of communication as described by linguist Deborah Tannen.
	LO7 Cite a major criticism of the assumption that men and women communicate differently.
	LO8 Explain the influence of same-sex play groups on the differences in the rules and assumptions about communication learned by girls and boys.
2.3 Other Communication Differences and Similarities 38	**LO9** Explain why persons from an individualistic and collectivist culture might have difficulty communicating.
	LO10 Identify two differences in the communication styles of heterosexual and same-sex couples.
2.4 Nonverbal Communication 40	**LO11** Define nonverbal communication and explain how it can change the meaning of verbal communication.
	LO12 List the three variables that affect our use of nonverbal communication.
	LO13 Compare the advantages and disadvantages of verbal and nonverbal communication during sex.

Online Activities

Key Terms	Video	Animation	Readings	Assessment
	Perspectives on Communication	Goals of Communication		Check Your Learning Quiz 2.1
genderlects, tag question, disclaimer, question statement, hedge word	Why does my girlfriend get angry when I try to offer solutions to her problems?		Gossiping and Complaining	Check Your Learning Quiz 2.2
	Maid Cafés			Check Your Learning Quiz 2.3
nonverbal communication	Do you think it's cheating when I walk in and see my boyfriend's checking out another girl's Facebook page?			Check Your Learning Quiz 2.4

Measure ^Your Learning

Online Activities

Key Terms	Video	Animation	Readings	Assessment
computer-mediated communication, emoticons, avatar	Teens and Sexting		Social Networks	Check Your Learning Quiz 2.5
self-disclosure	What can I do to make my partner more attracted to me? How can I overcome my fear of talking about sex?		Obstacles to Sexual Communication	Check Your Learning Quiz 2.6
active listening, nondefensive listening		Are You Listening?		Check Your Learning Quiz 2.7
overgeneralization, overkill, name-calling		Key Terms Exercise	Healthy and Unhealthy Approaches to Disagreements	Check Your Learning Quiz 2.8
				I Love Peanut Butter!

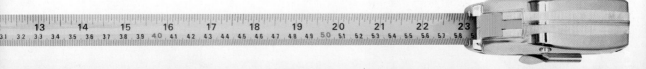

Gender Development, Gender Roles, and Gender Identity

3

8th week, the external genitalia of females—the clitoris, labia minora, vestibule, and labia majora—begin to develop (Figure 3.2). In males, the testes begin **androgen** secretion, which stimulates the development of male genitalia—the penis, in which lies the urethra, and the scrotum, where the testicles will ultimately rest when they descend.

Hormonal Development and Influences

Hormones play an important role in human development. The table in the online reading "The Roles of Sex Hormones" lists the various sex hormones and the roles they play. Endocrine glands, such as the gonads, secrete hormones directly into the bloodstream to be carried to the target organs. The ovaries, for example, produce the two major female hormones, estrogen and progesterone. Estrogen is an important influence in the development of female sexual characteristics throughout fetal development and later life, whereas progesterone regulates the menstrual cycle and prepares the uterus for pregnancy. The testicles produce androgens, which are quite important to the male, because even a genetically male embryo will develop female characteristics if androgens are not secreted at the right time or if the fetus is insensitive to androgens.

Brain Differentiation

Most hormonal secretions are regulated by the brain—in particular, by the hypothalamus, which is the body's single most important control center. Yet, hormones also affect the development of the brain itself, both in the uterus and after birth (Savic et al., 2010). Male and female brains have different tasks and thus undergo different development. For example, female brains control menstruation and, therefore, must signal the release of hormones in a monthly cycle, whereas male brains signal release continuously. With the brain, as with sexual organs, the presence of androgens during the appropriate critical stage of development may be the factor that programs the central nervous system to develop male sexual behaviors (Bocklandt & Vilain, 2007; Garcia-Falgueras & Swaab, 2010; Juntti et al., 2010).

The Roles of Sex Hormones

Hormonal Development and Influence

Check Your Learning Quiz 3.2

Go to **login.cengagebrain.com** and take the online quiz.

Prenatal development depends on carefully orchestrated developmental stages. At any stage, sex chromosome or hormone disorders can result in disorders of sex development. The result can be a child born with ambiguous genitals or with the external genitals of one sex and the genetic makeup of the other sex.

Chromosomal Disorders of Sex Development

Sometimes a person's sex chromosomes will include an extra X or Y chromosome, or will be missing one. Although medical researchers have identified more than 70 such abnormalities of the sex chromosomes, the most common are Klinefelter syndrome and Turner syndrome.

Klinefelter syndrome

Klinefelter syndrome occurs when an ovum containing an extra X chromosome is fertilized by a Y sperm (designated XXY), giving a child 47 chromosomes in all (Giltay & Maiburg, 2010). The Y chromosome triggers the development of male genitalia, but the extra X prevents them from fully developing. Klinefelter syndrome occurs in roughly 1 of every 750 live male births (Forti et al., 2010; Giltay & Maiburg, 2010). As adults, men with Klinefelter syndrome typically have feminized body contours, small testes, low levels of testosterone, **gynecomastia**, and possible verbal deficits (Forti et al., 2010; Giltay & Maiburg, 2010). Although two thirds of men with Klinefelter syndrome are never diagnosed, those who are diagnosed are typically identified during an evaluation for infertility (Forti et al., 2010). Men with Klinefelter syndrome may still be able to father children through sperm retrieval (Forti et al., 2010).

Turner Syndrome

Turner syndrome is a chromosomal disorder that occurs in 1 of every 2,500 live female births. Turner syndrome results from an ovum without any sex chromosome being fertilized by an X sperm (designated XO), which gives the child only 45 chromosomes in all. Although the external genitalia develop to look like a normal female's, the woman's ovaries do not develop fully, causing **amenorrhea** (aye-men-uh-REE-uh) and probable infertility. In addition, Turner syndrome is characterized by short stature, a relatively high-pitched voice, immature breast development, and abnormalities of certain internal organs (Menke et al., 2010; Moreno-Garcia et al., 2005). Although the majority of girls with Turner syndrome will never undergo

gynecomastia Abnormal breast development in the male.

amenorrhea The absence of menstruation.

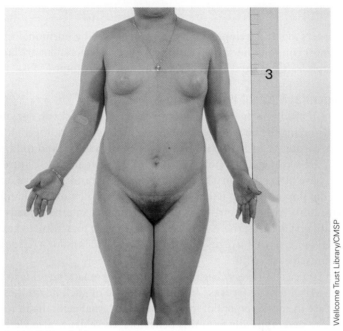

3

Wellcome Trust Library/CMSP

Femaie with Turner Syndrome.

puberty, those who do may be capable of pregnancy. However, pregnancies in women with Turner syndrome have a high risk for chromosomal abnormalities and fetal loss (Bouchlariotou et al., 2011).

XYY Syndrome and Triple X Syndrome

XYY syndrome and Triple X syndrome are rare conditions. As the names imply, these conditions occur when a normal ovum is fertilized by a sperm that has two Y chromosomes or two X chromosomes, or when an ovum with two X chromosomes is fertilized by a normal X sperm. The XYY individual may grow up as a normal male and the XXX as a normal female, and so often their unusual genetic status is not detected. However, many do suffer from some genital abnormalities, fertility problems, and possible learning difficulties later in life. There is no effective treatment for XYY or Triple X syndrome.

Sex in Real Life

Disorders of sex development in depth.

Hormonal Disorders of Sex Development

Disorders of sex development can also be caused by hormonal irregularities. The two most common hormonal disorders of sex development are congenital adrenal hyperplasia (CAH) and androgen-insensitivity syndrome (AIS).

Congenital Adrenal Hyperplasia

Congenital adrenal hyperplasia occurs when a child lacks an enzyme in the adrenal gland, forcing the body to produce higher amounts of androgen. It is estimated that approximately 1 in 15,000 infants are born with CAH, and today almost all newborns are screened for it (Johannsen et al., 2010; Roan, 2010). The excess androgens often have little effect on a developing male fetus and may have only a small effect on a developing female fetus, such as an enlarged clitoris (Johannsen et al., 2010; Roan, 2010). Although girls with CAH have female internal gonads (uterus and ovaries), in severe cases, these girls may be born with masculinized external genitalia, as well as menstrual irregularities, early body hair, and/or a deepening of the voice (Johannsen et al., 2010).

In 2010, a controversy began over the use of prenatal steroids to decrease the risk for CAH in female fetuses. Although the use of such hormones was thought to decrease the development of masculinized external genitalia in female fetuses and increase stereotypically feminine behaviors, these drugs also were found to potentially decrease the chances that the fetuses would be lesbian (Begley, 2010; Dreger et al., 2010; Roan, 2010).

Androgen-Insensitivity Syndrome

Approximately 1 in 20,000 boys are born each year with androgen-insensitivity syndrome (AIS) (Oakes et al., 2008). Although the gonads develop into testes and produce testosterone normally, for some reason, the cells of individuals with AIS cannot absorb it; in other words, the testosterone is there but has no effect on the body. Because the Wolffian ducts did not respond to testosterone during the sexual differentiation phase, no male genitalia develop; however, because the gonads are male, the Müllerian ducts do not develop into normal female internal organs either. Individuals with AIS are raised as females and end up with no internal reproductive organs except two testes, which remain in the abdomen producing testosterone that the body cannot use.

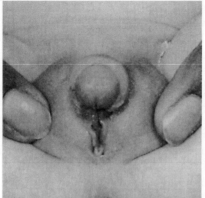
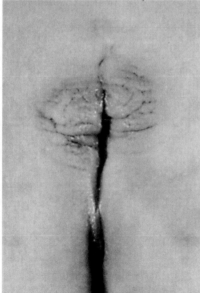

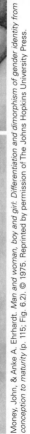
Money, John, & Anke A. Ehrhardt. *Man and woman, boy and girl: Differentiation and dimorphism of gender identity from conception to maturity* (p. 115; Fig. 6.2). © 1975. Reprinted by permission of The Johns Hopkins University Press.

Genitalia of a fetally androgenized female and an androgen-insensitive male with feminized genitals.

Check Your Learning Quiz 3.3

Go to **login.cengagebrain.com** and take the online quiz.

Societal expectations are that men will act like men and women like women, and we become confused and uncomfortable when we are denied knowledge of a person's gender. It is difficult to know how to interact with someone whose gender we do not know because we are so programmed to react to people first according to their gender. Even our language is constructed around gender. Every time you refer to a person, you must write either "he" or "she." Therefore, every sentence you write about a person reveals his or her gender, even if it reveals nothing else about that person.

Nevertheless, many of our basic assumptions about gender are open to dispute. A key question asked by researchers is: Which of our gender-specific behaviors are **gender roles** (i.e., culturally determined), and which are **gender traits** (i.e., innate or biologically determined)?

Masculinity and femininity refer to the ideal cluster of traits that society attributes to each gender. Models of masculinity and femininity are changing rapidly in modern American society. It's not uncommon today to see female police officers on crime scenes or stay-at-home dads at the park with their kids. Yet, gender role change can also result in confusion, fear, and even hostility in society. When things change, determining stereotypically correct behaviors becomes more difficult.

As gender stereotypes evolve, a trait may no longer be seen as the exclusive domain of a single gender. For example, many people have been trying to change our current stereotypes of men as "unemotional" and women as "emotional." For many centuries, these types of gender traits were seen as innate, immutable, and part of the biological makeup of the sexes. Few scientists suggested that the differences between men and women were primarily social; most believed that women and men were fundamentally different.

Not only did scientists believe that the differences in the sexes were innate, they also believed that men were superior—having developed past the "emotional" nature of women (Gould, 1981). Although science has moved forward, these outdated attitudes still exist, both subtly in cultures like our own and overtly in cultures where women are allowed few of the rights granted to men.

Biologically Based Gender Differences

gender roles Culturally defined ways of behaving seen as appropriate for males and females.

gender traits Innate or biologically determined gender-specific behaviors.

Some gender differences are considered purely biological. Physically, males tend to be larger and stronger, with more of their body weight in muscle and less in body fat compared with females (Angier, 1999). Females, however, are born more neurologically advanced than males, and they mature faster. Females are also biologically heartier than males; more male fetuses miscarry, more males are stillborn, the male infant mortality rate is higher, males acquire more hereditary diseases and remain more susceptible to disease throughout life, and men die at younger ages than women. Males are also more likely to have developmental problems such as learning disabilities (Martin et al., 2008). It has long been believed that males are better at mathematics and spatial problems, whereas females are better at verbal tasks; for example, female children learn language skills earlier than males (Weatherall, 2002).

There has always been evidence that men's and women's brains are different; autopsies have shown that men's brains are more asymmetrical than women's, and women seem to recover better from damage to the left hemisphere of the brain (as in strokes), where language is situated. Yet, it has always been unclear what these facts mean. Recently, newer techniques in brain imaging have provided evidence that women's and men's brains not only differ in size, but that women and men use their brains differently during certain activities (DeBellis et al., 2001; Hamberg, 2000; Menzler et al., 2010; Sánchez & Vilain, 2010; F. Schneider et al., 2000). Although it is too early to know what these differences mean, future studies may be able to provide clearer pictures of the different ways men and women think, and shed some light on the biological and social influences of these differences.

Culturally Based Gender Differences

Even when modern science suggests a certain gender trait that seems to be based on innate differences between the sexes, culture can contradict that trait or even deny it. For example, most researchers accept the principle that males display more aggression than females; adult males certainly demonstrate this tendency, which is probably the result, in part, of higher levels of testosterone. When female bodybuilders, for example, take steroids, they often find themselves acquiring male traits, including losing breast tissue, growing more body hair, and becoming more aggressive. However, the difference is also demonstrated in early childhood, when boys are more aggressive in play, whereas girls tend to be more compliant and docile.

Margaret Mead's (1935/1988/2001) famous discussion of the Tchambuli tribe of New Guinea shows that such traits need not determine gender roles. Among the Tchambulis, the women performed the "aggressive" occupations such as fishing, commerce, and politics, whereas the men were more sedentary and artistic, and took more care of domestic life. The women assumed the dress appropriate for their activities—plain clothes and short hair—whereas the men dressed in bright colors. So even if we accept biological gender differences, societies such as the Tchambuli show that human culture can transcend biology.

The Fear of Men

Men, the media, and our perceptions

Check Your Learning Quiz 3.4

Go to **login.cengagebrain.com** and take the online quiz.

We must be careful not to suggest that there are no innate differences between the sexes. Many of these differences remain controversial, such as relative levels of activity and curiosity, and facial recognition skills. These are relatively minor differences, however. Even if it turns out, for example, that female infants recognize faces earlier than male infants, as has been suggested, or that male children are more active than female children, would that really account for the enormous gender role differences that have developed over time? The answer depends on which theory of gender role development you accept.

Social Learning Theory: Learning from Our Environment

Social learning theory suggests that we learn gender roles from our environment, from the same system of rewards and punishments that we learn our other social roles. For example, research shows that many parents commonly reward gender-appropriate behavior and disapprove of (or even punish) gender-inappropriate behavior. Taking a Barbie away from a boy and handing him Spider-Man, making girls help with cooking and cleaning and boys take out the trash—these little, everyday actions build into powerful messages about gender. Gender stereotypes can also influence our perceptions of a person's abilities. In one study, mothers were asked to guess how steep a slope their 11-month-old sons and daughters could crawl down. Although no gender differences were found in the abilities of the babies to climb the slopes, mothers were significantly more likely to underestimate the ability of their daughters (Eliot, 2009).

Children also learn to model their behavior after the same-gender parent to win parental approval. They may learn about gender-appropriate behavior from parents even if they are too young to perform the actions themselves; for example, they see that Mommy is more likely to make dinner, whereas Daddy is more likely to pay the bills. Children also see models of the "appropriate" ways for their genders to behave in their books, on television, and when interacting with others.

Cognitive Development Theory: Age-Stage Learning

Cognitive development theory assumes that all children go through a universal pattern of development, and there really is not much parents can do to alter it. As children's brains mature and grow, they develop new abilities and concerns; at each stage, their understanding of gender changes in predictable ways. This theory follows the ideas of Piaget (1951), the child development theorist who suggested that social attitudes in children are mediated through their processes of cognitive development.

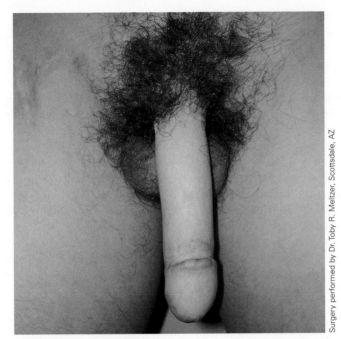

A completed female-to-male transsexual.

Medical and Surgical Methods of Sex Reassignment

Some transsexuals who believe they were "born into the wrong body" may select hormone therapy as a way to alter their physical appearance. Others who wish to have their genitals surgically altered to resemble those of the other biological sex may undergo sex reassignment surgery.

Transmen, or female-to-male transsexuals (FtoM), were assigned female at birth, whereas transwomen, or male-to-female transsexuals (MtoF), were assigned male at birth. A variety of different options are available, and although some transsexuals proceed through all the stages to eventual surgery, many do not. Treatment often begins with psychotherapy, which helps explore options, establish realistic life goals, and identify points of conflict that have been interfering with life happiness. They are encouraged to take on the role of the desired gender through cross-dressing, hair removal, body padding, vocal training, or various other behaviors.

Teo: A Transman

An interview with a transman about his experiences.

Liz: A Transwoman

A transwoman discusses her experiences and challenges.

▶ **LO23** Describe expressions of gender diversity in two non-Western cultures.

For some tranpeople, the next step typically involves cross-sex hormone therapy, in which androgens are given to biological females and estrogens (and possibly testosterone-blockers) are given to biological males. Taking these drugs significantly changes the physical appearance of a man or woman, typically within about 2 years.

Transwomen who take estrogens (and testosterone-blockers) will develop breasts, a redistribution of body fat, decreased upper body strength, a softening of the skin, a decrease in body hair, a slowing or stopping of hair loss in the scalp, decreased testicular size, and fewer erections (World Professional Organization for Transgender Health, 2001). However, if they stop taking these drugs, most of these effects will be reversible, with the exception of the breast tissue. Transmen who take testosterone will develop several permanent changes, including a deeper voice, clitoral enlargement, increased facial and body hair, and possible baldness (World Professional Organization for Transgender Health, 2001). They may also experience several reversible changes including increased sexual interest, upper body strength, weight gain, and a redistribution of body fat (World Professional Organization for Transgender Health, 2001). For some transpeople, these changes are enough and they do not feel the need to undergo additional surgical interventions.

Gender Diversity in Other Cultures

Some cultures challenge our notions of gender and even have a gender category that encompasses both aspects of gender. Two-spirits (or *berdache*) have been found in many cultures throughout the world, including American Indian, Indian, and Filipino cultures. A two-spirit was usually (but not always) a biological male who was effeminate or androgynous in behavior and who took on the social role of female (Blackwood, 1994; Jacobs et al., 1997; W. L. Williams, 1986). Being a two-spirit was considered a vocation, like being a hunter or warrior, which was communicated to certain boys in their first adult vision. In all social functions, the two-spirit was treated as a female. They held a respected, sacred position in society and were believed to have special powers.

Biologically female two-spirits began showing interest in boys' activities and games during childhood (Blackwood, 1984; Jacobs et al., 1997). Adults, recognizing this desire, would teach the girls the same skills the boys were learning. (In one tribe, a family with all girl children might select one daughter to be their "son," tying dried bear ovaries to her belt to prevent conception!)

women have historically been valued for their reproductive ability, they may be viewed as old once they lose the ability to reproduce, whereas men are valued for their achievements and are not viewed as old until they are physically incapacitated or unable to work. Overall, although both men and women have been found to value physical appearance, women have been found to be more concerned about the effects of aging on their physical appearance (Cash, 2000; Slevin, 2010).

However, it is important to keep in mind that attitudes about aging vary by race, ethnicity, and sexual orientation. Black and Latina women have less rigid aging stereotypes than white women (Schuler et al., 2008), as do lesbian women, who are more positive about aging and looking old compared with heterosexual women (Slevin, 2010; Wolf, 1991). Gay men, however, tend to have more negative attitudes about aging compared with heterosexual men because American gay culture places more emphasis on young and youthful bodies (Slevin, 2010).

Cross-culturally, negative attitudes about seniors and aging persist. In fact, a cross-cultural sample of college students from six countries found negative attitudes about senior citizens and support for the belief that seniors are "incompetent" (Cuddy et al., 2005). Other studies have found significant fears of aging in South Korea (Yun & Lachman, 2006) and Israel (Bodner & Lazar, 2008).

© imagebroker/Alamy

Check Your Learning Quiz 3.7

Go to **login.cengagebrain.com**
and take the online quiz.

Think Critically

Challenge Your Thinking

Consider these questions:

1. Do you think it is possible to create a society that avoids gender stereotypes, a society of total gender equality?
2. If you could design such a society, what would it be like? For example, does your vision of a gender-equal society include unisex bathrooms and gender-neutral dormitories, or is it something subtler, referring to a sense of equal opportunity and respect?
3. Would you want to live in such a society?
4. If you were running for President of the United States on a platform of building a gender-equal society, what would you say in your speeches to convince people to elect you?
5. What might your opponent say in his or her speeches to convince people not to elect you?

Different, But Not Less Than: Toward Gender Equality

Epstein (1986, 1988) believes that gender distinctions begin with basic human dichotomous thinking—the splitting of the world into opposites such as good–bad, dark–light, soft–hard, male–female, and gay–straight. This very basic human process tends to exaggerate differences between things, including the sexes, and society invests a lot of energy in maintaining those distinctions.

Many religious and cultural systems clearly define gender roles. Advocates of such systems deny that differentiating gender roles means that one gender is subordinate to the other. For example, Susan Rogers (1978) has argued that we cannot apply Western notions of gender equality to countries with fundamentally different systems. She argues that inequality can exist in society only when women and men are seen in that society as fundamentally similar.

In Oman, for example, women are subject to strict social rules that we in the West would clearly see as subordination. Yet, Rogers argues that women in Oman see themselves as quite different from men and are uninterested in the male role and male definitions of power. Is it appropriate for us to impose our categories on their society and suggest that women in Oman are exploited and subordinate even though they themselves do not think so? Such questions go to the heart of the discussion of power in society.

The goal for many is not a society without gender distinctions; a world without differences is boring. Yet, a world that restricts people's ability to express difference because of the color of their skin, their religious beliefs, the type of genitalia they happen to have (or not have!), or their sexual orientation is unjust. It is the content of gender roles, not their existence, that societies can alter to provide each person an opportunity to live without being judged by stereotypes of gender.

Think Critically

This article and its questions are available in interactive format online.

GO to your Psychology CourseMate at login.cengagebrain.com and take the Chapter Post-Test to see which Learning Objectives you've mastered and which need more review. Use the chapter review guide below and the online activities—including flashcards to review key terms—to measure your learning.

Measure ^Your Learning

Module		Learning Objectives	
3.1	What Is Gender? 60	LO1	Differentiate between coeducational, single-sex, and gender-neutral housing.
		LO2	Differentiate between the terms *sex* and *gender*.
		LO3	Identify how gender stereotypes can affect sexuality.
3.2	Prenatal Development 62	LO4	Explain the primary difference in the ways that simple and complex organisms reproduce.
		LO5	Explain how the sex chromosomes combine to determine the sex of a child during the fertilization of an ovum by a sperm.
		LO6	Summarize the sequence of events from undifferentiated zygote to a sexually differentiated male or female embryo.
		LO7	Identify the two key hormones responsible for the development of female and male organs at the embryonic stage of development.
		LO8	Explain why certain male and female external sex organs, such as the penis and clitoris, are called *homologous*.
3.3	Disorders of Sex Development 68	LO9	Identify the two most common chromosomal disorders of sex development and describe their physical manifestations.
		LO10	Identify the two most common hormonal disorders of sex development and describe their physical manifestations.
3.4	Gender Roles and Gender Traits 72	LO11	Explain why many people find it difficult to interact with someone without knowing that person's gender.
		LO12	Differentiate between gender roles and gender traits.
		LO13	Differentiate between biologically and culturally based gender differences.

Key Terms	Video	Animation	Readings	Assessment
gender			A Case of a Boy Being Raised as a Girl	Check Your Learning 3.1
sexual reproduction, gamete, germ cell, autosomes, sex chromosomes, fertilization, zygote, mitosis, gestation, gonads, testes, ovaries, Müllerian duct, Wolffian duct, endocrine glands, estrogen, progesterone, homologous, androgens	Does the father's sperm really determine the sex of the child?	Internal Sex Organs External Sex Organs	The Roles of Sex Hormones	Check Your Learning 3.2
disorders of sex development, Klinefelter syndrome, gynecomastia, Turner syndrome, amenorrhea, congenital adrenal hyperplasia (CAH), androgen-insensitivity syndrome (AIS)			Disorders of Sex Development in Depth	Check Your Learning 3.3
gender roles, gender traits, masculinity, femininity			The Fear of Men	Check Your Learning 3.4

Measure ^Your Learning

 Think Critically 88

Key Terms	Video	Animation	Readings	Assessment
schemas, gender schema		Gender Role Theories		Check Your Learning 3.5
androgyny, gender spectrum, gender diverse, transgender, transyouth, transsexuals, transwomen, transmen, gender dysphoria, queer, genderqueer, gender fluidity, sex reassignment surgery, two-spirits	Why do straight women never give the nice guys a chance? Teo: A Transman Liz: A Transwoman		Transsexuality in Iran	Check Your Learning 3.6
socialization, gender-identity disorder, homosocial play	Early Childhood Gender Roles Middle Childhood Gender Roles Why do so many parents discourage boys from playing with guns?			Check Your Learning 3.7
				Different, But Not Less Than: Toward Gender Equality

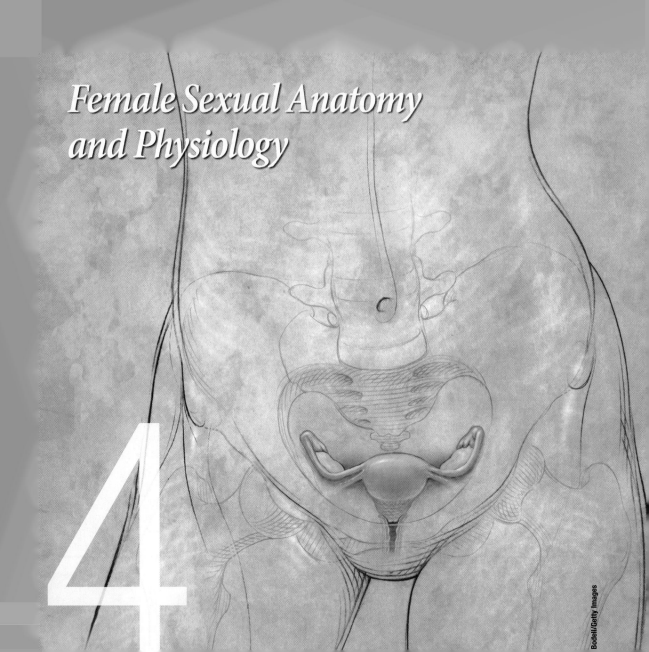

Female Sexual Anatomy and Physiology

4

Prepare to Learn 96

Chapter Pre-Test

Online Activities 97

4.1 External Sexual and Reproductive System 98

LO1 Identify and describe the function of each of the six female external sex organs.

LO2 Identify each of the three structures found in the vestibule.

4.2 Internal Sexual and Reproductive System 102

LO3 Locate and describe the structure and functions of the vagina.

LO4 Locate and describe the structure and functions of the uterus.

LO5 Locate and describe the structure and functions of the Fallopian tubes.

LO6 Locate and describe the structure and functions of the ovaries.

4.3 The Breasts 106

LO7 Describe how the female breasts can be used for infant nourishment as well as an erogenous zone.

4.4 Menstruation 108

LO8 Identify the four phases of the menstrual cycle and summarize the sequence of changes that take place during each phase.

LO9 Define *menopause* and explain why it occurs.

LO10 Identify the purpose, benefits, and potential drawbacks of hormone replacement therapy.

4.5 Menstruation and Lifestyle Issues 112

LO11 Summarize the two main reasons for a woman to consider menstrual manipulation or suppression.

LO12 Summarize the range of attitudes people have about sexual behavior during menstruation.

4.6 Menstrual Concerns and Problems 114

LO13 Differentiate between primary and secondary amenorrhea and give one cause of each.

LO14 Define *dysmenorrhea* and list two or three possible causes.

LO15 List the primary and 1–2 secondary causes of dysfunctional uterine bleeding.

LO16 Differentiate between premenstrual syndrome and premenstrual dysphoric disorder.

4.7 Female Reproductive and Sexual Health Concerns 118

LO17 Define *endometriosis* and discuss risk factors for the development of endometriosis.

LO18 Define *menstrual toxic shock syndrome* and discuss risk factors for the development of menstrual toxic shock syndrome.

LO19 Discuss douching as a risk factor for vaginal infections.

LO20 Identify and describe two female genital pain disorders.

4.8 Cancer of the Female Reproductive Organs 122

LO21 Discuss the importance and primary method of early detection of cervical cancer.

LO22 Identify and explain two or three risk factors for endometrial cancer.

LO23 Explain why ovarian cancer is difficult to detect early.

4.9 Breast Cancer 126

LO24 Discuss the importance of detecting breast cancer early.

LO25 List three key measures for early detection of breast cancer.

LO26 Describe the three approaches to treating breast cancer.

4.10 Female Sexual Health Maintenance 128

LO27 Identify the reasons why proper hygiene is important in women.

LO28 Discuss the importance of genital self-examination.

LO29 Discuss the importance of breast self-examination.

LO30 Discuss the importance of regular gynecological examinations.

Think Critically   132

Measure Your Learning   134

Chapter Post-Test

Prepare ^ to Learn

1 **GO** to your **Psychology CourseMate** at **login.cengagebrain.com** and take the **Chapter Pre-Test** to introduce yourself to this chapter's topics and see what you may already know.

2 **READ** the **Learning Objectives** (LOs, in the left sidebars) and begin the chapter.

3 **COMPLETE** the **Online Activities** (in the right sidebars) *as you read each module.* Activities include **videos, animations, readings,** and **quizzes.**

4 **CHECK Your Learning** by going online to take the quiz at the end of each module and review material as necessary.

5 **MEASURE Your Learning** after reading the chapter by taking the online **Chapter Post-Test.** Use the chapter review guide at the end of the chapter as needed.

WATCH for these **Online Activities** icons as you read:

Video

Animation

Reading

Assessment

Think Critically

These Online Activities are essential to mastering this chapter. Go to login.cengagebrain.com.

 Videos Explore diverse perspectives on sex as well as common questions:

- Is it possible to change the size of my vaginal lips?
- Will I have a problem breastfeeding if I have my nipples pierced?
- Breast Augmentation and Cosmetic Surgery
- First Periods
- Do women who live together really get their periods at the same time every month?
- PMS: Real or Imagined?
- If you have uterine fibroids can you have a baby?
- Breast Cancer Survivor

 Animations Interact with and visualize important processes, timelines, and concepts:

- The External Genital Structures of the Mature Female
- The Female Internal Reproductive System
- Ovulation
- The Female Breast
- Hormonal Control of the Menstrual Cycle
- Feedback Loops During the Menstrual Cycle
- Endometriosis
- Key Terms Exercises

 Readings Delve deeper into key content:

- Discovering the Complete Clitoris
- A Symbol of "Purity"
- Breast Cancer Risk Factors

 Assessment Measure your mastery:

- Chapter Pre-Test
- Check Your Learning Quizzes
- Chapter Post-Test

 Think Critically Challenge your thinking about data and accepted norms:

- Female Genital Mutilation

▶ **LO1** Identify and describe the function of each of the six female external sex organs.

ALL OF THE WOMEN in these photos have "normal" bodies. Individual differences in weight and size and shape of hips, breasts, and thighs, and even pubic hair are normal.

▼

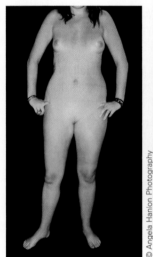
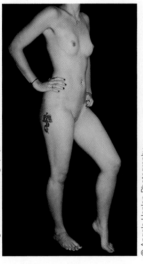
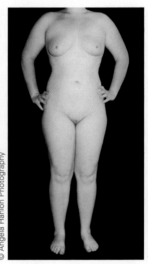

© Angela Hanlon Photography

It may seem surprising that the majority of questions that students ask about human sexuality are fundamental, biological questions. Yet, it becomes less surprising when we realize that many parents are still uncomfortable discussing sexual biology with their children, and younger people often do not know whom to approach or are embarrassed about the questions they have. Questions about sexual biology are natural, however, for the male and female reproductive systems are complex, and there are probably more myths and misinformation about sexual biology than any other single part of human functioning. It is important for both women and men to understand the structure of the female reproductive system, which is really a marvel of biological engineering. In this chapter and in Chapter 5, we explore female and male sexual anatomy and physiology.

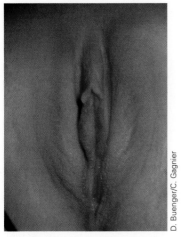
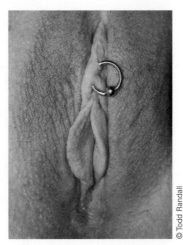
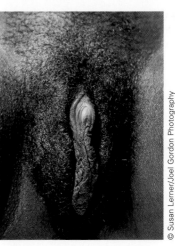

D. Buenger/C. Gagnier

© Todd Randall

© Susan Lerner/Joel Gordon Photography

Although many people refer to the female's external sex organs collectively as the "vagina," this is technically incorrect; the more accurate term for the whole region is vulva. The vulva comes in various sizes and shapes, and the color and quantity of pubic hair vary as well.

The structures that comprise the vulva are the mons veneris, the labia majora and labia minora, the vestibule, the perineum, and the clitoris (see Figure 4.1).

The Mons Veneris

The fatty cushion resting over the front surface of the pubic bone is called the mons veneris or mons pubis. The mons veneris becomes covered with pubic hair after puberty, and although it is considered a stimulating place to caress during lovemaking, it serves largely as a protective cushion for the genitals, especially during sexual activity.

The Labia Majora

The labia majora (LAY-bee-uh muh-JOR-uh) (outer lips) are two longitudinal folds of fatty tissue that extend downward and backward from the mons pubis, frame the rest of the female genitalia, and meet at the perineum (the tissue between the vagina and the anus). The skin of the outer labia majora is pigmented and covered with hair, whereas the inner surface is hairless and contains sebaceous (oil) glands. Dur-

The External Genital Structures of the Mature Female

Take a closer look.

▸ **LO2** Identify each of the three structures found in the vestibule.

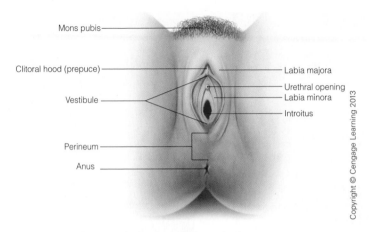

Figure 4.1 The female external reproductive system.

ing sexual excitement, the labia majora fill with blood and engorge, which makes the entire pubic region seem to swell.

The Labia Minora

The labia minora (LAY-bee-uh muh-NOR-uh) (inner lips) are two smaller pink skin folds inside the labia majora that join at the clitoris to form the **prepuce** (PREE-peus), the "hood" over the clitoris. The labia minora contain no hair follicles, although they are rich in sebaceous glands. They also contain some erectile tissue and serve to protect the vagina and urethra.

The Clitoris

prepuce A loose fold of skin that covers the clitoris.

Bartholin's glands A pair of glands on either side of the vaginal opening that open by a duct into the space between the hymen and the labia minora.

hymen A thin fold of vascularized mucous membrane at the vaginal opening.

Homologous to the penis, the clitoris is richly supplied with blood vessels, as well as nerve endings. The clitoral glans is a particularly sensitive receptor and transmitter of sexual stimuli. The body, bulbs, and crura enlarge and engorge with blood in much the same way as the penis does during physical arousal. Unlike the penis, however, the sole function of the clitoris is to bring sexual pleasure.

The clitoral glans is difficult to see in many women unless the prepuce is pulled back, although in some women the glans may swell enough during sexual excitement to emerge from under the prepuce. It is easy to feel the clitoral glans, however, by gently grasping the prepuce and rolling it between the fingers. In fact, most women do not enjoy direct stimulation of the glans and prefer stimulation through the prepuce.

The Vestibule

The vestibule is the name for the entire region between the labia minora. It contains the openings of the urethra and vagina, and the ducts of **Bartholin's glands**. The area of tissue between the vestibule and the anus is called the perineum.

The Urethral Meatus

The opening to the urethra, or urethral meatus, lies between the vagina and the clitoris. The urethra, which is much shorter in women than in men, allows bacteria greater access into the urinary tract, making women much more susceptible to urinary tract infections (UTIs; Azam, 2000; Kunin, 1997). Common symptoms for UTIs include pain or burning in the urethra or bladder and an increased urge to urinate. Antibiotics are necessary to cure the infection, and consuming cranberry products (i.e., drinks, breads) can help reduce the likelihood of UTIs (Epp et al., 2010).

The Introitus

The entrance, or introitus (in-TROID-us), of the vagina also lies in the vestibule. The introitus is usually covered at birth by a fold of tissue known as the **hymen** (HIGH-men). The hymen varies in thickness and extent, and is sometimes absent. The center of the hymen is usually perforated, and it is through this perforation that the menstrual flow leaves the vagina and that a tampon is inserted. If the hymen is intact, it will usually rupture easily and tear at several points when a woman first begins engaging in penetrative sexual behavior. This is often accompanied by a small amount of blood. If the woman is sexually aroused and well lubricated, the rupture of the hymen usually does not cause more than a brief moment's discomfort.

Bartholin's Glands

The "greater vestibular glands," or Bartholin's (BAR-tha-lenz) glands, are bean-shaped glands with ducts that empty into the vestibule in the middle of the labia minora. Historically, Bartholin's glands have been presumed to provide vaginal lubrication during sexual arousal; however, research by Masters and Johnson (see Chapter 1) found that lubrication is a result of vaginal transudation. The Bartholin's glands can become infected and form a cyst or abscess, causing pain and swelling in the labial and vaginal areas. Bartholin gland cysts are most common in women of reproductive age and are typically treated with antibiotics, surgery, or both (Bhide et al., 2010).

Discovering the Complete Clitoris

Eighteen structures, some visible, some not.

A Symbol of "Purity"

The hymen and the virginity myth.

On Your Mind

Is it possible to change the size of my vaginal lips?

Check Your Learning Quiz 4.1

Go to **login.cengagebrain.com** and take the online quiz.

▶ **LO3** Locate and describe the structure and functions of the vagina.

▶ **LO4** Locate and describe the structure and functions of the uterus.

Now that we've covered the female's external sex organs, let's move inside and explore the internal sex organs. These include the vagina, uterus, Fallopian tubes, and ovaries (see Figures 4.2 and 4.3).

The Vagina

The vagina is a thin-walled tube extending from the cervix of the uterus to the external genitalia and serves as the female organ of intercourse, a passageway for the arriving sperm, and a canal through which menstrual fluid and newborns can pass from the uterus. Approximately 4 inches in length when relaxed, the vagina contains numerous folds that allow it to expand to accommodate a penis or dildo during penetration, and it can stretch four to five times its normal size during childbirth.

The vagina does not contain glands but lubricates through small openings on the vaginal walls during engorgement (almost as if the vagina is sweating) and by mucus produced from glands on the cervix. Although the first third of the vaginal

Gräfenberg spot (G-spot) A structure that is said to lie on the anterior (front) wall of the vagina and is reputed to be a seat of sexual pleasure when stimulated.

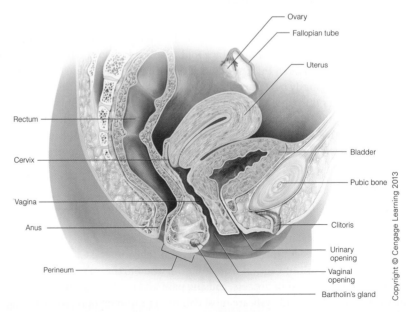

Copyright © Cengage Learning 2013

Figure 4.2 The female internal reproductive system (side view).

ers to compare racial and ethnic differences in the onset of menstruation. On average, menarche age is significantly earlier in Black, non-Hispanic girls than White or Hispanic girls (Chumlea et al., 2003; Freedman et al., 2002; Kaplowitz et al., 2001) and significantly later in Asian girls (Adair & Gordon-Larsen, 2001). In less-developed countries, the age of menarche is later.

In some cultures in the past, as soon as a girl reached menarche, she was considered ready to marry and begin bearing children. In American culture most people believe that there is a difference between being physiologically capable of bearing children and being psychologically ready for sexual intercourse and childbearing.

The Menstrual Cycle

The menstrual cycle lasts from 24 to 35 days, but the average is 28 (meaning there are 28 days from the first day of bleeding to the next first day of bleeding; see Figure 4.5). During the cycle, the lining of the uterus builds up and prepares for a pregnancy. When there is no pregnancy, menstruation occurs, and the lining of the uterus is released in the form of blood and tissue. A cycle of hormones controls the buildup and the release. The biological purpose of menstrual cycles is to enable a woman to become pregnant. The menstrual cycle can be divided into four general phases: follicular, ovulatory, luteal, and menstrual.

The Follicular Phase

The follicular phase begins after the last menstruation has been completed and lasts anywhere from 6 to 13 days. Only a thin layer of endometrial cells remains from the last menstruation. As the follicles in the ovaries begin to ripen with the next cycle's ova, estrogen released by the ovaries stimulates regrowth of the endometrium's outer layer, to about 2 to 5 millimeters in thickness.

The Ovulatory Phase

During the ovulatory phase, an ovum is released, usually about the 14th day of the cycle. The particulars of ovulation have been described in the preceding section on the ovaries and Fallopian tubes.

The Luteal Phase

The third phase of the menstrual cycle is the luteal phase. Immediately after ovulation, a small, pouchlike gland, the **corpus luteum**, forms on the ovary. The corpus luteum secretes additional progesterone and estrogen for 10 to 12 days, which

Hormonal Control of the Menstrual Cycle

See how hormones affect the menstrual and ovarian cycles.

Feedback Loops During the Menstrual Cycle

Take a closer look at underlying functions.

First Periods

Explores teens' reactions and thoughts about menarche.

4.4 Menstruation

▶ **LO9** Define *menopause* and explain why it occurs.

▶ **LO10** Identify the purpose, benefits, and potential drawbacks of hormone replacement therapy.

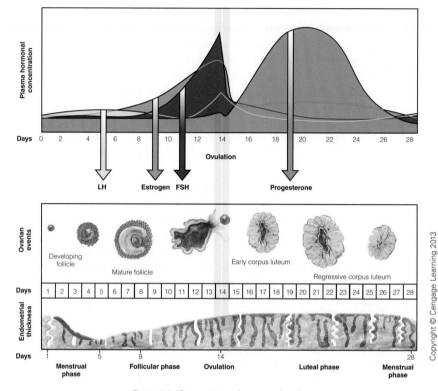

Figure 4.5 The ovarian and menstrual cycles.

menses The blood and tissue discharged from the uterus during menstruation.

anemia A deficiency in the oxygen-carrying material of the blood, often causing symptoms of fatigue, irritability, dizziness, memory problems, shortness of breath, and headaches.

hot flashes A symptom of menopause in which a woman feels sudden heat, often accompanied by a flush.

causes further growth of the cells in the endometrium and increases the blood supply to the lining of the uterus. The endometrium reaches a thickness of 4 to 6 millimeters during this stage (about a quarter of an inch) in preparation to receive and nourish a fertilized egg. If fertilization does not occur, however, the high levels of progesterone and estrogen signal the hypothalamus to decrease LH and other hormone production. The corpus luteum begins to degenerate as LH levels decline. Approximately 2 days before the end of the normal cycle, the secretion of estrogen and progesterone decreases sharply as the corpus luteum becomes inactive, and the menstrual phase begins.

The Menstrual Phase

In the menstrual phase, the endometrial cells shrink and slough off (this flow is referred to as **menses** [MEN-seez]). The uterus begins to contract in an effort to expel the dead tissue together with a small quantity of blood. (It is these contractions that cause menstrual cramps, which can be painful in some women). During menstruation, approximately 35 milliliters of blood, 35 milliliters of fluid, some mucus, and the lining of the uterus (about 2–4 tablespoons of fluid in all) are expelled from the uterine cavity through the cervical os and ultimately the vagina. Some women lose too much blood during their menstruation and may develop **anemia**. Menses usually stops about 3 to 7 days after the onset of menstruation.

Menopause

The term menopause is used to refer to the cessation of menstrual cycling, which typically occurs sometime between the age of 40 and 58 (Steiner et al., 2010). In most cases, menstruation does not stop suddenly. Periods become irregular and intervals between periods become longer.

Decreasing estrogen can lead to several possible adverse effects, including **hot flashes,** forgetfulness, mood swings, sleep disorders, bone loss, menstrual irregularities, vaginal dryness, decreased sexual interest, and joint aches (Pinkerton & Stovall, 2010). However, most American women go through menopause with few problems, and many find it to be a liberating time, signaling the end of their childbearing years and a newfound freedom from contraception.

In the past, hormone replacement therapy (HRT) was used to help maintain vaginal elasticity and lubrication, restore regular sleep patterns, and reduce hot flashes and depression. It was also helpful in decreasing the risks for development of osteoporosis, cardiovascular disease, and colorectal and lung cancers (Brinton & Schairer, 1997; Mahabir et al., 2008; Parry, 2008). However, in 2002, after the publication of results from the Women's Health Initiative that linked HRT to an increased rate of breast cancer, the use of HRT declined significantly.

Today, the use of HRT remains controversial (Pluchino et al., 2011; Yang & Reckelhoff, 2010). Although some health care providers continue to prescribe it for some patients, others have stopped prescribing it altogether; and some prescribe hormone replacement only for those women with severe menopausal symptoms (Tsai et al., 2010).

Check Your Learning Quiz 4.4

Go to **login.cengagebrain.com** and take the online quiz.

▶ **LO11** Summarize the two main reasons for a woman to consider menstrual manipulation or suppression.

▶ **LO12** Summarize the range of attitudes people have about sexual behavior during menstruation.

Sometimes menstruation may come when a woman least wants it to—during examinations, a vacation, or a romantic weekend getaway. This section discusses menstrual manipulation, suppression, and also sexual behavior during menstruation.

Menstrual Manipulation and Suppression

Over the last few years, **menstrual manipulation** has become more popular, and in the future, it is likely that **menstrual suppression** will make periods optional (Hicks & Rome, 2010). Women with painful periods, intense cramps, heavy menses, migraines, premenstrual syndrome (PMS), epilepsy, asthma, rheumatoid arthritis, irritable bowel syndrome, and diabetes all can benefit from menstrual suppression (F. D. Anderson et al., 2006; Freeman, 2008; Merki-Feld et al., 2008; A. L. Nelson, 2007; Stacey, 2008). In addition, menstrual disorders are the number one cause of gynecological disease and affect millions of American women yearly (Clayton, 2008). Some experts suggest that amenorrhea may be healthier than monthly periods because menstrual suppression also avoids the sharp hormonal changes that occur throughout the menstrual cycle.

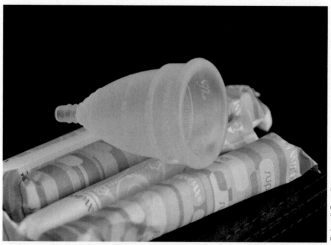

© Janell Carroll

The Diva Cup is a silicone menstrual cup that can be used as an alternative to disposable menstrual products such as tampons.

menstrual manipulation The ability to plan and schedule the arrival of menstruation.

menstrual suppression The elimination of menstrual periods.

Overall, there is no medical evidence that women need to have a monthly menstrual period, and studies conclude that continuous use of U.S. Food and Drug Administration (FDA)–approved pills to stop periods is a safe and effective option for preventing pregnancy and reducing menstrual-related symptoms (Anderson et al., 2006; Merki-Feld et al., 2008; A. L. Nelson, 2007; Stacey, 2008). Users of the new FDA-approved oral contraceptives Seasonale and Seasonique experience only 4 periods a year, compared with the usual 13. Lybrel is taken for 365 days, allowing a woman to stop menstruating altogether.

Although many women are excited about the option of reducing the number of menstrual periods, many other women link having their period with health and fertility. Bleeding has "psychological importance" to many women; it lets a woman know that her body is working the way it should. In fact, abnormal bleeding (spotting or clotting) or an absence of bleeding is an important event that should be reported to a health care provider promptly.

Menstruation and Sexual Behavior

Many cultures have taboos about engaging in sexual intercourse, or any sexual behaviors, during menstruation. Orthodox Jewish women are required to abstain from sexual intercourse for 1 week after their menstrual period. After this time, they engage in a mikvah bath, after which sexual activity can be resumed.

Although many heterosexual couples report avoiding sexual intercourse during menstruation (Hensel et al., 2004), research has found that this might have to do with personal comfort. Heterosexual couples who are more comfortable with their sexuality report higher levels of sexual intercourse during menstruation than couples who are less comfortable (Rempel & Baumgartner, 2003). Menstruation can make things a little messy, so a little preplanning is often needed. Some women use specially designed products, such as the Instead Softcup, to contain menstrual fluid.

Heterosexual and lesbian couples should talk about this issue and decide what they are comfortable with. As mentioned earlier, however, menstrual suppression might make this question obsolete.

On Your Mind

Do women who live together really get their periods at the same time every month?

Check Your Learning Quiz 4.5

Go to **login.cengagebrain.com** and take the online quiz.

Several concerns and problems are associated with menstruation, some common and others less so. This section discusses amenorrhea, dysmenorrhea, dysfunctional uterine bleeding, and PMS.

Amenorrhea

Amenorrhea (Aye-men-oh-REE-uh), the absence of menstruation, can take two forms: In *primary amenorrhea*, a woman never even begins menstruation, whereas in *secondary amenorrhea*, previously normal menses stop before the woman has gone through menopause. Primary amenorrhea may result from malformed or underdeveloped female reproductive organs, glandular disorders, general poor health, emotional factors, or excessive exercise. The most common cause of secondary amenorrhea is pregnancy, although it can also occur with emotional factors, certain diseases, surgical removal of the ovaries or uterus, hormonal imbalance (caused naturally or through the ingestion of steroids), or excessive exercise. It's important for women to maintain a healthy weight, especially those involved in athletics. Sports that require high energy may lead to a significant reduction in body fat, interfering with menstrual regularity. Eating disorders can also lead to amenorrhea. In fact, almost all women with anorexia nervosa experience amenorrhea (Pinheiro et al., 2007). When they regain weight, they often will not begin ovulating and menstruating, and may need drugs to induce ovulation and start their periods again (Ayala, 2009). If amenorrhea persists, a physician should be consulted.

Dysmenorrhea

Menstrual cramps are caused by prostaglandins, which stimulate the uterus to contract and expel the endo-

While regular exercise is a good thing, it's important for female athletes to maintain a healthy weight. Females who significantly reduce their body fat may stop menstruating.

© Todd Randall

metrial lining during menstruation. The uterine muscles are powerful (remember that the muscles help push an infant out at birth), and the menstrual contractions can be strong and sometimes quite painful. Although the majority of women experience mild-to-moderate cramping during menstruation, some experience dysmenorrhea (dis-men-uh-REE-uh), or extremely painful menstruation. Dysmenorrhea may be caused by a variety of inflammations, constipation, or even psychological stress. Poor eating habits, an increase in stress, alcohol use, insufficient sleep, and a lack of exercise can aggravate the problem. Reducing salt, sugar, and caffeine intake; moderate exercise; relaxation; warm baths; yoga; and gentle massage of the lower back sometimes help, as do antiprostaglandin pain relievers, such as ibuprofen. Newer research has found that acupressure may also be effective in reducing dysmenorrhea (Liu et al., 2010; Mirbagher-Ajorpaz et al., 2010).

Dysfunctional Uterine Bleeding

Dysfunctional uterine bleeding includes irregular periods or unusually heavy periods, and is a common complaint among women (Maness et al., 2010). Dysfunctional uterine bleeding is most common in women at both ends of the age spectrum (younger and older women) and typically occurs when the body does not respond to key hormones, such as estrogen and progesterone, resulting in anovulatory cycles (Tibbles, 2009). Causes include stress, excessive exercise, significant weight loss, vaginal injury, hormonal imbalances, and/or chronic illness (Estephan & Sinert, 2010).

Dysfunctional uterine bleeding can affect a woman's quality of life and can lead to both medical and social complications (Frick et al., 2009). Some women suffer from excessive menstrual flow, known as menorrhagia (men-or-RAY-gee-uh). Oral contraceptives may be prescribed to make menses lighter and more regular (Read, 2010).

Premenstrual Syndrome

The term premenstrual syndrome (PMS) refers to physical or emotional symptoms that appear in some women during the latter half of the menstrual cycle. Estimates of the numbers of women who experience PMS vary widely depending on how it is defined, but only a small number of women find it debilitating. Research has found that the majority of women experience emotional, behavioral, or physical premenstrual symptoms (Boyle et al., 1987; Shulman, 2010). Common complaints include feelings of sadness, irritability, restlessness, and sleep problems (including trouble falling asleep and also excessive sleepiness; Strine et al., 2005).

The existence of PMS has been controversial (Knaapen & Weisz, 2008). The term became well-known in the early 1980s when two separate British courts reduced the sentences of women who had killed their husbands on the grounds that severe PMS reduced their capacity to control their behavior (Rittenhouse, 1991). Although this defense never succeeded in a U.S. trial, publicity over the British trials led to much discussion about this syndrome. Some women objected to the idea of PMS, suggesting that it would reinforce the idea that women were "out of control" once a month and were slaves to their biology, whereas others supported it as an important biological justification of the symptoms they were experiencing each month. The extreme views of PMS have been tempered somewhat, and women who suffer from it can now find sympathetic physicians and a number of suggestions for coping strategies.

In 1994, the American Psychiatric Association introduced the diagnosis of premenstrual dysphoric disorder (PMDD), used to identify the most debilitating cases of PMS (Rapkin & Winer, 2008). PMDD will be listed in the DSM-5, the latest guide to accepted disorders of the American Psychiatric Association. It is estimated that approximately 3% to 8% of women meet the criteria for PMDD (Breech & Braverman, 2010; Rapkin et al., 2011).

There are four main groups of PMDD symptoms: mood, behavioral, somatic, and cognitive. Mood symptoms include depression, irritability, mood swings, sadness, and hostility. Behavioral symptoms include becoming argumentative, increased eating, and a decreased interest in activities. Somatic symptoms include abdominal bloating, fatigue, headaches, hot flashes, insomnia, backache, constipation, breast tenderness, and a craving for carbohydrates (Yen et al., 2010). Cognitive symptoms include confusion and poor concentration. PMDD symptoms seem to have both biological and lifestyle components, and so both medication and lifestyle changes can help.

Causes and Treatments of Premenstrual Dysphoric Disorder

While the exact causes for PMDD remains unclear, it is often blamed on physiological factors, such as hormones, neurotransmitters, and brain mechanisms (Shulman, 2010). Hormonal fluctuations are related to mood disorders associated with PMDD, such as depression and hopelessness (Zukov et al., 2010), while neurotransmitters, such as serotonin, have been found to be involved in the expression of irritability, anger, depression, and specific food cravings (Rapkin & Winer, 2008). Brain imaging has revealed that increased activity in certain areas of the brain may also contribute to PMDD (Rapkin et al., 2010).

Once documented, the first treatment for PMS or PMDD usually involves lifestyle changes. Dietary and vitamin/nutritional changes such as decreasing caffeine, salt, and alcohol intake; maintaining a low-fat diet; increasing calcium, magnesium, and vitamin E (to decrease negative mood and fluid retention) and various herbal remedies (such as *vitex agnus castus* [chasteberry]; Dante and Facchinetti, 2010) have been found to be helpful. Stress management, increased regular exercise, improved coping strategies, and drug therapy can also help (Shulman, 2010).

Women who have a history of major depression, post-traumatic stress disorder, sexual abuse, or those who smoke cigarettes tend to be more at risk for developing PMS or PMDD (L. Cohen et al., 2002; Koci, 2004; Wittchen et al., 2002). One of the most promising pharmacological treatments has been the SSRIs, such as fluoxetine (Prozac; Rendas-Baum et al., 2010; Clayton, 2008). Fluoxetine has yielded some promising results in the treatment of PMDD, although it can cause side effects, such as headaches and sexual dysfunction (Carr & Ensom, 2002). Overall, the majority of women who suffer from PMS and PMDD do respond well to treatment.

PMS: Real or Imagined?

Young women and men discuss their thoughts and experiences with premenstrual syndrome (PMS).

Check Your Learning Quiz 4.6

Go to **login.cengagebrain.com** and take the online quiz.

▶ **LO17** Define *endometriosis* and discuss risk factors for the development of endometriosis.

▶ **LO18** Define *menstrual toxic shock syndrome* and discuss risk factors for the development of menstrual toxic shock syndrome.

▶ **LO19** Discuss douching as a risk factor for vaginal infections.

Several conditions can interfere with gynecological health. The most prevalent include endometriosis, toxic shock syndrome, vaginal infections, and genital pain disorders.

Endometriosis

Endometriosis is a common gynecological condition that occurs when endometrial cells begin to migrate to places other than the uterus (Brown et al., 2010). Endometrial cells may implant on any of the reproductive organs or other abdominal organs and then engorge and atrophy every month with the menstrual cycle, just like the endometrium does in the uterus. The disease ranges from mild to severe, and women may experience a range of symptoms or none at all.

Endometriosis is most common in women aged between 25 and 40 years who have never had children; it has been called the "career woman's disease" because it is more common in professional women (Simsir et al., 2001). Women who have not had children and those who experience short and heavy menstrual cycles have also been found to be at greater risk for endometriosis (Vigano et al., 2004). Among women of childbearing age, the estimated prevalence rate of endometriosis is as high as 10%, and among infertile women, between 20% and 40% (Frackiewicz, 2000; Vigano et al., 2004). If you or someone you know has had symptoms of endometriosis, it is important that complaints are taken seriously.

The cause of endometriosis is still unknown, although some have suggested that it is due to retrograde menstrual flow (a process in which parts of the uterine lining are carried backward during the menstrual period into the Fallopian tubes and abdomen; Frackiewicz, 2000; Leyendecker et al., 2004). The symptoms of endometriosis depend on where the endometrial tissue has invaded but commonly include painful menstrual periods, pelvic or lower back pain, and pain during penetrative sex; some women also experience pain on defecation (Prentice, 2001). Symptoms often wax and wane with the menstrual cycle, starting a day or two before menstruation, becoming worse during the period, and gradually decreasing for a day or two afterward. The pain is often sharp and can be mistaken for menstrual cramping. Many women discover their endometriosis when they have trouble becoming pregnant. The endometrial cells can affect fertility by infiltrating the ovaries or Fallopian tubes and interfering with ovulation or ovum transport through the Fallopian tube.

laparoscope A small instrument through which structures within the abdomen and pelvis can be viewed.

douching A method of vaginal rinsing or cleaning that involves squirting water or other solutions into the vagina.

Traditionally, endometriosis is diagnosed through biopsy or the use of a **laparoscope**. Researchers are working on a urine test to aid in diagnosing endometriosis (Tokushige et al., 2011). Treatment consists of hormone therapy, surgery, or laser therapy to try to remove endometrial patches from the organs (Brown et al., 2010). Endometriosis declines during pregnancy and disappears after menopause.

Menstrual Toxic Shock Syndrome

Menstrual toxic shock syndrome (mTSS) is an acute inflammatory disease that develops when *Staphylococcus aureus* bacteria are allowed to grow in the vagina. It is most commonly associated with the use of high-absorbency tampons and forgetting to remove a tampon, which becomes a breeding ground for bacteria.

Menstrual toxic shock syndrome is a fast-developing disease that can cause multiple organ failure. Symptoms of mTSS usually include fever, sore throat, diarrhea, vomiting, muscle ache, and a scarlet-colored rash. It may progress rapidly from dizziness or fainting to respiratory distress, kidney failure, shock, and heart failure, and can be fatal if medical attention is not received immediately.

Despite the risks, it is estimated that more than 70% of women in the United States, Canada, and much of Western Europe use tampons during their periods (Parsonnet et al., 2005). Although any woman who uses tampons is at risk for development of mTSS, Black women have been found to be more susceptible than White women (Parsonnet et al., 2005). Regularly removing tampons and using less absorbent tampons or using only pads reduces the risk for development of mTSS. Ongoing research continues to explore whether the addition of various fibers to tampons can decrease the risk for mTSS (Strandberg et al., 2009).

Vaginal Infections

Concern about vaginal odor and cleanliness is typically what drives women to use a variety of feminine hygiene products. However, not all of these products are safe. For example, **douching** may put a woman at risk for vaginal infections because it changes the vagina's pH levels and can destroy healthy bacteria. A delicate balance in the levels of good and bad bacteria in the vagina is necessary to maintain an acidic environment. Many health care providers, as well as the American College of Obstetricians and Gynecologists, recommend that women do not douche.

Endometriosis

Learn about causes and treatments.

▶ **LO20** Identify and describe two female genital pain disorders.

In fact, numerous kinds of infections can afflict the female genital system. Some are sexually transmitted, and they are discussed in Chapter 12. However, some infections of the female reproductive tract are not necessarily sexually transmitted. For example, as we discussed earlier in this chapter, the Bartholin's glands and the urinary tract can become infected, just as any area of the body can become infected when bacteria get inside and multiply. These infections may happen because of certain hygiene practices and are more frequent in those who engage in frequent sexual intercourse. When infected, the glands can swell and cause pressure and discomfort, and can interfere with walking, sitting, or sexual intercourse. Usually a physician will need to drain the infected glands with a catheter and will prescribe a course of antibiotics (H. Blumstein, 2001).

Polycystic Ovarian Syndrome

Polycystic ovarian syndrome (PCOS) is an endocrine disorder that affects approximately 7% of premenopausal women worldwide (Diamanti-Kandarakis, 2007). PCOS causes cyst formation on the ovaries during puberty, which causes estrogen levels to decrease and androgen levels (including testosterone) to increase. A girl with PCOS typically experiences irregular or absent menstruation; a lack of ovulation; excessive body and facial hair or hair loss; obesity; acne, oily skin, or dandruff; infertility; or any combination of these. Many women with PCOS experience fertility issues, and research is ongoing to find ways to help them achieve successful pregnancies (Nader, 2010).

Uterine Fibroids

pubococcygeus muscle A muscle that surrounds and supports the vagina.

dilators A graduated series of metal rods used in the treatment of vaginismus.

vulvar vestibulitis syndrome Syndrome that causes pain and burning in the vaginal vestibule and often occurs during sexual intercourse, tampon insertion, gynecological examinations, bicycle riding, and wearing tight pants.

Uterine fibroids are noncancerous growths that occur in the myometrium layer of the uterus. It is estimated that 3 out of 4 women have uterine fibroids but because of the lack of symptoms, many women are unaware of them. If there are symptoms, a woman might experience pelvic pain and pressure, constipation, abdominal tenderness or bloating, frequent urination, heavy cramping, prolonged or heavy bleeding, and/or painful penetrative sex. It is important to point out that the majority of uterine fibroids are not cancerous and do not cause any problems.

Vulvodynia

At the beginning of the 21st century, many physicians were unaware that a condition known as vulvodynia (vull-voe-DY-nia) existed. Vulvodynia refers to chronic vulval pain and soreness, and it's estimated that 16% of women experience such pain (Danby and Margesson, 2010). Although a burning sensation is the most common symptom, women also report itching, burning, rawness, stinging, or stabbing vaginal/vulval pain (Danby and Margesson, 2010; Goldstein & Burrows, 2008). Pain can be either intermittent or constant and can range from mildly disturbing to completely disabling. Over the years, many women with vulvodynia were undiagnosed and left untreated because of a lack of understanding about the condition (Groysman, 2010). Because of this, women who suffer from vulvodynia experienced high levels of psychological distress and depression (Danby and Margesson, 2010; Jelovsek et al., 2008; Plante & Kamm, 2008).

Genital Pain Disorders

The *Diagnostic and Statistical Manual of Mental Disorders* is revising the terminology of genital pain disorders, and it is likely they will all be subsumed under one category and referred to as *genito-pelvic pain/penetration disorders* in the DSM-5. Historically, genital pain disorders have included vaginismus (vadg-ih-NISS-muss) and dyspareunia (diss-par-ROON-ee-uh).

Vaginismus involves involuntary contractions of the **pubococcygeus** (pub-oh-cock-SIGH-gee-us) **muscle,** which can make vaginal penetration impossible (Ozdemir et al., 2008). Past studies have found both physical and psychological causes for vaginismus, and women with strong conservative values or a history of sexual abuse have been found to be at increased risk (Borg et al., 2011). Women with insecure childhood attachments are more susceptible to pain during intercourse (Granot et al., 2011). **Dilators** are often used to help open and relax the vaginal muscles.

Dyspareunia involves slight to extreme pain before, during, or after sexual behavior. Physical and psychological issues may contribute to pain; therefore, a full diagnosis from a health professional is imperative. Chronic pain in the vulva, or vulvodynia, can be another cause of dyspareunia. **Vulvar vestibulitis** (vess-tib-u-LITE-is) **syndrome,** a type of vulvodynia, is considered one of the most common causes of dyspareunia today (Perrigouard et al., 2008).

Check Your Learning Quiz 4.7

Go to **login.cengagebrain.com** and take the online quiz.

▶ **LO21** Discuss the importance and primary method of early detection of cervical cancer.

▶ **LO22** Identify and explain two or three risk factors for endometrial cancer.

▶ **LO23** Explain why ovarian cancer is difficult to detect early.

Cancer is a disease in which certain cells in the body do not function properly—they divide too quickly or produce excessive tissue that forms a tumor, or both. A number of cancers can affect the female reproductive organs. This section examines uterine and ovarian cancers.

Uterine Cancer

Different types of cancer can affect the uterus. Here we discuss cervical, endometrial, and ovarian cancers.

Cervical Cancer

The American Cancer Society estimated that there were approximately 12,200 new cases of cervical cancer in the United States in 2010. The rates of cervical cancer have decreased over the past several decades. A Pap smear, taken during routine pelvic examinations, can detect early changes in the cervical cells, which may indicate cervical cancer. Early diagnosis can lead to more effective treatment and higher cure rates. During a Pap smear, a few cells are painlessly scraped from the cervix and are examined under a microscope for abnormalities. The majority of cervical cancers develop slowly, so if a woman has regular Pap tests, nearly all cases can be successfully treated (American Cancer Society, 2010).

Causes and Symptoms

The main cause of cervical cancer is an infection with certain types of human papillomavirus (HPV), which is discussed further in Chapter 12. Women who begin having sex at a young age or who have multiple sex partners are at an increased risk for HPV infection and cervical cancer (American Cancer Society, 2010). In addition, long-term use of birth control pills and cigarette smoking are also associated with an increased risk for cervical cancer.

Unfortunately, few symptoms are associated with cervical cancer until the later stages of the disease. When the cervical cells become cancerous and invade nearby cells, a woman may experience abnormal bleeding during the month, after penetrative sex, or after a pelvic examination.

Treatment

Cervical cancer has high cure rates because it starts as an easily identifiable lesion, called a cervical intraepithelial neoplasia, which usually progresses slowly into cervical cancer. Better early detection of cervical cancer has led to a sharp decrease in

hysterectomy The surgical removal of the uterus.

dilation and curettage (D&C) The surgical scraping of the uterine wall with a spoon-shaped instrument.

the numbers of serious cervical cancer cases. For some poor or uninsured women in the United States and for many women abroad, routine pelvic examinations and Pap smears are not available. It is for this reason that approximately 80% of the 500,000 new cases of cervical cancer are diagnosed every year in poor countries such as sub-Saharan Africa and Latin America (Nebehay, 2004).

Cervical lesions can be treated with surgery, radiation, chemotherapy, or a combination of these treatments, which has resulted in cure rates up to 90% in early-stage disease and a dramatic decline in mortality rate for cervical cancer. If the disease has progressed, treatment commonly includes a **hysterectomy** followed by radiation and chemotherapy. The FDA has approved two vaccines for the prevention of most types of HPV that cause cervical cancer: Gardasil and Cervarix (see Chapter 12 for further discussion of these vaccines).

Endometrial Cancer

The American Cancer Society estimated that there were approximately 43,500 new cases of uterine cancer in 2010, most of which involved the endometrial lining. Incidence rates have been decreasing over the last few years. Symptoms include abnormal uterine bleeding or spotting and pain during urination or penetrative sex. Because a Pap smear is rarely effective in detecting early endometrial cancer, a **dilation and curettage (D&C)** is more reliable. Endometrial cancer is typically treated with surgery, radiation, hormones, and chemotherapy, depending on the stage of the disease.

Causes and Treatments

Estrogen is a risk factor for endometrial cancer. Women who have been exposed to high levels of estrogen for HRTs, those who are overweight, experienced late menopause, never had children, or who have a history of polycystic ovarian syndrome are at increased risk for endometrial cancer (American Cancer Society, 2010). Because unexpected and heavy bleeding are possible indications of endometrial cancer, women who experience changes in menstrual bleeding should report this to their health care providers. If detected at an early stage, endometrial cancer has high survival rates (American Cancer Society, 2010).

Ovarian Cancer

The American Cancer Society estimated there were approximately 22,000 new cases of ovarian cancer in 2010. Ovarian cancer is more common in northern European and North American countries than in Asia or developing countries. Overall rates

On Your Mind

If you have uterine fibroids can you have a baby?

of ovarian cancer have been decreasing over the last few years. Although not as common as uterine or breast cancer, ovarian cancer causes more deaths than any other cancer of the female reproductive system because it invades the body silently, with few warning signs or symptoms until it reaches an advanced stage (American Cancer Society, 2010). Because the ovary floats freely in the pelvic cavity, a tumor can grow undetected without producing many noticeable symptoms (i.e., there is little pressure on other organs).

Causes and Symptoms

Although few symptoms of ovarian cancer exist, some women experience abdominal bloating, pelvic pain, difficulty eating or feeling full quickly, and an increased need to urinate (American Cancer Society, 2010). Because these symptoms are similar to other conditions (such as irritable bowel syndrome), it is important for a woman to check with her health care provider should she experience such symptoms for more than a week or two. The most important factor in the survival rate from ovarian cancer is early detection and diagnosis. It is estimated that two thirds of cases of ovarian cancer are diagnosed late (Mantica, 2005). A woman in whom an ovarian lump is detected need not panic, however, for most lumps turn out to be relatively harmless **ovarian cysts**.

The cause of ovarian cancer is unknown. Like other cancers, an increased incidence is found in women who have not had children, undergo early menopause, or eat a high-fat diet. Women who are lactose-intolerant or who use talc powder (especially on the vulva) have also been found to have higher rates of ovarian cancer. Women who take birth control pills, who were pregnant at an early age, or who had several pregnancies have particularly low rates of ovarian cancer. One study demonstrated that women who undergo tubal ligation (have their tubes tied to prevent pregnancy) also reduce the risk for ovarian cancer (Narod et al., 2001).

Treatment

Although no 100% accurate test for ovarian cancer is available, health care providers can use blood tests, pelvic examinations, and ultrasound to screen for the cancer. Women who are at high risk for ovarian cancer may be given an ultrasound and pelvic examination, along with a CA-125 blood test. However, some controversy exists over the usefulness of these tests, because they have fairly high false negatives (Mantica, 2005; Rettenmaier et al., 2010; U.S. Preventive Services Task Force, 2005).

ovarian cysts Small, fluid-filled sacs, which can form on the ovary, that do not pose a health threat under most conditions.

This is why many women with ovarian cancer are diagnosed after the cancer has spread beyond the ovary.

Treatment for ovarian cancer is removal of the ovaries and possibly the Fallopian tubes and uterus. Chemotherapy may also be used. In women who have not yet had children, the uterus may be spared, although chemotherapy is more successful after these have been removed (American Cancer Society, 2010).

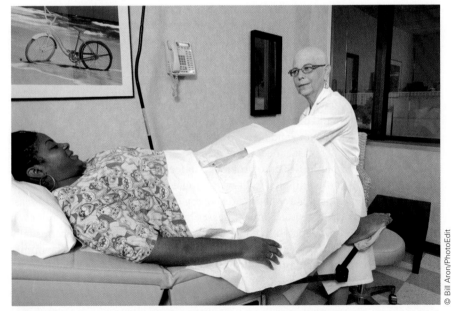

During a pelvic examination, a woman lies on her back with her feet in stirrups. A speculum is used during the pelvic exam to view the cervix.

© Bill Aron/PhotoEdit

Check Your Learning Quiz 4.8

Go to **login.cengagebrain.com** and take the online quiz.

Breast cancer is one of the most common cancers among American women and the second leading cause of cancer death in women, after lung cancer (American Cancer Society, 2010). The American Cancer Society estimated that approximately 207,100 new cases of invasive breast cancer occurred in the United States in 2010. However, after continuously increasing for more than two decades, the breast cancer rates among American women have been decreasing over the past few years. This may be because of a reduction in the use of HRT, which was discussed earlier in this chapter.

Measures for Early Detection

There is no known way to prevent breast cancer; however, the sooner it is detected, the more successfully it can be treated. Therefore, it is extremely important to detect it as early as possible. Every woman should regularly perform breast self-examinations (BSEs), especially after age 35. In addition, women should have their breasts examined during routine gynecological checkups, which is a good time to ask for instruction on self-examination if you have any questions about the technique.

Another important preventive measure is **mammography**, which can detect, on average, 80% to 90% of breast cancer in women without symptoms (American Cancer Society, 2010). Mammography can detect cancer at early stages when treatment is more effective and cures are more likely (Narod, 2011). The American Cancer Society advises women to have regular mammograms taken, beginning at the age of 40. However, you should discuss with your health care provider whether mammography is appropriate for you, and if so, how often.

The earliest sign of breast cancer is often an abnormality seen on a mammogram before a woman or her health care provider can feel it. However, sometimes there are symptoms, including nipple discharge, changes in nipple shape, and skin dimpling. It should be noted here that the discovery of a lump or mass in your breast does not mean you have cancer; most masses are benign, and many do not even need treatment. If it is malignant and left untreated, however, breast cancer usually spreads throughout the body, which is why it is important that any lump be immediately brought to the attention of your physician or other medical practitioner.

Treatment

In the past, women with breast cancer usually had a **radical mastectomy**. Today, few women need such drastic surgery. More often, a partial or modified mastectomy is performed, which leaves many of the underlying muscles and lymph nodes in

mammography A procedure for internal imaging of the breasts to evaluate breast disease or screen for breast cancer.

radical mastectomy A surgical procedure that involves removal of the breast, its surrounding tissue, the muscles supporting the breast, and underarm lymph nodes.

radiation A procedure that uses high-energy radiation to kill cancer cells by damaging their DNA.

chemotherapy A procedure that uses chemicals to kill rapidly dividing cancer cells.

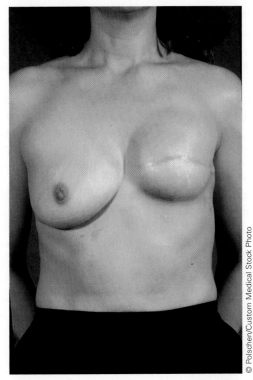

Partial or modified mastectomies are more common today than radical mastectomies.

place. If the breast must be removed, many women choose to undergo breast reconstruction, in which a new breast is formed from existing skin and fat or breast implants (Bellino et al., 2010).

If it appears that the tumor has not spread, a lumpectomy may be considered. A lumpectomy involves the removal of the tumor, together with some surrounding tissue, but the breast is left intact. Survival rates from lumpectomies are similar to the rates for mastectomies (American Cancer Society, 2010). **Radiation, chemotherapy,** or both are often used in conjunction with these surgeries.

Breast Cancer Survivor

A survivor discusses her journey though the discovery and treatments for breast cancer.

Breast Cancer Risk Factors

Genetics, environment, and other possible causes.

Check Your Learning Quiz 4.9

Go to **login.cengagebrain.com** and take the online quiz.

Female Hygiene

Although many women might believe that it is necessary to thoroughly wash the vagina with soap or various fragranced cleaning products, this is not true. In fact, these products are extremely drying and can strip beneficial oils from the vagina, leading to irritation, dryness, or both. Frequent bubble baths can also contribute to vaginal irritation. Experts recommend using only water to rinse out the vaginal area. By spreading the labia, the clitoral area can be gently rinsed. A pasty, white substance, known as smegma, may accumulate around the clitoris. This substance consists of epidermal cells that collect in moist areas of the genitals, especially under the clitoral hood in women. If this area is not properly cleaned, a buildup of smegma can cause itching and irritation.

It is also important for women to be aware of the fact that certain types of toilet paper contain chemicals that can irritate the vagina (Majerovich et al., 2010). Bisphenol A and formaldehyde have both been found in various types of toilet paper, and these chemicals can cause significant vaginal dryness and irritation when used excessively (and may be related to the development of various cancers; Gehring et al., 2006). Women who experience chronic vulvar irritation should be checked by a health care provider and might also benefit from using unbleached toilet paper and avoiding using soap in the vaginal area.

Female Genital Self-Examination

Many female health problems can be identified when changes are detected in the internal or external sexual organs; therefore, self-examination has an important health function as well. If you are female, it will serve you well to follow this simple procedure once a month. If you are male, understanding this procedure will help you better understand why it is so important for females to examine their genitals regularly.

Begin by examining the outside of your genitals; using a hand mirror can help. Using your fingers to spread open the labia majora, try to identify the other external structures—the labia minora, the prepuce, the introitus (opening) of the vagina, and the urethral opening. Look at the way your genitals look while sitting, lying down, standing up, squatting. Feel the different textures of each part of the vagina, and look carefully at the coloration and size of the tissues you can see. Both coloration and size can change with sexual arousal, but such changes are temporary, and the genitals should return to normal within a couple of hours after sexual activity.

Key Terms	Video	Animation	Readings	Assessment
amenorrhea, dysmenorrhea, dysfunctional uterine bleeding, menorrhagia, premenstrual syndrome (PMS), premenstrual dysphoric disorder (PMDD), hot flashes	PMS: Real or Imagined?			Check Your Learning 4.6
endometriosis, laparoscope, menstrual toxic shock syndrome (mTSS), douching, vaginismus, dyspareunia, pubococcygeus muscle, dilators, vulvodynia, vulvar vestibulitis syndrome		Endometriosis		Check Your Learning 4.7
cervical intraepithelial neoplasia, hysterectomy, dilation and curettage (D&C), polycystic ovarian syndrome, ovarian cysts, false negatives	If you have uterine fibroids can you have a baby?			Check Your Learning 4.8
mammography, benign, malignant, radical mastectomy, lumpectomy, radiation, chemotherapy	Breast Cancer Survivor		Breast Cancer Risk Factors	Check Your Learning 4.9
smegma, speculum, Papanicolaou (Pap) smear		Key Terms Exercise		Check Your Learning 4.10
				Female Genital Mutilation

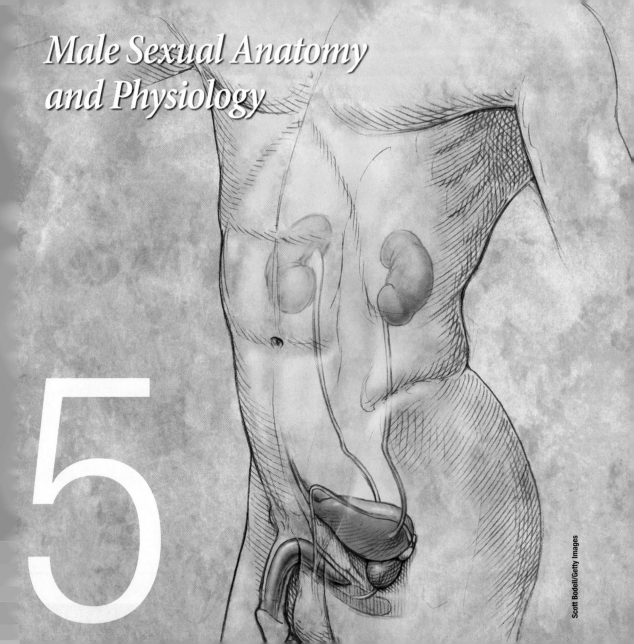

Male Sexual Anatomy and Physiology

5

Prepare to Learn 140

Chapter Pre-Test

Online Activities 141

5.1 External Sexual and Reproductive System 142

LO1 Identify and locate the two external sex organs of the human male.

LO2 Identify and locate the cylinders in the penis responsible for erection.

LO3 Identify and locate the three parts of the glans penis.

LO4 Summarize the role of blood flow in the process of penile erection.

LO5 Describe the effects of temperature on sperm production and the role of the scrotum in temperature regulation.

5.2 Internal Sexual and Reproductive System 148

LO6 Identify and locate the six internal male sex organs.

LO7 Identify the two organs involved in spermatogenesis.

LO8 Describe the process of spermatogenesis.

LO9 Identify and locate the seven organs involved in the ejaculatory pathway.

LO10 Describe the process of ejaculation and the composition of the ejaculate.

5.3 Male Maturation 154

LO11 Identify the two main functions of the testes and describe the feedback system that regulates male hormone and sperm production.

LO12 Summarize the changes to the male reproductive system that occur with puberty.

LO13 Summarize the changes to the male reproductive system that occur with age.

5.4 Male Reproductive and Sexual Health Concerns 156

LO14 Identify four disorders of the male reproductive organs and describe the main symptoms of each of these disorders.

LO15 Compare the perceived benefits and risks of anabolic-androgenic steroid use.

5.5 Cancer of the Male Reproductive Organs 160

LO16 Identify the three main cancers of the male reproductive organs and the primary symptoms of each.

LO17 Define and differentiate between benign prostatic hypertrophy and prostate cancer.

5.6 Male Sexual Health Maintenance 164

LO18 Identify the reasons why proper hygiene is important in men.

LO19 Explain the importance of testicular self-examination.

Think Critically 166

 Measure Your Learning 168

Chapter Post-Test

Prepare to Learn

1 **GO** to your **Psychology CourseMate** at **login.cengagebrain.com** and take the **Chapter Pre-Test** to introduce yourself to this chapter's topics and see what you may already know.

2 **READ** the **Learning Objectives** (LOs, in the left sidebars) and begin the chapter.

3 **COMPLETE** the **Online Activities** (in the right sidebars) *as you read each module.* Activities include **videos, animations, readings,** and **quizzes.**

4 **CHECK Your Learning** by going online to take the quiz at the end of each module and review material as necessary.

5 **MEASURE Your Learning** after reading the chapter by taking the online **Chapter Post-Test.** Use the chapter review guide at the end of the chapter as needed.

WATCH for these **Online Activities** icons as you read:

Video

Animation

Reading

Assessment

Think Critically

These Online Activities are essential to mastering this chapter. Go to login.cengagebrain.com:

 Videos Explore diverse perspectives on sex as well as common questions:

- Close Up: Growing Up Male
- Why do guys wake up with erections?
- Laptops and Sperm Quality
- Does what a guy eats actually affect the taste of his cum?
- Would it hurt a guy if he didn't cum regularly?
- Is it possible for a guy to have an orgasm without an ejaculation?
- Fighting Against Aging
- If a guy's penis curves to the right, does this mean he masturbated a lot as a kid?
- Don't Die Young
- Can a man who has been treated for testicular cancer still have children?

 Animations Interact with and visualize important processes, timelines, and concepts:

- The Internal Structure of the Penis
- The Male Reproductive Organs
- Hormones and the Male Reproductive System
- Internal Structure of the Testicle
- Spermatogenesis
- Ejaculatory Pathway
- Parts of a Sperm
- Testicular Descent
- Testicular Torsion
- Key Terms Exercise

 Readings Delve deeper into key content:

- Sperm, Toxins, Cell Phones, and Tofu
- Lance Armstrong's Battle with Testicular Cancer

 Assessment Measure your mastery:

- Chapter Pre-Test
- Check Your Learning Quizzes
- Chapter Post-Test

 Think Critically Challenge your thinking about data and accepted norms:

- Ethnicity, Religion, and Circumcision

▶ **LO1** Identify and locate the two external sex organs of the human male.

▶ **LO2** Identify and locate the cylinders in the penis responsible for erection.

THE PREVIOUS CHAPTER discussed female anatomy and physiology, and although there are many similarities between female and male anatomy, there are also many important differences. One obvious difference is the fact that the male gonads (the testes) lie outside of the body, whereas the female gonads (ovaries) are located deep within the abdomen. Because of the location of the male genitalia, boys are often more comfortable and familiar with their genitalia compared with girls. This chapter explores the male reproductive system, maturation, and sexual health issues.

▼

The external sex organs of the male include the penis (which consists of the glans and root) and the scrotum. This section discusses these organs and the process of penile erection.

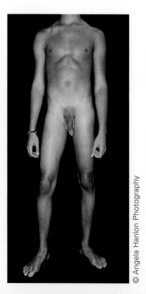

© Angela Hanlon Photography

© Angela Hanlon Photography

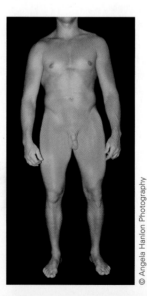

© Angela Hanlon Photography

© Angela Hanlon Photography

The Penis

The penis is the male sexual organ. It contains the urethra, which carries urine and semen to the outside of the body (see Figure 15.1a). The penis has the ability to engorge with blood and erect and has been defined as the symbol of male sexuality throughout history. Men have often been plagued by concerns about penis function and size—especially size. Many men assume that there is a correlation between penis size and masculinity, or sexual prowess, and many men assume that their partners prefer a large penis. Others worry about their size and fear that they are not "normal." Although there may be a psychological preference for large penises among some partners (just as some partners desire women with large breasts), penis size has no correlation with the ability to excite a partner sexually during sex.

The average flaccid penis is between 3 and 4 inches long, and the average erect penis is 6 inches. Gary Griffen, the author of *Penis Size and Enlargement,* has found that only 15% of men have an erect penis measuring over 7 inches, and fewer than 5,000 erect penises worldwide measure 12 inches (Griffen, 1995). In the end, penis size has been found to be largely dependent on heredity—fathers' penis sizes correlate well with their sons' (T. Hamilton, 2002).

The opinion most men have that the average penis size is greater than it really is comes from pornographic films (which tend to use the largest men they can find); from men's perspective on their own penis (which, from the top, looks smaller than from the sides); and from overestimates of actual penis size (researchers consistently find that people's estimation of the size of penises they have just seen is exaggerated; Shamloul, 2005).

It is erroneous beliefs such as these that cause some men to be anxious about their penis size. Some succumb to the advertisements for devices promising to enlarge their penises. Men who purchase these devices are bound to be disappointed, for there is no nonsurgical way to enlarge the penis, and many of these techniques (most of which use suction) can do significant damage to the delicate penile tissue (D. Bagley, 2005). Other men with size anxiety refrain from sex altogether, fearing they cannot please a partner or will be laughed at when their partner sees them naked. Yet the vast majority of women and men report that penis size is not a significant factor in the quality of a sex partner.

Close Up: Growing Up Male

Conversation with a young man about masculinity and pressures related to penis size.

▸ **LO3** Identify and locate the three parts of the glans penis.

▸ **LO4** Summarize the role of blood flow in the process of penile erection.

▸ **LO5** Describe the effects of temperature on sperm production and the role of the scrotum in temperature regulation.

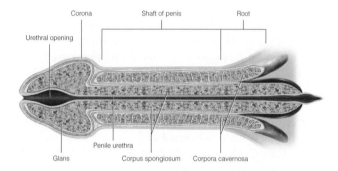

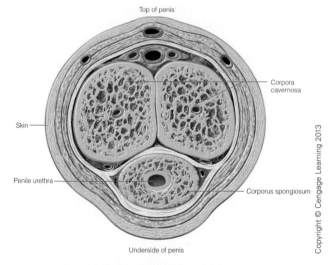

Figure 5.1 The internal structure of the penis.

semen A thick, whitish secretion of the male reproductive organs, containing spermatozoa and secretions from the seminal vesicles, prostate, and bulbourethral glands.

corpora cavernosa Plural of corpus cavernosum (cavernous body); areas in the penis that fill with blood during erection.

corpus spongiosum Meaning "spongy body," the erectile tissue in the penis that contains the urethra.

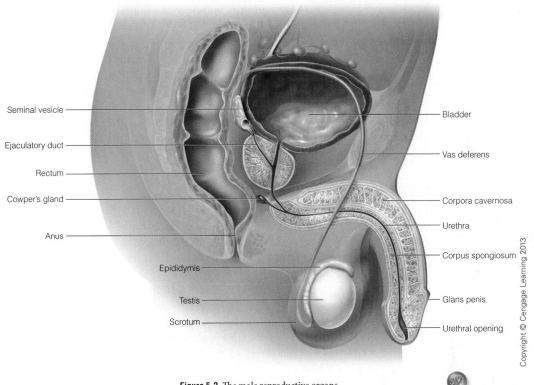

Seminal vesicle

Ejaculatory duct

Rectum

Cowper's gland

Anus

Epididymis

Testis

Scrotum

Bladder

Vas deferens

Corpora cavernosa

Urethra

Corpus spongiosum

Glans penis

Urethral opening

Figure 5.2 The male reproductive organs.

The Internal Structure of the Penis

Side and front cross-sections.

The Male Reproductive Organs

Take a closer look.

On Your Mind

Why do guys wake up with erections?

The Root

The root of the penis enters the body just below the pubic bone and is attached to internal pelvic muscles. The root of the penis goes farther into the body than most men realize; it can be felt in the perineum (between the scrotum and anus), particularly when the penis is erect.

Although there is no bone and little muscle in the human penis, the root of the penis is attached to a number of muscles that help eject **semen** and allow men to move the penis slightly when erect.

The root of the penis is composed of three cylinders, each containing erectile tissue—spongelike tissue that fills with blood to cause erection. Two lateral **corpora cavernosa** lie on the upper sides of the penis, and the central **corpus spongiosum** lies on the bottom and contains the urethra (see Figure 15.1b). The three are bound together with connective tissue to give the outward appearance of a single cylinder and are permeated by blood vessels and spongy tissues that fill with blood when the penis is erect.

The Glans Penis

The corpus spongiosum ends in a conelike expansion called the *glans penis* (see Figures 5.1a and 5.2). The **glans penis** is made up of the **corona**, the **frenulum**, and the **urethral opening**, or **meatus**. The glans is very sensitive to stimulation, and some males find direct or continuous stimulation of the glans irritating.

The prepuce of the glans penis is a circular fold of skin usually called the foreskin. The foreskin is a continuation of the loose skin that covers the penis as a whole to allow it to grow during erection. The foreskin can cover part or all of the glans and retracts back over the corona when the penis is erect. In many cultures, the foreskin is removed surgically through a procedure called a circumcision.

Erection

Erections can occur with any form of stimulation the individual perceives as sexual—visual, tactile, auditory, olfactory, or cognitive. In addition, involuntary sleep-related erections occur several times each night in healthy men (Hirshkowitz and Schmidt, 2005). During an erection nerve fibers swell the arteries of the penis, allowing blood to rush into the corpora cavernosa and corpus spongiosum, while veins are compressed to prevent the blood from escaping. The erectile tissues thus will fill with blood, causing the penis to become erect. The penis returns to its flaccid state when the arteries constrict, the pressure closing off the veins is released, and the sequestered blood is allowed to drain. Drugs for erectile dysfunction, such

glans penis The flaring, enlarged region at the end of the penis.

corona The ridge of the glans penis.

frenulum Fold of skin on the underside of the penis.

urethral opening (or meatus) The opening of the penis through which urine and semen are expelled.

as Viagra, work in a similar way by regulating blood flow in the penis and inhibiting blood loss (Eardley, 2010).

Erection is basically a spinal reflex, and men who have spinal injuries can sometimes achieve reflex erections, in which their penis becomes erect even though they can feel no sensation there. These erections generally occur without cognitive or emotional excitement.

The Scrotum

The scrotum is a loose, wrinkled pouch beneath the penis, covered with sparse pubic hair. The scrotum contains the testicles, each in a sac, separated by a thin layer of tissue. Chapter 4 discussed how a woman's gonads (the ovaries) are located in her abdomen. This is different from the male gonads (the testicles), which sit outside the body. This is because the production and survival of sperm require a temperature that is a few degrees lower than the body's temperature, so the scrotum is actually a kind of cooling tank for the testicles.

When the testicles become too hot, sperm production is halted; in fact, soaking the testicles in hot water has been used as a form of birth control. (Of course, such a technique is highly unreliable, and it takes only a few hardy sperm to undo an hour of uncomfortable soaking. I do not recommend you try it!) Likewise, after a prolonged fever, sperm production may be reduced for as long as 2 months. It has also been suggested that men who are trying to impregnate their partner wear loose-fitting underwear, because tight jockstraps or briefs have been shown to reduce sperm counts somewhat, although the effects are reversible (Shafik, 1991).

The scrotum is designed to regulate testicular temperature using two mechanisms. First, the skin overlying the scrotum contains many sweat glands and sweats freely, which cools the testicles when they become too warm. Second, the cremaster muscle of the scrotum contracts and expands: When the testicles become too cool, they are drawn closer to the body to increase their temperature; when they become too warm, they are lowered away from the body to reduce their temperature. Men often experience the phenomenon of having the scrotum relax and hang low when taking a warm shower, only to tighten up when cold air hits it after exiting the shower. The scrotum also contracts and elevates the testicles in response to sexual arousal, which may be to protect the testicles from injury during sexual behavior.

Laptops and Sperm Quality

Learn about findings that heat from laptops can affect sperm quality in men.

Check Your Learning Quiz 5.1

Go to **login.cengagebrain.com** and take the online quiz.

▶ **LO6** Identify and locate the six internal male sex organs.

▶ **LO7** Identify the two organs involved in spermatogenesis.

▶ **LO8** Describe the process of spermatogenesis.

The internal sex organs of the male include the testes, epididymis, vas deferens, seminal vesicles, prostate gland, and Cowper's glands. All of these organs play important roles in testosterone production, spermatogenesis, and the process of ejaculation.

Testosterone Production

Testosterone is produced in the testicles in the Leydig or interstitial cells and is synthesized from cholesterol. Testosterone is the most important male hormone; we discuss its role when we examine male puberty later in this chapter.

Spermatogenesis

Spermatogenesis is the process by which sperm is produced. Before we look at the process, we will consider the organs involved in the process.

Organs Involved in Spermatogenesis

The two organs involved in the process of spermatogenesis are the testicles and the epididymis (see Figure 5.3). The testicles (also referred to as the testes) are egg-shaped glands that rest in the scrotum, each about 2 inches long and 1 inch in diameter. The left testicle usually hangs lower than the right in most men (T. Hamilton, 2002), although this can be reversed in left-handed men. Having one testicle lower than the other helps one slide over the other instead of crushing together when compressed. The epididymis is a comma-shaped organ that sits atop the testicle and can be easily felt if the testicle is gently rolled between the fingers. If uncoiled, the epididymis would be about 20 feet in length.

epididymis A comma-shaped organ that sits atop the testicle and holds sperm during maturation.

spermatozoon A mature sperm cell.

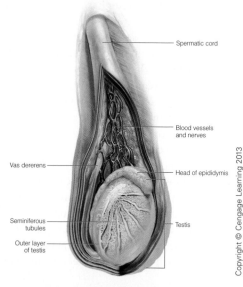

Spermatic cord

Blood vessels and nerves

Vas dererens

Head of epididymis

Seminiferous tubules

Testis

Outer layer of testis

Copyright © Cengage Learning 2013

Figure 5.3 The internal structure of the testicle.

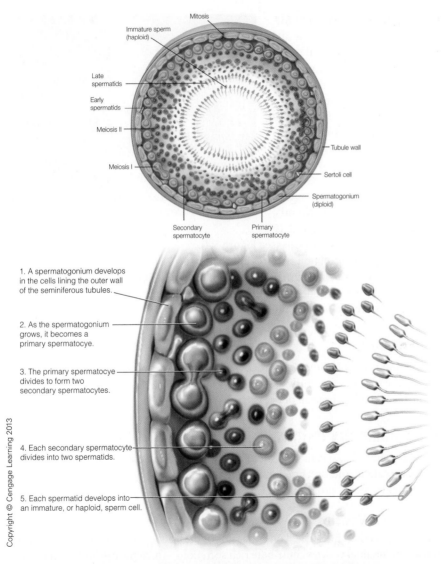

Mitosis

Immature sperm (haploid)

Late spermatids

Early spermatids

Meiosis II

Meiosis I

Tubule wall

Sertoli cell

Spermatogonium (diploid)

Secondary spermatocyte

Primary spermatocyte

1. A spermatogonium develops in the cells lining the outer wall of the seminiferous tubules.

2. As the spermatogonium grows, it becomes a primary spermatocye.

3. The primary spermatocye divides to form two secondary spermatocytes.

4. Each secondary spermatocyte divides into two spermatids.

5. Each spermatid develops into an immature, or haploid, sperm cell.

Figure 5.4 Spermatogenesis is a continuous process throughout the testes.

Hormones and the Male Reproductive System

See the role hormones play.

Internal Structure of the Testicle

Take a closer look at underlying structures.

Spermatogenesis

Take a closer look at this process.

▶ **LO9** Identify and locate the seven organs involved in the ejaculatory pathway.

▶ **LO10** Describe the process of ejaculation and the composition of the ejaculate.

Process of Spermatogenesis

Sperm are produced in some 300 microscopic tubes located in the testicles, known as seminiferous tubules. Uncoiled, this network of tubes would extend over a mile.

As sperm cells develop into immature, or haploid, sperm cells, they progressively move from the lining toward the center of the seminiferous tubules. Once formed, immature sperm cells migrate to the **epididymis**, where they mature for about 10 to 14 days into **spermatozoons** (see Figure 5.4).

© CNRI/Science Photo Library

Colored scans of seminiferous tubules each containing a swirl of sperm cells (in blue).

Human sperm formation requires approximately 72 days, yet because sperm is in constant production, the human male produces about 300 million sperm per day. After sperm have matured, the epididymis pushes them into the vas deferens, where they can be stored for several months.

Ejaculation

Ejaculation is the physiological process whereby the seminal fluid, or semen, containing the sperm is forcefully ejected from the penis. This is typically accompanied by the pleasurable sensation of orgasm.

The Ejaculatory Pathway

During ejaculation, sperm pass successively through the epididymis, vas deferens, ejaculatory duct, and urethra, picking up fluid along the way from three glands—the seminal vesicles, prostate, and Cowper's gland.

The Seminal Vesicles

vas deferens One of two long tubes that convey the sperm from the testes and in which other fluids are mixed to create semen.

The seminal vesicles are located on either side of the bladder and open into the **vas deferens**. The seminal vesicles contribute rich secretions, which provide nutrition for the traveling sperm and make up about 60% to 70% of the volume of the ejaculate. The vas deferens and the duct from the seminal vesicles merge into a common ejaculatory duct, a short, straight tube that passes into the prostate gland and opens into the urethra.

The Prostate Gland

The prostate gland, a walnut-sized gland at the base of the bladder, produces several substances that are thought to aid sperm in their attempt to fertilize an ovum. The vagina maintains an acidic pH to protect against bacteria, yet an acidic environment slows down and eventually kills sperm. Prostatic secretions, which comprise about 25% to 30% of the ejaculate, effectively neutralize vaginal acidity almost immediately after ejaculation.

The prostate is close to the rectum, so a health care provider can feel the prostate during a rectal examination. The prostate gland can cause a number of physical problems in men, especially older men, including prostate enlargement and the development of prostate cancer. Prostate cancer is discussed later in this chapter.

The Cowper's Glands

The Cowper's or bulbourethral glands are two pea-sized glands that flank the urethra just beneath the prostate gland. The glands have ducts that open right into the urethra and produce a fluid that cleans and lubricates the urethra for the passage of sperm, neutralizing any acidic urine that may remain in the urethra. The drop or more of pre-ejaculatory fluid that many men experience during arousal is the fluid from the Cowper's glands. Although in the past researchers believed there was no sperm in the pre-ejaculatory fluid, newer research has found that the fluid may contain live sperm, so heterosexual men should use condoms if pregnancy is not desired (Killick et al., 2010).

Process of Ejaculation

Earlier in this chapter, we discussed erection as a spinal reflex. Ejaculation, like erection, also begins in the spinal column; however, unlike erection, there is seldom a "partial" ejaculation. Once the stimulation builds to the threshold, ejaculation usually continues until its conclusion. When the threshold is reached, the first stage of ejaculation begins: the epididymis, seminal vesicles, and prostate all empty their contents into the urethral bulb, which swells up to accommodate the semen. The bladder is closed off by an internal sphincter so that no urine is expelled with the semen. Once these stages begin, some men report feeling that ejaculation is

Ejaculatory Pathway

Take a closer look at this process.

Sperm, Toxins, Cell Phones, and Tofu

What's the relationship?

On Your Mind

Does what a guy eats actually affect the taste of his cum?

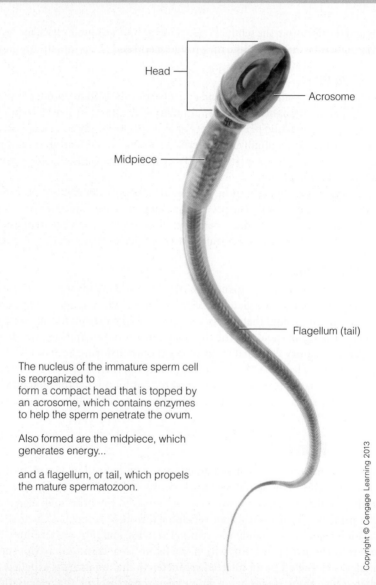

Head

Acrosome

Midpiece

Flagellum (tail)

The nucleus of the immature sperm cell is reorganized to
form a compact head that is topped by an acrosome, which contains enzymes to help the sperm penetrate the ovum.

Also formed are the midpiece, which generates energy...

and a flagellum, or tail, which propels the mature spermatozoon.

imminent, that they are going to ejaculate and nothing can stop it; however, others report that this feeling of inevitability can be stopped by immediately ceasing all sensation.

If stimulation continues, strong, rhythmic contractions of the muscles at the base of the penis squeeze the urethral bulb, and the ejaculate is propelled from the body, usually accompanied by the pleasurable sensation of orgasm. Most men have between 5 and 15 contractions during orgasm, and many report enjoying strong pressure at the base of the penis during orgasm. From an evolutionary standpoint, this may be a way of encouraging deep thrusting at the moment of ejaculation to deposit semen as deeply as possible within the vagina.

Once orgasm subsides, the arteries supplying the blood to the penis narrow, the veins taking the blood out enlarge, and the penis usually becomes limp. Depending on the level of excitement, the person's age, the length of time since the previous ejaculation, and his individual physiology, a new erection can occur anywhere from immediately to several hours later.

Ejaculate

The male ejaculate, or semen, averages about 2 to 5 milliliters—about 1 or 2 teaspoons. Semen normally contains secretions from the seminal vesicles and the prostate gland, and about 50 to 150 million sperm per milliliter. If there are less than 20 million sperm per milliliter, the male is likely to be infertile—even though the ejaculate can have up to 500 million sperm altogether. Sperm is required in such large numbers because during procreation only a small fraction of them ever reaches the ovum during procreation. Also, the sperm work together to achieve fertilization; for example, many die and block the os of the cervix for the other sperm, and the combined enzyme production of all sperm are necessary for a single spermatozoon to fertilize the ovum.

Directly after ejaculation, the semen initially coagulates into a thick mucus-like liquid, probably an evolutionary development to aid in procreation by decreasing the chances it would leak back out of the vagina. After 5 to 20 minutes, the prostatic enzymes contained in the semen cause it to thin out and liquefy. If it does not liquefy normally, coagulated semen from heterosexual men may be unable to complete its movement through the cervix and into the uterus.

Parts of a Sperm

Take a closer look.

On Your Mind

Would it hurt a guy if he didn't cum regularly?

Check Your Learning Quiz 5.2

Go to **login.cengagebrain.com** and take the online quiz.

▶ **LO11** Identify the two main functions of the testes and describe the feedback system that regulates male hormone and sperm production.

▶ **LO12** Summarize the changes to the male reproductive system that occur with puberty.

▶ **LO13** Summarize the changes to the male reproductive system that occur with age.

Now that we've discussed the male sexual and reproductive system, let's explore the physical changes that occur as the male reproductive and sexual systems mature during male puberty.

Male Puberty

During a boy's early life, the two major functions of the testes—to produce male sex hormones and to produce sperm—remain dormant. No one knows exactly what triggers the onset of puberty or how a boy's internal clock knows that he is reaching the age in which these functions of the testes will be needed. Still, at an average of 10 years of age, the hypothalamus begins releasing gonadotropin-releasing hormone (GnRH), which stimulates the anterior pituitary gland to send out luteinizing hormone (LH) and follicle-stimulating hormone (FSH).

These flow through the circulatory system to the testes, where LH stimulates the production of the male sex hormone, testosterone, which, together with FSH, stimulates sperm production. A negative feedback system regulates hormone production; when the concentration of testosterone in the blood increases to a certain level, GnRH release from the hypothalamus is inhibited, causing inhibition of LH and FSH production and resulting in decreased testosterone and sperm production. Alternately, when testosterone levels decrease below a certain level, this stimulates GnRH production by the hypothalamus, which increases the pituitary's LH and FSH production and testosterone and sperm production increases.

As puberty progresses, the testicles grow, and the penis begins to grow about a year later. The epididymis, prostate, seminal vesicles, and Cowper's glands also grow over the next several years. Increased testosterone stimulates an overall growth spurt in puberty, as bones and muscles rapidly develop. This spurt can be dramatic; teenage boys can grow 3 or 4 inches within a few months. The elevation of testosterone affects a number of male traits: the boy develops longer and heavier bones, larger muscles, thicker and tougher skin, a deepening voice because of growth of the voice box, pubic hair, facial and chest hair, increased sex drive, and increased metabolism.

nocturnal emissions Involuntary ejaculation during sleep, also referred to as a wet dream.

andropause The hormonal changes accompanying old age in men that correspond to menopause in women.

anemia A condition in which there is a deficiency in the oxygen-carrying material of the blood.

Spermatogenesis begins at about 12 years of age, but ejaculation of mature sperm usually does not occur for about another 1 to 1.5 years. At puberty, follicle-stimulating hormone begins to stimulate sperm production in the seminiferous tubules, and the increased testosterone induces the testes to mature fully. The development of spermatogenesis and the sexual fluid glands allows the boy to begin to experience his first **nocturnal emissions**, although at the beginning, they tend to contain a very low live sperm count.

Andropause

As men age, their blood testosterone concentrations decrease. Hormone levels in men have been found to decrease by about 1% each year after age 40 (Daw, 2002). Men do not go through an obvious set of stages, as menopausal women do, but some experience a less well-defined set of symptoms in their 70s or 80s called **andropause** (Makrantonaki et al., 2010). It is estimated that 2% of elderly men experience symptoms related to andropause (Pines, 2010). Although men's ability to ejaculate viable sperm is often retained past age 80 or 90, spermatogenesis decreases, the ejaculate becomes thinner, and ejaculatory pressure decreases. The reduction in testosterone production results in decreased muscle strength, decreased libido, easy fatigue, and mood fluctuations (Bassit & Morley, 2010; Seidman, 2007). Men can also experience osteoporosis and **anemia** from the decreasing hormone levels (Bain, 2001). For some men, androgen replacement therapy can increase sexual interest and functioning, as well as improve bone density, muscle mass, and overall mood (Bassil & Morley, 2010).

However, the use of androgen replacement therapy is controversial due to possible risks and limited long-term studies (Pines, 2010; Wu et al., 2010). One of the largest controversies revolves around the risks involved in taking testosterone, especially the possibility of an increased risk for prostate cancer, although there has been no evidence to support this risk (Bassil & Morley, 2010). Even so, androgen replacement therapy is commonly used in the United States today (Cunningham & Toma, 2011).

On Your Mind

Is it possible for a guy to have an orgasm without an ejaculation?

Fighting Against Aging

See how one group uses hormones to combat the effects of aging.

Check Your Learning Quiz 5.3

Go to **login.cengagebrain.com** and take the online quiz.

▶ **LO14** Identify four disorders of the male reproductive organs and describe the main symptoms of each of these disorders.

It is a good idea for every man to examine and explore his own sexual anatomy. A regular genital self-examination can help increase a man's comfort with his genitals. It can also help a man know what his testicles feel like just in case something were to change. This section first discusses various disorders that may affect the male reproductive organs, then turns to cancer of the male reproductive organs, its diagnosis, and its treatment.

Disorders of the Male Reproductive Organs

Several conditions can affect the male reproductive organs, including cryptorchidism, testicular torsion, priapism, and Peyronie's disease. It's important for both men and women to have a good understanding of what these conditions are and what symptoms they might cause.

Cryptorchidism

Cryptorchidism, or undescended testes, is the most common genital disorder in boys. One third of male infants who are born prematurely have cryptorchidism, whereas 2% to 5% of full-term male infants have at least one undescended testicle (Mathers et al., 2011). The testicles of a male fetus begin high in the abdomen near the kidneys and, during fetal development, descend into the scrotum through the **inguinal canal** (Hutson et al., 1994; see Figure 5.5).

Newborn boys with cryptorchidism may be given testosterone to help with testicular descent. However, if the testes have not descended by 6 months of age, surgery is often required to relocate the undescended tes-

inguinal canal Canal through which the testes descend into the scrotum.

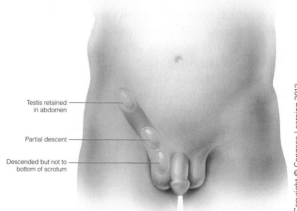

Testis retained in abdomen

Partial descent

Descended but not to bottom of scrotum

Copyright © Cengage Learning 2013

Figure 5.5 Although the testicles of a fetus begin high in the abdomen, if they do not descend into the scrotum during fetal development, the male may become infertile.

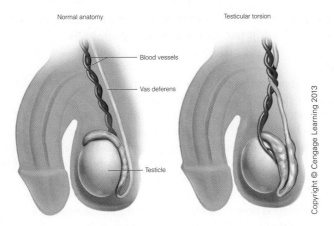

Figure 5.6 Testicular torsion.

tis to the scrotum (Hutson & Hasthorpe, 2005). It is estimated that 90% of men with untreated cryptorchidism will be infertile, because excessive heat in the abdomen impairs the ability to produce viable sperm (AbouZeid et al., 2011). Men with a history of cryptorchid testes also have an increased risk for testicular cancer (Robin et al., 2010; Thorup et al., 2010; Toppari et al., 2010).

Testicular Torsion

Testicular torsion refers to a twisting of a testis on its spermatic cord (see Figure 5.6). Usually it occurs when there is abnormal development of the spermatic cord or the membrane that covers the testicle (Wampler & Llanes, 2010). It is most common in men under the age of 25, and approximately 1 in 4,000 men are affected by testicular torsion each year (Ringdahl & Teague, 2006). Testicular torsion can occur after exercise, penetrative sex, or even while sleeping.

Acute scrotal pain and swelling are two of the most common symptoms, although there can also be abdominal pain, nausea, and vomiting (Kapoor, 2008). Testicular torsion should be considered a medical emergency, and any man who experiences a rapid onset of scrotal pain should immediately have this pain checked by a health care provider. An ultrasound is often used to help diagnose this condition, but because the twisted cord can cut off blood supply to the testicle, the condition must be diagnosed very quickly (Cokkinos et al., 2010). Restoration of blood flow to the testicle, through

Testicular Descent

The journey from abdomen to scrotum.

Testicular Torsion

Compare normal anatomy to testicular torsion.

On Your Mind

If a guy's penis curves to the right, does this mean he masturbated a lot as a kid?

▶ **LO15** Compare the perceived benefits and risks of anabolic-androgenic steroid use.

manipulation of the spermatic cord or surgery, must be made within 6 hours of the onset of symptoms or the testicle may be lost (Kapoor, 2008).

Priapism

Priapism is an abnormally prolonged and painful erection that is not associated with sexual desire or excitement (Cakin-Memik et al., 2010). It is primarily a vascular condition that causes blood to become trapped in the erectile tissue of the penis. Men with certain conditions, such as sickle cell disease, leukemia, and/or spinal cord injuries, are at greater risk for development of priapism (Mi et al., 2008). In some cases, drug use (erection drugs, cocaine, marijuana, or anticoagulants) is to blame. Like testicular torsion, priapism is considered a medical emergency because it can damage erectile tissue if left untreated (Mi et al., 2008). Treatment may involve pharmaceutical agents to reduce blood flow or stents to remove the built-up blood. If there is a neurological or other physiological cause for the priapism, surgery may be necessary.

Peyronie's Disease

Every male has individual curves to his penis when it becomes erect. These curves are quite normal. However, in approximately 1% of men, painful curvature makes penetration impossible, leading to a diagnosis of a condition known as Peyronie's disease (Perovic & Djinovic, 2010). Typically, this happens between the ages of 45 and 60, although younger and older men can also experience Peyronie's disease.

Peyronie's disease occurs in the connective tissue of the penis, and although some cases are asymptomatic, others develop plaques or areas of hardened tissue, which can cause severe erectile pain (Gelbard, 1988). In extreme cases, penetrative sex is impossible because of the curvature.

Usually this disease lasts approximately 2 years and may go away just as suddenly as it appears. It is treated in a variety of ways, including medication, surgery, or both (Seveso et al., 2010). Research has found that penile curvature can be successfully reduced with treatment, and many men find they are able to engage in penetrative sex again after treatment (Heidari et al, 2010).

Anabolic-Androgenic Steroid Abuse

Over the past few years, steroids have become a controversial topic as more and more male athletes disclose past steroid use. In 2005, congressional hearings began to evaluate steroid abuse in major league baseball. Anabolic-androgenic steroids

Jeff Hixon/Allsport/Getty Images

© Reuters/Corbis

Accusations of steroid use in Major League Baseball circulated in 2005. Before and after photos supported these claims. Photos above are of Barry Bonds in 1989 (left) and 2005 (right).

(AASs), also known as synthetic testosterone, have been used by elite athletes since the 1950s, but it wasn't until the 1980s that these types of drugs started being abused by nonathletes as well (Kanayama et al., 2010).

Some steroids occur naturally in the body, and they are known as androgens. During puberty in males, the release of androgens increases weight and muscle size, and can also increase endurance and aggressiveness. We know that millions of boys and men, primarily in Western countries, use AAS to enhance their appearance or athletic performance (Brennan et al., 2011). Women have also been found to abuse these drugs, although at lower levels than men (Gruber & Pope, 2000). The actual number of people abusing AAS is unknown.

Anabolic-androgenic steroid use comes at a high price. It has been associated with many damaging changes in the physiological characteristics of organs and body systems. The best documented effects are to the liver, serum lipids, and the reproductive system, including shrinkage of the testicles (Sato et al., 2008). In younger athletes, steroids can cause early fusion of the bone-growth plates, resulting in permanently shortened stature. AAS users have also been found to be more at risk for illicit drug use, particularly opioid use (Kanayama et al., 2010).

Check Your Learning Quiz 5.4

Go to **login.cengagebrain.com** and take the online quiz.

▶ **LO16** Identify the three main cancers of the male reproductive organs and the primary symptoms of each.

▶ **LO17** Define and differentiate benign prostatic hypertrophy and prostate cancer.

As discussed in Chapter 4, cancer is a disease in which certain cells in the body don't function properly—they divide too fast or produce excessive tissue that forms a tumor (or both). A number of cancers can affect the male reproductive organs. Let's now look at testicular, penile, and prostate cancers. This section also reviews preventive measures for detecting and/or avoiding common male health problems.

Penile Cancer

A wide variety of cancers involving the skin and soft tissues of the penis can occur, although cancer of the penis is rare (Mosconi et al., 2005). Any lesion on the penis must be examined by a health care provider, for benign and malignant conditions can be very similar in appearance, and sexually transmitted infections can appear as lesions. Even though most men handle and observe their penis daily, there is often significant delay between a person's recognition of a lesion and seeking medical attention. Fear and embarrassment are common reasons for avoiding medical attention, even though the majority of these lesions are treatable if caught early.

Testicular Cancer

The American Cancer Society (2011) estimated that 8,500 cases of testicular cancer were diagnosed in 2010. Testicular cancer is the most common malignancy in men aged 25 to 34 (Garner et al., 2008). Typically, there are few symptoms until the cancer is advanced, which is why early detection is so important. Most men first develop testicular cancer as a painless testicular mass. If there is pain or a sudden increase in testicular size, it is usually due to bleeding into the tumor.

Risk factors for testicular cancer include family history, cryptorchidism, increased height, body size, age at puberty, and dairy consumption

Lance Armstrong, who has won the Tour de France a record number of times, was diagnosed with testicular cancer when he was 25, by which time the cancer had spread to his lungs and brain. Had he known about the importance of early detection, he would have never ignored the swelling and pain in his testicles. Armstrong underwent aggressive surgery and chemotherapy. One year later, he began racing again and was still able to have five children through in vitro fertilization.

benign prostatic hypertrophy (BPH) The common enlargement of the prostate that occurs in most men after about age 50.

(McGlynn et al., 2007). In addition, newer research has found that frequent marijuana use (daily or greater) increases a man's risk for testicular cancer (Trabert et al., 2011).

Although the incidence of testicular cancer has continuously increased during the last few decades, cure rates have significantly improved. In fact, testicular cancer is one of the most curable forms of the disease (American Cancer Society, 2005). Treatment may involve radiation, chemotherapy, or the removal of the testicle (although radiation and chemotherapy can affect future fertility, the removal of a testicle does not). If removal of the testicle is necessary, many men opt to get a prosthetic testicle implanted, which gives the appearance of having two normal testicles. Early diagnosis is very important, because cure rates are higher early on and treatments are less severe.

Prostate Cancer

Earlier, we discussed how the prostate gland can enlarge and cause a number of physical problems in men as they age. In most cases, this natural occurrence, **benign prostatic hypertrophy (BPH)**, causes few problems. Because of its anatomical position surrounding the urethra, BPH may block urination, and surgeons may need to remove the prostate if the condition continues to worsen. Of far more concern than BPH is prostate cancer, which is the most frequently diagnosed cancer in men, besides skin cancer (American Cancer Society, 2007b). The American Cancer Society (2010) estimates that 1 in 6 men will be diagnosed with prostate cancer in their lifetime, and 1 in 36 will die of this cancer. Approximately 218,000 new cases of prostate cancer were diagnosed in 2010.

Although men of all ages can get prostate cancer, it is found most often in men older than age 50. In fact, risk for prostate cancer increases in men up until the age of 70 and then begins to decline. For reasons not clearly understood, prostate cancer is about twice as common among Black men as it is among White men. In addition, because the disease is more likely to be aggressive and advanced when it's caught, the risk for dying of prostate cancer is higher in Black men. Other ethnic and racial groups have lower rates of prostate cancer than either White or Black men. Worldwide, the incidence of prostate cancer varies, with the majority of cases diagnosed in economically developed countries (American Cancer Society, 2011).

We don't know exactly what causes prostate cancer, but we do know that several risk factors have been linked to prostate cancer. Men with a first-degree relative, such as a father or brother, with prostate cancer are two to three times more likely to experience development of prostate cancer, whereas men with more than one

Don't Die Young

Male reproductive organs.

On Your Mind

Can a man who has been treated for testicular cancer still have children?

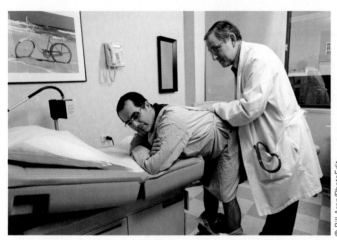

At some point in their lives men will be offered a prostate exam to help detect prostate cancer in its early stages. A man may be asked to either lean over or lie on his side while the health care provider inserts a gloved finger into the man's rectum to check the size of the prostate gland.

first-degree relative are three to five times more likely to experience development of the cancer (American Cancer Society, 2011). In addition, men with the BRCA gene are also at increased risk for development of prostate cancer. Other risk factors include race/ethnicity, age, and a diet high in fat. Studies have shown that men whose diets include high levels of calcium and consumption of red and processed meats have higher risks (American Cancer Society, 2011).

Early signs of prostate cancer may include lower back, pelvic, or upper thigh pain; inability to urinate; loss of force in the urinary stream; urinary dribbling; pain or burning during urination; and frequent urination, especially at night. Many deaths from prostate cancer are preventable, because a simple 5- or 10-second rectal examination by a physician, to detect hard lumps on the prostate, detects more than 50% of cases at a curable stage. Digital rectal examinations are recommended for men each year beginning at the age of 50.

In 1986, the U.S. Food and Drug Administration approved the **prostate-specific antigen (PSA)** blood test that measures levels of molecules that are overproduced by prostate cancer cells. This enables physicians to identify prostate cancer and is recommended yearly for men older than 50, although Black men and those with a first-degree relative with prostate cancer are often advised to begin screening at 45 years old (American Cancer Society, 2011). The PSA test has been one of the most important advances in the area of prostate cancer (Madan & Gulley, 2010). Although not all tumors will show up on a PSA test, a high reading does indicate that something (such as a tumor) is releasing prostatic material into the blood, and a biopsy or further examination is warranted.

Many treatments for prostate cancer are available, and almost all are controversial. Some argue that, in older men especially, the best thing is "watchful waiting" in which the cancer is simply left alone, because this type of cancer is slow growing and most men will die of other causes before the prostate cancer becomes life-

prostate-specific antigen (PSA) Blood test that measures levels of molecules that are overproduced by prostate cancer cells, enabling health care providers to identify prostate cancer early.

threatening. Men who have a history of poor health, are older than 80 years, or are living in a geographically undesirable location for medical treatment often opt for watchful waiting (Harlan et al., 2001).

Male Breast Cancer

The American Cancer Society (2011) estimated there were approximately 2000 cases of breast cancer diagnosed in men in 2010. Even though breast cancer is rare in men, it has a higher mortality rate in men than in women, mainly because it is often diagnosed at a more advanced stage in men compared with women (Al-Saleh, 2011; Rosa & Masood, in press).

Risk factors for breast cancer in men are similar to some of the risk factors for women, including heredity, obesity, hormonal issues, and physical inactivity. Newer research has found that a history of a bone fracture is a risk for breast cancer in men probably because of the association with osteoporosis (Brinton et al., 2008). Exposure to environmental toxins may also increase a man's risk for breast cancer (Maffini et al., 2006).

In Chapter 4, we reviewed the research on cancer and the BRCA genes. The presence of these genes in men can also lead to a higher risk for the development of both breast and prostate cancer (Stromsvik et al., 2010). In fact, the presence of these genes doubles the normal risk for breast cancer by seven times (Tai et al., 2007). Today, some men opt for genetic testing to learn whether they have a BRCA mutation. Research has found that, like women, men experience strong emotional reactions to positive test results for the BRCA genes. However, few disclose this information to others (Stromsvik et al., 2010). If they do talk to friends about it, most men report females as their main source of support and find it difficult to talk to other men about their diagnosis.

Treatment for breast cancer for men involves radiation or chemotherapy, and if the cancer has spread to other parts of the body, surgical removal of the breasts may be necessary to eliminate the hormones that could support the growth of the cancer.

Check Your Learning Quiz 5.5

Go to **login.cengagebrain.com** and take the online quiz.

It is important for men to be proactive about their sexual health maintenance. Experts recommend that men practice proper hygiene techniques and perform regular testicular self-examinations. This section discusses both of these recommendations.

Male Hygiene

Regular washing and drying of the penis helps reduce the buildup of smegma, which can cause irritation and inflammation. Uncircumcised men are advised to regularly retract the foreskin to clean the head of the penis. Poor hygiene may result in **balanitis**, an inflammation of the glans penis. Balanitis can also be caused by allergies to latex or certain skin care products used by the man or his partner. In addition, various medical conditions, such as psoriasis, yeast infections, or diabetes can also lead to balanitis. Symptoms include a redness of the foreskin or penis, itching, tenderness, a foul-smelling discharge, and/or penile pain. If you experience any of these symptoms, it is best to have them checked out by a health care provider.

Treatment depends on the cause, but typically antibiotics, antifungal drugs, or steroid creams are used. In severe cases, the foreskin of an uncircumcised man can adhere to the inflamed skin in a condition called **phimosis**. A circumcision may be recommended if this occurs. It's important to realize, however, that obsessive overwashing with soap and vigorous drying may also contribute to balanitis. It is best to use warm water and a gentle drying of the penis after cleaning.

Testicular Self-Examination

Although testicular cancer has no obvious symptoms, when detected early, it is treatable. The only early detection system for testicular cancer is testicular self-examination. However, a nationally representative sample of American men found that only 2% to 10% of men perform monthly testicular self-examinations and that various factors, such as gender roles and norms, may inhibit a man from performing a testicular self-examination (Reece et al., 2010). Just like breast self-examinations in women, men should examine their testicles at least monthly. This will enable them to have an understanding of what things feel like under normal conditions, which will help them find any lumps or abnormal growths, should they appear.

balanitis Inflammation of the glans penis.

phimosis An abnormal restriction of the foreskin that inhibits the ability to uncover the glans penis.

© Joel Gordon

Testicular self-exam.

To do a testicular examination, compare both testicles simultaneously by grasping one with each hand, using thumb and forefinger. This may be best done while taking a warm shower, which causes the scrotum to relax and the testicles to hang lower. Determine their size, shape, and sensitivity to pressure.

As you get to know the exact shape and feel of the testicles, you will be able to notice any swelling, lumps, or unusual pain. Report any such occurrence to your health care provider without delay, but do not panic; most lumps are benign and nothing to worry about.

Key Terms Exercise

Match the Key Terms with their definitions.

Lance Armstrong's Battle with Testicular Cancer

The importance of self-examination.

Check Your Learning Quiz 5.6

Go to **login.cengagebrain.com** and take the online quiz.

Think Critically

Challenge Your Thinking

Consider these questions:

1. Why do you think the practice of male circumcision has elicited such controversy? Where do you stand on this issue?
2. If the research was clear that uncircumcised men were at greater risk for sexually transmitted diseases, do you think the medical establishment has the right to make male circumcision mandatory? Why or why not?
3. Some experts suggest performing circumcision only when a man is old enough to decide that he wants to have it done. What do you think of performing circumcision at birth versus waiting until adulthood?
4. If you had a son, do you think you'd want to have him circumcised? Why or why not?
5. What do you think is the main reason parents might want to have their male children circumcised?

Ethnicity, Religion, and Circumcision

Male circumcision is practiced in many parts of the world. The World Health Organization (WHO) estimates that more than 664 million males—or 30%—are circumcised (Malone & Steinbrecher, 2007; WHO, 2007). Reasons for circumcision vary around the world but include religious, cultural, social, and/or medical reasons. Nonreligious circumcision became popular in the 1870s because it was thought to promote hygiene, reduce "unnatural" sexual behaviors, prevent syphilis and gonorrhea, and reduce masturbation (G. Kaplan, 1977; Wallerstein, 1980). An article published in 1947 sup-

porting circumcision reported that cancer was more common in laboratory mice that were not circumcised (Plaut & Kohn-Speyer, 1947). All of these medical reports and social considerations have influenced the incidence of male circumcision.

Circumcision can be done at any age, but it is most commonly done at birth up until the mid-20s. Infant circumcision is commonly done in the United States, Canada, Australia, New Zealand, the Middle East, Central Asia, and West Africa. Many parents cite hygiene and health reasons for circumcising their infants at birth. In other areas of the world, such as East and South Africa, male circumcisions are done in the mid-teens to early 20s and are viewed as rites of passage for boys and a transition from child to man (Crowley & Kesner, 1990). Some cultures believe that circumcision makes a boy a man because the foreskin is viewed as feminine (Silverman, 2004).

Various ethnic groups have different preferences concerning circumcising their male children. If circumcision is common in a particular ethnic group, parents may be inclined to circumcise their male children so their sons will look like other boys (Centers for Disease Control and Prevention, 2008). In addition, fathers who are circumcised often have their sons circumcised (Goldman, 1999). These social considerations have been found to outweigh the medical facts when parents are deciding whether to circumcise their sons (M. S. Brown & Brown, 1987). Medical reasons for circumcision are rare, and it is mainly practiced for religious and cultural reasons today (Malone & Steinbrecher, 2007).

The practice of male circumcision has elicited more controversy than any other surgical procedure in history (Alanis & Lucidi, 2004; Fox & Thomson, 2010; Hinchley & Patrick, 2007). Most of the controversy revolves around the risks and potential benefits of circumcision. A wide-scale study done in Africa found that male circumcision offered protection from HIV infection (M. S. Cohen et al., 2008; Drain et al., 2006; Morris, 2007; Thomson et al., 2007; Weiss et al., 2000). Male circumcision was found to reduce the risk for HIV in men by 60% (Smith et al., 2010; Weiss et al., 2010). Circumcision offered protection to both men who had sex with women, as well as men who had sex with men (Dinh et al., 2010; Fox & Thomson, 2010).

Circumcised men have also been found to have lower rates of infant urinary tract infections (Simforoosh et al., 2010) and sexually transmitted infections, such as herpes and human papillomavirus (see Chapter 12; Weiss et al., 2010). Female partners of circumcised men also have lower rates of certain types of vaginal infections and cervical cancer (Alanis & Lucidi, 2004; Drain et al., 2006; Morris, 2007; Weiss et al., 2010).

Even though there may be some medical benefits to circumcision, experts believe these benefits are not strong enough for health care providers to recommend routine circumcision (Kinkade & Meadows, 2005; Tobian et al., 2010). In 1999, the American Academy of Pediatrics stopped recommending routine male circumcision and suggested that parents make the decision to circumcise based on their own experiences, their family, and religious beliefs (American Academy of Pediatrics, 1999).

© John Warburton-Lee Photography/PhotoLibrary

A Samburu youth is circumcised in Kenya while his sponsors attend to him—one holding his leg, while the other turns his face away from the circumciser. Boys are not allowed to show any signs of fear or pain during the procedure. Even the blink of an eyelid is frowned upon.

Think Critically

This article and its questions are available in interactive format online.

GO to your Psychology CourseMate at login.cengagebrain.com and take the Chapter Post-Test to see which Learning Objectives you've mastered and which need more review. Use the chapter review guide below and the online activities—including flashcards to review key terms—to measure your learning.

Measure ^Your Learning

Module	Learning Objectives
5.1 External Sexual and Reproductive System 142	**LO1** Identify and locate the two external sex organs of the human male.
	LO2 Identify and locate the cylinders in the penis responsible for erection.
	LO3 Identify and locate the three parts of the glans penis.
	LO4 Summarize the role of blood flow in the process of penile erection.
	LO5 Describe the effects of temperature on sperm production and the role of the scrotum in temperature regulation.
5.2 Internal Sexual and Reproductive System 148	**LO6** Identify and locate the six internal male sex organs.
	LO7 Identify the two organs involved in spermatogenesis.
	LO8 Describe the process of spermatogenesis.
	LO9 Identify and locate the seven organs involved in the ejaculatory pathway.
	LO10 Describe the process of ejaculation and the composition of the ejaculate.
5.3 Male Maturation 154	**LO11** Identify the two main functions of the testes and describe the feedback system that regulates male hormone and sperm production.
	LO12 Summarize the changes to the male reproductive system that occur with puberty.
	LO13 Summarize the changes to the male reproductive system that occur with age.

Online Activities

Key Terms	Video	Animation	Readings	Assessment
penis, semen, erection, corpora cavernosa, corpus spongiosum, glans penis, corona, frenulum, urethral opening (or meatus), foreskin, circumcision, scrotum, cremaster muscle	Close Up: Growing Up Male Why do guys wake up with erections? Laptops and Sperm Quality	The Internal Structure of the Penis The Male Reproductive Organs		Check Your Learning 5.1
interstitial cells, Leydig cells, spermatogenesis, seminiferous tubules, epididymis, spermatozoon, ejaculation, vas deferens, ampulla, seminal vesicles, ejaculatory duct, prostate gland, Cowper's or bulbourethral gland	Does what a guy eats actually affect the taste of his cum? Would it hurt a guy if he didn't cum regularly?	Hormones and the Male Reproductive System The Internal Structure of the Testicle Spermatogenesis Ejaculatory Pathway Parts of a Sperm	Sperm, Toxins, Cell Phones, and Tofu	Check Your Learning 5.2
nocturnal emissions, andropause, anemia	Is it possible for a guy to have an orgasm without an ejaculation? Fighting Against Aging			Check Your Learning 5.3

Measure
>Your Learning
^

Online Activities

Key Terms	Video	Animation	Readings	Assessment
cryptorchidism, inguinal canal, testicular torsion, priapism, Peyronie's disease, androgen	If a guy's penis curves to the right, does this mean he masturbated a lot as a kid?	Testicular Descent Testicular Torsion		Check Your Learning 5.4
benign prostatic hypertrophy (BPH), prostate-specific antigen (PSA)	Don't Die Young Can a man who has been treated for testicular cancer still have children?			Check Your Learning 5.5
balanitis, phimosis		Key Terms Exercise	Lance Armstrong's Battle with Testicular Cancer	Check Your Learning 5.6
				Ethnicity, Religion, and Circumcision

Childhood and Adolescent Sexuality

Peter Cade/Getty Images

6

Chapter Outline and Learning Objectives

Prepare ^ to Learn

1 **GO** to your **Psychology CourseMate** at **login.cengagebrain.com** and take the **Chapter Pre-Test** to introduce yourself to this chapter's topics and see what you may already know.

2 **READ** the **Learning Objectives** (LOs, in the left sidebars) and begin the chapter.

3 **COMPLETE** the **Online Activities** (in the right sidebars) *as you read each module.* Activities include **videos, animations, readings,** and **quizzes.**

4 **CHECK Your Learning** by going online to take the quiz at the end of each module and review material as necessary.

5 **MEASURE Your Learning** after reading the chapter by taking the online **Chapter Post-Test.** Use the chapter review guide at the end of the chapter as needed.

WATCH for these **Online Activities** icons as you read:

Video

Animation

Reading

Assessment

Think Critically

These Online Activities are essential to mastering this chapter. Go to login.cengagebrain.com:

 Videos Explore diverse perspectives on sex as well as common questions:

- Would it destroy a child's life if they saw their parents naked or having sex?
- Cross-cultural Sex Talk: Children and Teens
- Puberty
- Gender Role Pressures in Childhood: A Male's Perspective
- It sounds like lots of kids have problems during adolescence, but mine was just fine. Is that weird?
- Why do guys masturbate so much more than girls?
- Why is there so much pressure for teens to have sex?
- Sex Education: The Dutch Approach

 Animation Interact with and visualize important processes, timelines, and concepts:

- Key Terms Exercise

 Readings Delve deeper into key content:

- Sexual Knowledge and Attitudes in Early Childhood
- Parents and Anxiety: Where Does It Come From?
- When Teens Are Sexually Exploited
- What Do Children Want to Know?
- Sexuality Education around the World

 Assessment Measure your mastery:

- Chapter Pre-Test
- Check Your Learning Quizzes
- Chapter Post-Test

 Think Critically Challenge your thinking about data and accepted norms:

- Evaluating the Results of Sexuality Education Programs

▸ **LO1** List three key aspects of physical and psychosexual development from birth to age 2.

▸ **LO2** Describe some of the typical behaviors related to sexual development in infancy.

THIS CHAPTER EXPLORES sexuality development from infancy through adolescence, including the influences of family and peers. It then examines contraception, pregnancy, parenthood, and sexually transmitted infections (STIs) as they apply specifically to adolescents and, finally, discusses the importance of sexuality education and the controversies surrounding it.

▼

Children are not just "little adults," and though they can be sexual, child sexuality is not adult sexuality (Gordon & Schroeder, 1995). Children want love, appreciate sensuality, and engage in behaviors that set the stage for the adult sexuality to come. Sexual growth in childhood and adolescence involves a host of factors: physical maturation of the sexual organs, psychological dynamics, familial relations, and peer relations, all within the social and cultural beliefs about gender roles and sexuality.

Let's first take a look at physical and psychosexual changes from birth to age 2. We would not label behavior as "sexual" during this time; however, many behaviors arise out of curiosity.

Physical and Psychosexual Development

Physical Development

Our sexual anatomy becomes functional even before we are born; ultrasound has shown male fetuses with erections in the uterus, and some newborns develop erections shortly after birth—even before the umbilical cord is cut (Masters et al., 1982). Female infants are capable of vaginal lubrication from birth (Martinson, 1981). Infant girls produce some estrogen from the adrenal glands before puberty, whereas infant boys have small testes that produce very small amounts of testosterone. Young children are even capable of orgasm.

Psychosexual Development

Throughout the book and online activities, we have discussed the importance of early relationships and the development of an attachment to a primary caregiver. Infants are helpless creatures, incapable of obtaining nourishment or warmth or relieving pain or distress. In fact, the bond between a mother and child is more than psychological; a baby's crying actually helps stimulate the secretion of the hormone *oxytocin* in the mother, which releases her milk for breast-feeding (Rossi, 1978).

Equally important as the infant's need for nourishment is the need for holding, cuddling, and close contact with caregivers. An infant's need for warmth and contact was demonstrated in Harlow's (1959) famous experiment, in which rhesus monkeys were separated at birth from their mothers. When offered two surrogate mothers, one a wire figure of a monkey equipped with milk bottles and one a terry-cloth–covered figure, the monkeys clung to the terry-cloth figure for warmth and security, and ventured over to the wire figure only when desperate for nourishment. The need for a sense of warmth and security in infancy overwhelms even the desire to eat.

Sexual Behavior

In infancy, children's bodies are busy making sure all of their organs work and learning to control them. The sexual system is no exception. Male infants sometimes have erections during breast-feeding (which can be very disconcerting to the mother), whereas girls have clitoral erections and lubrication (although that is less likely to be noticed). The infant's body (and mind) has not yet differentiated sexual functions from other functions, and the pleasure of breast-feeding, as well as the stimulation from the lips, mouth, and tongue, create a generalized neurological response that stimulates the genital response.

Genital touching is common in infancy, and many infants touch their genitals as soon as their hands are coordinated enough to do so (Casteels et al., 2004). Some infants only occasionally or rarely touch themselves, whereas others do it more regularly. Although infants clearly derive pleasure from this activity, it is not orgasm based. In fact, it is soothing to the infant and may serve as a means of tension reduction and distraction. Overall, genital touching is normal at this age, and parents should not be concerned about it.

Fabrizio Cacciatore/Index Stock Imagery/ Getty Images

Young girls and boys are curious about their bodies and bodily functions.

On Your Mind

Would it destroy a child's life if they saw their parents naked or having sex?

Check Your Learning Quiz 6.1

Go to **login.cengagebrain.com** and take the online quiz.

▶ **LO3** List three key aspects of physical and psychosexual development from ages 2 to 5.

▶ **LO4** Describe some behaviors that are indicative of young children's interest in their genitals.

Children continue to develop physically, and in early childhood they begin to understand what it means to be a boy or girl. Curiosity is still the basis for their sexuality during this time. Children also learn that their genitals are private during these years, and they often begin to associate sexuality with secrecy.

Physical and Psychosexual Development

Physical Development

Early childhood is a crucial period for physical development. Children of this age must learn to master the basic physical actions, such as eye–hand coordination, walking, talking, and generally learning to control their bodies. Think of all the new things a child must learn—all the rules of speaking and communicating; extremely complex physical skills such as self-feeding, walking, and running; how to interact with other children and adults; control of bodily wastes through toilet training; and handling all the frustrations of not being able to do most of the things they want to do when they want to do them. Although this period of childhood is not a particularly active one in terms of physical sexual development, children may learn more in the first few years of childhood about the nature of their bodies than they learn in the entire remainder of their lives. It is truly a time of profound change and growth.

Psychosexual Development

Chapter 3 discussed how infants begin to develop their gender identity (M. Lewis, 1987). After about age 2, it becomes increasingly difficult to change the child's gender identity (which is occasionally done when, for example, a female with an enlarged clitoris is mistakenly identified at birth as a boy). It takes a little longer to achieve **gender constancy**, whereby young children come to understand that they will not become a member of the other sex sometime in the future. Most children develop gender constancy by about age 6, and a strong identification with one gender typically develops that becomes a fundamental part of a child's self-concept (Warin, 2000).

In early childhood, children begin serious exploration of their bodies. It is usually during this period that children are toilet trained, and they go through a period of intense interest in their genitals and bodily wastes. They begin to ask the first, basic questions about sex, usually about why boys and girls have different genitals and what they are for. They begin to explore what it means to be "boys" or "girls" and turn to their parents, siblings, or television for models of gender behavior.

gender constancy The realization in the young child that one's gender does not normally change over the life span.

Sometimes children at this age will appear flirtatious or engage in sexual behaviors such as kissing in an attempt to understand gender roles.

Sexual Behavior and Awareness

Toddlers are not yet aware of the idea of sexuality or genital sexual relations. Like infants, toddlers and young children engage in many behaviors that involve exploring their bodies and doing things

Young boys develop strong relationships with same-sex and other-sex friends and relatives, and these relationships set the stage for adult intimate relationships.

that feel good. Both girls and boys at this age continue to engage in genital touching. More than 70% of mothers in one study reported that their children younger than age 6 touched themselves (Okami et al., 1997).

Genital Touching

Genital touching is actually more common in early childhood than in later childhood, although it picks up again after puberty (Friedrich et al., 1991). The act may be deliberate and obvious, and may even become a preoccupation. Boys at this age are capable of erection, and some proudly show it off to visitors. Parental reaction at this stage is important; strong disapproval may teach their children to hide the behavior and to be secretive and even ashamed of their bodies, whereas parents who are tolerant of their children's emerging sexuality can teach them to respect and take pride in their bodies. It is perfectly appropriate to make rules about the times and places that such behavior is acceptable, just as one makes rules about other childhood actions, such as the correct time and place to eat or to urinate.

Child sex play often begins with games exposing the genitals ("I'll show you mine if you show me yours....") and, by the age of 4, may move on to undressing and touching, followed by asking questions about sex around age 5. Sometimes young children will rub their bodies against each other, often with members of the same sex, which seems to provide general tactile pleasure.

Cross-cultural Sex Talk: Children and Teens

Explore sex talks with children and teens form around the world.

Check Your Learning Quiz 6.2

Go to **login.cengagebrain.com** and take the online quiz.

▶ **LO5** Describe the key physical changes that affect sexuality in middle childhood.

Between ages 6 and 12, the first outward signs of puberty often occur, and both boys and girls become more private about their bodies. Children begin building a larger knowledge base about sexual information—and acquire information from many sources, including their parents/caregivers, peers, and siblings. During the middle childhood to preteen years, children often play in same-sex groups and may begin masturbating, engaging in sexual fantasy, and/or sexual contact.

Physical Development

Puberty is one of the three major stages of physiological sexual development, together with prenatal sexual differentiation and menopause. Puberty marks the transition from sexual immaturity to maturity and the start of reproductive ability. Chapters 4 and 5 discussed the physiological and hormonal changes that accompany puberty, so this chapter reviews only those physical changes that have an effect on the nature of adolescent sexuality.

Until a child's body starts the enormous changes involved in puberty, the sexual organs grow in size only to keep up with general body growth and change very little in their physiological activity. Although the body begins internal changes to prepare for puberty as early as age 6 or 7, the first outward signs of puberty begin at 9 or 10. The physiological changes of puberty begin anywhere between the ages of 8 and 13 in most girls and 9 and 14 in most boys. As discussed in Chapter 4, research has found that girls are beginning puberty earlier than ever before (Biro et al., 2010). See Figure 6.1 for more information about signs of puberty in boys and girls. Overall, girls' maturation is about 1.5 to 2 years ahead of boys' (Gemelli, 1996).

In girls, **breast buds** appear, and pubic hair growth may begin. In boys, pubic hair growth generally starts a couple of years later than in girls, and, on average, girls experience menarche before boys experience their first ejaculation (often referred to as **semenarche**; SEM-min-ark). Preadolescent boys experience frequent erections, even to nonerotic stimuli. Common reactions to semenarche include surprise, curiosity, confusion, and pleasure—and typically, most boys don't tell anyone about this event (Frankel, 2002; J. H. Stein & Reiser, 1994). Pubertal changes can be frightening for both boys and girls if they are not prepared for them, and even if prepared, the onset of puberty can be emotionally, psychologically, and physically difficult for some children.

The physiological changes of puberty almost seem cruel. At the time when attractiveness to others begins to become important, the body starts growing in

breast buds The first swelling of the area around the nipple that indicates the beginning of breast development.

semenarche The experience of first ejaculation.

The Age Sequence of Pubertal Maturation in Boys and Girls

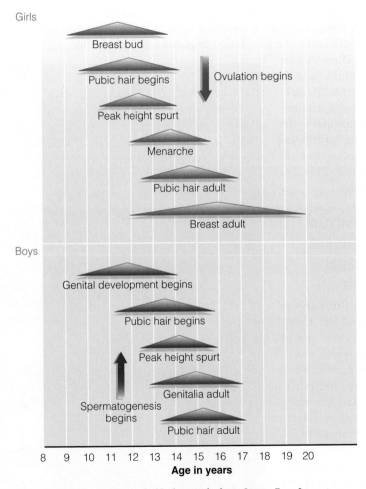

Figure 6.1 *Average ages of major bodily changes of puberty.* Source: From Lancaster, J. B., & B. A. Hamburg [Eds.]. [1986]. *School-age pregnancy and parenthood: Biosocial dimensions* [p. 20]. New York: Aldine DeGruyter. Reprinted by permission.

▶ **L06** Describe psychosexual development and sexual behaviors that occur in middle childhood.

disproportionate ways; fat can accumulate before muscles mature, feet can grow before the legs catch up, the nose may be the first part of the face to begin its growth spurt, and one side of the body may grow faster than the other (M. Diamond & Diamond, 1986). Add acne, a voice that squeaks at unexpected moments, and unfamiliarity with limbs that have suddenly grown much longer than one is accustomed to, and it is no wonder that adolescence is often a time of awkwardness and discomfort. Fortunately, the rest of the body soon catches up, so the awkward phase does not last too long.

Psychosexual Development and Sexual Behavior

Children through the middle and late childhood years continue to engage in genital touching and may explore both same- and other-sex contact. Curiosity drives some to display their genitals and seek out the genitals of other children. Prepubescence is the age of sexual discovery; most children learn about adult sexual behaviors such as sexual

gay (gā) **1.** there once was a time when all "gay" meant was "happy." then it meant "homosexual." now, people are saying "that's so gay" to mean dumb and stupid. which is pretty insulting to gay people (and we don't mean the "happy" people). **2.** so please, knock it off. **3.** go to ThinkB4YouSpeak.com

Ad Council

GLSEN

Negative language about GLBT people is common in schools today, although most of it may not be meant to be hurtful. The "Think B4 You Speak" campaign encourages people to understand what they are saying and to think about the consequences of the words they use.

intercourse at this age, and assimilate cultural taboos and prejudices concerning unconventional sexual behavior. For example, it is at this age that children (especially boys) first begin to use sexual insults with each other (using taunts like "you're so gay" or "you're a fag"), questioning their friends' desirability and/or sexual orientation. In 2010, a campaign was launched in the United States called "Think B4 You Speak" to help children and adolescents understand the negativity of such phrases and the potential consequences of the words they use.

Masturbation

Generally, by the end of this period, most children are capable of stimulating themselves to orgasm. Although orgasm is possible, not all children in this age range engage in genital touching for the purpose of orgasm. Boys often learn masturbation from peers, and as they get older, they may masturbate in groups. Girls, in contrast, typically discover masturbation by accident. When masturbation does begin, both boys and girls may stimulate themselves by rubbing their penis or vulva against soft objects like blankets, pillows, or stuffed animals. Many girls experience pleasure and even orgasm by rhythmically rubbing their legs together.

Sexual Contact

Children from age 6 to puberty engage in a variety of same- and other-sex play. Sex games, such as "spin the bottle" (spinning a bottle in a circle while asking a question such as, "Who is going to kiss Marie?"; then the person whom the bottle points to must perform the task), are common and allow children to make sexual contact under the guise of a game. Play, in a sense, is the "work" of childhood, teaching interpersonal and physical skills that will be developed as we mature. Children at this age have some knowledge about sex and are curious about it, but they often have incomplete or erroneous ideas. Both boys and girls exhibit a range of same-sex sexual behaviors as they move through childhood, from casual rubbing and contact during horseplay to more focused attention on the genitals.

Rates of sexual contact among school-age children are difficult to come by, and most experts still cite Kinsey's data of 1948 and 1953. Kinsey found that 57% of men and 46% of women remembered engaging in some kind of sex play in the preadolescent years. However, the problems with research in this area are that many studies are retrospective (i.e., they asked older adults to remember what they did when they were young), and there are many reasons to think people's recollections of childhood sexuality may not be entirely accurate.

Puberty

Personal experiences of puberty from various men and women.

Gender Role Pressures in Childhood: A Male's Perspective

Male student discusses childhood pressures to be masculine.

Check Your Learning Quiz 6.3

Go to **login.cengagebrain.com** and take the online quiz.

As we grow up, all of our experiences influence our sexuality in one way or another. We learn different aspects of sexuality from these varied influences; for example, we may learn values and taboos from our parents, information from our siblings, and techniques and behavior from our peers, television, and the Internet. All of these influences contribute to our developing sexuality.

© Creatas/Picturequest

Relationships with Parents and Caretakers

When it comes to childhood sexuality, many American parents feel conflicted. They may want their children to have a positive attitude toward sexuality, but many do not know how to go about fostering this attitude. Children have a natural curiosity about sex, and when parents avoid children's questions, they reinforce children's ideas that sex is secret, mysterious, and bad. As adolescents' bodies continue to change, they may feel anxious about these changes or their relationships with other people. Accurate knowledge about sex may lead to a more positive self-image and self-acceptance. The importance of sexuality education is discussed later in this chapter.

Parents may get upset and confused when they discover that their child engages in sexual play. Sex play in children is perfectly normal, and parents should probably be more concerned if their children show no interest in their own or other children's bodies than if they want to find out what other children have "down there."

Relationships with Peers and Siblings

As children age and try to determine how they will fare in the world outside the family, their peer groups increase in importance. Friendships are an essential part of adolescent social development (Ojanen et al., 2010). Learning acceptable peer-group sexual standards is as important as learning all the other attitudes and behaviors. Children learn acceptable attitudes and behaviors for common games, sports, and even the latest media trends.

Same-Sex Peers

During middle childhood, adolescents overwhelmingly prefer same-sex to other-sex friends (Hendrick & Hendrick, 2000; Mehta & Strough, 2010). Although other-sex friendships do develop, the majority of early play is done in same-sex groupings (Fabes et al., 2003). Early on these friendships tend to be activity-based (friends are made because of shared interests or proximity), but by early adolescence, affective qualities (such as trust, loyalty, honesty) replace the activity-based interests (Bigelow, 1977; Ojanen et al., 2010). With these qualities in place, friendships can tolerate differences in interests or activities and reasonable distance separations (such as not being in the same classroom). As a result, friendships in adolescence become more stable, supportive, and intimate than they were before this time.

Peers are a major catalyst in the decision to partake in voluntary sexual experimentation with others. Often initial sexual experimentation takes place among preadolescents of the same sex. Same-sex experimentation is quite common in childhood, even among people who grow up to be predominantly heterosexual.

Other-Sex Peers

For most American children, preadolescence is when they begin to recognize their sexual nature and to see peers as potential boyfriends or girlfriends. Although this does not happen until the very end of this period, children as young as 11 begin to develop interest in others and may begin pairing off within larger groups of friends or at parties. Preadolescence has traditionally been a time of early sexual contact, such as kissing and petting, but for many this does not occur until later.

Siblings

Another fairly common childhood experience is sexual contact with siblings or close relatives, such as cousins. Most of the time, this occurs in sex games or fondling, but it can also occur as abuse, with an older sibling or relative coercing a younger one into unwanted sexual activity. Greenwald and Leitenberg (1989) found that among a sample of college students, 17% reported having sibling sexual contact before age 13. Only a small percentage involved force or threat, and penetration was rare. Research on sexual contact between siblings suggests that it can be psychologically damaging when there is a large difference between the ages of siblings or coercive force is used (Finkelhor, 1980; Rudd & Herzberger, 1999).

Parents and Anxiety

Where does it come from?

Check Your Learning Quiz 6.4

Go to **login.cengagebrain.com** and take the online quiz.

▶ **LO10** Define *adolescence* and describe various rites of passage that might be celebrated around puberty.

▶ **LO11** Describe the key physical changes during adolescence.

▶ **LO12** Explore gender differences in reactions to the changes associated with puberty.

Adolescence begins after the onset of puberty and is, in part, our emotional and cognitive reactions to puberty. Adolescence ends when the person achieves "adulthood," signified by a sense of individual identity and an ability to cope independently with internal and external problems (Lovejoy & Estridge, 1987). People reach adulthood at different times; adolescence can end at around age 17 or 18, or it can stretch into a person's 20s. It is recognized the world over as a time of transition, as the entrance into the responsibilities and privileges of adulthood. Most societies throughout history have developed rites of passage around puberty; the Jewish Bar or Bat Mitzvah, Christian confirmation, and the Hispanic Quinceañera come to mind, and other cultures have other rites. The Quinceañera—a 15th birthday celebration for Latina girls—has traditionally been used as an opportunity to discuss female adolescent developmental tasks and challenges, including teenage pregnancy and sexuality (H. Stewart, 2005).

Many cultures have rituals of passage that signify the entry of the child into adulthood. Here, a young Jewish boy reads from the Torah at his Bar Mitzvah.

© Bill Aron/PhotoEdit

We know the most about this developmental period because there are ongoing research studies on adolescent sexual behavior. Overall, we know there is no other time in the life cycle that so many things happen at once: the body undergoes rapid change; the individual begins a psychological separation from the parents; peer relationships, dating, and sexuality increase in importance; and attention turns to job, career, or college choices.

Many young people have their first experience with partnered sex during this time. It is no wonder that many adults look back on their adolescence as both a time of confusion and difficulty and a time of fond memories.

body image A person's feelings and mental picture of his or her own body's beauty.

Physical Development

During early adolescence, parents are often shocked at the extreme changes that occur in their children; children can add 5 or 6 inches in height and gain 10 to 20 pounds in less than a year. Boys may develop a lower voice and a more decidedly adult physique, whereas girls develop breasts and a more female physique. Biological changes take place in virtually every system of the body and include changes in cardiovascular status, energy levels, sexual desire, mood, and personality characteristics (Hamburg, 1986).

Maturing early or late can also be awkward for boys or girls. Because girls' growth spurts happen earlier than boys', there is a period when girls will be at least equal in height and often taller than boys; this reversal of the cultural expectation of male height often causes both sexes to be embarrassed at dances. Girls who consider themselves to be "on time" in developing feel more attractive and positive about their bodies than those who consider themselves "early" or "late" (Hamburg, 1986).

Being the last boy (or the first) in the locker room to develop pubic hair and have the penis develop can be a humiliating experience that many remember well into adulthood. Similarly, girls who are the first or last to develop breasts often suffer the cruel taunts of classmates, although the messages can be mixed. It may be this combination of beginning of sexual exploration, changing bodies, and peer pressure that results in the average adolescent having a negative **body image** (Brumberg, 1997).

Females

Menarche is the hallmark of female puberty and is often viewed as one of the most important events in a woman's life (Ersoy et al., 2005; we discussed the physiology of menarche in Chapter 4). Menarche can be a scary time for a girl who is uninformed about what to expect and an embarrassing time if she is not taught how to use tampons or pads correctly.

The beginning of menstruation can mean different things to an adolescent girl depending on how her family or her culture explains it to her. It can signify the exciting beginning of adulthood, sexuality, and the ability to have babies—but with all the potential problems that brings as well. Girls who are prepared for menstruation and who are recognized for their intellectual or creative capabilities are more likely to describe pleasurable reactions to the onset of menstruation, whereas girls who are not recognized for other abilities often experience more fear and embarrassment associated with first menstruation (Teitelman, 2004).

Although boys' first sign of sexual maturity—ejaculation—is generally a pleasurable experience that is overtly associated with sexuality, girls' sign of maturity is not associated with sexual pleasure and may be accompanied by cramps and discomfort, as well as embarrassment if the onset is at an inopportune time (such as in the middle of school). Some girls begin menstruation with little idea of what is happening or with myths about it being bad to bathe, swim, exercise, or engage in sexual activities. Many are unfamiliar with their genital anatomy, making tasks such as inserting tampons difficult and frustrating (Carroll, 2009; M. Diamond & Diamond, 1986).

Males

Adolescent development in males differs in many ways from the development in girls. Boys' voices change more drastically than girls', and their growth spurts tend to be more extreme and dramatic, usually accompanied by an increase in appetite. Because boys' adolescent growth tends to be more uneven and sporadic than girls', the adolescent boy will often appear gangly or awkward. As boys continue to develop, the larynx enlarges, bones grow, and the frame takes on a more adult appearance.

For the most part, early development in boys is usually not as embarrassing as it is in girls; beginning to shave may be seen as a sign of maturity and adulthood. However, adolescent boys do experience frequent spontaneous erections, which may have no association with sexuality but are nonetheless quite embarrassing. Their increased sexual desire is often released through **nocturnal emissions** and increased masturbation.

Psychosexual Development

Adolescence is, by far, the most psychologically and socially difficult of the life cycle changes. Adolescents struggle with a number of tasks: achieving comfort with their bodies, developing an identity separate from their parents', trying to prove their capacity to establish meaningful intimate and sexual relationships, beginning to think abstractly and futuristically, and establishing emotional self-awareness (Gemelli, 1996). We now examine these life cycle changes.

In early adolescence, preteens begin to shift their role from child to adolescent, trying to forge an identity separate from their family by establishing stronger rela-

nocturnal emission Involuntary ejaculation during sleep, also referred to as a wet dream.

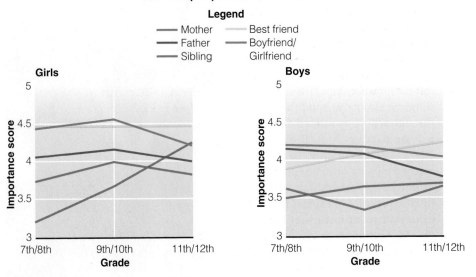

Figure 6.2 The age differences in mean ratings of the importance of each type of relationship to one's life during adolescence (1 = not at all important; 5 = extremely important). Source: From Brown et al. [1997]. Reprinted by permission of Cambridge University Press.

tionships with peers. Same-sex friendships are common by the eighth grade and may develop into first same-sex sexual contacts as well (L. M. Diamond, 2000; Lawlis & Lewis, 1987). The importance of a best friend grows as an adolescent matures. In fact, by the end of high school, both girls and boys rated their relationship with their best friend as their most important relationship (B. B. Brown et al., 1997; see Figure 6.2).

Early adolescence, as most of us remember, is often filled with "cliques," as people look to peers for validation and standards of behavior. Dating also often begins at this age, which drives many adolescents to become preoccupied with their bodily appearance and to experiment with different "looks." Young adolescents are often very concerned with body image at this time. Many young girls, in an attempt to achieve the perfect "model" figure, will endlessly diet, sometimes to the point of serious eating disorders. The Youth Risk Behavior Surveillance System found that

On Your Mind

It sounds like lots of kids have problems during adolescence, but mine was just fine. Is that weird?

many young boys and girls are developing eating disorders and may turn to drugs such as steroids to achieve the perfect body (Pisetsky et al., 2008).

By about age 14, most adolescents experience an increasing interest in intimate relationships. The social environment also helps build this interest through school-sponsored dances and private parties (B. B. Brown et al., 1997). Adolescents who have not yet reached puberty or those who feel they might be gay or lesbian often feel intense pressure to express interest in other-sex relationships at this time (K. M. Cohen & Savin-Williams, 1996). Many adolescents increase the frequency of dating as they try to integrate sexuality into their growing capacity for adult-to-adult intimacy.

For the average middle adolescent, dating consists of going to movies or spending time together after school or on weekends. Early dating is often quite informal, and going out in mixed groups is very popular. During this period, couples develop longer term and more exclusive relationships, and early sexual experimentation (deep kissing, fondling) may also begin.

In early and middle adolescence, teens try on different looks, from trendy to rebellious, as they develop an identity separate from their parents.

DreamPictures/Getty Images

have sexual intercourse, nearly 50% of women were motivated by affection for their partner, whereas only about 25% cited curiosity as their primary motivation. Twenty-four percent said they just went along with it (fewer than 8% of men said that); 4% of women reported being forced to have sex the first time, whereas only about 3 men in 1,000 (0.3%) reported being forced.

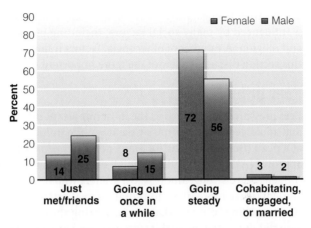

Figure 6.5 Relationship with partner at first intercourse among males and females aged 15 to 19: United States, 2006–2008. Source: Abma et al., 2010

First sexual intercourse is typically a monumental occasion. For many teens, this experience contributes to the redefining of self and the reconfiguration of relationships with friends, family members, and sexual partners (Upchurch et al., 1998).

Adolescent Same-Sex Sexual Behavior

We know that same-sex sexual behavior is common in adolescence, both for those who will go on to have predominantly heterosexual relationships and those who will have predominantly same-sex relationships. Some gay and lesbian adolescents experience sexual intercourse during their teenage years, before they identify themselves as lesbian or gay (Saewyc et al., 1998).

It is difficult to determine actual figures for adolescent same-sex sexual behavior. Studies of high-school students find that about 10% to 13% report being "unsure" about their sexual orientation, whereas 1% to 6% consider themselves homosexual or bisexual; still, anywhere from 8% to 12% report sexual contact with same-sex partners (Faulkner & Cranston, 1998). Such research, however, relies on self-reports; people may define homosexual differently, or they may not be comfortable being open about their experiences because of homosexual stigma. The NSSHB found that same-sex sexual activity was relatively uncommon in adolescence but increased in older age groups (Herbenick et al., 2010).

When Teens Are Sexually Exploited

Prostitution and pornography.

Check Your Learning Quiz 6.6

Go to **login.cengagebrain.com** and take the online quiz.

▶ **LO19** Identify two ways in which peers can influence teen sexual behavior.

▶ **LO20** Explain how religion can affect an adolescent's sexual behavior.

The decision to engage in sexual contact with another person is a personal one, yet it is influenced by many social factors, including peers, relationships with parents, and religion. A number of other social factors influence sexual behavior as well, and this section discusses a few of the more important ones.

Peer Influences

Peer pressure is often cited as the most important influence on teen sexual behavior, and adolescence is certainly a time when the influence of one's friends and peers is at a peak (Busse et al., 2010). Many adolescents base their own self-worth on peer approval (Akers et al., 2011; Rudolph et al., 2005). Even among preadolescents, peer influences are strong; among sixth graders who have engaged in sexual intercourse, students were more likely to initiate sexual intercourse if they thought that peers were engaging in it and that it would bring them some kind of social gain. Those who did not initiate sexual intercourse were more likely to believe that their behavior would be stigmatized or disapproved of by their peers (Grunbaum et al., 2002).

Remember, though, that people's perceptions of what their peers are doing has a greater influence on them than the peers' actual behavior. Among those subject to and applying peer pressure, many heterosexual adolescent males feel the need to "prove" their masculinity, leading to early sexual activity. Peer pressure is often rated as one of the top reasons that adolescents give for engaging in sexual intercourse.

Relationship with Parents

Good parental communication, an atmosphere of honesty and openness in the home, a two-parent home, and reasonable rules about dating and relationships are among the most important factors associated with adolescents delaying their first sexual intercourse (Akers et al., 2011; Hahm et al., 2008; Lam et al., 2008; Regnerus & Luckies, 2006). This may be attributed to the fact that close families are more likely to transmit their sexual values and integrate their children into their religious and moral views. Heterosexual children from these homes are also more likely to use contraception when they do engage in sexual intercourse (Halpern-Felsher et al., 2004; Zimmer-Gembeck & Helfand, 2008). This is the case among almost all races and ethnic groups (L. M. Baumeister et al., 1995; Brooks-Gunn & Furstenberg, 1989; Kotchick et al., 1999).

Research has found that many American parents do not discuss sex before an adolescent's first sexual experience (Beckett et al., 2010). If a parent does talk about sex, it is generally the mother who tends to be the primary communicator about sexuality to children; in one study of Latino youths, mothers did the majority of all communication about sexuality to their teenagers (L. M. Baumeister et al., 1995; Raffaelli & Green, 2003). Typically, mothers talk more to daughters about sexuality than to sons (Martin & Luke, 2010).

The ADD Health study (2002) has also found that there is a maternal influence on the timing of first sexual intercourse for heterosexual adolescents, especially for females. A mother's satisfaction with her relationship with her daughter, disapproval of her daughter having sex, and frequent communication about sex is related to a delay of first sexual intercourse (Lam et al., 2008; Tsui-Sui et al., 2010). Fathers are also important—in fact, girls who have a close relationship with their father are more likely to delay sex (Day & Padilla-Walker, 2009; Regnerus & Luchies, 2006; Wilson et al., 2010).

Religion

Although the relationship between religiosity and sexual activity is complex, in general, more religious heterosexual youths tend to delay first sexual intercourse, have fewer incidents of premarital sexual activity, and have fewer sexual partners (S. Hardy & Raffaelli, 2003; Hull et al., 2010; Nonnemaker et al., 2003). This correlation may be because young people who attend church frequently and who value religion in their lives are less sexually experienced overall (P. King & Boyatzis, 2004; S. D. White & DeBlassie, 1992). Not only do major Western religions and many other world religions discourage premarital sex, but religious adolescents also tend to develop friendships and relationships within their religious institutions, and thus have strong ties to people who are more likely to disapprove of early sexual activity. However, once teens begin engaging in sexual behaviors, religious affiliation and frequency of religious attendance have been found to have little impact on frequency of sexual behaviors (R. Jones et al., 2005).

On Your Mind

Why is there so much pressure for teens to have sex?

Check Your Learning Quiz 6.7

Go to **login.cengagebrain.com** and take the online quiz.

Although contraception, pregnancy, parenthood, and STIs are discussed further in other chapters, this chapter discusses these issues in relation to adolescents.

Approximately 80% of U.S. teens use a contraceptive method the first time they engage in sexual intercourse, and condoms are the most popular method (Abma et al., 2010; Figure 6.6). Adolescents who are able to talk to their mothers about sexuality are more likely to use contraception than adolescents who cannot talk to their mothers (Jaccard & Dittus, 2000; Lam et al., 2008; Meschke et al., 2000).

Of all the areas of adolescent sexual behavior, we probably know the most about teenage pregnancy because of its many impacts on the life of the teenager, the teenager's family, and society as a whole. The U.S. birthrate for female teens was 42.5 births per 1,000 females in 2007, which was higher than many other countries around the world (Abma et al., 2010; Brugman et al., 2010). For comparison, the teen birthrate in Canada was 13, Germany was 10, and Italy was 7. Teen birthrates

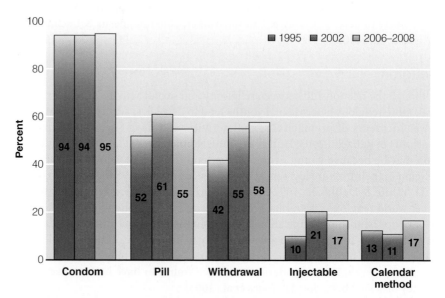

Figure 6.6 Ever-use of contraceptive methods among sexually experienced females aged 15 to 19. Source: From Centers for Disease Control and Prevention/National Center for Health Statistics, National Survey of Family Growth, 2006–2008.

© David J. Green–Lifestyle/Alamy

in the United States decreased steadily from 1991 to 2005, increased again until 2007, and then decreased in 2008 (Abma et al., 2010). Interestingly, although the majority of U.S. teens want to avoid a pregnancy, 70% of females and 50% of males say they would be accepting of a pregnancy outside of marriage (Abma et al., 2010).

The long-term consequences of teenage pregnancy may be difficult for the mother, child, and extended family. Teenage mothers are more likely to drop out of school, have poorer physical and mental health, and be on welfare than their non–childbearing peers, and their children often have lower birth weights, poorer health and cognitive abilities, more behavioral problems, and fewer educational opportunities (Meschke et al., 2000). Teen parenting also has an impact on others, such as the parents of the teens (who may end up having to take care of their children's children), and on society in general, because these parents are more likely to need government assistance.

Key Terms Exercise

Match the term with the definition.

▶ **LO23** Discuss the incidence of sexually transmitted infections in teens.

However, teen pregnancies do not always preclude teen mothers from living healthy, fulfilling lives. In fact, there are examples of teenagers who become pregnant and raise healthy babies while pursuing their own interests. However, the problems a teenage mother faces are many, especially if there is no partner participating in the child's care. A teen who has support from her partner, family, and friends, and who is able to stay in school has a better chance of living a fulfilling life.

In studies of teen pregnancy and birth, most of the focus has been on the mothers, who often bear the brunt of the emotional, personal, and financial costs of childbearing (Wei, 2000). Adolescent fathers are more difficult to study. Teenage fathers may not support their partners and become uninvolved soon after; thus, the problem of single mothers raising children can be traced, in part, to the lack of responsibility of teen fathers. Society asks little of the teenage male, and there are few social pressures on him to take responsibility for his offspring.

However, some adolescent fathers do accept their role in both pregnancy and parenthood, and realistically assess their responsibilities toward the mother and child. Ideally, teenage fathers should be integrated into the lives of their children and should be expected to take equal responsibility for them.

Adolescent parenthood affects every race, every income group, and every part of American society; it is not just a problem of the inner-city poor. Historically, White teenagers have had lower birthrates than Black or Latino adolescents, a trend that continued in the 1990s. Although through much of the 1990s, Black teenagers had the highest rates of pregnancy, birth, and abortion, all three rates declined by about 20% between 1990 and 1996. Because the birthrate declined more steeply among Black than White teenagers, the gap between these two groups narrowed. Unmarried mothers and their children of all races are more likely to live in poverty than any other segment of the population.

What is it about American society that seems to foster such high rates of teenage pregnancy? A complex series of factors is at work. American society is extremely conflicted about the issue of sexuality in general. Our teens are exposed to sexual scenes in movies and television, yet we hesitate to discuss sex frankly with them. We allow advertising to use blatantly sexual messages and half-dressed models, yet we will not permit advertising for birth control; there is also significant resistance to sex education in the schools.

Today, when teenagers do become pregnant, opportunities may be limited; it is difficult to have a baby and attend high school all day or work at a job. The United States is far behind most other Western countries in providing day-care services that would help single or young parents care for their children. Better counseling, birth control, day-care services, and hope for the future can help ensure that the teenagers who are at risk for unwanted pregnancies and the children of those unwanted pregnancies are cared for by our society.

Sexually Transmitted Infections

Although STIs are discussed in great detail in Chapter 12, this section briefly discusses adolescent STI rates. Sexually active teens are at greater risk for acquiring some STIs for behavioral, cultural, and biological reasons (Abma et al., 2010). Rates of chlamydia and gonorrhea are higher in 15- to 19-year-old females than any other age group (Abma et al., 2010). Although rates of other STIs are lower, they have been steadily increasing every year. Even though 15- to 24-year-olds account for only 25% of the sexually active population, they acquire approximately 50% of all new STIs (Weinstock et al., 2000).

Although gay, lesbian, and bisexual youths may not need contraception for birth control purposes, they do need it for protection from STIs. Research has found that gays and lesbians are less likely to use condoms or other barrier methods than their straight counterparts (S. M. Blake et al., 2001; Saewyc et al., 1998). Increasing condom use in all teens, regardless of sexual orientation, is imperative in decreasing STIs.

Preventing STIs and teenage pregnancy are both important goals of sex education programs. The following section discusses the importance of sexuality education and what is being taught in schools today.

Check Your Learning Quiz 6.8

Go to **login.cengagebrain.com** and take the online quiz.

Sexuality education inspires powerful emotions and a considerable amount of controversy. In fact, it may be one of the most heated topics in the field of sexuality, as different sides debate whether and how sexuality education programs should be implemented in the schools.

Why Sexuality Education Is Important

Although many people claim that knowledge about sexuality may be harmful, studies have found that it is the lack of sexuality education, ignorance about sexual issues, or unresolved curiosity that is harmful (S. Gordon, 1986). Students who participate in comprehensive sexuality education programs are less permissive about premarital sex than students who do not take these courses. Accurate knowledge about sex may also lead to a more positive self-image and self-acceptance. Sexuality affects almost all aspects of human behavior and relationships with other persons. Therefore, if we understand and accept our own sexuality and the sexuality of others, we will have more satisfying relationships. Some experts believe that not talking to children about sex before adolescence is a primary cause of sexual problems later in life (Calderone, 1983).

Another reason to support sexuality education is that children receive a lot of information about sex through the media, and much of it is not based on fact (Rideout et al., 2010). The media and peers are often primary sources of information about sexuality. Sex is present in the songs children listen to, the magazines they read, the shows they watch on television, and on the Internet. Although it is true that a growing number of educational sites on the Internet are dedicated to sexuality, there are also many poor sources of information on the web.

Proponents of sexuality education believe that sexual learning occurs even when there are no formalized sexuality education programs. When teachers or parents avoid children's questions or appear embarrassed or evasive, they reinforce children's ideas that sex is secret, mysterious, and bad (Milton et al., 2001). As adolescents approach puberty, they may feel anxious about their bodily changes or their relationships with other people. Many teenagers feel uncomfortable asking questions and may be pressured by their peers to engage in sexual activity when they do not feel ready. Giving teenagers information about sex can help them to deal with these changes. The majority of parents, teachers, and students want sexuality education to be taught in secondary schools and high schools, and favor comprehensive sex education (Bleakley et al., 2006).

comprehensive sexuality education programs Programs that often begin in kindergarten and continue through 12th grade, presenting a wide variety of topics to help students develop their own skills while learning factual information.

The History of Sexuality Education in the U.S.

Concern over skyrocketing rates of venereal diseases (what we now refer to as STIs) in the early 1900s resulted in the formation of two groups, the American Society of Sanitary and Moral Prophylaxis and the American Federation for Sex Hygiene. Although these groups helped to further the cause of sexuality education, they concentrated their attention on STIs. Their approach was to use sexuality education to explain biology and anatomy and to address adolescents' natural sexual curiosity. School sexuality education was very scientific and avoided all discussions of interpersonal sexuality.

Starting in the early 1900s, sexuality education was implemented by various national youth groups, including the YMCA, YWCA, Girl Scouts, Boy Scouts, and 4-H Clubs. These programs were developed mainly to demonstrate to young people the responsibilities required in parenting and to discourage early childbearing. More controversial, however, has been whether to include sexuality education as part of the public school curriculum.

In the United States, for example, the opposition to sexuality education has often been due to two attitudes: first, that sexuality is private, should be discouraged in children, and is best discussed in the context of a person's moral and religious beliefs; and second, that public schools are by their nature public, cannot discuss sex without giving children implicit permission to be sexual, and should not promote the moral or religious beliefs of any particular group. The result of these conflicting attitudes was the belief that sexuality education was best performed by parents in the home.

U.S. Sexuality Education Today

The majority of U.S. states either recommend or require sexuality education in public schools. Most place requirements on how abstinence or contraception information should be included, and overall, curriculums are heavily weighted toward stressing abstinence (Alan Guttmacher Institute, 2008). As of 2010, 27 states require that abstinence be stressed in school sexuality education, whereas 9 states required it be covered (Alan Guttmacher Institute, 2011).

Because each state is responsible for developing its own sexuality education program, the programs vary greatly. Overall, programs are typically either comprehensive or abstinence-based. **Comprehensive sexuality education programs** are those

What Do Children Want to Know?

And what are they ready for?

that begin in kindergarten and continue through 12th grade—they include a wide variety of topics and help students to develop their own skills and learn factual information. **Abstinence-only programs** emphasize abstinence from all sexual behaviors, and they typically do not provide information about contraception or disease prevention.

Comprehensive Sexuality Education Programs

Today, comprehensive sexuality education programs try to help students develop a positive view of sexuality. The Guidelines for Comprehensive Sexuality Education (Sexuality Information and Education Council of the United States, 2004) are a framework designed to help promote the development of comprehensive sexuality education programs nationwide. Originally developed in 1990, the guidelines were revised again in 2004 and include four main goals for sexuality education:

1. To provide accurate information about human sexuality
2. To provide an opportunity for young people to question, explore, and assess their sexual attitudes
3. To help young people develop interpersonal skills, including communication, decision making, peer refusal, and assertiveness skills that will allow them to create satisfying relationships
4. To help young people develop the ability to exercise responsibility regarding sexual relationships

The guidelines have also been adapted for use outside the United States and are being used in many countries to help design and implement a variety of sexuality education programs.

Abstinence-Only Sexuality Education Programs

Abstinence-only programs began in the early 1990s when there was a proliferation of sexuality education programs that used fear to discourage students from engaging in sexual behavior. These programs include mottos such as "Do the right thing—wait for the ring," or "Pet your dog—not your date." Important information about topics such as anatomy or STIs is often omitted from these programs, and there is an overreliance on the negative consequences of sexual behavior. These negative consequences are often exaggerated, portraying sexual behavior as dangerous and harmful. In 1996, the federal government also passed a law outlining the federal definition of abstinence education. These programs teach:

abstinence-only programs Sexuality education programs that emphasize abstinence from all sexual behaviors.

Online Activities

Key Terms	Video	Animation	Readings	Assessment
	Would it destroy a child's life if they saw their parents naked or having sex?			Check Your Learning Quiz 6.1
gender constancy	Cross-cultural Sex Talk: Children and Teens		Sexual Knowledge and Attitudes in Early Childhood	Check Your Learning Quiz 6.2
breast buds, semenarche	Puberty Gender Role Pressures in Childhood: A Male's Perspective			Check Your Learning Quiz 6.3
			Parents and Anxiety: Where Does It Come From?	Check Your Learning Quiz 6.4
body image, nocturnal emission	It sounds like lots of kids have problems during adolescence, but mine was just fine. Is that weird?			Check Your Learning Quiz 6.5

Measure ^Your Learning

Key Terms	Video	Animation	Readings	Assessment
abstinence	Why do guys masturbate so much more than girls?		When Teens Are Sexually Exploited	Check Your Learning Quiz 6.6
	Why is there so much pressure for teens to have sex?			Check Your Learning Quiz 6.7
		Key Terms Exercise		Check Your Learning Quiz 6.8
comprehensive sexuality education programs, abstinence-only programs			What Do Children Want to Know and What Are They Ready For? Sexuality Education around the World	Check Your Learning Quiz 6.9
	Sex Education: the Dutch Approach			Evaluating the Results of Sexuality Education Programs

Love, Intimacy,
and Sexual Relationships

7

© Max Wanger/Corbis

Prepare to Learn

1 **GO** to your **Psychology CourseMate** at **login.cengagebrain.com** and take the **Chapter Pre-Test** to introduce yourself to this chapter's topics and see what you may already know.

2 **READ** the **Learning Objectives** (LOs, in the left sidebars) and begin the chapter.

3 **COMPLETE** the **Online Activities** (in the right sidebars) *as you read each module.* Activities include **videos, animations, readings, and quizzes.**

4 **CHECK Your Learning** by going online to take the quiz at the end of each module and review material as necessary.

5 **MEASURE Your Learning** after reading the chapter by taking the online **Chapter Post-Test.** Use the chapter review guide at the end of the chapter as needed.

WATCH for these **Online Activities** icons as you read:

Video

Animation

Reading

Assessment

Think Critically

These Online Activities are essential to mastering this chapter. Go to login.cengagebrain.com.

 Videos Explore diverse perspectives on sex as well as common questions:

- Why is love so confusing?
- What is the difference between being in "love" and in "lust?"
- Love Science
- How can I tell the difference between being in love and just deeply liking someone?
- Forgive and Forget?
- Isn't it boring to stay with the same person your whole life?
- The Secret to Staying in Love
- Is it possible to take a hook-up relationship to the next level and become a "couple"?
- Living Together: Pros and Cons
- What is a "prenuptial" agreement?
- Dena and Lenny Are Getting Married

- Same-Sex Marriage
- Deciding Whether to Have Kids
- Divorce: Betrayal and Sadness

 Animations Interact with and visualize important processes, timelines, and concepts:

- The Love Triangle
- Attachment Styles
- Timeline: Same-Sex Relationships around the Globe

 Readings Delve deeper into key content:

- Love
- Love—It's All in Your Head
- Developing Intimacy Skills

- In the Men's Locker Room
- Arranged Marriages
- What Is Polyamory?
- Extramarital Sex in Other Cultures
- Sexuality in Same-Sex Relationships
- In Support of Same-Sex Marriage

 Assessment Measure your mastery:

- Chapter Pre-Test
- Check Your Learning Quizzes
- Chapter Post-Test

 Think Critically Challenge your thinking about data and accepted norms:

- Good Looks or a Good Prospect? Comparing Preferences across Cultures

▸ **LO1** Differentiate between romantic love and companionate love.

THIS CHAPTER EXAMINES love and sex in all forms of intimate relationships, both other sex and same sex, as people date, cohabit, marry, divorce, or remarry.

▼

One of the great mysteries of humankind is the capacity to love, to make attachments with others that involve deep feeling, selflessness, and commitment. Throughout history, literature and art have portrayed the saving powers of love. How many songs have been written about its passion, and how many films have depicted its power to change people's lives? We go through life trying to come to terms with loving, trying to figure out why we are attracted to certain types or why we fall in love with the people we do. The mystery of love is part of its attraction.

We are surrounded with images of love in the media and are taught from the time we first listen to fairy tales that love is the answer to most of life's problems. Movies, music, and television inundate us with stories of what love is, and these stories have a powerful impact on us (Griffin, 2006). Are there different, separate kinds of love—friendship, passion, love of parents—or are they all simply variations on one fundamental emotion? Does love really "grow"? What is the relationship between love and sexuality?

The Forms and Measures of Love

romantic love Idealized love, based on romance and perfection.

companionate love An intimate form of love that involves friendly affection and deep attachment based on a familiarity with the loved one. Also referred to as conjugal love.

We all love, and one of the characteristics of love is that we often believe that the intensity of the emotion is unique to us, that no one else has ever loved as we have loved. We can feel many different kinds of love, such as love of a friend, love of a parent, love of a child, love of a celebrity, or love of a pet. Philosophers, historians,

© JupiterImages/Creatas/Alamy

social scientists, and other scholars have all made attempts to untangle these types of love.

Romantic versus Companionate Love

Romantic love is the all-encompassing, passionate love of romantic songs and poetry, of tearjerker movies and romance novels, and it has become the prevailing model of sexual relationships and marriage in the Western world. Romantic love is also sometimes called *passionate love*, *infatuation*, *obsessive love*, and even *lovesickness*, and with it comes a sense of ecstasy and anxiety, physical attraction, and sexual desire. Those who experience romantic love tend to idealize the partner, ignoring faults during the newfound joy of the attachment. Passionate love blooms in the initial euphoria of a new attachment to a sexual partner, and it often seems as if we're swept away by it; that is why we say we "fall" in love, or even fall "head over heels" in love.

Unfortunately, perhaps, passion of that intensity fades after a time. If the relationship is to continue, romantic love usually develops into **companionate love**. Companionate love involves feelings of deep affection, attachment, intimacy, and ease with the partner, as well as the development of trust, loyalty, acceptance, and a willingness to sacrifice for the partner (Critelli et al., 1986; Regan, 2006; Shaver & Hazan, 1987). Although companionate love does not have the passionate high and

© Stockbyte/PictureQuest

Companionate love involves deep affection, trust, loyalty, attachment, and intimacy; although passion is often present, companionate love lacks the high and low swings of romantic love.

On Your Mind

Why is love so confusing?

▶ **LO2** Identify and define Lee's six styles of love.

▶ **LO3** Identify Sternberg's three building blocks of love and describe some of the ways in which they can be combined to form different types of love.

low swings of romantic love, passion is certainly present for many companionate lovers. Although some may see the mellowing of that passion as a loss of love rather than a development of a different kind of love, the mutual commitment to develop a new, more mature kind of love is, in fact, what we should mean by "true love."

Lee's Colors of Love

Psychologist John Alan Lee (1974, 1988, 1998) suggests that in romantic relationships, there are more forms of love than just romantic and companionate love. He identifies six basic ways to love, to which he gives Greek and Latin names.

- *Eros* is romantic love. Erotic lovers speak of their immediate attraction to their lover, to his or her eyes, skin, fragrance, or body. Most have the picture of an ideal partner in their mind, which a real partner cannot fulfill; that is why purely erotic love does not last.
- *Ludus* (LOO-diss) is playful love. Ludic lovers enjoy the act of seduction. Commitment, dependency, and intimacy are not valued, and ludic lovers will often juggle several relationships at the same time.
- *Storge* (STOR-gay) is a quiet, calm love that builds over time, similar to companionate love. Storgic lovers don't suddenly "fall in love" and do not dream of some idealized, romantic lover; marriage, stability, and comfort within love are the goal. Should the relationship break up, the storgic partners would probably remain friends, a status unthinkable to erotic lovers who have split.
- *Mania* is possessive and dependent love. Each encouraging sign from the lover brings joy; each little slight brings heartache, which makes their lives dramatic and painful. Manic lovers fear separation; they may sit by the phone waiting for the beloved to call, or they may call their beloved incessantly. They tend to wonder why all their relationships ultimately fail.
- *Pragma* is practical love. Pragmatic lovers have a "shopping list" of qualities they are looking for in a relationship. They are very practical about their relationship and lovers. Pragmatic lovers want a deep, lasting love but believe the best way to get it is to assess their own qualities and make the best "deal" in the romantic marketplace. They tend to be planners—planning the best time to get married, have children, and even when to divorce.
- *Agape (AH-ga-pay)* love is altruistic, selfless, never demanding, patient, and true. Never jealous, not needing reciprocity, agape love tends to happen in brief episodes. Lee found few long-term agape lovers. Lee gives the example

of a man whose lover was faced with a distressing choice between him and another man, and so he gracefully bowed out.

Lee points out that two lovers with compatible styles will be happier and more content with each other than two with incompatible styles. Couples who approach loving differently often cannot understand why their partners react the way they do or how they can hurt their partners unintentionally. Higher levels of manic and ludic love styles are associated with poorer psychological health, whereas higher levels of storge and eros love styles are associated with higher levels of psychological health (Blair, 2000).

Sternberg's Love Triangles

Robert Sternberg (1998, 1999) has suggested that different strategies of loving are really different ways of combining the basic building blocks of love: passion, intimacy, and commitment. Sternberg combines these elements into triangles, forming seven types of love (see Figure 7.1 on the next page).

- *Passion* is sparked by physical attraction and sexual desire and drives a person to pursue a romantic relationship. Passion instills a deep desire for union, and although it is often expressed sexually, self-esteem, nurturing, domination, submission, and self-actualization may also contribute to the experience. Passion is the element that identifies romantic forms of love; it is absent in the love of a parent for a child. Passion fires up quickly in a romantic relationship but is also the first element to fade (Ahmetoglu et al., 2010).
- *Intimacy* involves feelings of closeness, connectedness, and bondedness in a loving relationship. It is the emotional investment one has in the relationship and includes such things as the desire to support and help the other, happiness, mutual understanding, emotional support, and communication. The intimacy component of love is experienced in many loving relationships, such as parent–child, sibling, and friendship relationships.
- *Commitment,* in the short term, is the decision to love someone; in the long term, it is the determination to maintain that love. The marriage ceremony, for example, is a public display of a couple's commitment to each other. Unlike passion, which is quick to fire up and die out, commitment builds slowly and is often related to relationship length (Ahmetoglu et al., 2010). This element can sustain a relationship that is temporarily (or even permanently) going through a period without passion or intimacy.

The Love Triangle

Where does your relationship fall?

Love

From childhood to maturity.

On Your Mind

What is the difference between being in "love" and in "lust"?

▶ **LO4** Explain how Schachter and Singer's experiment using epinephrine with students provided valuable information on the relationship between physiological arousal and love.

The Physiology of Love

If you ask people how they know they are in love, most describe physiological sensations: "I felt so excited I couldn't breathe"; "My throat choked up"; "I felt tingling all over." If you look at those descriptions, couldn't they also be descriptions of fear,

Robert Sternberg, a professor of psychology at Yale University, believes that love is made up of three elements: passion, intimacy, and commitment, each of which may be present or absent in a relationship. The presence or absence of these components produces eight triangles (seven of these involve at least one component; the eighth represents the absence of any components, referred to as nonlove). Problems can occur in a relationship if one person's triangle differs significantly from the other's. This can happen when one person has more or less of one of the three elements of love. Following are the various types of love proposed by Sternberg.

 **Nonlove**		In most of our casual daily relationships, there is no sense of intimacy, passion, or commitment.
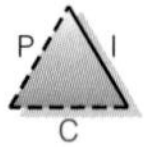 **Liking**		When there is intimacy without (sexual) passion and without strong personal commitment, we are friends. Friends can separate for long periods of time and resume the relationship as if it had never ended.
 **Infatuation**		Passion alone leads to infatuation. Infatuation refers to physiological arousal and a sexual desire for another person. Casual hookups and one-night stands would fall into this category. Typically, infatuation quickly fades, often to be replaced with infatuation for someone else!
 **Empty love**		Empty love involves only commitment, as in a couple who stays together even though their relationship long ago lost its passion and intimacy. However, relationships can begin with commitment alone and develop intimacy and passion.
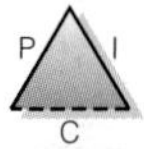 **Romantic love**		Passion and intimacy lead to romantic love, which is often the first phase of a relationship. Romantic love is often an intense, joyful experience.
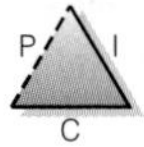 **Companionate love**		Companionate love ranges from long-term, deeply committed friendships to married or long-term couples who have experienced a decrease in the passionate aspect of their love.
 **Fatuous (FAT-you-us) love**		Love is fatuous (which means silly or foolish) when one does not really know the person to whom one is making a commitment. Hollywood often portrays two people who meet, become infatuated, and make a commitment by the end of the movie. However, a committed relationship continues even after passion fades, so it makes sense to know one's partner before making a commitment.
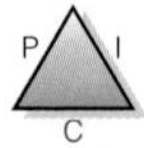 **Consummate love**		Consummate, or complete, love has all three elements in balance. Even after achieving consummate love, we can lose it: passion can fade, intimacy can stagnate, and commitment can be undermined by attraction to another. But it is consummate love we all strive for.

SOURCE: Sternberg, Robert J. (1986). "A Triangle Theory of Love," *Psychological Review, 93, 119–135.* Reprinted by permission of the author.

Figure 7.1 Steinberg's Triangular Theory of Love

anger, or excitement? Is there a difference between being in love and being on a roller-coaster?

Perhaps not. In a famous experiment, Schachter and Singer (1962) gave students a shot of epinephrine (adrenaline), which causes general arousal, including sweaty palms, increased heart rate, increased breathing, and so on. Some of the students were informed of what to expect from the epinephrine, others were not.

Each group was put into a waiting room with a student who was acting happy or a student who was acting angry. When they felt aroused, the informed students assumed they were feeling the effects of the epinephrine. However, the uninformed students tended to believe they were feeling happy or angry. Schachter and Singer concluded that an emotion happens when there is general physiological arousal for whatever reason and a label is attached to it—and that label might be any emotion.

So, is love just a label we give to a racing heart? The idea may explain why we tend to associate love and sex so closely; sexual excitement is a state of intense physiological arousal. Maybe that is why lust is so often confused with love.

Compulsiveness: Addicted to Love

Being in love can produce a sense of ecstasy, euphoria, and a feeling of well-being, much like a powerful drug. In fact, when a person is in love, his or her body releases the drug phenylethylamine, which produces these feelings (Sabelli et al., 1996). (Phenylethylamine is also present in chocolate, which may be why we love it so much, especially during a breakup!) Some people do move from relationship to relationship as if they were love addicted, trying to continually recreate that feeling, or else they obsessively hang on to a love partner long after his or her interest has waned.

Love addiction is reinforced by the popular media's portrayals (even as far back as Shakespeare's Romeo and Juliet) of passionate love as all-consuming. It fosters the belief that only one person is fated to be your "soul mate," that love is always mutual, and that you'll live "happily ever after." Some people feel the need to be in love because society teaches that only then are they really whole, happy, and fulfilled in their role as a woman or a man. Yet love based solely on need can never be truly fulfilling. In Peele and Brodsky's (1991) book Love and Addiction, they argue that love addiction is more common than most believe and that it is based on a continuation of an adolescent view of love that is never replaced as the person matures. Counseling or psychotherapy may help the person come to terms with his or her addiction to love.

Love—It's All in Your Head

Your brain's involvement in feelings of love and romance.

Love Science

Discussion of research using teenagers to analyze what happens in the brain during feelings of love.

Check Your Learning Quiz 7.1

Go to **login.cengagebrain.com** and take the online quiz.

Why do we love in the first place? What purpose does love serve? After all, most animals mate successfully without experiencing "love." Theories on why we form emotional bonds in the first place can be grouped into three categories: behavioral reinforcement, cognitive, and evolutionary. We will also explore the nature and quality of the bond with the caregiver and attachment styles.

Behavioral Reinforcement Theories

One group of theories suggests that we love because another person reinforces positive feelings in ourselves—they make us feel good. Lott and Lott (1961) suggested that a rewarding or positive feeling in the presence of another person makes us like them, even when the reward has nothing to do with the other person. For example, they found that children who were rewarded continually by their teachers came to like their classmates more than children who were not equally rewarded. The opposite is also true. Griffitt and Veitch (1971) found that people tend to dislike people they meet in a hot, crowded room, no matter what those people's personalities are like. Behavioral reinforcement theory suggests that we like people we associate with feeling good and love people if the association is very good. Love develops through a series of mutually reinforcing activities.

Cognitive Theories

Cognitive theories of loving are based on an interesting paradox: The less people are paid for a task, the more they tend to like it. In other words, a person tends to think, "Here I am washing this car, and I'm not even getting paid for it. Why am I doing this? I must love to wash cars!" The same goes for relationships. If we are with a person often and find our-

The behavioral reinforcement theory suggests that we love people we associate with feeling good. Our love for them grows out of doing things together that are mutually reinforcing.

selves doing things for them, we ask, "Why am I with her so often? Why am I doing her laundry? I must like her—I must even love her!" This theory suggests the action comes first and the interpretation comes later (Tzeng, 1992). Studies have also found that when we think certain people like us, we're more likely to be attracted to them (Ridge & Reber, 2002).

Evolutionary Theory

Evolutionary theorists try to understand the evolutionary advantages of human behaviors. Love, they believe, developed as the human form of three basic instincts: the need to be protected from outside threats, the instinct of the parent to protect the child, and the sexual drive. Love is an evolutionary strategy that helps us form the bonds we need to reproduce and pass our genes on to the next generation (Gonzaga & Haselton, 2008). We love to propagate the species.

To evolutionary theorists, that would explain why we tend to fall in love with people who we think have positive traits: we want to pass those traits along to our children. In fact, evolutionary theorists argue that their perspective can explain why heterosexual men look for attractive women, and why heterosexual women look for successful men, the world over (see the section on cultural influences on attraction later in this chapter). Heterosexual men want a fit, healthy woman to carry their offspring, and heterosexual women want a man with the resources to protect them and help care for the infant in the long period they devote to reproduction. For most of history, this included 9 months of pregnancy and more than a year of breast-feeding. Love creates the union that maximizes each partner's chance of passing on their genes to the next generation.

Attraction Chemicals: Pheromones

Research has shown that biological factors can also influence whom we fall in love with (Garver-Apgar et al., 2006; Rodriguez, 2004; Santos et al., 2005; Savic et al., 2005; Thorne & Amrein, 2003). We register the "smells" of people through their **pheromones** (FAIR-oh-moans)—odorless chemicals secreted by both humans and animals (Rodriguez, 2004; Thorne & Amrein, 2003). These pheromones are processed in the hypothalamus, and they influence our choice of sexual partner (Savic et al., 2005). Both men and women respond to pheromones. One study found that women reported their male partners to be more loving (and jealous) when they were ovulating (Hasleton et al., 2007).

In fact, pheromones have been found to influence attraction, mating, and bonding (Crawford et al., 2010; Wright, 1994) and have also been found to promote the love bond between a mother and her infant (Kohl & Francoeur, 2002). Research on pheromones and sexual orientation has found that homosexual men and heterosexual men respond differently to odors that

A strong and secure bond with a caregiver can have profound effects on the ability of the person to form attachments throughout life.

are involved in sexual attraction, with homosexual men responding in similar ways as heterosexual women (Savic et al., 2005).

Our odor preferences are influenced by our major histocompatibility complex (MHC), a group of genes that helps the body recognize invaders such as bacteria and viruses (Garver-Apgar et al., 2006; Herz, 2007; Santos et al., 2005). In order to pass a more complete MHC along to our offspring and protect them with the broadest array of disease resistance, heterosexual men and women may be programmed to mate with a partner whose MHC differs from their own (Crawford et al., 2010; Roberts & Roiser, 2010). We are more likely to be attracted and fall in love with someone whose MHC is different from our own (Garver-Apgar et al., 2006). Newer research has been exploring how the use of hormonal contraceptives, such as birth control pills, may alter MHC and odor preferences in women (Crawford et al., 2010; Ferdenzi et al., 2009; Roberts & Roiser, 2010; Roberts et al., 2008).

Finally, researchers have also been looking for love in neurotransmitters and various areas of the brain. Using magnetic resonance imaging (MRI), researchers have found that certain areas of the brain are stimulated when couples are in love (Aron et al., 2005; Fisher et al., 2010; H. Fisher, 2004). In addition, when these areas of the brain are stimulated, neurotransmitters, such as dopamine, create motivation and cravings to be with a particular partner (Fisher et al., 2010). So it appears there may be more to love and attraction than we thought. Certainly more research is needed in these areas.

Attachment Styles

When babies or young children feel sad, scared, or threatened, they seek out their mother. From an evolutionary perspective, the desire for closeness with the mother increases the infant's chances of survival (Mofrad et al., 2010). Bowlby (1969) proposed that infants develop an attachment, or an emotional bond, with their mother. Although Bowlby wrote about attachment as a mother–child bond, we know today that children can develop this bond with a mother, father, nanny, grandparent, or primary caregiver. However, it is the mother's response to her child that Bowlby felt was most important. If the mother responds in a sensitive, patient, and kind manner, the child is more likely to form a secure attachment (Prior & Glaser, 2006). However, if the mother responds in an inconsistent, angry, or dismissive manner, the child will form an insecure attachment.

Ainsworth and her colleagues (1978) built on Bowlby's research and suggested that infants form one of three styles of attachment:

- *Secure* infants tolerate caregivers being out of their sight because they believe the caregiver will respond if they cry out or need care.
- Inconsistent caregiving results in *anxious/ambivalent* infants, who cry more than secure infants and panic when the caregiver leaves them.
- *Avoidant* infants often have caregivers who are uncomfortable with hugging and holding them, and tend to force separation on the child at an early age.

Our childhood attachment styles stay with us as we grow up and may influence the type of loving relationships we form as adults (K. Burton, 2005; Mikulincer & Shaver, 2005). Adults who had a secure attachment in childhood report more positive childhood experiences, higher levels of self-esteem (Feeney & Noller, 1990), and have less anxiety (Diamond & Fagundes, 2010; Gentzler et al., 2010), shame, guilt, and loneliness (Akbag & Imamoglu, 2010). They also have a fairly easy time trusting and establishing loving relationships (Bartholomew & Horowitz, 1991; Neal & Frick-Horbury, 2001).

Adults who had anxious/ambivalent attachments with their caregivers often have a negative view of others as adults and tend to have a difficult time with trust. Finally, those with an avoidant attachment often have a negative view of others and are uncomfortable with intimacy. If you grew up in a family in which your caregiver was inconsistent or distant, it can be more challenging to allow yourself to love and be loved (Brumbaugh & Fraley, 2010; Dorr, 2001).

Attachment Styles

Match the attachment style with its description.

Check Your Learning Quiz 7.2

Go to **login.cengagebrain.com** and take the online quiz.

▸ **LO9** Identify three reasons why we are initially attracted to some people and not others.

Similarity and Proximity

Why are we attracted to certain people but not others? Researchers talk about the **field of eligibles** (Kerckhoff, 1964) to help explain why we are surrounded by hundreds of people but are attracted to only a handful of them. Our culture helps determine who is in our field of eligibles through social rules about acceptable and unacceptable partners. Because of these rules, we are more likely to be attracted to those who are similar to us in race, ethnicity, religion, socioeconomic group, and even age.

One of the most reliable predictors of attraction is proximity. Although we might want to believe that we could meet a complete stranger at a bar and fall madly in love, the research tells us this scenario is rare. People are most likely to find lovers among the people they know or meet through the people they know. We are much more likely to meet our romantic partners at a party, religious institution, or friend's house, where the people are similar to ourselves—in ethnicity, race, social class, religion, education, and even in attitudes and personality (Byrne & Murnen, 1988; Hitsch et al., 2010). Although folklore tells us both that "birds of a feather flock together" and that "opposites attract," the research supports only the first saying.

Physical Attractiveness

Although physical appearance tends to fade in importance over the life of a relationship, typically we are first attracted to another person based on physical factors. It might be their hair, eyes, body, or another physical feature. The "matching hypothesis" claims that people are drawn to others with similar levels of attractiveness. When considering a romantic

In the culture of the Longneck tribe of Thailand, an elongated neck is viewed as physically attractive.

© Corbis

field of eligibles The group of people from which it is socially acceptable to choose an intimate partner.

partner, both men and women may be willing to compromise on some qualities they are looking for in a partner but not on physical attractiveness (Sprecher & Regan, 2002).

Financial Stability

We also are attracted to partners who are financially stable. In the past, research on gender and attraction found that heterosexual women were more likely to rate financial stability in a partner as more important than heterosexual men did (Buss, 1989b). This was consistent across cultures. However, these gender differences have decreased, and both heterosexual men and women report being attracted to partners with financial resources (Buss et al., 2001; Sheldon, 2007).

What is it, finally, that we really look for in a partner? Although physical attractiveness is important, men and women around the world also report that mutual attraction, kindness, and reciprocal love are important factors (Buss et al., 2001; Pearce et al., 2010). In addition to this, people are in surprising agreement on what factors they want in an ideal partner. A study of homosexual, heterosexual, and bisexual men and women showed that, no matter what their sexual orientation, gender, or cultural background, all really wanted the same thing. They wanted partners who had similar interests, values, and religious beliefs, who were physically attractive, honest, trustworthy, intelligent, affectionate, warm, kind, funny, financially independent, and dependable (Amador et al., 2005; Toro-Morn & Sprecher, 2003). Now that doesn't seem to be too much to ask, does it?

Marli Forastieri/Getty Images

Both men and women report being attracted to partners who are financially secure.

On Your Mind

How can I tell the difference between being in love and just deeply liking someone?

Check Your Learning Quiz 7.3

Go to **login.cengagebrain.com** and take the online quiz.

▶ **LO10** Differentiate between love and intimacy.

▶ **LO11** Differentiate between male and female styles of intimacy.

Love relationships can last many years. As time goes by, love and relationships grow and change, and trying to maintain a sense of stability and continuity while still allowing for change and growth is probably the single greatest challenge of long-term love relationships.

Attaining intimacy is different from loving. We can love our cat, our favorite musician, or a great leader, but intimacy requires reciprocity—it takes two. Intimacy is a dance of two souls, each of whom must reveal a little, risk a little, and try a lot. In some ways, therefore, true intimacy is more difficult to achieve than true love because the emotion of love may be effortless, whereas the establishment of intimacy always requires effort.

Intimate Relationships

The word *intimacy* is derived from the Latin word *intimus,* meaning "inner" or "innermost" (Hatfield, 1988). Keeping our innermost selves hidden is easy; revealing our deepest desires, longings, and insecurities can be scary. As discussed in Chapter 2, intimate partners reveal beliefs and ideas to each other, disclose personal facts, share opinions, and admit to their fears and hopes. In fact, self-disclosure is so important to intimacy that early researchers thought that willingness to self-disclose was itself the definition of intimacy (M. S. Clark & Reis, 1988). True self-disclosure is a two-way street, and it involves both partners sharing feelings, fears, and dreams, not just facts and opinions. Individuals who can self-disclose have been found to have higher levels of self-esteem and confidence in their relationship, and rate their relationships as more satisfying (Macneil, 2004; Posey et al., 2010; Schiffrin et al., 2010; Sprecher & Hendrick, 2004).

Intimacy involves a sense of closeness, bondedness, and connectedness (Popovic, 2005; R. J. Sternberg, 1987). People who value intimacy tend to express greater trust in their friends; are more concerned for them; tend to disclose more emotional, personal, and relational content; and have more positive thoughts about others.

However, all types of disclosures are risky; the other person may not understand or accept the information offered or may not reciprocate. Thus, risk-taking and trust are crucial to the development of intimacy. Because intimacy makes us vulnerable and because we invest so much in the other person, intimacy can also lead to betrayal and disappointment, anger, and jealousy. We explore the dark side of intimacy later in this chapter.

We are often jealous when we think, fantasize, or imagine that another person has traits we ourselves want.

Michael Krasowitz/Getty Images

not be able to imagine a situation in which the relationship is really threatened. We are most jealous in a situation in which a person flirting with our partner has traits we ourselves want (or we fantasize that they do). Maybe we imagine our partner will find the other person more desirable than us, sexier, or funnier. A correlation has been found between self-esteem and jealousy: the lower the self-esteem, the more jealous a person feels and, in turn, the higher his or her insecurity (Knox et al., 1999, 2007). We imagine that the partner sees in the other person all those traits we believe that we lack.

Men and women experience similar levels of jealousy in intimate relationships, yet there is controversy over what triggers jealousy (Fleischmann et al., 2005). Some research supports the fact that heterosexual men are more jealous when they believe that their partner has had a sexual encounter with another man, whereas hetero-sexual women are often more focused on the emotional or relationship aspects of infidelity (Buss, 2003; Schützwohl, 2008).

People who do not experience jealousy have been found to be more secure, and this security in intimate relationships tends to increase as the couple's relationship grows (Knox et al., 1999, 2007). That is, the longer we are in a relationship with someone, the more our vulnerability to jealousy decreases.

Overall, jealousy is a demonstration of lack of trust and low self-esteem (Knox et al., 2007; Puente & Cohen, 2003). It can also be a self-fulfilling prophecy: jealous individuals can drive their mates away, which "proves" to them that they were right to be jealous in the first place. Jealousy can be contained by trying to improve one's own self-image, by turning it around into a compliment (not "she's flirting with other guys" but "look at how lucky I am—other guys also find her attractive") and by trusting one's partner. Communicating with your partner about your jealous feelings can often help to maintain your relationship (Guerrero & Aff, 1999). Opening up and talking about your uncertainty about the relationship or reassessing the relationship can help restore and strengthen the relationship.

Possessiveness

Because love also entails risk, dependency to some degree, and a strong connection between people, there is always the danger that the strength of the bond can be used by one partner to manipulate the other. Abusive love relationships exist when one partner tries to increase his or her own sense of self-worth or to control the other's behavior by withdrawing or manipulating love.

Possessiveness indicates a problem of self-esteem and personal boundaries, and can eventually lead to **stalking**. Most states have passed stalking laws, which enable the police to arrest a person who constantly shadows someone (usually, but not always, a woman) or makes threatening gestures or claims. Thinking about another person with that level of obsession is a sign of a serious psychological problem, one that should be brought to the attention of a mental health professional.

Intimacy in Different Cultures

Love seems to be a basic human emotion. Aren't "basic human emotions" the same everywhere? Isn't anger the same in Chicago and Timbuktu, and isn't sadness the same in Paris and Bombay? Although there is evidence that the majority of worldwide cultures experience romantic love, we do know that one's culture has been found to have a more powerful impact on love beliefs than one's gender (Sprecher & Toro-Morn, 2002). Culture affects how a person defines love, how easily he or she falls in love, with whom he or she falls in love, and how the relationship proceeds (Kim & Hatfield, 2004).

stalking Relentlessly pursuing someone, shadowing him or her, or making threatening gestures or claims toward the person when the relationship is unwanted.

As we discussed earlier, cultural differences in individual versus group needs can affect communication patterns (Cai et al., 2000). It should come as no surprise that these cultural differences can also affect patterns of intimacy. Passionate love is typically emphasized in individualistic cultures, but in collectivist cultures, passionate relationships are often viewed negatively because they may disrupt family traditions (Kim & Hatfield, 2004). For example, although Americans often equate love with happiness, the Chinese have equated love with sadness and jealousy (Shaver et al., 1992). This is because collectivist cultures, such as that of China or Japan, traditionally marry for reasons other than love. Passionate love dies and is not viewed as stable enough to base a marriage on. In a study of France, Japan, and the United States, intimacy style was directly related to whether the culture was individualistic, collectivistic, or mixed (France) and also to how much the culture had adopted stereotypical views of gender roles (how much it tended to see men as assertive and women as nurturing; Ting-Toomey, 1991). The Japanese, with a collectivistic culture and highly stereotypical gender roles, had lower scores in measures of attachment and commitment and were less likely to value self-disclosure than the French or Americans (Kito, 2005). Americans also have stereotypical gender roles, but because of the highly individualistic culture in the United States, Americans tend to have high levels of confusion and ambivalence about relationships. Interestingly, the French, who have a culture with high individual motivation yet with a strong group orientation, and who also have a more balanced view of masculine and feminine gender roles, had the lowest degree of conflict in intimate relationships.

Culture also affects one's sense of self. For example, in China, people's sense of self is entirely translated through their relationships with others. "A male Chinese would consider himself a son, a brother, a husband, a father, but hardly himself. It seems as if . . . there was very little independent self left for the Chinese" (Chu, 1985, quoted in Dion & Dion, 1988, p. 276). In China, love is thought of in terms of how a mate would be received by family and community, not in terms of one's own sense of romance. Because of this, the Chinese have a more practical approach to love than do Americans (Sprecher & Toro-Morn, 2002).

Finally, a cross-cultural study of college students from Brazil, India, Philippines, Japan, Mexico, Australia, the United States, England, Hong Kong, Thailand, and Pakistan studied the perceived significance of love for the building of a marriage. Researchers found that love is given highest importance in Westernized nations and the lowest importance in the less-developed Asian nations (R. Levine et al., 1995). Thus, culture plays a role in how we experience and express both love and intimacy.

Check Your Learning Quiz 7.4

Go to **login.cengagebrain.com** and take the online quiz.

▶ **LO14** Describe the two key differences in dating in traditional and contemporary American society.

▶ **LO15** Describe the role of sexuality in contemporary dating relationships.

The Changing Nature of Dating from Traditional to Contemporary Society

Changes in Dating Behavior

In traditional heterosexual dating, before the 1970s, the boy would pick up the girl at her house, the father and mother would meet or chat with the boy, and then the boy and girl would go to a well-defined event (e.g., a chaperoned, school-sponsored dance), and she would be brought home by the curfew her parents imposed (Benokraitis, 1993). Today, however, formal dating has given way to more casual dating. Teenagers still go to movies and dances, but just as often they will get together at someone's house.

Because of the risk for rejection, today's adolescents often use friend networks to find out if someone might be interested in them before asking them out. This way they can assess a potential partner's interest without the risk of rejection. It can be more difficult to meet potential partners as a person gets older. Socializing and going out to bars and clubs may work for some, but others are uncomfortable with

© Superstock/Photo Library

In the 1950s, traditional heterosexual dating involved going out together to share a fountain drink.

© Digital Vision/Picturequest

The dating years usually begin in high school in the United States.

Most older couples say their marriages have improved over time and that the later years are some of their happiest.

Sexuality is also an important component in older adult dating relationships. However, when we picture people engaging in sex, we rarely think of two people over the age of 60. Why is this? Why are we so averse to the idea that older people have healthy and satisfying sex lives? It is probably because we live in a society that equates sexuality with youth. Even so, the majority of older adults maintain an interest in sexuality, and many engage in sexual activity (Arena & Wallace, 2008; deVries, 2009; Waite et al., 2009). There are many similarities in aging among gay, lesbian, and heterosexual populations. In fact, the physical changes of aging affect all men and women, regardless of sexual orientation (Woolf, 2002).

A positive correlation was found between good health and sexual activity, with healthier people reporting higher levels of sexual activity (Holmberg & Blair, 2009; Trudel et al., 2010). A healthy sex life in the later years may keep aging adults happy and vibrant.

On Your Mind

Is it possible to take a hook-up relationship to the next level and become a "couple"?

Check Your Learning Quiz 7.5

Go to **login.cengagebrain.com** and take the online quiz.

Until fairly recently, there was little research on nonmarital **cohabitation**, or living together. In fact, researchers documented no increase in cohabitation rates between 1880 and 1970. This was probably because researchers had no labels for such relationships. In the mid-1990s, the Census and the Current Population Survey started allowing couples to identify themselves as "unmarried partner" of the homeowner (instead of a roommate), which allowed researchers to get more accurate statistics about cohabitation (Stevenson & Wolfers, 2007). Even so, researchers today believe that statistical data on cohabitation is skewed because of inadequate relationship labels. Some cohabitating heterosexual couples might not think of themselves as "unmarried partners" but rather as "boyfriend and girlfriend"; gay and lesbian couples might describe themselves as "roommates." You can see how this terminology can get a little tricky.

Cohabitation, or the number of cohabitating couples living together, has increased significantly over the last few years. Whereas 3.2 million unmarried heterosexual couples were living together in 1990, this number grew to 7.5 million heterosexual couples in 2010 (Bumpass & Lu, 2000; Pew Research Center, 2010). In 2009, more than 70% of U.S. heterosexual couples lived together before marriage (Rhoades et al., 2009). The number of unmarried same-sex couples living together also has increased, from approximately 358,400 in 2000 to 646,500 in 2010 (Kurtzleben, 2011). Overall, it is anticipated that the number of cohabiting couples will continue to increase. A recent study found that 60% of couples moved in together to spend more time together, 19% did so for financial reasons, and 14% did so to "test" the relationship (Rhoades et al., 2009).

Overall, cohabiting same-sex couples have higher rates of relationship dissolution than cohabiting heterosexual couples (Strohm, 2010). Among cohabiting same-sex couples, male couples have been found to have slightly higher dissolution rates than female couples.

Advantages and Disadvantages of Cohabitation

There are advantages and disadvantages to cohabitation. Cohabitation allows couples to learn more about each other's habits and idiosyncrasies, share finances, and mature in their relationship. Yet there are potential disadvantages. Parents and relatives may not support the union, and society as a whole tends not to recognize peo-

cohabitation Living together in a sexual relationship when not legally married.

ple who live together for purposes of health care or taxes. Also, the partners may want different things out of living together: One partner may view it as a stronger commitment to the relationship, whereas the other sees it as a way to have a more accessible sexual partner.

Some couples believe that living together can help them smooth out the rough spots in their relationships and see whether they would be able to take their relationship to the next level. Research indicates, however, that this might not be exactly true. Heterosexual couples who live together before marriage are more likely to get divorced than those who do not live together (Guzzo, 2009; Rhoades et al., 2009). However, there are several possible shortcomings of the foregoing findings. It may not be that living together itself increases the chance of divorce, but that heterosexual couples who choose to live together may have been more likely to divorce even if they didn't live together first (Stevenson & Wolfers, 2007). They may feel that they would not be happy in a marriage; they may be more accepting of divorce; they may be less religious and less traditional in the first place; or they may be less committed in the beginning of the relationship. Because we do not know about the samples in the studies on cohabiting couples, it is difficult to generalize their findings.

Breaking Up

How a person reacts to a breakup really depends on several factors, including who initiated the breakup, the amount of contact with the ex-partner after the breakup, and how much social support a person has. Typically, the person who initiated the breakup feels less distress but is more at risk for guilt (Locker et al., 2010). Those who were broken up with often feel rejection, experience more depression, and experience loss of self-esteem (Perilloux & Buss, 2008). Some rejected partners become obsessive about the lost relationship and engage in stalking behaviors such as repeated texting and/or calling (Fisher et al., 2010).

Earlier we discussed the importance of attachment styles, and it probably won't surprise you to learn that those with secure attachment styles often have the easiest time with breakups, whereas those with anxious attachment styles have the most difficulties (Locker et al., 2010; Svoboda, 2011). One of the most important factors in recovering from a breakup is support. Those who have friends to lean on and talk to have an easier time moving on after a breakup.

Living Together: Pros and Cons

Two heterosexual couples discuss the pros and cons of living together.

Check Your Learning Quiz 7.6

Go to **login.cengagebrain.com** and take the online quiz.

▶ **LO18** Summarize the current trends in marital rates and three factors that affect them.

In the mid-1960s, heterosexual marriage was nearly universal among 24- to 34-year-olds, with more than 80% of men and women marrying (Mather & Lavery, 2010). However, in the 1970s, many societal issues, such as the economy, an increased number of women in higher education and the labor force, and increasing rates of cohabitation, led to decreases in marriage rates. Today, couples are delaying marriage or even avoiding it altogether (Dougherty, 2010; Mather & Lavery, 2010). The following section discusses marriage statistics and trends, mixed marriages, marital satisfaction, sex within marriage, marriages in later life, and sex outside of marriage. Although same-sex marriage is discussed later in this chapter, this section focuses on heterosexual marriage.

Current Trends in Marital Rates

Marital Age

The average age at which a heterosexual man and woman marry today in the United States is the highest in recorded history. Whereas the median age for first marriage in the United States for men and women was 23 and 21, respectively, in 1970, these ages increased to 28 for men and 26 for women by 2010 (Mather & Lavery, 2010).

Overall, the proportion of married people older than 18 dropped from 57% in 2000 to 52% in 2009, which was the lowest percentage recorded since the U.S. Census Bureau began collecting data more than 100 years ago (Ruggles et al., 2009; see Figure 7.2). In fact, the number of unmarried women (single, separated, divorced, widowed) in 2009 outnumbered the number of married women for the first time in U.S. history (Mather & Lavery, 2010). Even so, it's important to point out that most young adults will get married at some point in their lives (Cherlin, 2009; Mather & Lavery, 2010).

In 2007, men and women older than 65 were much more likely to be married than at any other time in history (Stevenson & Wolfers, 2007). This is probably because the life expectancy for both men and women has improved. However, there is a higher percentage of married men than women—women live longer than men and widowhood is more common for them. Seventy-nine percent of men between the ages of 65 to 74 were married in 2004, whereas only 57% of women in the same age group were married. Although an estimated 500,000 people older than 65 remarry in the United States every year (M. Coleman et al., 2000), as discussed ear-

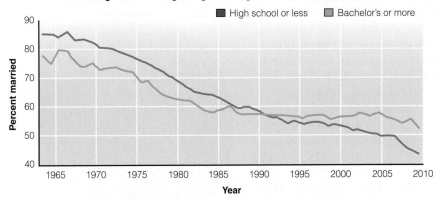

Figure 7.2 Marital rates have been decreasing among young adults since 1965. Source: U. S. Census Bureau, 2000 Census and American Community Survey.

lier in this chapter, more and more older couples decide to live together in place of marriage (S. L. Brown et al., 2006).

Research has found that many factors, such as education, ethnicity, and race, affect marital rates. Although before 1990, marriage rates for those with a high-school education were higher than for those with a college degree, today, college graduates are more likely to marry than those with less education (Mather & Lavery, 2010). From 1980 to 2008, female high school drop-outs went from "most likely to marry" to "least likely to marry" (Stevenson & Isen, 2010). Racial differences have also been found, with Blacks less likely to marry than Whites (Pew Research Center, 2010). In 2010, 37% to 44% of Blacks, 65% of Asians, 56% to 58% of Hispanics, and 58% to 62% of Whites were married (Bryant, 2010).

Mixed Marriages

Fewer than 1 in 1,000 new marriages were between a Black and a White spouse in 1961, but this number increased to 1 in 150 in 1980, and in 2010, 1 in 7 new marriages was between spouses of different races or ethnicities (Fincham & Beach, 2010; Lewis & Ford-Robertson, 2010; Passel et al., 2010; Saulny, 2010; Shibusawa, 2009;

On Your Mind

What is a "prenuptial" agreement?

Figure 7.3). Of the almost 4 million U.S. couples who married in 2008, 31% of Asians, 26% of Hispanics, 16% of Blacks, and 9% of Whites married someone whose race or ethnicity was different from their own (Passel et al., 2010).

Among Blacks and Asians, there are significant gender differences in marrying outside of one's race or ethnicity. Whereas 22% of Black male newlyweds in 2008 married outside their race, only 9% of Black females did (Passel et al., 2010). Gender differences were found in the opposite direction for Asians. Whereas 40% of Asian female newlyweds married outside their race, only 20% of Asian males did.

Marital Satisfaction

A survey in 2000 found that marriages in the United States are as happy today as they were 20 years ago (Amato et al., 2003). Marital satisfaction for men is related to the frequency of pleasurable activities (activities that involve doing fun things together) in the relationship, whereas for women is related to the frequency of pleasurable activities that focus on emotional closeness. Other important variables, including being able to talk to each other and self-disclose, physical and emotional intimacy, and personality similarities, are all instrumental in achieving greater relationship quality.

People who are married tend to be happier, healthier, and have longer lives than either widowed or divorced persons of the same age (Dush & Amato, 2005; Waldinger & Schulz, 2010). In fact, in a study of heterosexual couples, married couples had the

Mixed Marriage Types, 2008

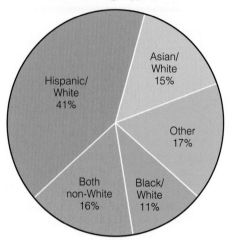

Note: "Newly married" refers to people who got married in the 12 months before the survey. All groups (other than Hispanic) are non-Hispanic. "Other" includes American Indian, mixed race, or "some other" race.

Source: Pew Research Center analysis of 2008 American Community Survey (ACS), based on Integrated Public-Use Microdata Series (IPUMS) samples.

Figure 7.3 Percentage of each type of newly married, mixed-race or -ethnicity couples in the United States, 2008.

Married couples have higher levels of well-being than couples who are dating or living together.

highest level of well-being, followed by (in order) cohabiting couples, steady dating relationships, casual dating relationships, and individuals who dated infrequently or not at all (Dush & Amato, 2005). Marriage has also been found to reduce the impact of several potentially traumatic events, including job loss, retirement, and illness (Waldinger & Schulz, 2010). In Black men and women, remaining single was found to be related to increased risk for health problems (Schwandt et al., 2010).

Although traditional marriages may have involved one partner staying home with children, whereas the other worked outside the home, today, more and more couples are both in the workforce, which has increased equality (Stevenson & Isen, 2010). These marriages have been found to be happier and more fulfilling than traditional marriages (Stevenson & Wolfers, 2008). Partners with more education report more happiness in their marriages (Stevenson & Isen, 2010).

Dena and Lenny Are Getting Married

Couple discusses their interracial relationship and engagement.

Arranged Marriages

How would you feel about someone else choosing a partner for you to marry?

Check Your Learning Quiz 7.7

Go to **login.cengagebrain.com** and take the online quiz.

Sexuality is an essential part of most marriages. Married men and women both report that sex is integral to a good marriage, although men often report higher sexual needs than women (Elliott & Umberson, 2008).

Current Trends in Marital Sex

However, a great deal of variation exists in who initiates sex, what behaviors a couple engages in, and how often they engage in it. Overall, the majority of married couples report satisfaction with their marital sex (Sprecher, 2002).

Frequency of Marital Sex

The National Survey of Sexual Health and Behavior found the majority of married couples have sex weekly or a few times per month, and that younger married couples engage in more frequent sex (Herbenick et al., 2010). Laumann and colleagues (1994) found that 40% of married couples have sexual intercourse two or more times a week, whereas 50% engage in it a few times each month. The frequency of sexual activity and satisfaction with a couple's sex life have been found to be positively correlated (Blumstein & Schwartz, 1983); that is, the more frequent the sexual behavior, the greater the relationship satisfaction. However, it is not known whether increased sexual frequency causes more satisfaction or whether increased relationship satisfaction causes increased sexual behavior.

Expectations of Sexual Exclusivity

Almost all couples, whether dating, living together, or married, expect sexual exclusivity from each other. When one partner violates this compact, it is considered "cheating." Not surprisingly, adults in the United States are more likely to cheat while living together than while married (Treas & Giesen, 2000). Those who cheat in intimate relationships have been found to have stronger sexual interests, more permissive sexual values, less satisfaction in their intimate relationship, and more opportunities for sex outside the relationship (Treas & Giesen, 2000). Studies on same-sex couples have found that gay men are more likely to cheat than lesbian women (Roisman et al., 2008).

Extramarital Sex

All societies regulate sexual behavior and use marriage as a means to control the behavior of their members to some degree. The United States is one of the few countries that has traditionally forbidden sexual contact outside of marriage; research estimates that less than 5% of all societies are as strict about forbidding extramarital sexual contact as the United States (Lance, 2007; Leslie & Korman, 1989).

Extramarital Sex in the United States

Laumann and colleagues (1994) found that 20% of women and 15% to 35% of men of all ages reported that they had engaged in extramarital sex while they were married. Even for those couples who never consider sex outside of marriage, the possibility looms and people wonder about it—what it would be like or whether their partners might be engaging in it. Typically, religiosity and church attendance are associated with a lower probability of engaging in extramarital sex (Burdette et al., 2007).

Although extramarital sex refers to sex outside of marriage, we are also referring here to extrarelationship sex, or sex outside of a committed, dating relationship. How does an extramarital affair typically begin? In the first stage, a person might become emotionally close to someone at school, work, a party, or even on the Internet. As they get to know each other, there is chemistry and a powerful attraction. This moves into the second stage, in which the couple decides to keep the relationship secret. They don't tell their closest friends about their attraction. This secret, in turn, adds fuel to the passion. In the third stage, the couple starts doing things together, even though they would not refer to it as "dating." Each still believes that the relationship is all about friendship. Finally, in the fourth stage, the relationship becomes sexual, leading to an intense emotional and sexual affair (Layton-Tholl, 1998).

Although many people think that sexual desire drives an extramarital affair, research has found that more than 90% of extramarital affairs occur because of unmet emotional needs within the relationship (Previti & Amato, 2004). Gender plays a role in both the type of extramarital affairs in which a person engages and a partner's acceptance of these affairs. Women are more likely than men to have emotional but not sexual affairs, whereas men are more likely to have sexual affairs. When it comes to accepting a partner's extramarital affair, women experience more emotional distress about affairs than men do, but they rate emotional affairs as more harmful than sexual affairs (Guerrero et al., 2004). Men, in contrast, rate sexual affairs as more harmful than emotional affairs. Extramarital affairs reduce marital happiness and increase the risk for divorce (Previti & Amato, 2004).

What Is Polyamory?

Unlike "swingers," the emphasis is on the relationships, rather than simply the sex.

Extramarital Sex in Other Cultures

From East to West.

Check Your Learning Quiz 7.8

Go to **login.cengagebrain.com** and take the online quiz.

7.9 *Same-Sex Relationships*

▶ **LO23** List and describe the three legal forms of same-sex relationships in the United States.

In many ways, gay and lesbian relationships have changed more than heterosexual relationships over the past few decades. First, these relationships came "out of the closet" in the 1960s and 1970s, when there was a blossoming and acceptance of a gay subculture. Then, the advent of AIDS resulted in fewer sexual partners and more long-term, monogamous relationships, especially in the gay community.

Heterosexual, gay, and lesbian men and women all hold similarly positive views of their intimate relationships (Roisman et al., 2008). Even so, there has been considerable debate throughout the years about what type of intimate relationships promote the healthiest psychological adjustment. One study by Blumstein and Schwartz (1983) compared same- and other-sex couples using interviews and questionnaires. Although this study is dated, it remains a classic because no other studies have undertaken such a large sample population comparing couples in a variety of different relationships (see Figure 7.4 for more information).

Although accurate statistics can be difficult to come by because some couples might not report being in a same-sex relationship, we know that in 2008, there were 565,000 same-sex couples—415,000 were unmarried and 150,000 were married (30,000–35,000 were legally married, and 80,000 were in nonmarital forms of legal recognition; Gates, 2008).

Forms of Same-Sex Relationships

The level of formality of their relationship depends a good deal on the laws of the state in which a same-sex couple resides. As we discussed earlier, many same-sex couples cohabit, and some choose **civil unions** (also referred to as domestic partnerships, civil partnerships, or registered partnerships), or, in the few states whereas it is available as an option, marriage. Legally recognized unions come with varying rights and benefits depending on the laws of each individual state. Legalized relationships are still unavailable to the majority of same-sex couples in the United States today.

Civil Unions and Domestic Partnerships

In 2000, Vermont was the first state to legalize civil unions, and by 2010, civil unions and domestic partnerships were available in several states, including California, Colorado, Connecticut, Hawaii, Illinois, Maine, Maryland, Nevada, New Jersey, Oregon, Vermont, Washington, Wisconsin, and the District of Columbia. Several other states are considering legislation for legal status of same-sex relationships. (See Figure 7.5 for more information.) Typically, civil unions and domestic

civil union A legal union of a same-sex couple, sanctioned by a civil authority.

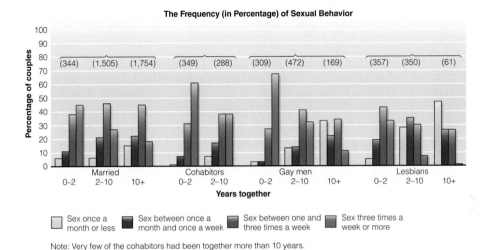

The Frequency (in Percentage) of Sexual Behavior

Years together

☐ Sex once a month or less
■ Sex between once a month and once a week
■ Sex between one and three times a week
■ Sex three times a week or more

Note: Very few of the cohabitors had been together more than 10 years.
Numbers in parentheses are the number of couples on which the percentages are based.

Figure 7.4 Frequency of sexual behavior in various types of relationships by years. The numbers above each category represent the total number of respondents. Source: From Blumstein, P., & Schwartz, P. (1983). *Frequency of sex in marriage from American couples* (p. 196). New York: HarperCollins Publishers. © 1983 by Philip B. Blumstein and Pepper S. Schwartz. Reprinted by permission of HarperCollins Publishers, Inc. and International Creative Management, Inc.

partnerships that are performed in one state are not recognized in other states, even if they have a civil union or domestic partnership law (Vestal, 2008).

Since 2000, there has been an increase in public support of legal recognition for same-sex couples. A 2010 CBS News Poll found that the majority of Americans think there should be some legal recognition of gay and lesbian couples—40% of respondents reported same-sex couples should be allowed to marry, whereas 30% thought they should be able to get civil unions (CBS, 2010). At the same time, however, about 25% of respondents reported same-sex couple should not have any legal recognition.

Same-Sex Marriage

In 1996, the U.S. Congress enacted the Defense of Marriage Act, which prohibits federal recognition of civil unions, domestic partnerships, and same-sex marriages. Even though individual U.S. states may offer these legal options, the federal government does not recognize these unions. In addition, based on the Defense of Marriage Act,

Sexuality in Same-Sex Relationships

Learn about common problems and positive aspects.

Timeline

Same-sex relationships around the globe.

each state can recognize or deny any relationship between same-sex couples, recognizing marriage as a "legal union of one man and one woman as husband and wife" or by referring to a "spouse" only as a person of the other sex. The Defense of Marriage Act also removes any federal spousal rights of civil unions, domestic partnerships, and same-sex marriage, including social security, federal tax law, and immigration rights for foreign same-sex spouses of American citizens (Mason et al., 2001). In early 2011, President Obama publicly declared that the Defense of Marriage Act was unconstitutional and directed the Justice Department to stop defending it.

As of 2011, same-sex marriage was legal in Massachusetts, Connecticut, Iowa, Vermont, New Hampshire, New York, and the District of Columbia. Same-sex marriages performed in states with legal same-sex marriage are typically not recognized outside of these states. Even with all this controversy, many gay and lesbian couples "marry" their partners in ceremonies that are not recognized by the states in which

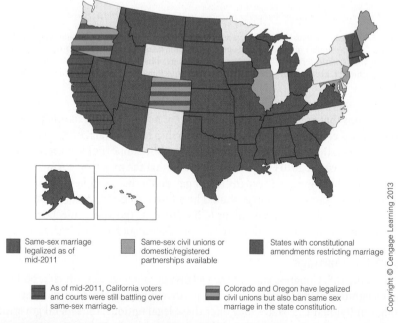

Same-sex marriage legalized as of mid-2011

Same-sex civil unions or domestic/registered partnerships available

States with constitutional amendments restricting marriage

As of mid-2011, California voters and courts were still battling over same-sex marriage.

Colorado and Oregon have legalized civil unions but also ban same sex marriage in the state constitution.

Figure 7.5 Laws regarding same-sex partnerships in the U.S. as of late 2011.

they live. As discussed earlier, approximately 1 of 4 same-sex couples (150,000 couples) refer to one another as "husband" or "wife," even though researchers estimate that approximately 32,000 of the couples have been legally married (Gates, 2008).

Same-sex couples who are married, or who identify as married, are similar to heterosexual couples in terms of age, income, and parenting (Gates, 2008). These relationships, whether legally recognized or not, often suffer from the same jealousies, power struggles, and "divorces" as heterosexual marriages (P. H. Collins, 1988). A study comparing same-sex couples who were married in Massachusetts, had domestic partnerships in California, and civil unions in Vermont found males were older and waited longer to legalize their relationships than women did, and males were less likely to have children (Rothblum et al., 2008).

Same-Sex Relationships in Other Cultures

Same-sex relationships outside the United States are supported in some countries and ignored in others. As of 2010, same-sex marriage was legal in Belgium, Canada, Denmark, the Netherlands, South Africa, Spain, Norway, Sweden, Portugal, Iceland, and Argentina. In addition, many other countries have proposed same-sex marriage legislation. Civil unions and domestic or registered partnerships have also been legalized in several countries.

Strongly religious countries, such as Italy, are not supportive of same-sex relationships. Even so, in the city of Padua, Italy, same-sex couples were allowed to have their relationships legally recognized, which met with strong criticism from the Vatican (Shoffman, 2006). Although homosexuality is outlawed in many countries in Africa, legal marriage rights were nonetheless extended to same-sex couples in 2006.

Rob Melynchuck/Getty Images

Same-sex marriages performed in states with legal same-sex marriage are typically not recognized outside of these states.

In Support of Same-Sex Marriage

A letter written by a 39-year-old gay man who lost his long-term partner.

Same-Sex Marriage

A lesbian woman discusses her commitment ceremony and personal views on same-sex marriage.

Check Your Learning Quiz 7.9

Go to **login.cengagebrain.com** and take the online quiz.

7.10 *Having Children or Remaining Childless*

▶ LO24 Discuss the impact of having children on intimate relationships.

The decision to have or raise children is one that most people face at one time or another—whether they are heterosexual or homosexual—and research shows that the timing of parenthood can affect a couple's relationship quality.

Heterosexual Relationships

In heterosexual relationships, children can be conceived and born at any time—while a couple is hooking up, dating, living together, or already married. Some couples decide to have children without a formal commitment to each other, some get married to have children, and others get married because the woman is pregnant. Although pregnancies can be experienced as unplanned events, ambivalence and uncertainty is common in many couples making decisions about parenthood (Pinquart et al., 2008).

Today's parents are more likely to be older, more educated, ethnically diverse, and less likely to be married (Koropeckyj-Cox et al., 2007; Livingston & Cohn, 2010). Although there were more teenage births in 1990, teenage births decreased and there were more births among older women by 2008. All of these changing trends are due to demographic and behavioral changes, such as population changes, delays in marriage, increases in education, and changing attitudes about marriage, pregnancy, and birth. Whereas several years ago having a child outside of wedlock might have seemed odd, today, most Americans know at least one woman who has had a baby without being married and at least one man who fathered a baby without being married (Livingston & Cohn, 2010).

Same-Sex Relationships

Unlike heterosexual couples, same-sex couples can't get pregnant by accident, but many do decide to become parents in a variety of ways, including surrogacy, adoption, foster care, arrangements with friends and family, or through a partner's biological children. Like heterosexual couples, same-sex couples may decide to have children while dating, living together, or married. Studies of lesbian and gay youths have found that about 66% of females and more than 50% of males are interested in raising children at some point in their lives (D'Augelli et al., 2006/2007). The 2008 Community Survey found that 31% of same-sex couples were raising children, compared with 43% of heterosexual couples (Gates, 2010).

The families of same-sex couples often include children and grandchildren.

Parenting and Relationship Satisfaction

Longitudinal research on heterosexual, gay, and lesbian couples has found the quality of intimate relationships declines when couples become parents (Campos et al., 2009; Claxton & Perry-Jenkins, 2008; Goldberg et al., 2010). Parents with children often experience decreases in leisure time and time to work on their relationship, which is why they often report lower relationship satisfaction than those without children. Relationship satisfaction continues to decline as the number of children increases. In fact, relationship happiness is higher before children come, declines steadily until it hits a low when children are in their teens, and then begins to increase once children leave the house (Papalia et al., 2002). This may be because of several factors, including reduced time for the relationship or disagreements about childcare responsibilities.

Deciding Whether to Have Kids

Hear from parents discussing their decision to have children and when.

Check Your Learning Quiz 7.10

Go to **login.cengagebrain.com** and take the online quiz.

There have been substantial changes in the institution of marriage over the past 30 years. During most of U.S. history, a married couple was viewed as a single, legal entity (M. A. Mason et al., 2001). Beginning in the late 1990s, marriage has been viewed more as a partnership. This shift in perception of marriage brought with it a shift in how marriage was dissolved. The liberalization of divorce laws made it easier to obtain a divorce and made it a less expensive process.

In a **no-fault divorce**, neither partner needs to be found guilty of a transgression (such as having sex outside marriage) to dissolve the marriage. No-fault divorce has been legal in all 50 states and the District of Columbia since 2010. Before this, most states required a partner to produce evidence of partner wrongdoing (such as extra-marital sex or abuse) to be granted a divorce. The availability of no-fault divorce contributed to skyrocketing divorce rates (Stevenson & Wolfers, 2007). In an attempt to reduce divorce rates, some states instituted **covenant marriages**, which revolve around restrictive agreed-on rules and regulations for ending a marriage, and also involve premarital counseling and an agreement to pursue additional counseling if marital problems develop. Covenant marriages also extend the wait time for a divorce, in some cases, to 2 years or more, unless domestic violence is involved.

Reasons for Divorce

What causes a couple to end their marriage? The question is complicated because not all unstable or unhappy marriages end in divorce. Couples stay together for many reasons—for the children, because of lack of initiative, because of religious prohibitions against divorce, or financial reasons—even though they have problems in their marriages. Similarly, couples with seemingly happy marriages separate and divorce, sometimes to the surprise of one of the partners who did not even know the marriage was in trouble.

A mutually shared decision to divorce is actually uncommon. Usually, one partner wants to terminate a relationship more than the other partner, who is still strongly attached to the marriage and who is more distraught at its termination. In fact, the declaration that a partner wants a divorce often comes as a shock to his or her spouse. When one partner is the initiator in a heterosexual divorce, it is usually the female. One study found that women initiated about 66% of all divorces (Brinig & Allen, 2000). The individual who wants his or her marriage to end is likely to view

no-fault divorce A divorce law that allows for the dissolution of a marriage without placing blame on either of the partners.

covenant marriage A marriage that is preceded by premarital counseling and has strict rules about divorce.

A personal story about the

Steve Grantz/WireImage/Getty Images

In the much publicized divorce between Sandra Bullock and Jesse James, infidelity by James was cited as the main cause of the divorce.

the marriage totally differently from the individual who wants the marriage to continue (H. Wang & Amato, 2000). In addition, the partner who initiated the divorce has often completed the mourning of the relationship by the time the divorce is complete, unlike the partner whose mourning begins once the divorce is finalized.

Heterosexual Divorce

Divorce rates for married heterosexuals increased sharply between 1970 and 1975, in part because of the liberalization of divorce laws (Kreider, 2005). Rates stabilized after this and began to decrease. By 2005, divorce rates were at the lowest level since 1970 (Stevenson & Wolfers, 2007). It is estimated that roughly 1 in 5 adults has divorced, and the U.S. Census Bureau reports that 50% of U.S. marriages end in divorce (Kreider, 2005; U.S. Census Bureau, 2007). However, research has found that marital stability has increased each decade. Whereas 23% of couples who married in the 1970s split within 10 years, only 16% of those who wed in the 1990s divorced (Parker-Pope, 2010). In 2008, the median duration of a marriage between a man and woman in the United States was 18 years (Cohn, 2009).

Same-Sex Divorce

Because same-sex marriage has been legalized for a short time in the United States, there is not a great deal of research on the reasons for same-sex divorce. We do know that many long-term same-sex couples typically dissolve their relationships privately, married or not. However, without divorce laws, these breakups can be difficult or unfair to one or both partners. If a same-sex couple married in Connecticut

Divorce: Betrayal and Sadness

A personal story about the dissolution of a marriage from a woman whose husband left the marriage and children.

▶ **LO25** Compare cultural attitudes toward divorce in the United States and other developed countries with those of predominantly Roman Catholic and Islamic countries.

▶ **LO26** Describe the two main types of personal problems resulting from divorce.

but moved to a state in which same-sex marriage is not recognized, they may not be able to divorce in that state (Haberman, 2011). Without a divorce, many couples experience problems with the division of property, children's visitation rights, and the ability to enter into other relationships (Chen, 2010).

Divorce in Other Cultures

Divorce is common in almost all societies, but cultural views are changing as societies develop. For example, in 2001, China's government revised its 20-year-old marriage law and included the concept of fault in marriage (Dorgan, 2001; Ruan & Lau, 2004). Before this law was implemented, Chinese couples had an equal division of family property regardless of the reasons for the divorce. Under this new law, however, if a partner is caught engaging in extramarital sex, he can lose everything (research has found that it is mostly men who cheat in China). In societies such as the United States, Sweden, Russia, and most European countries, divorce is relatively simple and has little stigma. The exceptions are countries that are largely Roman Catholic or Islamic.

The reasons that people get divorced are numerous, although different patterns emerge in different societies. In Egypt, the most common reason given for divorce is infidelity by the husband, whereas among the Hindus of India, the most common reason is cruelty (either physical or mental) from their partner (Pothen, 1989). Arab women's main reasons for divorce include the husband's physical, sexual, or verbal abuse; alcoholism; mental illness; and in-law interference (Savaya & Cohen, 2003). In China, more than 70% of divorces are initiated by women, and the main reason given is an extramarital affair of the husband (Ruan & Lau, 2004). This is also the main reason for divorce in Brazil and many other countries (de Freitas, 2004).

Adjusting to Divorce

How a person will adjust to a divorce depends on several factors, including who initiated the divorce, attitudes toward divorce, income levels, and the onset of a new relationship (Wang & Amato, 2000). Social connectedness is also an important factor in a person's adjustment (Moller et al., 2003).

Depression and sadness can surface when divorced men and women find that they have less in common with married friends as many friends. Older individuals experience more emotional and social problems because there are fewer options for

serial divorce The practice of divorce and remarriage, followed by divorce and remarriage.

forming new relationships in older age (H. Wang & Amato, 2000). Older divorced women are more likely to feel anger and loneliness than are younger divorced women.

Another area that is affected after heterosexual divorce is the couple's finances. Financial adjustment is often harder for women because after a divorce a woman's standard of living declines more than a man's (H. Wang & Amato, 2000). Research has found that after a divorce, a man's income increases by around one third, whereas a woman's income declines more than a fifth and remains low for years after the divorce (Jenkins, 2009). Many women who previously lived in a middle-class family find themselves slipping below the poverty line after divorce.

Dating after a divorce can be difficult for some. People may have been involved in committed relationships

Mary Kate Denny/Getty Images

Financial adjustment after a divorce is often more difficult for women.

for many years; consequently, they may find that the dating environment has changed drastically since they were younger. It is not uncommon for newly single people to feel frustrated or confused about this unfamiliar environment. The majority of divorced men and women remarry, and some remarry, divorce, and remarry again (often referred to as **serial divorce**). In fact, the median time between a divorce and a second marriage is about 3.5 years (U.S. Census Bureau, 2007). Overall, 13% to 14% of heterosexuals marry twice, 3% marry three or more times, and less than 1% marry four or more times (Kreider, 2005). Men remarry at higher rates than women, and Hispanics and Blacks remarry at lower rates than Whites (M. Coleman et al., 2000). Couples in second marriages report higher relationship satisfaction in their marriages than do couples in first marriages (McCarthy & Ginsberg, 2007).

Check Your Learning Quiz 7.11

Go to **login.cengagebrain.com** and take the online quiz.

Think Critically

Challenge Your Thinking

Consider these questions:

1. Why do you think men have traditionally been more interested in the physical attractiveness of a partner over the financial stability?

2. Do you want to marry a partner older or younger than yourself? Explain the reasons for your answer.

3. Give two reasons you believe women might prefer partners who are a few years older than themselves.

4. What reasons do you think contribute to the fact that women in Japan rate good looks in their partners as less important than women in the United States, France, or Brazil?

5. If these graphs were updated today what differences do you think you would find?

Good Looks or a Good Prospect?
Comparing Preferences across Cultures

In a classic study on cultural differences in what men and women look for in a mate, David Buss (1989b) found that, almost universally, men value good looks more in a mate, and women value good financial prospects. As for age, almost universally, men want their mates to be a few years younger than they are, and women want their mates to be a few years older.

In Figures 7.6 and 7.7, males and females from different countries rated the importance of a mate's looks and financial prospects. Participants rated the importance of "good looks" and "good financial prospects" from 0 (unimportant) to 3 (very important).

More recent research has found that, in the United States, good looks and financial stability are important partner qualities for both men and women (Amador et al., 2005; Lacey et al., 2004).

In Figure 7.8, male and female participants rated the importance of age difference in potential mates. A negative number refers to a desire for a mate who

How important is financial stability in a mate?

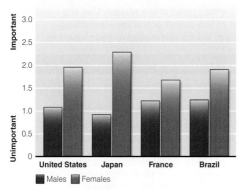

Figure 7.6 Source: Adapted from Buss (1989). Reprinted by permission of Cambridge University Press.

How important are good looks in a mate?

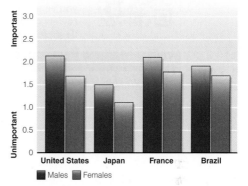

Figure 7.7 Source: Adapted from Buss (1989). Reprinted by permission of Cambridge University Press.

is younger by a certain number of years, whereas a higher number refers to a desire for a mate who is older by a certain number of years.

The author of this study, David Buss, believed that mate preferences in a particular culture could provide important clues about reproductive history. Differences in mate preferences help us understand more about different evolutionary pressures on males and females and also provides important cross-cultural information about reproductive strategies.

How many years older/younger do you want your partner to be?

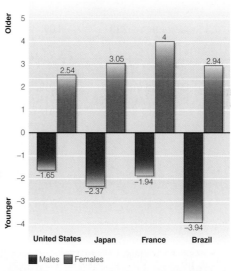

Figure 7.8 Source: Adapted from Buss (1989). Reprinted by permission of Cambridge University Press.

Think Critically

This article and its questions are available in interactive format online.

GO to your Psychology CourseMate at login.cengagebrain.com and take the Chapter Post-Test to see which Learning Objectives you've mastered and which need more review. Use the chapter review guide below and the online activities—including flashcards to review key terms—to measure your learning.

Measure ^Your Learning

Module			Learning Objectives
7.1	What Is Love?	218	**LO1** Differentiate between romantic love and companionate love.
			LO2 Identify and define Lee's six styles of love.
			LO3 Identify Sternberg's three building blocks of love and describe some of the ways in which they can be combined to form different types of love.
			LO4 Explain how Schachter and Singer's experiment using epinephrine with students provided valuable information on the relationship between physiological arousal and love.
7.2	Why Do We Love?	224	**LO5** Summarize the behavioral reinforcement theory of love.
			LO6 Summarize the cognitive theory of love.
			LO7 Summarize the evolutionary theory of love.
			LO8 Identify and briefly describe the three styles of attachment formed by infants.
7.3	Attraction	228	**LO9** Identify three reasons why we are initially attracted to some people and not others.
7.4	Love and Intimate Relationships	230	**LO10** Differentiate between love and intimacy.
			LO11 Differentiate between male and female styles of intimacy.
			LO12 Identify at least two questions related to personal values and motivations that an individual should consider before deciding to engage in a sexual relationship.
			LO13 Define *jealousy* and *possessiveness*, and explain the negative impact that these emotions can have on a relationship.

Online Activities

Key Terms	Video	Animation	Readings	Assessment
romantic love, companionate love	Why is love so confusing? What is the difference between being in "love" and in "lust"? Love Science	The Love Triangle	Love	Check Your Learning Quiz 7.1
		Attachment Styles	Love—It's All in Your Head	Check Your Learning Quiz 7.2
field of eligibles	How can I tell the difference between being in love and just deeply liking someone?			Check Your Learning Quiz 7.3
stalking	Forgive and Forget? Isn't it boring to stay with the same person your whole life? The Secret to Staying in Love		Developing Intimacy Skills In the Men's Locker Room	Check Your Learning Quiz 7.4

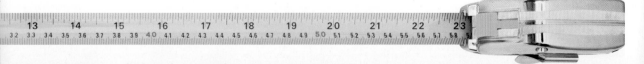

Measure ^ **Your Learning**

Online Activities

Key Terms	Video	Animation	Readings	Assessment
	Is it possible to take a hook-up relationship to the next level and become a "couple"?			Check Your Learning Quiz 7.5
cohabitation	Living Together: Pros and Cons			Check Your Learning Quiz 7.6
arranged marriage	What is a "prenuptial" agreement? Dena and Lenny Are Getting Married		Arranged Marriages	Check Your Learning Quiz 7.7
			What Is Polyamory? Extramarital Sex in Other Cultures	Check Your Learning Quiz 7.8
civil union	Same-Sex Marriage	Timeline: Same-Sex Relationships around the Globe	In Support of Same-Sex Marriage	Check Your Learning Quiz 7.9
	Deciding Whether to Have Kids			Check Your Learning Quiz 7.10
no-fault divorce, covenant marriage, serial divorce	Divorce: Betrayal and Sadness			Check Your Learning Quiz 7.11
				Good Looks or a Good Prospect? Comparing Preferences across Culture

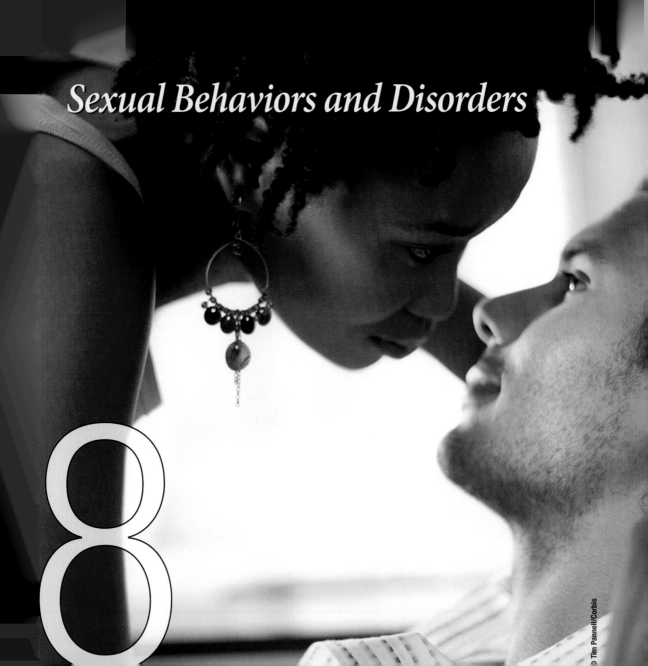

Sexual Behaviors and Disorders

8

1 **GO** to your **Psychology CourseMate** at **login.cengagebrain.com** and take the **Chapter Pre-Test** to introduce yourself to this chapter's topics and see what you may already know.

2 **READ** the **Learning Objectives** (LOs, in the left sidebars) and begin the chapter.

3 **COMPLETE** the **Online Activities** (in the right sidebars) *as you read each module.* Activities include **videos, animations, readings,** and **quizzes.**

4 **CHECK Your Learning** by going online to take the quiz at the end of each module and review material as necessary.

5 **MEASURE Your Learning** after reading the chapter by taking the online **Chapter Post-Test.** Use the chapter review guide at the end of the chapter as needed.

WATCH for these **Online Activities** icons as you read:

Video

Animation

Reading

Assessment

Think Critically

Online Activities

These Online Activities are essential to mastering this chapter. Go to login.cengagebrain.com.

 Videos Explore diverse perspectives on sex as well as common questions:

- Is Virtual Sex Cheating?
- Why do women fake orgasm?
- Are "blue balls" real?
- Is it weird to fantasize about having sex with lots of people watching?
- Is Monogamy for Everyone?
- Do women like their partners to kiss them right after they've had oral sex with them?
- Do guys want their partner to swallow after they get a blowjob?
- My girlfriend complains that I'm too big and I hurt her. What can I do?
- Japanese Love Hotels
- Oncosexology: Sex and Illness
- The Importance of Sexual Expression in People with Disabilities

- Helena: A Sex Worker for the Disabled
- No Sex for Me: Asexuality
- Are erection problems hereditary?
- Is it safe to use Viagra recreationally?

 Animations Interact with and visualize important processes, timelines, and concepts:

- Internal and External Changes in the Female Sexual Response Cycle
- Masters and Johnson's Sexual Response Cycle
- Breast Changes in the Female Sexual Response Cycle
- Internal and External Changes in the Male Sexual Response Cycle
- Female Sexual Response Cycle: Circular
- Key Terms Exercise

 Readings Delve deeper into key content:

- Meet Me in the Love Hotel
- What Is an Aphrodisiac?

 Assessment Measure your mastery:

- Chapter Pre-Test
- Check Your Learning Quizzes
- Chapter Post-Test

 Think Critically Challenge your thinking about data and accepted norms:

- Beyond the Medical Model

▶ **LO1** List three of the biggest influences on our sexual attitudes and behaviors.

THIS CHAPTER EXAMINES the human sexual response cycle, explores the various forms of sexual behavior, and considers psychologically and physiologically based challenges to sexual functioning. Our sexual attitudes and behaviors are shaped by many factors, including hormones, culture, ethnicity, religion, and the media. This section discusses three of the biggest influences: family background, ethnicity, and religion.

▼

Family Background, Ethnicity, and Religion

Our family of origin is our first reference group, and we internalize norms about sexual attitudes and behaviors from our interactions with our family (Davidson et al., 2008). Although the influence of our family is tied into our culture and religion,

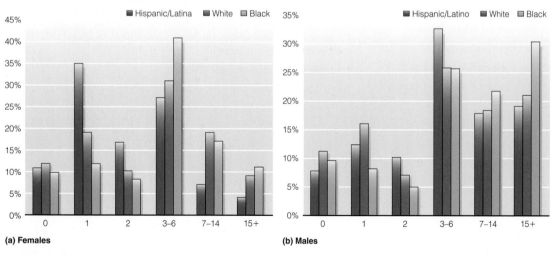

(a) Females

(b) Males

Figure 8.1 Number of other-sex partners in lifetime for (a) females and (b) males, 15- to 44-years-old in the U.S. by ethnicity/race, 2006–2008 Source: Chandra et al., 2011.

Side by Side

In the side-by-side position, the partners lie on their sides, and the woman lifts one leg to facilitate penile penetration. This is a good position for couples who want to take it slow and extend intercourse.

Disadvantages include the fact that there may be difficulties with penetration in this position. It can also be challenging to get momentum going and difficult to achieve deep penetration. Women may also have a difficult time maintaining contact with the male's pubic bone during intercourse, which may decrease the chance of orgasm.

Figure 8.16 The side-by-side position

Rear Entry

The rear-entry position of vaginal intercourse has many variations. Intercourse can be fast or slow depending on the variation chosen. One variation involves a woman on her hands and knees (often referred to as "doggie style"), while her partner is on his knees behind her. The female can also be lying on her stomach with a pillow under her hips while the male enters her from behind.

The rear-entry positions provide an opportunity for clitoral stimulation, either by the male or the female. It may also provide direct stimulation of the G-spot. The rear-entry position also can be good for women who are in the later stages of pregnancy or who are overweight.

Figure 8.17 The side rear-entry position

On Your Mind

My girlfriend complains that I'm too big and I hurt her. What can I do?

Check Your Learning Quiz 8.6

Go to **login.cengagebrain.com** and take the online quiz.

> ▶ **LO13** Identify common sexual behaviors used by gay couples.
>
> ▶ **LO14** Identify common sexual behaviors used by lesbian couples.

There are many similarities in the sexual behaviors of heterosexuals, gays, and lesbians. Like heterosexual couples, gays and lesbians report engaging in sexual behaviors to increase emotional and physical intimacy, feel accepted and supported, and to increase the positive view of self (Cohen et al., 2008). The following sections discuss sexual behaviors in same-sex couples.

Gay Men

Gay men use a variety of sexual techniques, including hugging, kissing, oral sex, mutual masturbation, and anal intercourse. Overall, gay and bisexual men engage in oral sex more often than heterosexual or lesbian couples. This is consistent with research that has shown men are more likely than women to have received oral sex (Brewster & Tillman, 2008).

Although many gay men report engaging in anal intercourse, not all gay men do. The NHSLS study found that found although 80% of gay men reported engaging in anal intercourse, 20% did not (Laumann et al., 1994). Some gay couples (and other couples, too) engage in fisting (also called "hand-balling"), which involves the insertion of the fist and even part of the forearm into the anus or vagina. Since the early 2000s, the use of rubber gloves during fisting has become more common (Richters et al., 2003).

Like many other couples, gay men enjoy hugging, kissing, and body caressing; **interfemoral** (in-ter-fem-OR-ull) **intercourse** (thrusting the penis between the thighs of a partner); and **buttockry** (BUT-ock-ree; rubbing of the penis in the cleft of the buttocks).

Gay male sexual behavior changed significantly in the 1980s after the arrival of AIDS. Undoubtedly because of the massive education efforts initiated in the gay community in the early 1990s, safe-sex practices increased (at least in the major cities) among gay men (Catania et al., 1989). However, researchers believe that sexually transmitted infection increases among sexually active gay men since the mid-2000s are due to a decreased fear of acquiring HIV, an increase in high-risk sexual behaviors (e.g., oral sex without a condom), a lack of knowledge

interfemoral intercourse Thrusting the penis between the thighs of a partner.

buttockry Rubbing of the penis in the cleft of the buttocks.

tribadism Rubbing genitals together with another person for sexual pleasure.

Figure 8.18 Gay men use a variety of sexual techniques

Figure 8.19 Lesbian couples often report higher levels of sexual satisfaction than heterosexual women

Copyright © Cengage Learning 2013

about diseases, and increased Internet access to sexual partners (Hughes, 2006).

Lesbians

Lesbians enjoy a wide range of sexual behaviors, including kissing, hugging, body rubbing, manual stimulation, oral sex, and the use of sex toys such as dildos or vibrators. Manual stimulation of the vulva is the most common sexual practice among lesbians, although lesbians tend to use a variety of techniques in their lovemaking. Lesbian couples kiss more than heterosexual couples, and gay couples kiss least of all.

After manual stimulation, the next most common practice in lesbian couples is cunnilingus, which many lesbians report is their favorite sexual activity. Another common practice is **tribadism** (TRY-bad-iz-um), also called *scissoring*, in which the women rub their genitals together. As noted earlier, some lesbians engage in fisting and also may use dildos or vibrators, often accompanied by manual or oral stimulation.

Lesbians in their 30s were twice as likely as other age groups to engage in anal stimulation (with a finger or dildo). Approximately 33% of women used vibrators, and there were a small number who reported using a variety of other sex toys, such as dildo harnesses, leather restraints, and handcuffs. Sexual play and orgasm are important aspects of lesbian sexuality (Bolso, 2005; Tomassilli et al., 2009).

Overall, lesbians have been found to be more sexually responsive and more satisfied with their sexual relationships, and to have lower rates of sexual problems than heterosexual women (Henderson et al., 2009; Kurdek, 2008). Although some studies have found decreased sexual activity among lesbian couples over time (Rosmalen-Noojjens et al., 2008), other studies have found no differences in sexual frequency between heterosexual and lesbian couples (Henderson et al., 2009; Matthews et al., 2003).

Key Terms Exercise

Match the key term with the correct definition.

Check Your Learning Quiz 8.7

Go to **login.cengagebrain.com** and take the online quiz.

▶ **LO15** Identify three or four physical changes in aging men and women that can affect sexual functioning, and suggest one way a couple might improve their functioning.

Today, older men and women are healthier and more active than previous generations, and many remain interested in sex and engage in several sexual behaviors. The NSSHB found that 20% to 30% of men and women remain sexually active well into their 80s (Schick et al., 2010). However, as men and women age, a variety of physical changes affects sexual functioning and behavior. This section discusses these physical changes and their effect on sexual behavior.

Physical Changes

As people age, they inevitably experience changes in their physical health, some of which can affect normal sexual functioning. Below are the most common physical changes related to sexual functioning experienced by aging men and women.

- *In men:*
  - Delayed and less firm erection
  - Extended refractory period (12–24 hours before rearousal can occur)
  - Reduced elevation of the testicles
  - Reduced vasocongestive response to the testicles and scrotum
  - Fewer expulsive contractions during orgasm
  - Less forceful expulsion of seminal fluid and a reduced volume of ejaculate
  - Rapid loss of erection after ejaculation
  - Less ejaculatory urgency
  - Decrease in size and firmness of the testes, changes in testicle elevation, less sex flush, and decreased swelling and erection of the nipples

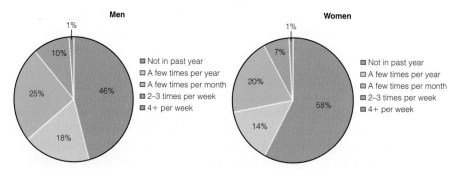

Figure 8.20 Percentage of men and women 50- to 80-years-old who reported engaging in vaginal intercourse within the past year. Source: National Survey of Sexual Health and Behavior, 2010

- *In women:*
  - Reduced or increased sexual interest
  - Possible pain during penetration because of menopausal changes
  - Decreased volume of vaginal lubrication
  - Decreased expansive ability of the vagina
  - Possible orgasmic pain because of less flexibility
  - Thinning of the vaginal walls
  - Shortening of vaginal width and length
  - Decreased sex flush, reduced increase in breast volume, and longer postorgasmic nipple erection

Changes in Sexual Behavior

Physical changes in aging men and women can lead to changes in sexual behavior. Frequent complaints among older adult women are decreases in sexual desire and pain during vaginal intercourse (Schick et al., 2010). Older men are more likely to report problems with erectile functioning and many turn to erectile drugs to enhance sexual functioning.

Many older adults continue to engage in vaginal intercourse (67% of men and 68% of women; Schick et al., 2010). Research on older gay men has found that they continue to be sexually active; however, they tend to engage in less anal intercourse than younger gay men (Van de Ven et al., 1997). Physical problems, such as arthritis, diabetes, and osteoporosis, can interfere with sexual functioning.

A key to sexual enjoyment later in life is for partners to be patient and understanding with each other. Physical fitness, good nutrition, adequate rest and sleep, a reduction in alcohol intake, and positive self-esteem can all enhance sexuality throughout the life span. In addition, many of these changes in sexual functioning later in life are exacerbated by sexual inactivity. In fact, research clearly indicates that older adults who have remained sexually active throughout their aging years have a greater potential for a more satisfying sex life later in life (Lindau & Gavrilova, 2010).

© Roy McMahon/Corbis

Check Your Learning Quiz 8.8

Go to **login.cengagebrain.com** and take the online quiz.

Sexual health is important to our overall health and quality of life. However, sexual problems are quite common and can happen to anyone—gay, straight, or bisexual. The following sections explore how psychological and physiological issues, together with chronic illnesses and disabilities, can challenge sexual functioning.

Psychological Challenges

Various psychological factors can challenge sexual functioning, including unconscious fears, ongoing stress, anxiety, depression, guilt, anger, fear of intimacy, dependency, abandonment, and concern over loss of control (Reynaert et al., 2010). Anxiety plays an important role in developing and maintaining sexual problems. When anxiety levels are high, physiological arousal may be impossible.

Performance fears, distractions, shifts in attention, or preoccupation during sexual arousal may interfere with the ability to respond sexually (see Figure 8.21;

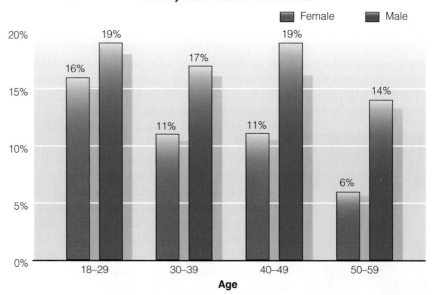

Anxiety About Sexual Performance

Figure 8.21 Percentage of Self-Reported Anxiousness about Performance during Sex by Gender and Age. Source: Laumann et al., 1999

performance fears The fear of not being able to perform during sexual behavior.

psychotropic medications Medications prescribed for psychological disorders, such as depression.

Bancroft et al., 2005; Kaplan, 1974; Masters & Johnson, 1970). Because sexual problems often occur within the context of intimate relationships, all of these issues can affect sexual functioning. Feeling unappreciated, anger, insecurity, resentment, conflict, or a lack of trust can lead to problems with sexual functioning. In addition, the pressures and time commitments of everyday life, together with a lack of privacy, can also affect sexual functioning.

© Masterfile

Physiological Challenges

Healthy sexuality depends on a fine interplay of vascular, hormonal, and neurological functioning. However, a variety of physiological factors can interfere with these functions including various injuries, disabilities, illnesses, and diseases.

Prescription drugs, such as **psychotropic medications** and birth control pills, can affect certain aspects of sexual functioning (see Chapter 11 for more information about birth control usage; Fava et al., 2011; Strohmaier et al., 2011; Yee, 2010). Nonprescription drugs such as tobacco, alcohol, marijuana, LSD, and cocaine may also affect sexual functioning. As discussed earlier, the common physical changes of aging can also affect sexual functioning.

Illness and Sexual Functioning

Sexual functioning involves a complex physiological process, which can be impaired by pain, immobility, changes in bodily functions, or medications (LeVay et al., 1981). Often, problems involve psychological issues as well. Sudden illness causes shock, anger, resentment, anxiety, and depression, all of which can adversely affect sexual desire and functioning.

Serious illness often puts strains on loving relationships. Still, many couples do enjoy loving, full relationships. Maintaining a healthy and satisfying sex life can

Japanese Love Hotels

Author takes a personal tour of a Japanese Love Hotel.

Oncosexology: Sex and Illness

Interview with European oncosexologist—Dr. Woet Gianotten.

Meet Me in the Love Hotel

What they are and why people use them.

increase personal happiness and satisfaction for those who are chronically ill or suffering from a variety of medical conditions.

Disabilities and Sexual Functioning

In the past, the needs of people who are mentally or physically disabled were neglected not because the disabled themselves were not interested in sexuality but because health care providers and other health care professionals were uncomfortable learning about their sexual needs and discussing them with their patients. Fortunately, this has been changing, and now sexuality counseling is a normal part of the recuperation from many diseases and injuries in many hospitals.

Defining a Sexual Problem

Defining a sexual problem can be difficult. To help clarify definitions, some sex therapists in the United States use the *Diagnostic and Statistical Manual and Mental Disorders (DSM),* which provides diagnostic criteria for the most common sexual problems. It is occasionally updated, and a revised, fifth edition of the *DSM (DSM-5)* is due to be released in 2013. However, since 2011, experts have been proposing diagnosis changes for the *DSM-5,* which we will discuss.

Although the *DSM* has been an important tool in helping to diagnose and classify sexual problems, some researchers criticize the *DSM* for strictly adhering to a physiological framing of sexual problems, which fails to acknowledge the relational aspects of sexual behavior (Basson, 2000; Tiefer, 1991). Although physiological functions, such as erection and vaginal lubrication, may be important aspects of sexual functioning, so, too, are relationship and gender issues. Psychological and physiological factors often overlap, as we will see in the following discussions of sexual desire, arousal, and orgasm problems.

Seeking Therapy

If you are experiencing problems with sexual functioning, it is important to seek help as soon as possible. Today, many therapists receive specific training in sexuality. One of the best training organizations in the United States is the American Association of Sexuality Educators, Counselors, and Therapists (AASECT). This organization offers certification programs in human sexuality for counselors, educators, and therapists, and it can also provide information on those who are certified as therapists or counselors.

Evaluating Sexual Problems

For a sex therapist to formulate a treatment plan for a sexual problem, it is important that the therapist understand more about how the patient experiences the problem. For example, how long has it been going on? Has it always happened or is it fairly new? A primary sexual problem is one that has always existed, whereas a secondary sexual problem is one that develops after a period of adequate functioning.

Therapists also need to know the context of the sexual problem: Does it occur all the time or just some of the time? A situational sexual problem is a problem that occurs during certain sexual activities or with certain partners (for instance, a man who can get an erection with his girlfriend but not his wife, or a woman who can have orgasms during masturbation but not during oral sex). A global sexual problem is a problem that occurs in every situation, during every type of sexual activity, and with every sexual partner. It is important to clarify these differences, for they may affect treatment strategies. For instance, primary problems tend to have more biological or physiological causes, whereas secondary problems tend to have more psychological causes.

Treating Sexual Problems

In the United States, treatment of most sexual problems begins with a medical history and workup to identify any physiological causes. In addition to a medical history and examination, it is also important to evaluate any past sexual trauma or abuse that may cause or contribute to the problem. After identifying potential causes, the next step is to determine a plan of treatment. Such treatment may be multimodal, involving more than one type of therapy.

Much of the current clinical research today focuses on developing new drugs to treat sexual problems (even though a number of problems may be caused by or worsened by other medications). The U.S. Food and Drug Administration (FDA) plays a major role in the approval of all new drugs in the United States. Many drug therapies used today for sexual problems, such as Viagra, were originally approved by the FDA to treat other diseases. There is also a brisk business in health supplements to aid in sexual functioning, including aphrodisiacs (see online reading "What Is an Aphrodisiac?").

The Importance of Sexual Expression in People with Disabilities

Interview with director of de schildpad, a Dutch organization that provides sex to the handicapped.

Helena: A Sex Worker for the Disabled

Interview with woman who works as a sex worker for de schildpad.

No Sex for Me: Asexuality

Hear from people who claim they are asexual, and listen to them explain their feelings about sexuality.

Check Your Learning Quiz 8.9

Go to **login.cengagebrain.com** and take the online quiz.

▸ **LO19** Compare hypoactive sexual desire disorder, sexual interest/arousal disorder, and sexual aversion.

▸ **LO20** Define *erectile disorder*, and discuss three of the available treatment options.

Problems with sexual desire include hypoactive sexual desire disorder (HSDD), sexual interest/arousal disorder, and sexual aversion. These problems involve a deficient or absent desire for sexual activity. Although experts have recommended dropping the diagnosis of sexual aversion in the *DSM-5*, it typically involves an extreme disgust, fear, or revulsion of sexuality.

Hypoactive Sexual Desire Disorder and Sexual Interest/Arousal Disorder

Hypoactive sexual desire disorder is a persistent or recurrent deficiency or absence of sexual fantasies and desire for sexual activity. Although both men and women have been diagnosed with HSDD in the past, many experts believe that women were disproportionately diagnosed, even though there were gender differences in how men and women experienced it. As a result, experts have recommended keeping HSDD for men in the *DSM-5*, but adding a new disorder specifically for women called *sexual interest/arousal disorder*. A nationally representative sample of U.S. women found 27% of premenopausal women and 52% of naturally menopausal women experienced problems with sexual interest and/or arousal (West et al., 2008).

Psychological factors that may contribute to either of these interest and

sexual aversion Persistent or recurring extreme aversion to and avoidance of all genital contact.

discrepancy in desire Differences in levels of sexual desire in a couple.

aphrodisiac A substance that increases, or is believed to increase, a person's sexual desire.

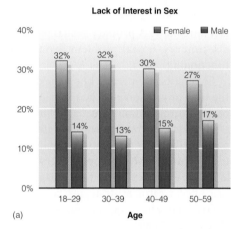

(a)

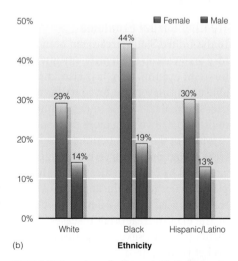

(b)

Figure 8.22 Percentage of self-reported lack of interest in sex, by gender, ethnicity, and age. Source: Laumann et al., 1999

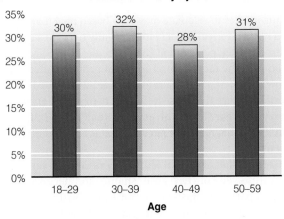

Problems with Early Ejaculation

Figure 8.25 Although early ejaculation is often associated with younger males, studies have found it can occur any any age.
Source: Laumann et al., 1999

soft stimulation should be. Some women worry about what their partners might think if they made sexual suggestions, or they feel uncomfortable receiving stimulation (such as cunnilingus or manual stimulation) without stimulating their partners at the same time.

Treating Female Orgasmic Disorder

Today, the majority of treatment programs for orgasmic disorder involve a combination of different treatment approaches, such as homework assignments, sex education, communication skills training, cognitive restructuring, desensitization, and other techniques (Meston et al., 2004). LoPiccolo and Lobitz (1972) developed the most effective treatment for female orgasmic disorder; it involves teaching a woman to masturbate to orgasm.

On a psychological level, masturbation also helps increase the pleasurable anticipation of sex. Education, self-exploration, communication training, and body awareness are also included in masturbation training for orgasmic problems. As a woman learns more about her body, she can teach her partner which areas are more sensitive than others.

Early Ejaculation

Although the time it takes to ejaculate may vary based on a man's age, sexual experience, health, and stress level, early ejaculation usually refers to a man reaching orgasm just before, or directly after, penetration (Althof et al., 2010; Feige et al., 2011).

Early ejaculation is the most common sexual problem affecting men (Linton & Wylie, 2010; Rowland et al., 2010; Serefoglu et al., 2011; Vardi et al., 2008). In the United States, estimates are that close to 30% of men report experiencing early ejaculation in the previous year (Laumann et al., 1994). Early ejaculation affects men of all ages and can lead to decreases in sexual satisfaction and quality of life for both men and their partners.

Psychological factors that have been found to contribute to early ejaculation include stress, anxiety, unresolved conflict, guilt, shame, and performance pressures (i.e., wanting to satisfy a partner). Masters and Johnson (1970) originally proposed that early ejaculation develops when a man's early sexual experiences are rushed because of the fear of being caught or discovered. These fears, they believed, could condition a man to ejaculate rapidly. Others have pointed out that early ejaculation occurs in men who are unable to accurately judge their own levels of sexual arousal, which would enable them to use self-control and avoid rapid ejaculation (H. S. Kaplan, 1989).

Potential physiological factors also may contribute to early ejaculation. Research has found that some men might have "hyperexcitability" or an "oversensitivity" of their penis, which prevents them from delaying orgasm. Nerves in the lumbar spine are related to ejaculation, and research continues to explore medications to decrease the increased sensitivity (Benson et al., 2009).

Treating Early Ejaculation

A variety of psychological, topical, and oral therapies have been used to treat early ejaculation, with varying levels of success (Hellstrom, 2006; Owen, 2009). A common treatment for early ejaculation has been the use of selective serotonin reuptake inhibitors, because a common negative side effect of these drugs is delayed ejaculation (Linton & Wylie, 2010; Rowland et al., 2010; Shindel et al., 2008).

Treatment may also include the use of behavioral techniques known as the **squeeze** or **stop–start techniques** (see Figure 8.26; Shindel et al., 2008). Both involve stimulating the penis to the point just before ejaculation. With the squeeze technique, sexual stimulation or masturbation is engaged in just short of orgasm; then stimulation is stopped. The man or his partner applies pressure to the frenu-

squeeze technique A technique in which the ejaculatory reflex is reconditioned using a firm grasp on the penis.

stop–start technique A technique in which the ejaculatory reflex is reconditioned using intermittent pressure on the glans of the penis.

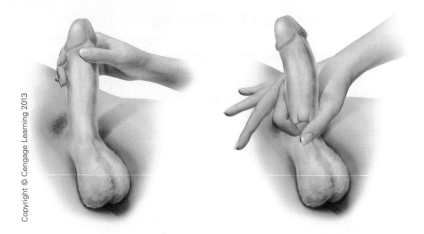

Copyright © Cengage Learning 2013

Figure 8.26 The squeeze technique is often recommended in the treatment of early ejaculation. Pressure is applied either at the top or to the base of the penis for several seconds until the urge to ejaculate subsides.

lum for 3 to 4 seconds until the urge to ejaculate subsides. With the stop–start technique, stimulation is simply stopped until the ejaculatory urge subsides. Using these methods, a man can usually gain some control over his erection within 2 to 10 weeks and can have excellent control within several months.

Delayed Ejaculation

In 2010, the American Psychiatric Association recommended renaming male orgasmic disorder to delayed ejaculation (Segraves, 2010). In this condition, ejaculation is delayed or absent, and this occurs in all, or almost all, sexual encounters for at least 6 months' duration. Delayed ejaculation is relatively rare—less than 3% of men report experiencing it (Perelman & Rowland, 2006).

Delayed ejaculation can be the result of both psychological and physiological factors. Psychological factors include stress, a lack of attraction to one's partner, a strict religious background, atypical masturbation patterns, or past traumatic events such as sexual abuse. Physiological factors include the use of certain drugs and various illnesses, nerve damage, and spinal cord injury.

Treatment for delayed ejaculation can include changing prescription medications, discontinuing the use of nonprescription drugs or alcohol, or sex therapy. Delayed ejaculation is often difficult to treat, and no evidence-based treatments have been proved to eliminate this dysfunction (Nelson et al., 2007; Richardson et al., 2006).

Key Terms Exercise

Match the correct term with each definition.

Check Your Learning Quiz 8.11

Go to **login.cengagebrain.com** and take the online quiz.

Think Critically

Challenge Your Thinking

Consider these questions:

1. Explain how the use of Masters and Johnson's model of sexual response, together with the *DSM,* might not be applicable to problems with sexual functioning in women.

2. Provide two reasons why feminist critics believe it is important to consider the psychosocial dimensions of sexual expression. Do you think this is a valid criticism? Why or why not?

3. How might a lack of sex education contribute to the development of a sexual problem?

4. Give one example of how betrayal or fear of a partner could interfere with adequate sexual functioning.

5. If you were to design a campaign to reduce "Sexual Problems Caused by Sociocultural, Political, or Economic Factors," what would you do to reduce these issues? Do you think it might work? Why or why not?

Beyond the Medical Model

Earlier in this chapter, Masters and Johnson's sexual response cycle was discussed. This model, together with the *DSM* classification system, has long been used as the foundation for treating sexual problems. However, critics challenge how these models apply to female sexuality and contend that they are incomplete by not encompassing psychosocial dimensions of sexual expression. In 2000, Leonore Tiefer, a leading sex therapist and feminist sexologist, and a group of colleagues proposed the *New View of Women's Sexual Problems* that included a revision in the classification system for female sexual dysfunction (Kaschak & Tiefer, 2001).

According to Tiefer and colleagues, most sexual problems occur when there is "discontent or dissatisfaction with any emotional, physical, or relational aspect of sexual experience" (Tiefer, 2001). The New View of Sexual Problems includes four categories that account for most of the limitations in women's sexual functioning:

I. **Sexual problems caused by sociocultural, political, or economic factors:** Issues include limited or no sex education, lack of access to reproductive health services, or other social constraints and pressures and cultural conflicts.

II. **Sexual problems relating to partner and relationship factors:** Issues may include inhibition, avoidance, or distress arising from betrayal, dislike, or fear of partner; communication issues; or discrepancies in desire.

III. **Sexual problems caused by psychological factors:** Issues include sexual aversion, mistrust, or inhibition of sexual pleasure because of past experiences of physical, sexual, or emotional abuse; depression and anxiety; or personality problems.

IV. **Sexual problems caused by medical factors:** Issues can include neurological, neurovascular, circulatory, endocrine, pregnancy-related, sexually transmitted diseases, or adverse effects of medications or medical treatments.

New View proponents believe that an overmedicalization of female sexuality has resulted in an obsessive focus on the genital aspect of sexuality, whereas ignoring psychological and social aspects (Tiefer, 1996, 2002). The medical approaches to women's sexual problems have evolved into an increasing emphasis on pills, creams, gels, and other pharmaceutical agents, to the dismay of those who believe sexual behavior is multidimensional, complex, and context dependent.

Think Critically

This article and its questions are available in interactive format online.

GO to your Psychology CourseMate at login.cengagebrain.com and take the Chapter Post-Test to see which Learning Objectives you've mastered and which need more review. Use the chapter review guide below and the online activities—including flashcards to review key terms—to measure your learning.

Measure ^Your Learning

Module		Learning Objectives	
8.1	Influences on Sexual Attitudes and Behaviors 270	LO1	List three of the biggest influences on our sexual attitudes and behaviors.
8.2	Masters and Johnson's Sexual Response Cycle 272	LO2	Describe the sexual response cycle in women, and identify the physical changes that occur.
		LO3	Describe the sexual response cycle in men, and identify the physical changes that occur.
8.3	Other Models of Sexual Response and Future Directions 278	LO4	Compare Kaplan's and Reed's models of sexual response with the Masters and Johnson model.
		LO5	Identify one to two criticisms of the existing sexual response models, and discuss proposals for future directions in sexual response research.
8.4	Sexual Fantasies and Masturbation 280	LO6	Explain gender differences in the use of sexual fantasy.
		LO7	Explain gender differences in masturbation.
8.5	Manual Sex, Oral Sex, and Anal Intercourse 282	LO8	Define *manual sex,* and discuss the popularity of this behavior.
		LO9	Define *oral sex,* and discuss the research on the frequency of this behavior.
		LO10	Define *anal intercourse,* and discuss the research on the frequency of this behavior.

Online Activities

Key Terms	Video	Animation	Readings	Assessment
	Is Virtual Sex Cheating?			Check Your Learning Quiz 8.1
excitement, plateau, orgasm, resolution, tenting effect, sex flush, orgasmic platform, tumescence, detumescence, refractory phase	Why do women fake orgasm? Are "blue balls" real?	Internal and External Changes in the Female Sexual Response Cycle Masters and Johnson's Sexual Response Cycle Breast Changes in the Female Sexual Response Cycle Internal and External Changes in the Male Sexual Response Cycle		Check Your Learning Quiz 8.2
		Female Sexual Response Cycle: Circular		Check Your Learning Quiz 8.3
	Is it weird to fantasize about having sex with lots of people watching?			Check Your Learning Quiz 8.4
sixty-nine, anal sphincter	Is Monogamy for Everyone? Do women like their partners to kiss them right after they've had oral sex with them? Do guys want their partner to swallow after they get a blow job?			Check Your Learning Quiz 8.5

Measure ^ Your Learning

Online Activities

Key Terms	Video	Animation	Readings	Assessment
premature ejaculation (PE)	My girlfriend complains that I'm too big and I hurt her. What can I do?			Check Your Learning Quiz 8.6
fisting, interfemoral intercourse, buttockry, tribadism		Key Terms Exercise		Check Your Learning Quiz 8.7
				Check Your Learning Quiz 8.8
performance fears, psychotropic medications	Japanese Love Hotels Oncosexology: Sex and Illness The Importance of Sexual Expression in People with Disabilities Helena: A Sex Worker for the Disabled No Sex for Me: Asexuality		Meet Me in the Love Hotel	Check Your Learning Quiz 8.9
hypoactive sexual desire disorders (HSDD), sexual interest/arousal disorder, sexual aversion, discrepancy in desire, aphrodisiac, erectile disorder, vacuum constriction device, prosthesis implantation, intracavernous injection	Are erection problems hereditary? Is it safe to use Viagra recreationally?		What Is an Aphrodisiac?	Check Your Learning Quiz 8.10
orgasmic disorder, delayed ejaculation, squeeze technique, stop–start technique		Key Terms Exercise		Check Your Learning Quiz 8.11
				Beyond the Medical Model

Sexual Orientation

9

Chapter Outline and Learning Objectives

Prepare ^ to Learn

1 **GO** to your **Psychology CourseMate** at **login.cengagebrain.com** and take the **Chapter Pre-Test** to introduce yourself to this chapter's topics and see what you may already know.

2 **READ** the **Learning Objectives** (LOs, in the left sidebars) and begin the chapter.

3 **COMPLETE** the **Online Activities** (in the right sidebars) *as you read each module.* Activities include **videos, animations, readings,** and **quizzes.**

4 **CHECK Your Learning** by going online to take the quiz at the end of each module and review material as necessary.

5 **MEASURE Your Learning** after reading the chapter by taking the online **Chapter Post-Test.** Use the chapter review guide at the end of the chapter as needed.

WATCH for these **Online Activities** icons as you read:

Video

Animation

Reading

Assessment

Think Critically

These Online Activities are essential to mastering this chapter. Go to login.cengagebrain.com.

 Videos Explore diverse perspectives on sex as well as common questions:

- Why are guys turned on by two girls having sex but turned off by two guys having sex?
- Do any animals engage in homosexual behavior or are they all straight?
- If I played sex games with a same-sex friend when I was 15, does that make me gay?
- Is there any therapy that can change a person's sexual orientation?
- Trying Not to Be Gay
- Discovering Bisexuality
- Are bisexuals really attracted to both men and women?
- Coming out as a Lesbian
- Coming out in the Workplace
- Peter and Stephan: A Dutch Couple
- Hate Crimes against Gays, Lesbians, and Bisexuals
- Homosexuality in Religion and Law

 Animations Interact with and visualize important processes, timelines, and concepts:

- The Kinsey Continuum
- Key Terms Exercise

 Readings Delve deeper into key content:

- Homosexuality in Other Times and Places
- Party Gay?
- A Model of Coming Out

 Assessment Measure your mastery:

- Chapter Pre-Test
- Check Your Learning Quizzes
- Chapter Post-Test

 Think Critically Challenge your thinking about data and accepted norms:

- Bisexuality: Playing Both Sides of the Fence?

Sexual orientation refers to the gender(s) that a person is attracted to emotionally, physically, sexually, and romantically. **Heterosexuals** are predominantly attracted to members of the other sex, **homosexuals** to members of the same sex, and **bisexuals** are attracted to both sexes.

The word *straight* is often used to refer to a heterosexual; *gay* is often used to refer to a male homosexual, and *lesbian* is often used to refer to a female homosexual. Although such distinctions may seem simple, human sexual behavior does not always fit easily into such neat boxes. Today, many people use the acronym GLBTQ to refer to people whose identity is gay, lesbian, bisexual, transgender, or questioning (or queer). Because we discussed transgender issues in earlier chapters and we focus on gay, lesbian, and bisexual (GLB) issues in this discussion, we will use the acronym GLB throughout this chapter.

▼

sexual orientation The gender(s) that a person is attracted to emotionally, physically, sexually, and romantically.

heterosexual Man or woman who is erotically attracted to members of the other sex.

homosexual Man or woman who is erotically attracted to members of the same sex.

bisexual Person who is erotically attracted to members of either sex.

What Determines Sexual Orientation?

How should we categorize a person's sexual orientation? The simplest way to categorize a person's sexual orientation seems to be through sexual behavior; that is, with whom does the person have sex? However, there are many other factors to consider. What

© Angela Hanlon

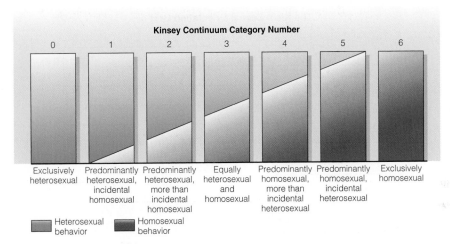

Kinsey Continuum Category Number

| 0 | 1 | 2 | 3 | 4 | 5 | 6 |

| Exclusively heterosexual | Predominantly heterosexual, incidental homosexual | Predominantly heterosexual, more than incidental homosexual | Equally heterosexual and homosexual | Predominantly homosexual, more than incidental heterosexual | Predominantly homosexual, incidental heterosexual | Exclusively homosexual |

Heterosexual behavior   Homosexual behavior

Figure 9.1 Source: From Kinsey et al. [1948]. Reprinted by permission of The Kinsey Institute for Research in Sex, Gender, and Reproduction, Inc.

about a person's sexual fantasies? If a man sometimes fantasizes about sex with men, even though he considers himself straight and has sex only with women, what is his sexual orientation?

Perhaps we should consider romantic love instead of sex to determine a person's sexual orientation. Who does the person love, or who could the person love? If a married man has sex with men but loves his wife romantically and would never consider an emotional attachment to the men he has sex with, would you consider him heterosexual just because he loves only his wife? Maybe we should just let people decide for themselves; if they believe they are heterosexual, they are, no matter how they behave. Yet when people's behavior and beliefs about themselves are in conflict, social scientists usually define them by their behavior.

The problem may be that we tend to think of sexual orientation in discrete categories: People are either homosexual or heterosexual (or, occasionally, bisexual). The full variety and richness of human sexual experience, however, cannot be easily captured in such restrictive categories. People can show enormous variety in their sexual behavior, sexual fantasies, emotional attachments, and sexual self-concept, and each contributes to a person's sexual orientation.

The Kinsey Continuum

See how the Kinsey continuum lines up with other models.

The Klein Sexual Orientation Grid

	Past	Present	Ideal
A. Sexual attraction			
B. Sexual behavior			
C. Sexual fantasies			
D. Emotional preference			
E. Social preference			
F. Self-identification			
G. Heterosexual/homosexual lifestyle			

0 = other sex only
1 = mostly other sex, incidental same sex
2 = mostly other sex, more than incidental same sex
3 = both sexes equally
4 = mostly same sex, more than incidental other sex
5 = mostly same sex, incidental other sex
6 = same sex only

Figure 9.2 Source: From Fritz [1990, p. 280]. Reprinted by permission of The Kinsey Institute for Research in Sex, Gender, and Reproduction, Inc.

Models of Sexual Orientation: Who Is Homosexual?

Kinsey and his colleagues (1948) believed that relying on the categories "homosexual" and "heterosexual" to describe sexual orientation was inadequate. They also suggested that using a category such as "homosexual" was not as helpful as talking about homosexual behavior. Trying to decide who is a homosexual is difficult; trying to compare amounts or types of homosexual behavior (including fantasies and emotions) is easier. Consequently, Kinsey introduced a seven-point scale (Figure 9.1) ranging from exclusively heterosexual behavior (0 points) to exclusively homosexual behavior (6 points).

The Kinsey continuum was the first scale to suggest that people engage in complex sexual behaviors that cannot be reduced to simply "homosexual" or "heterosexual." Many theorists agree that sexual orientation is a continuous variable rather than a categorical variable—that is, there are no natural cutoff points that would easily separate people into categories such as "heterosexual" or "homosexual" (Berkey et al., 1990; L. Ellis et al., 1987).

The Kinsey scale is not without its problems, however. First, Kinsey emphasized people's behavior (although he did consider other factors such as fantasies and emotions), but some researchers suggest that people's emotions and fantasies are the most important determinants of sexual orientation (Bell et al., 1981; F. Klein, 1993; Storms, 1980, 1981). Second, the scale is static in time; how recently must one have had homosexual contact to qualify for "incidents" of homosexual behavior? If a man slept with six men over the last year and had sex with his wife once a week, is he in category 5 (because he had sex with six men and only one woman) or category 2 (because he had 52 experiences with a woman, but only 6 with men; F. Klein, 1990)?

The Klein Sexual Orientation Grid (KSOG) takes the Kinsey continuum a step further by including seven dimensions—attraction, behavior, fantasy, emotional preference, social preference, self-identification, and lifestyle (Horowitz et al., 2001). Each of these dimensions is measured for the past, the present, and the ideal (Figure 9.2).

Measuring Sexual Orientation: How Prevalent?

How prevalent are homosexuality, heterosexuality, and bisexuality in society? Estimates for homosexuality range from 2% to 4% to more than 10% in males and 1% to 3% in females, whereas estimates for bisexuality are approximately 3% (M. Diamond, 1993; Hughes, 2006; Seidman & Rieder, 1994; Whitam et al., 1999). National studies in France, Britain, Norway, Denmark, and Canada all found same-sex behavior in 1% to 3% of men and a slightly lower percentage of women (Muir, 1993).

It is important to note, however, that those studies concentrated on same-sex behavior, not attraction, fantasies, or desires. One national population-based study measured both same-sex attraction and behavior and found that 16% to 20% of the adult population of the United States, United Kingdom, and France reported some same-sex attraction or behavior since age 15 (Sell et al., 1995). Although there is much work to be done in determining the prevalence of homosexuality, scholars generally agree that between 3% and 4% of males are predominantly gay, 1.5% to 2% of women are predominantly lesbian, and about 2% to 5% of people are bisexual (Jenkins, 2010; Laumann et al., 1994).

Check Your Learning Quiz 9.1

Go to **login.cengagebrain.com** and take the online quiz.

▶ **LO3** Summarize the findings of one or two studies that produced evidence for a substantial genetic component of sexual orientation.

▶ **LO4** Summarize the findings of one or two studies pointing to the possible influence of birth order on sexual orientation.

▶ **LO5** Summarize the findings of one or two studies that compared brain structure and function with other physical aspects of heterosexuals and homosexuals.

Early biological theories implied that homosexuality was an abnormality in development, which contributed to the argument that homosexuality was a sickness. More recently, gay and lesbian scholars, in an attempt to prove that homosexuality is not a "lifestyle choice" as antihomosexual forces have argued, have themselves been arguing that homosexuality is a biologically based sexual variation. Biological theories today claim that differing sexual orientations are due to differences in physiology. These differences can be because of genetics, hormones, birth order, or simple physical traits.

Genetics

J. Michael Bailey and his colleagues have performed a number of studies of twins to determine the genetic basis of homosexuality. They report that in homosexual males, 52% of identical twins, 22% of fraternal twins, and 11% of adoptive brothers were also gay, showing that the more closely genetically related two siblings were, the more likely they were to share a sexual orientation (J. M. Bailey & Pillard, 1995). Among females, 48% of identical twins, 16% of fraternal twins, and 6% of adoptive siblings of lesbians were also lesbians (J. M. Bailey et al., 1995). However, identical twins share much more than genetics. They also share many more experiences than do other kinds of siblings. Therefore, the studies cannot tell how much of the concordance is due to genetic factors and how much is due to the identical twins having grown up under similar environmental influences.

Some studies have found that sexual orientation is familial (i.e., runs in the family; Francis, 2008; Schwartz et al., 2010). Dean Hamer and colleagues (1993) found that gay males tended to have more gay relatives on their mother's side, and they traced that to the existence of a gene that they found in 33 of 40 gay brothers. This gene is inherited from the mother's, but not the father's, side (Keller, 2005). Gay men also have more gay brothers than lesbian sisters, whereas lesbians have more lesbian sisters than gay brothers (Bogaert, 2005; Pattatucci, 1998). Other studies support the familial link but have found that male sexual orientation is inherited from the father's, and not the mother's, side (Schwartz et al., 2010). In this study, gay men were found to have more homosexual male relatives than heterosexual men, and sisters of gay men were more likely to be lesbians than sisters of heterosexual men (Schwartz et al., 2010).

If homosexuality were solely a genetic trait, it should have disappeared long ago. Because homosexuals have been less likely than heterosexuals to have children, each successive generation of homosexuals should have become smaller, until genes for homosexuality disappeared from the gene pool. Yet, rates of homosexuality have remained constant. Concordance rates for siblings, twins, and adoptees reveal that genes account for at least 50% of the variance in sexual orientation (Pillard & Bailey, 1998). Even so, Bailey and his colleagues agree that environmental factors are also important.

Hormones

Hormonal theories can concentrate either on hormonal imbalances before birth or on hormone levels in adults. In this section, we examine both prenatal and adult hormonal levels.

Prenatal Factors

When certain hormones are injected into pregnant animals, such as rats or guinea pigs, at critical periods of fetal development, the offspring can be made to exhibit homosexual behavior. Some researchers have found evidence that sexual orientation may be influenced by levels of prenatal hormones in human beings as well (Berenbaum & Snyder, 1995; Cohen-Bendahan et al., 2005; Jenkins, 2010; Rahman, 2005; Swaab, 2004). Hormonal levels can be affected by stress during pregnancy, and research has explored how this stress can influence the sexual orientation of a fetus (L. Ellis, 1988; Hall & Schaeff, 2008).

Although many of the hormonal studies have focused on deficiencies in certain hormones, there is also research indicating that excess hormonal exposure during prenatal development may be related to sexual orientation. For example, females who were exposed to diethylstilbestrol (DES; synthetic estrogen) in the womb are more likely to identify as bisexual or lesbian compared with those females not exposed to DES (Meyer-Bahlburg et al., 1985).

Overall, the evidence for the effect of prenatal hormones on both male and female homosexuality is weak (Gooren, 2006; Hall & Schaeff, 2008; Whalen et al., 1990). In other words, even prenatal hormones that have yielded the most interesting research have been on finger lengths, which we will discuss in the upcoming physiology section. Finger-length ratios have been found to be related to prenatal hormonal levels (Hall & Schaeff, 2008).

On Your Mind

Why are guys turned on by two girls having sex but turned off by two guys having sex?

Adult Hormone Levels

Many studies have compared blood androgen levels in adult male homosexuals with those in adult male heterosexuals, and most have found no significant differences (Green, 1988; Mbugua, 2006). Of five studies comparing hormone levels in lesbians and straight women, three found differences between the two groups in testosterone, estrogen, or other hormones, and the other two found higher levels of testosterone in lesbians (and one found lower levels of estrogen; Dancey, 1990). Thus, studies so far do not support the idea of adult hormone involvement.

Birth Order

Gay men have more older brothers than do heterosexual men (Blanchard, 2008; McConaghy et al., 2006). This is often explained by the **maternal immune hypothesis**, which proposes there is a progressive immunization to male-specific antigens after the birth of successive sons in some mothers, which increases the effects of anti-male antibodies on the sexual differentiation of the brain in the developing fetus (this has also been referred to as the fraternal birth order effect; R. Blanchard, 2008; Bogaert & Skorska, 2011; Schwartz et al., 2010; Valenzuela, 2010). Research has found that in families with multiple brothers, later born brothers from the same mother are more likely to be homosexual (R. Blanchard, 2004; Bogaert & Skorska, 2011; Camperio-Ciani et al., 2004; Francis, 2008). Each older brother increases a man's chance of being gay by about 33% (Blanchard, 2008; Francis, 2010). However, the presence of older sisters from the same biological mom decreases the likelihood of homosexuality (Francis, 2008). Having siblings from different mothers does not have an effect on sexual orientation (Blanchard, 1997).

Although most of the research on birth order has been done on men, limited research on women has found that having an older brother or any sisters decreases the likelihood of homosexuality in women (Francis, 2008). This research is controversial, but nonetheless research in this direction continues to look for possible interactions.

maternal immune hypothesis Theory of sexual orientation that proposes that the fraternal birth order effect of gay brothers reflects the progressive immunization of some mothers to male-specific antigens by each succeeding male fetus.

Physiology

Two articles in the early 1990s reported differences between the brains of homosexual and heterosexual men (S. LeVay, 1991; Swaab & Hofman, 1990). Both studies found that certain areas of the hypothalamus, known to play a strong role in sexual urges, were either larger or smaller in gay men than in straight men. More recent studies have also found brain differences—specifically in the cerebral hemispheres—of heterosexual and homosexual men and women (Hu et al., 2008; Ponseti et al., 2006, 2009; Savic & Lindström, 2008). Another study found that straight men and lesbian women have similar brain structures, as do gay men and straight women (Savic & Lindström, 2008). Brain research has found that gay men use both sides of their brain, a pattern similar to heterosexual women (Brewster et al., 2010). However, it has not yet been determined whether brain differences were there from birth or developed later in life, and the research cannot prove that the differences were primarily due to sexual orientation (Kinnunen et al., 2004; Swaab, 2004).

Physiology studies have also looked at differences between heterosexuals and homosexuals for a variety of factors, such as the amount of facial hair, size of external genitalia, ear structure, hair whorls (a cowlick in the back of a hair part), hearing, body shape, eye-blink startle responses, and spatial ability (A. Bailey & Hurd, 2005; Beaton & Mellor, 2007; Hall & Schaeff, 2008; Johnson et al., 2007; McFadden, 2011; Rahman et al., 2010; Rahman & Koerting, 2008). Gay men and heterosexual women have similar spatial learning and memory abilities that differ from heterosexual men (Rahman & Koerting, 2008). Research on handedness has found that gay men are more likely than straight men to be left-handed (R. Blanchard et al., 2006, 2008; Brewster et al., 2010; Martin et al., 2008; Schwartz et al., 2010; Valenzuela, 2008).

However, the most physiological research has been done on finger lengths. The typical male-type finger pattern is a longer ring finger than index finger, whereas the typical female-type pattern is similar index and ring finger lengths, or a longer index finger. Lesbian women are more commonly found to have a typical male-type finger length pattern, whereas gay men are more likely to have a typical female-type finger length pattern (Galis et al., 2010; Grimbos et al., 2010; Hall & Schaeff, 2008; Martin et al., 2008; Schwartz et al., 2010).

Given the complexity of biological factors, it is impossible to make accurate individual predications because of the randomness of neural connections during development (Pillard, 1998). Because of this, it appears that sexual orientation is the result of an interaction of genetic, biological, and social influences (Schuklenk et al., 1997).

On Your Mind

Do any animals engage in homosexual behavior or are they all straight?

Check Your Learning Quiz 9.2

Go to **login.cengagebrain.com** and take the online quiz.

▸ **LO6** Explain how psychoanalytic theory became the basis for the view of homosexuality as a mental illness.

▸ **LO7** Summarize Storms's developmental theory of homosexuality, and indicate how it is contradicted by a study conducted in Papua New Guinea.

▸ **LO8** Summarize the behaviorist theories of homosexuality.

Psychoanalytic Theories

Sigmund Freud (1953) saw male heterosexuality as the result of normal maturation and male homosexuality as the result of an unresolved Oedipal complex. An intense attachment to the mother coupled with a distant father could lead the boy to fear revenge by the father through castration. Female genitalia, lacking a penis, could then represent this castration and evoke fear throughout his life. After puberty, the child might shift from desire for the mother to identification with her and begin to look for the love objects she would look for—men.

Like Freud's view of female sexuality in general, his theories on lesbianism were less coherent, but he basically argued that it resulted from an unresolved Electra complex, in which the young girl becomes angry when she discovers she lacks a penis and blames her mother. Unable to have her father, she defensively rejects him and all men and minimizes her anger at her mother by eliminating the competition between them for male affection.

Freud's generally tolerant attitude toward homosexuality was rejected by some later psychoanalysts, especially Sandor Rado. Rado (1949) claimed that humans were not innately bisexual and that homosexuality was a mental illness. This view (not Freud's) became standard for the psychiatric profession until at least the 1970s.

Another influential researcher who followed Rado's perspective was Irving Bieber. Bieber and colleagues (1962) claimed that all boys had a normal, erotic attraction to women. However, some had overly close and possessive mothers who were also overintimate and sexually seductive. Their fathers, in contrast, were hostile or absent, and this drove the boy to the arms of his mother, who inhibited his normal masculine development. Bieber and his colleagues blamed homosexuality on a seductive mother who puts the fear of heterosexuality in her son.

The psychoanalytic views of homosexuality dominated for many years. Evelyn Hooker, a clinical psychologist, was a pioneer in gay studies who tried to combat the psychoanalytic view that homosexuality was an illness (see Chapter 1). Hooker (1957) used psychological tests, personal histories, and psychological evaluations to show that homosexuals were as well adjusted as heterosexuals and that no real evidence existed that homosexuality was a psychological disorder. Although it took many years for her ideas to take hold, many modern psychoanalysts eventually shifted away from the pathological view of homosexuality. Lewes (1988) demonstrated that psychoanalytic theory itself could easily portray homosexuality as a result of healthy development, and that previous psychoanalytic interpretations of homosexuality were based more on prejudice than on science.

Storms's Developmental Theory

Storms (1981) suggests a purely developmental theory of homosexuality. Noting that a person's sex drive begins to develop in adolescence, Storms suggests that those who develop early begin to become sexually aroused before they have significant contact with the other sex. Because dating usually begins around age 15, boys who mature at age 12 still play and interact in predominantly same-sex groupings, so their emerging erotic feelings are more likely to focus on boys.

Boys of the Sambia tribe in Papua New Guinea.

Storms's theory is supported by the fact that homosexuals do tend to report earlier sexual contacts than heterosexuals. Also, men's sex drive may emerge at a younger age than women's, if such things as frequency of masturbation are any measure, which may explain why there are fewer lesbians than gay men.

However, Storms's theory is contradicted by a study of the Sambia tribe of Papua New Guinea, where boys live communally and have sex with other boys from an early age until they are ready to marry (Stoller & Herdt, 1985). If Storms is correct and a male becomes homosexual because only males are available at the time of sexual awakening, then all male Sambians should be gay. However, almost all go on to lead heterosexual lives.

Behaviorist Theories

Behaviorists consider homosexuality a learned behavior, brought about by the reinforcement of homosexual behaviors or the punishing of heterosexual behavior (Masters & Johnson, 1979). For example, a person may have a same-sex encounter that is pleasurable, coupled with an encounter with the other sex that is frightening; in his or her fantasies, that person may focus on the same-sex encounter, reinforcing its pleasure with masturbation. Masters and Johnson (1979) believed that even in adulthood, some men and women move toward same-sex behaviors if they have negative heterosexual encounters and pleasant same-sex ones.

It is interesting to point out, however, that in a society like ours that tends to view heterosexuality as the norm, it would seem that few men and women would be societally reinforced for homosexual behavior. Yet homosexuality exists even without this positive reinforcement from society.

On Your Mind

If I played sex games with a same-sex friend when I was 15, does that make me gay?

On Your Mind

Is there any therapy that can change a person's sexual orientation?

Check Your Learning Quiz 9.3

Go to **login.cengagebrain.com** and take the online quiz.

▶ **LO9** Compare the sociological and interactional theories of sexual orientation.

Sociological Theories

Sociological theories examine how social forces produce homosexuality in a society. They suggest that concepts such as homosexuality, bisexuality, and heterosexuality are products of our social fabric and are dependent on how we as a society decide to define things. In other words, we learn our culture's way of thinking about sexuality; then we apply it to ourselves.

The idea of "homosexuality" is a product of a particular culture at a particular time; the idea did not even exist before the 19th century (although the behavior did). Some have argued that the use of the term homosexuality as a way to think about same-sex behavior arose only after the Industrial Revolution freed people economically from the family unit and urbanization allowed them to choose new lifestyles in the cities (Adams, 1987). Thus, the idea that people are either "heterosexual" or "homosexual" is not a biological fact but simply a way of thinking that evolves as social conditions change. In other countries, as we note later, these terms are not used, and a person's sexuality is not defined by the gender of his or her partners.

Sociologists are interested in the models of sexuality that society offers its members and how individuals come to identify with one model or another. For example, maybe effeminate young boys begin to behave as homosexuals because they are labeled homosexual, are called "faggot" by their peers, are ridiculed by their siblings, and even witness the worry and fear on the faces of their parents. They begin to doubt themselves, search for homosexuality in their own behavior, and eventually find it. If American society did not split the sexual world into "homosexual" and "heterosexual" categories, perhaps these boys would move fluidly through same-sex and other-sex contacts without having to choose between the "gay" and "straight" communities.

Interactional Theory

Finally, interactional theory proposes that homosexuality results from a complex interaction of biological, psychological, and social factors. Perhaps a child is born after being exposed to prenatal hormones that could predispose him or her toward a particular sexual orientation, but this predisposition, in conjunction with social experiences, either facilitates or inhibits a particular sexual orientation.

Social psychologist Daryl Bem (2000) proposes an interactional theory that combines both biology and sociological issues. Bem suggests that biological variables, such as genetics, hormones, and brain neuroanatomy, do not cause certain sexual orientations; rather, they contribute to childhood temperaments that influence a child's preferences for sex-typical or sex-atypical activities and peers.

Bem believes that males who engage in "male-typical activities," such as rough-and-tumble play or competitive team sports, prefer to be with other boys who also like these activities. In contrast, girls who prefer "female-typical activities," such as socializing quietly or playing jacks, prefer the company of other girls who like to do the same activities. Gender-conforming children (those who engage in activities typical for their gender) prefer the other gender for romantic interests, whereas nonconforming children prefer the same gender. Bem's "exotic-becomes-erotic" theory suggests that sexual feelings evolve from experiencing heightened arousal in situations in which one gender is viewed as more exotic, or different from oneself (Bem, 1996). Bem asserts that gay and lesbian children had playmates of the other sex while growing up, and this led them to see the same sex as more "exotic" and appealing. However, his research has been contradictory and hasn't been supported by other research (Peplau et al., 1998). Many gay and lesbian children report playmates of both the same sex and the other sex while growing up.

Homosexuality in Other Times and Places

Across time periods and continents.

Check Your Learning Quiz 9.4

Go to **login.cengagebrain.com** and take the online quiz.

The Presumption of Heterosexuality

Imagine what it must be like to be an adolescent and either to believe or know that you are gay, lesbian, or bisexual (a number of you reading this book do not have to imagine it). All your life, from the time you were a toddler, you were presented with a single model of sexual life: You were expected to be attracted to the other sex, to go on dates, and eventually to marry. No other scenario was seriously considered; if you are heterosexual, you probably have never even reflected on how powerfully this "presumption of heterosexuality" (Herdt, 1989) was transmitted by your parents, your friends, television and movies, newspapers and magazines, even the government. Advertisements on television and in magazines always show heterosexual couples; your friends probably played house, doctor, or spin the bottle, assuming everyone was attracted to the other sex; your grade school, parties, and social activities were organized around this presumption of heterosexuality. There were open questions about many things in your life—what career you would pursue, where you might live, what college you would attend. However, one thing was considered certain: You were going to marry (or at least date) someone of the other sex.

Growing up and Feeling Different

Imagine that while all your friends were talking about the other sex, dating, and sex, you were experiencing a completely different set of emotions. Why, you wondered, can't I join in on these conversations? Why can't I feel the attractions that all my friends feel? Then, at some point in your early teens, you began to realize why you felt differently from your friends. All of a sudden you understood that all the models you had taken for granted your whole life did not apply to you. You began to look for other models that described your life and your feelings—and they simply were not there. In fact, in hundreds of subtle and not-so-subtle ways, society taught you that you were different—and possibly perverted, sinful, illegal, or disgusting. Now what are you supposed to do? Whom do you turn to? How can you possibly tell anyone your deep, painful secret?

The experiences of many GLBs, at least until recently, followed this scenario, although the timing and intensity varied with individual cases. For example, many gay men grew up with close male friends, enjoyed sports, and differed only in their secret attraction to other boys, whereas others remember feeling and acting differently from their friends as early as 4 or 5 years old (H. P. Martin, 1991).

biphobia Strongly negative attitudes toward bisexuals and bisexuality.

Bisexuality: A Separate Identity

Although we have been discussing bisexuality throughout this chapter, bisexuality has really emerged more recently as a separate identity from lesbian, gay, or heterosexual identities, and we are still learning more each year. Social and political bisexual groups began forming in the 1970s, but it wasn't until the late 1980s that an organized bisexual movement achieved visibility in the United States (Herek, 2002).

Girl-girl sexual contact between heterosexual women on college campuses typically occurs in front of friends in public places where the men and women have been drinking alcohol.

We do know that people who identify as bisexual often first identified as heterosexuals, and their self-labeling generally occurs later in life than either gay or lesbian self-labeling (Weinberg et al., 1994). It is interesting to note that for many years few people noticed the absence of research on bisexuality. This absence stemmed from the fact that researchers believed that sexuality was composed of only two opposing forms of sexuality: heterosexuality and homosexuality (Herek, 2002; Rust, 2000).

Homosexuals have tended to see bisexuals either as on their way to becoming homosexual or as people who want to be able to "play both sides of the fence" by being homosexual in the gay community and heterosexual in straight society. Heterosexuals have tended to lump bisexuals in with homosexuals. Sexuality scholars have suggested that bisexuality is a myth, or an attempt to deny one's homosexuality; identity confusion; or an attempt to be "chic" or "trendy" (Rust, 2000). Some studies claim that bisexuals are men and women who are ambivalent about their homosexual behavior (Carey, 2005a; Rieger et al., 2005). Bisexuals themselves have begun to speak of **biphobia**, which they suggest exists in both the straight and gay and lesbian communities (Eliason, 1997; Galupo, 2006; Mulick & Wright, 2002; L. Wright et al., 2006). Like gays and lesbians, bisexuals experience hostility, discrimination, and violence in response to their sexual orientation (Herek, 2002). Some researchers suggest that bisexuals experience "double discrimination" because they may experience discrimination from both the heterosexual and homosexual communities (Mulick & Wright, 2002). Compared with gays and lesbians, bisexuals have been found to have decreased social well-being, more barriers to health care, and increased sadness and suicidal thoughts (Conron et al., 2010; Kertzner et al., 2009).

Party Gay?

Sexual behavior between women is more acceptable than sexual behavior between men.

Trying Not to Be Gay

Hear a gay man describe his struggle to come to terms with his attraction to men.

Discovering Bisexuality

Hear a woman describe how she gradually realized that she was bisexual.

On Your Mind

Are bisexuals really attracted to both men and women?

Check Your Learning Quiz 9.5

Go to **login.cengagebrain.com** and take the online quiz.

▶ **LO13** Describe the typical conflicts that gay, lesbian, and bisexual individuals experience in their decision to come out to others.

▶ **LO14** Describe the range of reactions commonly exhibited by families when children come out to them.

One of the most important tasks of adolescence is to develop and integrate a positive adult identity. This task is an even greater challenge for gay and lesbian youth because they learn from a very young age the stigma of being different from the heterosexual norm (C. Ryan & Futterman, 2001). Special challenges confront the person who believes he or she is gay, lesbian, or bisexual, including the need to establish a personal self-identity and communicate it to others, known as **coming out**. A number of models have been offered to explain how this process proceeds (see, for example, Cass, 1979, 1984; E. Coleman, 1982; H. P. Martin, 1991; M. Schneider, 1989; Troiden, 1989).

Acknowledging One's Own Sexual Identity

Coming out refers, first, to acknowledging one's sexual identity to oneself, and many GLB individuals have their own negative feelings about homosexuality to overcome. The often difficult and anxiety-ridden process of disclosing the truth to family, friends, and eventually the public at large comes later. Disclosure of identity plays an important role in identity development and psychological adjustment for GLB men and women.

Although first awareness of sexual orientation typically occurs between the ages of 8 and 9, men and women vary in when they share this information with others. Some may come out early in their lives, whereas others remain closeted into adulthood (Savin-Williams & Diamond, 2000; H. E. Taylor, 2000). Coming out does not happen overnight; being homosexual for some may mean a lifetime of disclosing different amounts of information to family, friends, and strangers in different contexts (Hofman, 2005). Deciding whether and how to tell friends and family are difficult decisions. To minimize the risk for rejection, gay and lesbian adolescents choose whom they come out to very carefully (Vincke & van Heeringen, 2002).

Today's teens are coming out earlier than any other time in history. Although in the 1970s many people waited until adulthood to come out, in the 1980s and 1990s they began coming out in their teens (Ryan et al., 2009). By 2007, teens began coming out as early as middle school (Denizet-Lewis, 2009; Elias, 2007). A more accepting social climate and increased acceptance of homosexuality are responsible for these changes. In addition, increases in gay support groups in middle and high schools, and a more positive portrayal of gay role models in the popular media have also contributed to early ages in coming out (Elias, 2007). Years ago, many GLB men and women worked hard to hide their sexual orientation for fear of discrimination, harassment, and violence (Hudson, 2010). However, the changing social cli-

coming out The process of establishing a personal self-identity and communicating it to others.

mate has also lessened the pressure to "fit in." Today, many more GLB men and women live openly as gay, lesbian, or bisexual.

Family Reactions to Coming Out

Some parents of GLB youths initially react with disappointment, shame, and shock when they learn about a son or daughter's sexual orientation (D'Augelli, 2005; LaSala, 2000). They may feel responsible and believe they did something to "cause" their child's sexual orientation. In one study, more than 50% of gay and lesbian teens experienced a negative reaction from their parents when they came out (Martin et al., 2010; Ray, 2007). The family must go through its own "coming out," as parents and siblings slowly try to accept the idea and then tell their own friends. The importance of positive resolution in the family has prompted the formation of a national organization, the Federation of Parents, Families, & Friends of Lesbians and Gays (PFLAG), which helps parents learn to accept their children's sexual orientation and gain support from other families experiencing similar events.

Gay and lesbian youths who have a positive coming-out experience have higher self-confidence, lower rates of depression, and better psychological adjustment than those who have negative coming-out experiences (Needham & Austin, 2010; Ryan & Futterman, 2001). Compared with GLB teens with no or low levels of family rejection, GLB teens who reported high levels of family rejection were:

- 8.4 times more likely to attempt suicide
- 6 times more likely to report high levels of depression
- 3.4 times more likely to use illegal drugs
- 3.4 times more likely to report engaging in unprotected sexual behavior (Ryan et al., 2009)

At least 50% of gay teens experienced negative reactions from their parents when they came out, and 26% were kicked out of their homes (Brown & Trevethan, 2010; Remafedi, 1987). In fact, the number one cause for homelessness for GLB teens is family conflict (Ray, 2006). It is estimated that between 20% and 40% of homeless youths are gay, lesbian, or bisexual (Lockwood, 2008; Ray, 2006). Homeless GLB youths are also at greater risk than homeless heterosexual youths to abuse drugs and alcohol, and experience physical and sexual abuse (Chakraborty et al., 2011; Cochran et al., 2002; Gaetz, 2004; Needham & Austin, 2010; Ray, 2006). Today, homeless shelters that cater specifically to GLB youths have been set up across the United States.

A Model of Coming Out

There may be a need to redefine one's own concept of gay and lesbian behavior...

Coming out as a Lesbian

Listen to one woman describe coming out as a lesbian at age 38 and how it affected her family and children.

Check Your Learning Quiz 9.6

Go to **login.cengagebrain.com** and take the online quiz.

▶ **LO15** Discuss the impact of stigmatization on the mental and physical health of gay, lesbian, and bisexual individuals.

▶ **LO16** Discuss the economic and psychological effects of discrimination on gay, lesbian, and bisexual individuals.

Many gay and male bisexual youths report a history of feeling unattached and alienated—most probably because heterosexual dating was often a focal point in peer group bonds (Bauermeister et al., 2010; Herdt, 1989). The same is true of young lesbians and female bisexuals, although the pressure and alienation may be felt slightly later in life because same-sex affection and touching is more accepted for girls and because lesbians tend to determine their sexual orientation later than gay men. GLB youths have been found to experience high levels of stigmatization and discrimination (Bauermeister et al., 2010; Chakraborty et al., 2011; Cox et al., 2010).

Effects of Stigmatization

For many years, psychiatrists and other therapists argued that homosexual and bisexual groups had greater psychopathology than heterosexuals. Research has found they are more likely than heterosexuals to experience stress and tension, and are more at risk for the development of chronic diseases and mental health issues (Conron et al., 2010). GLB youths have higher levels of depression and are more likely than heterosexual youths to think about and commit suicide (Bauermeister et al., 2010; Chakraborty et al., 2011; Cox et al., 2010; D'Augelli et al., 2005; Doty et al., 2010; Espelage et al., 2008; Hegna & Rossow, 2007; Newcomb & Mustanski, 2010). They also have higher rates of substance abuse and alcohol-related problems (Conron et al., 2010; Rivers & Noret, 2008; D. F. Roberts et al., 2005), together with more widespread use of marijuana and cocaine (Rosario et al., 2004; Ryan & Futterman, 2001), and higher rates of truancy, homelessness, and sexual abuse (D'Augelli et al, 2006; H. E. Taylor, 2000) compared with heterosexual youths and adults. Overall, bisexuals are more likely than heterosexuals, gays, and lesbians to experience sadness, have thoughts of suicide, engage in binge drinking, and have experienced intimate partner violence (Conron et al., 2010; S. T. Russell et al., 2002).

In fact, the problems of GLB life may not be because of psychopathology, but rather the enormous pressures of living in a society that discriminates against them (Kertzner et al., 2009; Lock & Steiner, 1999; Roberts et al., 2010). Vulnerable and stigmatized groups in general have higher rates of these types of behaviors, and these problems often result from coping with stigma-related stress. In addition, homosexuals and bisexuals are particularly vulnerable to harassment and other forms of risk, further compounding their stress (Mishna et al., 2008).

Effects of Discrimination

Workplace discrimination also adds stress to the lives of GLB individuals. Gay men have been found to earn 23% less than married heterosexual men and 9% less than single heterosexual men who are living with a woman (Elmslie & Tebaldi, 2007). However, lesbians were not discriminated against when compared with heterosexual women. Lesbian workers earn more than their heterosexual female peers, perhaps because employers may believe lesbian women are more career oriented and less likely to leave the workforce to raise children (Elmslie & Tebaldi, 2007; Peplau & Fingerhut, 2004).

As of 2011, 21 states and the District of Columbia have laws that prohibit workplace discrimination based on sexual orientation. Although no federal law protects GLB individuals from employment discrimination, the Employment Non-Discrimination Act, which would provide protections to all GLB employees throughout the United States, has been included in every session of the U.S. Congress since 1994 (Human Rights Campaign, 2011). As of late-2011, it had not been passed. Around the world, many countries, such as France, Canada, and the Netherlands, offer such protections to their employees.

© Yuri Arcurs/Shutterstock

Coming out in the Workplace

Interviews with men and women who describe their experiences being "out" in the workplace.

Check Your Learning Quiz 9.7

Go to **login.cengagebrain.com** and take the online quiz.

▸ **LO17** List three or four ways in which gay, lesbian, and bisexual individuals typically find same-sex partners.

▸ **LO18** Identify some of the options that gay and lesbian couples have for becoming parents, and compare the advantages and disadvantages of these options.

Looking for Partners

Meeting other same-sex partners in the heterosexual world can be difficult, so the gay community has developed its own social institutions to help people meet one another and socialize. Today, many schools and universities have clubs, support groups, and meeting areas for GLB students. Whereas in the mid-1990s there were only a handful of gay–straight alliance clubs in U.S. high schools, as of 2008, there were more than 4,000 such clubs, as well as a handful of clubs in middle schools (Eckholm, 2011).

Today, adults can meet others at gay bars or clubs that cater primarily to GLB couples, mainstream bars that offer gay or lesbian nights, through GLB support or discussion groups, churches, and GLB organizations. Gay magazines such as *The Advocate* carry personal ads and ads for dating services, travel clubs, resorts, bed and breakfasts, theaters, businesses, pay phone lines, sexual products, and other services to help gays and lesbians find partners. And of course, gay individuals are introduced through gay and straight friends.

Gay and Lesbian Parenting

Gay men and lesbian women can become parents in a variety of ways, including artificial insemination, adoption, or surrogacy (these options are discussed in more detail in Chapter 10). Over the past few years, gay and lesbian parenting has become more mainstream as popular gay and lesbian celebrities, such as Ricky Martin, Rosie O'Donnell, Elton John, and Melissa Etheridge, have all become parents. Many gay and lesbian couples become parents, and they cite most of the same reasons for wanting to be parents that straight parents do (D'Augelli et al., 2006). Although fewer lesbian women have children than heterosexual women (18% vs. 50%; Elmslie & Tebaldi, 2007), it is estimated that more than one in three lesbians has given birth and one in six gay men has fathered or adopted a child (Gates et al., 2007).

Sexuality in gay and lesbian couples can be an expression of deep love, affection, or lust.

© Uwe Krejci/zefa/Corbis

In 2010, pop singer Ricky Martin came out of the closet, announcing that he was a "fortunate homosexual man." He is the proud father of two sons who were born via a surrogate mother.

Gay and lesbian couples who wish to be parents may encounter many problems that heterosexual couples do not face. Parenting is seldom an individual or couple decision for them and often involves several negotiations with others (Berkowitz & Marsiglio, 2007). In addition, because same-sex marriages are not yet legally recognized nationally in the United States, gay couples may have trouble gaining joint custody of a child, and employers may not grant nonbiological parents parental leave or benefits for the child. For the most part, our society assumes a heterosexist view of parenting. However, it has slowly been changing over the last couple of years. The majority of Americans today say that their definition of a family includes same-sex couples with children (Roberts, 2010).

Many gay and lesbian couples adopt children. However, adoption is regulated by state law, and each state has specific rules about who can adopt. Although many states allow same-sex couples to adopt, others do not specifically mention gay or lesbian adoption, and decisions about legality are done on a case-by-case basis or by court rulings. For many years, Florida had laws against same-sex couple adoption, even though a single gay man or lesbian woman in Florida could legally adopt (or foster a child). However, laws against same-sex adoption were struck down in Florida in 2010.

Throughout the United States, organizations such as PFLAG and Lambda (a national organization committed to the civil rights of GLB individuals) support gay and lesbian parents, and are helping to make it easier for them to adopt.

No significant differences have been found in the psychological adjustment and social relationships between the children of same-sex and heterosexual couples (Bos & Gartrell, 2010; Farr et al., 2010; Greenfeld, 2005; Hicks, 2005). All of the scientific evidence suggests that children who grow up with one or two gay and/or lesbian parents do as well emotionally, cognitively, socially, and sexually as children from heterosexual parents (American Psychological Association, 2005; Bos & Gartrell, 2010;

Peter and Stephan: A Dutch Couple

Dutch gay couple discusses their relationship and struggles along the way.

▶ **LO19** Identify two or three issues faced by aging gay, lesbian, and bisexual seniors.

Greenfeld, 2005; Perrin, 2002). Even so, some gay and lesbian couples find minimal support to parent children and experience a social stigmatization of children that they do have (Pawelski et al., 2006).

Gay and Lesbian Seniors

Coming out before the senior years often helps a gay or lesbian senior to feel more comfortable with his or her life and sexuality. Gay and lesbian seniors who have not come out or have not come to terms with their sexual orientation may feel depressed or alone as they continue to age. In addition, they may experience depression and isolation from the years of internalized homophobia (Altman, 2000; Gross, 2007). For some, hiding their sexual orientation when they are ready for a nursing home is their only choice. One gay man who had been in a relationship with his partner for more than 20 years said, "When I'm at the gate of the nursing home, the closet door is going to slam shut behind me" (Gross, 2007).

Many issues confront aging gay and lesbian seniors. Studies have found that nursing home staff often report intolerant or condemning attitudes toward GLB residents (Cahill et al., 2000; Gross, 2007; Röndahl et al., 2004). Because of this, many retirement homes for aging gays, lesbians, bisexual, and transgender (GLBT) individuals have been established. In 2010, the National Resource Center on GLBT Aging was launched by Services and Advocacy for GLBT Elders (SAGE) with the help of a federal grant from the U.S. Department of Health and Human Services. This organization will help connect aging providers and GLB organizations around the country to provide better services to aging GLB members.

Gay, Lesbian, and Bisexual Organizations

Because many organizations misunderstand the needs of homosexuals and bisexuals, gay and lesbian social services, medical, political, entertainment, and even religious organizations have formed. For example, the National Gay and Lesbian Task Force (NGLTF) and its associated Policy Institute advocate for gay civil rights, lobby Congress for such things as a Federal Gay and Lesbian Civil Rights Act, health care reform, AIDS policy reform, and hate-crime laws. In 1987, they helped establish the Hate Crimes Statistics Act, which identifies and records hate crimes. Also well known are the Lambda Legal Defense and Education Fund, which pursues litigation issues for the gay and lesbian community, and the Human Rights Campaign Fund, which lobbies Capitol Hill on gay and lesbian rights, AIDS, and privacy issues.

Since the arrival of the AIDS epidemic, many organizations have formed to help GLB men and women obtain medical, social, and legal services. Local GLB organizations—including counseling centers, hotlines, legal aid, and AIDS information—have been established in almost every reasonably sized city in the United States.

The Harvey Milk School in New York City is the first and largest accredited public school in the world devoted to the educational needs of lesbian, gay, bisexual, transgendered, and questioning youth. The school was named after a gay elected official from San Francisco who was murdered in 1978. Fourteen- to eighteen-year-old students from across the country come to the Harvey Milk School to study in an environment in which their sexual orientation is accepted and where they will not be ridiculed, ostracized, or assaulted, as many were in the schools they came from. Universities and colleges have also begun to offer gay and lesbian students separate housing, and, as we discussed earlier, many high schools provide gay–straight alliances that help encourage tolerance and provide a place for students to meet.

Gay and lesbian media, including countless magazines and newspapers across the country, have also developed over the past 30 years. The largest and best-known magazine, *The Advocate,* is a national publication that covers news of interest, entertainment reviews, commentaries, gay- and lesbian-oriented products and services, and hundreds of personal ads. Many other specialty magazines are available for GLB men and women, including parenting magazines (such as *Gay Parent* and *Proud Parenting*), travel magazines (such as *Out and About*), and religious magazines (such as *Whosoever*). Most major cities now have their own gay newspaper, some of which get national exposure.

Check Your Learning Quiz 9.8

Go to **login.cengagebrain.com** and take the online quiz.

When homosexuality as an illness was removed from the *Diagnostic and Statistical Manual of Mental Disorders* in 1973, negative attitudes toward homosexuality persisted. It was at this time that researchers began to study these negative attitudes and behaviors.

What Is Homophobia?

Many terms have been proposed to describe the negative, often violent, reactions of many people toward homosexuality—antihomosexualism, homoerotophobia, homosexism, homonegativism, and **homophobia**. The popularity of the term *homophobia* is unfortunate, for phobia is a medical term describing an extreme, anxiety-provoking, uncontrollable fear accompanied by obsessive avoidance. We use this term here to refer to strongly negative attitudes toward homosexuals and homosexuality.

Are people really homophobic? Some might accept homosexuality intellectually and yet still dislike being in the presence of homosexuals, whereas others might object to homosexuality as a practice and yet have personal relationships with individual homosexuals whom they accept (Forstein, 1988). When compared with people who hold positive views of GLBs, people with negative views are less likely to have had contact with homosexuals and bisexuals, and they are more likely to be older and less well educated; be religious and subscribe to a conservative religious ideology; have more traditional attitudes toward sex roles and less support for equality of the sexes; be less permissive sexually; and be authoritarian (Herek, 1984). Overall, heterosexual men, compared with heterosexual women, have been found to have significantly more negative attitudes toward gay men (Davies, 2004; Verweij et al., 2008).

Why Are People Homophobic?

What motivates people to be homophobic? A number of theories have been suggested. Because rigid, authoritarian personalities are more likely to be homophobic, it may be a function of personality type; for such people, anything that deviates from their view of "correct" behavior elicits disdain (K. T. Smith, 1971). Another common suggestion is that heterosexual people fear their own suppressed homosexual desires or are insecure in their own masculinity or femininity (H. E. Adams et al., 1996). Others believe that this explanation is too simplistic (Rosser, 1999). Perhaps people are simply ignorant about homosexuality and would change their

homophobia Irrational fear of homosexuals and homosexuality.

heterosexism The "presumption of heterosexuality" that has sociological implications.

Getty Images

Lesbians, gay men, and bisexual people who also belong to other minority groups must deal with the prejudices of society toward both groups, as well as each group's prejudices toward the other.

attitudes with education. Most likely, all of these are true to some degree in different people.

Heterosexism

An even bigger problem for most gay men and lesbians is **heterosexism**. Heterosexism describes the "presumption of heterosexuality" discussed earlier and the social power used to promote it (Neisen, 1990). Because heterosexual relationships are seen as "normal," a heterosexist person feels justified in suppressing or ignoring those who do not follow that model.

For example, even those with no ill feelings toward homosexuality are often unaware that businesses will not provide health care and other benefits to the partners of homosexuals. In other words, heterosexism can be passive rather than active, involving a lack of awareness rather than active discrimination. Furthermore, GLB individuals who also belong to other minority groups must deal with the prejudices of society toward both groups, as well as each group's prejudices toward the other.

The gay rights movement has been successful at changing some of these assumptions, especially in larger cities, but today heterosexism still dictates a large part of the way the average American considers his or her world. Heterosexism can lead to a lack of awareness of issues that can harm GLB individuals today.

How Can We Combat Homophobia and Heterosexism?

Heterosexism is widespread and subtle and therefore difficult to combat. Adrienne Rich (1983), a prominent scholar of lesbian studies, uses the term *heterocentrism* to describe the neglect of homosexual existence, even among feminists. Perhaps we can learn from the history of a similar term: ethnocentrism. Ethnocentrism refers to the belief that all standards of correct behavior are determined by one's own cultural background, leading to racism, ethnic bigotry, and even sexism and heterosexism. Although ethnocentrism is still rampant in American society, it is slowly being eroded by the passage of new laws, the media's spotlight on abuses, and improved education. Perhaps a similar strategy can be used to combat heterosexism.

Key Terms Exercise

Match the descriptions to the definitions.

Check Your Learning Quiz 9.9

Go to **login.cengagebrain.com** and take the online quiz.

▶ **LO22** List and discuss two important strategies for counteracting homophobia and heterosexism in a society.

▶ **LO23** Define *hate crimes,* and list three key federal laws aimed at combating hate crimes.

What Are Hate Crimes?

Hate crimes are those crimes motivated by hatred of someone's religion, sex, race, sexual orientation, disability, gender identity, or ethnic group. They are known as "message crimes" because they send a message to the victim's affiliated group (American Psychiatric Association, 1998). Typically, hate crimes involve strong feelings of anger (Parrott & Peterson, 2008).

The number of victims of hate crimes based on sexual orientation continues to increase. In 2010, there were 8,208 hate crimes reported to the Federal Bureau of Investigation, and more than 19% of these were motivated by the victims' sexual orientation (U.S. Department of Justice, 2011). These crimes involved an anti-male homosexual, anti-homosexual, anti-female homosexual, anti-heterosexual, and anti-bisexual biases (see the nearby figure for more information). The American Psychological Association (APA) reports that hate crimes against homosexuals are the most socially acceptable form of hate crimes.

Approximately 80% of GLB youths report verbal victimization, whereas 11% report physical and 9% report sexual victimization (D'Augelli et al., 2006). Victimization begins, on average, at age 13, although some verbal attacks began as early as age 6, physical attacks as early as age 8, and sexual attacks as early as age 9 (D'Augelli et al., 2006). Overall, rates of victimization are higher for boys.

Legislating against Hate Crimes

Hate crimes legislation targets violence that is committed in response to a victim's identity, including sexual orientation. The Hate Crimes Statistics Act was enacted by Congress in 1990. This law requires the compilation of data on hate crimes so that there is a comprehensive picture of these crimes. In 1997, the Hate Crimes Right to Know Act was passed, which requires college campuses to report all hate crimes. In 2009, the Matthew Shepard and James Byrd, Jr. Hate Crimes Prevention Act was signed into law, which provided the Justice Department with jurisdiction over hate crimes and enabled the department to help in the investigation of such crimes (Human Rights Campaign, 2009).

hate crime A criminal offense, usually involving violence, intimidation, or vandalism, in which the victim is targeted because of his or her affiliation with a particular group.

Promoting Positive Change through the Media

The representation of the GLB community is increasing in the media today (Draganowski, 2004; Freymiller, 2005). Shows such as *The L Word, Ellen, Gossip Girl,* and *Brothers and Sisters* have helped pave the way for GLBs on television, resulting in vastly different programming from just a few years ago. Before this, homosexuality was portrayed negatively, with images of GLBs as psychopaths or murderers.

Another important development in the media is the explosion of music, fiction, nonfiction, plays, and movies that portray gay and lesbian life in America more realistically. Whereas once these types of media were shocking and hidden, now they appear on radio stations and in mainstream bookstores and movie theaters.

George Pimentel/WireImage/Getty Images

In 2011, Lady Gaga, a prominent and long-time supporter of GLB rights, pulled the plug on a lucrative marketing deal with Target because of the company's inadequate support of GLB rights.

Promoting Positive Change through Education

Another important step to stopping heterosexism is education. Homosexuality remains a taboo subject in many schools, and most proposals to teach sexuality in general—nevermind homosexuality in particular—encounter strong opposition by certain parent groups. When sexuality education is taught in schools, there is often very little information included about sexual orientation. Educating today's students about homophobia and heterosexism can help reduce negative attitudes, gay bashing, and hate crimes.

Hate Crimes Against Gays, Lesbians, and Bisexuals

Learn about the degree of sexual prejudice in our society, the variables associated with sexual prejudices, and some suggested mechanisms for reducing this prejudice.

Check Your Learning Quiz 9.10

Go to **login.cengagebrain.com** and take the online quiz.

▶ **LO24** Compare the range of conservative and liberal attitudes toward homosexuality in various religions.

▶ **LO25** Cite two key legal events that occurred in the last 10 years that have had a positive impact on gay, lesbian, and bisexual rights in the United States.

Religion has generally been considered a bastion of antihomosexual teachings and beliefs, and these beliefs have often helped shape laws that prohibit homosexual behaviors. This section discusses both of these powerful influences.

Homosexuality and Religion

Since the early 1980s, a great deal of negativity has surrounded homosexuality in religion, and changes in social attitudes toward homosexuality have provoked conflict over homosexual policies in many religious denominations. Traditionally, both Judaism and Christianity have strongly opposed homosexual behavior.

Some Christian religions are more tolerant, such as the United Church of Christ. This church and its members have welcomed GLB members, worked for equal rights, and ordained GLB clergy. They generally view homosexuality as neither a sin nor a choice, and they believe that it is unchangeable. One of the most accepting churches, the Metropolitan Community Churches, promotes itself as the world's largest organization with a primary, affirming ministry to GLBT persons (Metropolitan Community Churches, 2005). Other Christian religions, such as Presbyterians, Methodists, Lutherans, and Episcopalians, have more conflict over the issue of sexual orientation, resulting in both liberal and conservative views.

In recent years, a number of Christian denominations have voted to allow noncelibate gays to serve as clergy if they are in a committed relationship (Condon, 2010). This includes the Evangelical Lutheran Church in America, the U.S. Episcopal Church, and the United Church of Christ.

In many churches and synagogues, most of the more conservative views, including the idea that homosexuality can be changed through prayer and counseling, come from older members and those living in the southern part of the United States. The conservative Christian faiths, such as Catholics, Southern Baptists, and the Assemblies of God, view homosexuality as a sin and work to restrict GLB rights.

Controversy also exists over sexual orientation in Jewish synagogues throughout the United States. Although Orthodox Jews believe that

© AP/World Wide Photos

homosexuality is an abomination forbidden by the Torah, reform congregations are more likely to welcome all sexual orientations. A Reform movement in 1990 allowed the ordaining of gay rabbis (Albert et al., 2001). In 2010, a Statement of Principles was signed and released by a group of Orthodox rabbis that supports the acceptance of homosexual members (Nahshoni, 2010).

Homosexuality and the Law

Throughout history, laws have existed in the Western world that prohibited same-sex sexual behavior, even on pain of death. In the United States, sodomy has been illegal since colonial days, and it was punishable by death until the late 18th century (Boswell, 1980). Homosexual acts were illegal in all 50 states until 1961.

The Supreme Court overturned the Texas antisodomy law, which made consensual sex between same-sex couples illegal, in 2003. Before 2003, under Texas homosexual conduct law, for example, individuals who engaged in "deviate sexual intercourse" with a person of the same sex (even if the partner was consenting) could be charged with a misdemeanor punishable by up to $500 in fines (Lambda, 2001).

Homosexuals are often denied equal housing rights through exclusionary zoning, rent control, and rent stabilization laws. Even in long-term, committed, same-sex couples, partners are routinely denied the worker's compensation and health care benefits normally extended to a spouse or dependents. In addition, without legal marriage, gay and lesbian couples are denied tax breaks, Social Security benefits, and rights of inheritance, all of which are available to married heterosexual couples.

Over the last few years, the legal landscape for gay rights has been changing in the United States. In 2010, President Obama signed a bill ending the military's "don't ask, don't tell" policy, which was one of the first moves toward equality for gays and lesbians. In 2011, he reversed his stance on the Defense of Marriage Act (DOMA), concluding that his administration could no longer defend the federal law that defines marriage as between a man and a woman. DOMA was enacted in 1996 and was supported by the Clinton, Bush, and most of Obama's administration. Dismantling DOMA was a major victory for gay rights advocates and one of the first steps toward a federal legal recognition of same-sex marriage in the United States. As a variety of legal cases that challenge the federal government's denial of same-sex marriage and marriage-related benefits make their way to the Supreme Court, it is likely that support for these issues will continue to grow. We are hopeful that this momentum for support of gay rights will continue in the future.

Homosexuality in Religion and Law

Gay men discuss the Mormon viewpoint on homosexuality and grapple with the implications for their lives.

Check Your Learning Quiz 9.11

Go to **login.cengagebrain.com** and take the online quiz.

Think Critically

Challenge Your Thinking

Consider these questions:

1. Many scholars believe that we may have been born with the ability to be attracted to everyone but as we are socialized, we learn what partners are socially acceptable for us. Do you think it is possible that we could have all been born with this potential? Why or why not?

2. Some men and women are introduced to bisexuality through intimate involvement with a close friend of the same sex, even if they have never had a same-sex attraction before. If they engaged in this behavior only once, in your opinion, does this behavior make them bisexual? Why or why not?

3. Provide two reasons why research on bisexuality lags so far behind the research on other sexual orientations. What do you think would improve this situation and why?

4. The research has found that bisexuals often do not self-identify as bisexuals. Give two reasons why you think this might be so.

Bisexuality: Playing Both Sides of the Fence?

Many bisexuals see themselves as having the best of both worlds. As one bisexual put it, "The more I talk and think about it, and listen to people, I realize that there are no fences, no walls, no heterosexuality or homosexuality. There are just people and the electricity between them" (quoted in Spolan, 1991). In our society, no matter what your sexual orientation, one gender or another is always taboo—your sexual intimacy is always restricted (F. Klein, 1978). From that perspective, bisexuality is simply lack of prejudice and full acceptance of both sexes.

More people in American society exhibit bisexual behavior than exclusively homosexual behavior (F. Klein, 1990). In *sequential bisexuality,* the person has sex exclusively with one gender, followed by sex exclusively with the other; *contemporaneous bisexuality* refers to having male and female sexual partners during the same period (J. P.

Paul, 1984). Numbers are hard to come by because bisexuality itself is so difficult to define. How many encounters with both sexes are needed for a person to be considered bisexual? One? Fifty? And what of fantasies? It is difficult to determine what percentage of people is bisexual because many who engage in bisexual behavior do not self-identify as bisexual (Weinberg et al., 1994).

Some people experience bisexuality through intimate involvement with a close friend of the same sex, even if they have not had same-sex attractions before. Others come to it through group sex or swinging, in which in the heat of passion, a body is a body and distinctions between men and women easily blur. The new bisexual movement may succeed in breaking through the artificial split of the sexual world into homosexuals and heterosexuals. Perhaps we fear the fluid model of sexuality offered by bisexuals because we fear our own cross-preference encounter fantasies and do not want to admit that most of us, even if hidden deep in our fantasies, are to some degree attracted to both sexes.

Think Critically

This article and its questions are available in interactive format online.

GO to your Psychology CourseMate at **login.cengagebrain.com** and take the Chapter Post-Test to see which Learning Objectives you've mastered and which need more review. Use the chapter review guide below and the online activities—including flashcards to review key terms—to measure your learning.

Measure ^**Your Learning**

Module		Learning Objectives	
9.1	**What Determines Sexual Orientation?** 316	**LO1**	Compare the Kinsey and Klein sexual orientation continuums.
		LO2	Discuss the percentage ranges that most sexuality scholars agree represent the prevalence of gays, lesbians, and bisexual individuals in the U.S. population and the controversy surrounding these statistics.
9.2	**Biological Theories of Sexual Orientation** 320	**LO3**	Summarize the findings of one or two studies that produced evidence for a substantial genetic component of sexual orientation.
		LO4	Summarize the findings of one or two studies pointing to the possible influence of birth order on sexual orientation.
		LO5	Summarize the findings of one or two studies that compared brain structure and function with other physical aspects of heterosexuals and homosexuals.
9.3	**Psychoanalytic, Developmental, and Behaviorist Theories** 324	**LO6**	Explain how psychoanalytic theory became the basis for the view of homosexuality as a mental illness.
		LO7	Summarize Storms's developmental theory of homosexuality, and indicate how it is contradicted by a study conducted in Papua New Guinea.
		LO8	Summarize the behaviorist theories of homosexuality.
9.4	**Sociological and Interactional Theories** 326	**LO9**	Compare the sociological and interactional theories of sexual orientation.
9.5	**Growing up Gay, Lesbian, or Bisexual** 328	**LO10**	Identify three ways in which children and adolescents are impacted by the presumption of heterosexuality.
		LO11	Identify two ways in which adolescents typically become aware of their differences in sexual orientation.
		LO12	Explain the typical process of self-identity in bisexuals.

Online Activities

Key Terms	Video	Animation	Readings	Assessment
sexual orientation, straight, heterosexual, homosexual, bisexual		The Kinsey Continuum		Check Your Learning Quiz 9.1
maternal immune hypothesis	Why are guys turned on by two girls having sex but turned off by two guys having sex? Do any animals engage in homosexual behavior or are they all straight?			Check Your Learning Quiz 9.2
	If I played sex games with a same-sex friend when I was 15, does that make me gay? Is there any therapy that can change a person's sexual orientation?			Check Your Learning Quiz 9.3
			Homosexuality in Other Times and Places	Check Your Learning Quiz 9.4
biphobia	Trying Not to Be Gay Discovering Bisexuality Are bisexuals really attracted to both men and women?		Party Gay?	Check Your Learning Quiz 9.5

Measure ∧ Your Learning

Key Terms	Video	Animation	Readings	Assessment
coming out	Coming out as a Lesbian		A Model of Coming Out	Check Your Learning Quiz 9.6
	Coming out in the Workplace			Check Your Learning Quiz 9.7
	Peter and Stephan: A Dutch Couple			Check Your Learning Quiz 9.8
homophobia, heterosexism		Key Terms Exercise		Check Your Learning Quiz 9.9
hate crime	Hate Crimes Against Gays, Lesbians, and Bisexuals			Check Your Learning Quiz 9.10
	Homosexuality in Religion and Law			Check Your Learning Quiz 9.11
				Bisexuality: Playing Both Sides of the Fence

Pregnancy and Birth

10

Prepare to Learn

1 **GO** to your **Psychology CourseMate** at **login.cengagebrain.com** and take the **Chapter Pre-Test** to introduce yourself to this chapter's topics and see what you may already know.

2 **READ** the **Learning Objectives** (LOs, in the left sidebars) and begin the chapter.

3 **COMPLETE** the **Online Activities** (in the right sidebars) *as you read each module.* Activities include **videos, animations, readings, and quizzes.**

4 **CHECK Your Learning** by going online to take the quiz at the end of each module and review material as necessary.

5 **MEASURE Your Learning** after reading the chapter by taking the online **Chapter Post-Test.** Use the chapter review guide at the end of the chapter as needed.

WATCH for these **Online Activities** icons as you read:

Video

Animation

Reading

Assessment

Think Critically

These Online Activities are essential to mastering this chapter. Go to login.cengagebrain.com.

 Videos Explore diverse perspectives on sex as well as common questions:

- Love Makes a Family
- Can guys ever get pregnant?
- I Didn't Know I Was Pregnant!
- Designer Babies
- Can I be pregnant if I've missed my period for 2 months?
- IVF and Multiple Births
- Do physicians ever mix up ova or embryos during embryo transplants?
- How much weight do women gain during pregnancy?
- Weight and Pregnancy
- What determines how long a woman is in labor?

- Is it safe to use drugs to lessen the pain of labor?
- Unintended Pregnancy: A Man's Perspective

 Animations Interact with and visualize important processes, timelines, and concepts:

- Timeline: The History of Assisted Reproduction
- Ovulation to Implantation
- Ectopic Pregnancy
- Key Terms Exercise
- Breech Position

 Readings Delve deeper into key content:

- Is It a Boy or a Girl?
- "I Want to Have a Baby!"
- Stillbirth
- Postpartum Sexuality for New Parents

 Assessment Measure your mastery:

- Chapter Pre-Test
- Check Your Learning Quizzes
- Chapter Post-Test

 Think Critically Challenge your thinking about data and accepted norms:

- Breast-feeding

▶ **L01** Describe the process of conception.

▶ **L02** Describe the process in which an ovum is fertilized and implants in the uterine wall.

A sperm.

© Dennis Kunkel Microscopy, Inc./Visuals Unlimited/Corbis

An ovum.

Derek Berwin/Getty Images

mucus plug A collection of thick mucus in the cervix that prevents bacteria from entering the uterus.

MOST PARENTS, sooner or later, must confront the moment when their child asks, "Where did I come from?" The answer they give depends on the parent, the child, the situation, and the culture. Every culture has its own traditional explanations for where babies come from. The Australian Aborigines, for instance, believe that babies are created by the mother earth and, therefore, are products of the land. The spirits of children rest in certain areas of the land, and these spirits enter a young woman as she passes by (Dunham et al, 1992). Women who do not want to become pregnant either avoid these areas or dress up like old women to fool the spirits. In Malaysia, the Malay people believe that because man is the more rational of the two sexes, babies come from men. Babies are formulated in the man's brain for 40 days before moving down to his penis for eventual ejaculation into a woman's womb.

In American culture, we take a more scientific view of where babies come from, and so it is important to understand the biological processes involved in conceiving a child, being pregnant, and giving birth. The biological answer to the question, "Where did I come from?" is that we are created from the union of an ovum and a spermatozoon. You may recall from the sexual anatomy and physiology chapters that fertilization and conception are dynamic processes that result in the creation of new life, a process so complex it is often referred to as "the incredible journey."

▼

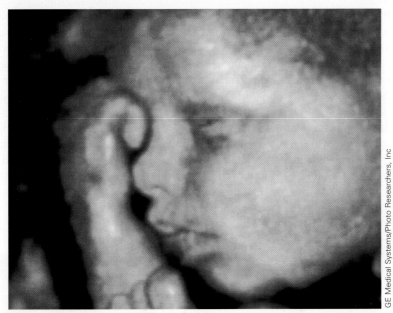

GE Medical Systems/Photo Researchers, Inc

Newer ultrasounds can produce both three- and four-dimensional ultrasounds like this one.

wall, supplies nutrients to the developing fetus, aids in respiratory and excretory functions, and secretes hormones necessary for the continuation of the pregnancy. The umbilical cord connects the fetus to the placenta. Toward the end of pregnancy, approximately 75 gallons of blood will pass through the placenta daily.

By the end of the first month of pregnancy, the fetal heart is formed and begins to pump blood. In fact, the circulatory system is the first organ system to function in the embryo (Rischer & Easton, 1992). In addition, many of the other major systems develop, including the digestive system, beginnings of the brain, spinal cord, nervous system, muscles, arms, legs, eyes, fingers, and toes.

By 14 weeks, the liver, kidneys, intestines, and lungs have begun to develop. In addition, the circulatory and urinary systems are operating, and the reproductive organs have developed. By the end of the first trimester, the fetus weighs 0.5 ounce and is approximately 3 inches long.

Ovulation to Implantation

Take a closer look at underlying structures and functions.

▶ **LO10** Describe the development of the fetus and changes in the mother during the second trimester.

▶ **LO11** Describe the development of the fetus, changes in the mother, and the experience of the mother's partner during the third trimester.

Changes in the Pregnant Mother

During the first few weeks of pregnancy, a woman's body adjusts to increased levels of estrogen and progesterone. This can cause fatigue, breast tenderness, constipation, increased urination, and nausea or vomiting. Some women experience nausea and vomiting so severe during pregnancy that they must be hospitalized because of weight loss and malnutrition (Sheehan, 2007). Specific food cravings are normal, as is an increased sensitivity to smells and odors.

Although some women feel physically uncomfortable because of all these changes, many also feel excited and happy about the life growing within them. The final, confirming sign of pregnancy—a fetal heartbeat—can usually be heard through ultrasound by the end of the first trimester. After the heartbeat is heard, the probability of miscarriage declines significantly.

Ultrasounds help to confirm a pregnancy, rule out abnormalities, indicate gestational age, and confirm multiple pregnancies. Newer three-dimensional and even four-dimensional ultrasounds, like the one in the nearby photo, allow parents to view almost lifelike fetal images, including yawns and facial expressions.

However, the standard two-dimensional images may still offer better diagnostic information than either three- or four-dimensional ultrasounds because they allow physicians to see inside of structures (Handwerk, 2005).

Second Trimester

The second trimester includes the second 15 weeks of pregnancy (weeks 14–28). The fetus looks noticeably more human. At 5 months, the fetus is becoming more and more lively. It can turn its head, move its face, and make breathing movements. The fetus in the nearby photo is approximately 5 months old and 9 inches long.

Neil Bromhall/Photo Researchers, Inc.

At 5 months, the fetus is becoming more and more lively. It can turn, move its head, move its face, and make breathing movements. This 5-month fetus is approximately 9 inches long.

Fetal Development

The fetus grows dramatically during the second trimester and is 13 inches long by the end of the trimester. The fetus has developed tooth buds and reflexes, such as sucking and swallowing. Although the sex of the fetus is determined at conception, it is not immediately apparent during development. If the fetus is positioned correctly during ultrasound, sex may be determined as early as 12-13 weeks, although most of the time it is not possible until sometime between the 18th -20th weeks.

During the second trimester, soft hair, called lanugo (lan-NEW-go), and a waxy substance, known as vernix, cover the fetus's body. These may develop to protect the fetus from the constant exposure to the amniotic fluid. By the end of the second trimester, the fetus will weigh about 1.75 pounds. If birth takes place at the end of the second trimester, the newborn may be able to survive with intensive medical care. Premature birth is discussed later in this chapter.

Changes in the Pregnant Mother

During the second trimester, nausea begins to subside as the body adjusts to the increased hormonal levels. Breast sensitivity also tends to decrease. However, fatigue may continue, as well as an increase in appetite, heartburn, edema (ankle or leg swelling), and a noticeable vaginal discharge. Skin pigmentation changes can occur on the face. As the uterus grows larger and the blood circulation slows down, constipation and muscle cramps bother some women. Internally, the cervix turns a deep red, almost violet color because of increased blood supply.

As the pregnancy progresses, the increasing size of the uterus and the restriction of the pelvic veins can cause more swelling of the ankles. Increased problems with varicose veins and hemorrhoids may also occur. Fetal movement is often felt in the second trimester, sometimes as early as the 16th week. Usually women can feel movement earlier in their second or subsequent pregnancies because they know what fetal movement feels like.

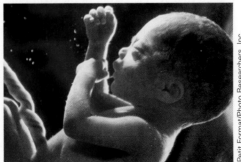

The fetus at 9 months, ready for birth.

Petit Format/Photo Researchers, Inc.

The second trimester of pregnancy is usually the most positive time for the mother. The early physiological signs of pregnancy such as morning sickness and fatigue lessen, and the mother-to-be finally feels better physically. Feeling better physically often leads to an increase in psychological feelings including excitement, happiness, and a sense of well-being. Many women report an increased sex drive during the second trimester, and for many couples, it is a period of high sexual satisfaction.

As the developing fetus begins to move around, many women feel reassured after anxiously wondering whether the fetus was developing at all. In fact, many women report that the kicking and moving about of the developing fetus is very comforting. Finally, the transition to maternity clothes often results in more positive feelings, probably because it is now obvious and public knowledge that the woman is pregnant.

Third Trimester

The third trimester includes the final weeks of pregnancy (weeks 28–40) and ends with the birth of a child. The fetus gains both fat deposits and muscle mass during this period.

Fetal Development

By the end of the seventh month, the fetus begins to develop fat deposits. The fetus can react to pain, light, and sounds. Some fetuses develop occasional hiccups or begin to suck their thumb. If a baby is born at the end of the seventh month, there is a good chance of survival. In the eighth month, the majority of the organ systems are well developed, although the brain continues to grow. By the end of the eighth month, the fetus is 15 inches long and weighs about 3 pounds. During the third trimester, there is often stronger and more frequent fetal movement, which will slow down toward the ninth month (because the fetus has less room to move around). At 9 months, the fetus in the nearby photo is ready for birth. At birth, an infant, on average, weighs 7.5 pounds and is 20 inches long.

Changes in the Pregnant Mother

Braxton–Hicks contractions Intermittent contractions of the uterus after the third month of pregnancy.

Many of the symptoms from the second trimester continue, with constipation and heartburn increasing in frequency. Backaches, leg cramps, increases in varicose veins, hemorrhoids, sleep problems, shortness of breath, and **Braxton–Hicks con-**

tractions often occur. At first these contractions are scattered and relatively pain-less (the uterus hardens for a moment and then returns to normal). In the eighth and ninth months, the Braxton–Hicks contractions become stronger. A thin, yellowish liquid called colostrum (kuh-LAHS-trum) may be secreted from the nipples as the breasts prepare to produce milk for breast-feeding. Toward the end of the third trimester, many women feel an increase in apprehension about labor and delivery; impatience and restlessness are common.

The Partner's Experience

In the United States today, partners are allowed and encouraged to participate in the birth. However, this was not always the case. For many years, fathers were told to go to the waiting room and sit until the baby was born. In some other cultures, such as in Bang Chan, Thailand, the father aids in the actual birth of his child (Dunham et al., 1992). The role of the father in pregnancy varies among cultures. Some fathers are required to remain on a strict diet during the course of the pregnancy or to cater to their partner's food cravings at all times.

Pregnancy can be a time of joy and anticipation for the partner of a pregnant woman, but it can also be a time of stress and anxiety. Feelings about parenting in combination with the many changes their partners are undergoing can all add to increased vulnerability.

© Sean Justice/Corbis/GlowImages

Check Your Learning
Quiz 10.4

Go to **login.cengagebrain.com**
and take the online quiz.

▶ **LO12** List and discuss two things a pregnant mother should do and two things she should not do to ensure her own health and the healthiest outcome for her baby.

▶ **LO13** Explain the recommendations for sexual behavior during pregnancy.

Staying Healthy

Exercise and Nutrition

A pregnant woman can do many things to be healthy during her pregnancy, including participating in physical exercise, getting good nutrition, and avoiding drugs and alcohol. Women often maintain sexual interest during pregnancy, although it may begin to decrease during the third trimester.

During the second trimester, an average-weight woman is advised to increase her caloric intake by 300 calories per day, and protein requirements increase. For vegetarians and vegans, it is necessary to increase consumption of vegetables, whole grains, nuts, and seeds and also to include a protein supplement to ensure adequate protein intake. An increase in calcium is also necessary to help with bone calcification of the growing fetus. Because a woman's blood volume increases as much as 50% during pregnancy, iron may be diluted in the blood; thus, many pregnant women are advised to take prenatal vitamins, which include iron supplements.

Drugs and Alcohol

Physicians recommend avoiding several substances during pregnancy,

fetal alcohol syndrome A disorder involving physical and mental deficiencies, nervous system damage, and facial abnormalities found in the offspring of mothers who consumed large quantities of alcohol during pregnancy.

Fabio Cardoso/PhotoLibrary

including caffeine, nicotine, alcohol, marijuana, and other drugs. All of these substances are teratogens that can cross the placenta, enter into the developing fetus's bloodstream, and cause physical or mental deficiencies. **Fetal alcohol syndrome**, a condition associated with alcohol intake, occurs when a woman drinks heavily during pregnancy, producing an infant with irreversible physical and mental disabilities. Experts agree that there is no safe level of alcohol use during pregnancy (Sayal et al., 2007).

Smoking during pregnancy has been associated with spontaneous abortion, low birth weight, prematurity, and low iron levels (R. P. Martin et al., 2005; Pandey et al., 2005). It has also been found to increase the risk for vascular damage to the developing fetus's brain and potentially interfere with a male's future ability to manufacture sperm (Storgaard et al., 2003). Children whose mothers smoked during pregnancy have been found to experience an increased aging of the lungs and a greater risk for lung damage later in life (Maritz, 2008). Second-hand smoke has negative effects, too, and partners, fathers, friends, relatives, and strangers who smoke around a pregnant woman jeopardize the future health of a developing baby.

Sex during Pregnancy

In an uncomplicated pregnancy, sexual behavior during pregnancy is safe for most mothers and the developing fetus up until the last several weeks of pregnancy. During a woman's first trimester, sexual interest is often decreased because of physical changes, including nausea and fatigue. Orgasm during pregnancy is also safe in an uncomplicated pregnancy, but occasionally it may cause painful uterine contractions, especially toward the end of pregnancy. Cunnilingus can also be safely engaged in during pregnancy; however, air should never be blown into the vagina of a pregnant woman because it could cause an air embolism, which could be fatal to both the mother and baby (Hill & Jones, 1993; Kaufman et al., 1987; Nicoll & Skupski, 2008; Sánchez et al., 2008).

Sexual interest usually begins to subside as the woman and fetus grow during the third trimester (Gokyildiz & Beji, 2005). The increasing size of the abdomen puts pressure on many of the internal organs and also makes certain sexual positions for vaginal intercourse difficult.

On Your Mind

How much weight do women gain during pregnancy?

Weight and Pregnancy

A look at the benefits of exercise during pregnancy and the importance of weight control.

Check Your Learning Quiz 10.5

Go to **login.cengagebrain.com** and take the online quiz.

The majority of women go through their pregnancy without any problems. However, understanding how complex the process of pregnancy is, it should not come as a surprise that occasionally things go wrong.

Ectopic Pregnancy

Most zygotes travel through the Fallopian tubes and end up in the uterus. In an ectopic pregnancy, the zygote implants outside of the uterus (Figure 10.2). Ninety-five percent of ectopic pregnancies occur when the fertilized ovum implants in the Fallopian tube (Hankins, 1995). These are called *tubal pregnancies.* The remainder occur in the abdomen, cervix, or ovaries.

Approximately 2% (1 in 50) of all U.S. pregnancies are ectopic, and this number has been steadily increasing primarily because of increases in the incidence of pelvic inflammatory disease caused by chlamydia infections (Tay et al., 2000).

The effects of ectopic pregnancy can be serious. Because the Fallopian tubes, cervix, and abdomen are not designed to support a growing fetus, when one is implanted in these places, they can rupture, causing internal hemorrhaging and possibly death. Possible symptoms include abdominal pain (usually on the side of the body that has the tubal pregnancy), cramping, pelvic pain, vaginal bleeding, nausea, dizziness, and fainting (Levine, 2007; Seeber & Barnhart, 2006; Tay et al., 2000).

Women who smoke and those who have had a sexually transmitted infection are at greater risk for an ectopic pregnancy (Ankum et al., 1996). Smoking cigarettes has been found to change the tubal contractions and muscular tone of the

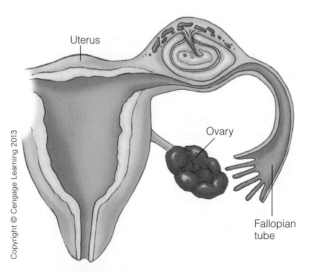

Copyright © Cengage Learning 2013

Figure 10.2 An ectopic pregnancy.

Fallopian tubes, which may lead to tubal inactivity, delayed ovum entry into the uterus, and changes in the tubes' ability to transport the ovum (Albers, 2007; Handler et al., 1989; Seeber & Barnhart, 2006).

Spontaneous Abortion

A spontaneous abortion, or miscarriage, is a natural termination of a pregnancy before the time that the fetus can live on its own. Approximately 15% to 20% of all diagnosed pregnancies end in miscarriage (Friebe & Arck, 2008). Miscarriages can occur anytime during a pregnancy, although the percentage declines dramatically after the first trimester.

In a significant number of miscarriages, there is some chromosomal abnormality (Christiansen, 1996; Vorsanova et al., 2010). In other cases, in which there are no chromosomal problems, the uterus may be too small, too weak, or abnormally shaped, or the miscarriage may be caused by maternal stress, nutritional deficiencies, drug exposure, or pelvic infection.

Common symptoms of miscarriage include vaginal bleeding, cramps, and lower back pain. Usually a normal menstrual period returns within 3 months after a miscarriage, and future pregnancies may be perfectly normal. However, some women experience repeated miscarriages, often caused by anatomic, endocrine, hormonal, genetic, or chromosomal abnormalities (Bick et al., 1998), as well as problems with defective sperm (Carrell et al., 2003). Tests are being developed to try to predict when a miscarriage will occur.

Toxemia

In the last 2 to 3 months of pregnancy, 6% to 7% of women experience toxemia (tock-SEE-mee-uh), or preeclampsia (pre-ee-CLAMP-see-uh). Symptoms include rapid weight gain, fluid retention, an increase in blood pressure, and protein in the urine. If toxemia is allowed to progress, it can result in eclampsia, which involves convulsions, coma, and, in approximately 15% of cases, death. Even though preeclampsia typically occurs at the end of pregnancy, research indicates that it may actually be caused by defective implantation or placental problems at the beginning of pregnancy (Urato & Norwitz, 2011). Screening tests to identify at-risk women are being evaluated (Huppertz, 2011; Urato & Norwitz, 2010).

Ectopic Pregnancy

Take a closer look.

Check Your Learning Quiz 10.6

Go to **login.cengagebrain.com** and take the online quiz.

The average length of a pregnancy is 40 weeks, but a normal birth can occur 3 weeks before or 2 weeks after the due date. Early delivery may occur in cases in which the mother has exercised throughout the pregnancy, the fetus is female, or the mother has shorter menstrual cycles (R. Jones, 1984).

As the birthing day comes closer, many women (and their partners) become anxious, nervous, and excited about what is to come. This is probably why the tradition of baby showers started. These gatherings enable women (and more recently, men) to gather and discuss the impending birth. Increasing knowledge and alleviating anxiety about the birth process are the main concepts behind childbirth classes. In these classes, women and their partners are taught what to expect during labor and delivery and how to control the pain through breathing and massage.

Choosing a Birthplace Location

In nonindustrialized countries, nearly all babies are born at home; worldwide, approximately 80% of babies are (Dunham et al., 1992). For low-risk pregnancies, home birth has been found to be as safe as a hospital delivery (K. C. Johnson & Daviss, 2005). Although the American College of Obstetricians and Gynecologists believes the risks associated with home births are low, women need to make medically informed decisions about birthplace choices.

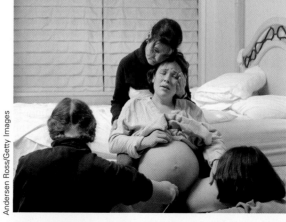

The majority of home births are done with the help of a **midwife** (Macdorman et al., 2011). Same-sex couples are more likely to use midwives in their birthing experience, even if they deliver in a hospital setting. This is primarily because many same-sex couples feel that midwives are more accepting of nontraditional families (L. E. Ross et al., 2006b).

midwife A person who assists women during childbirth.

A midwife assisting with a home birth.

Andersen Ross/Getty Images

Postpartum Challenges for Parents

Postpartum Physical Changes for the Mother

Many women report painful contractions for a few days after birth. These contractions are caused by the secretion of oxytocin, which is produced when a woman breast-feeds and is responsible for the shrinking of the uterus. The uterus returns to its original size about 6 weeks postpartum in breast-feeding women, which is sooner than in non–breast-feeding women. A bloody discharge can persist for anywhere from a week to several weeks after delivery. After the bleeding stops, the discharge is often yellow–white and can last for a couple of weeks in mothers who breast-feed and up to a month or so in women who do not.

©LWA-Dann Tardif/Corbis

A child with Down syndrome.

Women may experience an increase in frequency of urination, which can be painful if an episiotomy was performed or natural tearing occurred. Women may be advised to take sitz baths, in which the vagina and perineum are soaked in warm water to reduce the pain and to quicken the healing process. Until the cervix returns to its closed position, full baths are generally not advised.

Postpartum Emotional Changes for the Mother

Many women experience an onset of intense emotions after the birth of a baby. One study found that 52% of new mothers felt excited and elated, 48% reported feeling like they did not need sleep, 37% reported feeling energetic, and 31% reported being more chatty (Heron et al., 2008). At the same time, many women report feeling overwhelmed and exhausted. Minor sadness is a common emotion after the birth of a baby (Howard et al., 2005). However, for some, it is a difficult time with endless crying spells and anxiety.

Research has found that 1 in 8 women experience postpartum depression (Storm, 2011). Physical exhaustion, physiological changes, and an increased responsibility of child rearing all contribute to these feelings, coupled with postpartum hormonal changes (including a sudden decline in progesterone). Women with premature infants are at greater risk for postpartum depression because of the increased stress involved in these births (Storm, 2011). Male and female partners may also experience postpartum depression after the birth of a baby (Davé et al., 2010).

Partner support has been found to decrease postpartum depression in both heterosexual and same-sex couples (Misri et al., 2000; L. E. Ross, 2005, Storm, 2011). In the most severe cases, mental disturbances, called postpartum psychosis, occur: in rare cases, women have killed or neglected their babies after delivery (Rammouz et al., 2008).

Postpartum Sexuality for New Parents

Explore some common changes.

Unintended Pregnancy: A Man's Perspective

A young father discusses his feelings and experience with an unintended pregnancy.

Check Your Learning Quiz 10.10

Go to login.cengagebrain.com and take the online quiz.

Think Critically

Challenge Your Thinking

Consider these questions:

1. In 2010, supermodel Gisele Bündchen created a controversy when she said there should be a "worldwide law" requiring women to breast-feed for 6 months. Explain your reactions to her comment and reasons why you think this comment created such controversy.

2. Explore the pros and cons of breast-feeding, and discuss why you think many women choose not to breast-feed. If you had to design a campaign to encourage more breast-feeding, what would you concentrate on in your campaign?

3. Many controversies have surrounded public breast-feeding in the United States. In 2006, a flight attendant asked a 27-year-old woman to exit an airplane when the woman refused to put a blanket over her breast-feeding child. Why do you think many Americans view breast-feeding as "indecent"? Why do you think European countries are more open and accepting of public breast-feeding?

4. In 2011, the IRS announced that breast pumps and other breast-feeding supplies are tax deductible. Do you think these supplies should be tax deductible? Explain why or why not. Do you think this ruling encourages more women to breast-feed?

5. How do you think most Americans would respond if a woman decided to breast-feed her child up until the age of 2? What if she wanted to breast-feed longer than this? How long do you think a woman should breast-feed and why?

Breast-feeding

Within an hour after birth, the newborn usually begins a rooting reflex, which signals hunger. The baby's sucking triggers the flow of milk from the breast. This is done through receptors in the nipples, which signal the pituitary to produce prolactin, a chemical necessary for milk pro-duction. Another chemical, oxytocin, is also produced, which helps increase contractions in the uterus to shrink it to its original size. In the first few days of breast-feeding, the breasts release a fluid called *colostrum,* which is very important in strengthening the baby's immune system. This is one of the reasons that breast-feeding is recommended to new mothers.

Breast-feeding rates in the United States increased significantly between 1993 and 2006. Whereas 60% of newborns were breast-fed in 1993–1994, 77% were breast-fed in 2005–2006 (McDowell et al., 2008). In 2010, 3 of every 4 new mothers in the United States started out breast-feeding; however, rates of breast-feeding decreased significantly by time the infants were 6 months old (Centers for Disease Control and Prevention, 2010b).

Benefits of breast-feeding include strengthening of the infant's immune system and cognitive development, and a reduction in infant allergies, asthma, diarrhea, tooth decay, and ear, urinary tract, and respiratory infections (Daniels & Adair, 2005; Duijts et al., 2010; Khadivzadeh & Parsai, 2005). One study found that breast-fed children attain higher IQ scores than non–breast-fed children (Caspi et al., 2007). Benefits to the mother include an earlier return to pre-pregnancy weight and a lower risk for breast cancer and osteoporosis (Stuebe et al., 2009). In addition, the body-to-body contact during breast-feeding has been found to decrease stress and improve mood for both mother and child (Groer, 2005).

For some women, however, breast-feeding is not physically possible. Time constraints and work pressures may also prevent breast-feeding. It is estimated that a baby's primary caregiver loses between 450 and 700 hours of sleep in the first year of the baby's life, and overall, breast-feeding mothers lose the most sleep (Brizendine, 2006; Maas, 1998).

Some women who want to breast-feed but who also wish to return to work use a breast pump. This allows a woman to express milk from her breasts that can be given to her child through a bottle while she is away. Breast milk can be kept in the refrigerator or freezer, but it must be heated before feeding. In early 2011, the Internal Revenue Service (IRS) announced that breast pumps and other breast-feeding supplies were tax deductible (Belkin, 2011). This reversed an earlier decision by the IRS stating that breast-feeding did not contribute sufficient medical benefits to qualify for such a deduction.

There have been some heated debates about when a child should be weaned from breast-feeding. The American Academy of Pediatrics recommends exclusive breast-feeding (no other fluids or food) for 6 months and then continued breast-feeding for a minimum of 1 year, whereas the World Health Organization recommends exclusive breast-feeding for the first 4 to 6 months of life and continued breast-feeding until at least age 2.

© David Young-Wolff/Alamy

Think Critically

This article and its questions are available in interactive format online.

Measure ^Your Learning

GO to your Psychology CourseMate at login.cengagebrain.com and take the Chapter Post-Test to see which Learning Objectives you've mastered and which need more review. Use the chapter review guide below and the online activities—including flashcards to review key terms—to measure your learning.

Online Activities

Key Terms	Video	Animation	Readings	Assessment
mucus plug, spontaneous abortion, zygote, blastocyst	Love Makes a Family			Check Your Learning Quiz 10.1
miscarriage, morning sickness, human chorionic gonadotropin (hCG), false negative, false positive, amniocentesis	Can guys ever get pregnant? I Didn't Know I Was Pregnant! Designer Babies Can I be pregnant if I've missed my period for 2 months?		Is It a Boy or a Girl?	Check Your Learning Quiz 10.2
infertility, cesarean section (C-section), artificial insemination, sperm cryopreservation, embryo cryopreservation, ova cryopreservation, in vitro fertilization (IVF), test-tube baby, intracytoplasmic sperm injection, surrogate parenting, surrogate mother	IVF and Multiple Births Do physicians ever mix up ova or embryos during embryo transplants?	Timeline: The History of Assisted Reproduction	"I Want to Have a Baby!"	Check Your Learning Quiz 10.3
trimester, sonography, ultrasound, embryo, amnion, placenta, umbilical cord, lanugo, vernix, Braxton-Hicks contractions, colostrum		Ovulation to Implantation		Check Your Learning Quiz 10.4

Measure ^ Your Learning

Online Activities

Key Terms	Video	Animation	Readings	Assessment
fetal alcohol syndrome	How much weight do women gain during pregnancy? Weight and Pregnancy			Check Your Learning Quiz 10.5
ectopic pregnancy, toxemia, preeclampsia, eclampsia		Ectopic Pregnancy		Check Your Learning Quiz 10.6
due date, midwife	What determines how long a woman is in labor? Is it safe to use drugs to lessen the pain of labor?			Check Your Learning Quiz 10.7
engagement, cervical effacement, dilation, transition, endorphins, episiotomy, crowning		Key Terms Exercise		Check Your Learning Quiz 10.8
breech position, premature birth, placenta previa, fetal distress, stillbirth		Breech Position	Stillbirth	Check Your Learning Quiz 10.9
chorionic villus sampling, maternal-serum alpha-fetoprotein screening, spina bifida, anencephaly, Down syndrome, postpartum depression	Unintended Pregnancy: A Man's Perspective		Postpartum Sexuality for New Parents	Check Your Learning Quiz 10.10 Breast-feeding
				Breast-Feeding

Contraception and Abortion

11

Chapter Outline and Learning Objectives

1 **GO** to your **Psychology CourseMate** at **login.cengagebrain.com** and take the **Chapter Pre-Test** to introduce yourself to this chapter's topics and see what you may already know.

2 **READ** the **Learning Objectives** (LOs, in the left sidebars) and begin the chapter.

3 **COMPLETE** the **Online Activities** (in the right sidebars) *as you read each module.* Activities include **videos, animations, readings,** and **quizzes.**

4 **CHECK Your Learning** by going online to take the quiz at the end of each module and review material as necessary.

5 **MEASURE Your Learning** after reading the chapter by taking the online **Chapter Post-Test.** Use the chapter review guide at the end of the chapter as needed.

WATCH for these **Online Activities** icons as you read:

Video

Animation

Reading

Assessment

Think Critically

Online Activities

These Online Activities are essential to mastering this chapter. Go to login.cengagebrain.com.

 Videos Explore diverse perspectives on sex as well as common questions:

- Condoms and the Catholic Church
- Does wearing a condom make it harder for a guy to have an erection?
- Is it okay to borrow someone else's diaphragm if I can't find mine?
- I usually take my birth control pill every morning at 7 a.m. Should I continue taking it at 7 a.m. after daylight saving time?
- Permanent Contraception
- Morning After Pill
- Abortion before *Roe v. Wade*
- Will abortion eventually become illegal?
- How much does an abortion cost?
- Can women who've had an abortion still have children later in life?

 Animations Interact with and visualize important processes, timelines, and concepts:

- Timeline: History of Contraceptives in the United States
- Virtual Contraceptive Kit
- Insertion of a Female Condom
- Insertion of a Diaphragm
- Insertion of a Contraceptive Sponge
- Key Terms Exercise
- Insertion of an IUD
- Essure
- Vasectomy

 Readings Delve deeper into key content:

- A Brief History of Contraception
- Contraceptive Use around the World

- What to Do If You Forget
- Drugs and Herbs That Interact with Oral Contraceptives
- State Laws Regulating Abortion

 Assessment Measure your mastery:

- Chapter Pre-Test
- Check Your Learning Quizzes
- Chapter Post-Test

 Think Critically Challenge your thinking about data and accepted norms:

- Teens and Abortion

College students take risks when it comes to contraception, even though they are intelligent and educated about birth control. Many factors increase one's motivation to use contraception, including the ability to communicate with a partner, cost of the method, effectiveness rates, frequency of vaginal intercourse, motivation to avoid pregnancy, the contraceptive method's side effects, and one's openness about sexuality (Frost et al., 2008; Hatcher et al., 2011).

▼

Although many people believe that contraception is a modern invention, its origins actually extend back to ancient times. Today, the typical American woman spends about 30 years trying *not* to get pregnant and only a couple of years trying to become pregnant (Boonstra et al., 2006; see Figure 11.1).

Contraceptive use has increased in the United States over the last few years, and today, more than 99% of sexually active women 15 to 44 years old have used at least one contraceptive method (Mosher & Jones, 2010). Condom use continues to

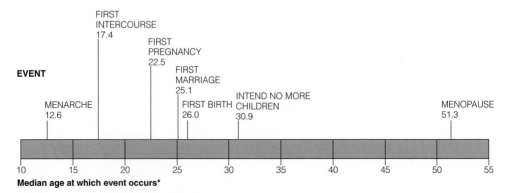

Figure 11.1 Timeline of reproductive events for the typical American woman. Source: Boonstra et al., 2006

Table 11.1
Contraceptive Method Use among U.S. Women Who Practice Contraception, 2006–2008

Method	No. of Users (in millions)	Users (%)
Pill	10.7	28.0
Tubal sterilization	10.4	27.1
Male condom	6.2	16.1
Vasectomy	3.8	9.9
Intrauterine device	2.1	5.5
Withdrawal	2.0	5.2
Three-month injectable (Depo-Provera)	1.2	3.2
Vaginal ring (NuvaRing)	.9	2.4
Implant (Implanon or Norplant), one-month injectable (Lunelle) or patch (Evra)	.4	1.1
Periodic abstinence (calendar)	.3	0.9
Other[†]	.2	0.4
Periodic abstinence (natural family planning)	.1	0.2
Diaphragm	‡	‡
Total	38.2	100.0

[†]Includes emergency contraception, female condom or vaginal pouch, foam, cervical cap, Today sponge, suppository or insert, jelly or cream (without diaphragm), and other methods.
‡Figure does not meet standards of reliability or precision.
SOURCE: Alan Guttmacher Institute. (2010, June). Facts on Contraceptive Use in the United States. New York: Alan Guttmacher Institute. Retrieved from http://www.guttmacher.org/pubs/fb_contr_use.html.

increase, which has helped decrease sexually transmitted infections (STIs). Overall, the most popular contraceptive methods in the United States are birth control pills (used by close to 11 million women) and female sterilization (used by approximately 10 million women; Mosher & Jones, 2010). See Table 11.1 for information on the use of various contraceptive methods in the United States.

A Brief History of Contraception

From ancient times to the present.

Timeline: History of Contraceptives in the United States

Put key dates in order.

▶ **LO1** List four or five factors that should be taken into account when choosing a method of contraception.

Choosing a Method of Contraception

The majority of women in the United States use some form of contraception. Figure 11.2 shows the percentage of women who used each major form of contraception in 2008.

Choosing the Best Method

The best method of birth control is one that you and your partner will use correctly every time you have vaginal intercourse. Choosing a contraceptive method is an important decision and one that must be made with your lifestyle in mind. Important issues include your own

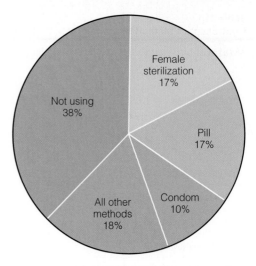

Figure 11.2 Distribution of women aged 15 to 44 years by contraceptive status in the United States, 2006–2008. Source: Jones, 2010

personal health and health risks, the number of sexual partners you have, frequency of vaginal intercourse, your risk for acquiring an STI, how responsible you are, the cost of the method, and the method's advantages and disadvantages. As shown in Figure 11.3, certain factors put a woman at greater risk for unintended pregnancy.

Avoiding Unreliable Methods

Unfortunately, many men and women rely on myths and false information when it comes to contraception. They may keep their fingers crossed in hopes of not getting pregnant, have sex standing up to try and invoke gravity, or even jump up and down after sex in an attempt to dislodge sperm from swimming up the vagina. We know these techniques won't work, but for many years, people thought they would. In the mid-1800s, physicians recommended douching as a contraceptive. However, we know today that douching is also not an effective contraceptive method. As we've learned, douching can increase the risk for pelvic infections and STIs. Another ineffective method is the lactational amenorrhea method (LAM), which is based on the

typical use Refers to the probability of contraceptive failure for less than perfect use of the method.

perfect use Refers to the probability of contraceptive failure for use of the method without error.

postpartum infertility that many women experience when they are breastfeeding (Hatcher et al., 2007). During breast-feeding, the cyclic ovarian hormones are typically suspended, which may inhibit ovulation. However, this is an ineffective contraceptive method because ovulation may still occur (Kennedy & Trussell, 2011).

The following sections discuss various effective methods of contraception, including barrier, hormonal, chemical, intrauterine, natural, permanent, and emergency contraception. For each of these methods, we consider how they work, their costs, their advantages and disadvantages, and their effectiveness rates in **typical use** (which includes user error) and **perfect use** (when a method is used without error).

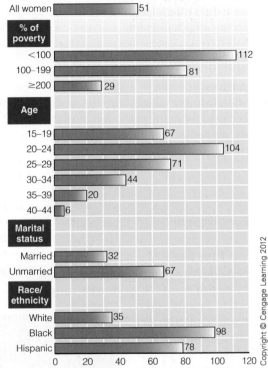

Unintended Pregnancies per 1,000 Women Aged 15–44

Copyright © Cengage Learning 2012

Figure 11.3 Unintended pregnancy rates vary dramatically based on income, age, marital status, and race/ethnicity. *Note: Poverty levels are defined by government standards of income. Groupings are <100 (making less income than the poverty level), 100–199 (earning more than poverty but less than 2X the poverty level), and >200 (earning more than 2X the poverty level).* Source: Alan Guttmacher Institute, 2006

Virtual Contraceptive Kit

Collection of various birth control methods.

Contraceptive Use around the World

Many factors can affect contraceptive use.

Check Your Learning Quiz 11.1

Go to **login.cengagebrain.com** and take the online quiz.

▶ **L02** Explain how spermicides work and identify their effectiveness rates, advantages, and disadvantages.

Spermicides can be used either alone or in conjunction with another contraceptive method—most often with one of the barrier methods, which work by preventing the sperm from entering the uterus. This section discusses various spermicides, as well as barrier methods including condoms, cervical barriers, and the contraceptive sponge.

Spermicides

Spermicides come in a variety of forms, including creams, suppositories, gels, foams, foaming tablets, capsules, and films. Nonoxynol-9 is a spermicide that has been used for many years. It is available over the counter in many forms (creams, gels, suppositories, film, and condoms with spermicide).

	Effectiveness Rates		
	Typical Use	**Perfect Use**	**Average Cost**
Spermicides (alone)	71%	82%	$5–$10

How They Work

Spermicides contain two components: one is an inert base such as jelly, cream, foam, or film that holds the spermicide close to the cervix; the second is the spermicide itself. Foam, jelly, cream, and film are usually inserted into the vagina with either an applicator or a finger. Vaginal contraceptive film contains nonoxynol-9 and comes in a variety of package sizes. The film is wrapped around the index finger and inserted into the vagina.

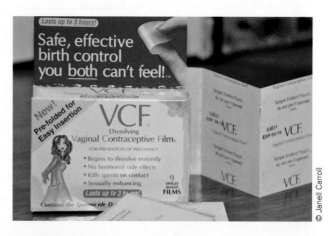

© Janell Carroll

Suppositories are inserted in the vagina 10 to 30 minutes before intercourse to allow time for the outer covering to melt. It is important to read manufacturer's directions for spermicide use carefully. Douching and tampon use should be avoided for 6 to 8 hours after the use of spermicides because they interfere with effectiveness rates.

Effectiveness Rates

Effectiveness rates for spermicides range from 71% to 82%. However, effectiveness depends on the types of spermicide and how consistently it is used. Overall, foam is more effective than jelly, cream, film, or suppositories.

Advantages

Spermicides do not require a prescription and can be easily purchased in drugstores, can be discreetly carried in a pocket or purse, do not interfere with a woman's hormones, can be inserted during foreplay, provide lubrication during intercourse, have minimal adverse effects, and can be used by a woman who is breast-feeding.

Disadvantages

Spermicides must be used each time a couple engages in vaginal intercourse, which may be expensive depending on frequency of intercourse. In addition, there is an increase in postcoital drip, and some couples may be allergic or have adverse reactions. Spermicides often have an unpleasant taste, and they may cause vaginal skin irritations or an increase in urinary tract infections (Cates & Harwood, 2011).

Cross-Cultural Use

Spermicides are widely used in some countries, including Argentina, Australia, Colombia, Costa Rica, Cuba, and many European and Scandinavian countries (Francoeur & Noonan, 2004). However, in many other countries, including Botswana, Brazil, Canada, China, Hong Kong, Japan, Kenya, and Puerto Rico, spermicides are not widely used, probably because of the relatively high cost or required genital touching.

Male Condoms

Male condoms are one of the most inexpensive and cost-effective contraceptive methods, providing not only high effectiveness rates but also added protection from STIs and HIV (Warner & Steiner, 2011). Male condoms are made of either latex or plastic and are the most widely available and commonly used barrier contraceptive method in the United States today (Figure 11.4).

A condom should be placed on an erect penis prior to any penetration.

	Effectiveness Rates		
	Typical Use	**Perfect Use**	**Average Cost**
Male condoms	85%	98%	$1.00 each

How They Work

The male condom is placed on an erect penis before vaginal penetration. Condoms must be put on before there is any vaginal contact by the penis because sperm may be present in the urethra. Some condom manufacturers recommend leaving space at the tip of the condom to allow room for the ejaculation, but others do not. To prevent tearing the condom, the vagina should be well lubricated. Although some condoms come prelubricated, if extra

postcoital drip A vaginal discharge (dripping) that occurs after sexual intercourse.

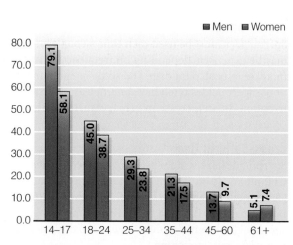

Figure 11.4 Condom use rates by age and gender. Source: National Survey of Sexual Health and Behavior. Source: Reece et al., 2010b

lubrication is needed, water, spermicidal jelly or cream, or a water-based lubricant such as K-Y jelly should be used. Oil-based lubricants such as hand or body lotion, petroleum jelly (e.g., Vaseline), baby oil, massage oil, or creams for vaginal infections (e.g., Monistat and Vagisil) should not be used with latex condoms because they may damage the latex and cause the condom to break.

To avoid the possibility of semen leaking out of the condom, withdrawal must take place immediately after ejaculation, while the penis is still erect, and the condom should be grasped firmly at the base to prevent its slipping off into the vagina during withdrawal.

Many types of male condoms are on the market, including dry, lubricated, colored, spermicidal, reservoir tip, and ribbed texture condoms. Condom users should always remember to check expiration dates before using condoms.

Effectiveness Rates

Effectiveness rates for male condoms range from 85% to 98%. Studies have demonstrated that when used correctly, the over-all risk for condom breakage is very low (Warner & Steiner, 2011). Using a condom after the expiration date is the leading cause of breakage.

Advantages

Male condoms allow men to help prevent pregnancy, can be discreetly carried in a pocket or purse, offer some protections from many STIs, can be purchased without a prescription, are relatively inexpensive, have minimal adverse effects, may reduce the incidence of premature ejaculation, reduce **postcoital drip**, can be used in conjunction with other contraceptive methods, and can be used during oral or anal sex to reduce the risk for STIs. Polyurethane condoms are more resistant to damage than latex condoms, have a longer shelf life, and can be used with both oil- and water-based lubricants (Warner & Steiner, 2011).

Disadvantages

The male condom decreases spontaneity, may pose sizing and erection problems, and may reduce male sensation. In one study, more than 75% of men and nearly 40% of women reported decreased sexual sensation with condom use (Crosby et al., 2008). Condoms may not be comfortable for all men, and some who use polyurethane condoms report slipping or bunching up during use (Hollander, 2001).

Condoms and the Catholic Church

Pope Benedict says condom use might be justified to prevent infection.

On Your Mind

Does wearing a condom make it harder for a guy to have an erection?

▶ **L04** Explain how female condoms work and identify their effectiveness rates, advantages, and disadvantages.

Finally, some men may feel uncomfortable interrupting foreplay to put on a condom.

Cross-Cultural Use

Worldwide, male condoms are the fourth most popular contraceptive method (behind female sterilization, IUDs, and birth control pills), with 6% of couples reporting relying on this method ("World Contraceptive Use: 2009"). Condoms are popular in more developed regions of the world, such as Europe and North America. Usage rates of between 20% to 40% have been reported in Argentina, Demark, Finland, Greece, Ireland, Jamaica, Singapore, Spain, Ukraine, the United Kingdom, and Uruguay.

In many other countries, however, male condoms are not widely used. This may be because of embarrassment, lack of availability, or religious prohibition. In Botswana, for example, many couples are embarrassed to purchase condoms (Mookodi et al., 2004), and a similar attitude is found in Brazil, especially among women (de Freitas, 2004). However, these attitudes are slowly changing because of increased condom availability. In Costa Rica, where religious prohibitions discourage condom use, men report not wanting to use condoms and prohibit their partners from using protection as well (Arroba, 2004).

Female Condoms

The first female condom, the Reality Vaginal Pouch (often referred to as "FC"), became available in the United States in 1993. It is made of polyurethane and is about 7 inches long with two flexible polyurethane rings. The inner ring serves as an insertion device, and the outer ring stays on the outside of the vagina. In 2005, a newer female condom (the "FC2") made of a softer and more flexible material became available in the United States.

	Effectiveness Rates		
	Typical Use	Perfect Use	Average Cost
Female condoms	79%	95%	$3.50 each

How They Work

A female condom is inserted into the vagina before penile penetration. The inner ring (or sponge, depending on which type of female condom used) is squeezed between the thumb and middle finger, making it long and thin, and then inserted into the vagina. Once this is done, an index finger inside the condom can push the inner ring/sponge up close to the cervix (Figure 11.5). The outer ring sits on the outside of the vulva. During intercourse, the penis is placed within the female condom, and care should be taken to make sure it does not slip between the condom and the vaginal wall. It is important that the vagina is well-lubricated so that the female condom stays in place. Effectiveness rates for female condoms range from 79% to 95%.

A female condom.

Advantages

Like male condoms, female condoms can be discreetly carried in a purse, offer some STI protection, can be purchased without a prescription, reduce postcoital drip, can be used by those with latex allergies, can be used with oil-based lubricants, and have minimal adverse effects. Unlike male condoms, female condoms do not require a male erection to put on and will stay in place if a man loses his erection. Finally, the external ring of the female condom may provide extra clitoral stimulation during vaginal intercourse, enhancing female sexual pleasure. Female condoms can also be used in the anus during anal sex.

Disadvantages

Female condoms can be difficult to insert, uncomfortable to wear, expensive, may decrease sensations, and slip during vaginal intercourse (Kerrigan et al., 2000; Lie, 2000). One study found that 57% of women and 30% of men reported difficulties with insertion, discomfort during sex, and/or excess lubrication with use (Kerrigan et al., 2000). Finally, some women may feel uncomfortable interrupting foreplay to put one in.

 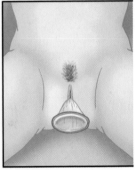

Figure 11.5 Female condoms are inserted into the vagina and the inner ring is pushed up inside until it reaches the cervix, while the outer ring hangs about an inch outside the vagina.

Insertion of a Female Condom

Take a closer look.

11.2 Spermicides and Barrier Methods

▶ **LO5** Identify two types of cervical barriers, explain how they work, and identify their effectiveness rates, advantages, and disadvantages.

Cross-Cultural Use

Female condoms have not been popular in developing countries. Several issues may contribute to this, including the fact that they are expensive and difficult to insert. Many women in other cultures are not comfortable touching the vagina or inserting anything into it (in fact, tampon use is also much lower in countries outside the United States). However, there are signs that female condom use is increasing in some countries. For example, in Zimbabwe, although acceptance of the female condom was low when the female condom was first introduced in 1997, after a creative media campaign about female condoms using billboards, television, and radio commercials, condom use increased six-fold (Helmore, 2010). The media campaign helped increase knowledge levels and broke down the stigma associated with female condoms.

Cervical Barriers

Cervical barriers include **diaphragms** (DIE-uh-fram) and **cervical caps**. These devices are inserted into the vagina before intercourse and fit over the cervix, creating a barrier so that sperm and ova cannot meet. Both types require the addition of spermicidal cream or jelly. We will discuss traditional diaphragms, Lea's Shield, and the FemCap. Although these methods work in similar ways, they are designed and function a bit differently from each other.

The diaphragm is a dome-shaped cup, made of either latex or silicone, with a flexible rim. It comes in several sizes and shapes, and it must be fitted by a health care provider. Like latex condoms, latex diaphragms should not be used with oil-based lubricants because these can damage the latex.

Lea's Shield is a silicone, one-size-fits-all diaphragm that works like a regular diaphragm. The biggest difference is that it has a one-way valve that allows the flow of cervical fluids and air. Although Lea's Shield is often available without a prescription around the world, as of 2011, it has to be prescribed by a health care provider in the United States.

FemCap, the only cervical cap currently available in the United States, works like the other cervical barriers. Cervical caps are much smaller than diaphragms and are designed to sit more snugly on the cervix. They are made of silicone and come in three sizes—small for women who have never been pregnant, medium for women who have been pregnant but have not had a vaginal delivery, and large for women who have had a vaginal delivery of a full-term baby.

diaphragm A birth control device consisting of a latex dome on a flexible spring rim; used with spermicidal cream or jelly.

cervical cap A birth control device similar to a diaphragm, but smaller.

Effectiveness Rates			
	Typical Use	**Perfect Use**	**Average Cost**
Cervical barrier	84%	94%	$60–$75

Diaphragms come in a variety of different shapes and sizes and must be fitted by a health care professional.

How They Work

Cervical barriers work by blocking the entrance to the uterus and deactivating sperm through the use of spermicidal cream or jelly. Before insertion, spermicidal cream or jelly should be placed inside the device and rubbed on the rim. They are folded and inserted into the vagina while a woman is standing with one leg propped up, squatting, or lying on her back (Figure 11.6). The device should be pushed downward toward the back of the vagina, while the front rim or lip is tucked under the pubic bone. After insertion, a woman must check to see that the device is covering her cervix. Once in place, a woman should not be able to feel the device; if she does, it is improperly inserted.

These methods can be inserted before intercourse but should be left in place for at least 8 hours after intercourse. Users of the Lea's Shield and FemCap can have repeated intercourse without applying additional spermicidal cream or jelly, although health care providers recommend diaphragm users insert additional spermicide into the vagina without removing the device. The diaphragm should not be left in place for longer than 24 hours, whereas Lea's Shield and the FemCap can be left in for up to 48 hours. After use, all the devices should be washed with soap and water and allowed to air-dry.

The FemCap is a silicone cup that fits securely over the cervix.

Effectiveness Rates

Effectiveness rates for these devices range from 84% to 94%. Women who have not had children have higher effectiveness rates than women who have given birth.

Lea's Shield is a silicone cup with a one-way valve and a loop for easier removal.

Insertion of a Diaphragm

Take a closer look.

Advantages

Cervical barriers can be discreetly carried in a purse, are immediately effective, do not affect spontaneity or hormonal levels, allow couples to engage in intercourse multiple times, and may reduce the risk for cervical dysplasia (Cates & Harwood, 2011).

Disadvantages

Cervical barriers require a prescription, do not offer protection from STIs, may be difficult to insert and/or remove, require genital touching, increase postcoital drip, may shift during vaginal intercourse, cannot be used during menstruation, and may develop a foul odor if left in place too long. In addition, some women experience allergic reactions to the spermicidal cream or jelly.

Cross-Cultural Use

Cervical barriers are widely used in England and in some countries—including Germany, Austria, Switzerland, and Canada—Lea's Shield has been available without a prescription since 1993 (Long, 2003). However, similar to cervical barriers, they are used infrequently in less-developed countries. This is possibly related to a shortage of health care providers, limited availability of spermicidal cream or jelly, high cost, and required genital touching.

The Contraceptive Sponge

The Today contraceptive sponge is a one-size-fits-all combination of a cervical barrier and spermicide.

	Effectiveness Rates		
	Typical Use	**Perfect Use**	**Average Cost**
Contraceptive sponge	84%	91%	$13–$17 for 3

How It Works

A contraceptive sponge works in three ways: as a barrier, blocking the entrance to the uterus; absorbing sperm; and deactivating sperm through the use of a spermicide. Before vaginal insertion, the sponge is moistened with water, which activates

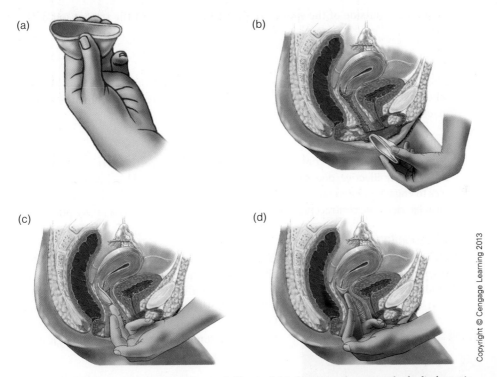

Figure 11.6 Insertion of a diaphragm (and other cervical barriers): (a) after placing the spermicide, the diaphragm is folded in half, rim to rim and (b) inserted into the vagina (c) as far as it will go, (d) check to feel the cervix is covered by the diaphragm.

Copyright © Cengage Learning 2013

the spermicide. It is then folded in half and inserted deep into the vagina (Figure 11.7).

Like the diaphragm and cervical cap, the sponge must be checked to make sure it is covering the cervix. Intercourse can take place immediately after insertion or at any time during the next 24 hours and can occur as many times as desired without adding additional spermicidal jelly or cream. However, the sponge must be left in place for 6 hours after intercourse. Because of the risk for toxic shock syndrome, the sponge should not be worn for more than 30 hours in a row. For removal, a cloth

On Your Mind

Is it okay to borrow someone else's diaphragm if I can't find mine?

loop on the outside of the sponge is grasped to gently pull the sponge out of the vagina.

Effectiveness Rates

Effectiveness rates for the contraceptive sponge range from 84% to 91%. Women who have not had children have higher effectiveness rates than women who have given birth.

Advantages

Like cervical barriers, a contraceptive sponge can be discreetly carried in a purse, is immediately effective, does not affect spontaneity or hormonal levels, and allows couples to engage in intercourse multiple times during a 24-hour period. Unlike the cervical barriers, the contraceptive sponge can be purchased without a prescription.

Disadvantages

The contraceptive sponge does not offer protection from STIs, may be difficult to insert and/or remove, requires genital touching, increases postcoital drip, cannot be used during menstruation, may cause a foul odor if left in place too long, and may increase the risk for toxic shock syndrome and urinary tract infections (Trussell & Guthrie, 2011). In addition, some women experience allergic reactions to the spermicidal cream or jelly.

Cross-Cultural Use

Contraceptive sponges have been fairly popular in European countries. In fact, women in France have used vaginal sponges dipped in various chemicals to avoid pregnancy for years. These sponges are washed and used over and over. This practice is not recommended, however, because of the risk of infection and toxic shock syndrome.

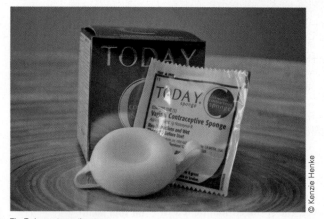

© Kenzie Henke

The Today contraceptive sponge.

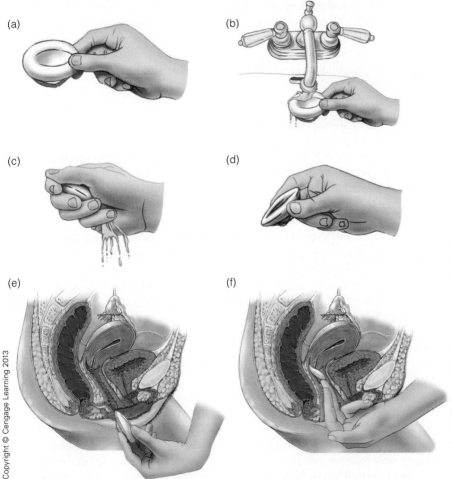

Figure 11.7 Insertion of a contraceptive sponge: (a) take it out of the packaging, (b) moisten with water, (c) wring out extra water, (d) fold in half, (e) insert the sponge into the vagina as far as it will go, (f) check to feel the cervix is covered by the sponge.

Copyright © Cengage Learning 2013

Insertion of a Contraceptive Sponge

Take a closer look.

Check Your Learning Quiz 11.2

Go to **login.cengagebrain.com** and take the online quiz.

▶ **L07** Explain how birth control pills work and identify their effectiveness rates, advantages, and disadvantages.

Combined-hormone methods use a blend of hormones to suppress ovulation and thicken the cervical mucus to prevent sperm from joining the ovum. We will discuss birth control pills, vaginal rings, and patches. Combined hormone methods have been found to be effective, safe, reversible, and acceptable to most women. However, for protection against STIs, condoms must also be used.

Birth Control Pills

After more than 50 years on the market, **oral contraceptives** still remain the most popular contraceptive method not only in the United States, but around the world as well (Frost et al., 2008; Nelson & Cwiak, 2011). The birth control pill was approved as a contraceptive method in the United States in 1960. At first, the pill was much stronger than it needed to be. In the search for the most effective contraception, researchers believed that higher levels of hormones were more effective. Today's birth control pills have less than half the doses of hormones the first pills had.

Combination birth control pills, which contain synthetic estrogen and progestin (a type of progesterone), are the most commonly used contraceptive method in the United States. They require a prescription and a medical office visit, and typically cost between $30 and $60 per month. Chapter 4 discussed menstrual manipulation and menstrual suppression. Typical birth control pills have been designed to mimic an average menstrual cycle, which is why a woman takes them for 21 days and then has 1 week off, when she usually starts her period (these pills are often referred to as 21/7 pills). Originally, this 3-week-on/1-week-off regimen was developed to convince women that the pill was "natural," which pill makers believed would make the product more acceptable to potential users and reassure them that they were not pregnant every month (Clarke & Miller, 2001; Thomas & Ellertson, 2000).

Extended-cycle birth control pills became available in 2003 with the U.S. Food and Drug Administration (FDA) approval of Seasonale, which uses a continuous 84-day active pill with a 7-day placebo pill (an 84/7 pill). Seasonale enabled women to have only four periods per year. In 2006, Seasonique, a similar extended-cycle pill, was approved by the FDA. The difference between Seasonale and Seasonique is in the placebo pills—whereas they are inactive in Seasonale, Seasonique placebo pills contain a low dose of estrogen that has been found to cause less spotting during the active pills. Another continuous birth control pill that completely stops menstrual periods, Lybrel, was approved by the FDA in 2007. Lybrel contains lower levels of estrogen than other pills but is taken daily for 365 days a year.

oral contraceptive The "pill"; a preparation of synthetic female hormones that blocks ovulation.

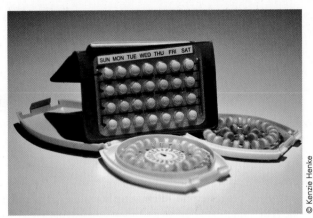

Combination birth control pills.

Today, more than 70 brands of birth control pills are on the market in the United States. They vary with the amount of estrogen (low, regular, high, or varied levels) and the type of progestin (there are eight different types of progestin hormones). Recent studies have found that one type of progestin, *drospirenone,* may increase the risk for cardiovascular problems (Jick & Hernandez, 2011; Reid, 2010; Sehovic & Smith, 2010; Shapiro & Dinger, 2010). It is important to talk to a healthcare provider to determine which pills are right for you.

There has been a very vocal debate in recent years about the relationship between oral contraceptive use and cancer. Although research has found that birth control pill use offers possible protection from breast and cervical cancers (Althuis et al., 2003; Deligeoroglou et al., 2003; Franceschi, 2005; Gaffield et al., 2009; Nelson & Cwiak, 2007, 2011; Marchbanks et al., 2002; Moreno et al., 2002; Vessey et al., 2010), the research on other cancers has been less clear-cut. According to some studies, birth control pill use *increases* the risks for endometrial and ovarian cancers (Burkman et al., 2004; Emons et al., 2000; Greer er al., 2005; Modan et al., 2001; Schildkraut et al., 2002); however, more recent studies have found that use decreases the risks (Grimbizis & Tarlatzis, 2010; Ness et al., 2011; Schindler, 2010; Vessey et al., 2010). In fact, recent studies have found that the use of birth control pills may provide significant protective effect from both ovarian and endometrial cancer, and protection may increase the longer birth control pills are taken (Cibula et al., 2010; Grimbizis & Tarlatzis, 2010; Mueck et al., 2010; Schindler, 2010).

	Effectiveness Rates		
	Typical Use	**Perfect Use**	**Average Cost**
Combination birth control pills	92%	99.7%	$15–$60 per month

How They Work

The hormones estrogen, progesterone, luteinizing hormone (LH), and follicle-stimulating hormone (FSH) fluctuate during a woman's menstrual cycle. These fluctuations control the maturation of an ovum, ovulation, the development of the endometrium, and menstruation. The synthetic hormones replace a woman's own natural hormones but in different amounts. The increase in estrogen and progesterone prevent the pituitary gland from sending hormones to cause the ovaries to begin maturation of an ovum. Hormone levels while taking birth control pills are similar to when a woman is pregnant, and this is what interferes with ovulation. Birth control pills also work by thickening the cervical mucus (which inhibits the mobility of sperm) and by reducing the buildup of the endometrium.

Combination birth control pills can be monophasic, biphasic, or triphasic (try-FAY-sic). Monophasic pills contain the same amount of hormones in each pill, whereas biphasic and triphasic pills vary the hormonal amount. Biphasic pills change the level of hormones once during the menstrual cycle, whereas triphasic pills contain three sets of pills for each week during the cycle. Each week, the hormonal dosage is increased, rather than keeping the hormonal level consistent, as with monophasic pills. **Breakthrough bleeding** is more common in triphasic pills because of the fluctuating hormone levels.

Traditionally, birth control pills have been used on a monthly cycling plan that involved either a 21- or 28-day regimen and started on the first or fifth day of menstruation or on the first Sunday after menstruation. **Start days** vary depending on the pill manufacturer. The majority of manufacturers recommend a Sunday start day, which enables a woman to avoid menstruating during a weekend. Each pill must be taken every day at approximately the same time. This is important because

breakthrough bleeding Slight blood loss from the uterus that may occur when a woman is taking oral contraceptives.

start day The actual day that the first pill is taken in a pack of oral contraceptives.

they work by maintaining a certain hormonal level in the bloodstream. If this level declines, ovulation may occur.

In most 28-day birth control pill packs, the last seven pills are placebo pills. The placebo pills do not contain hormones, and because of this, a woman usually starts menstruating while taking them. In fact, some low-dose pill brands extended usage to 24 days with a reduced 2- or 4-day placebo pill regimen (a 24/2 or 24/4 pill; Nelson & Cwiak, 2011). Women on these extended-cycle regimens report higher levels of satisfaction than women on traditional 21/7 regimens (Caruso et al., 2011; Cremer et al., 2010; Davis et al., 2010; Dinger et al., 2011). Women who take birth control pills usually have lighter menstrual periods and decreased cramping because the pills decrease the buildup of the endometrium.

Before starting on birth control pills, a woman must have a full medical examination. Women with a history of circulatory problems, strokes, heart disease, breast or uterine cancer, hypertension, diabetes, and undiagnosed vaginal bleeding are generally advised not to take oral contraceptives (Nelson & Cwiak, 2011). Although migraine headaches have typically been a reason for not using birth control pills, some women may experience fewer migraines while taking birth control pills, especially if used continuously without placebo pills (Nelson & Cwiak, 2011). If a woman can use birth control pills, health care providers usually begin by prescribing a low-dose estrogen pill, and they increase the dosage if breakthrough bleeding or other symptoms occur.

There are several potential adverse effects to the use of birth control pills. Because the hormones in birth control pills are similar to those during pregnancy, many women experience signs of pregnancy. These may include nausea, increase in breast size, breast tenderness, water retention, increased appetite, fatigue, and high blood pressure (Nelson & Cwiak 2011; see Chapter 10). Symptoms usually disappear within a couple of months, after a woman's body becomes used to the hormonal levels. Other possible adverse effects include migraines, weight gain, depression, and decreases in sexual desire and bone density (Nelson & Cwiak, 2011; Pitts & Emans, 2008). Possible serious adverse effects include blood clots, strokes, or heart attacks.

Effectiveness Rates

Effectiveness rates for oral contraceptives range from 92% to 99.7% (Nelson & Cwiak, 2011). However, women who are significantly overweight may experience lower effectiveness rates using oral contraceptives (Brunner-Huber & Toth, 2007; Gardner, 2004; Nelson & Cwiak, 2011).

What to Do If You Forget

For women using a 21- or 28-day combination birth control pill.

▶ **LO8** Explain how hormonal rings work and identify their advantages and disadvantages.

▶ **LO9** Explain how the hormonal patch works and identify its effectiveness rates, advantages, and disadvantages.

Advantages

Oral contraceptives offer one of the highest effectiveness rates; do not interfere with spontaneity; increase menstrual regularity; and reduce the flow of menstruation, menstrual cramps, premenstrual syndrome, and facial acne (Hatcher et al., 2011). They also provide important degrees of protection against ovarian cysts, uterine and breast fibroids, certain cancers, and **pelvic inflammatory disease**. They may increase sexual enjoyment because fear of pregnancy is reduced, and they have rapid reversibility (the majority of women who stop taking the pill return to ovulation within 2 weeks; Nelson & Cwiak, 2011).

Disadvantages

Oral contraception requires a prescription, provides no protection from STIs, and has several potential adverse effects, including nausea, increase in breast size, headaches, and decreased sexual desire. In addition, oral contraceptives can be expensive, and a woman must remember to take them every day.

Cross-Cultural Use

Worldwide, birth control pills are the third most popular contraceptive method (behind female sterilization and the IUD), with 9% of women relying on this method ("World Contraceptive Use: 2009"). However, usage is higher in more developed countries. Contraceptive pill use is high in Europe but lower in Asian countries. For example, 60% of women use birth control pills in France (Schuberg, 2009), whereas approximately 1% of women in Japan use them (Hayashi, 2004). By comparison, approximately 28% of women in the United States use birth control pills (Alan Guttmacher Institute, 2010).

Birth control pill use is high in Asia, Latin America, Belgium, France, Germany, Morocco, the Netherlands, Portugal, and Zimbabwe ("World Contraceptive Use: 2009"). In some countries, birth control pills are available over-the-counter, without a prescription (Arroba, 2004; Ng & Ma, 2004).

Fears about safety and reliability issues in countries such as Japan and Russia reduce birth control pill use (Hayashi, 2004; Kon, 2004). Birth control pills were not approved for use in Japan until 1999. However, they have remained unpopular because of safety concerns, negative side effects, required daily pill taking, country-wide conservatism, and a lack of advertising (Hayashi, 2004).

pelvic inflammatory disease
Widespread infection of the female pelvic organs.

Hormonal Ring

NuvaRing is a hormonal method of birth control that was approved by the FDA in 2001. It is a one-size-fits-all plastic ring that is inserted into the vagina once a month and releases a constant dose of estrogen and progestin. The amount of hormones released into the bloodstream with the NuvaRing is lower than in both oral contraceptives and the patch (we will talk more about the patch later in this chapter; Nanda, 2011; van den Heuvel et al., 2005).

The Nuva Ring.

	Effectiveness Rates		
	Typical Use	Perfect Use	Average Cost
Hormonal ring	92%	99.7%	$15–$70 per month

How It Works

Like birth control pills, NuvaRing works chiefly by inhibiting ovulation, but it is also likely to increase cervical mucus and changes the uterine lining (Nanda, 2011). The ring is inserted deep inside the vagina, where the vaginal muscles hold it in place, and moisture and body heat activate the release of hormones. Each ring is left in place for 3 weeks and then taken out for 1 week, during which a woman typically has her period. The used ring is disposed of and a new ring is put back in after the week break.

Effectiveness Rates

Effectiveness rates for the NuvaRing range from 92% to 99.7% (Nanda, 2011). Effectiveness rates may be lower when other medications are taken, when the unopened package is exposed to high temperatures or direct sunlight, or when the ring is left in the vagina for more than 3 weeks.

Advantages

The NuvaRing is highly effective, does not interfere with spontaneity, increases menstrual regularity, and reduces the flow of menstruation, menstrual cramps, and premenstrual syndrome (Nanda, 2011). It is easy to use and provides lower levels of hormones than some of the other combined hormone methods. In addition, NuvaRing may also offer some protection from pelvic inflammatory disease and various cancers.

On Your Mind

I usually take my birth control pill every morning at 7 a.m. Should I continue taking it at 7 a.m. after daylight saving time?

Drugs and Herbs That Interact with Oral Contraceptives

When you take medications, you should always let your health care provider know that you are taking birth control pills.

Disadvantages

A prescription is necessary to use NuvaRing, and it offers no protection against STIs. In addition, it requires genital touching and may cause a variety of adverse effects, including breakthrough bleeding, weight gain or loss, breast tenderness, nausea, mood changes, headaches, decreased sexual desire, increased vaginal irritation and discharge, and a risk for toxic shock syndrome (Nanda, 2011; Lopez et al., 2008). It may also take up to 1 to 2 months for a woman's periods to return after she stops using the vaginal ring, and periods may not be regular for up to 6 months.

Cross-Cultural Use

NuvaRing was first approved in the Netherlands in 2001 and has since been approved by many other European countries. Australia approved the NuvaRing in 2007, which brought the total number of countries using NuvaRing to 32 ("NuvaRing now available," 2007). In some countries, usage levels may be low because the NuvaRing requires genital touching. Even so, cross-cultural research has found that the NuvaRing is highly effective and users report high levels of satisfaction with this method (Brucker et al., 2008; Bruni et al., 2008; Merki-Feld & Hund, 2007; Novák et al., 2003).

Hormonal Patch

The Ortho Evra patch is a hormonal method of birth control that was approved by the FDA in 2001. It is a thin, peach-colored patch that sticks to the skin and time-releases hormones into the bloodstream.

	Effectiveness Rates		
	Typical Use	**Perfect Use**	**Average Cost**
Hormonal patch	92%	99.7%	$15–$70 per month

How It Works

Like other hormonal methods, the Ortho Evra patch uses synthetic estrogen and progestin to inhibit ovulation, increase cervical mucus, and render the uterus inhospitable to implantation. The patch is placed on the buttock, stomach, upper arm, or torso (excluding the breast area) once a week for 3 weeks, followed by a patch-free week (break week), which usually causes a woman to have her period. A woman can maintain an active lifestyle with the patch in place—she can swim, shower, use saunas, and exercise without the patch falling off (Burkman, 2002; Zacur et al., 2002).

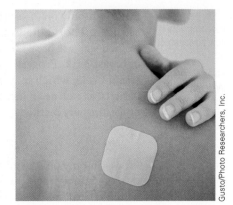

The Ortho Evra contraceptive patch.

Gusto/Photo Researchers, Inc.

Effectiveness Rates

Effectiveness rates for the Ortho Evra patch range from 92% to 99.7% (Nanda, 2011). It may be less effective in women who are significantly overweight (Nanda, 2011; Zieman et al., 202), and as with other hormonal methods, certain medications can decrease effectiveness.

Advantages

The Ortho Evra patch is highly effective, does not interfere with spontaneity, increases menstrual regularity, and reduces menstrual flow, menstrual cramps, and premenstrual syndrome (Nanda, 2011). Unlike other hormonal methods, the patch has a more than 90% perfect dosing level because it is applied directly to the skin (Burkman, 2002).

Disadvantages

The Ortho Evra patch has been found to expose women to higher levels of estrogen than typical birth control pills (Hitti, 2008; U.S. Food and Drug Administration, 2008); offers no protection from STIs; and may cause a variety of adverse effects, including breakthrough bleeding, breast tenderness, nausea, mood changes, changes in sexual desire, skin reactions, or headaches (Nanda, 2011). Users of the hormonal patch may also be more at risk for the development of blood clots (Hitti, 2008; U.S. Food and Drug Administration, 2008).

Cross-Cultural Use

We don't know a lot about Ortho Evra's use outside of the United States because it is fairly new. However, early estimates have found that approximately 2 million women worldwide use the contraceptive patch (Bestic, 2005).

Check Your Learning Quiz 11.3

Go to **login.cengagebrain.com** and take the online quiz.

11.4 *Progestin-Only Hormone Methods*

▸ **LO10** Explain how progestin-only pills work and identify their effectiveness rates, advantages, and disadvantages.

▸ **LO11** Explain how subdermal implants work and identify their effectiveness rates, advantages, and disadvantages.

Progestin-only birth control methods are hormonal methods that do not contain estrogen. The methods can be used by women who cannot take estrogen or by women who are breast-feeding, because the hormones do not affect the production of breast milk. Progestin-only birth control works by changing a woman's menstrual cycle, which may result in changes in menstrual flow and frequency of periods, as well as an increase in breakthrough bleeding. Over time, many users of progestin-only methods report having no periods at all.

Progestin-Only Pills

Progestin-only pills (minipills) are similar to combination birth control pills, except they contain a progestin hormone and no estrogen. Minipills are taken every day with no hormone-free days (Raymond, 2011).

	Effectiveness Rates		
	Typical Use	**Perfect Use**	**Average Cost**
Minipills	92%	99.7%	$15–$60 per month

How They Work
Similar to combination birth control pills, minipills work by inhibiting ovulation, thickening cervical mucus, and decreasing Fallopian tube cilia movement and the buildup of the endometrial lining.

Effectiveness Rates
Effectiveness rates for minipills range from 92% to 99.7% (Raymond, 2011).

Advantages
Minipills contain a lower overall hormone level than combination birth control pills and can be safely used by almost all women, including those who are older than 35, are overweight, smoke, have high blood pressure, have a history of blood clots, or are breast-feeding (Raymond, 2011). They also reduce menstrual symptoms and may eliminate periods altogether. Once discontinued, fertility is quickly restored.

subdermal contraceptive implant Contraceptive implant that time-releases a constant dose of progestin to inhibit ovulation.

Disadvantages
Because minipills contain lower hormone levels, they require obsessive regularity in pill taking (Raymond, 2011). They offer no protection from STIs and may cause sev-

eral adverse effects, including menstrual cycle disturbances (such as breakthrough bleeding or spotting), headaches, nausea, weight gain or loss, breast tenderness, decreased sexual desire, and an increased risk for ovarian cysts (Raymond, 2011).

Subdermal Implants

Subdermal contraceptive implants involve surgically inserting under the skin a matchstick-sized rod that time-releases progestin. Norplant was the first such method introduced in the United States in 1990. However, because of multiple lawsuits and court battles, Norplant was withdrawn from the U.S. market in 2002. As of 2010, the only implant available in the United States is a system called Implanon, which was approved by the FDA in 2006. Several other versions are currently in development both within and outside the United States.

	Effectiveness Rates		
	Typical Use	Perfect Use	Average Cost
Subdermal implant	99%	99%	$400–$800

How They Work

A subdermal contraceptive implant is inserted during the first 5 days of a woman's menstrual cycle (to ensure she is not pregnant). The implant time-releases progestin, and like other hormonal methods, it works by suppressing ovulation, thickening cervical mucus, and changing the endometrial lining. The Implanon implant can be left in place for 3 years. Once removed, ovulation usually returns within approximately 6 weeks (Makarainen et al., 1998).

Effectiveness Rates

Effectiveness rates for Implanon are approximately 99%. Like other hormonal methods, effectiveness rates may be lower in women who are significantly overweight.

Advantages

Implanon is a highly effective, long-lasting, easily reversible contraceptive method with a rapid onset of protection (Raymond, 2011b). It can decrease menstrual flow, cramping, and risk for endometrial cancer, and can be used by women who are

▶ **LO12** Explain how hormonal injectables work and identify their effectiveness rates, advantages, and disadvantages.

unable to take estrogen. In addition, Implanon can be left in place for up to 3 years and can be removed any time before this.

Disadvantages

Implanon requires a prescription and medical office visit, which may be expensive depending on where it is done. Possible adverse effects include irregular or heavy bleeding, especially within the first 6 to 12 months of usage. Other possible adverse effects include headaches, dizziness, nausea, weight gain, development of ovarian cysts, decreases in sexual desire, vaginal dryness, arm pain, and bleeding from the injection site (Raymond, 2011b). Removal may be difficult and generally takes longer than insertion. Researchers are working on a system that involves self-dissolving cylinders so that removal is unnecessary.

Cross-Cultural Use

Subdermal implants are more commonly used in less-developed regions of the world. They are approved in more than 60 countries and have been used by more than 11 million women worldwide (Hatcher et al., 2007; Meirik et al., 2003). Prior to U.S. FDA approval, Norplant and Implanon had been used throughout Europe, Latin America, Australia, and Asia.

In the United Kingdom, healthcare providers have switched from Implanon to a new contraceptive implant, Nexplanon (Mansour, 2010; Rowlands et al., 2010). Nexplanon is easier to insert than Implanon, is good for three years, and has a rapid return to fertility after use.

Hormonal Injectables

The most commonly used hormonal injectable is depo-medroxyprogesterone acetate (DMPA, or Depo-Provera; DEP-poe PRO-vair-uh), which was approved by the FDA for contraceptive use in 1992 (Bartz & Goldberg, 2011).

	Effectiveness Rates		
	Typical Use	Perfect Use	Average Cost
Hormone injectable	97%	99.7%	$35–$70 every 3 months

How They Work

Depo-Provera is a progestin injected into the muscle of a woman's arm or buttock. It begins working within 24 hours. Like other hormonal methods, it works by suppressing ovulation, thickening cervical mucus, and changing the endometrial lining.

Effectiveness Rates

Effectiveness rates for Depo-Provera range from 97% to 99.7% (Bartz & Goldberg, 2011).

Advantages

Depo-Provera is highly effective; does not interfere with spontaneity; reduces menstrual flow, cramping, and premenstrual syndrome; does not contain estrogen; lasts for 3 months; is only moderately expensive; and is reversible (Bartz & Goldberg, 2011). In addition, users need only four shots per year.

Disadvantages

Women who use Depo-Provera must schedule office visits every 3 months for their injections, and they experience a range of adverse effects, including irregular bleeding and spotting, fatigue, dizzy spells, weakness, headaches or migraines, weight gain (it is estimated that a woman will gain an average of 5.4 pounds in the first year of Depo-Provera use), and a decrease in bone density (Bartz & Goldberg, 2011). More recent studies have found that bone loss is reversible after a woman stops using Depo-Provera (Kaunitz et al., 2008; Pitts & Emans, 2008). In addition, it may take a couple months to restore fertility after the last injection (Bartz & Goldberg, 2011; Kaunitz, 2002).

Cross-Cultural Use

Like implants, injectable contraception is more commonly used in less-developed countries. In some regions, such as Eastern and Southern Africa, injectable contraception is the most popular method, accounting for almost half of all contraceptive use. Depo-Provera has been approved for use in more than 80 countries, including Botswana, Denmark, Finland, Great Britain, France, Sweden, Mexico, Norway, Germany, New Zealand, South Africa, and Belgium (Francoeur & Noonan, 2004; Hatcher et al., 2004). In addition, another combination injectable, Lunelle, is popular cross-culturally but is not available within the United States.

Key Terms Exercise

Match the key terms with their definitions.

Check Your Learning Quiz 11.4

Go to **login.cengagebrain.com** and take the online quiz.

An intrauterine device (IUD) is a small device made of flexible plastic that is placed in the uterus to prevent pregnancy (Figure 11.8). The Dalkon Shield was a popular type of IUD up until 1975, when the A. H. Robins Company recommended that it be removed from all women who were using them. Users experienced severe pain, bleeding, and pelvic inflammatory disease, which led to sterility in some cases. The problems with the Dalkon Shield were primarily caused by the multifilament string that allowed bacteria to enter into the uterus through the cervix. As of late 2011, only two IUDs were available in the United States, the ParaGard and Mirena.

Data from the 2006–2008 National Survey of Family Growth (NSFG) found that more than 2 million women in the United States (or 5.5% of women who use contraception) use an IUD, which is the highest level of use since the early 1980s (Mosher & Jones, 2010). Increases in use are due to many factors, including higher safety standards, more physicians and health care providers being trained in insertion and removal techniques, immigration from areas where IUDs are popular (e.g., Mexico), increased advertising, and positive word of mouth from other users (Hubacher et al., 2010).

	Effectiveness Rates		
	Typical Use	**Perfect Use**	**Average Cost**
IUDs	99.2%	99.9%	$500–$1,000 for medical examination, insertion, and follow-up visits

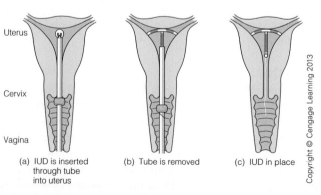

(a) IUD is inserted through tube into uterus
(b) Tube is removed
(c) IUD in place

Uterus
Cervix
Vagina

Copyright © Cengage Learning 2013

Figure 11.8 Insertion of an intrauterine device.

How They Work

The ParaGard IUD is placed in the uterus and causes an increase in copper ions and enzymes, which impairs sperm function and prevents fertilization (Dean & Schwarz, 2011). It can be left in place for up to 12 years. The Mirena IUD time-releases progestin, which thickens the cervical mucus, inhibits sperm survival, and suppresses the endometrium (Dean & Schwarz, 2011). It can be left in place for up to 5 years. The IUD string hangs down from the cervix, and a woman can check the string to make sure the IUD is still properly in place. Both IUDs may also interfere with the implantation of a fertilized ova.

Effectiveness Rates

Effectiveness rates for IUDs range from 99.2% to 99.9% (Dean & Schwarz, 2011).

Advantages

Intrauterine devices are the least expensive method of contraception over time, and they do not interfere with spontaneity. In addition, they have long-lasting contraceptive effects. The Mirena IUD also reduces or eliminates menstrual flow and cramping. IUDs can also be used as emergency contraception (we will discuss emergency contraception later in this chapter). Once the IUD is removed, fertility is quickly restored. IUDs can be used during breast-feeding.

Disadvantages

IUDs require moderately painful insertion and removal procedures, may cause irregular bleeding patterns and spotting (and heavier periods if using the ParaGard IUD), offer no protection from STIs, and carry a small risk for uterine perforation. The IUD may also be felt by a sexual partner.

Cross-Cultural Use

Worldwide, IUDs are the second most popular contraceptive method (behind female sterilization), with 14% of women relying on this method ("World Contraceptive Use: 2009"). However, they are more popular in less developed regions of the world. Whereas 5.5% of women in the United States use IUDs, 15% of women in Western Europe, 12% in Northern Europe, and 9% in Southern Europe use IUDs (Hubacher et al., 2010). The IUD has high usage rates in many Asian countries, Israel, Cuba, Egypt, and Estonia ("World Contraceptive Use: 2009"). The newer Mirena IUD has been available in Europe for more than 10 years, and it is estimated that millions of women have used it throughout the world. Overall, IUD usage rates vary depending on how much the devices are marketed and advertised.

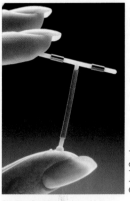

© Joel Gordon

The ParaGard is a T-shaped intra-uterine device (IUD) made of flexible plastic; it contains copper and can be left in place for up to 12 years.

© Joel Gordon

The Mirena is a T-shaped IUD made of flexible plastic; it continuously releases a small amount of progestin and can be left in place for up to 5 years.

Insertion of an IUD

Take a closer look.

Check Your Learning Quiz 11.5

Go to **login.cengagebrain.com** and take the online quiz.

Natural methods of contraception do not alter any physiological function. They include fertility awareness–based methods, natural family planning, withdrawal, and abstinence.

Fertility Awareness–Based Methods

Fertility awareness–based methods involve identifying a woman's fertile period and either abstaining from vaginal intercourse or using another contraceptive method during this time. With the **rhythm method**, a couple simply keeps track of a woman's cycle; other, more intensive methods involve charting and recording physical fertility signs (such as monitoring daily **basal body temperature (BBT)** and checking cervical mucus; Jennings & Burke, 2011). Typically, these intensive methods are referred to as natural family planning, or the symptothermal method.

	Effectiveness Rates		
	Typical Use	Perfect Use	Average Cost
Symptothermal method	88%	97%	Not applicable

rhythm method A contraceptive method that involves calculating the period of ovulation and avoiding sexual intercourse around this time.

basal body temperature (BBT) The body's resting temperature used to calculate ovulation in the symptothermal method of contraception.

CycleBeads can be used with fertility awareness-based methods to help determine fertile days. A ring is moved over a series of color-coded beads that represent low- and high-fertility days.

© Kenzie Henke

How They Work

With the symptothermal method, a woman takes her BBT every morning before she gets out of bed and records it on a BBT chart. Changes in hormonal levels cause body temperature to increase 0.4° to 0.8°F (0.2°–0.4°C) immediately before ovulation, and it remains elevated until menstruation begins. A woman using this method monitors her cervical mucus, which becomes thin and stretchy during ovulation to help transport sperm. At other times of the month, cervical mucus is thicker. After 6 months of consistent charting, a woman will be able to estimate the approximate time of ovulation, and she can then either abstain from vaginal intercourse or use contraception during her high-risk times (usually this period is between 1 and 2 weeks). Some women use CycleBeads to help determine their fertile days.

Effectiveness Rates

Effectiveness rates for fertility awareness-based methods range from 88% to 97% (Jennings & Burke, 2011). However, effectiveness rates depend on the accuracy of identifying a fertile period and a couple's ability to avoid intercourse (or use another contraceptive method) during this time.

Advantages

Fertility awareness–based methods are an acceptable form of birth control for those who cannot use another method for religious reasons. They can teach couples about the menstrual cycle, are inexpensive, may encourage couples to communicate more about contraception, can involve the male partner, and have no medical side effects. This method can also be helpful when a woman is ready to get pregnant because she may be familiar with when she is ovulating. Couples who use these methods often use a variety of sexual expressions when they avoid intercourse during the fertile period.

Disadvantages

Fertility awareness–based methods restrict spontaneity and provide no protection from STIs. In addition, they take time and commitment to learn, and require several cycles of records before they can be used reliably. The majority of failures with this method are due to couples engaging in intercourse too close to ovulation. A woman may ovulate earlier or later than usual because of diet, stress, or alcohol use. These methods are often best suited for those needing to space pregnancies, rather than for those who want to avoid pregnancy.

Cross-Cultural Use

Fertility awareness-based contraceptive methods are popular around the world. This is mostly because they are inexpensive and do not require much assistance from health care providers. These methods are commonly used parts of Africa, Western Asia, and Eastern Europe. These methods may be the only form of acceptable contraception in predominantly Catholic countries such as Ireland, Brazil, and the Philippines. In the Philippines, natural family planning and the rhythm method are thought to improve a couple's relationship because they need to work together to use the method (remember our earlier discussion about pressure from the Church against using modern methods of contraception in the Philippines; Leyson, 2004). Societal issues and marketing may also affect the use of this method. For example, cultural resistance to condom use has increased the popularity of these methods in Kenya, where it is the most commonly used contraceptive method (Brockman, 2004). Today, many women's groups from the United States travel to developing countries to teach fertility awareness-based methods.

Withdrawal and Abstinence

Withdrawal (or coitus interruptus) involves withdrawing the penis from the vagina before ejaculation. Although withdrawal is a popular contraceptive method, many couples use it because of convenience and dissatisfaction with other methods (Whittaker et al., 2010). When women in the National Survey of Family Growth study (see Chapter 1) were asked about using withdrawal, 59% reported they had used it as a contraceptive method (Kowal, 2011). However, many couples express anxiety about using it because it relies on the male to pull out in time. Withdrawal can be used alone or in conjunction with another contraceptive method.

	Effectiveness Rates		
	Typical Use	**Perfect Use**	**Average Cost**
Coitus interruptus	73%	96%	Not applicable

How It Works

Withdrawal does not require any advance preparation. A couple engages in vaginal intercourse; before ejaculation, the male withdraws his penis away from the vaginal opening of the woman. The ejaculate does not enter the vagina.

Effectiveness Rates

Effectiveness rates for withdrawal range from 73% to 96% (Kowal, 2011).

Advantages

Withdrawal is an acceptable method of birth control for those who cannot use another method for religious reasons. It is free, does not require any devices or chemicals, and is better than using no method at all (Kowal, 2011). In addition, it may be a good method for couples who don't have another method available.

Disadvantages

Withdrawal provides no protection from STIs, may contribute to ejaculatory problems, and can be difficult and stressful to use. Many men experience a mild-to-extreme "clouding of consciousness" just before orgasm when physical movements become involuntary (Kowal, 2011). This method also requires trust from the female partner.

Cross-Cultural Use

Withdrawal is a popular contraceptive method throughout the world. It is one of the most frequently used methods in Austria, the Czech Republic, Greece, Ireland, and Italy (Francoeur & Noonan, 2004). In Azerbaijan, 64% of contraceptive users rely on withdrawal ("World Contraceptive Use: 2009"). Overall, it is a popular contraceptive method for couples with limited contraceptive choices or for those who are reluctant to use modern methods of contraception. In many countries, such as Iran, a lack of education and misconceptions about withdrawal has led to low usage rates (Rahnama et al., 2010). Many Iranian men and women believe that withdrawal does not work and will lead to multiple health problems, which it does not.

Abstinence

Withdrawal is a decision made during vaginal intercourse, whereas abstinence is the decision not to engage in vaginal intercourse at all. It is the only 100% effective contraceptive method (Kowal, 2011). It has probably been the most important factor in controlling fertility throughout history. Abstinence may be primary (never having engaged in vaginal intercourse) or secondary (not currently engaging in vaginal intercourse). Couples may choose abstinence to prevent pregnancy, to protect against STIs, or for many other reasons.

Key Terms Exercise

Match the key terms with their definitions.

Check Your Learning Quiz 11.6

Go to **login.cengagebrain.com** and take the online quiz.

Male and female **sterilization** methods are the most commonly used contraceptive methods in the United States (Roncari & Hou, 2011). The National Survey of Family Growth study (see Chapter 1) reported that 16.7% of all women aged 15 to 44 years who were using contraception relied on tubal sterilization, whereas 6.1% relied on a partner's vasectomy (Mosher & Jones, 2010).

	Effectiveness Rates		
	Typical Use	**Perfect Use**	**Average Cost**
Female sterilization	99%	99.9%	$2,000–$5,000
Male sterilization	99%	99.9%	$300–$1,000

The primary difference between sterilization and other methods of contraception is that sterilization is typically considered irreversible. Although some people have been able to have their sterilizations reversed, this can be expensive and time-consuming (Peterson, 2008). The majority of people who request sterilization reversals do so because they have remarried and desire children with their new partners.

Female Sterilization

sterilization Surgical contraceptive method that causes permanent infertility.

cauterization A sterilization procedure that involves burning or searing the Fallopian tubes or vas deferens for permanent sterilization.

ligation A sterilization procedure that involves the tying or binding of the Fallopian tubes or vas deferens.

laparoscope A tiny scope that can be inserted through the skin and allows for the viewing of the uterine cavity.

vasectomy A surgical procedure in which each vas deferens is cut, tied, or cauterized for permanent contraception.

Female sterilization, or tubal sterilization, is the most widely used method of birth control in the world (Roncari & Hou, 2011). In a tubal sterilization, a health care provider may close or block both Fallopian tubes so that the ovum and sperm cannot meet. Blocking the tubes can be done with **cauterization**; a ring, band, or clamp (which pinches the tube together); or **ligation**; or nonsurgical procedures that involve placing inserts to block the Fallopian tubes. In the United States, female sterilization procedures are generally done with the use of a **laparoscope** through a small incision either under the navel or lower in the abdomen. After the procedure, a woman continues to ovulate, but the ovum does not enter the uterus.

One nonsurgical sterilization method for women is Essure, which was approved in the United States in 2002. Essure is a tiny, springlike device that is threaded into the Fallopian tubes (Figure 11.9). Within 3 months, the body's own tissue grows around the device, blocking fertilization. A woman using this method must

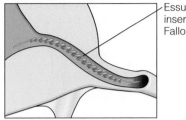
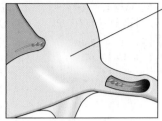

Essure is inserted into the Fallopian tube

Body tissue grows into the Essure micro-insert, blocking the Fallopian tube

Figure 11.9 Insertion of Essure, a permanent contraceptive method.

undergo testing to make sure that the Fallopian tubes are fully blocked. Essure is considered an irreversible method of female sterilization (Roncari & Hou, 2011; Ledger, 2004).

Another nonsurgical sterilization method, Adiana, was approved by the FDA in 2009. This sterilization method involves placing small, silicone inserts in the Fallopian tubes that stimulate the body's own tissue to grow around the inserts, blocking the tubes. Both of these methods require follow-up visits with a health care provider to ensure the tubes are blocked.

Overall, the majority of women who choose permanent sterilization are content with their decision to do so (although the risk for regret is highest in women who undergo these procedures before age 30; Jamieson et al., 2002; Peterson, 2008). No hormonal changes occur, and ovaries continue to work and produce estrogen. Women maintain their levels of sexual interest and desire after permanent sterilization and report more positive than negative sexual side effects (Costello et al., 2002).

Male Sterilization

Male sterilization, or **vasectomy**, blocks the flow of sperm through the vas deferens. Typically, this procedure is simpler, less expensive, and has lower rates of complications than female sterilization (Shih et al., 2011). Even so, vasectomies are performed at less than 50% the rate of female sterilizations (Shih et al., 2011). It is also the least used in Black and Latino populations, which have the highest rates of female sterilization.

After a vasectomy, the testes continue to produce viable sperm cells, but with nowhere to go, they die and are absorbed by the body. Semen normally contains

Permanent Contraception

A new permanent contraceptive procedure involves the injection of an insert into each Fallopian tube.

Essure

Take a closer look.

Vasectomy

Take a closer look.

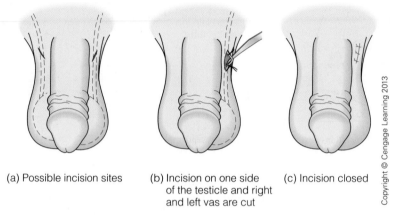

(a) Possible incision sites

(b) Incision on one side of the testicle and right and left vas are cut

(c) Incision closed

Copyright © Cengage Learning 2013

Figure 11.10 In a vasectomy, each vas deferens is clipped, cut, or cauterized.

approximately 98% fluid and 2% sperm; after a vasectomy, the man still ejaculates semen, but the semen contains no sperm (there is no overall change in volume or texture of the semen after a vasectomy). All other functions, such as the manufacturing of testosterone, erections, and urination, are unaffected by a vasectomy procedure.

The surgery for a vasectomy is performed as outpatient surgery with local anesthesia. Two small incisions about a 0.25 to 0.5 inch long are made in the scrotum, and the vas deferens is clipped or cauterized (Figure 11.10).

Men are advised to use another form of contraception for 12 weeks after a vasectomy to ensure that there is no sperm left in the ejaculate (Roncari & Hou, 2011). Typically, one or two repeat semen analyses are required to evaluate whether there is viable sperm in the sample. Semen samples can be collected during masturbation or through the use of a special condom during vaginal intercourse. In 2008, the FDA approved a postvasectomy home sperm test called SpermCheck, which allows a man to test his semen sample at home rather than returning to a medical facility (Coppola et al., 2010).

After a vasectomy, a man may experience swelling, bleeding, bruising, or pain, but generally these subside within 2 weeks (Roncari & Hou, 2011). The cost for the procedure varies widely depending on where it is done.

Effectiveness Rates

Effectiveness rates for both male and female sterilization procedures range from 99% to 99.9% (Roncari & Hou, 2011). Tubal sterilizations are effective immediately, whereas vasectomies require semen analysis for 12 weeks after the procedure to ensure no viable sperm remains.

Advantages

Sterilization is a highly effective, permanent method of contraception. It does not interfere with hormones, offers few long-term adverse effects, and, once completed, does not interfere with spontaneity (Shih et al., 2011).

Disadvantages

Sterilization requires medical intervention and/or surgery, can be expensive, provides no protection from STIs, and is considered irreversible.

Cross-Cultural Use

Worldwide, female sterilization is used by more women than any other contraceptive method. However, this procedure is more popular in less developed regions of the world. Overall, female sterilizations are more popular than male sterilizations, even though these procedures are often expensive and have more potential risks. In China, although 32% of women go under sterilization, only 6% of men do (Wu, 2010).

In Brazil and India, nearly two-fifths of women elect sterilizations, and most women do this early in their reproductive life (Brazilian women have the surgery at about 30 years old, whereas Indian women have it at about 26 years old; Leone & Padmadas, 2007). The Essure method has been used outside of the United States in many countries in Europe, as well as in Mexico, Brazil, Venezuela, Chile, and Uruguay.

In countries where family planning clinics are sparse, many women travel long distances to be sterilized. In some countries, female sterilization procedures are outpatient procedures using local anesthesia (Hatcher et al., 2007). As we have discussed, access to and promotion of a certain method also contribute to its popularity. In addition, cultural acceptance of female sterilization has also led to higher rates of usage (Leone & Padmadas, 2007).

**Check Your Learning
Quiz 11.7**

Go to **login.cengagebrain.com**
and take the online quiz.

▶ **L019** Discuss the primary reasons for the use of emergency contraception and explain the outcome of taking an emergency contraceptive pill.

Emergency contraception can prevent pregnancy when taken shortly after unprotected vaginal intercourse. It is designed to be used in cases in which no contraception was used, contraception was used improperly (such as missed or delayed birth control pills, hormonal injections, replacement vaginal rings or patches), a male condom slipped or broke, a female condom or barrier device was improperly inserted or dislodged during intercourse, an IUD was expelled, or a sexual assault occurred (Trussell & Schwarz, 2011). There are some misconceptions about emergency contraception. Although it is referred to as the "morning after pill," this is misleading because the pill can be used 3 to 5 days after unprotected intercourse, not just the morning after. In addition, it is important to point out that emergency contraception does *not* cause an abortion. Emergency contraception is birth control in that it works to *prevent* pregnancy (we will talk more about abortion later in this chapter).

Plan B is the only progestin-only method of emergency contraception approved by the FDA. (Next Choice is the generic equivalent to Plan B.) This method works by inhibiting ovulation, thickening cervical mucus, and reducing endometrial buildup. If taken within 3 days (72 hours) of vaginal intercourse, Plan B or Next Choice can reduce the likelihood of pregnancy by 81% to 90%. It is available without a prescription to men and women who are older than 17 and costs $35 to $60 (Kavanaugh & Schwarz, 2008).

Concerns about emergency contraception being available without a prescription have raised fears about increased sexual risk taking in women. However, research has shown this is not the case; having available emergency contraception has not been found to increase sexual risk taking (M. Gold et al., 2004; Hu et al., 2005; Raymond et al., 2006).

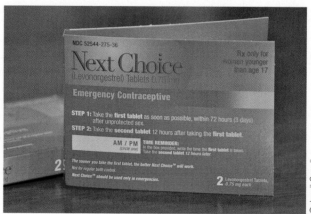

Emergency contraception, such as Next Choice, must be taken within 72 hours to prevent pregnancy.

© Janell Carroll

In mid-2010, the FDA approved ella, a new, nonhormonal form of emergency contraception. Ella is a single-dose pill that can prevent pregnancy up to 5 days after unprotected intercourse. However, as of late 2011, ella was available only by prescription. The benefit of ella over Plan B is that it has a higher effectiveness rate (98%) and a longer window in which it can be used (5 versus 3 days).

Other options for emergency contraception include the use of ordinary birth control pills or the insertion of a copper-releasing IUD (Trussell & Schwarz, 2011; Jensen, 2008). However, using birth control pills as emergency contraception can lead to adverse effects of nausea, vomiting, cramping, breast tenderness, headaches, abdominal pain, fatigue, and dizziness (Trussell & Schwarz, 2011). The incidence of these side effects is significantly lower in women who use Plan B or Next Choice, since they do not contain estrogen. The IUD insertion method is used much less frequently than other methods of emergency contraception. Adverse effects for emergency insertion of a copper-releasing IUD include abdominal discomfort and vaginal bleeding or spotting (Trussell & Schwarz, 2011).

Studies have found that 10% (or 5.1 million) of U.S. women aged 15 to 44 years have used emergency contraception at least once between 2006 and 2008 (Mosher & Jones, 2010). The typical user of emergency contraception in the United States is single, educated, without children, and between the ages of 15 and 25 (Phipps et al., 2008). Outside the United States, emergency contraception has been available in many countries throughout the world, including Australia, Belgium, Canada, China, Denmark, Finland, France, Greece, Iceland, India, Israel, Jamaica, Libya, New Zealand, the Netherlands, Norway, Portugal, Senegal, South Africa, Sri Lanka, Sweden, Switzerland, Tunisia, the United Kingdom, and many other countries. Emergency contraception is registered in 134 countries around the world, and in 63 of these countries, women have access to emergency contraception without a prescription (Wanja, 2010). It can be purchased without a prescription in countries such as France (since 1999), Norway (since 2000), Sweden (since 2001), the Netherlands (since 2004), and India (since 2005). In France, emergency contraception is free of charge.

Research on global users of emergency contraception found that 24- to 25-year-old Kenyan women are the major users of emergency contraception (Wanja, 2010). High usage was noted during weekends and holidays. In 2009, Europe approved ella, and today it is available in many countries around the world, including Austria, Belgium, Bulgaria, the Czech Republic, Denmark, Finland, France, Germany, Greece, Guadeloupe, Hungary, Iceland, Lithuania, Monaco, Netherlands, Norway, Poland, Portugal, Romania, Spain, Sweden, and the United Kingdom.

Morning After Pill

Program exploring the possible impact of the pill on sexual health and abortion rates.

Check Your Learning Quiz 11.8

Go to **login.cengagebrain.com** and take the online quiz.

Because family planning involves controlling conception and birth, there are two main methods to achieve these goals: contraception and **abortion** (Leonard, 2006). Many believe that the ability to determine whether and when to have a child is a necessity today (Boonstra et al., 2006). At the beginning of this chapter, we pointed out that the typical American woman spends at least 30 years trying *not* to get pregnant. Although the majority of women have used contraception, we know that many methods are difficult to use consistently and/or effectively, and no method is 100% effective. Unintended pregnancies do occur when a woman is using effective contraception, even though they are much more likely to occur when a woman uses no contraception. In fact, 52% of unintended pregnancies occur in the 11% of the women who use no contraception (Boonstra et al., 2006). For women with stable relationships or the resources to raise a child, or both, an unintended pregnancy might not present much of a hardship. However, for many women, an unintended pregnancy can lead to serious consequences.

Abortion Statistics

In the United States, women who have abortions are most likely to be in their 20s, poor or with a low income, unmarried, and from ethnic or racial minorities (Cohen, 2008; Jones et al., 2010). In 2008, 36% of women having abortions were non-Hispanic White women, 30% were non-Hispanic Black women, 25% were Hispanic women, and 9% were non-Hispanic women of other races (Jones et al., 2010). Higher abortion rates are directly related to rates of unintended pregnancy, which is typically a result of the lack of access to high-quality contraception, as well as a lack of consistency in using certain methods (Cohen, 2008).

Although many believe that young teenagers are the ones most likely to have abortions, the largest group of women having abortions is in their 20s, followed by women in their 30s (Jones et al., 2010). Although most of these women were unmarried and not living with their partners at the time of the abortion, the majority were in relationships (Jones et al., 2010).

The Abortion Debate

Today, abortion is the moral issue of the times in the United States. It is an issue that leads many people to question the role that the government should play in their lives. Disagreements about this issue have been very emotional and, at times, even violent. In 2009, Dr. George Tiller, one of only a few doctors who provided abortions late in a pregnancy, was murdered (Stumpe & Davey, 2009). He had received

abortion Induced termination of a pregnancy before fetal viability.

Chapter Outline and Learning Objectives

Prepare to Learn

1 **GO** to your **Psychology CourseMate** at **login.cengagebrain.com** and take the **Chapter Pre-Test** to introduce yourself to this chapter's topics and see what you may already know.

2 **READ** the **Learning Objectives** (LOs, in the left sidebars) and begin the chapter.

3 **COMPLETE** the **Online Activities** (in the right sidebars) *as you read each module.* Activities include **videos, animations, readings,** and **quizzes.**

4 **CHECK Your Learning** by going online to take the quiz at the end of each module and review material as necessary.

5 **MEASURE Your Learning** after reading the chapter by taking the online **Chapter Post-Test.** Use the chapter review guide at the end of the chapter as needed.

WATCH for these **Online Activities** icons as you read:

| Video | Animation | Reading | Assessment | Think Critically |

These Online Activities are essential to mastering this chapter. Go to login.cengagebrain.com.

 Videos Explore diverse perspectives on sex as well as common questions:

- Can I get a sexually transmitted infection by having oral sex?
- What sexually transmitted infections do gynecologists check for during a regular exam?
- Can crabs be spread through casual contact, such as sleeping on the same sheets?
- Should I get an "over-the-counter" cream if I have an itchy vaginal discharge?
- Testing Positive for HSV: Why Me?
- My Side of the Story
- Can people still transmit herpes if they don't have any blisters or symptoms?

- Irregular Pap Smears, LEEPs, and the HPV Vaccine
- How does the HPV vaccine work?
- HIV/AIDS: Orel's Story

 Animations Interact with and visualize important processes, timelines, and concepts:

- Key Terms Exercise

 Readings Delve deeper into key content:

- High-Risk Sexual Behaviors
- Global Aspects of AIDS
- Microbicides

 Assessment Measure your mastery:

- Chapter Pre-Test
- Check Your Learning Quizzes
- Chapter Post-Test

Think Critically Challenge your thinking about data and accepted norms:

- Preventing Sexually Transmitted Infections

▶ **L01** Discuss the attitudes and risk factors that contribute to the incidence of sexually transmitted infections in the United States.

MORE THAN 19 MILLION CASES of sexually transmitted infections (STIs) are reported each year in the United States, and almost 50% of these are in young people aged 15 to 24 (Centers for Disease Control and Prevention, 2009d). However, because many STIs are either unreported or undiagnosed, the actual numbers are much higher. We live in a society that is often reluctant to openly discuss issues related to sexuality; as a result, communication about STIs is difficult for many of us.

▼

Attitudes about Sexually Transmitted Infections

Sexually transmitted infections have historically been viewed as symbols of corrupt sexuality (P. L. Allen, 2000). When compared with other illnesses, such as cancer or diabetes, attitudes about STIs have been considerably more negative, and many people believe that people so afflicted "got what they deserved." This has been referred to as the punishment concept of disease. It was generally believed that, to acquire an STI, one must break the silent moral code of sexual responsibility. Those who become infected, therefore, have done something bad, for which they are being punished.

High-Risk Groups and Sexually Transmitted Infections

Gender and racial/ethnic disparities also exist in STI rates. Women are at greater risk for long-term complications from STIs than men because the tissue of the vagina is much more fragile than penile skin. Heterosexual women have another additional risk because semen often remains in the female reproductive tract (Bolton et al., 2008; CDC, Division of STD Prevention, 2007). Women are also more likely to be **asymptomatic**; therefore, they do not know that they are infected. Some infections, such as herpes and HIV, also have properties of **latency**. As a result, infected individuals may be unaware that they are infecting others. This is why it is important to tell all sexual partners about an STI if you are infected. In fact, in 2008, the CDC formally recommended testing for men and women whose partners have been infected with HIV, syphilis, chlamydia, or gonorrhea (Dooley, 2008).

asymptomatic Without recognizable symptoms.

latency A period in which a person is infected with a sexually transmitted infection but does not test positive for it.

Overall, Black communities have higher rates of many STIs than other groups in the United States (Barrow et al., 2008).

Over the past several decades, the rates of STIs in men who have sex with men (MSM) have been increasing. Compared with heterosexual men and women, MSM report significantly more sexual risk taking (i.e., inconsistent condom use and multiple sexual partners; Workowski & Berman, 2010). MSM are also at greater risk for anal cancer from engaging in anal sex with infected partners. Women who have sex with women (WSW) do have some level of risk for bacterial and viral STIs (Workowski & Berman, 2010). Transmission can occur with skin-to-skin contact, oral sex, or vaginal or anal sex using hands, fingers, or sex toys.

Birth Control, Pregnancy, and Sexually Transmitted Infections

In 1993, the Food and Drug Administration (FDA) approved labeling contraceptives for STI protection. Barrier methods, such as condoms, diaphragms, or contraceptive sponges, can decrease the risk of acquiring an STI, although the FDA recommended revised labeling on condom packaging in 2005 to indicate that condoms must be used "consistently and correctly" to decrease STI risk (Alonso-Zaldivar & Neuman, 2005).

When a woman does become pregnant, untreated STIs can adversely affect her pregnancy. Syphilis, gonorrhea, chlamydia, herpes, hepatitis B, and HIV, can cause miscarriage, stillbirth, early onset of labor, premature rupture of the amniotic sac, mental retardation, and fetal or uterine infection (Kimberlin, 2007; Su et al, 2010). Syphilis can cross the placenta and infect a developing fetus, whereas other STIs, such as gonorrhea, chlamydia, and herpes, can infect a newborn as he or she moves through the vagina during delivery. HIV can cross the placenta, infect a newborn at birth, or, unlike other STIs, be transmitted during breast-feeding (Salazar-Gonazalez, et al., 2011).

Bacterial STIs can be treated during pregnancy with antibiotics, and if treatment is begun immediately, there is less chance the newborn will become infected. Antiviral medications can be given to pregnant women to lessen the symptoms of viral infections (Bardeguez et al., 2008; Kriebs, 2008). If there are active vaginal lesions or sores from an STI at the time of delivery, a health care provider may recommend a cesarean section. Women who do not know their partner's STI history should always use latex condoms during pregnancy.

High-Risk Sexual Behaviors

Certain sexual behaviors increase your risk of acquiring a sexually transmitted infection.

On Your Mind

Can I get a sexually transmitted infection by having oral sex?

On Your Mind

What sexually transmitted infections do gynecologists check for during a regular exam?

Check Your Learning Quiz 12.1

Go to **login.cengagebrain.com** and take the online quiz.

Ectoparasitic infections are those that are caused by parasites that live on the skin's surface. The two ectoparasitic infections that are sexually transmitted are pubic lice and scabies.

Pubic Lice

Pubic lice (or "crabs") are a parasitic STI; the lice are very small, wingless insects that can attach themselves to pubic hair with their claws. They feed off the tiny blood vessels just beneath the skin and are often difficult to detect on light-skinned people. Under closer observation, it is possible to see the movement of their legs. They may also attach themselves to other hairy parts of the body, although they tend to prefer pubic hair. When not attached to the human body, pubic lice cannot survive more than 24 hours. However, they reproduce rapidly, and the female cements her eggs to the sides of pubic hair. The eggs hatch in 7 to 9 days, and the newly hatched nits (baby pubic lice) reproduce within 17 days.

Pubic lice attach to pubic hair and feed off the tiny blood vessels beneath the skin.

The Wellcome Medical Photo Library, London

Incidence

Pubic lice are common and regularly seen by health clinics and various health care providers. Although there are no mandated reporting laws, pubic lice affect millions of people worldwide.

Symptoms

The most common symptom is a mild to unbearable itching, which often increases during the evening hours. This itching is thought to be a result of an allergic reaction to the saliva that the lice secrete during their feeding. People who are not allergic to this saliva may not experience any itching.

Diagnosis

The itching usually forces a person to seek treatment, although some people detect the lice visually first. Diagnosis is usually made fairly quickly because the pubic lice and eggs can be seen with the naked eye.

Treatment

To treat pubic lice, it is necessary to kill both the insects and their eggs. In addition, the eggs must be destroyed on sheets and clothing. Health care providers can prescribe *Kwell* ointment, which comes in a shampoo or cream. The cream must be applied directly to the pubic hair and left on for approximately 12 hours, whereas the shampoo can be applied and directly rinsed off. There are also some fairly effective over-the-counter products that can be purchased in drugstores; however, these products are usually not as effective as *Kwell*. Sheets and all articles of clothing should be either dry cleaned, boiled, or machine washed in very hot water. As with other STIs, it is important to tell all sexual partners to be checked for lice because they are highly contagious.

Scabies

Scabies is an ectoparasitic infection of the skin with the mite *Sarcoptes scabiei*. It is spread during skin-to-skin contact, both during sexual and nonsexual contact. The mites can live for up to 48 hours on bed sheets and clothing and are impossible to see with the naked eye.

Incidence

Infection with scabies occurs worldwide and among all races, ethnic groups, and social classes. Like pubic lice, there are no mandated reporting laws, but scabies affects millions of people worldwide.

Symptoms

Usually the first symptoms include a rash and intense itching. The first time a person is infected, the symptoms may take between 4 and 6 weeks to develop. If a person has been infected with scabies before, the symptoms usually develop more quickly.

Diagnosis

A diagnosis can usually be made on examination of the skin rash. A skin scraping can be done to confirm the diagnosis. A delay in diagnosis can lead to a rapid spread of scabies, so immediate diagnosis and treatment are necessary (Tjioe & Vissers, 2008).

Treatment

Topical creams are available to treat scabies. All bed sheets, clothing, and towels must be washed in hot water, and all sexual partners should be treated. Usually itching continues for 2 to 3 weeks after infection, even after treatment.

On Your Mind

Can crabs be spread through casual contact, such as sleeping on the same sheets?

Check Your Learning Quiz 12.2

Go to **login.cengagebrain.com** and take the online quiz.

Gonorrhea, syphilis, and chlamydia are STIs caused by a bacterial infection.

Gonorrhea

Gonorrhea (the "clap" or "drip") is caused by the bacterium *Neisseria gonorrhoeae*. The bacteria can survive only in the mucous membranes of the body, such as the cervix, urethra, mouth, throat, rectum, and even the eyes. Transmission of gonorrhea occurs when mucous membranes come into contact with each other; this can occur during vaginal intercourse, oral sex, vulva-to-vulva sex, and anal sex.

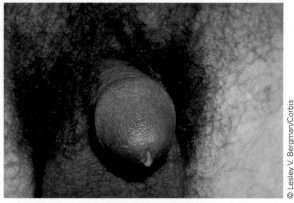

The majority of men infected with gonorrhea experience symptoms and will seek out treatment. However, this may not happen until they have already infected others.

© Lesley V. Bergman/Corbis

Incidence

In 2010, there were 309,341 cases of gonorrhea reported in the United States, although the CDC estimates the actual number of cases was probably much higher (Centers for Disease Control and Prevention, 2011). As shown in Figure 12.1, gonorrhea rates in 2010 were higher in women than in men and highest in those aged 15 to 24 years.

Research has also found racial differences. As shown in Figure 12.2, the rate of gonorrhea in Black men was 26 times greater than in White men in 2010, whereas the rate in Black women was 17 times greater than in White women.

Symptoms and Diagnosis

Most men who are infected with gonorrhea experience symptoms, although they can infect others before the onset of symptoms (Workowski & Berman, 2010). Symptoms typically appear between 2 and 6 days after infection and may include urethral discharge, painful urination, and an increase in the frequency and urgency of urination.

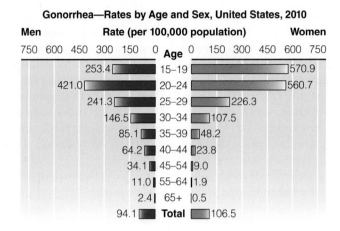

Figure 12.1 Gonorrhea rates by age and sex, United States, 2010. Source: Centers for Disease Control and Prevention, 2011

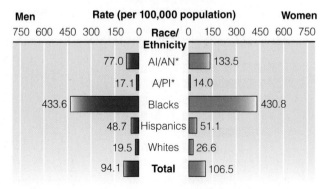

Figure 12.2 Gonorrhea rates by race, ethnicity, and sex: United States, 2010. Source: Centers for Disease Control and Prevention, 2011

▶ **LO4** Identify the cause of syphilis, and summarize the incidence, symptoms, diagnosis, and treatment of this sexually transmitted infection.

Unlike men, the majority of women do not experience symptoms until complications develop, such as pelvic inflammatory disease (PID). If symptoms do develop, they typically begin within 3 to 5 days and include an increase in urinary frequency, abnormal uterine bleeding, and bleeding after vaginal penetration, which results from an irritation of the cervix. The cervical discharge can irritate the vaginal lining, causing pain and discomfort. Urination can be difficult and painful.

Rectal gonorrhea, which can be transmitted to men and women during anal intercourse, may cause bloody stools and pus-like discharge. If left untreated, gonorrhea can move throughout the body and settle in various areas, including the joints, causing swelling, pain, and pus-filled infections.

Testing for gonorrhea involves collecting a sample of the discharge from the cervix, urethra, or another infected area with a cotton swab.

Treatment

The recommended treatment for gonorrhea infection is antibiotics—typically an injection of Ceftriaxone (one dose) or a variety of other antibiotic combinations (Workowski & Berman, 2010). Because patients with gonorrhea are often co-

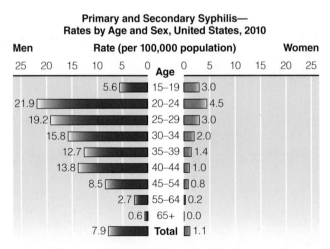

**Primary and Secondary Syphilis—
Rates by Age and Sex, United States, 2010**

Men	Rate (per 100,000 population)	Age		Women
5.6		15–19	3.0	
21.9		20–24	4.5	
19.2		25–29	3.0	
15.8		30–34	2.0	
12.7		35–39	1.4	
13.8		40–44	1.0	
8.5		45–54	0.8	
2.7		55–64	0.2	
0.6		65+	0.0	
7.9		**Total**	1.1	

congenital syphilis A syphilis infection acquired by an infant from the mother during pregnancy.

Figure 12.3 Primary and secondary syphilis rates by age and sex, 2010.
Source: Centers for Disease Control and Prevention, 2011

infected with other STIs, such as chlamydia, dual treatment is possible. All sexual partners should also be tested for gonorrhea, regardless of whether they are experiencing symptoms. Patients should be retested 3 months after treatment. Typically, becoming infected again after treatment is most likely caused by the failure of sex partners to get tested or receive treatment.

Syphilis

Syphilis is caused by an infection with the bacterium *Treponema pallidum*. Syphilis is transmitted during sexual contact, and it usually first infects mucous membranes in the cervix, penis, anus, lips, or other area of the body. **Congenital syphilis** may also be transmitted through the placenta during the first or second trimester of pregnancy.

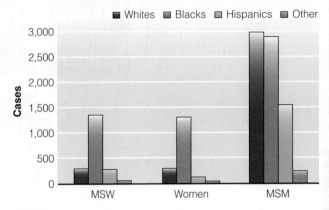

Figure 12.4 Primary and secondary syphilis, reported cases by sex, sexual behavior, and race/ethnicity, United States, 2010. Source: Centers for Disease Control and Prevention, 2011

Incidence

In 2010, there were 13,774 cases of primary and secondary syphilis reported to the CDC, which was the first decrease in rates in 10 years (Centers for Disease Control and Prevention, 2011). As shown in Figure 12.3, primary and secondary syphilis rates in 2010 were greatest among younger people and higher in men and in women in the United States. As shown in Figure 12.4, the increased rates in men are due, in part, to increased numbers of MSM.

In 2010, syphilis rates were eight times higher in Blacks than in Whites (CDC, 2011). During 2006 to 2010, syphilis rates increased 75% among Black men aged 15 to 19 years and 134% in those aged 20 to 24 years (CDC, 2011).

Symptoms and Diagnosis

Infection with syphilis is divided into three stages. During the primary stage (typically within 2 to 6 weeks after infection), there may be one or more small, red–brown sores, called chancres, that appear on the vulva, penis, vagina, cervix, anus, mouth, or lips. If left untreated, the chancre will heal in 3 to 8 weeks. However, during this time, the person can still transmit the disease to other sexual partners.

▶ **L05** Identify the cause of chlamydia, and summarize the incidence, symptoms, diagnosis, and treatment of this sexually transmitted infection.

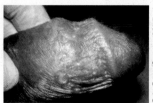

Syphilis chancres on penis.

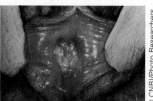

Syphilis chancres on female labia.

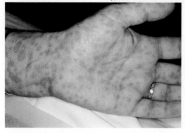

Secondary syphilis infection.

The second stage, known as secondary syphilis, begins 3 to 6 weeks after the chancre has healed. During this stage, the syphilis invades the central nervous system. The infected person develops reddish patches on the skin that look like a rash or hives (D. L. Brown & Frank, 2003). Other symptoms may include enlarged lymph glands in the groin, armpit, or neck; headaches; fevers; anorexia; flulike symptoms; and fatigue.

In the third stage, tertiary or late syphilis, the disease goes into remission. The rash, fever, and other symptoms go away, and the person usually feels fine. The infected individual is still able to transmit the disease for about 1 year, but after this time, the individual is no longer infectious. Left untreated, however, tertiary or late syphilis can cause neurological, sensory, muscular, and psychological difficulties and is eventually fatal.

A syphilis diagnosis can be made by culturing and evaluating the lesion or through a blood test. Blood tests check for the presence of antibodies, which develop after a person is infected with the bacteria.

Treatment

In its early stages, syphilis is relatively easy to treat. If a person has been infected for less than a year, treatment typically involves a single injection of an antibiotic. However, if syphilis is allowed to progress to the later stages, it is no longer treatable.

infection in their lifetime, and about 40% to 45% will have two or more episodes in their lifetime (C. Wilson, 2005; Workowski & Berman, 2010). Typically, the organism multiplies when the pH balance of the vagina is disturbed because of douching, pregnancy, oral contraceptive or antibiotic use, diabetes, or careless wiping after defecation. Although yeast infections are usually not sexually transmitted during vaginal intercourse, if a woman experiences multiple infections, all partners should be evaluated and treated.

Symptoms of a yeast infection include burning, itching, and an increase in vaginal discharge. Treatment includes either an antifungal prescription or over-the-counter drugs (such as Monistat, Gyne-Lotrimin), which are applied topically on the vulva and can be inserted into the vagina. Like BV, probiotics have also been used in the treatment of yeast infections (Falagas et al., 2006; Watson & Calabretto, 2007). In addition, eating one cup of yogurt daily may help reduce yeast infections (Falagas et al., 2006; Watson & Calabretto, 2007).

Pelvic Inflammatory Disease

Pelvic inflammatory disease is associated with some bacterial STIs, especially chlamydia and gonorrhea (Workowski & Berman, 2010). PID infects the female genital tract, including the endometrium, Fallopian tubes, and the lining of the pelvic area. Although the exact rates of PID are unknown, the CDC estimates that 750,000 women experience acute cases of PID each year. Long-term complications of PID include ectopic and tubal pregnancies, chronic pelvic pain, and infertility. Between 10% and 15% of women with PID become infertile each year because of the disease (CDC, 2011). Women with multiple sexual partners are at greatest risk for the development of PID.

Symptoms of PID vary from none to severe. The most common symptom is lower abdominal pain. Severe symptoms may include acute pelvic pain, fever, painful urination, and an abnormal vaginal bleeding or discharge. There are a variety of treatment approaches to PID, and treatment is usually dependent on how progressed the infection is. For women with mildly to moderately severe PID, treatment is typically done with antibiotics. Women with acute cases may be required to undergo injections or intravenous treatments. Sexual partners should be treated if they have had sexual contact with the woman during the 60 days before the onset of her symptoms.

On Your Mind

Should I get an "over-the-counter" cream if I have an itchy vaginal discharge?

Check Your Learning Quiz 12.4

Go to **login.cengagebrain.com** and take the online quiz.

▸ **LO10** Identify and differentiate between the two most common herpes viruses.

▸ **LO11** Discuss the contagious
nature of herpes simplex virus
(HSV) and explain the differences in the ways that HSV-1
and HSV-2 are transmitted.

▸ **LO12** Describe the common
symptoms associated with herpes simplex virus infection and
factors that may affect the frequency and severity of
symptoms.

Sexually transmitted infections can also be
caused by viruses. Herpes is a viral infection. Two
of the most common viral STIs are **herpes simplex I (HSV-1)** and **herpes simplex II (HSV-2)**.
HSV-1 is often transmitted through kissing or
sharing eating or drinking utensils and causes
cold sores or blisters on the face and mouth.

Although HSV-1 can lead to genital herpes—
if an infected person performs oral sex on
someone—the majority of cases of genital herpes are caused by an infection with HSV-2
(Workowski & Berman, 2010). When the virus
infects a nonpreferred site (i.e., HSV-1 infects
the genitals or HSV-2 infects the mouth or lips),
symptoms are often less severe.

Contagion and Incidence

Herpes simplex virus is highly contagious, and
the virus may be released between outbreaks
from the infected skin (often referred to as **viral
shedding**). Because of this,
it is possible to transmit the
virus even when the
infected partner does not
have any active symptoms
(Mertz, 2008; Wald et al.,
2000). Viral shedding is
more common in genital
HSV-2 infection than genital HSV-1 infection, especially during the first year
after infection (Workowski
& Berman, 2010). Infected
individuals can also **auto-**

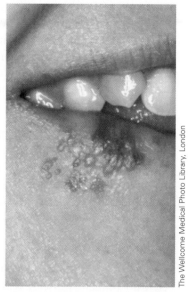

Typical patch of HSV-1 blisters near the mouth and
lips.

The Wellcome Medical Photo Library, London

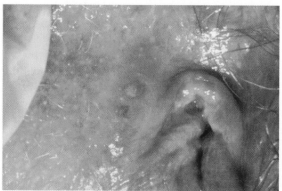

HSV-2 blisters on the vulva.

© Luis M. de la Maza, Ph.D. M.D./Phototake

herpes simplex I (HSV-I) A viral infection that is usually transmitted through kissing or sharing eating or drinking utensils and can
cause cold sores or blisters on the
face and mouth.

herpes simplex II (HSV-2) A
viral infection that is often sexually
transmitted and is responsible for
genital ulcerations and blisters.

viral shedding The release of viral infections between outbreaks
from infected skin.

autoinoculate To cause a secondary infection in the body from an
already existing infection.

inoculate themselves by touching a cold sore or blister and then rubbing another part of their body.

Whereas HSV-2 is almost always sexually transmitted, HSV-1 is usually transmitted during childhood through nonsexual contact (Usatine & Tinitigan, 2010; Xu et al., 2006). In fact, studies suggest that by adolescence, 62% of people have been infected

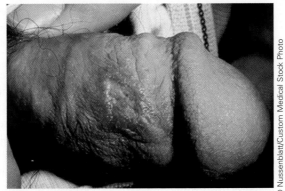

Herpes simplex 2 blisters appear on the penis.

© Nussenblatt/Custom Medical Stock Photo

with HSV-1, and by the age of 60, 85% have been infected. Pregnant mothers can pass HSV-2 on to their infants while the baby is in the uterus, during delivery from exposure to active sores in the birth canal, or directly after birth (Corey & Handsfield, 2000).

No federal mandatory reporting regulations for HSV in the United States exist, but it is known to be a common virus. It is also estimated that one of every five Americans is infected with HSV-2 (Tirabassi et al., 2011). However, because many men and women might have mild or unrecognized infections, the majority of people with HSV-2 infections have never been diagnosed, mainly because many infected men and women do not experience blisters or ulcers (Workowski & Berman, 2010). In fact, most people who have been infected with genital herpes were infected by others who didn't even know they had it.

Symptoms

Although many people infected with herpes do not experience the classic blisters associated with herpes, if they do have symptoms, the symptoms usually appear within 2 to 12 days after infection. If blisters are present, the first episode is generally the most painful (Workowski & Berman, 2010).

At the onset, there is usually a tingling or burning feeling in the affected area, which can grow into an itching and a red, swollen appearance of the genitals (this period is often referred to as the prodromal phase). The sores usually last anywhere

Testing Positive for HSV: Why Me?

Female college student discusses becoming infected with genital herpes when her long-term boyfriend cheated.

My Side of the Story

Male who infected his girlfriend tells his side of the story.

On Your Mind

Can people still transmit herpes if they don't have any blisters or symptoms?

▶ **LO13** Identify at least three treatments for herpes simplex virus.

from 8 to 10 days, and the amount of pain they cause can range from mild to severe. Pain is usually most severe at the onset of the infection and improves thereafter. Other symptoms of HSV include a fever, headaches, pain, itching, vaginal or urethral discharge, and general fatigue.

The frequency and severity of recurrent episodes of herpes depend on several things, including how much of the virus was contained in the original infection, the type of herpes, and the timing of treatment (Mark et al., 2008). Men and women who experience symptoms during their first outbreak of genital HSV-2 infection will most likely experience recurrent episodes of blisters, but those infected with genital HSV-1 infections may not have recurrences (Workowski & Berman, 2010). Over time, the frequency of recurrent outbreaks diminishes. Certain triggers may increase the likelihood of an HSV outbreak, including exposure to sunlight (natural or tanning beds), lip trauma or chapping, sickness, menstruation, fatigue, and persistent anxiety and stress (F. Cohen et al., 1999). After several years, individuals may no longer experience outbreaks, although they may still be contagious and able to infect others.

Psychological reactions to herpes outbreaks can include anxiety, guilt, anger, frustration, helplessness, a decrease in self-esteem, and depression. Persons with supportive partners and social relationships tend to have better emotional reactions. In addition, those who receive psychological support services experience a greater reduction in recurrent episodes of herpes and an improvement in their emotional health (Swanson et al., 1999).

Diagnosis

During the first several weeks after infection, antibodies to HSV develop and will remain in the body indefinitely. Blood tests are often used to diagnose HSV infection and also to distinguish between HSV-1 and HSV-2. The presence of blisters caused by the herpes virus is often enough to diagnose the disease. Oftentimes, however, health care providers will take a scraping of the blisters to evaluate for the presence of HSV (Whitley & Roizman, 2001). No tests for the detection of HSV-1 or HSV-2 are 100% accurate because tests depend on the amount of infectious agent and the stage of the disease. Success rates for detecting HSV-2 antibodies vary from

80% to 98%, and there are high false-negative results, mainly because the tests are performed too early.

Treatment

Unlike bacteria, which can be killed by antibiotics, once a virus invades a body cell, it is able to reproduce, so most of the time people will have the virus for the rest of their lives. Antiviral drugs are a standard treatment for HSV infection, and they can be taken as needed to reduce an outbreak or as suppressive therapy to reduce recurrences (Workowski & Berman, 2010). These drugs also shorten the duration of outbreaks, prevent complications (such as itching or scarring), and reduce viral shedding. Suppressive therapy has been found to reduce the risk for infecting sexual partners with genital HSV-2. Once a person stops taking these drugs, however, HSV symptoms will return.

Natural remedies for herpes outbreaks include applying an ice pack to the affected area during the prodromal phase and applying cooling or drying agents such as witch hazel. Increasing intake of foods rich in certain amino acids, such as L-lysine, which includes fish or yogurt, and decreasing the intake of sugar and nuts (which are high in another amino acid, arginine) may also help reduce recurrences (Griffith et al., 1987; Vukovic, 1992). Lysine can also be purchased from the vitamin section of any drugstore. Herbal treatments have also been used, including lemon balm (to dry cold sores), aloe (to decrease healing time of blisters), and peppermint oil (to inhibit the virus from replicating). It is recommended that natural remedies be used under medical supervision.

Support groups, relaxation training, hypnosis, and individual therapy have also been found to reduce the stress associated with HSV infections. Reducing stress can also reduce the frequency and severity of outbreaks. Research continues to explore the development of a vaccine for HSV, although it may be a few more years before an effective vaccine is available (Brans & Yao, 2010; Hu et al., 2011; Kask et al., 2010; Morello et al., 2011; Pouriayevali et al., 2011; Tirabassi et al., 2011). Several studies have also been exploring antiviral therapy to decrease viral shedding, but as of early 2011, no medications have been found to effectively reduce viral shedding (Bernstein et al., 2011; Tan et al., 2011; Schiffer et al., 2010).

Check Your Learning
Quiz 12.5

Go to **login.cengagebrain.com** and take the online quiz.

▶ **LO14** Differentiate between high-risk and low-risk types of human papillomavirus and explain the importance of a strong immune system.

▶ **LO15** Explore the incidence of human papillomavirus in men and women in the United States.

▶ **LO16** Identify symptoms associated with human papillomavirus and explain the importance of regular Pap smears in women.

There are more than 40 types of human papillomaviruses (HPVs) that can infect the genitals, anus, mouth, and throat during various sexual behaviors, including vaginal and anal intercourse, oral sex, and vulva-to-vulva contact. The majority of people who are infected do not know they have it. "Low-risk" HPV (types 6 and 11) can cause genital warts (condyloma acuminata, venereal warts), which are different from warts that appear on other parts of the body. "High-risk" HPV (types 16 and 18) can cause abnormal Pap tests and increase cancer risks, especially cervical cancer in women (Grce & Davies, 2008; Tovar et al., 2008).

Almost all cervical cancers can be attributed to HPV infection (Smith & Travis, 2011; Wattleworth, 2011). HPV is also a risk factor for several other types of cancer, including oral, penile, and anal cancer (Dietz & Nyberg, 2011). In fact, the incidence of anal cancer in MSM is greater than the incidence of cervical cancer among WSW (Chin-Hong et al., 2008; Dietz & Nyberg, 2011; Goodman et al., 2008; Palefsky, 2008).

One important aspect of HPV infection that sets it apart from other viruses is the fact that research has found that in more than 90% of cases, a person's immune system can clear HPV within 2 years (CDC, 2009c).

Incidence

Human papillomavirus is the most common viral STI in the United States today. Approximately 20 million men and women in the United States are currently infected with HPV, and 6 million more become infected each year (CDC, 2009c). It is estimated that at least 50% of all sexually active men and women will get HPV at some point in their lives. Because of the contagious nature of genital warts, approximately 65% of sexual partners of people with cervical warts develop warts within 3 to 4 months of contact (Krilov, 1991).

Studies have found that many lesbians believe that HPV cannot be spread by female-to-female sex and/or do not identify HPV as a

© Science VU/Visuals Unlimited

Warts that appear on the penis are usually flesh-colored and may have a bumpy appearance.

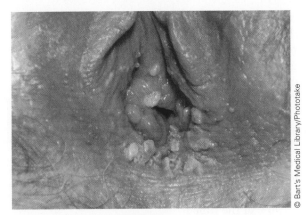

Genital warts can grow on the outside of the vulva.

© Bart's Medical Library/Phototake

cancer risk (Polek & Hardie, 2010). However, HPV is prevalent in both WSW and MSM (Dunne et al., 2006; Marrazzo et al., 2001). A study evaluating HPV prevalence in all men in the United States, Mexico, and Brazil found an overall prevalence rate of 65%, which was higher in Brazil (72%) than in the United States (61%) and Mexico (62%; Giuliano et al., 2008b). In gay men, HPV infections have been found to co-occur with HIV infection (Pierangeli et al., 2008).

Symptoms and Diagnosis

Symptoms for HPV depend on the type of HPV infection. Although several types may cause genital warts, the two most common types associated with genital warts are types 6 and 11 (Workowski & Berman, 2010). These types are also related to the development of warts in the throat, nose, and mouth. Warts are usually flesh colored, with a bumpy surface. In some areas, warts may grow together and have a cauliflower-like appearance. Warts develop in women on the vagina, vulva, introitus, or cervix, and in men on the penile shaft or under the foreskin in an uncircumcised penis. Warts can also appear on the anus in both men and women. Warts are generally asymptomatic, and unless they are large, many people do not notice them and unknowingly infect other sexual partners. If warts grow in the throat (referred to as *recurrent respiratory papillomatosis*), they can potentially block the airway, causing breathing difficulties and/or a hoarse voice.

Typically, cervical cancer and other HPV-related cancers do not have symptoms until they are very advanced. Regular Pap smears can help health care providers to monitor precancerous changes in the cervical cells (often referred to as **cervical dysplasia**). Identifying problems early can significantly reduce the risk for the infection developing into cancer.

HPV may show up on Pap testing, but 80% to 90% of the time it does not (Kassler & Cates, 1992). Today, high-risk HPV DNA testing is available for women (Huang et al., 2011). Cervical magnification (called *colposcopy*) and biopsies can also be used.

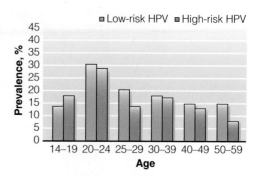

Prevalance of high-risk and low-risk types of human papillomavirus in females 14 to 59 years old, 2003–2004. Source: National Health and Nutrition Examination Survey, 2007

Treatment

It is important to seek treatment immediately for genital warts because they can quickly grow and multiply. Genital warts can be treated in several ways, and no treatment method is superior to another or best for all patients with HPV. Important factors for a health care provider to consider when deciding treatment options include the number and size of the warts, patient preference, treatment costs, convenience, and adverse effects.

Treatment alternatives include chemical topical solutions (to destroy external warts), cryotherapy (freezing the warts with liquid nitrogen), electrosurgical interventions (removal of warts using a mild electrical current, often referred to as a LEEP, or "loop electrosurgical excision procedure"), or laser surgery (high-intensity lasers to destroy the warts). It may be necessary to try several treatment methods, and repeat applications are common.

Although the majority of sexual partners of those infected with HPV are already infected, if they are not, an infected person should use condoms during sexual behavior for at least 6 months after treatment (Lilley & Schaffer, 1990). Some couples decide to use condoms long term because of the possibility of transmitting the virus when no warts are present. It is possible that a low-risk type infection may be

cervical dysplasia Disordered growth of cells in the cervix, typically diagnosed with Pap testing.

cleared up by the immune system over time (Corneanu et al., 2011; Dunne, 2007). Women who have been diagnosed with a high-risk type of HPV may be encouraged to have pelvic examinations and Pap tests more frequently.

Currently, two vaccines are available in the United States, Gardasil and Cervarix. Gardasil protects from four HPV types—6, 11 (which cause 90% of genital warts), and 16 and 18 (which cause 70% of cervical cancer and many anal, vaginal, and penile cancers)—whereas Cervarix protects from two HPV types—16 and 18. Both vaccines are given as shots and require three injections. They are approved for use in women aged 9 to 26. Gardasil can also protect boys and men against most genital warts, although as of late 2011, no formal recommendations had been made by the U.S. Food and Drug Administration (Giuliano et al., 2011; Workowski & Berman, 2010). Research also indicates that MSM can benefit from HPV vaccination (Dietz & Nyberg, 2011).

Ideally, the HPV vaccine should be given before an individual is sexually active, although there is evidence that sexually active individuals may also benefit from the vaccine (National Cancer Institute, 2009). The vaccines can protect sexually active individuals from HPV types they have not been exposed to, and may offer some protection from types they have already been exposed to (National Cancer Institute, 2009). In addition to the reduced risk of cervical cancer in women and genital warts in both men and women, these vaccines may also reduce the risk of anal and mouth/throat cancers, as well as cancer of the penis in men (National Cancer Institute, 2009).

Since the vaccines are relatively new, the actual duration of immunity is unknown. Research continues to evaluate immunity duration but it appears the vaccines are effective for at least four years (National Cancer Institute, 2009). At some point, it is possible that booster vaccinations (additional doses of a vaccine) will be necessary. Since the HPV vaccine does not protect against all types of HPV that can cause cancer, it's important that women continue to have regular Pap tests (Tovar et al., 2008).

In women, vaccine side effects include arm soreness, possible joint and muscle pain, fatigue, and general weakness. In males, the most common side effect has been soreness at the site of the injection (Garnock-Jones and Giuliano, 2011). Some women have reported feeling lightheaded after the injection, and health care providers recommend waiting 15 minutes after the vaccine is given before leaving a health care provider's office (National Cancer Institute, 2009).

As of early 2011, the HPV vaccine was still fraught with controversy, mostly surrounding the safety and long-term side effects of the vaccine as well as issues surrounding who should get the vaccine (Lechuga et al., 2011).

Irregular Pap Smears, LEEPs, and the HPV Vaccine

A 26-year-old woman discusses her reaction to an irregular Pap smear.

On Your Mind

How does the HPV vaccine work?

Check Your Learning Quiz 12.6

Go to **login.cengagebrain.com** and take the online quiz.

Viral hepatitis is an infection that causes impaired liver function. The three main types of viral hepatitis include hepatitis A virus (HAV), hepatitis B virus (HBV), and hepatitis C virus (HCV). HAV and HBV can be sexually transmitted, whereas HCV is commonly passed on through intravenous drug use or unscreened blood transfusions. HCV is rarely passed on from infected sexual partners or from mother to child during birth.

HAV is primarily transmitted through contact with fecal material during oral–anal sex (such as licking or "rimming" the anus) with an infected partner. However, it can also be transmitted through oral contact with contaminated food or water (which is one of the main reasons people who work in restaurants are advised to wash their hands after using the restroom). HBV is commonly spread through contact with infected semen, vaginal secretions, saliva, urine, or blood. This can happen during sexual activity, but also from sharing toothbrushes or razors with an infected person. HBV can also be spread through the use of contaminated needles during tattooing, ear piercing, or acupuncture. Health care providers recommend using only reputable providers that sterilize their instruments for tattoos and body piercings.

Incidence

In 2009, approximately 1,987 acute cases of HAV were reported in the United States, which was one of the lowest rates ever recorded (Centers for Disease Control, 2010). This is probably a result of the HAV vaccine, which became available in 1995. However, after adjusting for asymptomatic cases and underreporting, the total number of HAV cases was probably closer to 21,000 cases (CDC, 2010). Rates are highest in males, among American Indian/Alaska Natives, and in Western regions of the United States.

Rates of HBV have also been declining; in 2009, approximately 3,371 acute cases of HBV were reported in the United States (CDC, 2010). However, after adjusting for asymptomatic cases and underreporting, the total number of HBV cases was probably closer to 38,000. Rates are highest in males, among non-Hispanic Blacks, and in Western and Southern regions of the United States.

Finally, in 2009, there were only 781 acute cases of HCV reported in the United States. However, after adjusting for asymptomatic cases and underreporting, the total number of HCV cases was probably closer to 16,000 in 2009 (CDC, 2010). However, HCV is the most common chronic blood-borne infection in the United States, with an estimated 3.2 million people chronically infected (CDC, 2010d).

Symptoms

Symptoms of HAV usually occur within 4 weeks and include fatigue, abdominal pain, loss of appetite, and diarrhea. Symptoms of HBV usually occur anywhere from 6 weeks to 6 months after infection, although infection with HBV is usually asymptomatic. Possible symptoms may include nausea, vomiting, jaundice, headaches, fever, a darkening of the urine, moderate liver enlargement, and fatigue. Finally, most people infected with HCV are asymptomatic or have a mild illness, and this illness develops within 8 to 9 weeks. The CDC estimates that between 60% and 70% of those infected with HCV will experience development of a chronic liver infection (Workowski & Berman, 2010).

Diagnosis and Treatment

Blood tests are used to identify viral hepatitis infections, and antiviral therapies are available for the treatment and management of hepatitis. These therapies have been designed to reduce viral load by interfering with the life cycle of the virus and also causing the body to generate an immune response against the virus (Guha et al., 2003). Health care providers generally recommend bed rest and adequate fluid intake so that a person doesn't develop dehydration. Usually after a few weeks, an infected person feels better, although this can take longer in persons with severe and chronic infections.

Vaccines are available for the prevention of both hepatitis A and B, and persons at high risk of contracting either of these should have the vaccine. Young children are often routinely vaccinated against both hepatitis A and B (CDC, 2010d). High-risk individuals include health care workers who may be exposed to blood products, intravenous drug users and their sex partners, people with multiple sexual partners, people with chronic liver disease, men who have sex with men, and housemates of anyone with hepatitis (CDC, 2010d). Research continues to explore a vaccine for hepatitis C (Hwu et al., 2011; Ruhl et al., 2011).

**Check Your Learning
Quiz 12.7**

Go to **login.cengagebrain.com**
and take the online quiz.

12.8 *HIV and AIDS*

▶ **LO21** Discuss the ways in which HIV is transmitted and identify the relationship between the HIV and AIDS.

▶ **LO22** Summarize the Centers for Disease Control and Prevention's findings regarding age, gender, race/ethnicity, and geographical differences in the incidence of HIV in the United States.

acquired immune deficiency syndrome (AIDS) A condition of increased susceptibility to opportunistic diseases; results from an infection with HIV, which destroys the body's immune system.

human immunodeficiency virus (HIV) The retrovirus responsible for the development of AIDS; can be transmitted during vaginal or anal intercourse.

opportunistic disease Disease that occurs when the immune system is depressed; often fatal.

perinatal HIV infections HIV transmission from mother to child during pregnancy, labor and delivery, or breast-feeding.

Acquired immune deficiency syndrome (AIDS) is caused by a viral infection with the **human immunodeficiency virus (HIV)**, a virus primarily transmitted through body fluids, including semen, vaginal fluid, breast milk, and blood. During vaginal or anal intercourse, this virus can enter the body through the vagina, penis, or rectum. Intravenous drug use can also transmit the virus by sharing needles. Oral sex may also transmit the virus, although the research has shown that the risk for HIV transmission from unprotected oral sex is lower than that of unprotected vaginal or anal sex (Kohn et al., 2002; E. D. Robinson & Evans, 1999). Kissing has been found to be low risk for transmitting HIV, especially when there are no cuts in the mouth or on the lips.

Like most viruses, HIV never goes away; it remains in the body for the rest of a person's life. However, unlike the herpes virus, an untreated HIV infection is often fatal. After a person is infected, the virus may remain dormant and cause no symptoms. This is why some people who are infected may not realize that they are infected. However, a blood test can be taken to reveal whether a person is HIV-positive. Even individuals who do not know that they have been infected can transmit the virus to other people immediately after infection.

HIV attacks the T lymphocytes (tee-LIM-foe-sites; T helper cells) in the blood, leaving fewer of them to fight off infection. When there is a foreign invader in our bloodstream, antibodies develop that are able to recognize the invader and destroy it. These antibodies can be detected in the bloodstream anywhere from 2 weeks to 6 months after infection, which is how the screening test for HIV works.

HIV attaches itself to the T helper cells and injects its infectious RNA into the fluid of the helper cell. The RNA contains an enzyme known as reverse transcriptase (trans-SCRIPT-ace), which is capable of changing the RNA into DNA. The new DNA takes over the T helper cell and begins to manufacture more HIV.

The attack on the T helper cells causes the immune system to be less effective in its ability to fight disease, and so many **opportunistic diseases** infect people with AIDS that a healthy person could easily fight off. No one knows exactly why some people acquire the virus from one sexual encounter, whereas others may not be infected even after repeated exposure. Research has shown that a person who has an STI is at greater risk for acquiring HIV (Gilson & Mindel, 2001; Hader et al., 2001; Pialoux et al., 2008).

Incidence

The CDC estimate that there are approximately 1.1 million adults and teens living with HIV in the United States, with an additional 50,000 to 60,000 more Americans becoming infected each year (Hall et al., 2011; Figure 12.7). However, one in five people living with HIV in the United States is unaware of their infection.

Like other STIs, there are age, gender, race/ethnicity, and geographical differences in the prevalence of HIV. From 2006 to 2009, the highest rate of HIV—15% of diagnoses—was in persons 20 to 24 years old (CDC, 2010b). Although the rate of HIV in females decreased from 2006 to 2009, rates in males remained stable—males accounted for 76% of all HIV diagnoses (CDC, 2010b). Racial and ethnicity factors were also important during this period. In 2009, Blacks accounted for 52% of all HIV diagnoses; the rates were 66.6 per 100,000 population in Blacks, 23 in Hispanic/Latinos, 21 in Native Hawaiian or other Pacific Islanders, 17 in those reporting multiple races, 10 in American Indian or Alaskan Natives, 7 in Whites, and 6.4 in Asians (CDC, 2010b; Figure 12.8).

Overall, the majority of people infected with HIV in 2009 were MSM (57%), followed by heterosexuals (31%; CDC, 2010b; Figure 12.9). In 2008, MSM were 64 times more likely than heterosexual men to become infected with HIV (Hall et al., 2011). This was the largest relative difference among groups and represented a 1,218% increase from 2005 to 2008 (Hall et al., 2011).

Although **perinatal HIV infections** have declined in the United States since 2000, it is estimated that 8,700 HIV-infected women gave birth in 2006 (Whitmore et al., 2011). Worldwide, it is estimated that 2.1 million children younger than 15 are living with HIV, and every year, 430,000 new HIV infections occur in newborns,

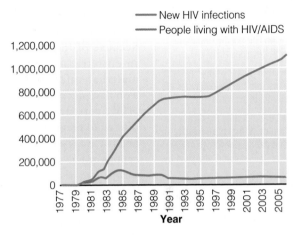

Figure 12.7 HIV and AIDS in the United States, 1977–2005. Source: Hall et al. 2009b; Centers for Disease Control 2006

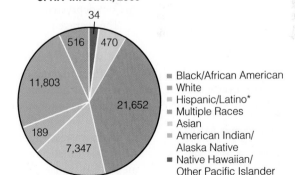

*Hispanics/Latinos can be of any race.

Figure 12.8 Estimated number of HIV diagnoses by race/ethnicity, 2009. Source: Center for Disease Control and Prevention, 2009b

viral load The measure of the severity of a viral infection calculated by estimating the amount of virus in body fluid.

oral candidiasis An infection in the mouth caused by the excess growth of a fungus that naturally occurs in the body.

***Pneumocystis carinii* pneumonia** A rare type of pneumonia; an opportunistic disease that often occurs in people with AIDS.

toxoplasmosis A parasite that can cause headache, sore throat, seizures, altered mental status, or coma.

cryptococcosis An acute or chronic infection that can lead to pulmonary or central nervous system infection.

cytomegalovirus A virus that can lead to diarrhea, weight loss, headache, fever, confusion, or blurred vision.

mostly in Africa (Fowler et al., 2010). Fortunately, because of improvements in obstetric care, rates of maternal–infant transmission have decreased. Today, HIV tests are routinely offered to pregnant women, and if a test is positive, medications can be used to reduce **viral load**; also, a planned cesarean section can be done to reduce the risk for transmission to the infant during delivery.

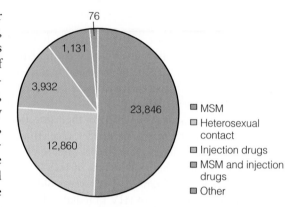

Figure 12.9 Estimated diagnoses of HIV infection by transmission category, 2009. Source: Centers for Disease Control and Prevention

Symptoms

HIV infection results in a gradual deterioration of the immune system through the destruction of T helper lymphocytes (Friedman-Kien & Farthing, 1990). For those who are not being treated, this decline in T helper lymphocytes takes an average of 3 years in those who are emotionally depressed and more than 5 years in those who are not depressed (B. Bower, 1992).

The average person who is HIV-positive and is not on any type of treatment will experience development of AIDS within 8 to 10 years. Flulike symptoms such as fever, sore throat, chronic swollen lymph nodes in the neck or armpits, headaches, and fatigue may appear. Later symptoms may include significant dizziness, blurring of vision or hearing, weight loss, severe diarrhea, skin rashes, night sweats, **oral candidiasis**, gingivitis, oral ulcers, and persistent fever (Friedman-Kien & Farthing, 1990).

In an untreated person, the deterioration of the immune system makes it easier for opportunistic diseases to develop. In general, the incidence of opportunistic illnesses (i.e., those that can make people sick when their immune systems are compromised) are similar in men and women with a few exceptions. In women, cervical cancer may develop as an AIDS-defining condition (Hader et al., 2001). ***Pneumocystis carinii* pneumonia** is one type of opportunistic illness that may develop in

The lesions on this 26-year-old woman in Saveto, South Africa, are caused by Kaposi's sarcoma, an AIDS-defining cancer which is often less common in women with AIDS.

© Jon Hrusa/epa/Corbis

untreated men and women who are infected with HIV. PCP is a type of pneumonia that was uncommon before 1980. Other opportunistic diseases include **toxoplasmosis**, **cryptococcosis**, **cytomegalovirus**, and Kaposi's sarcoma (KS). KS is a rare type of blood vessel cancer that occurs in gay men but is rarely seen in other populations. Lesions from KS frequently occur around the ankle or foot, or they may be on the tip of nose, face, mouth, penis, eyelids, ears, chest, or back. Without treatment, about 66% of all men with AIDS experience development of KS lesions (Alkhuja et al., 2001).

Diagnosis

Tests for HIV can either identify the virus in the blood or, more commonly, detect whether the person's body has developed antibodies to fight HIV. The most widely used test for antibodies is the ELISA (enzyme-linked immunoabsorbent assay). To check for accuracy, if an ELISA test result is positive, a second test, known as the Western blot, is used to check for accuracy.

Global Aspects of AIDS

Prevalence around the world.

HIV/AIDS: Orel's Story

Orel describes his initial diagnosis and the struggle with coming to terms with being HIV positive.

▶ **LO26** Discuss the primary factors that contribute to the prevention of further spread of HIV.

Since the mid-2000s, the biggest development in diagnosis has been the development of rapid HIV testing (Greenwald et al., 2006). Both the ELISA and Western blot HIV tests require as long as 2 weeks before a result is possible. Results from the OraQuick Rapid HIV Antibody test are available within 20 minutes. However, it is recommended that these tests be followed up by confirmatory testing.

Treatment

Since 1995, there has been a tremendous decrease in HIV- and AIDS-related deaths, primarily because of the development of **highly active antiretroviral therapy** (**HAART**; Crum et al., 2006; M. H. Katz et al., 2002; Venkatesh et al., 2008). HAART is the combination of three or more HIV drugs, often referred to as "drug cocktails." This development, in conjunction with the development of HIV RNA testing (which allows health care providers to monitor the amount of virus in the bloodstream), has allowed for better control of HIV and has slowed the disease progression.

HAART has also significantly increased the life expectancy of children infected with HIV at birth (Davies et al., 2008; Ghosh et al., 2011). Without treatment, one in three HIV-positive African newborns die before the age of 1, one in two die before their second birthday, and the majority die by the age of 5 (Newell et al., 2004).

Finally, it is also important to point out that the advent of HAART in the late 1990s brought with it a substantial increase in high-risk behavior among HIV-positive gay men (Elford et al., 2000; M. H. Katz et al., 2002; Stephenson et al., 2003; Wolitski et al., 2001). These behavioral changes were thought to be due to increased feelings of optimism and reduced levels of HIV. Research has found that since 2005, risky sexual behaviors in HIV-positive gay men have been increasing again (Bezemer et al., 2008; Hart & Elford, 2010; Sullivan et al., 2007).

Prevention

To prevent the further spread of HIV, people's behavior must change. Many programs have been started to achieve this goal, including educational programs, advertising, and mailings. Public service announcements about AIDS have increased on radio stations, and many television programs have agreed to address HIV/AIDS in upcoming episodes. A variety of television shows have also included the topic of HIV/AIDS in their programming. Schools are also working to help pre-

highly active antiretroviral therapy (HAART) A combination of antiretroviral drugs for the treatment of infections by retroviruses, primarily HIV.

Prepare to Learn ^

1 **GO** to your **Psychology CourseMate** at **login.cengagebrain.com** and take the **Chapter Pre-Test** to introduce yourself to this chapter's topics and see what you may already know.

2 **READ** the **Learning Objectives** (LOs, in the left sidebars) and begin the chapter.

3 **COMPLETE** the **Online Activities** (in the right sidebars) *as you read each module.* Activities include **videos, animations, readings,** and **quizzes.**

4 **CHECK Your Learning** by going online to take the quiz at the end of each module and review material as necessary.

5 **MEASURE Your Learning** after reading the chapter by taking the online **Chapter Post-Test.** Use the chapter review guide at the end of the chapter as needed.

WATCH for these **Online Activities** icons as you read:

Video

Animation

Reading

Assessment

Think Critically

These Online Activities are essential to mastering this chapter. Go to login.cengagebrain.com.

 Videos Explore diverse perspectives on sex as well as common questions:

- If I fantasize about being spanked, does that mean I have a paraphilia?
- Why do men have more paraphilias than women?
- Kiki and Kink
- The Professional Dominatrix
- BDSM
- The Sexual Offender Registry
- Sex Addiction
- If I think about sex all the time, does that mean I'm addicted to it?

 Animations Interact with and visualize important processes, timelines, and concepts:

- Key Terms Exercise

 Readings Delve deeper into key content:

- Paraphilias throughout the World
- Dutch Pedophilia Party?
- The Story of Megan's Law
- Obscene Phone Calls, Texts, and Emails
- Paraphilia Treatment Options

 Assessment Measure your mastery:

- Chapter Pre-Test
- Check Your Learning Quizzes
- Chapter Post-Test

 Think Critically Challenge your thinking about data and accepted norms:

- Internet Sexual Addiction

13.1 *What Is "Typical" Sexual Expression?*

▶ **LO1** Discuss the changing societal attitudes toward sexual variations throughout history.

HUMAN SEXUALITY can be expressed in many ways. We tend to celebrate individual and cultural differences in most aspects of human life—in what people eat, how they dress, or how they dance, for example. Yet we have been less tolerant of sexual diversity, and we have historically considered such behavior "deviant" or "perverted" (Laws & O'Donohue, 1997). More modern views of sexuality, however, do not categorize people as "deviant" versus "normal." For example, the sexual world is not really split into those who become sexually excited from looking at others naked or having sex and those who do not; most people get aroused to some degree from visual sexual stimuli. Some people get more aroused than others, and at the upper limits are those who can get aroused only when watching sexual scenes; such people have taken a normal behavior to an extreme. In this chapter, we explore variations of sexual behavior, including differences in sexual desire and the paraphilias.

▼

Many undergraduate texts discuss these behaviors in chapters that includes words such as "abnormal," "unusual," or "atypical" sexual behavior in their titles. Yet how exactly do we decide whether a behavior is "normal"? Where do we draw the line? Do we call it "atypical" if 5% of sexually active people do it? Ten percent? Twenty-five percent?

Throughout history, sexual behaviors have increased and decreased in popularity; oral sex, for example, was once considered a perversion, but now it is a commonly reported sexual behavior, even in adolescent populations (Dake et al., 2011; Song & Halpern-Felsher et al., 2011). Perhaps, then, we should consider as "deviant" only behaviors that may be harmful in some way. Masturbation was once believed to lead to mental illness, acne, and stunted growth; now it is considered a normal, healthy part of sexual expression. If many of these desires exist to some degree in all of us, then any such desire itself is not atypical, just the degree of the desire.

Social value judgments, not science, primarily determine which sexual behaviors are considered "normal" by a society. For example, in 1906, Krafft-Ebing defined sexual deviance as "every expression of (the sexual instinct) that does not correspond with the purpose of nature—i.e., propagation" (J. C. Brown, 1983, p. 227). Certainly, most people would not go so far today.

The author talks with a convicted pedophile about his sexual attractions to children.

Freud himself stated that the criterion of normalcy was love and that defenses against "perversion" were the bedrock of civilization because perversion trivializes or degrades love (A. M. Cooper, 1991). Note that Freud's objections to perversion are not medical, as they were to most other mental disturbances, but moral.

Even "modern" definitions can contain hidden value judgments: "The sexually variant individual typically exhibits sexual arousal or responses to inappropriate people (e.g., minors), objects (e.g., leather, rubber, garments), or activities (e.g., exposure in public, coercion, violence)" (Gudjonsson, 1986, p. 192). "Appropriate" or "inappropriate" people, objects, or activities of sexual attention differ in different times, in different cultures, and for different people. Despite these objections, certain groups of behaviors are considered the most common deviations from conventional heterosexual or homosexual behavior.

Society may view these behaviors as either solely the business of the individual in the privacy of his or her bedroom (e.g., sexual excitement from pain or certain clothing), as a sign that the person is mentally ill (e.g., having sex with animals), or as dangerous and illegal (e.g., sex with underage children). The United States Department of Justice coordinates the National Sex Offender Registry, which enables individuals to search for the identity and location of known sex offenders. In this chapter, we explore variations in sexual behaviors, theories of why people are attracted to unusual sexual objects, and how therapists have tried to help those who are troubled by their sexual desires.

On Your Mind

If I fantasize about being spanked, does that mean I have a paraphilia?

Check Your Learning Quiz 13.1

Go to **login.cengagebrain.com** and take the online quiz.

© Amardeep Kaleka

▶ **LO2** Define *paraphilia* and list the essential features of a paraphilia as suggested by the *Diagnostic and Statistical Manual of Mental Disorders*.

▶ **LO3** Compare two to three theories about the development of paraphilias.

Defining Paraphilia

The word *paraphilia* (pear-uh-FILL-ee-uh) is derived from the Greek "para" (besides) and "philia" (love or attraction). In other words, **paraphilias** are sexual behaviors that involve a craving for an erotic object that is unusual or different. According to the *Diagnostic and Statistical Manual of Mental Disorders* (*DSM*), the essential features involved in a paraphilia are recurrence and intensity of the sexual behavior that involves a nonhuman object, or the suffering or humiliation of oneself or one's partner, a child, or a nonconsenting person. This behavior causes significant distress and interferes with a person's ability to work, interact with friends, and other important areas of one's life. Experts have recommended differentiating between paraphilias (which would be consensual) and paraphiliac disorders (which may be coercive) and have suggested paraphilic coercive disorder, in which a person seeks stimulation by forcing sexual behaviors on various persons.

Although many people view their behaviors as exciting aspects of their sexuality, others may be uncomfortable with their sexual interests or behaviors. However, discomfort or distress about certain sexual interests or behaviors may arise from the fact that their sexual desires are in conflict with current social standards (Wright, 2010). If a person enjoys sexual behaviors that society views as pathological, distress can occur. Because of this, there has been a movement to depathologize unusual sexual behaviors (Wright, 2010). Of course, some paraphiliac behaviors can be dangerous or can threaten others. Men who expose themselves to young girls, people who violate corpses, strangers who rub against women on buses, or adults who seduce underage children must not be allowed to continue their behavior. There can even be legal problems with the paraphilias that are not in themselves dangerous; some **fetishists** resort to stealing the object of interest to them, and occasionally a voyeur will break into people's homes.

Individuals who engage in paraphiliac behaviors are a heterogeneous group with no true factors that set them apart from nonparaphiliacs, with the exception of gender—the majority of those with paraphilias are men. Other than this, people with paraphilias come from every socioeconomic bracket, every ethnic and racial group, and every sexual orientation (Seligman & Hardenburg, 2000).

Theories about Paraphilias

Many researchers have theorized why and how paraphilias develop, but little consensus has been reached. Paraphilias are undoubtedly complex behavior patterns, which may have biological, psychological, or social origins—or aspects of all three.

paraphilia Clinical term used to describe types of sexual expressions that are seen as unusual and potentially problematic. A person who engages in paraphilias is often referred to as a paraphiliac.

fetishist A person who engages in a fetishistic behavior.

Biological Theories

Biological researchers have found that a number of conditions can initiate paraphiliac behavior, such as illnesses, disturbances of brain structure and brain chemistry, and higher levels of certain hormones, such as testosterone (Giotakos et al., 2005; Rahman & Symeonides, 2008; Sartorius et al., 2008). However, this does not mean that everyone with a paraphilia has one of these conditions. At most, these conditions are factors that may lead some people to be more likely to develop a paraphilia, but they do not explain the majority of such behaviors.

Psychoanalytic Theory

Psychoanalytic thought suggests that paraphilias can be traced back to the difficult time the infant has in negotiating his way through the Oedipal crisis and castration anxiety. This can explain why paraphilias are more common among men because both boys and girls identify strongly with their mothers, but girls can continue that identification, whereas boys must, painfully, separate from their mothers to establish a male identity.

Louise Kaplan, a psychoanalyst, suggests that every paraphilia involves issues of masculinity or femininity; as she writes, "every male perversion entails a masquerade or impersonation of masculinity and every female perversion entails a masquerade or impersonation of femininity" (1991, p. 249). For example, a man who exposes himself in public may be coping with castration anxiety by evoking a reaction to his penis from women. The exhibitionist in this view is "masquerading" as a man to cover up feelings of nonmasculinity; he is saying, in effect, *Let me prove that I am a man by showing that I possess the instrument of masculinity.* He even needs to demonstrate that his penis can inspire fear, which may be why exhibitionists disproportionately choose young girls, who are more likely to display a fear reaction (Kline, 1987). This confirms to the exhibitionist the power of his masculinity.

In contrast, voyeurs, who are excited by looking at others nude or having sex, may be fixated on the experience that aroused their castration anxieties as children—the sight of genitals and sexuality (Kline, 1987). Looking allows the person to gain power over the fearful and hidden world of sexuality while safe from the possibility of contact. The visual component of castration anxiety occurs when the boy sees the power and size of the father's genitals and the lack of a penis on his mother or sisters. The act of looking initiates castration anxiety, and in the voyeur, the looking has never ceased. Yet looking itself cannot really relieve the anxiety permanently, and so the voyeur is compelled to peep again and again.

Paraphilias throughout the World

Explore what we know of paraphilias in a variety of countries.

On Your Mind

Why do men have more paraphilias than women?

Developmental Theories

Freud suggested that children are polymorphously perverse; that is, at birth we have a general erotic potential that can be attached to almost anything. We learn from an early age what sexual objects society deems appropriate for us to desire, but society's messages can get off track. For example, advertising tries to "sexualize" its products—we have all seen shoe commercials, for example, that emphasize the long, sexy legs of the model while focusing on the shoes she wears. Some boys may end up focusing on those shoes as objects of sexual fantasy, which can develop into a fetish.

A theory that builds on similar ideas is John Money's (1984, 1986, 1990) **lovemaps**. Money suggests that the auditory, tactile, and (especially) visual stimuli we experience during childhood sex play form a template in our brain that defines our ideal lover and ideal sexual situation. If our childhood sex play remains undisturbed, development goes on toward heterosexual desires. If, however, the child is punished for normal sexual curiosity or if there are traumas during this stage, such as sexual abuse, the development of the lovemap can be disrupted in one of three ways.

In hypophilia (high-po-FILL-ee-uh), negative stimuli prevent the development of certain aspects of sexuality, and the genitals may be impaired from full functioning. Overall, females are more likely to experience hypophilia than men, resulting in an inability to orgasm, vaginal pain, or lubrication problems later in life. A lovemap can also be disrupted to cause a condition called hyperphilia (high-per-FILL-ee-uh), in which a person defies the negative sexual stimulus and becomes overly sexually active, even becoming compulsively sexual. Finally, a lovemap can be disrupted when there is a substitution of new elements into the lovemap, and a paraphilia can develop. Because normal sexual curiosity has been discouraged or made painful, the child redirects erotic energy toward other objects that are not forbidden, such as shoes or rubber, or just looking; in other cases, the child turns his or her erotic energy inward and becomes excited by pain or humiliation.

Once this lovemap is set, it becomes very stable, which explains why changing it is so difficult. For example, Money (1984) suggests that sexual arousal to objects may arise when a parent makes a child feel shame about interest in an object. For example, a boy may be caught with his mother's panties in the normal course of curiosity about the woman's body, but when he is severely chastised, the panties become forbidden, dirty, and promising of sexual secrets, and he may begin to seek them out.

Another theory about how these fixations occur is the idea of courtship disorders (K. Freund & Blanchard, 1986; K. Freund et al., 1983, 1984). Organizing paraphilias

lovemap Term coined by John Money to refer to the template of an ideal lover and sexual interest we develop as we grow up.

into "courtship" stages suggests that the paraphiliac's behavior becomes fixed at a preliminary stage of mating that would normally lead to vaginal intercourse. Thus, a person becomes fixated on a particular person, object, or activity and does not progress to typical mating behaviors.

Behavioral Theories

Behaviorists suggest that paraphilias develop because some behavior becomes associated with sexual pleasure through conditioning (G. D. Wilson, 1987). For example, imagine that a boy gets a spanking. While receiving it, the boy has an erection, either by coincidence or because he finds the stimulus of the spanking pleasurable (it becomes a reinforcement). Later, remembering the spanking, he becomes excited and masturbates. As he repeats his masturbatory fantasy, a process called conditioning occurs, whereby sexual excitement becomes so associated with the idea of the spanking that he has trouble becoming excited in its absence.

You can imagine how similar situations could lead to other types of fetishes: A boy lies naked on a fur coat, takes a "pony" ride on his aunt's leg while she's wearing her black leather boots, puts on his sister's panties, or spies on a female houseguest through the bathroom keyhole. All of these behaviors become positively reinforced and thus are more likely to be repeated.

Sociological Theories

Another way of looking at the causes of paraphilias is to examine the ways society encourages certain behaviors. Feminists, for example, argue that in societies that treat women as sexual objects, it can be a natural development to replace the woman with another, inanimate sexual object. When men and their sexual organs are glorified, some men may need to reinforce their masculinity by exposing themselves and evoking fear.

American society is ruled by images, saturated with television, movies, commercials, advertisements, and magazines; most of these images have highly charged sexual imagery (R. Collins, 2005). The result, some argue, is a world where the image takes the place of the reality, where it becomes common to substitute fantasies for reality. Surrounded by media, the society experiences things vicariously, through reading about it or seeing it rather than actually doing it. In such a climate, representations of eroticism may be easily substituted for sex itself, and so paraphilias become common.

Check Your Learning Quiz 13.2

Go to **login.cengagebrain.com** and take the online quiz.

▸ **LO4** Explain how the intermittent use of certain objects or fantasies in lovemaking differs from a fetish.

▸ **LO5** Define *fetishistic disorder.*

▸ **LO6** Define *transvestic disorder.*

Many people enjoy using lingerie or other fabrics as part of their lovemaking without becoming dependent on them for arousal. It is common for young children to play around with clothing and sometimes dress as the other sex, but the majority of them do not develop an erotic attraction to the clothing.

A person with a fetish (a *fetishist*), in contrast, needs the presence or the fantasy of the object to achieve arousal and sometimes cannot achieve orgasm in its absence. Some fetishists integrate the object of their desire into their sexual life with a partner; for others it remains a secret fetish, with hidden collections of shoes, or panties, or photographs of a body part, over which they masturbate in secret, ever fearful of discovery.

Many fetishists see their sexual habits as a major part of their life, a source of their sense of identity. Yet, because fetishism is often regarded by society as shameful, they may be embarrassed to admit to their sexual desires. It is therefore rare to find individuals who are open about their fetishes.

Fetishism involves a person becoming sexually attracted to a symbol itself instead of what it represents. Put another way, for the fetishist, the object—unlike the living,

It is common for young children to play around with clothing and sometimes dress as the other sex. Above, a young boy dresses as a ballerina while a young girl dresses as a man.

breathing person—is itself erotic, rather than the person, which also eliminates having to deal with another person's feelings, wants, and needs. It can be a refuge from the complexity of interpersonal sexual relations. In that sense, all the paraphilias we discuss can be seen as a type of fetishism; pain and humiliation, or women's clothes, or looking at people having sex can each be a substitute for interpersonal sexuality.

A person with a foot fetish has an inability to experience sexual arousal or orgasm without contact or a sexual fantasy about feet.

© Zefa RF/Alamy

Fetishistic Disorder

A fetishistic (FEH-tish-is-tic) disorder is defined as recurrent and intense sexual arousal manifested in fantasies, urges, or behaviors that involve the use of nonliving objects (such as shoes, boots, panties, or bras; to a fabric, such as leather, silk, fur, or rubber) or focus on nongenital body parts (such as feet or hair). As with most paraphilias, the majority of fetishists are male (Darcangelo, 2008). The strength of the preference for the object varies from thinking about or holding the object to a need to use it during all sexual acts.

Transvestic Disorder

Chapter 3 discussed the transgender community, which includes a variety of gender diverse individuals. This is different from a transvestic (trans-VESS-tick) disorder, which involves wearing clothes of the other gender and recurrent and intense sexual arousal from the cross-dressing, which can cause significant distress or impairment in daily functioning (American Psychiatric Association, 2010).

Even so, transvestic disorder is usually harmless, and many transvestites are not anxious to seek out therapy to stop their behavior (Newring et al., 2008). Many times, treatment is sought only when a transvestite's partner is upset or the cross-dressing causes stress in the relationship (Dzelme & Jones, 2001). The goal of therapy is to cope with the anxieties and guilt of the transvestites and the way they relate interpersonally and sexually with their partner and family (Newring et al., 2008).

Kiki and Kink

A young woman explains her interest in sexual kink and describes various "scenes" she has been involved in.

Check Your Learning Quiz 13.3

Go to **login.cengagebrain.com** and take the online quiz.

13.4 Sadism and Masochism

▶ **L07** Define *sexual sadism disorder*.

▶ **L08** Define *sexual masochism disorder*.

▶ **L09** Discuss sadomasochistic behaviors and differentiate between dominant and submissive roles.

Sexual Sadism Disorder

Sexual sadism disorder refers to recurrent and intense sexual arousal from the physical or psychological suffering of another person, which can be manifested by fantasies or behaviors (American Psychiatric Association, 2010). Sadistic behaviors may include restraint, blindfolding, strangulation, spanking, whipping, pinching, beating, burning, and electrical shocks (Kleinplatz & Moser, 2006).

The term **sadism** is derived from a man named Donatien Alphonse François de Sade (1740–1814), known as the Marquis de Sade. De Sade believed that the highest form of sexual activity for women was pain, not pleasure, because pleasure could be too easily faked. Marquis De Sade spent much of his life in prison (Bullough, 1976).

Sexual Masochism Disorder

The *DSM* describes sexual masochism disorder (MASS-oh-kiz-um) as a recurrent and intense sexual arousal from the act of being humiliated, beaten, bound, or suffering in other ways (American Psychiatric Association, 2010). The *DSM* criteria specifies that these behaviors typically cause significant distress or impairment in life functioning for a period of at least six months. A professional dominatrix like the one shown in the nearby photo can be hired to assist a masochist in bondage and discipline fantasy play.

Sadomasochism

sadism Deriving sexual pleasure from administering or watching pain and humiliation.

masochism Deriving sexual pleasure from receiving pain or being humiliated.

sadomasochism Broad term that refers to the receiving of sexual pleasure from acts involving the infliction or receiving of pain and humiliation.

dominant Describes the active role in sadomasochistic sexuality.

submissive Describes the passive role in sadomasochistic activity.

Sadism and **masochism** both associate sexuality and pain, and most people who practice one are also involved with the other. Therefore, the phenomenon as a whole is often referred to as **sadomasochism** (say-doe-MASS-oh-kiz-um), or S&M. The acronym BDSM—bondage, discipline, sadism, and masochism—is commonly used today because it illustrates the diverse range of possible experiences (Kleinplatz & Moser, 2006; Wiseman, 2000). A sadomasochistic (or "kink") subculture exists for those who

A dominatrix.

© Joel Gordon

have adopted BDSM as a lifestyle. Sadomasochistic subcultures exist among gays, lesbians, and heterosexuals (Nordling et al., 2006; Sandnabba et al., 2002).

In most S&M encounters, one partner plays the **dominant** role ("master" or "top") and the other the **submissive** ("slave" or "bottom"). Female dominants are often referred to as Mistress, and male dominants are referred to as Master or Lord. Bondage and restraint are the most common expressions of BDSM, although it is power, rather than pain, that is the most important aspect of BDSM behaviors (Cross & Matheson, 2006; Seligman & Hardenburg, 2000). A "safe word" is usually agreed on so that the submissive partner can signal if he or she is in real distress.

Sadomasochists often use props, like leather clothes, studs, chains, and nipple clamps.

The BDSM subculture takes symbols of authority and dominance from the general culture, such as whips, uniforms, and handcuffs, and uses them in a safe erotic drama in which scripted roles take the place of "real self." It even mocks these symbols of authority by using them for erotic pleasure. Well-known social psychologist R. F. Baumeister (1988) suggests that sadomasochism is a reaction to modern society itself. Noting that sexual masochism proliferated when Western culture became highly individualistic, Baumeister suggests that it relieves the submissive partner of a sense of responsibility for the self by placing one's behavior completely under someone else's control. The majority of men and women who engage in BDSM behaviors are well adjusted and well educated (Allison et al., 2001; Kleinplatz & Moser, 2006; Santilla et al., 2000).

The Professional Dominatrix

Hear from a professional dominatrix about her job.

BDSM

A couple discusses their master/slave relationship.

Check Your Learning Quiz 13.4

Go to **login.cengagebrain.com** and take the online quiz.

▶ **LO10** Define *exhibitionism* and explain what exhibitionists are typically looking for when they flash an unsuspecting individual.

▶ **LO11** Define *voyeurism* and explain what voyeurs are typically looking for when they peep.

For some people, looking at nudity or sexual acts, or being seen naked or engaging in sex, become the paramount activities of sexuality. The person who becomes sexually aroused primarily from displaying his (or, more rarely, her) genitals, nudity, or sexuality to strangers is an *exhibitionist;* the person whose primary mode of sexual stimulation is to watch others naked or engaging in sex is called a *voyeur.* Langevin and Lang (1987) reviewed a number of studies that show that there is a close connection between **exhibitionism** and **voyeurism**; most exhibitionists engaged in voyeuristic habits before beginning to expose themselves.

Exhibitionism

Exhibitionism (or exhibitionistic disorder) involves recurrent and intense arousal from exposing one's genitals to an unsuspecting stranger (American Psychiatric Association, 2010). As such, this behavior is nonconsensual. The exhibitionist (or "flasher"), who is usually male, achieves sexual gratification from exposing his genitals in public or to unsuspecting people, who are usually female (Murphy & Page, 2008). What excites the exhibitionist is not usually the nudity itself but the lack of consent of the victim as expressed in her shocked or fearful reaction.

Exhibitionism is legally classified as "indecent exposure" and accounts for up to 33% of all sex convictions in the United States, Canada, and Europe (Bogaerts et al., 2006; Langevin & Lang, 1987; Murphy & Page, 2008). However, it is important to keep in mind that exhibitionists have a witness to their crimes, unlike some of the other paraphilias (such as voyeurism). As such, there is a higher likelihood of being caught. The majority of exhibitionists are shy and withdrawn, and many have been found to have borderline or avoidant personality disorders, or both (Murphy & Page, 2008). Although we don't know exactly how many exhibitionists there are, we do know that many women are "flashed"—in fact, 40% to 60% of female college students report having been flashed at some point (Murphy & Page, 2008).

Exhibitionism in women is rare, although cases of it are reported in the literature (Grob, 1985; Rhoads & Boekelheide, 1985). Perhaps, however, exhibitionism in women just takes a different form than in men. Women have more legitimate ways to expose their bodies than men do. After all, women exposing breast (and even buttock) cleavage is often acceptable by today's fashion standards.

exhibitionist A person who experiences recurrent and intense arousal from exposing his genitals to an unsuspecting stranger.

voyeur A person who experiences recurrent and intense arousal from observing unsuspecting persons undressing or engaging in sex acts.

AP/Wide World Photos

Although female exhibitionism is rare, it is interesting how much more acceptable it is for a woman to expose her body in U.S. society. Few people would call the police about this woman exposing her breasts in public.

Voyeurism

Voyeurism, or voyeuristic disorder, involves individuals whose main means of sexual gratification is watching unsuspecting persons undressing, naked, or engaging in sexual activity. Some would argue that we are a voyeuristic society; our major media—newspapers, television, movies, advertisements—are full of sexual images that are intended to interest and arouse us. In modern society, it seems we have all become casual voyeurs to some degree.

Clinical voyeurs, however, are those for whom watching others naked or viewing erotica is a compulsion. Voyeurs are often called "Peeping Toms," a revealing term because implicit in it are two important aspects of voyeurism. First, a "peeper" is one who looks without the knowledge or consent of the person being viewed, and true voyeurs are excited by the illicit aspect of their peeping. Second, voyeurs are usually male. Although it is becoming more acceptable for women in society to watch porn or to go to see male strippers, clinically speaking, there are few "Peeping Janes" (Lavin, 2008).

The Sexual Offender Registry

Student discusses learning her bus driver in middle school was a registered sex offender.

Check Your Learning Quiz 13.5

Go to **login.cengagebrain.com** and take the online quiz.

Throughout history **pedophilia** (pee-doh-FILL-ee-uh) has been called many things, including child-love, cross-generational sex, man–child (or adult–child) interaction, boy-love, pederasty, and Greek love (Bullough, 1990). The variety of terms shows how differently adult–child sexual interactions have been viewed in different periods of history; however, today, pedophilia is illegal in every country in the world (O'Grady, 2001).

Pedophilia involves recurrent and intense sexual arousal from prepubescent or pubescent children, which usually causes distress or impairment in important areas of functioning (American Psychological Association, 2010). Some pedophiles are unable to function sexually with an adult, whereas others also maintain adult sexual relationships (Seligman & Hardenburg, 2000). Some pedophiles only look at children and never touch, whereas others engage in a variety of sexual acts with their victims, with the most common behavior being fondling and exhibitionism, rather than penetration (Murray, 2000). Pedophiles are often 18 years or older and at least 5 years older than their victims.

Clinically speaking, pedophilia refers to sexual activity with a prepubescent child (younger than 14 years). Many times these behaviors are also referred to as child sexual abuse. In fact, it has been shown that heterosexual males in almost all cultures are attracted to younger females, and homosexual males are attracted to younger (or younger appearing) males (O'Grady, 2001). Many child abuse activists argue that the sexualization of children in the media contributes to this attraction.

Female pedophiles also exist, although they often abuse children in concert with another person, usually their male partner. They may act to please their adult sexual partners rather than to satisfy their own pedophilic desires. Although less common, female pedophiles have been found to have a higher incidence of psychiatric disorders than male pedophiles (Chow & Choy, 2002).

Pedophilia and the Law

Pedophiles often believe that their behavior does not cause any negative psychological or physical consequences for their victims (Miranda & Fiorello, 2002). Many threaten their victims and tell them they must keep their sexual activity secret. Unfortunately, some pedophiles, realizing the chance of the child reporting the act, kill their victims. After one such murder of a young New Jersey girl named Megan Kanka in July 1994, her parents spearheaded "Megan's Law," which was signed into state law in October 1994. This law made it mandatory for authorities in New Jersey to tell parents when a

pedophilia A paraphilia that involves recurrent and intense sexual arousal from prepubescent or pubescent children, which usually causes distress or impairment in important areas of functioning. People who engage in this behavior are called *pedophiles,* or *sexual offenders.*

recidivism A tendency to repeat crimes, such as sexual offenses.

Toys that sexualize girls, such as Bratz dolls, can encourage girls to think of and treat their bodies as sexual objects.

convicted child molester moved into the neighborhood and increased penalties for child molesters. In 1996, Megan's Law became federal law. Pedophiles have high **recidivism** (re-SID-iv-iz-um) rates, and for some unknown reason, these rates are higher in homosexual men (Murray, 2000). The recidivism rate is the main impetus for legislation such as Megan's Law (M. A. Alexander, 1999).

A number of small organizations in Western countries, usually made up of pedophiles, argue that man–boy love should be legalized, usually under the pretense of guarding "the sexual rights of children and adolescents" (Okami, 1990). In America, the North American Man–Boy Love Association (NAMBLA) supports the abolition of age-of-consent laws. NAMBLA believes that there is a difference between those who simply want to use children for sexual release and those who develop long-lasting, often exclusive, and even loving relationships with a single boy. In contrast, those who work with sexually abused children vehemently deny the claim, pointing to children whose lives were ruined by sex with adults.

Factors Associated with the Development of Pedophiles

Over the years, research has found that being a victim of sexual abuse in childhood is one of the most frequently reported risk factors for the development of pedophilia (Glasser et al., 2001; Langstrom et al., 2000; Seto, 2004). It is estimated that 35% of pedophiles were sexually abused as children (Keegan, 2001). Studies have also found that the choice of gender and age of victims often reflects the pattern of past sexual abuse in the pedophile's life (Pollock & Hashmall, 1991). Although past sexual abuse is a risk factor, it is important to point out that the majority of male victims of child sexual abuse do not become pedophiles (Salter et al., 2003). Other studies have found that pedophiles have brain abnormalities that contribute to their sexual behaviors (Eastvold et al., 2011).

Dutch Pedophilia Party?
Does everyone have the right to express themselves?
The Story of Megan's Law
Many convicted sex offenders have protested, claiming that the law violates their constitutional rights . . .

Check Your Learning Quiz 13.6
Go to **login.cengagebrain.com** and take the online quiz.

Scatolophilia

Scatolophilia (scat-oh-low-FILL-ee-uh), or obscene telephone calling, is when a person, almost always male, calls women and becomes excited as the victims react to his obscene suggestions. Most scatolophiliacs masturbate either during the call or afterward. Like exhibitionism, scatolophilia is nonconsensual, and the scatolophiliac becomes excited by the victim's reactions of fear, disgust, or outrage.

The obscene telephone caller may boast of sexual acts he will perform on the victim, may describe his masturbation in detail, may threaten the victim, or may try to entice the victim to reveal aspects of her sexual life or even perform sexual acts such as masturbating while he listens on the phone. Some callers are very persuasive; many have great success in talking women into performing sexual acts while posing as product representatives recalling certain products, as the police, or even as people conducting a sexual survey. (*Note:* No reputable sexuality researchers conduct surveys over the phone. If you receive such a call, do not answer any sexually explicit questions.) Others threaten harm to the victim or her family if she does not do what he asks.

Most scatolophiliacs have problems in their relationships and suffer from feelings of isolation and inadequacy. For many, scatolophilia is the only way they can express themselves sexually (Holmes, 1991). Scatolophiliacs often have coexisting paraphilias, such as exhibitionism or voyeurism (M. Price et al., 2002).

Frotteurism

Frotteurism (frah-TOUR-iz-um) involves a man rubbing his genitals against a woman's thighs or buttocks in a crowded place (such as a subway) where he can claim it was an accident and get away quickly. In some cases, he may fondle a woman's breasts with his hand while he is rubbing up against her. This is similar to toucheurism, which is the compulsive desire to touch strangers with one's hands for sexual arousal. This desire, usually in men, finds expression on buses, trains, in shopping malls, while waiting in line, at crowded concerts, anyplace where bodies are pressed together. Frotteurism, how-

A female-only subway car in Tokyo, Japan.

Koichi Kamoshida/Liaison/Getty Images

ever, does not usually appear in isolation but as one of a number of paraphilias in an individual (Langevin & Lang, 1987).

Problems with groping and frotteurism on public transportation has led to the establishment of women-only passenger cars in places such as Tokyo, Japan, and Seoul, South Korea.

Zoophilia

Zoophilia (zoo-uh-FILL-ee-uh; also referred to as bestiality), or sexual contact with animals, is rare, although Kinsey and his colleagues (1948, 1953) found that 1 man in every 13 engages in this behavior. Contact between people and animals has been both practiced and condemned since the earliest times.

Studies of people who engage in sex with animals have found that a male dog is the most popular animal sex partner for both men and women (Miletski, 2002). Sexual behaviors included masturbating the animal, submitting to anal sex performed by the animal, or active or passive oral sex with the animal (Miletski, 2002).

Necrophilia

Tales of necrophilia (neck-row-FILL-ee-uh), or having sex with corpses, have been found even in ancient civilizations. The Egyptians prohibited embalmers from taking immediate delivery of corpses of the wives of important men for fear that the embalmers would violate them (Rosman & Resnick, 1989). More recently, the legends of the vampires imply necrophilia in the highly sexual approaches of the "undead."

Rosman and Resnick (1989) identified three types of genuine necrophilia: necrophiliac fantasy, in which a person has persistent fantasies about sex with dead bodies without actually engaging in such behavior; "regular" necrophilia, which involves the use of already-dead bodies for sexual pleasure; and necrophiliac homicide, in which the person commits murder to obtain a corpse for sexual pleasure. However, necrophilia is rare and accounts for only a tiny fraction of murders (Milner et al., 2008).

An infamous case of necrophiliac homicide was that of serial killer Jeffrey Dahmer. Dahmer, who admitted to killing 17 men and having sex with their corpses, also mutilated their bodies, tried to create a "shrine" out of their organs that he thought would give him "special powers," and ate their flesh. Dahmer admitted his deeds but claimed he was insane. A jury found him sane and guilty, and he was sentenced to life in prison with no chance of parole. Dahmer was killed by another inmate in 1994.

Obscene Phone Calls, Texts, and Emails

Scatolophilia can be one of the most stressful and frightening invasions of privacy.

Key Terms Exercise

Match the key terms with their definitions.

Check Your Learning Quiz 13.7

Go to **login.cengagebrain.com** and take the online quiz.

13.8 *Sexual Addiction*

▶ **LO19** Discuss sexual addiction and the controversies involved in this disorder.

In the past, derogatory terms, mostly for women, were used to describe these people; an example is **nymphomaniac**. Terms for men were more flattering and included **Don Juanism, satyriasis**, or, in other cases, "studs." Perhaps nowhere else is the double standard between the sexes so blatant—women who enjoy frequent sexual encounters are considered "whores" or "sluts," whereas men who enjoy similar levels of sexual activity have been admired.

Although there is a great range in frequency of sexual contact in the general population, some argue that certain people cross over the line from a vigorous sex life to an obsessed sex life. Sexuality, like drugs, alcohol, gambling, and all other behaviors that bring a sense of excitement and pleasure, should involve some degree of moderation. Yet, for some people, the need for repeated sexual encounters, which often end up being fleeting and unfulfilling, becomes almost a compulsion (Bancroft & Vukadinovic, 2004; G. H. Golden, 2001). An addiction involves an uncontrollable craving and compulsive need for a specific object. A typical sexual addict is a married man whose obsession with masturbation increases to an obsession with pornography, cybersex, prostitute visits, or multiple sexual affairs (Keane, 2004).

Sexual addiction, or hypersexual disorder, involves recurrent and intense sexual fantasies, sexual urges, and sexual behavior, and excessive time spent on these behaviors and an inability to control these fantasies (American Psychiatric Association, 2010). Recent cases of possible sexual addiction involving celebrities such as Tiger Woods, Charlie Sheen, and Arnold Schwarzenegger have put the media spotlight on this disorder.

Hypersexual disorder typically interferes with a person's daily functioning and may include compulsive masturbation or an obsession with pornography, whereas for others it may progress to multiple sex partners or exhibitionistic behaviors. It can lead to emotional suffering and problems in one's occupational functioning and marital and family relationships (Bird, 2006; Miner et al., 2007). A number of self-help groups have been organized, including *Sexaholics Anonymous, Sex Addicts Anonymous, Sex and Love Addicts Anonymous,* and *Co-Dependents of Sexual Addicts.*

Although no definite numbers are available, the Society for the Advancement of Sexual Health estimates that 3% to 5% of Americans have a sexual addiction, with men outnumbering women 5 to 1 (Beck, 2008; Society for the Advancement of Sexual Health, 2008). However, these numbers are based only on those who seek treat-

nymphomaniac A pejorative term used to describe women who engage in frequent or promiscuous sex.

Don Juanism or **satyriasis** Terms used to describe men who engage in frequent or promiscuous sex.

WireImage/Getty Images

Recent cases of sexual addiction in the media involving celebrities such as Charlie Sheen and others have prompted experts to include "hypersexual disorder" in *DSM-5* due out in 2013.

ment, so actual numbers are probably much higher. The availability of sex on the Internet has increased the number of cases of sexual addiction (Landau, 2008).

Typically, treatment of sexual addiction involves individual or group therapy as part of a 12-step recovery process (similar to the Alcoholics Anonymous program), originated by Carnes (2001). Medications may also be used, especially if a person also has bipolar disorder or depression, both of which are commonly associated with compulsive sexual behavior.

Many have criticized the idea of hypersexuality. They argue that terms such as "sexual addiction" are really disguised social judgments. Before the sexual freedom of the 1960s, those who engaged in promiscuous sex were often considered physically, mentally, or morally sick. Some scholars suggest that there has been an attempt to return to a pathological model of sexuality using the concept of addiction (Irvine, 1995).

Sex Addiction

Defining sex addiction, the symptoms, who is susceptible, and whether or not Bill Clinton is considered a sex addict.

On Your Mind

If I think about sex all the time, does that mean I'm addicted to it?

**Check Your Learning
Quiz 13.8**

Go to **login.cengagebrain.com** and take the online quiz.

▶ **LO20** List and describe two assessments for paraphilias and discuss some of the issues involved in these assessments.

▶ **LO21** Explain the goals of behavioral therapies for paraphilia.

Although the majority of those with paraphilias and sexual variations do not seek treatment and are content with balancing the pleasure and guilt of their behaviors, others find their behaviors to be an unwanted disruption to their lives. Their sexual desires may get in the way of forming relationships, may get them into legal trouble, or may become such a preoccupation that they dominate their lives. For these people, a number of therapeutic solutions have been tried, with varying success.

Assessment

Although some people with paraphilias are referred to clinicians by law enforcement, for others, assessment is often done through self-report, behavioral observation, or by physiological tests or personality inventories (Laws & O'Donahue, 2008; Seligman & Hardenburg, 2000). Self-reports may not be reliable, however; individuals under court order to receive treatment for pedophilia may be highly motivated to report that the behavior has ceased. Also, people are not necessarily the best judge of their own desires and behavior; some may truly believe they have overcome their sexual desires when, in fact, they have not. The second technique, behavioral observation, is limited by the fact that it cannot assess fantasies and desires; also, most people can suppress these behaviors for periods of time.

Physiological tests may be a bit more reliable. The most reliable technique for men is probably **penile plethysmography**, which is often used with male sex offenders. For example, a pedophile can be shown films of nude children and the plethysmograph can record his penile blood volume. If he becomes excited at the pictures, then he is probably still having pedophilic desires and fantasies. A similar test is also available to test the sexual response of female offenders. However, both of these physiological tests have been found to be of limited use in this population because there are no outward signs of arousal (Laws & O'Donahue, 2008; Seligman & Hardenburg, 2000).

Personality inventories, such as the **Minnesota Multiphasic Personality Inventory (MMPI)**, can help establish personality patterns and determine whether there are additional psychological disorders (Seligman & Hardenburg, 2000). Other psychological inventories for depression and anxiety are often also used. In the future, the development of methodologies to assess these behaviors will be a priority in this field (Laws & O'Donahue, 2008).

penile plethysmography A test performed by measuring the amount of blood that enters the penis in response to a stimulus, which can indicate how arousing the stimulus is for the male.

Minnesota Multiphasic Personality Inventory (MMPI) Psychological test used to assess general personality characteristics.

Key Terms	Video	Animation	Readings	Assessment
	If I fantasize about being spanked, does that mean I have a paraphilia?			Check Your Learning Quiz 13.1
paraphilia, paraphilic coercive disorder, fetishist, lovemap, hypophilia, hyperphilia, courtship disorder, conditioning	Why do men have more paraphilias than women?		Paraphilias throughout the World	Check Your Learning Quiz 13.2
fetishistic disorder, transvestic disorder	Kiki and Kink			Check Your Learning Quiz 13.3
sexual sadism disorder, sadism, sexual masochism disorder, masochism, sadomasochism, dominant, submissive	The Professional Dominatrix BDSM			Check Your Learning Quiz 13.4
exhibitionist, voyeur	The Sexual Offender Registry			Check Your Learning Quiz 13.5

Measure Your Learning ^

Online Activities

Key Terms	Video	Animation	Readings	Assessment
pedophilia, recidivism			Dutch Pedophilia Party? The Story of Megan's Law	Check Your Learning Quiz 13.6
scatolophilia, frotteurism, toucheurism, zoophilia or bestiality, necrophilia		Key Terms Exercise	Obscene Phone Calls, Texts, and Emails	Check Your Learning Quiz 13.7
nymphomaniac, Don Juanism or satyriasis, hypersexual disorder	Sex Addiction If I think about sex all the time, does that mean I'm addicted to it?			Check Your Learning Quiz 13.8
penile plethysmography, Minnesota Multiphasic Personality Inventory (MMPI), orgasmic reconditioning, satiation therapy, obsessive–compulsive disorder (OCD)			Paraphilia Treatment Options	Check Your Learning Quiz 13.9
				Internet Sexual Addiction

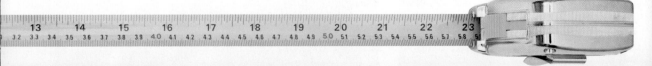

Power and Sexual Coercion

14

Prepare ^to Learn

1 **GO** to your **Psychology CourseMate** at **login.cengagebrain.com** and take the **Chapter Pre-Test** to introduce yourself to this chapter's topics and see what you may already know.

2 **READ** the **Learning Objectives** (LOs, in the left sidebars) and begin the chapter.

3 **COMPLETE** the **Online Activities** (in the right sidebars) *as you read each module.* Activities include **videos, animations, readings,** and **quizzes.**

4 **CHECK Your Learning** by going online to take the quiz at the end of each module and review material as necessary.

5 **MEASURE Your Learning** after reading the chapter by taking the online **Chapter Post-Test.** Use the chapter review guide at the end of the chapter as needed.

WATCH for these **Online Activities** icons as you read:

Video

Animation

Reading

Assessment

Think Critically

These Online Activities are essential to mastering this chapter. Go to login.cengagebrain.com.

 Videos Explore diverse perspectives on sex as well as common questions:

- Why do people rape?
- The Online Sexual Predator
- Is it rape if my ex-boyfriend forces me to have sex with him?
- What if I had sex with a girl when we were really drunk and then she called it rape the next morning?
- Rape and Post-traumatic Stress Disorder
- Can a woman who was raped eventually have a normal sex life?
- Can a man really be raped?
- Date Rape: Meg's Story
- Child Sexual Abuse
- Psychology of an Abusive Relationship

 Animations Interact with and visualize important processes, timelines, and concepts:

- Testing Your Beliefs in Rape Myths

 Readings Delve deeper into key content:

- Date Rape Drugs
- Corrective Rape
- Confronting the Incest Offender
- Domestic Violence in Lesbian Relationships

 Assessment Measure your mastery:

- Chapter Pre-Test
- Check Your Learning Quizzes
- Chapter Post-Test

 Think Critically Challenge your thinking about data and accepted norms:

- Sexual Harassment

▶ **LO1** Define *rape* and *sexual assault,* and explain how certain factors can make defining these crimes difficult.

IN 2009, there were 125,910 cases of rape or sexual assault reported in the United States, which was significantly less than the 203,830 cases that were reported in 2008 (Truman & Rand, 2010). Although both women and men can be raped, by far the majority of victims are female (Figure 14.1). We will primarily discuss the rape of women by men here and will explore the rape of men later in this chapter. In the majority of rape or sexual assault cases, the victims know their assailants (Lawyer et al., 2010; Figure 14.2).

▼

Defining Rape and Sexual Assault

The line that separates **rape** from other categories of sexual activity can be blurry because of the fine distinctions between forced and consensual sex, as well as societal patterns of female passivity and male aggression (LaFree, 1982). For instance, societal and cultural rules often dictate that among heterosexuals, men, not women,

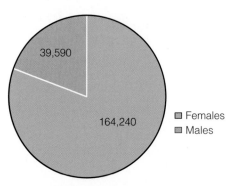

Figure 14.1 Reported rapes by sex of victim in the United States, 2008. Source: U.S. Department of Justice, Bureau of Justice Statistics, 2008

rape Forced sexual behavior without a person's consent.

should initiate sexual activity. These beliefs about how sex is supposed to be can make defining rape a difficult task. Defining rape is also complicated by the fact that sometimes unwanted sex is consensual (meaning that one or both parties said yes when they wished they had said no or regretted sex afterwards). Studies have found that a significant percentage of college students engage in unwanted sexual activity in dating relationships (Brousseau et al., 2011; O'Sullivan & Allgeier, 1998).

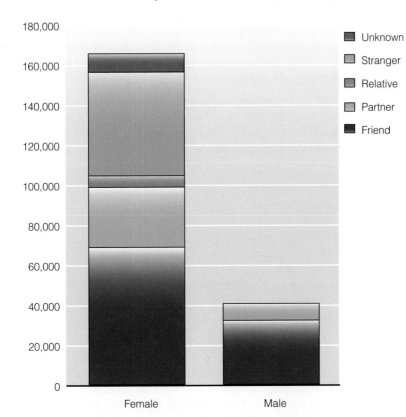

Figure 14.2 Number of rapes/sexual assaults by relationship with offender. Source: U.S. Department of Justice, Bureau of Justice Statistics. Criminal Victimization, 2008

On Your Mind

Why do people rape?

The Online Sexual Predator

The psychology of an online predator is explored through an interview with him and the woman he married in order to have access to her daughter.

On Your Mind

Is it rape if my ex-boyfriend forces me to have sex with him?

The U.S. Department of Justice defines rape as forced sexual penetration that can include psychological and physiological coercion. This would include forced vaginal, anal, or oral penetration. Psychological coercion would include pressuring someone who has not consented to sexual activity or taking advantage of someone because of their intellectual abilities, intoxication, or age. **Sexual assault** is defined as any type of sexual contact or behavior that occurs without the consent of the recipient of the unwanted sexual activity. Behaviors that are included in the definition of sexual assault are unwanted penetration, forced oral sex, masturbation, touching, fondling, or kissing. It would also include forcing someone to view sexually explicit materials, such as pornography. These definitions apply to both male and female victims, and include heterosexual and homosexual rape and sexual assault.

Common Myths about Rape

Martha Burt (1980) defined rape myths as prejudicial and stereotyped beliefs about rape, rape victims, and rapists. They often lead people to justify rape by rationalizing what happened and who might be at fault. Frequently, they shift the blame for rape to the victims. Some common myths are:

- Only "bad" women get raped.
- Women make false reports of rape.
- Women fantasize about rape.
- Men can't be raped.
- You can tell a rapist by the way he looks.
- People cannot be raped against their will.
- A man can't rape his wife.
- Rape happens only to young, attractive women.
- Most rapists rape only once.
- Women who are raped usually have a bad reputation.

Characteristics of Rapists

sexual assault Coercion of a non-consenting victim to have sexual contact.

intimate partner violence (IPV) A pattern of coercive behavior designed to exert power and control over a person in an intimate relationship through the use of intimidation, threats, or harmful or harassing behavior.

What is your image of a "rapist"? Who is it that rapes? A stranger who jumps out of a bush? A drunk at a fraternity party? Rapists are primarily male, single, and between the ages of 15 and 30 (Amir, 1971; D. E. H. Russell, 1984). They have been found to have high levels of impulsivity and aggression, sexist views about women, and high levels of rape myth acceptance (Beech et al., 2006; Giotakos et al., 2005; Lalumière et al., 2005d; Langevin et al., 2007; Masser et al., 2006). Men who commit sexual assault and rape often have histories of personal violence, such as child physical abuse, child sexual abuse, dating violence, or **intimate partner violence** (**IPV**; Cavanaugh et al., 2011; Lisak & Miller, 2002). Even so, despite the assumption that rapists are psychologically disturbed individuals, research does not support the belief that they are very different from nonoffenders (Oliver et al., 2007; Voller & Long, 2010).

Rapists often have multiple victims. In fact, research has found that the majority of rapes against women are perpetrated by serial offenders, each of whom has had an average of six victims (Lisak & Miller, 2002). Thus, a relatively small number of men are responsible for a large number of rapes, which explains the disparities between the number of men who say they rape and the number of women who say they have been raped (Lisak & Miller, 2002). Within this group of men, there are a variety of rapist "types," including the power, anger, and sadistic rapists, which differentiate motivations for rape (J. Douglas & Olshaker, 1998; Hazelwood & Burgess, 1987; McCabe & Wauchope, 2005; Pardue & Arrigo, 2008). Power rapists are motivated by domination and control; anger rapists are motivated by anger and use it in overt ways (i.e., force or weapons); and sadistic rapists are motivated by sexual and aggressive fantasies.

Variations in Attitudes toward Rape

Studies have found gender and ethnic variations in attitudes about rape. In addition, cultural issues can affect how a society defines rape and the attitudes toward it. These issues are discussed in the following sections.

Gender Differences in Attitudes about Rape

Overall, men are less empathetic and sensitive than women toward rape (Black & Gold, 2008; Davies et al., 2009; Earnshaw et al., 2011; Schneider et al., 2009). Men are more likely than women to believe rape myths and blame victims (Earnshaw et al., 2011; Franiuk et al., 2008). Studies have found that heterosexual men are more likely than heterosexual women to believe that a man should expect sexual intercourse if he pays for an expensive date (Basow & Minieri, 2011; Emmers-Sommer et al., 2010); however, there were no expectations when the expenses were split.

However, some hope exists about changing these attitudes about rape. Men who take rape education workshops or college courses on violence against women have less rape-myth acceptance than men who do not take such workshops or courses (Currier & Carlson, 2009; Foubert & Cremedy, 2007).

Testing Your Beliefs in Rape Myths

Myth or reality?

Ethnic Differences in Attitudes about Rape

Overall, ethnic minorities have been found to have more traditional attitudes toward women, which have been found to affect rape attitudes. For example, among college students, non-Hispanic Whites are more sympathetic than Blacks to women who have been raped (Nagel et al., 2005). However, Blacks are more sympathetic than either Hispanic or Japanese American college students (Fischer, 1987; Littleton et al., 2007; Yamawaki & Tschanz, 2005). Asian American students have the least sympathy for women who have been raped and are more likely to hold a rape victim responsible for the rape and excuse the rapist (Devdas & Rubin, 2007; J. Lee et al., 2005; Yamawaki & Tschanz, 2005).

Cultural Differences in Attitudes about Rape

Rape is defined differently around the world, so the incidence of rape varies depending on a culture's definition. One culture might accept sexual behavior that is considered rape in another culture. For example, rape has been accepted as a punishment in some cultures throughout history. Among the Cheyenne Indians, a husband who suspected his wife of infidelity could put her "out to field," where other men were encouraged to rape her (Hoebel, 1954). In the Marshall Islands of the Pacific Ocean, women were seen as the property of the males, and any male could force sexual intercourse upon them (Sanday, 1981). In Kenya, the Gusii people view intercourse as an act in which males overpower their female partners and cause them considerable pain. In fact, if she has difficulty walking the next morning, the man is seen as a "real man" and will boast of his ability to make his partner cry (Bart & O'Brien, 1985). In 2002, an 11-year-old Pakistani boy was found guilty of walking unchaperoned with a girl from a different tribe. His punishment involved the gang raping of his 18-year-old sister, which was done to shame his family. The gang rape took place in a mud hut while hundreds of people stood by and laughed and cheered (Tanveer, 2002).

Rape has also been used for initiation purposes. In East Africa, the Kikuyu used to have an initiation ritual in which a young boy was expected to rape to prove his manhood (Broude & Greene, 1976). Until he did this, he could not engage in sexual intercourse or marry a woman. In Australia, among the Arunta, rape serves as an initiation rite for girls. After the ceremonial rape, she is given to her husband, and no one else has access to her (Broude & Greene, 1976).

Many cultural beliefs and societal issues are responsible for the high rape rates in South Africa, including the fact that South African women have a difficult time say-

Rapex, an anti-rape condom worn by women, was unveiled in South Africa in 2005. The South African inventor, shown here, advises women to insert the device as part of their daily security routine. During a rape, metal barbs in the condom will hook into the skin of the penis and immediately disable the man, allowing the woman to get away. The barbs must be surgically removed, so a rapist will need to seek medical attention, enabling the police to identify him.

ing no to sex; many men believe they are entitled to sex and believe that women enjoy being raped (Meier, 2002). In 2005 an anti-rape female condom was unveiled in South Africa (Dixon, 2005; see nearby photo). This device was controversial, with some believing that it put the responsibility for the problem on the shoulders of South African women and others believing that the device was a valuable tool in decreasing the climbing rape rates in South Africa.

In Asian cultures there are often more conservative attitudes about sex; because of this, there is often more tolerance for rape myths (M. A. Kennedy & Gorzalka, 2002; Uji et al., 2007; Yamawaki, 2007). Research by Sanday (1981) indicates that the primary cultural factors that affect the incidence of rape in a society include relations between the sexes, the status of women, and male attitudes in the society. Societies that promote male violence have higher incidences of rape because men are socialized to be aggressive and dominating and to use force to get what they want.

Check Your Learning
Quiz 14.1

Go to **login.cengagebrain.com** and take the online quiz.

Female college students are at greater risk for rape than their noncollege peers (Gonzales et al., 2005). It is estimated that 1 of every 5 college women will experience a rape during college. The majority of these rapes will be perpetrated by someone the women know, which is why most cases are never reported (B. S. Fisher et al., 2000).

Alcohol and Rape

On college campuses, alcohol use is one of the strongest predictors of rape—up to 66% of rape victims have voluntarily consumed alcohol before an assault (Lawyer et al., 2010; Littleton et al., 2009a). Women who are drunk are more likely to be viewed as "loose" or sexually "easy" (Parks & Scheidt, 2000). For men, alcohol seems to "sexualize" the environment around them. Cues that might be taken as neutral if the men were not drunk (such as a certain woman talking to them or dancing with them) may be seen as an indication of sexual interest (Abbey et al., 2005; Montemurro & McClure, 2005; Peralta, 2008). Alcohol also reduces inhibitions, which increases the chances of engaging in risky sexual behaviors for both men and women (Klein et al., 2007; Maisto et al., 2004; O'Hare, 2005). Being impaired or incapacitated during a rape has been associated with self-blame, stigma, and problematic alcohol use in victims post-assault (Littleton et al., 2009a). In addition, many women might not even label the event as a rape even when it clearly was (L. G. Hensley, 2002).

Fraternities and Rape

Initially, Greek organizations were established to help students join together to participate in social issues that they felt were largely ignored by their respective universities (Bryan, 1987). Today, however, many fraternities and sororities operate primarily for socializing. Although rape does occur in residence halls and off-campus apartments, there are several ways in which fraternities create a riper environment for rape. Many fraternities revolve around an ethic of masculinity. Values that the members see as important include competition, dominance, willingness to drink alcohol, and sexual prowess. There is considerable pressure to be sexually successful, and the members gain respect from other members through sex (Flanagan, 2011; Murnen & Kohlman, 2007). The emphasis on masculinity, secrecy, and the protection of the group often provides a fertile environment for coercive sexuality (Adams-Curtis & Forbes, 2004). In addition, fraternity men have been found to be more accepting of rape myths (Bleecker & Murnen, 2005).

Athletes and Rape

Over the last few years, it has become increasingly more common to hear stories in the news about college and professional athletes who are accused of rape or sexual assault (Farr & Kern, 2010; Lundstrom & Walsh, 2010; Namuo, 2010; Tramel,

Alcohol can sexualize the environment for men, making neutral comments seem sexual in nature.

2011). Participation in athletics has been found to be associated with rape-supportive attitudes and, to a lesser degree, sexually aggressive behavior (Murnen & Kohlman, 2007). In addition, athletes who participate on teams that produce revenue have higher rates of sexually abusive behavior than athletes on teams that do not produce revenue (McMahon, 2004). Researchers suggest that perhaps it is the sense of privilege that contributes to a view of the world in which rape is legitimized. Playing sports may also help connect aggression and sexuality.

Some researchers suggest that all male groups may foster "hypermasculinity," which promotes the idea that violence and aggression are "manly" (Muehlenhard & Cook, 1988). The need to be aggressive and tough while playing sports may also help create problems off the field (Boeringer, 1999; T. J. Brown et al., 2002). Many male athletes may also have a distorted view of women, which often revolves around views expressed in the locker room. Locker room talk often includes derogatory language about women (including the use of words such as "sluts" or "bitches" to describe them), whereas those athletes who are not playing well are referred to as "girls" (McMahon, 2004; Murnen & Kohlman, 2007).

On Your Mind

What if I had sex with a girl when we were really drunk and then she called it rape the next morning?

Date Rape Drugs

Names, Slang, and Effects

**Check Your Learning
Quiz 14.2**

Go to **login.cengagebrain.com** and take the online quiz.

▶ **LO8** Describe and compare the physical effects of rape on younger and older women.

▶ **LO9** Discuss the range of psychological and emotional reactions to rape experienced by victims and by victims' partners.

Rape is an emotionally, physically, and psychologically shattering experience for the victim. Some deny that the rape occurred at all, to avoid the pain of dealing with it. Others express self-blame, disbelief, anger, vulnerability, and increased feelings of dependency. As time goes by, the healing process begins, and feelings may shift to self-pity, sadness, and guilt. Anxiety attacks, nightmares, and fear slowly begin to decrease, although the incident is never forgotten. Some women never return to prior functioning levels and must create an entirely new view of themselves.

Physical Effects of Rape

Physical symptoms after a rape include general body soreness, bruises, nausea, throat soreness and difficulties swallowing (if there was oral sex), genital itching or burning, and rectal bleeding or pain (if there was anal sex). In women, the emotional stress of the rape may also cause menstrual irregularities. However, some of these symptoms (nausea and menstrual irregularities) are also signs of pregnancy, which is why a pregnancy test is of utmost importance after a victim has been raped.

Although it is true that younger women are at greater risk for rape, older women are likely to be even more traumatized by rape than younger women because they have undergone physical changes in the genitals (lack of lubrication and/or thinning of the walls of the vagina) that can increase the severity of physical injury. In addition, many have very conservative attitudes about sexuality and have less social support after a rape, which reinforces and intensifies their sense of vulnerability (Burgess & Morgenbesser, 2005).

rape trauma syndrome (RTS) A two-stage stress response pattern that occurs after a rape.

post-traumatic stress disorder (PTSD) Anxiety disorder that can develop after a life-threatening or anxiety-producing event and can cause ongoing emotional and psychological symptoms, such as insomnia, depression, flashbacks, and nightmares.

long-term reorganization The second stage of the rape trauma syndrome, which involves a restoration of order in the victim's lifestyle and reestablishment of control.

Mel Curtis/Getty Images

The majority of women who are raped know their assailant.

Psychological and Emotional Reactions to Rape

Emotional reactions also vary depending on whether the victims knew their assailants. Women who report being raped by strangers experience more anxiety, fear, and startle responses, whereas those raped by acquaintances usually report more depression and guilt, and decreased self-confidence (Sorenson & Brown, 1990). The majority of women who have been raped know their assailant and may have initially trusted him and agreed to be with him. After the rape, they may second-guess themselves, wondering how they could have had such bad judgment or why they didn't see it coming. Many also feel a sense of betrayal. Women who feel guilty or responsible for a rape have lower levels of psychological well-being than women who do not feel responsible or guilty (Glenn & Byers, 2009).

Rape Trauma Syndrome

Researchers Burgess and Holmstrom (1974) coined the term **rape trauma syndrome (RTS)**, which describes the effects of rape. RTS is a two-stage stress response pattern characterized by physical, psychological, behavioral, or sexual problems, or a combination of these, and it occurs after forced, nonconsenting sexual activity. Although the *Diagnostic and Statistical Manual of Mental Disorders* does not recognize RTS, the symptoms are similar to **post-traumatic stress disorder (PTSD)**, which occurs after a traumatic event. Research has found that a significant number of rape survivors experience development of PTSD within 2 weeks after the rape (Littleton & Henderson, 2009; Taft et al., 2009).

During the first stage of RTS, most victims fear being alone, strangers, or even their bedroom or their car if that is where the rape took place. Other emotional reactions to rape include anger (at the assailant, the rape, health care workers, family, oneself, court), anxiety, depression, confusion, shock, disbelief, incoherence, guilt, humiliation, shame, and self-blame (Frazier, 2000). A victim may also experience wide mood fluctuations. Difficulties with sleeping, including recurrent nightmares, are common. This phase begins immediately after the assault, may last from days to weeks, and involves several stress-related symptoms. Talking to a counselor can be very helpful in working through these feelings.

Long-term reorganization, stage two of RTS, involves restoring order in the victim's lifestyle and reestablishing control. Many victims report that changing some aspect of their lives, such as changing addresses, roommates, universities, or even phone numbers, helped them to gain control.

Rape and Post-traumatic Stress Disorder

Listen to a young woman describe her symptoms of post-traumatic stress disorder after being raped.

On Your Mind

Can a woman who has been raped eventually have a normal sex life?

© David Buffington/Photodisc/Picturequest

Talking with a counselor can help rape victims work through their emotional reactions, such as anger, depression, self-blame, guilt, and/or humiliation.

silent rape reaction A type of rape trauma syndrome in which a victim does not talk to anyone after the rape.

rape crisis centers Organizations that offer support services to victims of sexual assault, their families, and friends. Many offer information, referrals, support groups, counseling, educational programs, and workshops.

Silent Rape Reaction

Some victims never discuss their rape with anyone and carry the burden of the assault alone. Burgess and Holmstrom (1974) call this the **silent rape reaction**, and in many ways, it is similar to RTS. Feelings of fear, anger, and depression and physiological symptoms still exist; however, they remain locked inside. In fact, those who take longer to confide in someone usually suffer a longer recovery period (L. Cohen & Roth, 1987). The silent rape reaction occurs because some victims deny and repress the incident until a time when they feel stronger emotionally. This may be months or even years later.

Partners' Reactions to Rape

When a man or woman's sexual partner is raped, the partner often feels anger, frustration, and intense feelings of revenge (M. E. Smith, 2005). Many partners express a strong desire to "kill him" (the rapist), "make him pay," and the like. In addition, some partners experience a sense of loss, guilt, self-blame, and jealousy. Emotional reactions to the rape may affect their feelings about their partner and their view of men in the world (M. E. Smith, 2005). In cases of acquaintance rape, people may lose trust in their partner, feeling that because the partner knew the assailant, she may have expressed sexual interest in him. Overall, after a date rape experience, negative judgments and reactions by a rape victim's partner are common (A. Brown & Testa, 2008). These reactions further isolate the victim and reinforce her feelings of guilt.

All in all, rape places a great deal of stress on a relationship. Couples often avoid dealing with rape entirely, believing that talking about it would be too stressful. Many men feel uncomfortable sharing their feelings about a rape because they worry about burdening their partners. However, open communication is extremely beneficial and should be encouraged. Even though dealing with a rape in a relationship can be traumatic, it has been found that women who have a stable and supportive partner recover from a rape more quickly than those who do not. In addition, **rape crisis centers** offer valuable support services to victims of rape and sexual assault.

Partners of rape victims often experience feelings of anger, frustration, guilt, and self-blame.

Check Your Learning Quiz 14.3

Go to **login.cengagebrain.com** and take the online quiz.

Although we have learned from the research that certain groups of people (such as female college students) are at greater risk for rape and sexual assault, we also know that there are special populations who are also at risk.

Marital Rape

Since 1993, marital rape has been a crime in all 50 states. However, 30 states have exemptions for husbands when they force sex under certain conditions (e.g., while the wife is unconscious, asleep, or mentally impaired; Bergen, 2006). It has been estimated that 10% to 14% of all married women have been raped by their husbands, although this percentage is much higher in battered women (D. E. H. Russell & Howell, 1983; Yllo & Finkelhor, 1985).

Although their symptoms are similar to those who are victims of nonmarital rape, many of these women report feeling extremely betrayed and may lose the ability to trust others, especially men. In addition, there is often little social support for wives who are raped, and those who stay with their husbands often endure repeated attacks (Bergen & Bukovec, 2006). Unfortunately, marital rape may be one of the least discussed types of rape.

Lesbian and Bisexual Rape

Rape is a common experience in both lesbian and bisexual women. In fact, adult sexual assault by men is slightly higher in lesbian and bisexual women compared with heterosexual women (Balsam et al., 2005). Like heterosexual women, lesbian and bisexual women experience RTS after a rape. However, there may be more intense emotional repercussions compared with heterosexual women (Campbell, 2008; Long et al., 2007). Lesbians may also experience difficulties in assimilating the experience of rape into their own self-image (Long et al., 2007). Some lesbians may have never experienced vaginal intercourse with a man and may be unaccustomed to dealing with the fear of pregnancy, let alone the extreme feelings of being violated and abused. Although little research is available on this topic, lesbians can also be raped by women (Campbell, 2008).

Women with Disabilities and Rape

Women with disabilities are assaulted, raped, and abused at a rate two times greater than women without disabilities (Cusitar, 1994; Sobsey, 1994; Wacker et al., 2008).

They may be more vulnerable because of their diminished ability to fight back. In addition, mentally handicapped persons may have a more difficult time reading the preliminary cues that would alert them to danger. In many cases, women with severe mental disabilities who have been sexually assaulted may not realize that their rights have been violated and therefore may not report the crime. Because of these factors, the intensity and length of time of RTS is usually prolonged (Foster & Sandel, 2010). Educational interventions, together with solid support networks, have been found to help women with disabilities cope with sexual assaults (Foster & Sandel, 2010).

Prostitute Rape

Studies have found that between 68% and 70% of female prostitutes have been victims of rape (Farley & Barkan, 1998; Silbert, 1998). Sexual assaults on prostitutes by their pimps are also common. Because a prostitute's job is to provide sex in exchange for payment, the question of consent is often difficult to judge. People tend not to believe that she was raped or may think that she is angry because she was not paid. Also, because of the general disapproval of prostitution, a prostitute who reports rape is often treated with disdain.

Prison Inmates and Rape

The Prison Rape Elimination Act, a federal law that reduces tolerance for prison sexual assault, became effective in 2003. It mandated the collection of national data on the incidence of prison rape, and provides funding for research and program development. This law has helped reduce prison rape and support those who have been raped in prison. Studies have found that approximately 18% of prison inmates report sexual threats from other prisoners, whereas 8.5% report sexual assaults in prison (C. Hensley et al., 2005).

Although prison rape occurs most frequently in the male population, it also occurs between female inmates using a variety of different objects to penetrate the vagina or anus. Women who are in U.S. prisons are often victims of sexual harassment, molestation, coercive sexual behaviors, and forced intercourse, with the majority of this abuse being perpetuated by prison staff (Struckman-Johnson & Struckman-Johnson, 2002). Female inmates also experience sexual pressure in their interactions with other female inmates (Alarid, 2000). Like male victims, the majority of women who are raped in prison never report the crime for fear of retaliation.

Corrective Rape

Sexual entitlement and the rape of women and children in South Africa.

Check Your Learning Quiz 14.4

Go to **login.cengagebrain.com** and take the online quiz.

14.5 *When Men Are Rape Victims*

L015 Discuss how men can be raped and common long-term effects of rape in men.

Can a man be raped? Although male rape is more underreported than female rape in the United States, it is estimated that 1 of every 33 men has been a victim of a completed or attempted rape (Tewksbury, 2007; U.S. Department of Justice, 2006). One study found a lifetime prevalence rate of sexual assault in men of 13% (Masho & Anderson, 2009). Male rape accounts for approximately 8% of all noninstitutional rapes in the United States (Masho & Anderson, 2009).

The majority of men who are sexually assaulted are assaulted for the first time before the age of 18 (Masho & Anderson, 2009). Male victims of rape are more likely to be Black (Scarce, 1997). However, the higher frequency of rape in Black men may be because much of the research on male rape has been done in African American communities.

Although the long-term effects of rape are common in men and can include depression, anger, anxiety, self-blame, and increased vulnerability, few men ever seek out medical care or counseling (Masho &Anderson, 2009; J. Walker et al., 2005). Like for women, sexual problems are common in male rape victims and can continue for years after the rape (Walker et al., 2005).

Rape of Men by Women

Students often dismiss the idea that a man could be raped by a woman because they believe that because men are always willing to have sex, a woman would never need to rape a man. However, this belief actually serves to make male rape more humiliating and painful for many men.

Female rapists have been found to engage in a wide range of sexually aggressive behaviors, including forced sex and the use of verbal coercion (P. B. Anderson & Savage, 2005). In a study of male college students, 34% reported coercive sexual contact: 24% from women, 4% from men, and 6% from both sexes (Struckman-Johnson & Struckman-Johnson, 1994). The majority of male rapes by women use psychological or pressured contact, such as verbal persuasion or emotional manipulation, rather than physical force. Although the majority of college men had no reaction, or a very mild negative reaction, to the unwanted female contact, 20% of the men experienced strong negative reactions. Because men who are raped by women are often unwilling to define themselves as victims, many do not report these rapes even though physical and psychological symptoms are common (P. B. Anderson & Savage, 2005).

Rape of Men by Men

Gay men have been found to be raped at a higher rate than heterosexual men (Scarce, 1997). Hickson and colleagues (1994) found that in a sample of 930 gay men, close to 30% claimed they had been sexually assaulted at some point in their lives. Close to 33% of the victims had been sexual with the perpetrator before the sexual assault. The victims reported forced anal and oral sex, and masturbation to ejaculation. The most common type of activity in the sexual assault of men by men is anal penetration, followed by oral penetration (N. Groth & Burgess, 1980; Scarce, 1997).

As in the case of female rape, male rape is an expression of power, a show of strength and masculinity that uses sex as a weapon. The most common emotional reactions to the rape of men by men include shame, embarrassment, self-blame, hostility, and depression (Scarce, 1997; Tewksbury, 2007). Like women, men who have been raped may go through the RTS. Many victims question their sexual orientation and feel that the rape makes them less of a "real man." Fearing others will think they are gay is a barrier to reporting for some men (Sable et al., 2006).

© Enrico Fianchini/iStockphoto

Common emotional reactions to male rape include shame, embarrassment, self-blame, hostility, and depression.

On Your Mind

Can a man really be raped?

Check Your Learning
Quiz 14.5

Go to **login.cengagebrain.com** and take the online quiz.

The majority of rape victims are unsure how to cope during a rape and do not report the rape to the police after the episode. We now explore a variety of coping strategies, reporting statistics, reasons for nonreporting, and the process of telling the police and pressing charges.

Coping with Rape

Rape is the only violent crime in which the victim is expected to fight back. If a woman does not struggle, people question whether she wanted to have sex. Only with visible proof of a struggle (bruises and cuts) does society seem to have sympathy. Some victims of rape have said that at the time of the rape, they felt frozen with fear, unable to move because they just could not believe what was happening to them.

How do people know when to fight back? What should their strategies be? If you are confronted with a potential or attempted rape, the first and best strategy is to try to escape. However, this may not be possible if you are in a deserted area, if there are multiple attackers, or if your attacker has a weapon. If you cannot escape, effective strategies include verbal strategies such as screaming, dissuasive techniques ("I have my period" or "I have herpes"), empathy (listening or trying to understand), negotiation ("Let's discuss this"), and stalling for time. However, if the rapist does not believe the victim, these techniques may cause more harm than good.

Prentky and Knight (1986) assert that the safest strategy is to attempt to talk to the attacker and try to make yourself a real person to the attacker ("I'm a stranger; why do you want to hurt me?"). Self-defense classes can help people feel more confident in their ability to fight back.

Reporting a Rape

It is estimated that about 1 in 7 rapes is reported (Resnick et al., 2005); the likelihood of reporting is increased if the assailant was a stranger, if there was violence, or if a weapon was involved (U.S. Department of Justice, Office of Justice Programs, 2002). This probably has to do with the fact that victims are clearer about intent under these conditions.

Gender differences in reporting are also common. Women are less likely to report a rape if they know the attacker, whereas men are less likely to report if it jeopardizes their masculine self-identity (Pino & Meier, 1999). Women who report their rapes to the police have been subsequently found to have a better adjustment and fewer emotional symptoms than those who do not report it (Sable et al., 2006).

It is also important for a victim to write out exactly what happened in as much detail as possible. When did the rape occur? Where was the victim? What time was it? Who was with the victim? What did the rapist look like? What was the rapist wearing? Exactly what happened? Was alcohol involved? Was anyone else present? Victims should keep this for their own records, for if they decide to press charges, it will come in handy. Over time memories fade, and victims can lose the important small details.

Telling the Police

On college campuses, campus police are often notified before the local police. Campus police may be able to take disciplinary action, such as fines or dismissal if the assailant is a student, but they are not able to press formal charges. Pressing charges with the local police may be important for

Reliving a rape during a legal trial can be emotionally draining.

two reasons. First, it alerts the police to a crime, and thus may prevent other women from being victimized. Second, if the victim decides to take legal action, he or she will need to have a formal report from the local police (not the campus police).

Although police officers have become more sensitive to the plight of rape victims in the past few years, some victims still report negative experiences (Monroe et al., 2005). Society's victim-precipitated view of rape also affects the attitudes of the police. To make sure that a crime did indeed occur, police must interrogate each case completely, which can be very difficult for a victim who has just been through a traumatic experience. Still, many report that taking such legal action makes them feel back in control, that they are doing something about their situation.

Pressing Charges

The decision to press official charges is a difficult one that takes much consideration. It has often been said that rape victims go through a second rape because they tend to be put on trial more than the accused rapist. Court proceedings take up a great deal of time and energy, and they create considerable anxiety.

Victims of rape report that they pressed charges because they were angry, to protect others, or because they wanted justice to be served. Reasons for refusing to press charges include being afraid of revenge, wanting to just forget, feeling sorry for the rapist, or feeling as though it would not matter anyway because nothing would be done. Victims of rape can also file a civil lawsuit and sue the assailant for monetary damages. Civil lawsuits are generally easier to prove than criminal lawsuits (Wagner, 1991). If a victim is undecided about whether to press charges, it may be helpful to sit in on a rape trial. Rape trials can be extremely difficult for all involved, so it is important to prepare oneself and to gather support from friends and family.

Date Rape: Meg's Story

College student describes a date rape experience.

Check Your Learning Quiz 14.7

Go to **login.cengagebrain.com** and take the online quiz.

▶ **LO18** Define *child sexual abuse* and identify the key factor that characterizes the typical child sexual abuser.

▶ **LO19** Define *incest* and discuss the incest taboo.

▶ **LO20** Explain the psychological and emotional effects of child sexual abuse.

Child sexual abuse is defined as sexual behavior that occurs between an adult and a minor. One important characteristic of child sexual abuse is the dominant, powerful position of the adult or older teen that allows him or her to force a child into sexual activity. The sexual activity can include inappropriate touch, removing a child's clothing, genital fondling, masturbation, digital penetration with fingers or sex toys, oral sex, vaginal intercourse, or anal intercourse (Valente, 2005).

Chapter 13 discussed pedophilia, a paraphilia that involves recurrent and intense sexual arousal from prepubescent or pubescent children. In this section, we first look at incest, a type of child sexual abuse, and then examine child sexual abuse, or molestation, in general.

Incest

Incest is sexual abuse of a child or adolescent who is related to the abuser. Although there are various types of incest, father–daughter and sibling incest are the most common (Caffaro & Conn-Caffaro, 2005; Thompson, 2009).

Because most children look to their parents for nurturing and protection, incest involving a parent, guardian, or someone else the child trusts can be extremely traumatic. The incestuous parents exploit this trust to fulfill sexual or power needs of their own. The particularly vulnerable position of children in relation to their parents has been recognized in every culture. The **incest taboo**—the absolute prohibition of sex between family members—is universal (J. L. Herman, 1981).

It is estimated that 1 of every 4 girls and 1 of every 10 boys experiences sexual abuse as a child (Fieldman & Crespi, 2002; Valente, 2005). The median age for sexual abuse of both girls and boys is around 8 or 9 years old. Boys are more likely to be sexually abused by strangers, whereas girls are more likely to be sexually abused by family members (Feinauer, 1988; Finkelhor et al., 1990).

Many victims are scared to reveal the abuse, because of shame, fear of retaliation, belief that they themselves are to blame, or fear that they will not be believed. Victims of incest with a biological father delay reporting the longest, whereas those who have been victims of stepfathers or live-in partners are more likely to tell someone (Faller, 1989).

Many siblings play sex games with each other while growing up, and the line between harmless sex play and incest can be difficult to ascertain. Sex play often involves siblings who are no more than 5 years apart, is nonabusive, is mutually desired, and often involves experimentation (Kluft, 2010). Sibling incest, in contrast,

child sexual abuse Sexual contact with a minor by an adult.

incest Sexual contact between persons who are related or have a caregiving relationship.

incest taboo The absolute prohibition of sex between family members.

often involves siblings with a large age difference, repeated sexual contact, and motivations other than curiosity (Kluft, 2010; Rudd & Herzberger, 1999; Thompson, 2009).

Although the majority of incest offenders are male, some women do engage in such behaviors. Mother–son incest is more likely to be subtle, including behaviors that may be difficult to distinguish from normal mothering behaviors (including genital touching; R. J. Kelly et al., 2002). Men who have been sexually abused by their mothers often experience more trauma symptoms than do other sexually abused men.

Psychological and Emotional Reactions to Child Sexual Abuse

Sexual abuse can be devastating for a child and often causes feelings of betrayal, powerlessness, fear, anger, self-blame, low self-esteem, and problems with intimacy and relationships later in life (Martens, 2007; Thompson, 2009; Valente, 2005). Many children who were sexually abused experience antisocial behavior, drug abuse, and prostitution later in life (Hardt et al., 2008; Jonas et al., 2011; Lu et al., 2008; Thompson, 2009). Overall, incest behaviors are the most traumatic when they occur over a long period, the offender is a person who is trusted, penetration occurs, and there is aggression (A. N. Groth, 1978). Children who hide their sexual abuse often experience shame and guilt, and fear the loss of affection from family and friends (Seymour et al., 2000). They also feel frustrated about not being able to stop the abuse.

Regardless of whether they tell someone about their sexual abuse, many victims experience psychological symptoms such as depression, increased anxiety, nervousness, emotional problems, and personality and intimacy disorders. Similar to reactions of rape victims, PTSD and depression are common symptoms, and may occur more often in victims who are abused repeatedly (Jonas et al., 2011; Thompson, 2009). Guilt is usually severe, and many children blame themselves for the sexual abuse (Thompson, 2009; Valente, 2005). Victims of sexual abuse are also more likely than nonabused children to abuse alcohol and drugs, experience eating disorders, and contemplate suicide (Jonas et al., 2011).

The most devastating emotional effects occur when the abuser is someone the victim trusts. In a study of the effects of sexual abuse by relatives, friends, or strang-

Child Sexual Abuse

Watch this short clip featuring surprising statistics about sexual abusers.

▶ **LO21** List three or four long-term effects of child sexual abuse.

▶ **LO22** List and describe two approaches to treating victims of child sexual abuse.

▶ **LO23** Discuss some of the proposed approaches to preventing child sexual abuse.

ers, it was found that the stronger the emotional bond and trust between the victim and the assailant, the more distress the victim experienced (Feinauer, 1989).

Long-Term Effects of Child Sexual Abuse

Although it has long been a controversial issue in psychology, there is research to support the claim that some abuse victims are unable to remember past abuse (Malmo & Laidlaw, 2010). Some experts claim that although the memories are classified as bad, disgusting, and confusing, many times they are not "traumatic." Because of this, the memories are simply forgotten and not repressed (McNally et al., 2004, 2005).

It is not uncommon for children who are sexually abused to display what Finkelhor and Browne (1985) refer to as **traumatic sexualization**. Children may begin to exhibit compulsive sex play or masturbation and show an inappropriate amount of sexual knowledge. When they enter adolescence, they may begin to show promiscuous and compulsive sexual behavior, which may lead to sexually abusing others in adulthood (Rudd & Herzberger, 1999; Valente, 2005). Both antisocial and promiscuous sexual behaviors have been related to a history of childhood sexual behavior (Deliramich & Gray, 2008; Valente, 2005). A large proportion of patients who seek sex therapy have histories of incest, rape, and other forms of sexual abuse (Maltz, 2002).

Research demonstrates a connection between eating disorders and past sexual abuse (Kong & Berstein, 2009; Ross, 2009; Steiger et al., 2010; Vrabel et al., 2010). Gay and bisexual men who experience childhood sexual abuse are significantly more likely to have an eating disorder than men without a history of sexual abuse (Feldman & Meyer, 2007). Women and men who can discuss the sexual abuse are often able to make significant changes in their eating patterns.

Problems with drug and alcohol addiction are also more common in adults with a history of child sexual abuse. In fact, high rates of alcohol and drug use have been found even as early as age 10 (Valente, 2005). Finkelhor and Browne (1985) hypothesize that because of the stigma that surrounds the early sexual abuse, the children believe they are "bad," and the thought of "badness" is incorporated into their self-concept (Kluft, 2010). As a result, they often gravitate toward behaviors that society sees as deviant.

It is not unusual for adults who had been abused as children to confront their offenders later in life, especially among those who have undergone some form of coun-

traumatic sexualization A common result of sexual abuse in which a child displays compulsive sex play or masturbation and shows an inappropriate amount of sexual knowledge.

seling or psychotherapy to work through their own feelings about the experience. They may feel a strong need to deal with the experience and often get help to work through it.

Helping Child Abuse Victims Heal

Currently, the most effective treatments for victims of child sexual abuse include a combination of cognitive and behavioral psychotherapies, which teach victims how to understand and handle the trauma of their assaults more effectively. Many victims of sexual abuse also have difficulties developing and maintaining intimate relationships. Being involved in a relationship that is high in emotional intimacy and low in expectations for sex is beneficial (W. Maltz, 1990). Learning that they have the ability to say no to sex is very important and usually develops when they establish relationships based first on friendship, rather than sex. Many times the partners of victims of sexual abuse are confused; they do not fully understand the effects of abuse in the lives of their mates, and so they may also benefit from counseling (L. Cohen, 1988).

Preventing Child Sexual Abuse

How can we prevent child sexual abuse? One program that has been explored is the "just say no" campaign, which teaches young children how to say no to inappropriate sexual advances by adults. This program has received much attention. How effective is such a strategy? Even if we can teach children to say no to strangers, can we also teach them to say no to their fathers or sexually abusive relatives? Could there be any negative effects of educating children about sexual abuse? Future research will need to address several questions.

Increasing the availability of sex education has also been cited as a way to decrease the incidence of child sexual abuse. Children from traditional, authoritarian families who have no sex education are at greater risk for sexual abuse. Education about sexual abuse—teaching that it does not happen to all children—may help children to understand that it is wrong. Telling children where to go and whom to talk to is also important.

Another important factor in prevention is adequate funding and staffing of child welfare agencies. Social workers may be among the first to become aware of potentially dangerous situations. Physicians and educators must also be adequately trained to identify the signs of abuse.

Confronting the Incest Offender

A letter from an 18-year-old college student to her father.

Check Your Learning Quiz 14.7

Go to **login.cengagebrain.com** and take the online quiz.

Intimate partner violence (IPV, which may also be referred to as domestic violence) is coercive behavior that uses threats, harassment, or intimidation. It can involve physical (shoving, hitting, hair pulling), emotional (extreme jealousy, intimidation, humiliation), or sexual (forced sex, physically painful sexual behaviors) abuse. Some offenders even are violent toward pets, especially pets that are close to the victim. Generally there is a pattern of abuse rather than a single isolated incident.

Scope of the Problem

Intimate partner violence is found among all racial, ethnic, and socioeconomic classes. It is estimated that close to 5 million women and men are victims of IPV each year (Armour et al., 2008; Centers for Disease Control and Prevention, 2011a). However, the numbers of unreported IPV incidents are much higher. In fact, national studies have found that 29% of both women and men have experienced IPV in their lifetime (Reid et al., 2008).

Many women and men are killed by their violent partners (known as *intimate partner homicide* [IPH])—76% of IPH victims were women, whereas 24% were men (Fox & Zawitz, 2004). Studies on men who commit IPH have found that 42% have past criminal charges, 15% have a psychiatric history, and 18% have both (Eke et al., 2011).

Although IPV is common in adolescent and college-age populations, it can happen to men and women at any age (Bonomi et al., 2007; Forke et al., 2008). It is often related to stress (Harville et al., 2011). Studies have found that women with disabilities are significantly more likely to report experiencing IPV in their life-time compared with women without disabilities (Armour et al., 2008; Friedman et al., 2011).

IPV in same-sex relationships looks similar to IPV in heterosexual relationships (Eaton et al., 2008; St Pierre & Senn, 2010). However, in same-sex relationships, additional issues may arise, including fewer social supports, less availability of med-ical and psychological services, and the fear of being "outed" when seeking help (C. Brown, 2008; St Pierre & Senn, 2010).

Although we know less about IPV in gay relationships, studies have found that 1 in 3 men in same-sex relationships has been abused (Houston & McKirnan, 2008). Unfortunately, many gay and bisexual men are reluctant to seek help for violence in intimate relationships because there is often little social support to do so (Cruz, 2003).

Reactions to Intimate Partner Violence

Victims of IPV experience both physical and psychological symptoms, and the symptoms depend on both the frequency and severity of the violence (Beeble et al., 2011; J. C. Campbell et al., 2002). Common psychological symptoms, similar to those experienced by victims of other coercive sexual behaviors, include depression, antisocial behavior, increased anxiety, low self-esteem, and a fear of intimacy (Cavanaugh et al., 2011; Tjaden & Thoennes, 2000). PTSD is also common (Cavanaugh et al., 2011). Physical symptoms may include headaches, back pain, broken bones, gynecological disorders, and stomach problems.

Many women in abusive relationships claim their relationship started off well and that they believed the first incidence of violence was a one-time occurrence that would not happen again. They often excuse their partner's behavior and accept their partner's apologies. In time, abusers convince their partners that they are responsible for the abuse and if they change, it won't happen again. Most victims begin to believe that the problems are indeed their fault, so they stay in the abusive relationship. Many actually believe that it is safer in the relationship than outside of it. Issues that may make it more difficult for some victims to leave include finances, low self-esteem, fear, or isolation.

© Joel Gordon

Women who experience intimate partner violence from other women often experience a wide range of emotional and psychological responses to the assault but may never tell anyone about the violence.

Psychology of an Abusive Relationship

A teenager deals with the repercussions of an abusive relationship.

Domestic Violence in Lesbian Relationships

One woman's story about the violence in her relationship.

Check Your Learning Quiz 14.8

Go to **login.cengagebrain.com** and take the online quiz.

Think Critically

Challenge Your Thinking

Consider these questions:

1. Researchers have found gender differences in how certain behaviors may be interpreted. For example, where a woman may interpret a behavior as sexual harassment, a man may interpret it as flattery. Why do you think this is the case?

2. Most victims of sexual harassment are women and most of them never say anything to authorities. Why do you think this is? Identify factors that you think might contribute to women keeping silent about these behaviors.

3. Have you ever personally experienced sexual harassment? If so, how did you deal with it? Would you use the same strategies again in the future or would you handle it differently?

4. Many corporations have implemented "sensitivity training" programs to educate employees about sexual harassment. Studies have shown that such programs can reduce the occurrence of coercive behaviors. Do you think colleges and universities should also make this type of training available? Should it be mandatory? Why or why not?

Sexual Harassment

We have seen in rape, child abuse, and intimate partner violence how power can be used to degrade and oppress others. Situations also exist in which a person with more power coerces, pressures, or intimidates another person with less power, using behaviors such as unwanted glances, comments, and jokes—in the work environment or in e-mails—to unwanted "friendly" or "accidental" touching, to unwanted sexual advances, to coerced sexual contact. This is *sexual harassment*. Because of the wide variety of actions that fall under this definition, many people are confused about what exactly constitutes sexual harassment.

In the United States, the courts recognize two types of sexual harassment. In *quid pro quo* (meaning "this for that") *harassment,* a person is coerced by a superior, such as a boss, supervisor, or teacher, to behavior that ranges from putting up with the superior's unwanted verbal abuse and/or touching behavior to being submitted to some type of sexual conduct, all under the stated or implied threat of being fired, or failed a course, or denied any opportunity for advancement. In *hostile environment harassment,* a person is repeatedly subjected by peers at work or in school to unwelcome sexual comments or visually offensive material. Federal law prohibits sexual harassment in both work and educational settings, and victims of sexual harassment can sue their companies or schools for damages (Hogan, 2005).

Sexual harassment has increased in recent years in the United States, probably in relation to the increase in women in education and the workforce. A survey by the American Association of University Women found that among college students, 62% of females and 61% of males reported experiencing sexual harassment in college (Hill & Silva, 2005). Lesbian, gay, bisexual, and transgender college students were more likely than heterosexual students to experience sexual harassment (Hill & Silva, 2005).

It may seem that sexual harassment is not as shocking as other forms of sexual coercion, but the effects of harassment on the victim can be traumatic and often cause long-term difficulties. Fitzgerald and Ormerod (1991) claim, "There are many similarities between sexual harassment and other forms of sexual victimization, not only in the secrecy that sur-

© First Light/Alamy

rounds them but also in the [myth] that supports them" (p. 2). Severe or chronic sexual harassment can cause psychological side effects similar to those of rape and sexual assault, and in extreme cases, it has been known to contribute to suicide.

The first step in reducing sexual harassment is to acknowledge the problem. The majority of college students who admit to sexually harassing another student claim they did so because they thought it was funny, the person wanted attention, or just because everyone did it (Hill & Silva, 2005). However, because sexual harassers usually have more power, it is difficult for victims to come forward to disclose their victimization. If you are being sexually harassed by someone in a college or university setting, the best advice is to talk to a counselor or your advisor about it. Remember that you are protected by federal law. Colleges and universities today will not tolerate the sexual harassment of any student, regardless of gender, ethnicity, religion, or sexual orientation.

Think Critically

This article and its questions are available in interactive format online.

GO to your Psychology CourseMate at login.cengagebrain.com and take the Chapter Post-Test to see which Learning Objectives you've mastered and which need more review. Use the chapter review guide below and the online activities—including flashcards to review key terms—to measure your learning.

Measure ^Your Learning

Module		Learning Objectives	
14.1	Rape and Sexual Assault 526	LO1	Define *rape* and *sexual assault*, and explain how certain factors can make defining these crimes difficult.
		LO2	Identify five to six of the common myths about rape and sexual assault, and discuss how these myths affect perceptions of these crimes.
		LO3	Describe the profile of the typical individual who commits rape.
		LO4	Discuss gender, ethnic, and cultural differences in attitudes toward rape.
14.2	Rape and Sexual Assault on Campus 532	LO5	Identify two ways in which alcohol is a strong predictor of rape on college campuses.
		LO6	Discuss the ways in which fraternities might create a ripe environment for rape.
		LO7	Discuss some of the reasons for the higher rates of rape-supportive attitudes and sexually aggressive behavior among college and professional athletes.
14.3	Effects of Rape 534	LO8	Describe and compare the physical effects of rape on younger and older women.
		LO9	Discuss the range of psychological and emotional reactions to rape experienced by victims and by victims' partners.

Online Activities

Key Terms	Video	Animation	Readings	Assessment
rape, sexual assault, intimate partner violence (IPV)	Why do people rape? The Online Sexual Predator Is it rape if my ex-boyfriend forces me to have sex with him?	Testing Your Beliefs in Rape Myths		Check Your Learning Quiz 14.1
	What if I had sex with a girl when we were really drunk and then she called it rape the next morning?		Date Rape Drugs	Check Your Learning Quiz 14.2
rape trauma syndrome (RTS), post-traumatic stress disorder (PTSD), long-term reorganization, silent rape reaction, rape crisis centers	Rape and Post-Traumatic Stress Disorder Can a woman who was raped eventually have a normal sex life?			Check Your Learning Quiz 14.3

Online Activities

Key Terms	Video	Animation	Readings	Assessment
			Corrective Rape	Check Your Learning Quiz 14.4
	Can a man really be raped?			Check Your Learning Quiz 14.5
	Date Rape: Meg's Story			Check Your Learning Quiz 14.6
child sexual abuse, incest, incest taboo, traumatic sexualization	Child Sexual Abuse		Confronting the Incest Offender	Check Your Learning Quiz 14.7
	Psychology of an Abusive Relationship		Domestic Violence in Lesbian Relationships	Check Your Learning Quiz 14.8
				Sexual Harassment

abortion Induced termination of a pregnancy before fetal viability.

abstinence Refraining from intercourse and often other forms of sexual contact.

abstinence-only programs Sexuality education programs that emphasize abstinence from all sexual behaviors.

acquired immune deficiency syndrome (AIDS) A condition of increased susceptibility to opportunistic diseases; results from an infection with HIV, which destroys the body's immune system.

active listening Communication and listening technique in which the listener uses nonverbal communication, such as nodding or eye contact, to signal that he or she is attentive to the speaker.

amenorrhea The absence of menstruation.

amniocentesis A procedure in which a small sample of amniotic fluid is analyzed to detect chromosomal abnormalities in the fetus or to determine the sex of the fetus.

amnion A thin, tough, membranous sac that encloses the embryo or fetus.

ampulla Base of the vas deferens, where the vas hooks up over the ureter of the bladder.

anal sphincter A ringlike muscle that surrounds the anus; it usually relaxes during normal physiological functioning.

anal stage A psychosexual stage in which the anal area is the primary erogenous zone.

androgen A hormone that promotes the development of male genitals and secondary sex characteristics. It is produced by the testes in men and by the adrenal glands in both men and women. Also, the general name for male hormones such as testosterone and androsterone.

androgen-insensitivity syndrome (AIS) A condition in which a genetic male's cells are insensitive to androgens, resulting in the development of female external genitalia (but no internal reproductive organs). People with AIS are raised as females.

androgyny Having high levels of both masculine and feminine characteristics.

andropause The hormonal changes accompanying old age in men that correspond to menopause in women.

anemia A condition in which there is a deficiency in the oxygen-carrying material of the blood, often causing symptoms of fatigue, irritability, dizziness, memory problems, shortness of breath, and headaches.

anencephaly Congenital absence of most of the brain and spinal cord.

anilingus Oral stimulation of the anus.

antimiscegenation laws Laws forbidding sexuality, marriage, or breeding among members of different races.

aphrodisiac A substance that increases, or is believed to increase, a person's sexual desire.

areola The pigmented ring around the nipple of the breast.

arranged marriage Marriage that is arranged by parents or relatives and is often not based on love.

artificial insemination Artificially introducing sperm into a woman's reproductive tract.

asceticism The practice of a lifestyle that rejects sensual pleasures such as drinking alcohol, eating rich food, or engaging in sex.

asymptomatic Without recognizable symptoms.

autoinoculate To cause a secondary infection in the body from an already existing infection.

autosome Any chromosome that is not a sex chromosome.

avatar A computer user's online representation of himself or herself presented in two- or three-dimensional art.

back-alley abortion Illegal abortion, which was all that was available before the legalization of abortion in the 1970s.

bacterial vaginosis (BV) Bacterial infection that can cause vaginal discharge and odor but is often asymptomatic.

balanitis Inflammation of the glans penis.

Bartholin's glands A pair of glands on either side of the vaginal opening that open by a duct into the space between the hymen and the labia minora; also referred to as the greater vestibular glands.

basal body temperature (BBT) The body's resting temperature used to calculate ovulation in the symptothermal method of contraception.

behaviorists Theorists who believe that behavior is learned and can be altered.

benign A nonmalignant, mild case of a disease that is favorable for recovery.

benign prostatic hypertrophy (BPH) The common enlargement of the prostate that occurs in most men after about age 50.

biphasic pill A type of oral contraceptive that contains two different doses of hormones in the active pills.

biphobia Strongly negative attitudes toward bisexuals and bisexuality.

birth control Another term for *contraception*.

bisexual Person who is erotically attracted to members of either sex.

blastocyst The hollow ball of embryonic cells that enters the uterus from the Fallopian tube and eventually implants.

body image A person's feelings and mental picture of his or her own body's beauty.

Braxton–Hicks contractions Intermittent contractions of the uterus after the third month of pregnancy.

breakthrough bleeding Slight blood loss from the uterus that may occur when a woman is taking oral contraceptives.

breast buds The first swelling of the area around the nipple that indicates the beginning of breast development.

breech position An abnormal and often dangerous birthing position in which the baby's feet, knees, or buttocks emerge before the head.

buttockry Rubbing of the penis in the cleft of the buttocks.

cannula A tube, used in an abortion procedure, through which the uterine contents are emptied.

case study A research methodology that involves an in-depth examination of one participant or a small number of participants.

cauterization A sterilization procedure that involves burning or searing the Fallopian tubes or vas deferens for permanent sterilization.

celibacy The state of remaining unmarried; often used today to refer to abstaining from sex.

cervical barrier A plastic or rubber cover for the cervix that provides a contraceptive barrier to sperm.

cervical cap A birth control device similar to a diaphragm, but smaller.

cervical dysplasia Disordered growth of cells in the cervix, typically diagnosed with Pap testing.

cervical effacement The stretching and thinning of the cervix in preparation for birth.

cervical intraepithelial neoplasia A change in the cells on the surface of the cervix that may signal early beginnings of cervical cancer; sometimes referred to as *cervical dysplasia*.

cervical laceration Cuts or tears on the cervix.

cervix The doughnut-shaped bottom part of the uterus that protrudes into the top of the vagina.

cesarean section (C-section) A surgical procedure in which the woman's abdomen and uterus are surgically opened and a child is removed.

chancre A small, red–brown sore that results from syphilis infection; the sore is actually the site at which the bacteria entered the body.

chastity The quality of being sexually pure, either through abstaining from intercourse or by adhering to strict rules of sexuality.

chemotherapy A procedure that uses chemicals to kill rapidly dividing cancer cells.

child sexual abuse Sexual contact with a minor by an adult.

chlamydia A bacterial sexually transmitted infection (STI); although often asymptomatic, it is thought to be one of the most damaging of all the STIs.

chorionic villus sampling The sampling and testing of the chorion for fetal abnormalities.

circumcision The surgical removal of the penile foreskin.

civil union A legal union of a same-sex couple, sanctioned by a civil authority.

clitoris An erectile organ of the female located under the prepuce; an organ of sexual pleasure.

cognitive theory A theory proposing that our thoughts are responsible for our behaviors.

cohabitation Living together in a sexual relationship when not legally married.

colostrum A thin, yellowish fluid, high in protein and antibodies, secreted from the nipples at the end of pregnancy and during the first few days after delivery.

combination birth control pill An oral contraceptive that contains synthetic estrogen and progesterone.

coming out The process of establishing a personal self-identity and communicating it to others.

companionate love An intimate form of love that involves friendly affection and deep attachment based on a familiarity with the loved one. Also referred to as *conjugal love*.

comprehensive sexuality education programs Programs that often begin in kindergarten and continue through 12th grade, presenting a wide variety of topics to help students develop their own skills while learning factual information.

computer-mediated communication Communication produced when people interact with one another by transmitting messages via networked computers.

conditioning In behaviorism, a type of associative learning in which a person associates a particular behavior with a positive response.

condom A latex, animal membrane, or polyurethane sheath that fits over the penis and is used for protection against pregnancy and STIs; female condoms made of either polyurethane or polymer, which protect the vaginal walls, are also available.

confidentiality Assurance that all materials collected in a research study will be kept private and confidential.

congenital adrenal hyperplasia (CAH) A disorder involving overproduction of androgen in the adrenal glands that can affect males and females. Females born with this condition frequently have masculinized genitals because of excess prenatal androgen exposure, whereas males typically experience early pubertal changes.

congenital syphilis A syphilis infection acquired by an infant from the mother during pregnancy.

contraception Prevention of pregnancy.

contraceptive sponge Polyurethane sponge impregnated with spermicide, inserted into the vagina for contraception.

corona The ridge of the glans penis.

corpora cavernosa Plural of *corpus cavernosum* (cavernous body); areas in the penis that fill with blood during erection.

corpus luteum A yellowish endocrine gland in the ovary formed when a follicle has discharged its secondary oocyte.

corpus spongiosum Meaning "spongy body," the erectile tissue in the penis that contains the urethra.

correlation A statistical measure of the relationship between two variables.

correlational study A type of research that examines the relationship between two or more variables.

courtship disorder Theory that asserts that paraphilias develop from abnormalities in the normal courtship process, which involves looking for sexual partners, interacting with partners, touching or embracing them, and sexual intercourse.

covenant marriage A marriage that is preceded by premarital counseling and has strict rules about divorce.

Cowper's or bulbourethral gland One of a pair of glands located under the prostate gland on either side of the urethra that secretes a fluid into the urethra.

cremaster muscle The "suspender" muscle that raises and lowers the scrotum to control scrotal temperature.

crowning The emergence of a baby's head at the opening of the vagina at birth.

cryptococcosis An acute or chronic infection that can lead to pulmonary or central nervous system infection.

cryptorchidism A condition in which the testes fail to descend into the scrotum.

cunnilingus The act of sexually stimulating the female genitals with the mouth.

cytomegalovirus A virus that can lead to diarrhea, weight loss, headache, fever, confusion, or blurred vision.

delayed ejaculation A delayed or absent ejaculation.

Depo-Provera Depo-medroxyprogesterone, an injectable contraceptive that prevents ovulation and thickens cervical mucus.

detumescence The return of an erect penis to the flaccid state.

diaphragm A birth control device consisting of a latex dome on a flexible spring rim; used with spermicidal cream or jelly.

dilation The expansion of the opening of the cervix in preparation for birth.

dilation and curettage (D&C) The surgical scraping of the uterine wall with a spoon-shaped instrument.

dilation and evacuation (D&E) A second-trimester abortion procedure that involves cervical dilation and vacuum aspiration of the uterus.

dilation rods A series of graduated metal rods that are used to dilate the cervical opening during an abortion procedure.

dilators A graduated series of metal rods used in the treatment of vaginismus.

direct observation A research methodology that involves actual participation in the event being researched.

disclaimer A way of speaking in which speakers renounce or deny the validity of what they are saying by including a negative statement.

discrepancy in desire Differences in levels of sexual desire in a couple.

disorders of sex development Medical term referring to hormonal and chromosomal conditions that may lead to disorders of sex development.

dominant Describes the active role in sadomasochistic sexuality.

Don Juanism or **satyriasis** Terms used to describe men who engage in frequent or promiscuous sex.

douching A method of vaginal rinsing or cleaning that involves squirting water or other solutions into the vagina.

Down syndrome A problem occurring on the 21st chromosome of the developing fetus that can cause mental retardation and physical challenges.

dysfunctional uterine bleeding Menstrual bleeding for long periods of time or intermittent bleeding throughout a cycle.

dysmenorrhea Painful menstruation.

dyspareunia Genital pain associated with sexual behavior.

eclampsia A progression of toxemia with similar, but worsening, conditions.

ectopic pregnancy The implantation of the fertilized egg outside the uterus, such as in the Fallopian tubes or abdomen.

effectiveness rates Estimated rates of the number of women who do not become pregnant each year using each method of contraception.

ego The part of the personality that mediates between environmental demands (reality), conscience (superego), and instinctual needs (id).

ejaculation The reflex ejection or expulsion of semen from the penis.

ejaculatory duct A tube that transports spermatozoa from the vas deferens to the urethra.

ejaculatory inevitability A feeling that ejaculation can no longer be controlled.

ELISA (enzyme-linked immunoabsorbent assay) The screening test used to detect HIV antibodies in blood samples.

embryo The developing organism from the second to the eighth week of gestation.

embryo cryopreservation The freezing of embryos for later use.

emergency contraception Contraception that is designed to prevent pregnancy after unprotected vaginal intercourse.

emoticons Facial symbols used when sending electronic messages online; an example would be :-).

endocrine gland A gland that secretes hormones into the blood.

endometriosis The growth of endometrial tissue outside the uterus.

endometrium The mucous membrane lining the uterus.

endorphins Neurotransmitters, concentrated in the pituitary gland and parts of the brain, that inhibit physical pain.

engagement When the fetus moves down toward the birth canal before delivery.

epididymis A comma-shaped organ that sits atop the testicle and holds sperm during maturation.

episiotomy A cut made with surgical scissors to avoid tearing of the perineum at the end of the second stage of labor.

erectile disorder (ED) Diminished or absent ability to attain or maintain, until completion of the sexual activity, an adequate erection.

erection The hardening of the penis caused by blood engorging the erectile tissue.

estrogen A hormone that produces female secondary sex characteristics and affects the menstrual cycle.

excitement The first stage of the sexual response cycle, in which an erection occurs in males and vaginal lubrication occurs in females.

exhibitionist A person who experiences recurrent and intense arousal from exposing his genitals to an unsuspecting stranger.

Fallopian tubes Two ducts that transport ova from the ovary to the uterus; also referred to as *oviducts.*

false negative Incorrect result of a medical test or procedure that wrongly shows the lack of a finding.

false positive Incorrect result of a medical test or procedure that wrongly shows the presence of a finding.

family of origin The family into which one is born and raised.

fellatio The act of sexually stimulating the male genitals with the mouth.

FemCap Reusable silicone barrier vaginal contraceptive that comes in three sizes.

femininity The ideal cluster of traits that society attributes to females.

fertility awareness Basal body temperature charting used in conjunction with another method of contraception.

fertility awareness–based methods Contraceptive or family planning method that involves identifying a fertile period in a woman's cycle and either avoiding intercourse or using contraception during this time.

fertilization The union of two gametes, which occurs when a haploid sperm and a haploid egg join to produce a diploid zygote, containing 46 chromosomes.

fetal alcohol syndrome A disorder involving physical and mental deficiencies, nervous system damage, and facial abnormalities found in the offspring of mothers who consumed large quantities of alcohol during pregnancy.

fetal distress Condition in which a fetus has an abnormal heart rate or rhythm.

fetishist A person who engages in a fetishistic behavior.

fetishistic disorder A recurrent and intense sexual arousal manifested in fantasies, urges, or behaviors involving the use of nonliving objects or nongenital body parts.

field of eligibles The group of people from which it is socially acceptable to choose an intimate partner.

fimbriae The branched, finger-like border at the end of each Fallopian tube.

first-trimester surgical abortion (or vacuum aspiration) Termination of pregnancy within the first 16 weeks of pregnancy by using suction to empty the contents of the uterus.

fisting Sexual technique that involves inserting the fist and even part of the forearm into the anus or vagina.

follicular phase First phase of the menstrual cycle that begins after the last menstruation has been completed.

foreskin The fold of skin that covers the glans penis; also called the *prepuce*.

free love movement A movement of the early 19th century that preached love should be the factor that determines whether one should have sex (not to be confused with the free love movement of the 1960s).

frenulum Fold of skin on the underside of the penis.

frotteurism A paraphiliac behavior that involves recurrent and intense sexual arousal from fantasies or behaviors that involve touching and/or rubbing the genitals against a nonconsenting person in a crowded place.

gamete A male or female reproductive cell—the spermatozoon or ovum; also referred to as a *germ cell.*

gender The behavioral, psychological, and social characteristics associated with being biologically male or female.

gender constancy The realization in the young child that one's gender does not normally change over the life span.

gender diverse An individual whose gender identity or gender expression lies outside of the socially accepted gender norms.

gender dysphoria A condition in which a person feels extreme confusion and/or discomfort between his or her biological sex and gender identity.

gender fluidity A flexible range of gender expression, which can change day-to-day and allows for less restrictive and stereotypical gender expectations.

gender roles Culturally defined ways of behaving seen as appropriate for males and females.

gender schema A cognitive mechanism that helps us to understand gender roles.

gender spectrum The continuum of possibilities of biological gender, gender identity, gender expression, and sexual orientation.

gender traits Innate or biologically determined gender-specific behaviors.

gender-identity disorder A disorder in which a child has a strong and persistent identification with the other sex or the gender role of the other sex and is uncomfortable with his or her own biological sex or gender role.

genderlect Coined by Deborah Tannen, this term refers to the fundamental differences between the way men and women communicate.

generalizability If findings are generalizable, they can be taken from a particular sample and applied to the general population.

genital stage Final psychosexual stage in which a person develops the ability to engage in adult sexual behavior.

genital wart Wartlike growth on the genitals; also called *venereal wart, condylomata,* or *papilloma.*

germ cell A male or female reproductive cell—the spermatozoon or ovum; also referred to as a *gamete.*

gestation The period of intrauterine fetal development.

glans penis The flaring, enlarged region at the end of the penis.

gonads The male and female sex glands—ovaries and testes.

gonorrhea A bacterial sexually transmitted infection that causes a puslike discharge and frequent urination in men; many women are asymptomatic.

Gräfenberg spot (G-spot) A structure that is said to lie on the anterior (front) wall of the vagina and is reputed to be a seat of sexual pleasure when stimulated.

gynecologist A physician who specializes in the study and treatment of disorders of the female reproductive system.

gynecomastia Abnormal breast development in the male.

hate crime A criminal offense, usually involving violence, intimidation, or vandalism, in which the victim is targeted because of his or her affiliation with a particular group.

hedge word A way of speaking in which speakers renounce or deny the validity of what they are saying by using certain words to decrease their perceived assertiveness.

herpes A highly contagious viral infection that causes eruptions of the skin or mucous membranes.

herpes simplex I (HSV-I) A viral infection that is usually transmitted through kissing or sharing eating or drinking utensils and can cause cold sores or blisters on the face and mouth.

herpes simplex II (HSV-2) A viral infection that is often sexually transmitted and is responsible for genital ulcerations and blisters.

heterosexism The "presumption of heterosexuality" that has sociological implications.

heterosexual Man or woman who is erotically attracted to members of the other sex.

highly active antiretroviral therapy (HAART) A combination of antiretroviral drugs for the treatment of infections by retroviruses, primarily HIV.

HIV RNA testing Test that allows health care providers to monitor the amount of virus in the bloodstream.

homoerotic The representation of same-sex love or desire.

homologous Corresponding in structure, position, or origin but not necessarily in function.

homophobia Irrational fear of homosexuals and homosexuality.

homosexual Man or woman who is erotically attracted to members of the same sex.

homosocial play Gender-segregated play.

hormone replacement therapy (HRT) Medication containing one or more female hormones, often used to treat symptoms of menopause.

hot flashes A symptom of menopause in which a woman feels sudden heat, often accompanied by a flush.

human chorionic gonadotropin (hCG) The hormone that stimulates production of estrogen and progesterone to maintain pregnancy.

human immunodeficiency virus (HIV) The retrovirus responsible for the development of AIDS; can be transmitted during vaginal or anal intercourse.

human papillomavirus (HPV) A sexually transmitted viral infection that can infect the genitals, anus, mouth, and throat, causing genital warts, cervical, anal, oral, and penile cancer.

human sexuality A general term for the feelings and behaviors of human beings concerning sex.

hymen A thin fold of vascularized mucous membrane at the vaginal opening.

hyperphilia Compulsive sexuality caused by overcompensating for negative reactions to childhood sexuality.

hypersexual disorder Recurrent and intense sexual fantasies, sexual urges, and sexual behaviors, and excessive time spent on these behaviors and an inability to control these fantasies.

hypoactive sexual desire disorder (HSDD) Diminished or absent sexual interest or desire.

hypophilia Lack of full functioning of the sexual organs because of missing stages of childhood development.

hysterectomy The surgical removal of the uterus.

id The collection of unconscious urges and desires that continually seek expression.

in vitro fertilization (IVF) A procedure in which a woman's ova are removed from her body, fertilized with sperm in a laboratory, and then surgically implanted back into her uterus.

incest Sexual contact between persons who are related or have a caregiving relationship.

incest taboo The absolute prohibition of sex between family members.

infertility The inability to conceive (or impregnate).

informed consent Informing participants about what will be expected of them before they agree to participate in a research study.

inguinal canal Canal through which the testes descend into the scrotum.

interfemoral intercourse Thrusting the penis between the thighs of a partner.

interstitial cells Cells responsible for the production of testosterone; also referred to as *Leydig cells.*

interviewer bias The bias of a researcher caused by his or her own opinions, thoughts, and attitudes about the research.

intimate partner violence (IPV) A pattern of coercive behavior designed to exert power and control over a person in an intimate relationship through the use of intimidation, threats, or harmful or harassing behavior.

intracavernous injection A treatment method for erectile disorders in which vasodilating drugs are injected into the penis for the purpose of creating an erection.

intracytoplasmic sperm injection Fertility procedure that involves mechanically injecting a sperm into the center of an ovum.

intrauterine device (IUD) Small plastic contraceptive device that is inserted into a woman's uterus.

introitus Entrance to the vagina.

Kama Sutra Famous ancient Indian sex manual.

Kaposi's sarcoma (KS) A rare form of cancer that often occurs in untreated men with AIDS.

karma The idea that there is a cycle of birth, death, and rebirth, and that deeds in one's life affect one's status in a future life.

Klinefelter syndrome A genetic disorder in men in which there are three sex chromosomes, XXY, instead of two; characterized by small testes, low sperm production, breast enlargement, and absence of facial and body hair.

Koran The holy book of Islam. Also spelled Quran or Qur'an.

labia majora Two longitudinal folds of skin extending downward and backward from the mons pubis of the female.

labia minora Two small folds of mucous membrane lying within the labia majora of the female.

lactation The collective name for milk creation, secretion, and ejection from the nipple.

Lactobacillus Bacteria in the vagina that helps maintain appropriate pH levels.

laminaria Seaweed used in second-trimester abortion procedures to dilate the cervix. Used dried, it can swell three to five times its original diameter.

lanugo The downy covering of hair over a fetus.

laparoscope A small instrument through which structures within the abdomen and pelvis can be viewed.

latency A period in which a person is infected with a sexually transmitted infection but does not test positive for it.

latency stage A psychosexual stage in which libido and sexual interest are repressed.

Lea's Shield Reusable silicone barrier vaginal contraceptive that contains a one-way valve.

Leydig cells The cells in the testes that produce testosterone; also referred to as *interstitial cells*.

ligation A sterilization procedure that involves the tying or binding of the Fallopian tubes or vas deferens.

long-term reorganization The second stage of the rape trauma syndrome, which involves a restoration of order in the victim's lifestyle and reestablishment of control.

lovemap Term coined by John Money to refer to the template of an ideal lover and sexual situation we develop as we grow up.

lumpectomy A modern surgical procedure for breast cancer in which only the tumorous lump and a small amount of surrounding tissue are removed.

luteal phase Third phase of the menstrual cycle, following ovulation, when the corpus luteum forms.

malignant A cancerous growth that tends to spread into nearby normal tissue and travel to other parts of the body.

mammography A procedure for internal imaging of the breasts to evaluate breast disease or screen for breast cancer.

manual sex The physical caressing of the genitals during solo or partner masturbation.

masculinity The ideal cluster of traits that society attributes to males.

masochism Deriving sexual pleasure from receiving pain or being humiliated.

maternal immune hypothesis Theory of sexual orientation that proposes that the fraternal birth order effect of gay brothers reflects the progressive immunization of some mothers to male-specific antigens by each succeeding male fetus.

maternal-serum alpha-fetoprotein screening A blood test used during early pregnancy to determine neural tube defects such as spina bifida or anencephaly.

menarche The start of menstrual cycling, usually during early puberty.

menopause The cessation of menstrual cycling.

menorrhagia Excessive menstrual flow.

menses The blood and tissue discharged from the uterus during menstruation.

menstrual manipulation The ability to plan and schedule the arrival of menstruation.

menstrual phase Final stage of the general menstrual cycle, when the endometrial cells shrink and slough off.

menstrual suppression The elimination of menstrual periods.

menstrual toxic shock syndrome (mTSS) A bacteria-caused illness, associated with tampon use, that can lead to high fever, vomiting, diarrhea, sore throat and shock, loss of limbs, and death if left untreated.

midwife A person who assists women during childbirth.

mifepristone Drug used in medication abortion procedures; it blocks development of progesterone, which causes a breakdown in the uterine lining. Referred to as RU-486 when it was in development.

minipills A type of birth control pill that contains only synthetic progesterone and no estrogen.

Minnesota Multiphasic Personality Inventory (MMPI) Psychological test used to assess general personality characteristics.

miscarriage A pregnancy that terminates on its own; also referred to as *spontaneous abortion*.

mitosis The division of the nucleus of a cell into two new cells such that each new daughter cell has the same number and kind of chromosomes as the original parent.

monophasic pill A type of oral contraceptive that contains one level of hormones in all the active pills.

mons veneris or **mons pubis** The mound of fatty tissue over the female pubic bone, also referred to as *mons pubis,* meaning "pubic mound."

morning sickness The nausea and vomiting that some women have when they become pregnant; typically caused by the increase in hormones. Can occur at any point in the day.

mucus plug A collection of thick mucus in the cervix that prevents bacteria from entering the uterus.

Müllerian duct One of a pair of tubes in the embryo that will develop, in female embryos, into the fallopian tubes, uterus, and part of the vagina.

multiple orgasms More than one orgasm experienced within a short period.

mutual masturbation Simultaneous masturbation of sexual partners by each other.

myometrium The smooth muscle layer of the uterus.

myotonia Involuntary contractions of the muscles.

name-calling Using negative or stereotyping words when in disagreement.

natural family planning A contraceptive method that involves calculating ovulation and avoiding sexual intercourse during ovulation and at other unsafe times.

necrophilia A paraphiliac behavior that involves recurrent and intense sexual arousal from fantasies or behaviors involving sexual contact with dead bodies.

nipple A pigmented, wrinkled protuberance on the surface of the breast that contains ducts for the release of milk.

nocturnal emission Involuntary ejaculation during sleep, also referred to as a *wet dream.*

no-fault divorce A divorce law that allows for the dissolution of a marriage without placing blame on either of the partners.

nondefensive listening Listening strategy in which the listener focuses attention on what his or her partner is saying without being defensive.

nongonococcal urethritis Urethral infection in men that is usually caused by an infection with chlamydia.

nonverbal communication Communication without words (includes eye contact, head nodding, touching, and the like).

Norplant A hormonal method of birth control using doses that are implanted in a woman's arm and that can remain in place for up to 5 years.

NuvaRing A small plastic contraceptive ring that is inserted into the vagina once a month and releases a constant dose of estrogen and progestin.

nymphomaniac A pejorative term used to describe women who engage in frequent or promiscuous sex.

obsessive–compulsive disorder (OCD) A psychological disorder in which a person experiences recurrent and persistent thoughts, impulses, or images that are intrusive and inappropriate, and that cause marked anxiety and repetitive behaviors.

oocyte A cell from which an ovum develops.

opportunistic disease Disease that occurs when the immune system is depressed; often fatal.

oral candidiasis An infection in the mouth caused by the excess growth of a fungus that naturally occurs in the body.

oral contraceptive The "pill"; a preparation of synthetic female hormones that blocks ovulation.

oral stage A psychosexual stage in which the mouth, lips, and tongue are the primary erogenous zone.

orgasm The third stage of the sexual response cycle, which involves an intense sensation during the peak of sexual arousal and results in a release of sexual tension.

orgasmic disorder A delay or absence of orgasm after a normal phase of sexual excitement.

orgasmic platform The thickening of the walls of the lower third of the vagina.

orgasmic reconditioning A sex therapy technique in which a person switches fantasies just at the moment of masturbatory orgasm to try to condition himself or herself to become excited by more conventional fantasies.

Ortho Evra patch A thin, peach-colored patch that sticks to the skin and time-releases synthetic estrogen and progestin into the bloodstream to inhibit ovulation, increase cervical mucus, and render the uterus inhospitable; also referred to as the "patch."

outpatient surgery Surgery performed in the hospital or doctor's office, after which a patient is allowed to return home; inpatient surgery requires hospitalization.

ova cryopreservation The freezing of ova for later use.

ovarian cysts Small, fluid-filled sacs that can form on the ovary and do not pose a health threat under most conditions.

ovaries Female gonads that produce ova and sex hormones.

overgeneralization Making statements that tend to exaggerate a particular issue.

overkill A common mistake that couples make during arguments, in which one person threatens the worst but does not mean what he or she says.

oviducts Another name for the Fallopian tubes.

ovulation The phase of the menstrual cycle in which an ovum is released.

ovulatory phase The second stage of the general menstrual cycle, when the ovum is released.

ovum The female reproductive cell or gamete; plural is *ova*.

oxytocin A hormone secreted by the hypothalamus that stimulates contraction of both the uterus for delivery of the newborn and the mammary gland ducts for lactation.

Papanicolaou (Pap) smear A microscopic examination of cells scraped from the cervix. Named after its inventor.

paraphilia Clinical term used to describe types of sexual expressions that are seen as unusual and potentially problematic. A person who engages in paraphilias is often referred to as a paraphiliac.

paraphilic coercive disorder A paraphilia that involves recurrent and intense sexual arousal from fantasies or behaviors involving sexual coercion.

participant observation A research methodology that involves actual participation in the event being researched.

patriarchal A society ruled by the male as the figure of authority, symbolized by the father's absolute authority in the home.

pedophilia A paraphilia that involves recurrent and intense sexual arousal from prepubescent or pubescent children, which usually causes distress or impairment in important areas of functioning. People who engage in this behavior are called *pedophiles,* or *sexual offenders*.

pelvic inflammatory disease Widespread infection of the female pelvic organs.

penile plethysmography A test performed by measuring the amount of blood that enters the penis in response to a stimulus, which can indicate how arousing the stimulus is for the male.

penis The male copulatory and urinary organ, used both to urinate and move spermatozoa out of the urethra through ejaculation; it is the major organ of male sexual pleasure and is homologous to the female clitoris.

perfect use Refers to the probability of contraceptive failure for use of the method without error.

performance fears The fear of not being able to perform during sexual behavior.

perimetrium The outer wall of the uterus.

perinatal HIV infections HIV transmission from mother to child during pregnancy, labor and delivery, or breast-feeding.

perineum Area between the vagina and the anus.

Peyronie's disease Abnormal calcifications or fibrous tissue buildup in the penis, which may cause painful curvature, often making penetrative sex impossible.

phallic stage A psychosexual stage in which the genital region is the primary erogenous zone and in which the Oedipus or Electra complex develops.

phimosis An abnormal restriction of the foreskin that inhibits the ability to uncover the glans penis.

placebo pills In a pack of 28-day oral contraceptives, the seven pills at the end; these pills are sugar pills and do not contain any hormones; they are used to help a woman remember to take a pill every day.

placenta The structure through which the exchange of materials between fetal and maternal circulations occurs.

placenta previa A condition in which the placenta is abnormally positioned in the uterus so that it partially or completely covers the opening of the cervix.

plateau The second stage of the sexual response cycle, occurring before orgasm, in which vasocongestion builds up.

Pneumocystis carinii **pneumonia** A rare type of pneumonia; an opportunistic disease that often occurs in people with AIDS.

polycystic ovarian syndrome An endocrine disorder in women that can affect the menstrual cycle, fertility, hormones, a woman's appearance, and long-term health.

polygamy The practice of men or women marrying more than one partner.

postcoital drip A vaginal discharge (dripping) that occurs after sexual intercourse.

postpartum depression A woman's clinical depression that occurs after childbirth.

post-traumatic stress disorder (PTSD) Anxiety disorder that can develop after a life-threatening or anxiety-producing event and can cause ongoing emotional and psychological symptoms, such as insomnia, depression, flashbacks, and nightmares.

preeclampsia A condition of hypertension during pregnancy, typically accompanied by leg swelling and other symptoms.

premature birth Any infant born before the 37th week of pregnancy.

premature ejaculation (PE) Pattern of ejaculating with minimal sexual stimulation before, on, or shortly after penetration and before the person wishes it.

premenstrual dysphoric disorder (PMDD) The most debilitating and severe cases of premenstrual syndrome.

premenstrual syndrome (PMS) A group of physiological and psychological symptoms related to the postovulation phase of the menstrual cycle.

prepuce A loose fold of skin that covers the clitoris.

priapism A condition in which an erection is long-lasting and often painful.

pro-choice supporter Individual who believes that the abortion decision should be left up to the woman and not regulated by the government.

prodromal phase The tingling or burning feeling that precedes the development of herpes blisters.

progesterone A hormone that is produced by the ovaries and helps to regulate the menstrual cycle.

progestin-only birth control method Contraceptive hormonal method that does not contain estrogen and works by changing a woman's menstrual cycle.

prolactin A hormone secreted by the pituitary gland that initiates and maintains milk secretion.

pro-life supporter Individual who believes that abortion should be illegal or strictly regulated by the government.

prostaglandin Oral or injected drug taken to cause uterine contractions.

prostate gland A doughnut-shaped gland that wraps around the urethra as it comes out of the bladder, contributing fluid to the semen.

prostate-specific antigen (PSA) Blood test that measures levels of molecules that are overproduced by prostate cancer cells, enabling health care providers to identify prostate cancer early.

prosthesis implantation A treatment method for erectile disorder in which a prosthesis is surgically implanted into the penis.

psychosexual development The childhood stages of development during which the id's pleasure-seeking energies focus on distinct erogenous zones.

psychotropic medications Medications prescribed for psychological disorders, such as depression.

pubic lice A parasitic sexually transmitted infection that infests the pubic hair and can be transmitted through sexual contact; also called *crabs.*

pubococcygeus muscle A muscle that surrounds and supports the vagina.

punishment concept The idea that people who had become infected with certain diseases, especially sexually transmitted infections, did something wrong and are being punished.

Puritans Refers to members of a 16th- and 17th-century Protestant group from England that wanted to purge the church of elaborate ceremonies and simplify worship. It has come to mean any person or group that is excessively strict in regard to sexual matters.

queer or **genderqueer** Umbrella terms in the gender diverse community that refer to a range of different sexual orientations, gender behaviors, or ideologies.

question statement A way of speaking in which speakers renounce or deny the validity of what they are saying by adding a question at the end of their statement.

radiation A procedure that uses high-energy radiation to kill cancer cells by damaging their DNA.

radical mastectomy A surgical procedure that involves removal of the breast, its surrounding tissue, the muscles supporting the breast, and underarm lymph nodes.

random sample A number of people taken from the entire population in such a way to ensure that any one person has as much chance of being selected as any other.

rape Forced sexual behavior without a person's consent.

rape crisis centers Organizations that offer support services to victims of sexual assault, their families, and friends. Many offer information, referrals, support groups, counseling, educational programs, and workshops.

rape trauma syndrome (RTS) A two-stage stress response pattern that occurs after a rape.

recidivism A tendency to repeat crimes, such as sexual offenses.

refractory phase The period after an ejaculation in which men cannot be stimulated to further orgasm.

reliability The dependability of a test as reflected in the consistency of its scores on repeated measurements of the same group.

repression A coping strategy by which unwanted thoughts or prohibited desires are forced out of consciousness and into the unconscious mind.

resolution The fourth stage of the sexual response cycle, in which the body returns to the prearoused state.

reverse transcriptase A chemical that is contained in the RNA of HIV; it helps to change the virus's DNA.

rhythm method A contraceptive method that involves calculating the period of ovulation and avoiding sexual intercourse around this time.

romantic love Idealized love, based on romance and perfection.

sadism Deriving sexual pleasure from administering or watching pain and humiliation.

sadomasochism Broad term that refers to the receiving of sexual pleasure from acts involving the infliction or receiving of pain and humiliation.

samples of convenience A research methodology that involves using samples that are easy to collect and acquire.

satiation therapy A therapy to lessen excitement to an undesired stimulus by masturbating to a desired stimulus and then immediately masturbating again, when desire is lessened, to an undesired stimulus.

scabies A parasitic sexually transmitted infection that affects the skin and is spread during skin-to-skin contact, both during sexual and nonsexual contact.

scatolophilia A paraphiliac behavior that involves making obscene phone calls.

schema A cognitive mechanism that helps to organize information.

scrotum External pouch of skin that contains the testicles.

second-trimester surgical abortion Termination of pregnancy between the 16th and 21st weeks of pregnancy.

self-actualization Fulfillment of an individual's potentialities, including aptitudes, talents, and the like.

self-disclosure Opening up, talking with your partner, and sharing feelings.

semen A thick, whitish secretion of the male reproductive organs, containing spermatozoa and secretions from the seminal vesicles, prostate, and bulbourethral glands.

semenarche The experience of first ejaculation.

seminal vesicles The pair of pouchlike structures lying next to the urinary bladder that secrete a component of semen into the ejaculatory ducts.

seminiferous tubules The tightly coiled ducts located in the testes, where spermatozoa are produced.

serial divorce The practice of divorce and remarriage, followed by divorce and remarriage.

sex chromosomes Rod-shaped bodies in the nucleus of a cell at the time of cell division that contain information about whether the fetus will become male or female.

sex flush A temporary reddish color change of the skin that sometimes develops during sexual excitement.

sex reassignment surgery A wide range of various surgical options to change genitalia on a transsexual; also referred to as *gender reassignment.*

sexologist A person who engages in the scientific study of sexual behavior. Sexologists can be scientists, researchers, or clinicians, and can hold a variety of different graduate degrees.

sexual assault Coercion of a nonconsenting victim to have sexual contact.

sexual aversion Persistent or recurring extreme aversion to and avoidance of all genital contact.

sexual cognitions Thoughts about sex.

sexual interest/arousal disorder A category of sexual problems that involves a lack of sexual interest or arousal in women.

sexual masochism disorder A paraphilia that involves recurrent and intense sexual arousal from fantasies or behaviors involving the act of being humiliated, beaten, bound, or suffering in other ways.

sexual orientation The gender(s) that a person is attracted to emotionally, physically, sexually, and romantically.

sexual reproduction The production of offspring from the union of two parents.

sexual response Series of physiological and psychological changes that occur in the body during sexual behavior.

sexual response cycle Four-stage model of sexual arousal proposed by Masters and Johnson.

sexual revolution Changes in sexual morality and sexual behavior that occurred throughout the Western world during the 1960s and 1970s.

sexual sadism disorder A paraphilia that involves a recurrent and intense sexual arousal from fantasies or behaviors involving the physical or psychological suffering of another person.

silent rape reaction A type of rape trauma syndrome in which a victim does not talk to anyone after the rape.

sixty-nine Oral sex that is performed simultaneously between two partners.

smegma A pasty white accumulation of epidermal cells that collects in moist areas of the genitalia, such as under the clitoral hood (in women) or foreskin (in men).

socialization The process in which an infant is taught the basic skills for functioning in society.

sonography Electronic monitoring; also called *ultrasound*.

speculum An instrument for dilating the vagina to examine the cervix and other internal structures.

sperm cryopreservation The freezing of sperm for later use.

spermatogenesis The production of sperm in the testes.

spermatozoon A mature sperm cell.

spermicide Chemical method of contraception, including creams, gels, foams, suppositories, and films, that works to reduce the survival of sperm in the vagina.

spina bifida A congenital defect of the vertebral column in which the halves of the neural arch of a vertebra fail to fuse in the midline.

spontaneous abortion A natural process through which the body expels a developing embryo.

squeeze technique A technique in which the ejaculatory reflex is reconditioned using a firm grasp on the penis.

stalking Relentlessly pursuing someone, shadowing him or her, or making threatening gestures or claims toward the person when the relationship is unwanted.

start day The actual day that the first pill is taken in a pack of oral contraceptives.

sterilization Surgical contraceptive method that causes permanent infertility.

stillbirth An infant who is born dead.

stop–start technique A technique in which the ejaculatory reflex is reconditioned using intermittent pressure on the glans of the penis.

straight Slang for heterosexual.

subdermal contraceptive implant Contraceptive implant that time-releases a constant dose of progestin to inhibit ovulation.

submissive Describes the passive role in sadomasochistic activity.

superego The social and parental standards an individual has internalized; the conscience.

surrogate mother A woman who donates her ovum (which is fertilized by the father's sperm) and then carries the zygote to term.

surrogate parenting Use of a woman who, through artificial insemination or in vitro fertilization, gestates a fetus for another woman or man.

symptothermal method A contraceptive method that involves monitoring both cervical mucus and basal body temperature to determine ovulation.

syphilis A bacterial sexually transmitted infection that is divided into primary, secondary, and tertiary stages.

T lymphocyte (T helper cell) Type of white blood cell that helps to destroy harmful bacteria in the body.

tag question A way of speaking in which speakers renounce or deny the validity of what they are saying by adding a questioning statement at the end of their statement.

tenting effect During sexual arousal in females, the cervix and uterus pull up, and the upper third of the vagina balloons open, making a larger opening in the cervix.

testes Male gonads inside the scrotum that produce testosterone.

testicular torsion The twisting of a testis on its spermatic cord, which can cause severe pain and swelling.

test-tube baby A slang term for any zygote created by mixing sperm and egg outside a woman's body.

theory A set of assumptions, principles, or methods that helps a researcher understand the nature of a phenomenon being studied.

toucheurism A paraphiliac behavior that involves recurrent and intense sexual arousal from fantasies or behaviors involving compulsively touching strangers.

toxemia A form of blood poisoning caused by kidney disturbances.

toxoplasmosis A parasite that can cause headache, sore throat, seizures, altered mental status, or coma.

transgender or **trans** A general term referring to a person or group of people who identify or express their gender in a variety of different ways, typically in opposition to their biological sex.

transition The last period in labor, in which contractions are strongest and the periods in between contractions are the shortest.

transmen A label that may be used by female-to-male transsexuals to signify they are male with a female history.

transsexual A person who identifies with a gender other than the one he or she was given at birth.

transudation The lubrication of the vagina during sexual arousal.

transvestic disorder A paraphilia that involves recurrent and intense sexual arousal from fantasies or behaviors involving cross-dressing, which often causes significant distress.

transwomen A label that may be used by male-to-female transsexuals to signify they are female with a male history.

transyouth A label often used to describe youths who are experiencing issues related to gender identity or expression.

traumatic sexualization A common result of sexual abuse in which a child displays compulsive sex play or masturbation and shows an inappropriate amount of sexual knowledge.

tribadism Rubbing genitals together with another person for sexual pleasure.

trichomoniasis A vaginal infection that may result in discomfort, discharge, and inflammation.

trimester Three periods of 12–15 weeks each; typically refers to the division of the nine months of pregnancy.

triphasic model A model of sexual response, proposed by Helen Singer Kaplan, which includes three phases.

triphasic pill A type of oral contraceptive that contains three different doses of hormones in the active pills.

tubal sterilization A surgical procedure in which the Fallopian tubes are cut, tied, or cauterized for permanent contraception.

tumescence The swelling of the penis because of vasocongestion, causing an erection.

Turner syndrome A genetic disorder in females in which there is only one X sex chromosome instead of two, characterized by lack of internal female sex organs, infertility, short stature, and mental retardation.

two-spirit A term used in Native American culture and other parts of the world for a male or female who is thought to possess both masculine and feminine spirits. (In Native American culture, also referred to as a *berdache*.)

typical use Refers to the probability of contraceptive failure for less than perfect use of the method.

ultrasound The use of ultrasonic waves to monitor a developing fetus; also called *sonography*.

umbilical cord The long, ropelike structure that connects the fetus to the placenta.

unconditional positive regard Acceptance of another without restrictions on their behaviors or thoughts.

urethral opening (or meatus) The opening of the penis through which urine and semen are expelled.

urinary tract infection (UTI) Infection of the urinary tract, often resulting in a frequent urge to urinate, painful burning in the bladder or urethra during urination, and fatigue.

uterine perforation Tearing a hole in the uterus.

uterus The hollow muscular organ in females that is the site of menstruation, implantation of the fertilized ovum, and labor; also referred to as the *womb*.

vacuum aspirator A vacuum pump that is used during abortion procedures.

vacuum constriction device Treatment device for erectile disorders used to pull blood into the penis.

vagina A thin-walled muscular tube that leads from the uterus to the vestibule and is used for sexual intercourse and as a passageway for menstrual fluid, sperm, and a newborn baby.

vaginal contraceptive film Spermicidal contraceptive film that is placed in the vagina.

vaginismus Involuntary spasms of the muscles around the vagina in response to attempts at penetration.

validity The property of a device measuring what it is intended to measure.

vas deferens One of two long tubes that convey the sperm from the testes and in which other fluids are mixed to create semen.

vasectomy A surgical procedure in which each vas deferens is cut, tied, or cauterized for permanent contraception.

vasocongestion An increase in the blood concentrated in the male and female genitals, as well as in the female breasts, during sexual activity.

vernix Cheeselike substance that coats the fetus in the uterus.

vestibule The entire region between the labia minora, including the urethra and introitus.

viral hepatitis A viral infection; three main types of viral hepatitis include hepatitis A, B, and C.

viral load The measure of the severity of a viral infection calculated by estimating the amount of virus in body fluid.

viral shedding The release of viral infections between outbreaks from infected skin.

volunteer bias A slanting of research data caused by the characteristics of participants who volunteer to participate.

voyeur A person who experiences recurrent and intense arousal from observing unsuspecting persons undressing or engaging in sex acts.

vulva The collective designation for the external genitalia of the female.

vulvar vestibulitis syndrome Syndrome that causes pain and burning in the vaginal vestibule and often occurs during sexual intercourse, tampon insertion, gynecological examinations, bicycle riding, and wearing tight pants.

vulvodynia Chronic vulvar pain and soreness.

vulvovaginal candidiasis A vaginal infection that causes a heavy discharge; also referred to as a *yeast infection*.

Western blot A test used to confirm a positive ELISA test; more accurate than the ELISA test, but too expensive to be used as the primary screening device for infection.

withdrawal (or coitus interruptus) A contraceptive method that involves withdrawal of the penis from the vagina before ejaculation.

Wolffian duct One of a pair of structures in the embryo that, when exposed to testosterone, will develop into the male reproductive system.

women's suffrage The movement to get women the right to vote.

yeast infection Vaginal infection that causes an increase in vaginal discharge, burning, and itching, and may be sexually transmitted; also referred to as vulvovaginal candidiasis.

yin and yang According to a Chinese belief, the universe is run by the interaction of two fundamental principles: yin, which is negative, passive, weak, yielding, and female; and yang, which is positive, assertive, active, strong, and male.

zoophilia or **bestiality** A paraphiliac behavior that involves recurrent and intense sexual arousal from fantasies or behaviors involving sexual contact with animals (also referred to as *bestiality*).

zygote The single cell resulting from the union of sperm and egg cells; the fertilized ovum.

Abbey, A., Zawacki, T., & Buck, P. O. (2005). The effects of past sexual assault perpetration and alcohol consumption on men's reactions to women's mixed signals. *Journal of Social & Clinical Psychology, 24*(2), 129–155.

Abma, J. C., Martinez, G. M., & Copen, C. E. (2010). Teenagers in the United States: Sexual activity, contraceptive use, and childbearing, National Survey of Family Growth 2006–2008. National Center for Health Statistics. *Vital Health Statistics, 23*(30), 1–47.

Aboueh, A., & Clayton, A. (1999). Compulsive voyeurism and exhibitionism: A clinical response to paroxetine. *Archives of Sexual Behavior, 28*(1), 23–30.

AbouZeid, A. A., Mousa, M. H., Soliman, H. A., Hamza, A. F., & Hay, S. A. (2011). Intra-abdominal testis: Histological alterations and significance of biopsy. *Journal of Urology, 185*(1), 269–274.

Adams, H. E., Wright, L. W., Jr., & Lohr, B. A. (1996). Is homophobia associated with homosexual arousal? *Journal of Abnormal Psychology, 105,* 440–445.

Adams-Curtis, L. E., & Forbes, G. B. (2004). College women's experiences of sexual coercion: A review of cultural, perpetrator, victim, and situational variables. *Trauma, Violence, & Abuse, 5*(2), 91–122.

Add Health. (2002). Add Health and Add Health 2000: A national longitudinal study of adolescent health. Retrieved from http://www.cpc.unc.edu/addhealth

Adler, R. B., Rosenfeld, L. B., & Proctor, R. F. (2007). *Interplay: The process of interpersonal communication* (10th ed.). New York: Oxford University Press.

Ahmetoglu, G., Swami, V., & Chamorro-Premuzic, T. (2010). The relationship between dimensions of love, personality, and relationship length. *Archives of Sexual Behavior, 39*(5), 1181–1190.

Ainsworth, M. D. S., Blehar, M. C., Waters, E., & Wall, S. (1978). *Patterns of attachment: A psychological study of the strange situation.* Hillsdale, NJ: Erlbaum.

Akbag, M., & Imamoglu, S. (2010). The prediction of gender and attachment styles on shame, guilt, and loneliness. *Educational Sciences: Theory and Practice, 10*(2), 669–682.

Akers, A. Y., Gold, M. A., Bost, J. E., Adimora, A. A., Orr, D. P., & Fortenberry, J. D. (2011). Variation in sexual behaviors in a cohort of adolescent females: The role of personal, perceived peer, and perceived family attitudes. *Journal of Adolescent Health, 48*(1), 87–93.

Alan Guttmacher Institute. (2002). Facts in brief: Contraceptive use. Retrieved January 14, 2003, from http://www.agi-usa.org/pubs/fb_contr_use.html

Alan Guttmacher Institute. (2008a, January). Facts in brief: Facts on contraceptive use. Retrieved July 20, 2008, from http://www.guttmacher.org/pubs/fb_contr_use.html

Alan Guttmacher Institute. (2008b, July 1). State policies in brief: Abortion policy in the absence of Roe. Retrieved July 28, 2008, from http://www.guttmacher.org/statecenter/spibs/spib_APAR.pdf

Alan Guttmacher Institute. (2010, October 1). Media center: News in context: A key step forward in overhauling U.S. teen pregnancy prevention efforts. Retrieved January 24, 2011, from http://www.guttmacher.org/media/inthenews/2010/10/01/index.html

Alan Guttmacher Institute. (2011, January 1). State policies in brief: Sex and HIV education. Retrieved January 24, 2011, from http://www.guttmacher.org/statecenter/spibs/spib_SE.pdf

Alan Guttmacher Institute. (2011, March 1). State policies in brief: An overview of abortion laws. Retrieved January 24, 2011, from http://www.guttmacher.org/statecenter/spibs/spib_OAL.pdf

Alan Guttmacher Institute. (2011, March 1). State policies in brief: Abortion policy in the absence of Roe. Retrieved from http://www.guttmacher.org/statecenter/spibs/spib_APAR.pdf

Alan Guttmacher Institute. (2011, March 1). State policies in brief: Parental involvement in minors' abortions. Alan Guttmacher Institute. Retrieved from http://www.guttmacher.org/statecenter/spibs/spib_PIMA.pdf

Alanis, M. C., & Lucidi, R.S. (2004, May). Neonatal circumcision: A review of the world's oldest and most controversial operation. *Obstetrical & Gynecological Survey, 59*(5), 379–395.

Alarid, L. F. (2000). Sexual assault and coercion among incarcerated women prisoners: Excerpts from prison letters. *The Prison Journal, 80*(4), 391–406.

Albers, K. (2007). Comprehensive care in the prevention of ectopic pregnancy and associated negative outcomes. *Midwifery Today with International Midwife, (84),* 26–27, 67.

Albert, A., & Porter, J. R. (1988). Children's gender-role stereotypes: A sociological investigation of psychological models. *Sociological Forum, 3,* 184–210.

Albert, R. T., Elwell, S. L., & Idelson, S. (2001). *Lesbian rabbis: The first generation.* Piscataway, NJ: Rutgers University Press.

Alexander, M. A. (1999). Sexual offender treatment efficacy revisited. *Sexual Abuse: A Journal of Research and Treatment, 11,* 101–116.

Alexandre, B., Lemaire, A., Desvaux, P., & Amar, E. (2007). Intracavernous injections of prostaglandin E1 for erectile dysfunction: Patient satisfaction and quality of sex life on long-term treatment. *Journal of Sexual Medicine, 4,* 426–431.

Alkhuja, S., Mnekel, R., Patel, B., & Ibrahimbacha, A. (2001). Stridor and difficult airway in an AIDS patient. *AIDS Patient Care and Sexually Transmitted Diseases, 15*(6), 293–295.

Allen, P. L. (2000). *The wages of sin: Sex and disease, past and present.* Chicago: University of Chicago Press.

Allison, L., Santilla, P., Sandnabba, N., & Nordling, N. (2001). Sadomasochistically oriented behavior: Diversity in practice and meaning. *Archives of Sexual Behavior, 30,* 1–12.

Althaus, F. (1997). Most Japanese students do not have intercourse until after adolescence. *Family Planning Perspectives, 29*(3), 145–147.

Althof, S., Abdo, C., Dean, J., Hackett, G., McCabe, M., McMahon, C., … International Society for Sexual Medicine. (2010). International society for sexual medicine's guidelines for the diagnosis and treatment of premature ejaculation. *Journal of Sexual Medicine, 7*(9), 2947–2969.

Altman, C. (2000). Gay and lesbian seniors: Unique challenges of coming out in later life. *SIECUS Report, 4,* 14.

Amador, J., Charles, T., Tait, J., & Helm, H. (2005). Sex and generational differences in desired characteristics in mate selection. *Psychological Reports, 96*(1), 19–25.

Amato, P., Johnson, D., Booth, A., & Rogers, S. (2003). Stability and change in marital quality between 1980 and 2000. *Journal of Marriage and Family, 65,* 1–22.

American Academy of Pediatrics. (1999). Task force on circumcision. Circumcision policy statement (RE 9850), *Pediatrics, 103,* 686–693.

American Cancer Society. (2005). Testicular cancer has high cure rate—in America. Retrieved April 6, 2008, from http://www.cancer.org/docroot/NWS/content/update/NWS_1_1xU_Testicular_Cancer_Has_High_Cure_Rate_%E2%80%94_In_America. asp

American Cancer Society. (2007a). How to perform a breast self exam. Retrieved March 22, 2008, from http://www.cancer.org/docroot/CRI/content/CRI_2_6x_How_to_perform_a_breast_self_exam_5.asp

American Cancer Society. (2007b). Overview: Prostate cancer. Retrieved October 15, 2008, from http://www.cancer.org/docroot/CRI/CRI_2_1x.asp?dt=36

American Cancer Society. (2010). Cancer: Facts and figures, 2010. Atlanta, GA: American Cancer Society. Retrieved January 5, 2011, from http://www.cancer.org/acs/groups/content/@epidemiologysurveilance/documents/document/acspc-026238.pdf

American College of Obstetricians and Gynecologists. (2006). ACOG practice bulletin. Episiotomy. Clinical managment guidelines for obstetrician-gynecologists. *Obstetrics and Gynecology, 107*(4), 957–962.

American College of Obstetricians and Gynecologists. (2007). Screening for fetal chromosomal abnormalities. Washington, DC: American College of Obstetricians and Gynecologists (ACOG); 2007 Jan. 11 p. (*ACOG Practice Bulletin;* No. 77).

American Psychiatric Association. (1998). Media information: Position statement on hate crimes. Retrieved from http://www.apa.org/releases/hate.html

American Psychiatric Association. (2010). About the DSM. Retrieved June 18, 2011, from http://www.dsm5.org/about/Pages/Default.aspx

American Psychological Association. (2005). Lesbian and gay parenting. Committee on Lesbian, Gay, and Bisexual Concerns. Retrieved September 1, 2008, from http://www.apa.org/pi/lgbc/publications/lgparenting.pdf

Amir, M. (1971). *Patterns in forcible rape.* Chicago: University of Chicago Press.

Amis, D. (2007). Care practice #1: Labor begins on its own. *Journal of Perinatal Education, 16,* 16–20.

Anderson, F. D., Gibbons, W., & Portman, D. (2006). Long-term safety of an extended cycle oral contraceptive (Seasonale): A 2-year multimember open-label extension trial. *American Journal of Obstetrics and Gynecology, 195,* 92–96.

Anderson, P. B., & Savage, J. S. (2005). Social, legal, and institutional context of heterosexual aggression by college women. *Trauma, Violence, & Abuse, 6*(2), 130–140.

Angier, N. (1999). *Woman: An intimate geography.* New York: Anchor Books.

Antheunis, M., Valkenburg, P. M., & Peter, J. (2007). Computer-mediated communication and interpersonal attraction: An experimental test of two explanatory hypotheses. *CyberPsychology & Behavior, 10,* 831–836.

Arena, J. M., & Wallace, M. (2008). Issues regarding sexuality. In E. Capezuti, D. Zwicker, M. Mezey, T. Fuller, D. Gray-Miceli, & M. Kluger (Eds.), *Evidence-based geriatric nursing protocols for best practice* (3rd ed., pp. 629–647). New York: Springer Publishing Company.

Aries, E. (1996). *Men and women in interaction: Reconsidering the differences.* New York: Oxford University Press.

Armour, B.S., Wolf, L., Mitra, M., & Brieding, M. (2008, October 27). Differences in intimate partner violence among women with and without a disability. American Public Health Association's 136th Annual Meeting, San Diego, CA. Retrieved November 14, 2008, from http://apha.confex.com/apha/136am/webprogram/Paper182004.html

Atanackovic, G., Wolpin, J., & Koren, G. (2001). Determinants of the need for hospital care among women with nausea and vomiting of pregnancy. *Clinical and Investigative Medicine, 24*(2), 90–94.

Athenstaedt, U., Haas, E., & Schwab, S. (2004). Gender role self-concept and gender-typed communication behavior in mixed-sex and same-sex dyads. *Sex Roles, 50*(1–2), 37–52.

Ayala, M. (2009). Brain serotonin, psychoactive drugs, and effects on reproduction. *Central Nervous System Agents in Medical Chemistry, 9*(4), 258–276.

Azam, S. (2000). What's behind retro virginity? The Toronto Star life story. Retrieved December 29, 2002, from http://www.psurg.com/star2000.html

Back, M., Stopfer, J., Vazire, S., Gaddis, S., Schmukle, B., & Gosling, S. (2010). Facebook profiles reflect actual personality, not self-idealization. *Psychological Science, 21*(3), 372–374.

Bailey, A., & Hurd, P. (2005). Finger length ratio correlates with physical aggression in men but not in women. *Biological Psychology, 68*(3), 215–222.

Bailey, B. P., Gurak, L. J., & Konstan, J. A. (2003). Trust in cyberspace. In J. Ratner (Ed.), *Human factors and Web development* (2nd ed., pp. 311–321). Mahwah, NJ: Erlbaum.

Bailey, J. M., & Pillard, R. C. (1995). Genetics of human sexual orientation. *Annual Review of Sex Research, 6,* 126–150.

Bain, J. (2001). Testosterone replacement therapy for aging men. *Canadian Family Physician, 47,* 91–97.

Balaban, B., Yakin, K., Alatas, C., Oktem, O., Isiklar, A., & Urman, B. (2011). Clinical outcome of intracytoplasmic injection of spermatozoa morphologically selected under high magnification: A prospective randomized study. *Reproductive Biomedicine Online, 22*(5), 472–476.

Balsam, K., Rothblum, E., & Beauchaine, T. (2005). Victimization over the life span: A comparison of lesbian, gay, bisexual and heterosexual siblings. *Journal of Counseling and Clinical Psychology, 73,* 477–487.

Bancroft, J., Herbenick, D., Barnes, T., Hallam-Jones, R., Wylie, K., & Janssen, E. (2005). The relevance of the dual control model to male sexual dysfunction: The Kinsey Institute/BASRT collaborative project. *Sexual & Relationship Therapy, 20*(1), 13–30.

Bancroft, J., & Vukadinovic, Z. (2004). Sexual addiction, sexual compulsivity, or what? Toward a theoretical model. *Journal of Sex Research, 41*(3), 225–234.

Barbach, L. (1982). *For each other: Sharing sexual intimacy.* New York: Penguin Group.

Baron, N. S. (2004). See you online: Gender issues in college student use of instant messaging. *Journal of Language & Social Psychology, 23*(4), 397–423.

Barrow, R., Newman, L., & Douglas, J. (2008). Taking positive steps to address STD disparities for African-American communities. *Sexually Transmitted Diseases, 35*(12), S1–S3.

Bartholomew, K., & Horowitz, L. (1991). Attachment styles among young adults: A test of a four-category model. *Journal of Personality and Social Psychology, 61,* 226–244.

Bartz, D., Goldberg, A. (2011). Injectable contraceptives. In R. A. Hatcher, J. Trussell, A. L. Nelson, W. Cates, D. Kaval, M. S. Policar (Eds) *Contraceptive Technology,* 20th Edition. pp. 209-236. Ardent Media, New York, N.Y.

Basow, S., & Minieri, A. (2011). "You owe me": Effects of date cost, who pays, participant gender, and rape myth beliefs on perceptions of rape. *Journal of Interpersonal Violence, 26*(3), 479–497.

Bassil, N., & Morley, J. E. (2010). Late-life onset hypogonadism: A review. *Clinical Geriatric Medicine, 26*(2), 197–222.

Basson, R. (2000). The female sexual response: A different model. *Journal of Sex and Marital Therapy, 26,* 51–65.

Basson, R. (2005). Women's sexual dysfunction: Revised and expanded definitions. *Canadian Medical Association Journal, 172*(10), 1327–1333.

Bauermeister, J. A., Johns, M. M., Sandfort, T. G., Eisenberg, A., Grossman, A. H., & D'Augelli, A. R. (2010). Relationship trajectories and psychological well-being among sexual minority youth. *Journal of Youth and Adolescence, 39*(10), 1148–1163.

Baumeister, L. M., Flores, E., & Marin, B. V. (1995). Sex information given to Latina adolescents by parents. *Health Education Research, 10*(2), 233–239.

Baumeister, R. F. (1988). Masochism as escape from self. *Journal of Sex Research, 25,* 28–59.

Bearman, P., & Bruckner, H. (2001). Promising the future: Virginity pledges and first intercourse. *American Journal of Sociology, 106*(4), 859–912.

Beaton, A. A., & Mellor, G. (2007). Direction of hair whorl and handedness. *Laterality, 12,* 295–301.

Beck, M. (2008, September 30). Is sex addiction a sickness, or excuse to behave badly? *Wall Street Journal* (Eastern edition). New York, p. B.9.

Beckett, M. K., Elliott, M. N., Martino, S., Kanouse, D. E., Corona, R., Klein, D. J., & Schuster, M. A. (2010). Timing of parent and child communication about sexuality relative to children's sexual behaviors. *Pediatrics, 125*(1), 34–42.

Beeble, M., Sullivan, C., & Bybee, D. (2011). The impact of neighborhood factors on the well-being of survivors of intimate partner violence over time. *American Journal of Community Psychology, 47*(3–4), 287–306.

Beech, A., Ward, T., & Fisher, D. (2006). The identification of sexual and violent motivations in men who assault women: Implication for treatment. *Journal of Interpersonal Violence, 21,* 1635.

Begley, S. (2010, July 2). The anti-lesbian drug. *Newsweek.* Retrieved November 16, 2010, from http://www.newsweek.com/2010/07/02/the-anti-lesbian-drug.html

Belkin, L. (2011, February 11). The IRS, breast pumps, and other updates. *New York Times.* Retrieved May 30, 2011, from http://parenting.blogs.nytimes.com/2011/02/11/the-irs-breast-pumps-and-other-updates/

Bell, A. P., Weinberg, M. S., & Hammersmith, S. K. (1981). *Sexual preference: Its development in men and women.* Bloomington, IN: Indiana University Press.

Bellino, S., Renocchio, M., Zizzo, M., Rocca, G., Bogetti, P., & Bogetto, F. (2010). Quality of life of patients who undergo breast reconstruction after mastectomy: Effects of personality characteristics. *Plastic Reconstructive Surgery, 127*(1), 10–17.

Bem, D. J. (2000). Exotic becomes erotic: Interpreting the biological correlates of sexual orientation. *Archives of Sexual Behavior, 29*(6), 531–548.

Bem, S. L. (1974). The measurement of psychological androgyny. *Journal of Consulting and Clinical Psychology, 42,* 155–162.

Bem, S. L. (1977). On the utility of alternative procedures for assessing psychological androgyny. *Journal of Consulting and Clinical Psychology, 45,* 196–205.

Bem, S. L. (1981). Gender schema theory: A cognitive account of sex-typing. *Psychological Review, 88,* 354–364.

Benokraitis, N. V. (1993). *Marriages and families.* Englewood Cliffs, NJ: Prentice Hall.

Benson, A., Ost, L., Noble, M., & Laakin, M. (2009). Premature ejaculation. *Emedicine.* Retrieved March 25, 2010, from http://emedicine.medscape.com/article/435884-overview

Bergen, R. (2006). Marital rape: New research and directions. National Sexual Violence Resource Center. Retrieved June 26, 2011, from http://new.vawnet.org/Assoc_Files_VAWnet/AR_MaritalRapeRevised.pdf

Bergen, R., & Bukovec, P. (2006). Men and intimate partner rape: Characteristics of men who sexually abuse their partner. *Journal of Interpersonal Violence, 21,* 1375.

Bergmann, M. S. (1987). *The anatomy of living.* New York: Fawcett Columbine.

Berkey, B. R., Perelman-Hall, T., & Kurdek, L. A. (1990). The multidimensional scale of sexuality. *Journal of Homosexuality, 19,* 67–87.

Berkowitz, D., & Marsiglio, W. (2007). Gay men: Negotiating procreative, father, and family identities. *Journal of Marriage and Family, 69,* 366–382.

Bernstein, D. I., Earwood, J. D., Bravo, F. J., Cohen, G. H., Eisenberg, R. J., Clark, J. R., ... Cardin, R. D. (2011). Effects of herpes simplex virus type 2 glycoprotein vaccines and CLDC adjuvant on genital herpes infection in the guinea pig. *Vaccine, 29*(11), 2071–2078.

Bessede, T., Massard, C., Albouy, B., Leborgne, S., Gross-Goupil, M., Droupy, S., ... Escudier, B. (In press). Sexual life of male patients with advanced renal cancer treated with angiogenesis inhibitors. *Annals of Oncology.*

Bezemer, D., de Wolf, F., Boerlijst, M. C., van Sighem, A., Hollingsworth, T. D., Prins, M., ... Fraser, C. (2008). A resurgent HIV-1 epidemic among men who have sex with men in the era of potent antiretroviral therapy. *AIDS, 22*(9), 1071–1077.

Bhide, A., Nama, V., Patel, S., & Kalu, E. (2010). Microbiology of cysts/abscesses of Bartholin's gland: Review of empirical antibiotic therapy against microbial culture. *Journal of Obstetrics and Gynecology, 30*(7), 701–703.

Bialik, C. (2010a, October 8). Sex, and studying it, are complicated. *Wall Street Journal.*

Retrieved October 10, 2010, from http://blogs.wsj.com/numbersguy/sex-and-studying-it-is-complicated-998/.

Bialik, C. (2010b, October 9). Research into human sexuality leaves a lot to be desired. *Wall Street Journal,* p. A2.

Bick, R. L., Maden, J., Heller, K. B., & Toofanian, A. (1998). Recurrent miscarriage: Causes, evaluation, and treatment. *Medscape Women's Health, 3*(3), 2.

Bieber, I., Dain, H. J., Dince, P. R., Drellich, M. G., Grand, H. G., Gundlach, R. H., ... Bieber, Toby B. (1962). *Homosexuality: A psychoanalytic study.* New York: Basic Books.

Bigelow, B. J. (1977). Children's friendship expectations: A cognitive developmental study. *Child Development, 48,* 246–253.

Bird, M. H. (2006). Sexual addiction and marriage and family therapy: Facilitating individual and relationship healing through couple therapy. *Journal of Marital and Family Therapy, 32*(3), 297–310.

Biro, F., Galvez, M., Greenspan, L., Succop, P., Vangeepuram, N., Pinney, S., ... Wolff, M. (2010). Pubertal assessment method and baseline characteristics in a mixed longitudinal study of girls. *Pediatrics, 6*(11), 595.

Black, K., & Gold, D. (2008). Gender differences and socioeconomic status biases in judgments about blame in date rape scenarios. *Violence and Victims, 23*(1), 115–128.

Black, M., Shetty, A., & Bhattacharya, S. (2008). Obstetric outcomes subsequent to intrauterine death in the first pregnancy. *British Journal of Gynecology, 115,* 269–274.

Blackwood, E. (1994). Sexuality and gender in Native American tribes: The case of crossgender females. In A. C. Herrmann & A. J. Stewart (Eds.), *Theorizing feminism: Parallel trends in the humanities and social sciences* (pp. 301–315). Boulder, CO: Westview Press.

Blair, A. (2000) Individuation, love styles, and health-related quality of life among college students. *Dissertation Abstracts International,* University of Florida, #0-599-91381-9.

Blake, S. M., Ledsky, R., Lehman, T., Goodenow, C., Sawyer, R., & Hack, T. (2001). Preventing sexual risk behaviors among gay, lesbian, and bisexual adolescents: The benefits of gay-sensitive HIV instruction in schools. *American Journal of Public Health, 91,* 940–946.

Blakemore, J. E. (2003). Children's beliefs about violating gender norms: Boys shouldn't look like girls, and girls shouldn't act like boys. *Sex Roles, 48*(9–10), 411–419.

Blanchard, R. (1997). Birth order and sibling sex ratio in homosexual versus heterosexual males and females. *Annual Review of Sex Research, 8,* 27–67.

Blanchard, R. (2004). Quantitative and theoretical analyses of the relation between older brothers and homosexuality in men. *Journal of Theoretical Biology, 230*(2), 173–187.

Blanchard, R. (2008). Review and theory off-handedness, birth order, and homosexuality in men. *Laterality, 13,* 51–70.

Blanchard, R., Cantor, J. M., Bogaert, A., Breedlove, S., & Ellis, L. (2006). Interaction of fraternal birth order and handedness in the development of male homosexuality. *Hormones & Behavior, 49,* 405–414.

Bleakley, A., Hennessey, M., & Fishbein, M. (2006). Public opinion on sex education in U.S. schools. *Archives of Pediatrics and Adolescent Medicine, 160,* 1151–1156.

Blecher, S. R., & Erickson, R. P. (2007). Genetics of sexual development: A new paradigm. *American Journal of Medical Genetics, 143,* 3054–3068.

Bleecker, E., & Murnen, S. (2005). Fraternity membership, the display of degrading sexual images of women, and rape myth acceptance. *Sex Roles, 53,* 487–493.

Blumstein, H. (2001). Bartholin gland disease. Retrieved from http://www.emedicine.com/emeg/topic54.htm

Blumstein, P., & Schwartz, P. (1983). *American couples.* New York: William Morrow.

Bocklandt, S., & Vilain, E. (2007). Sex differences in brain and behavior: Hormones versus genes. *Advances in Genetics, 59,* 245–266.

Bodenmann, G., Meuwly, N., Bradbury, T., Gmelch, S., & Ledermann, T. (2010). Stress, anger, and verbal aggression in intimate relationships: Moderating effects of individual and dyadic coping. *Journal of Social and Personal Relationships, 27*(3), 408–424.

Bodner, E., & Lazar, A. (2008). Ageism among Israeli students: Structure and demographic influences. *International Psychogeriatrics, 20*(5), 1046–1058.

Boeringer, S. (1999). Associations of rape-supportive attitudes with fraternal and athletic participation. *Violence Against Women, 5*(1), 81–90.

Bogaert, A. F. (2005). Gender role/identity and sibling sex ratio in homosexual men. *Journal of Sex and Marital Therapy, 31,* 217–227.

Bogaert, A. F., Blanchard, R., & Crosthwait, L. (2007). Interaction of birth order, handedness, and sexual orientation in the Kinsey interview data. *Behavioral Neuroscience, 121,* 845–853.

Bogaert, A. F., & Skorska, M. (2011). Sexual orientation, fraternal birth order, and the mater-nal immune hypothesis: A review. *Frontiers in Neuroendocrinology, 32*(2), 247–254.

Bogaerts, S., Vanheule, S., Leeuw, F., & Desmet, M. (2006). Recalled parental bonding and personality disorders in a sample of exhibitionists: A comparative study. *Journal of Forensic Psychiatry & Psychology, 17*(4), 636–646.

Bolso, A. (2005). orgasm and lesbian sexuality. *Sex Education, 5*(1), 29–48.

Bolton, M., van der Straten, A., & Cohen, C. (2008). Probiotics: Potential to prevent HIV and sexually transmitted infections in women. *Sexually Transmitted Diseases, 35*(3), 214–225.

Bonomi, A., Anderson, M., Reid, R., Carrell, D., Fishman, P., Rivara, F., & Thompson, R. (2007). Intimate partner violence in older women. *The Gerontologist, 47,* 34–41.

Boomer, D. S. (1963). Speech disturbances and body movement in interviews. *Journal of Nervous and Mental Disease, 136,* 263–266.

Boonstra, H. D., Gold, R. B., Richards, C. L., & Finer, L. B. (2006). *Abortion in women's lives.* New York: Alan Guttmacher Institute.

Borg, C., de Jong, P. J., & Weijmar Schultz, W. (2011). Vaginismus and dyspareunia: Relationship with general and sex-related moral standards. *Journal of Sexual Medicine, 8*(1), 223–231.

Bos, H., & Gartrell, N. (2010). Adolescents of the USA National Longitudinal Lesbian Family Study: Can family characteristics counteract the negative effects of stigmatization? *Family Process, 49*(4), 559–572.

Boswell, J. (1980). *Christianity, social tolerance, and homosexuality: Gay people in western Europe from the beginning of the Christian era to the fourteenth century.* Chicago: The University of Chicago Press.

Bouchlariotou, S., Tsikouras, P., Dimitraki, M., Athanasiadis, A., Papoulidis, I., Maroulis, G., … Liberis, V. (2011). Turner's syndrome and pregnancy: Has the 45,X/47,XXX mosaicism a different prognosis? *Journal of Maternal and Fetal Neonatal Medicine, 24*(5), 668–672.

Boushey, H., & O'Leary, A. (2010, March 8). How working women are reshaping America's families and economy and what it means for policymakers. Center for American Progress. Retrieved December 20, 2010, from http://www.americanprogress.org/issues/2010/03/our_working_nation.html/print.html

Bower, B. (1992). Depression, early death noted in HIV cases. *Science News, 142,* 53.

Bowlby, J. (1969). *Attachment and loss: Attachment.* New York: Basic Books.

Boyd, L. (2000). Morning sickness shields fetus from bugs and chemicals. *RN, 63*(8), 18–20.

Boyle, C., Berkowitz, G., & Kelsey, J. (1987). Epidemiology of premenstrual symptoms. *American Journal of Public Health, 77*(3), 349–350.

Bradshaw, C., Kahn, A., & Saville, B. (2010). To hook up or date: Which gender benefits? *Sex Roles, 62*(9–10), 661–669.

Brans, R., & Yao, F. (2010). Immunization with a dominant-negative recombinant Herpes Simplex Virus (HSV) type 1 protects against HSV-2 genital disease in guinea pigs. *BMC Microbiology, 10,* 163.

Breech, L., & Braverman, P. (2010). Safety, efficacy, actions, and patient acceptability of drospirenone/ethinyl estradiol contraceptive pills in the treatment of premenstrual dysphoric disorder. *International Journal of Women's Health, 1,* 85–95.

Brennan, B. P., Kanayama, G., Hudson, J. I., & Pope, H. G., Jr. (2011). Human growth hormone abuse in male weightlifters. *American Journal of Addiction, 20*(1), 9–13.

Brewster, P., Mullin, C., Dobrin, R., & Steeves, J. (2010). Sex differences in face processing are mediated by handedness and sexual orientation. *Laterality, 9,* 1–13.

Brinig, M. F., & Allen, D. A. (2000). "These boots are made for walking": Why most divorce filers are women. *American Law and Economics Review, 2,* 126–169.

Brinton, L. A., & Schairer, C. (1997). Postmenopausal hormone-replacement therapy: Time for a reappraisal? *New England Journal of Medicine, 336*(25), 1821–1822.

Brizendine, L. (2006). *The female brain.* New York: Broadway Publishing.

Brizendine, L., & Allen, B. J. (2010). Are gender differences in communication biologically determined? In B. Slife (Ed.), *Taking sides: Clashing views on psychological issues* (16th ed., pp. 71–88). New York: McGraw-Hill.

Brooks-Gunn, J., & Furstenberg, F. F. (1989). Adolescent sexual behavior. *American Psychologist, 44,* 249–257.

Brousseau, M., Bergeron, S., & Hebert, M. (2011). Sexual coercion victimization and perpetration in heterosexual couples: A dyadic investigation. *Archives of Sexual Behavior, 40*(2), 363–372.

Brown, A., & Testa, M. (2008). Social influences on judgments of rape victims: The role of the negative and positive social reactions of others. *Sex Roles, 58,* 490–501.

Brown, B. B., Dolcini, M. M., & Leventhal, A. (1997). Transformations in peer relationships at adolescence: Implications for health-related behavior. In J. Schulenberg, J. L. Maggs, & K. Hurrelmann (Eds.), *Health risks and developmental transitions during adolescence* (pp. 161–189). Cambridge, England.: Cambridge University Press.

Brown, C. (2008). Gender-role implications on same-sex intimate partner abuse. *Journal of Family Violence, 23,* 457–463.

Brown, D. L., & Frank, J. E. (2003). Diagnosis and management of syphilis. *American Family Physician, 68*(2), 283–290.

Brown, J., Pan, A., & Hart, R. J. (2010). Gonadotrophin-releasing hormone analogues for pain associated with endometriosis. *Cochrane Database of Systematic Reviews, 12,* CD008475.

Brown, J., & Trevethan, R. (2010). Shame, internalized homophobia, identity formation, attachment style, and the connection to relationship status in gay men. *American Journal of Men's Health, 4*(3), 267–276.

Brown, M. S., & Brown, C. A. (1987). Circumcision decision: Prominence of social concerns. *Pediatrics, 80,* 215–219.

Brown, S. L., Lee, G. R., & Bulanda, J. R. (2006). Cohabitation among older adults: A national portrait. *Journals of Gerontology Series B: Psychological Sciences and Social Science, 61,* S71–S79.

Brown, T. J., Sumner, K. E., & Nocera, R. (2002). Understanding sexual aggression against women: An examination of the role of men's athletic participation and related variables. *Journal of Interpersonal Violence, 17*(9), 937–952.

Brubaker, L., Handa, V., Bradley, C., Connolly, A., Moalli, P., Brown, M., & Weber, A. (2008). Sexual function 6 months after first delivery. *Obstetrics and Gynecology, 111,* 1040–1044.

Brückner, H., & Bearman, P. (2005). After the promise: The STD consequences of adolescent virginity pledges. *Journal of Adolescent Health, 36*(4), 271–278.

Brugman, M., Caron, S., & Rademakers, J. (2010). Emerging adolescent sexuality: A comparison of American and Dutch college women's experiences. *International Journal of Sexual Health, 22*(1), 32–46.

Brumbaugh, C., & Fraley, C. (2010). Adult attachment and dating strategies: How do insecure people attract dates? *Personal Relationships, 17*(4), 599–614.

Brumberg, J. J. (1997). *The body project: An intimate history of American girls.* New York: Vintage Books.

Bryan, W. A. (1987). Contemporary fraternity and sorority issues. *New Directions for Student Services, 40,* 37–56.

Bryant, C. (2010). Understanding the intersection of race and marriage: Does one model fit all? *Psychological Science Agenda.* Retrieved May 11, 2011, from http://www.apa.org/science/about/psa/2010/10/race-marriage.aspx

Bullivant, S., Sellergren, S., Stern, K., Spencer, N., Jacob, S., Mennella, J., & McClintock, M. (2004). Women's sexual experience during the menstrual cycle: Identification of the sexual phase by noninvasive measurement of luteinizing hormone. *Journal of Sex Research, 41*(1), 82–93.

Bullough, V. L. (1976). *Sexual variance in society and history.* New York: Wiley.

Bullough, V. L. (1990). History in adult human sexual behavior with children and adolescents in Western societies. In J. Feierman (Ed.), *Pedophilia biosocial dimensions* (pp. 69–90). New York: Springer-Verlag.

Bumpass, L., & Lu, H.-H. (2000). Trends in cohabitation and implications for children's family contexts in the United States. *Population Studies, 54*(1), 29–41.

Burdette, A. M., Ellison, C. G., Sherkat, D. E., & Gore, K. A. (2007). Are there religious variations in marital infidelity? *Journal of Family Issues, 28,* 1553.

Burgess, A. W., & Morgenbesser, L. I. (2005). Sexual violence and seniors. *Brief Treatment & Crisis Intervention, 5*(2), 193–202.

Burkman, R. T. (2002). The transdermal contraceptive patch: A new approach to hormonal contraception. *International Journal of Fertility and Women's Medicine, 47*(2), 69–76.

Burleson, B. R., Kunkel, A. W., Samter, W., & Werking, K. (1996). Men's and women's evaluations of communication skills in personal relationships: When sex differences make a difference—And when they don't. *Journal of Social and Personal Relationships, 13,* 201–224.

Burt, M. (1980). Cultural myths and support for rape. *Journal of Personality and Social Psychology, 38,* 217–230.

Burton, K. (2005). Attachment style and perceived quality of romantic partner's opposite-sex best friendship: The impact on romantic relationship satisfaction. *Dissertation Abstracts International, 65*(8-B), 4329, # 0419-4217.

Busby, D., Carroll, J., & Willoughby, B. (2010). Compatibility or restraint? The effects of sexual timing on marriage relationships. *Journal of Family Psychology, 24*(6), 766–774.

Buss, D. (1989). Sex differences in human mate preferences: Evolutionary hypotheses tested in 37 cultures. *Behavioral and Brain Sciences, 12,* 1–49.

Buss, D. M. (1994). *The evolution of desire: Strategies of human mating.* New York: Basic Books.

Buss, D. M. (2003). The dangerous passion: Why jealousy is as necessary as love and sex. *Archives of Sexual Behavior, 32*(1), 79–80.

Buss, D. M., Shackelford, T. K., Kirkpatrick, L., & Larsen, R. J. (2001). A half-century of mate preferences: The cultural evolution of values. *Journal of Marriage & the Family, 63*(2), 491–503.

Busse, P., Fishbein, M., Bleakley, A., & Hennessy, M. (2010). The role of communication with friends in sexual initiation. *Communication Research, 37*(2), 239–255.

Byers, E., Henderson, J., & Hobson, K. (2009). University students' definitions of sexual abstinence and having sex. *Archives of Sexual Behavior, 38*(5), 665–674.

Byrne, D., & Murnen, S. K. (1988). Maintaining loving relationships. In R. Sternberg & M. L. Barnes (Eds.), *Psychology of love* (pp. 293–310). New Haven, CT: Yale University Press.

Cado, S., & Leitenberg, H. (1990). Guilt reactions to sexual fantasies during intercourse. *Archives of Sexual Behavior 19*(1), 49–63.

Caffaro, J., & Conn-Caffaro, A. (2005). Treating sibling abuse families. *Aggression and Violent Behavior, 10*(5), 604–623.

Cahill, S., South, K., & Spade, J. (2000). *Outing age: Public policy issues affecting gay, lesbian, bisexual, and transgender elders.* Washington, DC: National Gay and Lesbian Task Force.

Cai, D., Wilson, S. R., & Drake, L. (2000). Culture in the context of intercultural negotiation: Individualism–collectivism and paths to integrative agreements. *Human Communication Research, 26*(4), 591–617.

Cakin-Memik, N., Yildiz, O., Sişmanlar, S. G., Karakaya, I., & Ağaoğlu, B. (2010). Priapism associated with methylphenidate: A case report. *Turkish Journal of Pediatrics, 52*(4), 430–434.

Calderone, M. (1983). On the possible prevention of sexual problems in adolescence. *Hospital and Community Psychiatry, 34,* 528–530.

Calzavara, L. M., Burchell, A. N., Lebovic, G., Myers, T., Remis, R. S., Raboud, J., … Hart, T. A. (2011). The impact of stressful life events on unprotected anal intercourse among gay and bisexual men. *AIDS Behavior.* Retrieved February 20, 2011 from http://www.ncbi.nlm.nih.gov/pubmed/21274612

Cameron, S., Glasier, A., Dewart, H., & Johnstone, A. (2010). Women's experiences of the final stage of early medical abortion at home: Results of a pilot survey. *Journal of Family Planning and Reproductive Health Care, 36*(4), 213–216.

Campbell, J., Jones, A. S., Dienemann, J., Kub, J., Schollenberger, J., O'Campo, P., Gielen, A.,

Wynne, C. (2002). Intimate partner violence and physical health consequences. *Archives of Internal Medicine, 162*(10), 1157–1163.

Campbell, P. P. (2008). Sexual violence in the lives of lesbian rape survivors. St. Louis, MO: Saint Louis University, AAT #3324148.

Camperio-Ciani, A., Corna, F., & Capiluppi, C. (2004). Evidence for maternally inherited factors favouring male homosexuality and promoting female fecundity. *Proceedings: Biological Sciences, 271*(1554), 2217–2221.

Carcopino, X., Shojai, R., & Boubli, L. (2004). Female genital mutilation: Generalities, complications, and management during obstetrical period. *Journal of Gynecology, Obstetrics, & Biological Reproduction, 33*(5), 378–383.

Carey, B. (2005). Straight, gay or lying? Bisexuality revisited. Retrieved July 5, 2005, from http://www.thetaskforce.org/downloads /07052005NYTBisexuality.pdf

Carlton, C. L., Nelson, E. S., & Coleman, P. K. (2000). College students' attitudes toward abortion and commitment to the issue. *Social Science Journal, 37*(4), 619–625.

Carnes, P. (2001). *Out of the shadows: Understanding sexual addiction.* Center City, MN: Hazelden Information Education.

Carrell, D. T., Wilcox, A. L., Lowry, L., Peterson, C. M., Jones, K. P., Erickson, L., … Hatasaka, H. H. (2003). Elevated sperm chromosome aneuploidy and apoptosis in patients with unexplained recurrent pregnancy loss. *Obstetrics and Gynecology, 101*(6), 1229–1235.

Carroll, J. (2009). *The day Aunt Flo comes to visit.* Avon, CT: Best Day Media.

Caruso, S., Iraci Sareri, M., Agnello, C., Romano, M., Lo Presti, L., Malandrino, C., & Cianci, A. (2011). Conventional vs. extended-cycle oral contraceptives on the quality of sexual life: Comparison between two regimens containing 3 mg drospirenone and 20 µg ethinyl estradiol. *Journal of Sexual Medicine, 8*(5), 1478–1485.

Casey, B., Getz, S., & Galvan, A. (2008). The adolescent brain. *Developmental Review, 28,* 62–77.

Caspi, A., Williams, B., Kim-Cohen, J., Craig, I., Milne, B., Poulton, R., … Moffitt, T. E. (2007). Moderation of breastfeeding effects on the IQ by genetic variation in fatty acid metabolism. *Proceedings of the National Academy of Sciences of the United States of America, 104,* 18860–18865.

Cass, V. C. (1979). Homosexual identity formation: A theoretical model. *Journal of Homosexuality, 4,* 219–235.

Cass, V. C. (1984). Homosexual identity formation: Testing a theoretical model. *The Journal of Sex Research, 20,* 143–167.

Casteels, K., Wouters, C., VanGeet, C., & Devlieger, H. (2004). Video reveals self-stimulation in infancy. *Acta Paediatrics, 93*(6), 844–846.

Catania, J. A., Coates, T. J., Kegeles, S. M., Ekstrand, M., Guydish, J. R., & Bye, L. L. (1989). Implications of the AIDS risk-reduction model for the gay community: The importance of perceived sexual enjoyment and help-seeking behaviors. In V. M. Mays, G. W. Albee, & S. F. Schneider (Eds.), *Primary prevention of AIDS: Psychological approaches* (pp. 242–261). Newbury Park, CA: Sage.

Cates, W., Harwood, B. (2011). Vaginal barriers and spermicides. In R. A. Hatcher, J. Trussell, A. L. Nelson, W. Cates, D. Kaval, M. S. Policar (Eds) *Contraceptive Technology,* 20th Edition. pp. 391-408. Ardent Media, New York, N.Y.

Cathcart, R. (2008, February 23). Boy's killing, labeled a hate crime, stuns a town. *New York Times.* Retrieved February 23, 2008, from http://www.nytimes.com/2008/02/23/us/23oxnard.html?ref=us

Cavanaugh, C., Messing, J., Petras, H., Fowler, B., LaFlair, L., Kub, J., … Campbell, J. (2011). Patterns of violence against women: A latent class analysis. *Psychological Trauma: Theory, Research, Practice, and Policy,* 3(1), 0–8.

CBS. (2010, August). CBS News Poll. Should gays be allowed to married? Retrieved January 31, 2011, from http://www.cbsnews.com/stories/2007/10/12/politics/main3362530.shtml?tag= featuredPostArea

Centers for Disease Control and Prevention. (2003). Can I get HIV from oral sex? Retrieved November 22, 2005, from http://www.cdc.gov/hiv/pubs/faq/faq19.htm

Centers for Disease Control and Prevention, Division of STD Prevention. (2007). Sexually transmitted disease surveillance, 2006. Retrieved from http://www.cdc.gov/STD/stats/toc2006. htm

Centers for Disease Control and Prevention. (2007a). 2005 assisted reproductive technology success rates: National summary and fertility clinic reports. Atlanta, GA: Author.

Centers for Disease Control and Prevention. (2007b). Chlamydia—CDC fact sheet. Retrieved September 18, 2008, from http://www.cdc.gov/std/Chlamydia/STDFact-Chlamydia.htm

Centers for Disease Control and Prevention. (2007c). Trends in reportable sexually transmitted diseases in the U.S., 2006. Retrieved September 18, 2008, from http://www.cdc.gov/STD/STATS/pdf/trends2006.pdf

Centers for Disease Control and Prevention. (2007d). Trichomoniasis—CDC fact sheet. Retrieved from http://www.cdc.gov/std/trichomonas/STDFact-Trichomoniasis.htm

Centers for Disease Control and Prevention. (2008a). Genital HPV infection—CDC fact sheet. Retrieved September 18, 2008, from http://www.cdc.gov/std/HPV/STDFact-HPV.htm

Centers for Disease Control and Prevention. (2008b). Hepatitis A. National Center for HIV/AIDS, Viral Hepatitis, STD, and TB Prevention, Division of Viral Hepatitis. Retrieved September 16, 2008, from http://www.cdc.gov/hepatitis/HAV/HAVfaq. htm#general

Centers for Disease Control and Prevention. (2008c). Hepatitis B. National Center for HIV/AIDS, Viral Hepatitis, STD, and TB Prevention, Division of Viral Hepatitis. Retrieved September 16, 2008, from http://www.cdc.gov/hepatitis/HBV/HBVfaq. htm#overview

Centers for Disease Control and Prevention. (2008d). Hepatitis C. National Center for HIV/AIDS, Viral Hepatitis, STD, and TB Prevention, Division of Viral Hepatitis. Retrieved September 16, 2008, from http://www.cdc.gov/hepatitis/HCV.htm

Centers for Disease Control and Prevention. (2008e). HIV and AIDS in the U.S.: A picture of today's epidemic. Retrieved on September 18, 2008, from http://www.cdc. gov/hiv/topics/surveillance/united_states. htm

Centers for Disease Control and Prevention. (2008f). HIV/AIDS among women. CDC HIV/AIDS fact sheet. Retrieved September 16, 2008, from http://www.cdc.gov/hiv/topics/women/resources/factsheets/pdf/women.pdf

Centers for Disease Control and Prevention. (2008g). HPV vaccine—Questions and answers. Retrieved September 18, 2008, from http://www.cdc.gov/vaccines/vpd-vac/hpv/vac-faqs.htm

Centers for Disease Control and Prevention. (2008h, February). Male circumcision and risk for HIV transmission and other health conditions: Implications for the United States. Department of Health and Human Services. Retrieved December 18, 2008, from http://www.cdc.gov/hiv/resources/factsheets/circumcision.htm

Centers for Disease Control and Prevention. (2008i). MMWR analysis provides new details on HIV incidence in U.S. populations. CDC HIV/AIDS Facts. Retrieved September 16, 2008, from http://www.cdc.gov/hiv/topics/

surveillance/resources/factsheets/pdf/
mmwr-incidence.pdf

Centers for Disease Control and Prevention. (2008j). Pelvic inflammatory disease—CDC fact sheet. Retrieved September 18, 2008, from http://www.cdc.gov/std/PID/STDFact-PID.htm

Centers for Disease Control and Prevention. (2008k). Syncope after vaccination—United States, January 2005–July 2007. *Morbidity and Mortality Weekly Report, 57*, 457–460.

Centers for Disease Control and Prevention. (2008l). Viral hepatitis. National Center for HIV/AIDS, Viral Hepatitis, STD, and TB Prevention, Division of Viral Hepatitis. Retrieved September 16, 2008, from http://www.cdc .gov/hepatitis/index.htm

Centers for Disease Control and Prevention. (2008m). Update on overall prevalence of major birth defects—Atlanta, Georgia, 1978–2005. *MMWR Morbidity and Mortality Weekly, 57*(1), 1–5.

Centers for Disease Control and Prevention. (2009a). Genital HPV infection—Fact sheet. Centers for Disease Control and Prevention. Retrieved April 1, 2011, from http://www.cdc .gov/std/HPV/STDFact-HPV.htm#common

Centers for Disease Control and Prevention. (2009b). HIV surveillance report, 2009 (Vol. 21). Retrieved March 26, 2011, from http:// www.cdc.gov/hiv/topics/surveillance/ resources/reports/

Centers for Disease Control and Prevention. (2009c). Oral sex and HIV risk. CDC HIV/AIDS facts. Retrieved April 1, 2011, from http://www.cdc.gov/hiv/resources/factsheets/PDF/oralsex.pdf

Centers for Disease Control and Prevention. (2009d). Sexually transmitted diseases in the United States, 2008: National surveillance data for chlamydia, gonorrhea, and syphilis. Atlanta, GA: U.S. Department of Health and Human Services. Retrieved April 1, 2011, from http://www.cdc.gov/std/stats08/trends.htm

Centers for Disease Control and Prevention. (2009e). Sexually transmitted disease surveillance, 2008. Atlanta, GA: U.S. Department of Health and Human Services.

Centers for Disease Control and Prevention. (2010a). 2008 Assisted reproductive technology success rates: National summary and fertility clinic reports. Atlanta, GA: U.S. Department of Health and Human Services. Retrieved March 1, 2011, from http://www.cdc .gov/art/ART2008/PDF/ART_2008_Full.pdf

Centers for Disease Control and Prevention. (2010b). Breastfeeding report card—United States, 2010. Department of Health and Human Services. Retrieved February 24, 2010, from http://www.cdc.gov/breastfeeding/pdf/BreastfeedingReportCard2010.pdf

Centers for Disease Control and Prevention. (2010c). Hepatitis A information for health professionals. Retrieved April 1, 2011, from http://www.cdc.gov/hepatitis/Statistics/2008Surveillance/Commentary.htm

Centers for Disease Control and Prevention. (2010d). HIV in the United States. National Center for HIV/AIDS, hepatitis, STD, and TB prevention. Retrieved March 30, 2011, from http://www.cdc.gov/hiv/topics/surveillance/resources/factsheets/pdf/us_overview.pdf

Centers for Disease Control and Prevention. (2010e). Sexually transmitted disease surveillance 2009. Atlanta, GA: U.S. Department of Health and Human Services.

Centers for Disease Control and Prevention. (2010f). Sexually transmitted diseases treatment guidelines, 2010. *Morbidity and Mortality Weekly Report: Recommendations and Reports, 59*(RR12), 1–110.

Centers for Disease Control and Prevention. (2010g). Viral hepatitis surveillance, United States, 2009. National Center for HIV/AIDS, Viral Hepatitis, STD and TB Prevention. Retrieved online November 30, 2011 from http://www.cdc.gov/hepatitis/Statistics/2009Surveillance/PDFs/2009HepSurveillanceBpt.pdf

Centers for Disease Control and Prevention. (2010h). Youth Risk Behavior Surveillance—United States, 2009. *Morbidity and Mortality Weekly Report Surveillance Summaries, 59*(5), 1–142.

Centers for Disease Control and Prevention. (2011a). Pelvic inflammatory disease—CDC fact sheet. Retrieved April 1, 2011, from http://www.cdc.gov/std/pid/stdfact-pid.htm

Centers for Disease Control and Prevention (2011b). Sexually transmitted disease prevalence, 2010. National Center for HIV/AIDS, Viral Hepatitis, STD, and TB Prevention, Division of STD Prevention. Retrieved online November 30, 2011 from http://www.cdc.gov/std/stats10/surv2010.pdf

Centers for Disease Control and Prevention. (2011c). Understanding intimate partner violence fact sheet. CDC Violence Prevention. Retrieved April 29, 2011, from http://www .cdc.gov/violenceprevention/pdf/IPV_factsheet-a.pdf

Chakraborty, A., McManus, S., Brugha, T. S., Bebbington, P., & King, M. (2011). Mental health of the non-heterosexual population of England. *British Journal of Psychiatry, 198*, 143–148.

Chang, S., Chen, K., Lin, H., Chao, Y., & Lai, Y. (2011). Comparison of the effects of episiotomy and no episiotomy on pain, urinary incontinence, and sexual function 3 months postpartum: A prospective follow-up study. *International Journal of Nursing Studies, 48*(4), 409–418.

Chavarro, J., Sadio, S. M., Toth, T. L., & Hauser, R. (2007a, October). Soy food and soy isoflavone intake in relation to semen quality parameters. Presentation at the Annual Meeting of the American Society for Reproductive Medicine. Washington, D.C.

Chavarro, J. E., Willett, W. C., & Skerrett, P. J. (2007b). *The fertility diet.* New York: McGraw Hill.

Chen, J., & Danish, S. (2010). Acculturation, distress disclosure, and emotional self-disclosure within Asian populations. *Asian American Journal of Psychology, 1*(3), 200–211.

Chen, S. (2010, May 3). Serious legal hurdles for gay divorce. CNN. Retrieved January 31, 2011, from http://articles.cnn.com/2010-05-03/living/texas.gay.divorce_1_gay-marriage-gay-divorce-same-sex-divorce?_s=PM:LIVING

Cheng, W., & Warren, M. (2001). She knows more about Hong Kong than you do isn't it: Tags in Hong Kong conversational English. *Journal of Pragmatics, 33*, 1419–1439.

Cherlin, A. (2009). The origins of the ambivalent acceptance of divorce. *Journal of Marriage and Family, 71*(2), 226–229.

Chin-Hong, P., Berry, J., Cheng, S., Catania, J., DaCosta, M., Darragh, T., … Palefsky, J. M. (2008). Comparison of patient- and clinician-collected anal cytology samples to screen for human papillomavirus-associated anal intraepithelial neoplasia in men who have sex with men. *Annals of Internal Medicine, 149*, 300–306.

Choi, N. (2004). Sex role group differences in specific, academic, and general self-efficacy. *Journal of Psychology: Interdisciplinary & Applied, 138*(2), 149–159.

Chopin-Marcé, M. J. (2001). Exhibitionism and psychotherapy: A case study. *International Journal of Offender Therapy & Comparative Criminology, 45*(5), 626–633.

Chow, E. W., & Choy, A. L. (2002). Clinical characteristics and treatment response to SSRI in a female pedophile. *Archives of Sexual Behavior, 31*(2), 211–215.

Christiansen, O. B. (1996). A fresh look at the causes and treatments of recurrent miscarriage, especially its immunological aspects. *Human Reproduction Update, 2*(4), 271–293.

Christofides, E., Muise, A., & Desmarais, S. (2009). Information disclosure and control on

Facebook: Are they two sides of the same coin or two different processes? *CyberPsychology & Behavior, 12*(3), 341–345.

Clark, M. S., & Reis, H. T. (1988). Interpersonal processes in close relationships. *Annual Review of Psychology, 39,* 609–672.

Clarke, A. K., & Miller, S. J. (2001). The debate regarding continuous use of oral contraceptives. *Annals of Pharmacotherapy, 35,* 1480–1484.

Clayton, A. H. (2008). Symptoms related to the menstrual cycle: Diagnosis, prevalence, and treatment. *Journal of Psychiatric Practices, 14,* 13–21.

Cochran, B. M., Ginzler, J., & Cauce, A. (2002). Challenges faced by homeless sexual minorities: Comparison of gay, lesbian, bisexual, and transgendered homeless sexual minorities with their heterosexual counterparts. *Journal of Public Health, 92,* 773–777.

Cochran, S. D., Mays, V. M., Alegria, M., Ortega, A. N., & Takeuchi, D. (2007). Mental health and substance use disorders among Latino and Asian American lesbian, gay, and bisexual adults. *Journal of Consulting and Clinical Psychology, 75*(5), 785–794.

Cohen, F., Kemeny, M., Kearney, K., Zegans, L., Neuhaus, J., & Conant, M. (1999). Persistent stress as a predictor of genital herpes recurrence. *Archives of Internal Medicine, 159,* 2430–2436.

Cohen, J., Byers, E., & Walsh, L. (2008). Factors influencing the sexual relationships of lesbians and gay men. *International Journal of Sexual Health, 20*(3), 162–176.

Cohen, K. M., & Savin-Williams, R. C. (1996). Developmental perspectives on coming out to self and others. In R. C. Savin-Williams & K. M. Cohen (Eds.), *The lives of lesbians, gays, and bisexuals: Children to adults* (pp. 113–151). Fort Worth, TX: Harcourt Brace.

Cohen, L. (1988). Providing treatment and support for partners of sexual-assault survivors. *Psychotherapy, 25,* 94–98.

Cohen, L., & Roth, S. (1987). The psychological aftermath of rape: Long-term effects and individual differences in recovery. *Journal of Social and Clinical Psychology, 5,* 525–534.

Cohen, M. S., Hellmann, N., Levy, J. A., Decock, K., & Lange, J. (2008). The spread, treatment, and prevention of HIV-1: Evolution of a global pandemic. *Journal of Clinical Investigation, 118,* 1244–1254.

Cohen, S. A. (2008, Summer). Abortion and women of color: The bigger picture. *Guttmacher Policy Review, 11*(3). Retrieved March 14, 2011, from http://www.guttmacher.org/pubs/gpr/11/3/gpr110302.html

Coker, A. L. (2007). Does physical intimate partner violence affect sexual health? A systematic review. *Trauma Violence Abuse, 8,* 149–177.

Cokkinos, D. D., Antypa, E., Tserotas, P., Kratimenou, E., Kyratzi, E., Deligiannis, I., ... Piperopoulos, P. N. (2011). Emergency ultrasound of the scrotum: A review of the commonest pathologic conditions. *Current Problems in Diagnostic Radiology, 40*(1), 1–14.

Coleman, E. (1982). Developmental stages of the coming-out process. *American Behavioral Scientist, 25,* 469–482.

Coleman, M., & Ganong, L. H. (1985). Love and sex role stereotypes: Do macho men and feminine women make better lovers? *Journal of Personality & Social Psychology, 49*(1), 170–176.

Coleman, M., Ganong, L., & Fine, M. (2000). Reinvestigating remarriage: Another decade of progress. *Journal of Marriage and Family, 62*(4), 1288–1308.

Coleman, P. (2002). *How to say it for couples.* New York: Prentice Hall Press.

Coleman, P. K. (2006). Resolution of unwanted pregnancy during adolescence through abortion versus childbirth: Individual and family predictors and psychological consequences. *Journal of Youth and Adolescence, 35,* 903–911.

Coles, M., Makino, K., Stanwood, N., Dozier, A., & Klein, J. (2010). How are restrictive abortion statutes associated with unintended teen birth? *Journal of Adolescent Health, 47*(2), 160–167.

Coles, R., & Stokes, G. (1985). *Sex and the American teenager.* New York, NY: Harper & Row.

Colley, A., Todd, Z., White, A., & Turner-Moore, T. (2010). Communication using camera phones among young men and women: Who sends what to whom? *Sex Roles, 63*(5/6), 348–360.

Collier, J. F., & Rosaldo, M. Z. (1981). Politics and gender in simple societies. In S. Ortner & H. Whitehead (Eds.), *Sexual meanings* (pp. 275–329). Cambridge, England: Cambridge University Press.

Collins, P. H. (1998). The tie that binds: Race, gender, and U.S. violence. *Ethnic and Racial Studies, 21*(5), 917–939.

Collins, R. (2005). Sex on television and its impact on American youth: Background and results from the RAND television and adolescent sexuality study. *Child & Adolescent Psychiatric Clinics of North America, 14*(3), 371–385.

Conron, K. J., Mimiaga, M. J., & Landers, S. J. (2010). A population-based study of sexual orientation identity and gender differences in adult health. *American Journal of Public Health, 100*(10), 1953–1960.

Cooksey, C., Berggren E., & Lee, J. (2010). Chlamydia trachomatis infection in minority adolescent women: A public health challenge. *Obstetrics and Gynecology Survey, 65*(11), 729–735.

Coppola, M. A., Klotz, K. L., Kim, K. A., Cho, H. Y., Kang, J., Shetty, J., ... Herr, J. C. (2010). SpermCheck Fertility, an immunodiagnostic home test that detects normozoospermia and severe oligozoospermia. *Human Reproduction, 25*(4), 853–861.

Corey, L., & Handsfield, H. (2000). Genital herpes and public health. *Journal of the American Medical Association, 283,* 791–794.

Corneanu, L. M., Stănculescu, D., & Corneanu, C. (2011). HPV and cervical squamous intraepithelial lesion: Clinicopathological study. *Romanian Journal of Morphology and Embryology, 52*(1), 89–94.

Cornelius, T., Shorey, R., & Beebe, S. (2010). Self-reported communication variables and dating violence: Using Gottman's marital communication conceptualization. *Journal of Family Violence, 25*(4), 439.

Corty, E. W., & Guardiani, J. M. (2008). Canadian and American sex therapists' perceptions of normal and abnormal ejaculatory latencies: How long should intercourse last? *Journal of Sexual Medicine, 5,* 1251–1256.

Costabile, R., Mammen, T., & Hwang, K. (2008). An overview and expert opinion on the use of alprostadil in the treatment of sexual dysfunction. *Expert Opinions in Pharmacotherapy, 9,* 1421–1429.

Costello, C., Hillis, S. D., Marchbanks, P. A., Jamieson, D. J., & Peterson, H. B. (2002). The effect of interval tubal sterilization on sexual interest and pleasure. *Obstetrics and Gynecology, 100*(3), 511–518.

Coulson, N. J. (1979). Regulation of sexual behavior under traditional Islamic law. In Al-Sayyid-Marsot & A. Lutfi (Eds.), *Society and the sexes in medieval Islam* (pp. 63–68). Malibu, CA: Undena Publications.

Courtenay, W. H. (2000). Behavioral factors associated with disease, injury, and death among men: Evidence and implications for prevention. *The Journal of Men's Studies, 9*(1), 81–142.

Cox, N., Vanden Berghe, W., Dewaele, A., & Vincke, J. (2010). Acculturation strategies and mental health in gay, lesbian, and bisexual youth. *Journal of Youth and Adolescence, 39*(10), 1199–1210.

Crawford, J. T., Leynes, P. A., Mayhorn, C. B., & Bink, M .L. (2004). Champagne, beer, or coffee? A corpus of gender-related and neutral words. *Behavior Research Methods, Instruments & Computers, 36*(3), 444–459.

Cremer, M., Phan-Weston, S., & Jacobs, A. (2010). Recent innovations in oral contraception. *Seminars in Reproductive Medicine, 28*(2), 140–146.

Crepaz, N., Hart, T. A., & Marks, G. (2004). Highly active antiretroviral therapy and sexual risk behavior: A meta-analytic review. *Journal of the American Medical Association, 292*(2), 224–236.

Critelli, J. W., Myers, E. J., & Loos, V. E. (1986). The components of love: Romantic attraction and sex role orientation. *Journal of Personality, 54*(2), 354–370.

Crosby, R., & Danner, F. (2008). Adolescents' STD protective attitudes predict sexually transmitted disease acquisition in early adulthood. *Journal of School Health, 78*, 310–313.

Crosby, R., Milhausen, R., Yarber, W., Sanders, S., & Graham, C. (2008). Condom "turnoffs" among adults: An exploratory study. *International Journal of STDs and AIDS, 19*, 590–594.

Cross, P., & Matheson, K. (2006). Understanding sadomasochism: An empirical examination of four perspectives. *Journal of Homosexuality, 50*, 133–166.

Crowley, I. P., & Kesner, K. M. (1990). Ritual circumcision (umkhwetha) amongst the Xhosa of the Ciskei. *British Journal of Urology, 66*(3), 318–321.

Crum, N., Riffenburgh, R., Wegner, S., Agan, B., Tasker, S., Spooner, K., … Triservice AIDS Clinical sortium. (2006). Comparisons of causes of death and mortality rates among HIV-infected patients. Analysis of the pre-, early, and late HAART (highly active antiretroviral therapy) eras. *Journal of Acquired Immune Deficiency Syndromes, 41*, 194–200.

Cruz, J. M. (2003). "Why doesn't he just leave?": Gay male domestic violence and the reasons victims stay. *Journal of Men's Studies, 11*, 309.

Cuddy, A. J. C., Norton, M. I., & Fiske, S. T. (2005) This old stereotype: The pervasiveness and persistence of the elderly stereotype. *Journal of Social Issues, 61*(2), 267–285.

Cunningham, G. R., & Toma, S. M. (2011). Why is androgen replacement in males controversial? *Journal of Clinical Endocrinological Metabolism, 96*(1), 38–52.

Currier, D., & Carlson, J. (2009). Creating attitudinal change through teaching: How a course on "women and violence" changes students' attitudes about violence against women. *Journal of Interpersonal Violence, 24*(10), 1735–1754.

Cusitar, L. (1994). *Strengthening the link: Stopping the violence*. Toronto, ON: Disabled Women's Network.

Dake, J. A., Price, J. H., Ward, B. L., & Welch, P. J. (2011). Midwestern rural adolescents' oral sex experience. *Journal of School Health, 81*(3), 159–165.

d'Amora, D., & Hobson, B. (2003). Sexual offender treatment. Retrieved from http://www.smith-lawfirm.com/ nsacs_offender_treatment.htm

Daniels, M. C., & Adair, L. S. (2005). Breastfeeding influences cognitive development in Filipino children. *Journal of Nutrition, 135*(11), 2589–2595.

Daniluk, J., & Browne, N. (2008). Traditional religious doctrine and women's sexuality reconciling the contradictions. *Women and Therapy, 31*(1), 129–142.

Darcangelo, S. (2008). Fetishism: Psychopathology and theory. In D. Laws & W. O'Donohue (Eds.), *Sexual deviance: Theory, assessment, and treatment* (2nd ed., pp. 108–118). New York: Guilford Press.

Dare, R. O., Oboro, V. O., Fadiora, S. O., Orji, E. O., Sule-Edu, A. O., & Olabode, T. O. (2004). Female genital mutilation: An analysis of 522 cases in South-Western Nigeria. *Journal of Obstetrics & Gynaecology, 24*(3), 281–283.

Das, A., Parish, W., & Laumann, E. (2009). Masturbation in urban China. *Archives of Sexual Behavior, 38*(1), 108–120.

Dattijo, L. M., Nyango, D. D., & Osagie, O. E. (2010). Awareness, perception, and practice of female genital mutilation among expectant mothers in Jos University Teaching Hospital Jos, north-central Nigeria. *Nigerian Journal of Medicine, 19*(3), 311–315.

D'Augelli, A. R. (2005). Stress and adaptation among families of lesbian, gay, and bisexual youth: Research challenges. *Journal of GLBT Family Studies, 1*, 115–135.

D'Augelli, A. R., Grossman, A., Salter, N., Vasey, J., Starks, M., & Sinclair, K. (2005). Predicting the suicide attempts of lesbian, gay, and bisexual youth. *Suicide and Life-Threatening Behavior, 35*, 646–660.

D'Augelli, A., Grossman, A., & Starks, M. (2005). Parents' awareness of lesbian, gay, and bisexual youths' sexual orientation. *Journal of Marriage & Family, 67*(2), 474–482.

D'Augelli, A. R., Grossman, A. H., & Starks, M. (2006). Childhood gender atypicality, victimization, and PTSD among lesbian, gay, and bisexual youth. *Journal of Interpersonal Violence, 21*, 1462–1482.

D'Augelli, A. R., Rendian, J., Sinclair, K., & Grossman, A. (2007). Lesbian and gay youth's

aspirations for marriage and raising children. *Journal of LGBT Issues in Counseling, 1*(4), 77–98.

Davé, S., Petersen, I., Sherr, L., & Nazareth, I. (2010). Incidence of maternal and paternal depression in primary care. *Archives of Pediatriac Adolescent Medicine, 164*(11), 1038–1044.

Davidson, J., Moore, N., Earle, J., & Davis, R. (2008). Sexual attitudes and behavior at four universities: Do region, race, and/or religion matter? *Adolescence, 433*(170), 189–220.

Davies, M., Boulle, A., Fakir, T., Nuttall, J., & Eley B. (2008). Adherence to antiretroviral therapy in young children in Cape Town, South Africa, measured by medication return and caregiver self-report: a prospective cohort study. *BMC Pediatrics, 4*(8), 34.

Davies, M., Rogers, P., & Whitelegg, L. (2009). Effects of victim gender, victim sexual orientation, victim response, and respondent gender on judgments of blame in a hypothetical adolescent rape. *Legal and Criminological Psychology, 14*(2), 331–338.

Davis, M. G., Reape, K. Z., & Hait, H. (2010a). A look at the long-term safety of an extended-regimen OC. *Journal of Family Practitioner, 59*(5), E3.

Daw, J. (2002). Hormone therapy for men? *Monitor on Psychology, 33*(9), 53.

Day, R. D., & Padilla-Walker, L. M. (2009). Mother and father connectedness and involvement during early adolescence. *Journal of Family Psychology, 23*(6), 900–904.

De Bellis, M. D., Keshavan, M. S., Beers, S. R., Hall, J., Frustaci, K., Masalehdan, A., … Boring, A. M. (2001) Sex differences in brain maturation during childhood and adolescence. *Cerebral Cortex, 11*(6), 552–557.

de Freitas, S. (2004). In R. T. Francoeur & R. J. Noonan (Eds.), *The Continuum complete international encyclopedia of sexuality* (pp. 98–113). New York/London: Continuum International.

de Vries, B. (2009). Brain sexuality and aging: A late blooming relationship. *Sexuality Research & Social Policy, 6*(4), 1–4.

D'Emilio, J., & Freedman, E. (1988). *Intimate matters: A history of sexuality in America*. New York: Harper & Row.

Dean, G., Schwarz, E. B. (2011). Intrauterine contraceptives. In R. A. Hatcher, J. Trussell, A. L. Nelson, W. Cates, D. Kaval, M. S. Policar (Eds) *Contraceptive Technology*, 20th Edition. pp. 147-191. Ardent Media, New York, N. Y.

DeJonge, A., Teunissen, D., van Diem, M., Scheepers, P., & Lagro-Janssen, A. (2008). Woman's positions during the second stage of labour: Views of primary care midwives. *Journal of Advanced Nursing, 63,* 347–356.

DeLamater, J. (1987). A sociological approach. In J. H. Geer & W. T. O'Donohue (Eds.), *Theories of human sexuality* (pp. 237–253). New York: Plenum Press.

DeLange, J. (1995). Gender and communication in social work education: A cross-cultural perspective. *Journal of Social Work Education, 31*(1), 75–82.

Deliramich, A., & Gray, M. (2008). Changes in women's sexual behavior following sexual assault. *Behavior Modification, 32*(5), 611–621.

Denizet-Lewis, B. (2009, September 23). Coming out in middle school. *New York Times.* Retrieved February 20, 2011, from http://www.nytimes.com/2009/09/27/magazine/27out-t.html?pagewanted=4&_r=1

Devdas, N., & Rubin, L. (2007). Rape myth acceptance among first- and second-generation South Asian American women. *Sex Roles, 56,* 701–705.

Diamanduros, T., Jenkins, S. J., & Downs, E. (2007). Analysis of technology ownership and selective use among undergraduates. *College Student Journal, 41,* 970–976.

Diamond, L. M. (2000). Sexual identity, attractions, and behavior among young sexual minority women over a 2-year period. *Developmental Psychology, 36*(2), 241–250.

Diamond, L. M., & Fagundes, C. (2010). Psychobiological research on attachment. *Personal Relationships, 27*(2), 218.

Diamond, M. (1993). Homosexuality and bisexuality in different populations. *Archives of Sexual Behavior, 22,* 291–310.

Diamond, M., & Diamond, G. H. (1986). Adolescent sexuality: Biosocial aspects and intervention. In P. Allen-Meares & D. A. Shore (Eds.), *Adolescent sexualities: Overviews and principles of intervention* (pp. 3–13). New York: Haworth Press.

Dietz, A., & Nyberg, C. (2011). Genital, oral, and anal human papillomavirus infection in men who have sex with men. *Journal of the American Osteopathic Association, 111*(3 Suppl. 2), S19–S25.

Dillow, M., Dunleavy, K., & Weber, K. (2009). The impact of relational characteristics and reasons for topic avoidance on relational closeness. *Communication Quarterly, 57*(2), 205.

Dimah, K., & Dimah, A. (2004). Intimate relationships and sexual attitudes of older African American men and women. *The Gerontologist, 44,* 612–613.

Dindia, K. & Canary, D. J. (Eds.). (2006). *Sex differences and similarities in communication* (2nd. ed.). Mahwah, NJ: Erlbaum.

Dinger, J., Minh, T. D., Buttmann, N., & Bardenheuer, K. (2011). Effectiveness of oral contraceptive pills in a large U.S. cohort comparing progestogen and regimen. *Obstetrics and Gynecology, 117*(1), 33–40.

Dinh, M., Fahrbach, K., & Hope, T. (2011). The role of the foreskin in male circumcision: An evidence-based review. *American Journal of Reproductive Immunlogy, 65*(3), 279–283.

Dixon, R. (2005). Controversy in South Africa over device to snare rapists. Retrieved October 19, 2005, from http://www.smh.com.au/news/world/controversy-in-south-africa-over-device-to-snare-rapists/2005/09/01/1125302683893.html

Dodge, B., Reece, M., Herbenick, D., Schick, V., Sanders, S. A., & Fortenberry, J. D. (2010). Sexual health among U.S. black and Hispanic men and women: A nationally representative study. *Journal of Sexual Medicine, 7*(Suppl. 5): 330–345.

Donnan, H. (1988). *Marriage among Muslims: Preference and choice in Northern Pakistan.* New York: E. J. Brill.

Dooley, S. W. (2008). Recommendations for partner services programs for HIV infection, syphilis, gonorrhea, and chlamydial infection. *Morbidity and Mortality Weekly, 57*(RR09), 1–63.

Dorgan, M. (2001, June 13). New divorce laws in China give rise to spying. *Hartford Courant,* A13.

Dorr, C. (2001). Listening to men's stories: Overcoming obstacles to intimacy from childhood. *Families in Society, 82,* 509–515.

Doty, N. D., Willoughby, B. L., Lindahl, K. M., & Malik, N. M. (2010). Sexuality related social support among lesbian, gay, and bisexual youth. *Journal of Youth and Adolescence, 39*(10), 1134–1147.

Dougherty, C. (2010, September 29). New vow: I don't take thee. *Wall Street Journal.* Retrieved October 5, 2010, from http://online.wsj.com/article/SB10001424052748703882404575519871444705214.html

Douglas, J., & Olshaker, M. (1998). *Obsession.* Sydney, Australia: Pocket Books.

Doyle, D. (2005). Ritual male circumcision: A brief history. *Journal of the Royal College of Physicians, 35,* 279–285. Retrieved April 8, 2008, from http://www.rcpe.ac.uk/publications/articles/journal_35_3/doyle_circumcision.pdf

Draganowski, L. (2004). Unlocking the closet door: The coming out process of gay male

adolescents. *Dissertation Abstracts International, 64*(11-B), #0419-4217.

Drain, P. K., Halperin, D. T., Hughes, J. P., Klausner, J. D., & Bailey, R. C. (2006). Male circumcision, religion, and infectious diseases: An ecologic analysis of 118 developing countries. *BMC Infectious Diseases, 6,* 172.

Dreger, A., Feder, E., & Tamar-Mattis, A. (2010, June 29). Preventing homosexuality (and uppity women) in the womb? The Hastings Center. Retrieved November 13, 2010, from http://www.thehastingscenter.org/Bioethicsforum/Post.aspx?id=4754

Dresner, E., & Herring, S. (2010). Functions of the nonverbal in CMC: Emoticons and illocutionary force. *Communication Theory, 20*(3), 249.

Drew, P. E. (2004). Iran. In R. T. Francoeur & R. J. Noonan (Eds.), *The Continuum international encyclopedia of sexuality* (pp. 554–568). New York/London: Continuum International.

Duijts, L., Jaddoe, V., Hofman, A., & Moll, H. (2010). Prolonged and exclusive breastfeeding reduces the risk of infectious diseases in infancy. *Pediatrics, 126,* e18–e25.

Dunham, C., Myers, F., McDougall, A., & Barnden, N. (1992). *Mamatoto: A celebration of birth.* New York: Penguin Group.

Dunne, E. (2007). *Genital warts.* U.S. Centers for Disease Control, Division of STD Prevention. Retrieved September 17, 2008, from http://www.cdc.gov/vaccines/recs/acip/downloads/mtg-slides-oct07/23HPV.pdf

Durex.com. (2007). *Sexual wellbeing global study 2007–2008.* Retrieved January 20, 2008, from http://durex.com/cm/sexual_wellbeing_globeflash.asp

Durham, L., Veltman, L., Davis, P., Ferguson, L., Hacker, M., Hooker, D., … Van Hout, G. (2008). Standardizing criteria for scheduling elective labor inductions. *American Journal of Maternal Child Nursing, 33,* 159–165.

Dush, C., & Amato, P. R. (2005). Consequences of relationship status and quality for subjective well-being. *Journal of Social and Personal Relationships, 22,* 607.

Dzelme, K., & Jones, R. A. (2001). Male cross-dressers in therapy: A solution-focused perspective for marriage and family therapists. *American Journal of Family Therapy, 29,* 293–305.

Eaker, E. D., Sullivan, L. M., Kelly-Hayes, M., D'Agostino, R. B., Sr., & Benjamin, E. J. (2007). Marital status, marital strain, and the risk of coronary heart disease or total mortality: The Framingham Offspring Study. *Psychosomatic Medicine, 69,* 509–513.

Eardley, I. (2010). Oral therapy for erectile dysfunction. *Archives of Españoles Urology, 63*(8), 703–714.

Earnshaw, V., Pitipitan, E., & Chaudoir, S. (2011). Intended responses to rape as functions of attitudes, attributions of fault, and emotions. *Sex Roles, 64*(5–6), 382–393.

Eastvold, A., Suchy, Y., & Strassberg, D. (2011). Executive function profiles of pedophilic and nonpedophilic child molesters. *Journal of the International Neuropyshochological Society, 17*(2), 295–308.

Eaton, D. K., Kann, L., Kinchen, S., Ross, J., Hawkins, J., Harris, W., … Wechsler, H. (2006, June 9). Youth risk behavior surveillance—United States, 2005. Surveillance Summaries. *Morbidity and Mortality Weekly Report, 55*(no. SS-5). Hyattsville, MD: U.S. Department of Health and Human Services, Centers for Disease Control. Retrieved September 2, 2008, from http://www.cdc.gov/mmwr/PDF/SS/SS5505.pdf

Eaton, L., Kaufman, M., Fuhrel, A., Cain, D., Cherry, C., Pope, H., & Kalichman, S. (2008). Examining factors co-existing with interpersonal violence in lesbian relationships. *Journal of Family Violence, 23,* 697–706.

Eckholm, E. (2011, January 1). In isolated Utah city, new clubs for gay students. *New York Times.* Retrieved February 16, 2011, from http://www.nytimes.com/2011/01/02/us/02utah.html

Eckstein, D., & Goldman, A. (2001). The couples' gender-based communication questionnaire. *Family Journal of Counseling and Therapy for Couples and Families, 9*(1), 62–74.

Edwards, R. (1998). The effects of gender, gender role, and values. *Journal of Language and Social Psychology, 17*(1),52–72.

Edwards, R., & Hamilton, M. A. (2004). You need to understand my gender role: An empirical test of Tannen's model of gender and communication. *Sex Roles, 50*(7–8), 491–504.

Eisenberg, M. (2001). Differences in sexual risk behaviors between college students with same-sex and opposite-sex experience. *Archives of Sexual Behavior, 30*(6), 575–589.

Eke, A., Hilton, N., Harris, G., Rice, M., & Houghton, R. (2011). Intimate partner homicide: Risk assessment and prospects for prediction. *Journal of Family Violence, 26*(3), 211–216.

Ekman, P., & Friesen, W. (1969). The repertoire of nonverbal behavior: Categories, origins, usage, and coding. *Semiotica, 1,* 49–98.

Eley, A., & Pacey, A. A. (In press). The value of testing semen for Chlamydia trachomatis in men of infertile couples. *International Journal of Andrology,* Retrieved May 29, 2011, from http://onlinelibrary.wiley.com/doi/10.1111/j.1365-2605.2010.01099.x/abstract

Elford, J. (2006). Changing patterns of sexual behaviour in the era of highly active antiretroviral therapy. *Current Opinions in Infectious Disease, 19*(1), 26–32.

Elford, J., Bolding, G., Maguire, M., & Sherr, L. (2000). Combination therapies for HIV and sexual risk behavior among gay men. *Journal of Acquired Immune Deficiency Syndrome, 23,* 266–271.

El-Helaly, M., Awadalla, N., Mansour, M., & El-Biomy, Y. (2010). Workplace exposures and male infertility: A case-control study. *International Journal of Occupational Medicine and Environmental Medicine, 23*(4), 331–338.

Elias, M. (2007, February 11). Gay teens coming out earlier to peers and family. *USA Today.* Retrieved October 2, 2008, from http://www.usatoday.com/news/nation/2007-02-07-gay-teens-cover_x.htm

Eliason, M. J. (1997). The prevalence and nature of biphobia in heterosexual undergraduate students. *Archives of Sexual Behavior, 26,*(3), 317–326.

Eliot, L. (2009). *Pink brains, blue brains: How small differences grow into troublesome gaps—and what we can do about it.* Orlando, FL: Houghton Mifflin Harcourt.

Elliott, S., & Umberson, D. (2008). The performance of desire: Gender and sexual negotiation in long-term marriages. *Journal of Marriage and Family, 70,* 392–407.

Ellis, D. G., & McCallister, L. (1980). Relational control sequences in sex-typed and androgynous groups. *Western Journal of Speech Communication, 44,* 35–49.

Ellis, L., Burke, D., & Ames, M. (1987). Sexual orientation as a continuous variable: A comparison between the sexes. *Archives of Sexual Behavior, 16,* 523–529.

Elmslie, B., & Tebaldi, E. (2007). Sexual orientation and labor market discrimination. *Journal of Labor Research, 28*(3), 436–453.

Ely, G., Flaherty, C., & Cuddeback, G. (2010). The relationship between depression and other psychosocial problems in a sample of adolescent pregnancy termination patients. *Child and Adolescent Social Work Journal, 27*(4), 269–282.

Emmers-Sommer, T., Farrell, J., Gentry, A., Stevens, S., Eckstein, J., Battocletti, J., & Gardener, C. (2010). First date sexual expectations: The effects of who asked, who paid, date location, and gender. *Communication Studies, 61*(3), 339–355.

Epps, J., & Kendall, P. C. (1995). Hostile attributional bias in adults. *Cognitive Therapy and Research, 19,* 159–178.

Epstein, C. F. (1986). Symbolic segregation: Similarities and differences in the language and non-verbal communication of women and men. *Sociological Forum, 1,* 27–49.

Epstein, C. F. (1988). *Deceptive distinctions: Sex, gender, and the social order.* New Haven, CT: Yale University Press.

Ersoy, B., Balkan, C., Gunay, T., & Egemen, A. (2005). The factors affecting the relation between the menarcheal age of mother and daughter. *Child: Care, Health, & Development, 31*(3), 303–308.

Eshbaugh, E. M., & Gute, G. (2008). Hookups and sexual regret among college women. *Journal of Social Psychology, 148,* 77–89.

Espelage, D. L., Aragon, S. R., Birkett, M., & Koenig, B. W. (2008). Homophobic teasing, psychological outcomes, and sexual orientation among high school students: What influence do parents and schools have? *School Psychology Review, 37,* 202–216.

Estephan, A., & Sinert, R. (2010, February 1). *Dysfunctional uterine bleeding.* Retrieved December 26, 2010, from http://emedicine.medscape.com/article/795587-overview

Evans, A., Scally, A., Wellard, S., & Wilson, J. (2007). Prevalence of bacterial vaginosis in lesbians and heterosexual women in a community setting. *Sexually Transmitted Infections, 83,* 424–425.

Fabes, R., Martin, C., & Hanish, L. (2003). Young children's play qualities in same-, other-, and mixed-sex peer groups. *Child Development, 74*(3), 921–932.

Falagas, M., Betsi, G., Athanasiou, S. (2006). Probiotics for prevention of recurrent vulvovaginal candidiasis: A review. *Journal of Antimicrobial Chemotherapy, 58*(2), 266–272.

Faller, K. C. (1989). The role relationship between victim and perpetrator as a predictor of characteristics of intrafamilial sexual abuse. *Child and Adolescent Social Work Journal, 6,* 217–229.

Farah, M. (1984). *Marriage and sexuality in Islam.* Salt Lake City, UT: University of Utah Press.

Farley, M., & Barkan, H. (1998). Prostitution, violence, and post-traumatic stress disorder. *Women and Health, 27*(3), 37–49.

Farr, R., Forssell, S., & Patterson, C. (2010). Parenting and child development in adoptive families: Does parental sexual orientation matter? *Applied Developmental Science, 14*(3), 164–178.

Farr, S., & Kern, M. (2010, November 24). Temple football players eyed in rape of student. *McClatchy-Tribune Business News.* Retrieved from http://articles.philly.com/2010-11-24/news/24955668_1_temple-students-temple-officials-al-golden

Faulkner, A. H., & Cranston, K. (1998). Correlates of same-sex sexual behavior in a random sample of Massachusetts high school students. *American Journal of Public Health, 88*(2), 262–266.

Faulkner, S., & Lannutti, P. (2010). Examining the content and outcomes of young adults' satisfying and unsatisfying conversations about sex. *Qualitative Health Research, 20*(3), 375.

Feeney, J. A., & Noller, P. (1990). Attachment style as a predictor of adult romantic relationships. *Journal of Personality & Social Psychology, 58*(2), 281–291.

Feige, A. M., Pinsky, M. R., & Hellstrom, W. J. (2011). Dapoxetine for premature ejaculation. *Clinical Pharmacology and Therapeutics, 89*(1), 125–128.

Feinauer, L. (1988). Relationship of long term effects of childhood sexual abuse to identity of the offender: Family, friend, or stranger. *Women and Therapy, 7,* 89–107.

Feinauer, L. (1989). Comparison of long-term effects of child abuse by type of abuse and by relationship of the offender to the victim. *American Journal of Family Therapy, 17,* 46–48.

Feldman, M., & Meyer. I. (2007). Childhood abuse and eating disorders in gay and bisexual men. *International Journal of Eating Disorders, 40*(5), 418–423.

Fergusson, D. M., Horwood, L. J., & Boden, J. M. (2009). Reactions to abortion and subsequent mental health. *British Journal of Psychiatry, 195*(5), 420–426.

Ferreira-Poblete, A. (1997). The probability of conception on different days of the cycle with respect to ovulation: An overview. *Advances in Contraception, 13*(2–3), 83–95.

Fieldman, J. P., & Crespi, T. D. (2002). Child sexual abuse: Offenders, disclosure, and school-based initiatives. *Adolescence, 37*(145), 151–160.

Fincham, F., & Beach, S. (2010). Marriage in the new millennium: A decade of review. *Journal of Marriage and Family, 72*(3), 630–650.

Finer, L., Frohwirth, L., Dauphinee, L., Singh, S., & Moore, A. (2006). Timing of steps and reasons for delays in obtaining abortions in the United States. *Contraception, 74*(4), 334–344.

Finer, L. B., & Henshaw, S. K. (2006). Disparities in rates of unintended pregnancy in the United States, 1994 and 2001. *Perspectives on Sexual and Reproductive Health, 38,* 90–96.

Fink, H. A., MacDonald, R., Rutks, I. R., & Nelson, D. B. (2002). Sildenafil for male erectile dysfunction: A systematic review and meta-analysis. *Archives of Internal Medicine, 162*(12), 1349–1360.

Finkelhor, D. (1980). Sex among siblings: A survey on prevalence, variety, and effects. *Archives of Sexual Behavior, 9,* 171–194.

Finkelhor, D., & Browne, A. (1985). The traumatic impact of child sexual abuse. *American Journal of Ortho-Psychiatry, 55,* 530–541.

Finkelhor, D., Hotaling, G., Lewis, I. A., & Smith, C. (1990). Sexual abuse in a national survey of adult men and women: Prevalence, characteristics, and risk factors. *Child Abuse and Neglect, 14,* 19–28.

Fischer, G. J. (1987). Hispanic and majority student attitudes toward forcible date rape as a function of differences in attitudes toward women. *Sex Roles, 17*(1–2), 93–101.

Fisher, H., Brown, L., Aron, A., Strong, G., & Mashek, D. (2010). Reward, addiction, and emotion regulation systems associated with rejection in love. *Journal of Neurophysiology, 104*(1), 51–60.

Fitzgerald, L. F., & Ormerod, A. J. (1991). Perceptions of sexual harassment: The influence of gender and academic context. *Psychology of Women Quarterly, 15,* 281–294.

Flanagan, C. (2011, April 23). Shutter fraternities for young women's good. *Wall Street Journal.* Retrieved April 24, 2011, from http://online.wsj.com/article/SB10001424052748704658704576275152354071470.html?mod=WSJ_WSJ_News_BlogsModule

Flanigan, C., Suellentrop, K., Albert, B., Smith, J., & Whitehead, M. (2005, September 15). Science says #17: Teens and oral sex. Retrieved September 17, 2005, from http://www.teenpregnancy.org/works/pdf/ScienceSays_17_OralSex.pdf

Fleischmann, A. A., Spitzberg, B. H., Andersen, P. A., Roesch, S. C., & Metts, S. (2005). Tickling the monster: Jealousy induction in relationships. *Journal of Social and Personal Relationships, 22*(1), 49–73.

Foldes, P., & Buisson, O. (2009). The clitoral complex: A dynamic sonographic study. *Journal of Sexual Medicine, 6*(5), 1223–1231.

Food and Drug Administration. (2008, January 18). *FDA approves update to label on birth control patch.* Retrieved October 28, 2008, from http://www.fda.gov/bbs/topics/NEWS/2008/NEW01781.html

Foote, W. E., & Goodman-Delahunty, J. (2005). Harassers, harassment contexts, same-sex harassment, workplace romance, and harassment theories. In W. E. Foote & J. Goodman-Delahunty (Eds.), *Evaluating sexual harassment: Psychological, social, and legal considerations in forensic examinations* (pp. 27–45). Washington, DC: American Psychological Association.

Forke, C., Myers, R., Catallozzi, M., & Schwarz, D. (2008). Relationship violence among female and male college undergraduate students. *Archives of Pediatric Adolescent Medicine, 162,* 634–641.

Forstein, M. (1988). Homophobia: An overview. *Psychiatric Annals, 18,* 33–36.

Fortenberry, J., Schick, V., Herbenick, D., Sanders, S., Dodge, B., & Reece, M. (2010). Sexual behaviors and condom use at least vaginal intercourse: A national sample of adolescents age 14 to 17 years. *Journal of Sexual Medicine, 7*(Suppl. 5), 305–314.

Forti, G., Corona, G., Vignozzi, L., Krausz, C., & Maggi, M. (2010). Klinefelter's syndrome: A clinical and therapeutical update. *Sex Development, 4*(4–5), 249–258.

Forti, G., & Krausz, C. (1998). Clinical review 100: Evaluation and treatment of the infertile couple. *Journal of Clinical Endocrinology Medicine, 83*(12), 4177–4188.

Foster, K., & Sandel, M. (2010). Abuse of women with disabilities: Toward an empowerment perspective. *Sexuality and Disability, 28*(3), 177–187.

Foubert, J., & Cremedy, B. (2007). Reactions of men of color to a commonly used rape prevention program. *Sex Roles, 57,* 137–144.

Fowers, B. J. (1998). Psychology and the good marriage. *American Behavioral Scientist, 41*(4), 516.

Fowler, M. G., Gable, A. R., Lampe, M. A., Etima, M., & Owor, M. (2010). Perinatal HIV and its prevention: Progress toward an HIV-free generation. *Clinical Perinatology, 37*(4), 699–719.

Fox, J. A., & Zawitz, M. W. (2004). Homicide trends in the United States. Retrieved October 23, 2005, from www.ojp.usdoj.gov/bjs/homicide/homtrnd.htm

Fox, M., & Thomson, M. (2010). HIV/AIDS and circumcision: Lost in translation. *Journal of Medical Ethics, 36*(12), 798–801.

Frackiewicz, E. J. (2000). Endometriosis: An overview of the disease and its treatment. *Journal of the American Pharmaceutical Association, 40*(5), 645–657.

Francis, A. (2008). Family and sexual orientation: The family-demographic correlates of homosexuality in men and women. *Journal of Sex Research, 45*(4), 371–377.

Franiuk, R., Seefelt, J., & Vandello, J. (2008). Prevalence of rape myths in headlines and their effects on attitudes toward rape. *Sex Roles, 58,* 790–802.

Frankel, L. (2002). "I've never thought about it": Contradictions and taboos surrounding American males' experiences of first ejaculation (semenarche). *Journal of Men's Studies, 11*(1), 37–54.

Frazier, P. A. (2000). The role of attributions and perceived control in recovery from rape. *Journal of Personal and Interpersonal Loss, 5*(2/3), 203–225.

Freedman, D. H. (2010, November). Lies, damned lies, and medical science. *The Atlantic.* Retrieved January 2, 2011, from http://www.theatlantic.com/magazine/archive/2010/11/lies-damned-lies-and-medical-science/8269/

Freeman, S. B. (2008). Continuous oral contraception. Strategies for managing breakthrough bleeding. *Advance for Nurse Practitioners 16*(8), 36–38.

Freud, S. (1953). Three essays on the theory of sexuality. In J. Strachey (Ed. & Trans.), *The standard edition of the complete psychological works of Sigmund Freud* (Vol. 7, pp. 130–243). London: Hogarth Press. (Original work published 1905).

Freymiller, L. (2005, May). Separate or equal?: Gay viewers respond to same-sex and gay/straight relationships on TV. Presented at the 2005 Annual Meeting of the International Communication Association. New York.

Frick, K. D., Clark, M. A., Steinwachs, D. M., Langenberg, P., Stovall, D., Munro, M. G., … STOP-DUB Research Group. (2009). Financial and quality-of-life burden of dysfunctional uterine bleeding among women agreeing to obtain surgical treatment. *Womens Health Issues, 19*(1), 70–78.

Friebe, A., & Arck, P. (2008). Causes for spontaneous abortion: What the bugs 'gut' to do with it? *International Journal of Biochemistry and Cell Biology, 40*(11), 2348–2352.

Friedman, S., Loue, S., Heaphy, E., & Mendez, N. (2011). Intimate partner violence victimization and perpetration by Puerto Rican women with severe mental illnesses. *Community Mental Health Journal, 47*(2), 156–163.

Friedman-Kien, A. E., & Farthing, C. (1990). Human immunodeficiency virus infection: A survey with special emphasis on mucocutaneous manifestations. *Seminars in Dermatology, 9,* 167–177.

Friedrich, W. N., Grambsch, P., Broughton, D., Kuiper, J., & Beilke, R. L. (1991). Normative sexual behavior in children. *Pediatrics, 88,* 456–464.

Frost, J. J., Darroch, J. E., & Remez, L. (2008). Improving contraception use in the United States. *In Brief, 1.* New York: Alan Guttmacher Institute.

Fryar, C. D., Hirsch, R., Porter, K. S., Kottiri, B., Brody, D., & Louis, T. (2007, June 28). Drug use and sexual behaviors reported by adults: United States, 1999–2002. Advance Data from Vital and Health Statistics, Centers for Disease Control, 384. Retrieved October 3, 2008, from http://www.cdc.gov/nchs/data/ad/ad384.pdf

Fu, Y. (2010). Interracial marriage formation: Entry into first union and transition from cohabitation to marriage. *Dissertation Abstracts International,* University of North Carolina at Chapel Hill, AAT #1483777.

Gaetz, S. (2004). Safe streets for whom? Homeless youth, social exclusion, and criminal victimization. *Canadian Journal of Criminology and Criminal Justice, 46,* 423–456.

Galis, F., Broek, C., Van Dongen, S., & Wijnaendts, L. (2010). Sexual dimorphism in the prenatal digit ratio (2D:4D). *Archives of Sexual Behavior, 39,* 57–62.

Galupo, M. P. (2006). Sexism, heterosexism, and biphobia: The framing of bisexual women's friendships. *Journal of Bisexuality, 6,* 35–45.

Gan, C., Zou, Y., Wu, S., Li, Y., & Liu, Q. (2008). The influence of medical abortion compared with surgical abortion on subsequent pregnancy outcome. *International Journal of Gynecology and Obstetrics, 101,* 231–238.

Garcia-Falgueras, A., & Swaab, D. F. (2010). Sexual hormones and the brain: An essential alliance for sexual identity and sexual orientation. *Endocrine Development, 17,* 22–35.

Garner, M., Turner, M. C., Ghadirian, P., Krewski, D., & Wade, M. (2008). Testicular cancer and hormonally active agents. *Journal of Toxicology and Environmental Health, 11,* 260–275.

Gates, G., Badgett, L., Macomber, J. E., & Chambers, K. (2007, March 27). Adoption and foster care by lesbian and gay parents in the United States. Urban Institute. Retrieved October 2, 2008, from http://www.urban.org/url.cfm?ID=411437

Gates, G. J. (2008). Same-sex couples: U.S. census and the American Community Survey. Retrieved from http://www2.law.ucla.edu/williamsinstitute/pdf/CensusPresentation_LGBT.pdf

Gehring, M., Vogel, D., Tennhardt, L., Weltin, D., & Bilitewski, B. (2006). Bisphenol A contamination of wastepaper, cellulose, and recycled paper products. Wessex Institute. Retrieved April 25, 2011, from http://library.witpress.com/pages/PaperInfo.asp?PaperID=14382

Gelbard, M. (1988). Dystrophic penile classification in Peyronie's disease. *Journal of Urology, 139,* 738–740.

Gemelli, R. J. (1996). *Normal child and adolescent development.* Arlington, VA: American Psychiatric Press.

Gentzler, A., Kerns, K., & Keener, E. (2010). Emotional reactions and regulatory responses to negative and positive events: Associations with attachment and gender. *Motivation and Emotion, 34*(1), 78.

Ghosh, M. K. (2005). Breech presentation: Evolution of management. *Journal of Reproductive Medicine, 50*(2), 108–116.

Ghosh, S., Neubert, J., Niehues, T., Adams, O., Morali-Karzei, N., Borkhardt, A., & Laws, H. J. (2011). Induction maintenance concept for HAART as initial treatment in HIV infected infants. *European Journal of Medical Research, 16*(6), 243–248.

Gibbs, J. L., Ellison, N. B., & Heino, R. D. (2006). Self-presentation in online personals: The role of anticipated future interaction, self-disclosure, and perceived success in Internet dating. *Communication Research, 33,* 152–177.

Gilmore, D. D. (1990). *Manhood in the making: Cultural concepts of masculinity.* New Haven, CT: Yale University Press.

Gilson, R. J., & Mindel, A. (2001). Sexually transmitted infections. *British Medical Journal, 322*(729S), 1135–1137.

Giltay, J. C., & Maiburg, M. C. (2010). Klinefelter syndrome: Clinical and molecular aspects. *Expert Review of Molecular Diagnostics, 10*(6), 765–776.

Giotakos, O., Markianos, M., & Vaidakis, N. (2005). Aggression, impulsivity, and plasma sex hormone levels in a group of rapists, in relation to their history of childhood attention-deficit/hyperactivity disorder symptoms. *Journal of Forensic Psychiatry & Psychology, 16*(2), 423–433.

Giuliano, A. R., Palefsky, J. M., Goldstone, S., Moreira, E. D., Jr., Penny, M. E., Aranda, C., … Guris, D. (2011). Efficacy of quadrivalent HPV vaccine against HPV infection and disease in males. *New England Journal of Medicine, 364*(5), 401–411.

Giuliano, A., Lu, B., Nielson, C., Flores, R., Papenfuss, M., Lee, J., … Harris, R. B. (2008). Age-specific prevalence, incidence, and duration of human papillomavirus infections in a cohort of 290 U.S. men. *Journal of Infectious Disease, 198,* 827–835.

Glasser, M., Kolvin, I., Campbell, D., Glasser, A., Leitch, I., & Farrelly, S. (2001). Cycle of child sexual abuse: Links between being a victim and becoming a perpetrator. *British Journal of Psychiatry, 179,* 482–494.

Glenn, N., & Marquardt, E. (2001). Hooking up, hanging out, and hoping for Mr. Right: College women on mating and dating today. Retrieved October 19, 2005, from http://www.americanvalues.org/Hooking_Up.pdf

Glenn, S., & Byers, E. (2009). The roles of situational factors, attributions, and guilt in the well-being of women who have experienced sexual coercion. *Canadian Journal of Human Sexuality, 18*(4), 201–220.

Gokyildiz, S., & Beji, N. K. (2005). The effects of pregnancy on sexual life. *Journal of Sex and Marital Therapy, 31*(3), 201–215.

Gold, M., Wolford, J., Smith, K., & Parker, A. (2004). The effects of advance provision of emergency contraception on adolescent women's sexual and contraceptive behaviors. *Journal of Pediatric and Adolescent Gynecology, 17,* 87–96.

Golden, G. H. (2001). Dyadic-dystonic compelling eroticism: Can these relationships be saved? *Journal of Sex Education & Therapy, 26*(1), 50.

Goldman, R. (1999). The psychological impact of circumcision. *British Journal of Urology International, 83,* 93–102.

Goleman, D. (1992, April 14). Therapies offer hope for sexual offenders. *The New York Times,* pp. C1, C11.

Golen, S. (1990). A factor analysis of barriers to effective listening. *Journal of Business Communication, 27,* 25–36.

Gómez, A. (2011). Testing the cycle of violence hypothesis: Child abuse and adolescent dating violence as predictors of intimate partner violence in young adulthood. *Youth and Society, 43*(1), 171–192.

Gonzales, A., Schofield, R., & Schmitt, G. (2005). Sexual assault on campus: What colleges and universities are doing about it. U.S. Department of Justice. Retrieved April 25, 2011, from http://www.publicintegrity.org/investigations/campus_assault/assets/pdf/Fisher_report_3.pdf

Goodman, M., Shvetsov, Y., McDuffie, K., Wilkens, L., Zhu, X., Ning, L., … Hernandez, B. Y. (2008). Acquisition of anal human papillomavirus infection in women: The Hawaii HPV cohort study. *Journal of Infectious Diseases, 197,* 957–966.

Gordon, B. N., & Schroeder, C. S. (1995). *Sexuality: A developmental approach to problems.* Chapel Hill, NC: Clinical Child Psychology Library.

Gordon, L. (2010, March 15). Mixed-gender dorm rooms are gaining acceptance. *Los Angeles Times.* Retrieved November 6, 2010, from http://articles.latimes.com/2010/mar/15/local/la-me-dorm-gender15-2010mar15

Gordon, S. (1986). What kids need to know. *Psychology Today, 20,* 22–26.

Gottman, J. M. (1994). *Why marriages succeed or fail.* New York: Simon & Schuster.

Gould, S. J. (1981). *The mismeasure of man.* New York: Norton.

Grce, M., & Davies, P. (2008). Human papillomavirus testing for primary cervical cancer screening. *Expert Review of Molecular Diagnostics, 8,* 599–605.

Greenfeld, D. A. (2005). Reproduction in same sex couples: Quality of parenting and child development. *Current Opinions in Obstetrics and Gynecology, 17,* 309–312.

Greenwald, E., & Leitenberg, H. (1989). Longterm effects of sexual experiences with siblings and nonsiblings during childhood. *Archives of Sexual Behavior, 18,* 289–400.

Greenwald, J. L., Burstein, G., Pincus, J., & Branson, G. (2006). A rapid review of rapid HIV antibody tests. *Current Infectious Disease Reports, 8,* 125–131.

Grenier, G., & Byers, E. (2001). Operationalizing premature or rapid ejaculation. *Journal of Sex Research, 38*(4), 369–378.

Griffin, S. A. (2006). A qualitative inquiry into how romantic love has been portrayed by contemporary media and researchers. *Dissertation Abstracts International Section A: Humanities and Social Sciences, 67,* 2272.

Griffith, R. S., Walsh, D. E., Myrmel, K. H., Thompson, R. W., & Behforooz, A. (1987). Success of L-lysine therapy in frequently recurrent herpes simplex infection. Treatment and prophylaxis. *Dermatologica, 175*(4), 183–190.

Griffiths, M. (2001). Sex on the Internet: Observations and implications for Internet sex addiction. *Journal of Sex Research, 38*(4), 333–343.

Griffitt, W., & Veitch, R. (1971). Hot and crowded: Influences of population density and temperature on interpersonal affective behavior. *Journal of Personality and Social Psychology, 17,* 92–98.

Grimbos T., Dawood K., Burriss R. P., Zucker K. J., & Puts D. A. (2010). Sexual orientation and the second to fourth finger length ratio: a meta-analysis in men and women. *Behavioral Neuroscience, 124*(2), 278–287.

Grob, C. S. (1985). Single case study: Female exhibitionism. *Journal of Nervous and Mental Disease, 173,* 253–256.

Groer, M. W. (2005). Differences between exclusive breastfeeders, formula-feeders, and controls: A study of stress, mood, and endocrine variables. *Biological Research for Nursing, 7*(2), 106–117.

Gross, J. (2007, October 9). Aging and gay, and facing prejudice in twilight. *New York Times.* Retrieved September 3, 2008, from http://www.nytimes.com/2007/10/09/us/09aged.html

Groth, A. N. (1978). Patterns of sexual assault against children and adolescents. In A. W. Burgess, A. N. Groth, L. L. Holmstrom, & S. M. Sgroi (Eds.), *Sexual assault of children and adolescents.* Toronto, ON: Lexington Books.

Groth, N., & Burgess, A. (1980). Male rape: Offenders and victims. *American Journal of Psychiatry, 137,* 806–810.

Grove, C., Gillespie, B., Royce, T., & Lever, J. (2011). Perceived consequences of casual online sexual activities on heterosexual relationships: A U.S. online survey. *Archives of Sexual Behavior, 40*(2), 429–439.

Gruber, A. J., & Pope, H. G. (2000). Psychiatric and medical effects of anabolic–androgenic steroid use in women. *Psychotherapy and Psychosomatics, 69*(1), 19–26.

Gruenbaum, E. (2006). Sexuality issues in the movement to abolish female genital cutting in Sudan. *Medical Anthropology Quarterly, 20,* 121.

Grunbaum, J. A., Kann, L., Kinchen, S. A., Williams, B., Ross, J. G., Lowry, R., & Kolbe, L. (2002). Youth risk behavior surveillance: United States, 2001. *Morbidity and Mortality Weekly Report, 51*(no. SS-4).

Gudjonsson, G. H. (1986). Sexual variations: Assessment and treatment in clinical practice. *Sexual and Marital Therapy, 1,* 191–214.

Guerrero, L., & Bachman, G. (2010). Forgiveness and forgiving communication in dating relationships: An expectancy–investment explanation. *Journal of Social and Personal Relationships, 27*(6), 801.

Guerrero, L. K., & Afifi, W. (1999). Toward a goal-oriented approach for understanding communicative responses to jealousy. *Western Journal of Communication, 63*(2), 216–248.

Guerrero, L. K., Spitzberg, B. H., & Yoshimura, S. M. (2004). Sexual and emotional jealousy. In J. H. Harvey, A. Wenzel, & S. Sprecher (Eds.), *The handbook of sexuality in close relationships* (pp. 311–345). Mahwah, NJ: Erlbaum.

Guffey, M. E. (1999). *Business communication: Process & product* (3rd ed.). Belmont, CA: Wadsworth.

Guha, C., Shah, S. J., Ghosh, S. S., Lee, S. W., Roy-Chowdhury, N., & Roy-Chowdhury, J. (2003). Molecular therapies for viral hepatitis. *BioDrugs, 17*(2), 81–91.

Gundersen, B. H., Melas, P. S., & Skar, J. E. (1981). Sexual behavior of preschool children: Teachers' observations. In L. L. Constantine & F. M. Martinson (Eds.), *Children and sex: New findings, new perspectives* (pp. 45–61). Boston: Little, Brown.

Gupta, J. K., & Nikodem, V. C. (2000). Woman's position during second stage of labour. *Cochrane Database of Systematic Reviews, 2,* CD002006.

Guzzo, K. (2009). Marital intentions and the stability of first cohabitations. *Journal of Family Issues, 30*(2), 179–205.

Hader, S. L., Smith, D. K., Moore, J. S., & Holmberg, S. D. (2001). HIV infection in women in the U.S.: Status at the millennium. *Journal of the American Medical Association, 285*(9), 1186–1192.

Haggerty, C. L., Gottlieb, S. L., Taylor, B. D., Low, N., Xu, F., & Ness, R. B. (2010). Risk of sequelae after chlamydia trachomatis genital infection in women. *Journal of Infectious Disease, 201*(Suppl. 2), S134–S155.

Hahlweg, K., Kaiser, A., Christensen, A., Fehm-Wolfsdorf, G., & Grother, T. (2000). Selfreport and observational assessment of couples' conflict. *Journal of Marriage and Family, 62*(1), 61.

Hahm, H., Lee, J., Zerden, L., & Ozonoff, A. (2008). Longitudinal effects of perceived maternal approval on sexual behaviors of Asian and Pacific Islander (API) young adults. *Journal of Youth and Adolescence, 37,* 74–85.

Hall, H., Hughes, D., Dean, H., Mermin, J., & Fenton, K. (2011). HIV infection—United States, 2005 and 2008. *Morbidity and Mortality Weekly Report, 60*(01), 87–89.

Hall, P., & Schaeff, C. (2008). Sexual orientation and fluctuating asymmetry in men and women. *Archives of Sexual Behavior, 37,* 158–165.

Hall, T., Hogben, M., Carlton, A., Liddon, N., & Koumans, E. (2008). Attitudes toward using condoms and condom use: Difference between sexually abused and nonabused African American female adolescents. *Behavioral Medicine, 34,* 45–54.

Halpern, C. J., Udry, J. R., Suchindran, C., & Campbell, B. (2000). Adolescent males' willingness to report masturbation. *Journal of Sex Research, 37*(4), 327–333.

Halpern-Felsher, B., Kropp, R., Boyer, C., Tschann, J., Ellen, J. (2004). Adolescents' self-efficacy to communicate about sex: Its role in condom attitudes, commitment, and use. *Adolescence, 39*(155), 443–457.

Hamberg, K. (2000). Gender in the brain: A critical scrutiny of the biological gender differences. *Lakartidningen, 97,* 5130–5132.

Hamburg, B. A. (1986). Subsets of adolescent mothers: Developmental, biomedical, and psychosocial issues. In J. B. Lancaster & B. A. Hamburg (Eds.), *School-age pregnancy and parenthood: Biosocial dimensions* (pp. 115–145). New York: Aldine DeGruyter.

Hamer, D. H., et al. (1993). A linkage between DNA markers on the X chromosome and male sexual orientation. *Science, 261,* 321–327.

Hamilton, L., & Armstrong, E. (2009). Gendered sexuality in young adulthood: Double binds and flawed options. *Gender and Society, 23*(5), 589–616.

Hamilton, T. (2002). *Skin flutes and velvet gloves.* New York: St. Martin's Press.

Handler, A., Davis, F., Ferre, C., & Yeko, T. (1989). The relationship of smoking and ectopic pregnancy. *American Journal of Public Health, 79,* 1239–1242.

Handwerk, B. (2005, February 25). 4-D ultrasound gives video view of fetuses in the womb. *National Geographic News.* Retrieved October 14, 2008, from http://news.nationalgeographic.com/news/pf/80752382.html

Hankins, G. (1995). *Operative obstetrics.* Stamford, CT: Appleton and Lange.

Hardt, J., Sidor, A., Nickel, R., Kappis, B., Petrak, P., & Egle, U. T. (2008). Childhood adversities and suicide attempts: A retrospective study. *Journal of Family Violence, 23,* 713–719.

Hardy, S., & Raffaelli, M. (2003). Adolescent religiosity and sexuality: An investigation of reciprocal influences. *Journal of Adolescence, 26*(6), 731–739.

Harlan, L. C., Potosky, A., Cilliland, F. D., Hoffman, R., Albertsen, P. C., Hamilton, A. S., … Stephenson, R. A. (2001). Factors associated with initial therapy for clinically localized prostate cancer: Prostate cancer outcomes study. *Journal of the National Cancer Institute, 93*(24), 1864–1871.

Harlow, H. F. (1959). Love in infant monkeys. *Scientific American, 200,* 68–70.

Hart, G. J., & Elford, J. (2010). Sexual risk behaviour of men who have sex with men: Emerging patterns and new challenges. *Current Opinions in Infectious Disease, 23*(1), 39–44.

Hartmann, K., Viswanathan, M., Palmieri, R., Gartlehner, G., Thorp, J., & Lohr, K. (2005). Outcomes of routine episiotomy: A systematic review. *Journal of the American Medical Association, 293*(17), 2141–2148.

Harville, E., Taylor, C., Tesfai, H., Xiong, X., & Buekens, P. (2011). Experience of hurricane Katrina and reported intimate partner violence. *Journal of Interpersonal Violence, 26*(4), 833–845.

Hatcher, R. A., Trussell, J., Stewart, F. H., Nelson, A. L., Cates, W., Guest, F., & Kowal, D. (2004). *Contraceptive technology* (18th rev. ed.). New York: Ardent Media.

Hatfield, E. (1988). Passionate and companionate love. In R. J. Sternberg & R. J. Barnes (Eds.), *Psychology of love* (pp. 191–217). New Haven, CT: Yale University Press.

Hathaway, J. E., Willis, G., Zimmer, B., & Silverman, J. G. (2005). Impact of partner abuse on women's reproductive lives. *Journal of the American Medical Women's Association, 60*(1), 42–45.

Hazelwood, R., & Burgess, A. (1987). *Practical aspects of rape investigation: A multidisciplinary approach.* New York: Elsevier.

Hegna, K., & Rossow, I. (2007). What's love got to do with it? Substance use and social integration for young people categorized by same-sex experience and attractions. *Journal of Drug Issues, 37,* 229–256.

Heidari, M., Nejadi, J., Ghate, A., Delfan, B., & Iran-Pour, E. (2010). Evaluation of intralesional inject of verapamil in treatment of Peyronie's disease. *Journal of the Pakistan Urological Association, 60*(4), 291–293.

Hellstrom, W. J. (2006). Current and future pharmacotherapies of premature ejaculation. *Journal of Sexual Medicine, 3*(Suppl. 4), 332–341.

Henderson, A., Lehavot, K., & Simoni, J. (2009). Ecological models of sexual satisfaction among lesbian/bisexual and heterosexual women. *Archives of Sexual Behavior, 38*(1), 50–66.

Hendrick, C., & Hendrick, S. S. (2000). *Close relationships: A sourcebook.* Thousand Oaks, CA: Sage.

Hensel, D. J., Fortenberry, J. D., Harezlak, J., Anderson, J. G., & Orr, D. P. (2004). A daily diary analysis of vaginal bleeding and coitus among adolescent women. *Journal of Adolescent Health, 34*(5), 392–394.

Hensley, C., Koscheski, M., & Tewksbury, R. (2005). Examining the characteristics of male sexual assault targets in a Southern maximum-security prison. *Journal of Interpersonal Violence, 20*(6), 667–679.

Hensley, L. G. (2002). Treatment of survivors of rape: Issues and interventions. *Journal of Mental Health Counseling, 24*(4), 331–348.

Herbenick, D., Reece, M., Schick, V., Sanders, S., Dodge, B., & Fortenberry, D. (2010a). Sexual behavior in the United States: Results from a national probability sample of men and women ages 14–94. *Journal of Sexual Medicine, 7*(Suppl. 5), 255–265.

Herbenick, D., Reece, M., Schick, V., Sanders, S., Dodge, B., & Fortenberry, J. D. (2010b). Sexual behaviors, relationships, and perceived health status among adults women in the U.S.: Results from a national probability sample. *Journal of Sexual Medicine, 7*(Suppl. 5), 277–290.

Herdt, G. (1989). Introduction: Gay and lesbian youth, emergent identities, and cultural scenes at home and abroad. In G. Herdt (Ed.), *Gay and lesbian youth* (pp. 1–42). New York: Harrington Park Press.

Herek, G. (2002). Heterosexuals' attitudes toward bisexual men and women in the United States. *Journal of Sex Research, 39*(4), 264–274.

Herek, G. M. (1984). Beyond "homophobia": A social psychological perspective on attitudes toward lesbians and gay men. In J. P. DeCecco (Ed.), *Homophobia: An overview* (pp. 1–21). New York: The Haworth Press.

Herman, J. L. (1981). *Father–daughter incest.* Cambridge, MA: Harvard University Press.

Heron, J., McGuinness, M., Blackmore, E., Craddock, N., & Jones, I. (2008). Early postpartum symptoms in puerperal psychosis. *British Journal of Obstetrics and Gynecology, 115*, 348–353.

Hicks, C. W., & Rome, E. S. (2010). Menstrual manipulation: Options for suppressing the cycle. *Cleveland Clinic Journal of Medicine, 77*(7), 445–453.

Hickson, F. C. I., Davies, P. M., & Hunt, A. J. (1994). Gay men as victims of nonconsensual sex. *Archives of Sexual Behavior, 23*(3), 281–294.

Hill, B. F., & Jones, J. S. (1993). Venous air embolism following orogenital sex during pregnancy. *American Journal of Emergency Medicine, 11*, 155–157.

Hill, C., & Silva, E. (2005). Drawing the line: Sexual harassment on campus. American Association of University Women Educational Foundation. Retrieved from http://www.aauw.org/learn/research/upload/DTLFinal.pdf

Hinshelwood, M. (2002). Early and forced marriage: The most widespread form of sexual exploitation of girls? Retrieved August 27, 2003, from http://www.kit.nl/ils/exchange_content/html/forced_marriage_-_sexual_healt.asp

Hirshkowitz, M., & Schmidt, M. H. (2005). Sleep-related erections: Clinical perspectives and neural mechanisms. *Sleep Medicine Reviews, 9*(4), 311–329.

Hitsch, G., Hortacsu, A., & Ariely, D. (2010). What makes you click? Mate preferences in online dating. *Quantitative Marketing and Economics, 8*(4), 393.

Hitti, M. (2008, January 18). *FDA strengthens warning on blood clot risk for users of Ortho Evra birth control skin patch.* WebMD. Retrieved October 28, 2008, from http://www.webmd.com/sex/birth-control/news/20080118/birth-control-patch-stronger-warning

"HIV/AIDS vaccine developed at the university of western Ontario proceeding to human clinical trials." Press Release, Fiere Biotech, Retrieved online December 25, 2011 from http://www.fiercebiotech.com/press-releases/hivaids-vaccine-developed-univerity-western-ontario-proceeding-human-clini

Hjelmstedt, A., Andersson, L., Skoog-Svanberg, A., Bergh, T., Boivin, J., & Collins, A. (1999). Gender differences in psychological reactions to infertility among couples seeking IVF and ICSI treatment. *Acta Obstetricia et Gynecologica Scandinavica, 78*(1), 42–48.

Ho, V. P., Lee, Y., Stein, S. L., & Temple, L. K. (2011). Sexual function after treatment for rectal cancer: A review. *Diseases of the Colon and Rectum, 54*(1), 113–125.

Hofman, B. (2005). "What is next?": Gay male students' significant experiences after coming out while in college. *Dissertation Abstracts International Section A: Humanities & Social Sciences, 65*(8-A), #0419–4209.

Hogan, H. (2005). Title IX requires colleges and universities to eliminate the hostile environment caused by campus sexual assault. Retrieved October 25, 2005, from http://www.securityoncampus.org/victims/titleixsummary.html

Hollander, D. (2001). Users give new synthetic and latex condoms similar ratings on most features. *Family Planning Perspectives, 33*(1), 45–48.

Holmberg, D., & Blair, K. (2009). Sexual desire, communication, satisfaction, and preferences of men and women in same-sex versus mixed-sex relationships. *Journal of Sex Research, 46*(1), 57–66.

Holmes, J. G., & Rempel, J. K. (1989). Trust in close relationships. In C. Hendrick (Ed.), *Close relationships* (Vol. 10, pp. 187–219). Newbury Park, CA: Sage.

Holmes, M. C. (2004). Reconsidering a "woman's issue:" Psychotherapy and one man's post-abortion experiences. *American Journal of Psychotherapy, 58*(1), 103–115.

Holmes, R. (1991). *Sex crimes.* Newbury Park, CA: Sage.

Hooker, E. (1957). The adjustment of the male overt homosexual. *Journal of Projective Techniques, 21*, 18–31.

Horowitz, S. M., Weis, D. L., & Laflin, M. T. (2001). Differences between sexual orientation behavior groups and social background, quality of life, and health behaviors. *Journal of Sex Research, 38*(3), 205–219.

Horrigan, J. B., Rainie, L., & Fox, S. (2001). Online communities: Networks that nurture long-distance relationships and local ties. Pew Internet and American Life Project. Retrieved April 26, 2008, from http://www.pewinternet.org/pdfs/pip_communities_report.pdf

Houston, E., & McKirnan, D. (2008). Intimate partner abuse among gay and bisexual men: Risk correlates and health outcomes. *Journal of Urban Health, 84*, 681–690.

Howard, L. M., Hoffb rand, S., Henshaw, C., Boath, L., & Bradley, E. (2005). Antidepressant prevention of postnatal depression. *The Cochrane Database of Systematic Reviews, 2*, art. no. CD004363.

Howe, N., Rinaldi, C., & Recchia, H. (2010). Patterns in mother–child internal state discourse across four contexts. *Merrill-Palmer Quarterly, 56*(1), 1–20.

Htay, T., Aung, K., Carrick, J., & Papica, R. (2009, September 29). *Premenstrual dysphoric disorder.* Retrieved January 4, 2011, from http://emedicine.medscape.com/article/293257-overview

Hu, K., He, X., Yu, F., Yuan, X., Hu, W., Liu, C., … Dou, J. (2011). Immunization with DNA vaccine expressing herpes simplex virus type 1 gD and IL-21 protects against mouse herpes keratitis. *Immunology Invest, 40*(3), 265–278.

Hu, S., Wei, N., Wang, Q., Yan, L., Wei, E., Zhang, M., … Xu, Y. (2008). Patterns of brain activation during visually evoked sexual arousal differ between homosexual and heterosexual men. *American Journal of Neuroradiology, 29*, 1890–1896.

Hu, X., Cheng, L., Hua, X., & Glasier, A. (2005). Advanced provision of emergency contraception to postnatal women in China makes no difference in abortion rates: A randomized controlled trial. *Contraception, 72*, 111–116.

Hubacher, D., Finerb, L., & Espeyc, E. (2010). Renewed interest in intrauterine contraception in the United States: Evidence and explanation. *Contraception, 83*(4), 291–294.

Hudson, D. J. (2010). Standing OUT/fitting IN: Identity, appearance, and authenticity in gay and lesbian communities. *Symbolic Interaction, 33*(2), 213–233.

Hughes, J. R. (2006). A general review of recent reports on homosexuality and lesbianism. *Sexuality and Disability, 24*, 195–205.

Hulbert, F. (1989). Barriers to effective listening. *Bulletin for the Association for Business Communication, 52*, 3–5.

Hull, S., Hennessy, M., Bleakley, A., Fishbein, M., & Jordan, A. (2010). Identifying the causal pathways from religiosity to delayed adolescent sexual behavior. *Journal of Sex Research, 19,* 1–11.

Human Rights Campaign. (2011). Employment non-discrimination act. Retrieved February 16, 2011, from http://www.hrc.org/laws_and_elections/enda.asp

Huppertz, B. (2011). Placental pathology in pregnancy complications. *Thombosis Research, 127*(Suppl. 3), S96–S99.

Hutson, J. M., Baker, M., Terada, M., Zhou, B., & Paxton, G. (1994). Hormonal control of testicular descent and the cause of cryptorchidism. *Reproduction, Fertility, and Development, 6*(2), 151–156.

Hutson J. M., & Hasthorpe S. J. (2005). Testicular descent and cryptorchidism: The state of the art in 2004. *Pediatric Surgery, 40*(2), 297–302.

Ignatius, E., & Kokkonen, M. (2007). Factors contributing to verbal self-disclosure. *Nordic Psychology, 59*(4), 362–391.

Irvine, J. (1990). *Disorders of desire, sex, and gender in modern American sexology.* Philadelphia: Temple University Press.

Irvine, J. (1995). Reinventing perversion: Sex addiction and cultural anxieties. *Journal of the History of Sexuality, 5*(3), 429–449.

Irving, C., Basu, A., Richmond, S., Burn, J., & Wren, C. (2008, July 2). Twenty-year trends in prevalence of survival of Down syndrome. *European Journal of Human Genetics.* Retrieved October 14, 2008, from http://www.nature.com/ejhg/journal/vaop/ncurrent/abs/ejhg2008122a.html

Jackman, L. P., Williamson, D. A., Netemeyer, R. G., & Anderson, D. A. (1995). Do weight-preoccupied women misinterpret ambiguous stimuli related to body size? *Cognitive Therapy and Research, 19,* 341–355.

Jacobs, S. E., Thomas, W., & Lang, S. (1997). *Two-spirit people: Native American gender identity, sexuality, and spirituality.* Chicago: University of Illinois Press.

Jamieson, D., Kaufman, S., Costello, C., Hillis, S., Marchbanks, P., & Peterson, H. (2002). A comparison of women's regret after vasectomy versus tubal sterilization. *Obstetrics and Gynecology, 99,* 1073–1079.

Jenkins, S. (2009). Marital splits and income changes over the longer term. In M. Brynin & J. Ermisch (Eds.), *Changing relationships.* London: Routledge.

Jenkins, W. (2010). Can anyone tell me why I'm gay? What research suggests regarding the origins of sexual orientation. *North American Journal of Psychology, 12*(2), 279–296.

Jennings, V., Burke, A. (2011). Fertility awareness-based methods. In R. A. Hatcher, J. Trussell, A. L. Nelson, W. Cates, D. Kaval, M. S. Policar (Eds) *Contraceptive Technology,* 20th Edition. pp. 417–434. Ardent Media, New York, N.Y.

Jha, A. (2010, October 4). British IVF pioneer Robert Edwards wins Nobel prize for medicine. Retrieved March 1, 2011, from http://www.guardian.co.uk/science/2010/oct/04/ivf-pioneer-robert-edwards-nobel-prize-medicine

Jick, S., & Hernandez, R. (2011). Risk of non-fatal venous thromboembolism in women using oral contraceptives containing drospirenone compared with contraceptives containing levonorgestrel. *British Medical Journal.* Retrieved June 5, 2011, from http://www.bmj.com/content/342/bmj.d2151.full

Johannsen, T., Ripa, C., Carlsen, E., Starup, J., Nielsen, O., Schwartrz, M., … Main, K. (2010). Long-term gynecological outcomes in women with congenital adrenal hyperplasia due to 21-hydroxylase deficiency. *International Journal of Pediatric Endocrinology.* Retrieved November 13, 2010, from http://www.ncbi.nlm.nih.gov/pmc/articles/PMC2963122/

Johnson, A. J. (2009). A functional approach to interpersonal argument: Differences between public-issue and personal-issue arguments. *Communication Reports, 22*(1), 13.

Johnson, A. M. (2001). Popular belief in gender-based communication differences and relationship success. *Dissertation Abstracts,* University of Massachusetts, Amherst, #0-599-95739-5.

Johnson, A. M., Mercer, C. H., Erens, B., Copas, A. J., McManus, S., Wellings, K., … Field, J. (2001). Sexual behaviour in Britain: Partnerships, practices, and HIV-risk behaviours. *Lancet, 358,* 1835–1842.

Johnson, K., Gill, S., Reichman, V., Tassinary, L. (2007). Swagger, sway, and sexuality: Judging sexual orientation from body motion and morphology. *Journal of Personality and Social Psychology, 93*(3), 321–334.

Johnson, K. C., & Daviss, B. A. (2005). Outcomes of planned home births with certified professional midwives: Large prospective study in North America. *British Medical Journal, 330*(7505), 1416–1420.

Johnson, L. A. (2005). Experts urge routine HIV tests for all. Retrieved February 11, 2005, from http://abcnews.go.com/Health/wireStory?id=485527

Jonas, S., Bebbington, P., McManus, S., Meltzer, H., Jenkins, R., Kuipers, E., … Brugha, T. (2011). Sexual abuse and psychiatric disorder in England: Results from the 2007 adult psychiatric morbidity survey. *Psychological Medicine, 41*(4), 709–720.

Jones, R. (1984). *Human reproduction and sexual behavior.* Englewood Cliffs, NJ: Prentice Hall.

Jones, R., Darroch, J., & Singh, S. (2005). Religious differentials in the sexual and reproductive behaviors of young women in the United States. *Journal of Adolescent Health, 36*(4), 279–288.

Jones, R., Finer, L., & Singh, S. (2010, May). Characteristics of U.S. abortion patients, 2008. New York: Alan Guttmacher Institute. Retrieved June 5, 2011, from http://www.guttmacher.org/pubs/US-Abortion-Patients.pdf

Jones, R., & Kooistra, K. (2011). Abortion incidence and access to services in the U.S., 2008. *Perspectives in Sex and Reproductive Health, 43*(1), 41–50.

Juntti, S. A., Tollkuhn, J., Wu, M. V., Fraser, E., Soderborg, T., Tan, S., … Shah, N. M. (2010). The androgen receptor governs the execution, but not the programming, of male sexual and territorial behavior. *Neuron, 66*(2), 167–169.

Kanayama, G., Hudson, J. I., & Pope, H. G., Jr. (2010). Illicit anabolic-androgenic steroid use. *Hormones and Behavior, 58*(1), 111–121.

Kaplan, G. (1977). Circumcision: An overview. *Current Problems in Pediatrics, 1,* 1–33.

Kaplan, H., Kohl, R., Pomeroy, W., Offit, A., & Hogan, B. (1974). Group treatment of premature ejaculation. *Archives of Sexual Behavior, 3*(5), 443–452.

Kaplan, H. S. (1974). *The new sex therapy.* New York: Bruner/Mazel.

Kapoor, S. (2008). Testicular torsion: A race against time. *International Journal of Clinical Practices, 62,* 821–827.

Karlsson, A., Sterlund, A., & Forss, N. (2011). Pharyngeal chlamydia trachomatis is not uncommon any more. *Scandinavian Journal of Infectious Disease, 43,* 344–348.

Kaschak, E., & Tiefer, L. (2001). *A new view of women's sexual problems.* Binghamton, NY: Haworth Press.

Kask, A. S., Chen, X., Marshak, J. O., Dong, L., Saracino, M., Chen, D., … Koelle, D. M. (2010). DNA vaccine delivery by densely-packed and short microprojection arrays to skin protects against vaginal HSV-2 challenge. *Vaccine, 28*(47), 7483–7491.

Kassler, W. J., & Cates, W. (1992). The epidemiology and prevention of sexually transmitted diseases. *Urologic Clinics of North America, 19,* 1–12.

Katz, M. H., Schwarcz, S. K., Kellogg, T. A., Klausner, J. D., Dilley, J. W., Gibson, S., &

McFarland, W. (2002). Impact of highly active antiretroviral treatment on HIV seroincidence among men who have sex with men. *American Journal of Public Health, 92*(3), 388–395.

Kaufman, B. S., Kaminsky, S. J., Rackow, E. C., & Weil, M. H. (1987). Adult respiratory distress syndrome following orogenital sex during pregnancy. *Critical Care Medicine, 15,* 703–704.

Kaunitz, A. (2002). Current concepts regarding use of DMPA. *Journal of Reproductive Medicine, 47*(9 Suppl.), 785–789.

Kaunitz, A. M., Arias, R., & McClung, M. (2008). Bone density recovery after depot medroxyprogesterone acetate injectable contraception use. *Contraception, 77,* 67–76.

Kayongo-Male, D., & Onyango, P. (1984). *The sociology of the African family.* London: Longman.

Keane, H. (2004). Disorders of desire: Addiction and problems of intimacy. *Journal of Medical Humanities, 25*(3), 189–197.

Keegan, J. (2001). The neurobiology, neuropharmacology, and pharmacological treatment of the paraphilias and compulsive sexual behavior. *Canadian Journal of Psychiatry, 46*(1), 26–33.

Keller, J. C. (2005). Straight talk about the gay gene. *Science & Spirit, 16,* 21.

Kelly, R. J., Wood, J., Gonzalez, L., MacDonald, V., & Waterman, J. (2002). Effects of mother–son incest and positive perceptions of sexual abuse experiences on the psychosocial adjustment of clinic-referred men. *Child Abuse and Neglect, 26*(4), 425–441.

Kempeneers, P., Andrianne, R., & Mormont, C. (2004). Penile prosthesis, sexual satisfaction, and representation of male erotic value. *Sexual & Relationship Therapy, 19*(4), 379–392.

Kennedy, K, Trussell, J. (2011). Postpartum contraception and lactation. In R. A. Hatcher, J. Trussell, A. L. Nelson, W. Cates, D. Kaval, M. S. Policar (Eds) *Contraceptive Technology,* 20th Edition, pp 483-511. Ardent Media, New York, N.Y.

Kennedy, M. A., & Gorzalka, B. B. (2002). Asian and non-Asian attitudes toward rape, sexual harassment, and sexuality. *Sex Roles, 46*(7–8), 227–238.

Kerckhoff, A. (1964). Patterns of homogamy and the field of eligibles. *Social Forces, 42*(3), 289–297.

Kerrigan, D., Mobley, S., Rutenberg, N., Fisher, A., & Weiss, E. (2000). The female condom: Dynamics of use in urban Zimbabwe. New York: The Population Council. Retrieved July 24, 2008, from http://www.popcouncil.org/pdfs/horizons/fcz.pdf

Kertzner, R. M., Meyer, I. H., Frost, D. M., & Stirratt, M. J. (2009). Social and psychological well-being in lesbians, gay men, and bisexuals: The effects of race, gender, age, and sexual identity. *American Journal of Orthopsychiatry, 79*(4), 500–510.

Khadivzadeh, T., & Parsai, S. (2005). Effect of exclusive breastfeeding and complementary feeding on infant growth and morbidity. *Eastern Mediterranean Health Journal, 10*(3), 289–294.

Killick, S., Leary, C., Trussell, J., & Guthrie, K. (2010). Sperm content of pre-ejaculatory fluid. *Human Fertility, 14*(1), 48–52.

King, M., Semlyen, J., Tai, S., Killaspy, H., Osborn, D., Popelyuk, D., & Nazareth, I. (2008). A systematic review of mental disorder, suicide, and deliberate self harm in lesbian, gay, and bisexual people. *BMC Psychiatry, 8,* 70. Retrieved January 24, 2011, from http://www.biomedcentral.com/1471-244X/8/70

King, P., & Boyatzis, C. (2004). Exploring adolescent spiritual and religious development: Current and future theoretical and empirical perspectives. *Applied Developmental Science, 8,* 2–6.

Kinkade, S., & Meadows, S. (2005). Does neonatal circumcision decrease morbidity? *The Journal of Family Practice, 54*(1), 81–82.

Kinnunen, L. H., Moltz, H., Metz, J., & Cooper, M. (2004). Differential brain activation in exclusively homosexual and heterosexual men produced by the selective serotonin reuptake inhibitor, fluoxetine. *Brain Research, 1024*(1–2), 251–254.

Kinsey, A., Pomeroy, W. B., & Martin, C. E. (1948). *Sexual behavior in the human male.* Philadelphia, PA: Saunders.

Kinsey, A. C., Pomeroy, W., Martin, C. E., & Gebhard, P. (1953). *Sexual behavior in the human female.* Philadelphia: Saunders.

Kirby, D. (2001, May). Emerging answers: Research findings on programs to reduce teen pregnancy. National Campaign to Prevent Teen Pregnancy. Retrieved from http://eric.ed.gov/PDFS/ED456171.pdf

Kirby, D. (2007). Emerging answers: 2007. *Research Findings on Programs to Reduce Teen Pregnancy and Sexually Transmitted Diseases.* Washington, DC: National Campaign to Prevent Teen and Unplanned Pregnancy. Retrieved May 29, 2008, from http://www.thenationalcampaign.org/EA2007/EA2007_full.pdf

Klausen, P. (2007). *Trends in birth defect research.* Hauppauge, NY: Nova Science Publishers.

Klein, F. (1990). The need to view sexual orientation as a multivariable dynamic process: A theoretical perspective. In D. P. McWhirter, S. A. Sanders, & J. M. Reinisch (Eds.), *Homosexuality/heterosexuality: Concepts of sexual orientation* (pp. 277–282). New York: Oxford University Press.

Klein, F. (1993). *The bisexual option* (2nd ed.). Philadelphia: Haworth Press.

Klein, W., Geaghan, T., & MacDonald, T. (2007). Unplanned sexual activity as a consequence of alcohol use: A prospective study of risk perceptions and alcohol use among college freshman. *Journal of American College Health, 56,* 317–323.

Kleinplatz, P., & Moser, C. (2006). *Sadomasochism: Powerful pleasures.* Routledge, NY: Haworth Press.

Kluft, R. (2010). Ramifications of incest. *Psychiatric Times, 27*(12), 48–56.

Knaapen, L., & Weisz, G. (2008). The biomedical standardization of premenstrual syndrome. *Studies in History and the Philosophy of Biology and Biomedical Science, 39,* 120–134.

Knapp, M. L., & Hall, J. A. (2005). *Nonverbal communication in human interaction* (6th ed.). Belmont, CA: Wadsworth.

Knox, D., Breed, R., & Zusman, M. (2007). College men and jealousy. *College Student Journal, 41,* 435–444.

Knox, D., Zusman, M. E., Buffington, C., & Hemphill, G. (2000). Interracial dating attitudes among college students. *College Student Journal, 434*(1), 69–72.

Knox, D., Zusman, M. E., & Mabon, L. (1999). Jealousy in college student relationships. *College Student Journal, 33*(3), 328–329.

Koda, T., Ishida, T., Rehm, M., & Andre, E. (2009). Avatar culture: Cross-cultural evaluations of avatar facial expressions. *Artificial Intelligence & Society, 24,* 237–250.

Kohler, P. K., Manhart, L. E., & Lafferty, W. E. (2008). Abstinence-only and comprehensive sex education and the initiation of sexual activity and teen pregnancy. *Journal of Adolescent Health, 42,* 344–351.

Kohn, C., Hasty, S., & Henderson, C. W. (2002, September 3). Study confirms infection from receptive oral sex occurs rarely. *AIDS Weekly,* 20–22.

Kolata, G. (2007, August 12). The myth, the math, the sex. *New York Times.* Retrieved October 14, 2010, from http://www.nytimes.com/2007/08/12/weekinreview/12kolata.html

Kong, S., & Bernstein, K. (2009). Childhood trauma as a predictor of eating psychopathology and its mediating variables in patients with eating disorders. *Journal of Clinical Nursing, 18*(13), 1897–1907.

Koropeckyj-Cox, T., Romano, V., & Moras, A. (2007). Through the lenses of gender, race, and class. Students' perceptions of childless/childfree individuals and couples. *Sex Roles, 56,* 415–428.

Kotchick, B. A., Dorsey, S., & Miller, K. S. (1999). Adolescent sexual risk-taking behavior in single-parent ethnic minority families. *Journal of Family Psychology, 13*(1), 93–102.

Kowal, D. (2011). Coitus interruptus. In R. A. Hatcher, J. Trussell, A. L. Nelson, W. Cates, D. Kowal, M. S. Policar (Eds) *Contraceptive Technology,* 20th Edition. pp 409-415. Ardent Media, New York, N.Y.

Kreider, R. M. (2005). Number, timing, and duration of marriages and divorces: 2001. *Current Population Reports* (P70-97). Washington, DC: U.S. Census Bureau.

Krilov, L. (1991). What do you know about genital warts? *Medical Aspects of Human Sexuality, 25,* 39–41.

Krone, N., Hanley, N. A., & Arlt, W. (2007). Age-specific changes in sex steroid biosynthesis and sex development. *Best Practice & Research: Clinical Endocrinology Metabolism, 21*(3), 393–401.

Kuliev, A., & Verlinsky, Y. (2008). Impact of pre-implantation genetic diagnosis for chromosomal disorders on reproductive outcome. *Reproductive Biomedical Online, 16,* 9–10.

Kunin, C. M. (1997) *Urinary tract infections: Detection, prevention, and management* (5th ed.). Baltimore: Williams & Wilkins.

Kunkel, A. W., & Burleson, B. R. (1998). Social support and the emotional lives of men and women: An assessment of the different cultures perspective. In D. Canary & K. Dindia (Eds.), *Sex differences and similarities in communication: Critical essays and empirical investigations of sex and gender in interaction* (pp. 101–125). Mahwah, NJ: Lawrence Erlbaum Associates.

Kurdek, L. A. (2008). Change in relationship quality for partners from lesbian, gay male, and heterosexual couples. *Journal of Family Psychology, 22*(5), 701–711.

Lacey, R. S., Reifman, A., Scott, J. P., Harris, S. M., & Fitzpatrick, J. (2004). Sexual–moral attitudes, love styles, and mate selection. *The Journal of Sex Research, 41*(2), 121–129.

LaFree, G. (1982). Male power and female victimization. *American Journal of Sociology, 88,* 311–328.

Lai, C. H. (2011). Major depressive disorder: Gender differences in symptoms, life quality, and sexual function. *Journal of Clinical Psychopharmacology, 31*(1), 39–44.

Lakoff, R. (1975). *Language and woman's place.* New York: Harper.

Lalumière, M. L., Harris, G. T., Quinsey, V., & Rice, M. E. (2005). Sexual interest in rape. In M. L. Lalumière & G. Harris (Eds.), *Causes of rape: Understanding individual differences in male propensity for sexual aggression* (pp. 105–128). Washington, DC: American Psychological Association.

Lam, A. G., Russell, S. T., Tan, T. C., & Leong, S. J. (2008). Maternal predictors of noncoital sexual behavior: Examining a nationally representative sample of Asian and White American adolescents who have never had sex. *Journal of Youth and Adolescence, 37,* 62–74.

Lance, L. M. (2007). College student sexual morality revisited: A consideration of premarital sex, extramarital sex, and childlessness between 1940 and 2000–2005. *College Student Journal, 41,* 727–734.

Landau, E. (2008, September 5). When sex becomes an addiction. CNN.com. Retrieved October 2, 2008, from http://www.cnn.com/2008/HEALTH/09/05/sex.addiction/

Langevin, R., & Lang, R. A. (1987). The courtship disorders. In G. D. Wilson (Ed.), *Variant sexuality: Research and theory* (pp. 202–228). Baltimore: Johns Hopkins University Press.

Langevin, R., Langevin, M., & Curnoe, S. (2007). Family size, birth order, and parental age among male paraphilics and sex offenders. *Archives of Sexual Behavior, 36,* 599–609.

Langstrom, N., Grann, M., & Lindblad, F. (2000). A preliminary typology of young sex offenders. *Journal of Adolescence, 23,* 319–329.

LaSala, M. C. (2000). Lesbians, gay men, and their parents: Family therapy for the coming out crisis. *Family Process, 39*(2), 257–266.

Laumann, E. O., Gagnon, J., Michael, R. & Michaels, S. (1994). *The social organization of sexuality: Sexual practices in the United States.* Chicago: University of Chicago Press.

Lavin, M. (2008). Voyeurism: Psychopathology and theory. In D. Laws & W. O'Donohue (Eds.), *Sexual deviance: Theory, assessment, and treatment* (2nd ed., pp. 305–319). New York: Guilford Press.

Laws, D., & O'Donohue, W. (2008). *Sexual deviance: Theory, assessment, and treatment.* New York: Guilford Press.

Lawyer, S., Resnick, H., Bakanic, V., Burkett, T., & Kilpatrick, D. (2010). Forcible, drug-facilitated, and incapacitated rape and sexual assault among undergraduate women. *Journal of American College Health, 58*(5), 453–461.

Layton-Tholl, D. (1998). Extramarital affairs: The link between thought suppression and level of arousal. *Dissertation Abstracts,* Miami Institute of Psychology of the Caribbean Center for Advanced Studies, #AAT9930425.

Lechuga, J., Swain, G., & Weinhardt, L. S. (In press). Perceived need of a parental decision aid for the HPV vaccine: Content and format preferences. *Health Promotions Practice.*

Ledbetter, A. (2010). Communication patterns and communication competence as predictors of online communication attitude: Evaluating a dual pathway model. *Journal of Family Communication, 10*(2), 99–115.

Ledermann, T., Bodenmann, G., Rudaz, M., & Bradbury, T. (2010). Stress, communication, and martial quality in couples. *Family Relations, 59*(2), 195–207.

Ledger, W. (2004). Implications of an irreversible procedure. *Fertility and Sterility, 82,* 1473.

Lee, J. A. (1974). The styles of loving. *Psychology Today, 8,* 43–51.

Lee, J. A. (1988). Love-styles. In R. Sternberg & M. Barnes (Eds.), *The Psychology of Love.* New Haven, CT: Yale University Press.

Lee, J. A. (1998). Ideologies of lovestyle and sexstyle. In V. de Munck (Ed.), *Romantic love and sexual behavior* (pp. 33–76). Westport, CT: Praeger.

Lee, J., Pomeroy, E. C., Yoo, S., & Rheinboldt, K. (2005). Attitudes toward rape: A comparison between Asian and Caucasian college students. *Violence Against Women, 11*(2), 177–196.

Leiblum, S., Koochaki, P., Rodenberg, X., Barton, I., & Rosen, R. (2006). Hypoactive sexual desire disorder in postmenopausal women: U.S. results from the women's international study of health and sexuality. *Menopause, 13,* 46–56.

Leitenberg, H., & Henning, K. (1995). Sexual fantasy. *Psychological Bulletin, 117*(3), 469–496.

Leo, S., & Sia, A. (2008). Maintaining labour epidural analgesia: What is the best option? *Current Opinions in Anesthesiology, 21,* 263–269.

Leonard, K. E. (2005). Editorial: Alcohol and intimate partner violence: When can we say that heavy drinking is a contributing cause of violence? *Addiction, 100*(4), 422–425.

Leonard, T. M. (2006). *Encyclopedia of the developing world* (Vol. 2). Philadelphia: Taylor & Francis.

Leslie, G. R., & Korman, S. K. (1989). *The family in social context.* New York: Oxford University Press.

LeVay, S. (1991). A difference in hypothalamic structure between heterosexual and homosexual men. *Science, 253*, 1034–1037.

Levine, D. (2007). Ectopic pregnancy. *Radiology, 245*, 385–397.

Lewes, K. (1988). *The psychoanalytic theory of male homosexuality.* New York: Meridian.

Lewis, M. (1987). Early sex role behavior and school age adjustment. In J. M. Reinish, L. A. Rosenblum, & S. A. Sanders (Eds.), *Masculinity/femininity: Basic perspectives* (pp. 202–226). New York: Oxford University Press.

Lewis, R., & Ford-Robertson, J. (2010). Understanding the occurrence of interracial marriage in the United States through differential assimilation. *Journal of Black Studies, 41*(2), 405–420.

Leyendecker, G., Kunz, G., Herbertz, M., Beil, D., Huppert, P., Mall, G., … Wildt, L. (2004, December). Uterine peristaltic activity and the development of endometriosis. *Annals of the New York Academy of Sciences, 1034*, 338–355.

Lie, D. (2000). Contraception update for the primary care physician. Retrieved May 17, 2001, from http://www.medscape.com/medscape/CNO/200/AAFP/AAFP-06.html

Lie, M. L., Robson, S. C., & May, C. R. (2008). Experiences of abortion: A narrative review of qualitative studies. *BMC Health Services Research, 8*, 150.

Lilley, L. L., & Schaffer, S. (1990). Human papillomavirus: A sexually transmitted disease with carcinogenic potential. *Cancer Nursing, 13*, 366–372.

Lindau, S., & Gavrilova, N. (2010). Sex, health, and years of sexually active life gained due to good health: Evidence from two U.S. population-based cross-sectional surveys of ageing. *British Medical Journal, 340*, c810. Retrieved from http://www.bmj.com/content/340/bmj.c810.full.pdf

Lindberg, L. D., Jones, R., & Santelli, J. S. (2008, July). Non-coital sexual activities among adolescents. *Journal of Adolescent Health.* Retrieved May 26, 2008, from http://www.guttmacher.org/pubs/JAH_Lindberg.pdf

Linton, K. D., & Wylie, K. R. (2010). Recent advances in the treatment of premature ejaculation. *Journal of Drug Design, Development, and Therapy, 18*(4), 1–6.

Lips, H. (2008). *Sex & gender: An introduction* (6th ed.). New York: McGraw-Hill.

Lipsky, S., Caetono, R., Field, C. A., & Larkin, G. (2005). Psychosocial and substance use risk factors for intimate partner violence. *Drug & Alcohol Dependence, 78*(1), 39–47.

Lisak, D., & Miller, P. (2002). Repeat rape and multiple offending among undetected rapists. *Violence and Victims, 17*(1), 73–84.

Litosseliti, L. (2006). *Gender and language: Theory and practice.* London: Arnold.

Littleton, H., Breitkopf, C., & Berenson, A. (2007). Rape scripts of low-income European American and Latina women. *Sex Roles, 56*, 509–516.

Littleton, H., Grills-Taquechel, A., & Axsom, D. (2009). Impaired and incapacitated rape victims: Assault characteristics and post-assault experiences. *Violence and Victims, 24*(4), 439–457.

Littleton, H., & Henderson, C. (2009). If she is not a victim, does that mean she was not traumatized? Evaluation of predictors of PTSD symptomatology among college rape victims. *Violence Against Women, 15*(2), 148–167.

Liu, D. F., Jiang, H., Hong, K., Zhao, L. M., Tang, W. H., & Ma, L. L. (2010). Influence of erectile dysfunction course on its progress and efficacy of treatment with phosphodiesterase type 5 inhibitors. *Chinese Medical Journal, 123*(22), 3258–3261.

Lock, J., & Steiner, H. (1999). Gay lesbian and bisexual youth risks for emotional, physical, and social problems: Results from a community-based survey. *Journal of American Academy of Child and Adolescent Psychiatry, 38*(3), 297–305.

Locker, L., McIntosh, W., Hackney, A., Wilson, J., & Wiegand, K. (2010). The breakup of romantic relationships: Situational predictors of perception of recovery. *North American Journal of Psychology, 12*(3), 565–578.

Lockwood, S. (2008, April 7). Homeless GLBT youths often face violent life on the streets. *Columbia Spectator.* Retrieved October 2, 2008, from http://www.columbiaspectator.com/node/30281

Loke, A., & Poon, C. (2011). The health concerns and behaviours of primigravida: Comparing advanced age pregnant women with their younger counterparts. *Journal of Clinical Nursing, 20*, 1141–1150.

Long, S., Ullman, S., Long, L., Mason, G., & Starzynski, L. (2007). Women's experiences of male-perpetrated sexual assault by sexual orientation. *Violence and Victims, 22*, 684–701.

Lopez, L., Grimes, D. A., Gallo, M., & Schulz, K. (2008). Skin patch and vaginal ring versus combined oral contraceptives for contraception. *Cochrane Database Systems Review, 23*, CD003552.

LoPiccolo, J., & Lobitz, W. C. (1972). The role of masturbation in the treatment of orgasmic dysfunction. *Archives of Sexual Behavior, 2*, 163–171.

Lott, A. J., & Lott, B. E. (1961). Group cohesiveness, communication level, and conformity. *Journal of Abnormal & Social Psychology, 62*, 408–412.

Lovejoy, F. H., & Estridge, D. (Eds.). (1987). *The new child health encyclopedia.* New York: Delacorte Press.

Lu, W., Mueser, K., Rosenberg, S., & Jankowski, M. (2008). Correlates of adverse childhood experiences among adults with severe mood disorders. *Psychiatric Services, 59*, 1018–1026.

Ludermir, A., Lewis, G., Valongueiro, S., de Araujo, T., & Araya, R. (2010). Violence against women by their intimate partner during pregnancy and postnatal depression: A prospective cohort study. *Lancet, 376*(9744), 903–910.

Lue, T. (2000). Erectile dysfunction. *New England Journal of Medicine, 342*(24), 1802–1813.

Lundstrom, M., & Walsh, D. (2010, November 14). Secrecy shrouds UOP sexual attack suit. *The Sacramento Bee.* Retrieved May 1, 2011, from http://www.sacbee.com/2010/11/14/v-mobile/3183395/secrecy-shrouds-sexual-assault.html

Maas, J. (1998). *Power sleep.* New York: Harper-Collins.

Maccoby, E. E., & Jacklin, C.N. (1987). Gender segregation in childhood. In H.W. Reese (Ed.), *Advances in child development and behavior,* (Vol. 20, pp. 239–287). San Diego, CA: Academic Press.

MacDorman, M. F., Declercq, E., & Menacker, F. (2011). Trends and characteristics of home births in the United States by race and ethnicity, 1990–2006. *Birth, 38*(1), 17–23.

MacDorman, M. F., Mathews, T. J., Martin, J. A., & Malloy, M. H. (2002). Trends and characteristics of induced labour in the U.S., 1989–1998. *Paediatric & Perinatal Epidemiology, 16*(3), 263–274.

Macklon, N., & Fauser, B. (2000). Aspects of ovarian follicle development throughout life. *Hormone Research, 52*, 161–170.

Macneil, S. (2004). It takes two: Modeling the role of sexual self-disclosure in sexual satisfaction. *Dissertation Abstracts International: Section B: The Sciences & Engineering, 65*(1-B), 481, #0419–4217.

Madan, R. A., & Gulley, J. L. (2010). The current and emerging role of immunotherapy in prostate cancer. *Clinical Genitourinary Cancer, 8*(1), 10–16.

Mahabir, S., Spitz, M. R., Barrera, S. L., Dong, Y. Q., Eastham, C., & Forman, M. R. (2008).

Dietary boron and hormone replacement therapy as risk factors for lung cancer in women. *American Journal of Epidemiology*. Epub ahead of print. Retrieved March 18, 2008, from http://www.ncbi.nlm.nih.gov/sites/entrez

Maisto, S. A., Carey, M. P., Carey, K. B., Gordon, C. M., Schum, J., & Lynch, K. (2004). The relationship between alcohol and individual differences variables on attitudes and behavioral skills relevant to sexual health among heterosexual young adult men. *Archives of Sexual Behavior, 33*(6), 571–584.

Majerovich, J., Canty, A., & Miedema, B. (2010). Chronic vulvar irritation: Could toilet paper be the culprit? *Canadian Family Physician, 56*(4), 350–352.

Makarainen, L., van Beek, A., Tuomivaara, L., Asplund, B., & Coelingh-Bennink, B. (1998). Ovarian function during the use of a single contraceptive implant: Implanon compared with Norplant. *Fertility and Sterility, 69*, 714–721.

Makrantonaki, E., Schönknecht, P., Hossini, A. M., Kaiser, E., Katsouli, M. M., Adjaye, J., … Zouboulis, C. C. (2010). Skin and brain age together: The role of hormones in the ageing process. *Experimental Gerontology, 45*(10), 801–813.

Malmo, C., & Laidlaw, T. (2010). Symptoms of trauma and traumatic memory retrieval in adult survivors of childhood sexual abuse. *Journal of Trauma and Dissociation, 11*(1), 22–43.

Malone, P., & Steinbrecher, H. (2007). Medical aspects of male circumcision. *British Medical Journal, 335*(7631), 1206–1290.

Maltz, D. W., & Borker, R. A. (1982). A cultural approach to male–female communication. In J. J. Gumperz (Ed.), *Language and social identity* (pp. 196–216). New York: Cambridge University Press.

Maltz, W. (1990, December). Adult survivors of incest: How to help them overcome the trauma. *Medical Aspects of Human Sexuality*, 38–43.

Maltz, W. (2002). Treating the sexual intimacy concerns of sexual abuse survivors. *Sexual and Relationship Therapy, 17*(4), 321–327.

Maltz, W., & Boss, S. (2001). *Private thoughts: Exploring the power of women's sexual fantasies*. Novato, CA: New World Library.

Maness, D. L., Reddy, A., Harraway-Smith, C. L., Mitchell, G., & Givens, V. (2010). How best to manage dysfunctional uterine bleeding. *Journal of Family Practice, 59*(8), 449–458.

Mantica, A. (2005). Better test for a stealthy cancer. *Prevention, 57*(3), 48–51.

Margolis, J. (2004). *O: The intimate history of the orgasm*. New York: Grove/Atlantic Press.

Marinakis, G., & Nikolaou, D. (2011). What is the role of assisted reproduction technology in the management of age-related infertility? *Human Fertility, 14*, 8–15.

Maritz, G. S. (2008). Nicotine and lung development. *Birth Defects Research, Part C., 84*, 45–53.

Mark, K., Wald, A., Mageret, A., Selke, S., Olin, L, Huang, M., & Corey, L. (2008). Rapidly cleared episodes of herpes simplex virus reactivation in immunocompetent adults. *Journal of Infectious Disease*. Epub ahead of print. Retrieved September 19, 2008, from http://www.ncbi.nlm.nih.gov/sites/entrez

Marrazzo, J., Cook, R., Wiesenfeld, H., Murray, P., Busse, B., Krohn, M., & Hillier, S. (2007). *Lactobacillus* capsule for the treatment of bacterial vaginosis. *Journal of Women's Health, 15*, 1053–1060.

Marrazzo, J., Koutsky L., Kiviat, N., Kuypers J., & Stine, K. (2001). Papanicolaou test screening and prevalence of genital human papillomavirus among women who have sex with women. *American Journal of Public Health, 91*, 947–952.

Marrazzo, J., Thomas, K., Fiedler, T., Ringwood, K., & Fredricks, D. (2008). Relationship of specific vaginal bacteria and bacterial vaginosis treatment failure in women who have sex with women. *Annals of Internal Medicine, 149*, 20–28.

Marrazzo, M., Thomas, K., Fiedler, T., Ringwood, K., & Fredricks, D. (2010). Risks for acquisition of bacterial vaginosis among women who report sex with women: A cohort study. *PLoS One, 5*(6), e11139.

Marshal, M. P., Friedman, M. S., Stall, R., & Thompson, A. L. (2009). Individual trajectories of substance use in lesbian, gay, and bisexual youth and heterosexual youth. *Addiction, 104*(6), 974–981.

Marshall, W. L. (1979). Satiation therapy: A procedure for reducing deviant sexual arousal. *Journal of Applied Behavior Analysis, 12*(3), 377–389.

Martens, W. (2007). Optimism therapy: An adapted psychotherapeutic strategy for adult female survivors of childhood sexual abuse. *Annals of the American Psychotherapy Association, 10*, 30–38.

Martin, D., Martin, M., & Carvalho, K. (2008a). Reading and learning-disabled children: Understanding the problem. *The Clearing House, 81*, 113–118.

Martin, H. P. (1991). The coming-out process for homosexuals. *Hospital and Community Psychiatry, 42*, 158–162.

Martin, J. T., Puts, D. A., & Breedlove, S. M. (2008b). Hand asymmetry in heterosexual and homosexual men and women: Relationship to 2D:4D digit ratios and other sexually dimorphic anatomical traits. *Archives of Sexual Behavior, 37*(1), 119–132.

Martin, K., Hutson, D., Kazyak, E., & Scherrer, K. (2010). Advice when children come out: The cultural tool kits of parents. *Journal of Family Issues, 31*(7), 960–991.

Martin, K., & Luke, K. (2010). Gender differences in the ABC's of the birds and bees: What mothers teach young children about sexuality and reproduction. *Sex Roles, 62*(3–4), 278–291.

Martin, R. P., Dombrowski, S. C., Mullis, C., Wisenbaker, J., & Huttunen, M. O. (2005, July 7). Smoking during pregnancy: Association with childhood temperament, behavior, and academic performance. *Journal of Pediatric Psychology*. Epub ahead of print. Retrieved July 17, 2005, from http://www.ncbi.nlm.nih.gov/entrez/query.fcgi?c md=Retrieve&db=pubmed&dopt=Abstract&list_uids=16002482&query_hl=23

Martinson, F. M. (1981). Eroticism in infancy and childhood. In L. L. Constantine & F. M. Martinson (Eds.), *Children and sex: New findings, new perspectives* (pp. 23–35). Boston: Little, Brown.

Masho, S., & Anderson, L. (2009). Sexual assault in men: A population-based study of Virginia. *Violence and Victims, 24*(1), 98–110.

Mason, M. A., Fine, M. A., & Carcochan, S. (2001). Family law in the new millennium: For whose families? *Journal of Family Issues, 22*(7), 859–882.

Masser, B., Viki, T., & Power, C. (2006). Hostile sexism and rape proclivity amongst men. *Sex Roles, 54*, 565–574.

Masters, W. H., & Johnson, V. E. (1966). *Human sexual response*. Boston: Little, Brown.

Masters, W. H., & Johnson, V. E. (1970). *Human sexual inadequacy*. Boston: Little, Brown.

Masters, W. H., & Johnson, V. E. (1979). *Homosexuality in perspective*. Boston: Little, Brown.

Masters, W. H., Johnson, V. E., & Kolodny, R. C. (1982). *Human sexuality*. Boston: Little, Brown.

Mather, M., & Lavery, D. (2010). In U.S., proportion married at lowest recorded levels. Population Reference Bureau. Retrieved May 11, 2011, from http://www.prb.org/Articles/2010/usmarriagedecline.aspx

Mathers, M., Degener, S., & Roth, S. (2011). Cryptorchidism and infertility from the perspective of interdisciplinary guidelines. *Urologe A, 50*(1), 20–25.

Matsumoto, D. (1996). *Culture and psychology.* Pacific Grove, CA: Brooks/Cole.

Matthews, A., Dowswell, T., Haas, D. M., Doyle, M., & O'Mathúna, D. P. (2010). Interventions for nausea and vomiting in early pregnancy. *Cochrane Database Systems Review, 8*(9), CD007575.

Matthews, A. K., Tartaro, J., & Hughes, T. L. (2003). A comparative study of lesbian and heterosexual women in committed relationships. *Journal of Lesbian Studies, 7,* 101–114.

Maynard, E., Carballo-Dieguez, A., Ventuneac, A., Exner, T., & Mayer, K. (2009). Women's experiences with anal sex: Motivations and implications for STD prevention. *Perspectives on Sexual and Reproductive Health, 41*(3), 142–149.

McAdams, M. (1996). Gender without bodies. Retrieved September 3, 2005, from http://www.december.com/cmc/mag/1996/mar/mcadams.html

McCabe, M., & Wauchope, M. (2005). Behavioral characteristics of men accused of rape: Evidence for different types of rapists. *Archives of Sexual Behavior, 34,* 241–253.

McCabe, S., Bostwick, W., Hughes, T., West, B., & Boyd, C. (2010). The relationships between discrimination and substance use disorders among lesbian, gay, and bisexual adults in the U.S. *American Journal of Public Health, 100*(10), 1946–1952.

McCarthy, B. W., & Ginsberg, R. L. (2007). Second marriages: Challenges and risks. *Family Journal, 15,* 119.

McConaghy, N., Hadzi-Pavlovic, D., Stevens, C., Manicavasagar, V., Buhrich, N., & Vollmer-Conna, U. (2006). Fraternal birth order and ratio of heterosexual/homosexual feelings in women and men. *Journal of Homosexuality, 51*(4), 161–174.

McDowell, M., Wang, C., & Kennedy-Stephenson, J. (2008). Breastfeeding in the United States: Findings from the National Health and Nutrition Examination Survey, 1999–2006. *NCHS Data Briefs,* no. 5. Hyattsville, MD: National Center for Health Statistics.

McFadden, D. (2011). Sexual orientation and the auditory system. *Front Neuroendocrinology.* Retrieved February 20, 2011, from http://www.ncbi.nlm.nih.gov/pubmed/21310172

McGrath, R. (1991). Sex offender risk assessment and disposition planning. *International Journal of Offender Treatment and Comparative Criminology, 35*(4), 328–350.

McMahon, S. (2010). Rape myth beliefs and bystander attitudes among incoming college students. *Journal of American College Health, 59*(1), 3–12.

McNally, R. J., Clancy, S. A., Barrett, H. M., & Parker, H. A. (2004). Inhibiting retrieval of trauma cues in adults reporting histories of childhood sexual abuse. *Cognition and Emotion, 18*(4), 479–493.

McNally, R. J., Clancy, S. A., Barrett, H. M., & Parker, H. A. (2005). Reality monitoring in adults reporting repressed, recovered, or continuous memories of childhood sexual abuse. *Journal of Abnormal Psychology, 114*(1), 147–152.

Mead, M. (1935/1988/2001). *Sex and temperament in three primitive societies.* New York: William Morrow.

Mehl, M. R., Vazire, S., Ramirez-Esparza, N., Slatcher, R. B., & Pennebaker, J. W. (2007). Are women really more talkative than men? *Science, 317,* 82.

Mehrabian, A. (2009). *Nonverbal communication.* Piscataway, NJ: Transaction Publishers.

Mehta, C., & Strough, J. (2010). Gender segregation and gender-typing in adolescence. *Sex Roles, 64*(3–4), 251–263.

Meier, E. (2002). Child rape in South Africa. *Pediatric Nursing, 28*(5), 532–535.

Ménard, K. S., Nagayama Hall, G., Phung, A., Erian Ghebrial, M., & Martin, L. (2003). Gender differences in sexual harassment and coercion in college students. *Journal of Interpersonal Violence, 18*(10), 1222–1239.

Menke, L., Sas, T., Keizer-Schrama, S., Zandwijken, G., de Ridder, M., Odink, R., … Wit, J. M. (2010). Efficacy and safety of oxandrolone in growth hormone-treated girls with Turner syndrome. *Journal of Clinical Endocrinology & Metabolism, 95*(3), 1151–1160.

Menon, R. (2008). Spontaneous preterm birth, a clinical dilemma: Etiologic, pathophysiologic, and genetic heterogeneities and racial disparity. *Acta Obstetrica Gynecologic Scandinavica, 87,* 590–600.

Merki-Feld, G. S., Seeger, H., & Mueck, A. O. (2008). Comparison of the proliferative effects of ethinylestradiol on human breast cancer cells in an intermittent and a continuous dosing regime. *Hormone and Metabolic Research.* Retrieved March 18, 2008, from http://www.thieme-connect.com/ejournals/abstract/hmr/doi/10.1055/s-2007-1004540

Mertz, G. (2008). Asymptomatic shedding of herpes simplex virus 1 and 2: Implications for prevention of transmission. *Journal of Infectious Diseases, 198*(8), 1098–1100.

Meschke, L. L., Bartholomae, S., & Zentall, S. R. (2000). Adolescent sexuality and parent–adolescent processes: Promoting healthy teen choices. *Family Relations, 49*(2), 143–155.

Meston, C. M., Hull, E., Levin, R., & Sipski, M. (2004). Disorders of orgasm in women. *Journal of Sexual Medicine, 1,* 66–68.

Meston, C. M., Trapnell, P. D., & Gorzalka, B. B. (1996). Ethnic and gender differences in sexuality: Variations in sexual behavior between Asian and non-Asian university students. *Archives of Sex Behavior, 25*(1), 33–71.

Mhloyi, M. M. (1990). Perceptions on communication and sexuality in marriage in Zimbabwe. *Women and Therapy, 10*(3), 61–73.

Mi, T., Abbasi, S., Zhang, H., Uray, K., Chunn, J., Wei, L., … Xia, Y. (2008). Excess adenosine in murine penile erectile tissues contributes to priapism via A2B adenosine receptor signaling. *Journal of Clinical Investigation, 118*(4), 1491–1501.

Mikulincer, M., & Shaver, P. (2005). Attachment theory and emotions in close relationships: Exploring the attachment-related dynamics of emotional reactions to relational events. *Personal Relationships, 12*(2), 149–168.

Miletski, H. (2002). *Understanding bestiality and zoophilia.* Bethesda, MD: East-West.

Miller, E., Decker, M. R., Reed, E., Raj, A., Hathaway, J. E., & Silverman, J. G. (2007). Male partner pregnancy-promoting behaviors and adolescent partner violence: Findings from a qualitative study with adolescent females. *Ambulatory Pediatrics, 7*(5), 360–366.

Milner, J., Dopke, C., & Crouch, J. (2008). Paraphilia not otherwise specified. In D. Laws & W. O'Donohue (Eds.), *Sexual deviance: Theory, assessment, and treatment* (2nd ed., pp. 384–418). New York: Guilford Press.

Miner, M.H., Coleman, E., Center, B., Ross, M., Simon Rosser, B. (2007). The compulsive sexual behavior inventory: Psychometric properties. *Archives of Sexual Behavior, 36*(4), 579–587.

Miranda, A., & Fiorello, K. (2002). The connection between social interest and the characteristics of sexual abuse perpetuated by male pedophilies. *Journal of Individual Psychology, 58,* 62–75.

Mirbagher-Ajorpaz, N., Adib-Hajbaghery, M., & Mosaebi, F. (2010). The effects of acupressure on primary dysmenorrheal: A randomized controlled trial. *Complementary Practices in Clinical Practices, 17*(1), 33–36.

Mishna, F., Newman, P., Daley, A., & Soloman, S. (2008, January 5). Bullying of lesbian and gay youth: A qualitative investigation. *British Journal of Social Work*. Retrieved October 2, 2008, from http://bjsw.oxfordjournals.org/cgi/content/abstract/bcm148

Misri, S., Kostaras, X., Fox, D., & Kostaras, D. (2000). The impact of partner support in the treatment of postpartum depression. *Canadian Journal of Psychiatry, 45*(6), 554–559.

Moen, V., & Irestedt, L. (2008). Neurological complications involving central neuraxial blockades in obstetrics. *Current Opinions in Anesthesiology, 21,* 275–280.

Mofrad, S., Abdullah, R., & Uba, I. (2010). Attachment patterns and separation anxiety symptom. *Asian Social Science, 6*(11), 148–153.

Moller, N. P., Fouladi, R. T., McCarthy, C. J., & Hatch, K. D. (2003). Relationship of attachment and social support to college students' adjustment following a relationship breakup. *Journal of Counseling & Development, 81,* 354–369.

Money, J. (1984). Paraphilias: Phenomenology and classification. *American Journal of Psychotherapy, 38,* 164–179.

Money, J. (1986). *Venuses penuses: Sexology, sexophy, and exigency theory.* Buffalo, NY: Prometheus Books.

Money, J. (1990). Pedophilia: A specific instance of new phylism theory as applied to paraphiliac lovemaps. In J. Feierman (Ed.), *Pedophilia: Biosocial dimensions* (pp. 445–463). New York: Springer-Verlag.

Monroe, L. M., Kinney, L., Weist, M., Dafeamekpor, D., Dantzler, J., & Reynolds, M. (2005). The experience of sexual assault: Findings from a statewide victim needs assessment. *Journal of Interpersonal Violence, 20*(7), 767–776.

Montemurro, B., & McClure, B. (2005). Changing gender norms for alcohol consumption. *Sex Roles, 52,* 279–288.

Montirosso, R., Peverelli, M., Frigerio, E., Crespi, M., & Borgatti, R. (2010). The development of dynamic facial expression recognition at different intensities in 4- to 18-year-olds. *Social Development, 19*(1), 71.

Moore, M. E. (2010). Communication involving long-term dating partners' sexual conversations: The connection between religious faith and sexual intimacy. *Dissertation Abstract International, 48*/05. University of Arkansas, AAT #1484652.

Morbidity and Mortality Weekly Report. (2008). Update on overall prevalence of major birth defects—Atlanta, Georgia, 1978–2005. Centers for Disease Control and Prevention. Retrieved from http://www.cdc.gov/mmwr/preview/mmwrhtml/mm5701a2.htm

Morello, C. S., Levinson, M. S., Kraynyak, K. A., & Spector, D. H. (2011). Immunization with herpes simplex virus 2 (HSV-2) genes plus inactivated HSV-2 is highly protective against acute and recurrent HSV-2 disease. *Journal of Virology, 85*(7), 3461–3472.

Moreno-Garcia, M., Fernandez-Martinez, F. J., & Miranda, E. B. (2005). Chromosomal anomalies in patients with short stature. *Pediatric International, 47*(5), 546–549.

Morris, B. J. (2007). Why circumcision is a biomedical imperative for the 21st century. *Bioessays, 29,* 1147–1158.

Morrison-Beedy, D., Carey, M. P., Cote-Arsenault, D., Seibold-Simpson, S., & Robinson, K. A. (2008). Understanding sexual abstinence in urban adolescent girls. *Journal of Obstetric, Gynecologic, and Neonatal Nursing, 37,* 185.

Mortenson, S. T. (2002). Sex, communication, values, and cultural values. *Communication Reports, 15*(1), 57–71.

Mosconi, A. M., Roila, F., Gatta, G., & Theodore, C. (2005). Cancer of the penis. *Critical Reviews in Oncology/Hematology, 53*(2), 165–178.

Mosher, W. D., & Jones, J. (2010). Use of contraception in the United States: 1982–2008. *Vital Health Statistics, 23*(29), 1–44.

Muehlenhard, C. L., & Cook, S. W. (1988). Men's self-reports of unwanted sexual activity. *Journal of Sex Research, 24,* 58–72.

Muir, J. G. (1993, March 31). Homosexuals and the 10% fallacy. *The Wall Street Journal,* p. A14.

Mulick, P. S., & Wright, L. W. (2002). Examining the existence of biphobia in the heterosexual and homosexual populations. *Journal of Bisexuality, 2,* 45–65.

Mulvaney, B. M. (1994). Gender differences in communication: An intercultural experience. Paper prepared by the Department of Communication, Florida Atlantic University.

Mumba, M. (2010). A phenomenological study of how college students communicate about anal sex and its implications for health. *Dissertation Abstracts,* Ohio University, AAT #3433979.

Munk-Olsen, T., Laursen, T. M., Pedersen, C. B., Lidegaard, Ø., & Mortensen, P. B. (2011). Induced first-trimester abortion and risk of mental disorder. *New England Journal of Medicine, 364*(4), 332–339.

Murnen, S., & Kohlman, M. (2007). Athletic participation, fraternity membership, and sexual aggression among college men: A meta-analysis review. *Sex Roles, 57,* 145–157.

Murphy, W., & Page, J. (2008). Exhibitionism: Psychopathology and theory. In D. Laws & W. O'Donohue (Eds.), *Sexual deviance: Theory, assessment, and treatment* (2nd ed., pp. 61–75). New York: Guilford Press.

Murray, J. (2000). Psychological profile of pedophiles and child molesters. *Journal of Psychology, 134*(2), 211–224.

Murray, K. M., Ciarrocchi, J. W., & Murray-Swank, N. A. (2007). Spirituality, religiosity, shame, and guilt as predictors of sexual attitudes and experiences. *Journal of Psychology and Theology, 35,* 222–234.

Nagel, B., Matsuo, H., McIntyre, K. P., & Morrison, N. (2005). Attitudes toward victims of rape: Effects of gender, race, religion, and social class. *Journal of Interpersonal Violence, 20*(6), 725–737.

Nagel, J. (2003). *Race, ethnicity and sexuality.* New York: Oxford University Press.

Nair, V. R., & Baguley, S. (2010). Tracking down chlamydia infection in primary care. *Practitioner, 254*(1732), 24–26, 3.

Namuo, C. (2010, October 8). UNH football player charged with rape. Manchester, NH: *The Union Leader,* p. A1.

Nanda, K. (2011). Contraceptive patch and vaginal contraceptive ring. In R. A. Hatcher, J. Trussell, A. L. Nelson, W. Cates, D. Kowal, M. S. Policar (Eds) *Contraceptive Technology,* 20th Edition. pp. 343-369. Ardent Media, New York, N.Y.

Nanda, S. (2001). *Gender diversity: Crosscultural variations.* Prospect Heights, IL: Waveland Press.

Narod, S. (2011). Age of diagnosis, tumor size, and survival after breast cancer: Implications for mammographic screening. *Breast Cancer Research and Treatment, 128,* 259–266.

Narod, S. A., Sun, P., Ghadirian, P., Lynch, H., Isaacs, C., Garber, J., … Neuhausen, S. L. (2001). Tubal ligation and risk of ovarian cancer in carriers of BRCA1 or BRCA2 mutations: A case-control study. *Lancet, 357*(9267), 843–844.

National Student GenderBlind. (2010). 2010 Campus Equality Index: Colleges and universities with inclusive rooming policies. Retrieved November 13, 2010, from http://www.genderblind.org/wp-content/uploads/2010/07/2010CampusEqualityIndex.pdf

Naziri, D. (2007). Man's involvement in the experience of abortion and the dynamics of the couple's relationship: A clinical study. *European Journal of Contraceptive and Reproductive Health Care, 12,* 168–174.

Neal, J., & Frick-Horbury, D. (2001). The effects of parenting styles and childhood attachment patterns on intimate relationships. *Journal of Instructional Psychology, 28*(3), 178–183.

Nebehay, S. (2004). Cervical cancer epidemic in poor countries. Retrieved December 12, 2004, from http://www.reuters.co.uk/printerFriendlyPopup.jhtml?type=healthN ews&storyID= 7114888

Needham, B. L., & Austin, E. L. (2010). Sexual orientation, parental support, and health during the transition to young adulthood. *Journal of Youth and Adolescence, 39*(10), 1189–1198.

Neisen, J. H. (1990). Heterosexism: Redefining homophobia for the 1990s. *Journal of Gay and Lesbian Psychotherapy, 1,* 21–35.

Nelson, A. L. (2007). Communicating with patients about extended-cycle and continuous use of oral contraceptives. *Journal of Women's Health, 16,* 463–470.

Nelson, A., Cwiak, C. (2011). Combined oral contraceptives (COCs). In R. A. Hatcher, J. Trussell, A. L. Nelson, W. Cates, D. Kowal, M. S. Policar (Eds) *Contraceptive Technology,* 20th Edition. pp. 249-341. Ardent Media, New York, N.Y.

Nelson, R. (2005). Gottman's sound medical house model. Retrieved September 3, 2005, from http://www.psychpage.com/family/library/gottman.html

Neri, Q., Takeuchi, T., & Palermo, G. (2008). An update of assisted reproductive technologies results in the U.S. *Annals of the New York Academy of Sciences, 1127,* 41–49.

Newcomb, M. E., & Mustanski, B. (2010). Internalized homophobia and internalizing mental health problems: A meta-analytic review. *Clinical Psychology Review, 30*(8), 1019–1029.

Newell, M., Coovadia, H., Cortina-Borja, M., Rollins, N., Gaillard, P., & Dabis, F. (2004). Mortality of infected and uninfected infants born to HIV-infected mothers in Africa: A pooled analysis. *The Lancet, 364*(9441), 1236–1243.

Newring, K., Wheeler, J., & Draper, C. (2008). Transvestic fetishism: Assessment and treatment. In D. Laws & W. O'Donohue (Eds.), *Sexual deviance: Theory, assessment, and treatment* (2nd ed., pp. 285–304). New York: Guilford Press.

Nicholas, D. R. (2000). Men, masculinity and cancer. *Journal of American College Health, 49*(1), 27–33.

Nicoll, L. M., & Skupski, D.W. (2008). Venous air embolism after using a birth-training device. *Obstetrics and Gynecology, 111,* 489–491.

Nilsson, L. (1990). *A child is born.* New York: Delacorte Press, Bantam Books.

Njus, D., & Bane, C. (2009). Religious identification as a moderator of evolved sexual strategies of men and women. *Journal of Sex Research, 46*(6), 546–557.

Noland, C. M. (2010). *Sex talk: The role of communication in intimate relationships.* Portland, OR: Praeger Publishing.

Nonnemaker, J., McNeely, C., & Blum, R. (2003). Public and private domains of religiosity and adolescent health risk behaviors: Evidence from the National Longitudinal Study of Adolescent Health. *Social Science & Medicine, 57*(11), 2049–2054.

Nordling, N., Sandnabba, N., Santtila, P., Alison, L. (2006). Differences and similarities between gay and straight individuals involved in the SM subculture. *Journal of Homosexuality, 50*(2–3), 41–67.

Nour, N. M. (2004). Female genital cutting: Clinical and cultural guidelines. *Obstetrical & Gynecological Survey, 59*(4), 272–279.

Nour, N. M. (2006). Health consequences of child marriage in Africa. *Emerging Infectious Diseases, 12*(11). Retrieved June 26, 2008, from http://www.cdc.gov/ncidod/EID/vol12no11/06-0510.htm

Oakes, M., Eyvazzadeh, A., Quint, E., & Smith, Y. (2008). Complete androgen insensitivity syndrome—A review. *Journal of Pediatric and Adolescent Gynecology, 21,* 305–310.

Ochsenkühn, R., Hermelink, K., Clayton, A. H., von Schönfeldt, V., Gallwas, J., Ditsch, N., ... Kahlert, S. (2011). Menopausal status in breast cancer patients with past chemotherapy determines long-term hypoactive sexual desire disorder. *Journal of Sexual Medicine, 8*(5), 1486–1494.

O'Connor, M. (2008). Reconstructing the hymen: Mutilation or restoration? *Journal of Law, Medicine, and Ethics, 16*(1), 161–175.

Ogletree, S. M., & Ginsburg, H. J. (2000). Kept under the hood: Neglect of the clitoris in common vernacular. *Sex Roles, 43*(11–12), 917–927.

O'Grady, R. (2001). Eradicating pedophilia toward the humanization of society. *Journal of International Affairs, 55*(1), 123–140.

O'Hare, T. (2005). Risky sex and drinking contexts in freshman first offenders. *Addictive Behaviors, 30*(1), 585–588.

Ojanen, T., Sijtsema, J., Hawley, P., & Little, T. (2010). Intrinsic and extrinsic motivation in early adolescents' friendship development: Friendship selection, influence, and prospective friendship quality. *Journal of Adolescence, 33*(6), 837.

Okami, P. (1990). Sociopolitical biases in the contemporary scientific literature on adult human sexual behavior with children and adolescents. In J. Feierman (Ed.), *Pedophilia* (pp. 91–121). New York: Springer Verlag.

Okami, P., Olmstead, R., & Abramson, P. R. (1997). Sexual experiences in early childhood: 18-year longitudinal data from the UCLA Family Lifestyles Project. *Journal of Sex Research, 34*(4), 339–347.

Oliver, C., Beech, A., Fisher, D., & Beckett, R. (2007). A comparison of rapists and sexual murderers on demographic and selected psychometric measures. *International Journal of Offender Therapy and Comparative Criminology, 51,* 298.

Oner, B. (2001). Factors predicting future time orientation for romantic relationships with the opposite sex. *Journal of Psychology: Interdisciplinary & Applied, 135*(4), 430–438.

O'Sullivan, L., & Allgeier, E. (1998). Feigning sexual desire: Consenting to unwanted sexual activity in heterosexual dating relationships. *Journal of Sex Research, 35,* 234–243.

Oswald, R., & Clausell, E. (2005). Same-sex relationships and their dissolution. In M. Fine & J. Harvey (Eds.), *Handbook of divorce and relationship dissolution* (pp. 499–513). New York: Routledge.

Owen, R. (2009). Dapoxetine: A novel treatment for premature ejaculation. *Drugs Today, 45*(9), 669–678.

Ozdemir, O., Simsek, F., Ozkardes, S., Incesu, C., & Karakoc, B. (2008). The unconsummated marriage: Its frequency and clinical characteristics in a sexual dysfunction clinic. *Journal of Sex and Marital Therapy, 34,* 268–279.

Palca, J. (1991). Fetal brain signals time for birth. *Science, 253,* 1360.

Palefsky, J. (2008). Human papillomavirus and anal neoplasia. *Current HIV/AIDS Report, 5,* 78–85.

Palomares, N., & Lee, E. (2010). Virtual gender identity: The linguistic assimilation to gendered avatars in computer-mediated communication. *Journal of Language and Social Psychology, 29*(1), 5.

Pandey, M. K., Rani, R., & Agrawal, S. (2005). An update in recurrent spontaneous abortion. *Archives of Gynecology & Obstetrics, 272*(2), 95–108.

Pardue, A., & Arrigo, B. (2008). Power, anger, and sadistic rapists: Toward a differentiated model of offender personality. *International Journal of Offender Therapy and Comparative Criminology, 52,* 378–400.

Parker, S. E., Mai, C. T., Canfield, M. A., Rickard, R., Wang, Y., Meyer, R. E., ... Correa, A. (2010).

Updated national birth prevalence estimates for selected birth defects in the United States, 2004–2006. National Birth Defects Prevention Network. *Birth Defects Research: Part A, Clinical and Molecular Teratology, 88*(12), 1008–1016.

Parker, S. K., & Griffin, M. A. (2002). What is so bad about a little name calling? *Journal of Occupational Health Psychology, 7*(3), 195–210.

Parker Pope, T. (2010). *For better: The science of marriage.* Boston, MA: Dutton.

Parks, K. A., & Scheidt, D. M. (2000). Male bar drinkers' perspective on female bar drinkers. *Sex Roles, 43*(11/12), 927–935.

Parrott, D., & Peterson, J. (2008). What motivates hate crimes based on sexual orientation? Mediating effects of anger on antigay aggression. *Aggressive Behavior, 34*, 306–318.

Parry, B. L. (2008). Perimenopausal depression. *American Journal of Psychiatry, 165*, 23–27.

Parsonnet, J., Hansmann, M., Delaney, M., Modern, P., Dubois, A., Wieland-Alter, W., … Onderdonk, A. (2005). Prevalence of toxic shock syndrome toxin 1-producing Staphylococcus aureus and the presence of antibodies to this superantigen in menstruating women. *Journal of Clinics in Microbiology, 43*(9), 4628–4634.

Passel, J., Wang, W., & Taylor, P. (2010). Marrying out: One in seven new U.S. marriages is interracial or interethnic. Pew Research Center. Retrieved May 11, 2011, from http://pewresearch.org/pubs/1616/american-marriage-interracial-interethnic

Pastor, Z. (2010). G spot—Myths and realities. *Czechoslovakian Gynecology, 75*(3), 211–217.

Pasupathy, D., & Smith, G. C. (2005). The analysis of factors predicting antepartum stillbirth. *Minerva Ginecology, 57*(4), 397–410.

Pattatucci, A. M. (1998). Molecular investigations into complex behavior: Lessons from sexual orientation studies. *Human Biology, 70*(2), 367–387.

Paul, B. (2009). Predicting internet pornography use and arousal: The role of individual difference variables. *Journal of Sex Research, 46*(4), 344–357.

Paul, B., & Shim, J. (2008). Gender, sexual affect, and motivations for internet pornography use. *International Journal of Sexual Health, 20*(3), 187–199.

Pearce, A., Chuikova, T., Ramsey, A., & Galyautdinova, S. (2010). A positive psychology perspective on mate preferences in the U.S. and Russia. *Journal of Cross-Cultural Psychology, 41*(5–6), 742.

Pearson, J. C., Turner, L. H., & Todd-Mancillas, W. (1991). *Gender and communication* (2nd ed.). Dubuque, IA: William C. Brown.

Pelosi, M., & Pelosi, M. (2010). Breast augmentation. *Obstetrics and Gynecology Clinics of North America, 37*(4), 533–546.

Peplau, L. A., & Fingerhut, A. (2004). The paradox of the lesbian worker. *Journal of Social Issues, 60*(4), 719–736.

Peplau, L. A., Garnets, L. D., & Spalding, L. R. (1998). A critique of Bem's "exotic becomes erotic" theory of sexual orientation. *Psychological Review, 105*(2), 387–394.

Peralta, R. L. (2008). "Alcohol allows you to not be yourself": Toward a structured understanding of alcohol use and gender difference among gay, lesbian, and heterosexual youth. *Journal of Drug Issues, 38*, 373–400.

Perelman, M., & Rowland, D. (2006). Retarded ejaculation. *World Journal of Urology, 24*, 645–652.

Perilloux, C., & Buss, D. (2008). Breaking up romantic relationships: Costs experienced and coping strategies deployed. *Evolutionary Psychology, 6*(1), 164–181.

Perovic, S. V., & Djinovic, R. P. (2010). Current surgical management of severe Peyronie's disease. *Archives of Españoles Urology, 63*(9), 755–770.

Perrigouard, C., Dreval, A., Cribier, B., & Lipsker, D. (2008). Vulvar vestibulitis syndrome: A clinicopathological study of 14 cases. *Annals of Dermatologie et de Venereologie, 135*, 367–372.

Perrin, E. C. (2002). Technical report: Coparent or second-parent adoption by same-sex parents. *Pediatrics, 109*(2), 341–345.

Peterson, H. B. (2008). Sterilization. *Obstetrics and Gynecology, 111*, 189–203.

Pew Research Center. (2010). The decline of marriage and rise of new families. Pew Research Center's Social and Demographic Trends Project. Retrieved May 12, 2011, from http://pewsocialtrends.org/files/2010/11/pew-social-trends-2010-families.pdf

Phipps, M. G., Matteson, K. A., Fernandez, G., Chiaverini, L., & Weitzen, S. (2008, March 19). Characteristics of women who seek emergency contraception and family planning services. *American Journal of Obstetrics and Gynecology, 199*(2), 111 (e1–5).

Piaget, J. (1951). *Play, dreams, and imitation in children.* New York: Norton.

Pialoux, G., Vimont, S., Moulignier, A., Buteux, M., Abraham, B., & Bonnard, P. (2008). Effect of HIV infection on the course of syphilis. *AIDS Review, 10*, 85–92.

Pillard, R. C. (1998). Biologic theories of homosexuality. *Journal of Gay and Lesbian Psychotherapy, 2*(4), 75–76.

Pillard, R. C., & Bailey, J. M. (1998). Human sexual orientation has a heritable component. *Human Biology, 70*(2), 347–366.

Pinheiro, A. P., Thorton, L., & Plotonicov, K. (2007). Patterns of menstrual disturbance in eating disorders. *International Journal of Eating Disorders, 40*(5), 424.

Pinkerton, J., & Stovall, D. (2010). Reproductive aging, menopause, and health outcomes. *Annals of the New York Academy of Science, 1204*, 169–178.

Pino, N. W., & Meier, R. F. (1999). Gender differences in rape reporting. *Sex Roles, 40*(11–12), 979–990.

Pinquart, M., Stotzka, C., & Silberreisen, R., (2008). Personality and ambivalence in decisions about becoming parents. *Social Behavior and Personality, 36*, 87–96.

Pisetsky, E. M., Chao, Y., Dierker, L. C., May, A. M., & Striegel-Moore, R. (2008). Disordered eating and substance use in highschool students: Results from the Youth Risk Behavior Surveillance System. *International Journal of Eating Disorders, 41*, 464.

Pitts, S. A., & Emans, S. J. (2008). Controversies in contraception. *Current Opinion in Pediatrics, 20*(4), 383–389.

Planned Parenthood Federation of America. (2005). Abstinence-only "sex" education. Retrieved May 30, 2005, from http://www.plannedparenthood.org/pp2/portal/medicalinfo/teensexualhealth/fact-abstinenceeducation.xml

Pluchino, N., Bucci, F., Cela, V., Cubeddu, A., & Genazzani, A. (2011). Menopause and mental well-being: Timing of symptoms and timing of hormone treatment. *Women's Health, 7*(1), 71–80.

Polek, C., & Hardie, T. (2010). Lesbian women and knowledge about human papillomavirus. *Oncology Nursing Forum, 37*(3), E191–E197.

Pollock, N. L., & Hashmall, J. M. (1991). The excuses of child molesters. *Behavioral Sciences and the Law, 9*, 53–59.

Ponseti, J., Bosinski, H., Wolff, S., Peller, M., Jansen, O., Mehdorn, H., … Siebner, H. (2006). A functional endophenotype for sexual orientation in humans. *Neuroimage, 33*(3), 825–833.

Ponseti, J., Granert, O., Jansen, O., Wolff, S., Mehdorn, H., Bosinski, H., & Siebner, H. (2009). Assessment of sexual orientation using the hemodynamic brain response to visual sexual stimuli. *Journal of Sexual Medicine, 6*(6), 1628–1634.

Popovic, M. (2005). Intimacy and its relevance in human functioning. *Sexual and Relationship Therapy, 20*(1), 31–49.

Posey, C., Lowry, P., Roberts, T., & Ellis, T. (2010). Proposing the online community self-disclosure model: The case of working professionals in France and the UK who use online communities. *European Journal of Information Systems, 19*(2), 181–196.

Pothen, S. (1989). Divorce in Hindu society. *Journal of Comparative Family Studies, 20*(3), 377–392.

Pouriayevali, M. H., Bamdad, T., Parsania, M., & Sari, R. (2011). Full-length antigen priming enhances the CTL epitope-based DNA vaccine efficacy. *Cell Immunology, 268*(1), 4–8.

Pozniak, A. (2002). Pink versus blue: The things people do to choose the sex of their baby. Retrieved June 3, 2002, from http://abcnews .go.com/sections/living/DailyNews/ choosingbabysex020603.html

Prentice, A. (2001). Endometriosis. *British Medical Journal, 323*(7304), 93–96.

Prentky, R. A., & Knight, R. A. (1986). Impulsivity: In the lifestyle and criminal behavior of sexual offenders. *Criminal Justice and Behavior, 13*(2), 141.

Previti, D., & Amato, P. (2004). Is infidelity a cause or a consequence of poor marital quality? *Journal of Social and Personal Relationships, 21*(2), 217–230.

Price, M., Kafka, M., Commons, M., Gutheil, T., & Simpson, W. (2002). Telephone scatologia: Comorbidity with other paraphilias and paraphilia-related disorders. *International Journal of Law & Psychiatry, 25*(1), 37–49.

Prior, V., & Glaser, D. (2006). *Understanding attachment and attachment disorders: Theory, evidence, and practice*. London: Jessica Kingsley.

Pryzgoda, J., & Chrisler, J. C. (2000). Definitions of gender and sex: The subtleties of meaning. *Sex Roles, 43*(7–8), 499–528.

Puente, S., & Cohen, D. (2003). Jealousy and the meaning (or nonmeaning) of violence. *Personality and Social Psychology Bulletin, 29*(4), 449–460.

Quadagno, D., Sly, D. F., & Harrison, D. F. (1998). Ethnic differences in sexual decisions and sexual behavior. *Archives of Sexual Behavior, 27*(1), 57–75.

Rabin, R. C. (2010, May 10). New spending for a wider range of sex education. *New York Times.* Retrieved January 24, 2011, from http://www .nytimes.com/2010/05/11/health/ policy/11land.html

Rabinowitz Greenberg, S. R., Firestone, P., Bradford, J., & Greenberg, D. M. (2002).

Prediction of recidivism in exhibitionists: Psychological, phallometric, and offense factors. *Sexual Abuse: Journal of Research & Treatment, 14*(4), 329–347.

Radestad, I., Olsson, A., Nissen, E., & Rubertsson, C. (2008). Tears in the vagina, perineum, spincter ani, and rectum and first sexual intercourse after childbirth: A nationwide follow up. *Birth, 35,* 98–106.

Rado, S. (1949, rev. 1955). An adaptional view of sexual behavior. *Psychoanalysis of behavior: Collected papers.* New York: Grune & Stratton.

Raffaelli, M., & Green, S. (2003). Parent–adolescent communication about sex; retrospective reports by Latino college students. *Journal of Marriage and the Family, 65,* 474–481.

Rahman, Q., & Koerting, J. (2008). Sexual orientation-related differences in allocentric spatial memory tasks. *Hippocampus, 18,* 55–63.

Rahman, Q., & Symeonides, D. (2008). Neurodevelopmental correlates of paraphilic sexual interests in men. *Archives of Sexual Behavior, 37,* 166–171.

Ramirez, A., & Zhang, S. (2007). When online meets offline: The effect of modality switching on relational communication. *Communication Monographs, 74,* 287.

Rand, M. R. (2009). Criminal victimization, 2008. National Crime Victimization Survey, Bureau of Justice Statistics. *Bureau of Justice Statistics Bulletin.* Retrieved April 13, 2011, from http://bjs.ojp.usdoj.gov/content/pub/ pdf/cv08.pdf

Rankin, P. T. (1952). The measurement of the ability to understand spoken language. *Dissertation Abstracts.* University of Michigan, 1953-06117-001.

Rapkin, A. J., & Winer, S. A. (2008). The pharmacologic management of premenstrual dysphoric disorder. *Expert Opinions in Pharmacotherapy, 9,* 429–445.

Ray, N. (2006). Lesbian, gay, bisexual and transgendered youth: An epidemic of homelessness. National Gay and Lesbian Task Force Policy Institute. Retrieved February 17, 2011, from http://www.thetaskforce.org/downloads/ reports/reports/HomelessYouth.pdf

Raymond, E., Stewart, F., Weaver, M., Monteith, C., & Van Der Pol, B. (2006). Impact of increased access to emergency contraception pills: A randomized controlled trial. *Obstetrics and Gynecology, 108,* 1098–1106.

Raymond, E. G. (2011). Progestin-only pills. In R. A. Hatcher, J. Trussell, A. L. Nelson, W. Cates., D. Kowal, M. S. Policar (Eds)

Contraceptive Technology, 20th Edition. pp. 237-247. Ardent Media, New York, N.Y.

Raymond, E. G. (2011b). Contraceptive Implants. In R. A. Hatcher, J. Trussell, A. L. Nelson, W. Cates, D. Kowal, M. S. Policar (Eds) *Contraceptive Technology,* 20th Edition. pp. 193-207. Ardent Media, New York, N.Y.

Read, C. M. (2010). New regimens with combined oral contraceptive pills—Moving away from traditional 21/7 cycles. *European Journal of Contraceptive and Reproductive Health Care, 15*(Suppl. 2), S32–S41.

Reece, M., Herbenick, D., Sanders, S., Dodge, B., Ghassemi, A., & Fortenberry, J. (2010a). Prevalence and predictors of testicular self-exam among a nationally representative sample of men in the U.S. *International Journal of Sexual Health, 22*(1), 1–4.

Reece, M., Herbenick, D., Schick, V., Sanders, S. A., Dodge, B., & Fortenberry, J. D. (2010b). Background and considerations on the National Survey of Sexual Health and Behavior (NSSHB). *Journal of Sexual Medicine, 7*(Suppl. 5), 243–245.

Reece, M., Herbenick, D., Schick, V., Sanders, S., Dodge, B., & Fortenberry, D. (2010c). Condom use rates in a national probability sample of males and females ages 14–94 in the United States. *Journal of Sexual Medicine, 7*(Suppl. 5), 266–276.

Reece, M., Herbenick, D., Schick, V., Sanders, S., Dodge, B., & Fortenberry, J. (2010d). Sexual behaviors, relationships, and perceived health among adult men in the United States: Results from a national probability sample. *Journal of Sexual Medicine, 7*(Suppl. 5), 291–304.

Regan, P. C. (2006). Love. In R. D. McAnulty & M. M. Burnette (Eds.), *Sex and sexuality: Sexual functions and dysfunctions* (pp. 87–113). Westport, CT: Praeger.

Regnerus, M. D., & Luchies, L. B. (2006). The parent–child relationship and opportunities for adolescents' first sex. *Journal of Family Issues, 27,* 159–183.

Rehman, U. S., & Holtzworth-Munroe, A. (2007). A cross-cultural examination of the relation of marital communication behavior to marital satisfaction. *Journal of Family Psychology, 21,* 759–763.

Reid, R., Bonomi, A., Rivara, F., Anderson, M., Fishman, P., Carrell, D., & Thompson, R. (2008). Intimate partner violence among men: Prevalence, chronicity, and health effects. *American Journal of Preventive Medicine, 34,* 478–485.

Reid, R., & Society of Obstetricians and Gynaecologists of Canada. (2010). SOGC clinical practice guideline. No. 252, December

2010. Oral contraceptives and the risk of venous thromboembolism: An update. *Journal of Obstetrics and Gynecology, 32*(12), 1192–1204.

Reilly, D. R., Delva, N. J., & Hudson, R. W. (2000). Protocols for the use of cyproterone, medroxyprogesterone, & leuprolide in the treatment of paraphilia. *Canadian Journal of Psychiatry, 45*(6), 559–564.

Remafedi, G. (1987). Male homosexuality: The adolescent perspective. *Pediatrics, 79*(3), 326–330.

Remez, L. (2000, November/December). Oral sex among adolescents: Is it sex or is it abstinence? *Family Planning Perspectives, 32*(6), 298–304.

Rempel, J. K., & Baumgartner, B. (2003). The relationship between attitudes towards menstruation and sexual attitudes, desires, and behavior in women. *Archives of Sexual Behavior, 32*(2), 155–163.

Renaud, C. A., & Byers, E. S. (1999). Exploring the frequency, diversity, and content of university students' positive and negative sexual cognitions. *Canadian Journal of Human Sexuality, 8*(1), 17–30.

Resnick, H., Acierno, R., Kilpatrick, D. G., & Holmes, M. (2005). Description of an early intervention to prevent substance abuse and psychopathology in recent rape victims. *Behavior Modification, 29*(1), 156–188.

Resnick, M. D., Bearman, P. S., Blum, R. W., Bauman, K. E., Harris, K. M., Jones, J., … Udry, J. R. (1997). Protecting adolescents from harm. Findings from the National Longitudinal Study on Adolescent Health. *Journal of the American Medical Association, 278*(10), 823–832.

Rettenmaier, N., Rettenmaier, C., Wojciechowski, T., Abaid, L., Brown, J., Micha, J., & Goldstein, B. (2010). The utility and cost of routine follow-up procedures in the surveillance of ovarian and primary peritoneal carcinoma: A 16-year institutional review. *British Journal of Cancer, 103*(11), 1657–1662.

Reynaert, C., Zdanowicz, N., Janne, P., & Jacques, D. (2010). Depression and sexuality. *Psychiatria Danubina, 22*(Suppl. 1), S111–S113.

Rhoades, G. K., Stanley, S. M., & Markman, H. J. (2009). The pre-engagement cohabitation effect: A replication and extension of previous findings. *Journal of Family Psychology, 23*(1), 107–111.

Rhoads, J. M., & Boekelheide, P. D. (1985). Female genital exhibitionism. *The Psychiatric Forum,* Winter, 1–6.

Richardson, C. T., & Nash, E. (2006). Misinformed consent: The medical accuracy of state-developed abortion counseling materials. *Guttmacher Policy Review, 9*(4). Retrieved March 18, 2011, from http://www.guttmacher.org/pubs/gpr/09/4/gpr090406.html

Richardson, D., Nalabanda, A., & Goldmeier, D. (2006). Retarded ejaculation: A review. *International Journal of STDs and AIDS, 17,* 143–150.

Richters, J., Hendry, O., & Kippax, S. (2003). When safe sex isn't safe. *Culture, Health, & Sexuality, 5*(1), 37–52.

Rideout, V. J., Foehr, U. G., & Roberts, D. F. (2010). *Generation M2: Media in the lives of 8- to 18-year-olds.* Menlo Park, CA: Kaiser Family Foundation.

Ridge, R. D., & Reber, J. S. (2002). "I think she's attracted to me": The effect of men's beliefs on women's behavior in a job interview scenario. *Basic and Applied Social Psychology, 24*(1), 1–14.

Rieger, G., Chivers, M. L., & Bailey, J. M. (2005). Sexual arousal patterns of gay men. *Psychological Science, 16*(8), 579–584.

Riordan, M., & Kreuz, R. (2010). Cues in computer-mediated communication: A corpus analysis. *Computers in Human Behavior, 26*(6), 1806–1817.

Rischer, C. E., & Easton, T. (1992). *Focus on human biology.* New York: HarperCollins.

Rittenhouse, C. A. (1991). The emergence of premenstrual syndrome as a social problem. *Social Problems, 38*(3), 412–425.

Rivers, I., & Noret, N. (2008). Well-being among same-sex- and opposite-sex-attracted youth at school. *School Psychology Review, 37,* 174–187.

Roan, S. (2010, August 15). Medical treatment carries possible side effect of limiting homosexuality. *Los Angeles Times.* Retrieved October 15, 2010, from http://articles.latimes.com/2010/aug/15/science/la-sci-adrenal-20100815

Roberts, A., Austin, S., Corliss, H., Vandermorris, A., & Koenen, K. (2010). Pervasive trauma exposure among U.S. sexual orientation minority adults and risk of posttraumatic stress disorder. *American Journal of Public Health, 100*(12), 2433–2441.

Roberts, D. F., Foehr, U. G., & Rideout, V. (2005). Generation M: Media in the lives of 8–18-year-olds. Retrieved November 3, 2005, from http://www.kff.org/entmedia upload/Generation-M-Media-in-the-Lives-of-8-18-Year-olds-Report.pdf

Roberts, S. (2010, September 15). Study finds wider view of family. *New York Times.* Retrieved September 15, 2010, from http://query.nytimes.com/gst/fullpage.html?res=9504E7DE163AF936A2575AC0A9669D8B63

Robin, G., Boitrelle, F., Marcelli, F., Colin, P., Leroy-Martin, B., Mitchell, V., …Rigot, J. M. (2010). Cryptorchidism: From physiopathology to infertility. *Gynecological Obstetrics and Fertility, 38*(10), 588–599.

Robinson, E. D., & Evans, B. G. I. (1999). Oral sex and HIV transmission. *AIDS, 16*(6), 737–738.

Rogers, S. C. (1978). Woman's place: A critical review of anthropological theory. *Comparative Studies in Society and History, 20,* 123–162.

Roisman, G., Clausell, E., Holland, A., Fortuna, K., & Elieff, C. (2008). Adult romantic relationships as contexts of human development: A multimethod comparison of same-sex couples with opposite-sex dating, engaged, and married dyads. *Developmental Psychology, 44,* 91–101.

Rome, E. (1998). Anatomy and physiology of sexuality and reproduction. In The Boston Women's Health Collective (Eds.), *The New Our Bodies, Ourselves* (pp. 241–258). Carmichael, CA: Touchstone Books.

Roncari, D., Hou, M. (2011) Female and male sterilization. In R. A. Hatcher, J. Trussell, A. L. Nelson, W. Cates, D. Kowal, M. S. Policar (Eds) *Contraceptive Technology,* 20th Edition. pp. 435-482. Ardent Media, New York, N.Y.

Röndahl, G., Innala, S., & Carlsson, M. (2004). Nurses' attitudes towards lesbians and gay men. *Journal of Advanced Nursing, 47,* 386–392.

Rosario, M., Schrimshaw, E., & Hunter, J. (2004). Predictors of substance use over time among gay, lesbian, and bisexual youths. An examination of three hypotheses. *Addictive Behaviors, 29*(8), 1623–1631.

Rosenblatt, P. C., Karis, T. A., & Powell, R. D. (1995). *Multiracial couples.* Thousand Oaks, CA: Sage.

Rosmalen-Noorjens, K., Vergeer, C., & Lagro-Janssen, A. (2008). Bed death and other lesbian sexual problems unraveled: A qualitative study of the sexual health of lesbian women involved in a relationship. *Women & Health, 48*(3), 339–362.

Rosman, J. P., & Resnick, P. J. (1989). Sexual attraction to corpses: A psychiatric review of necrophilia. *Bulletin of the American Academy of Psychiatry and the Law, 17,* 153–163.

Ross, C. A. (2009). Psychodynamics of eating disorder behavior in sexual abuse survivors. *American Journal of Psychotherapy, 63*(3), 211–227.

Ross, L. E. (2005). Perinatal mental health in lesbian mothers: A review of potential risk and protective factors. *Women Health, 41*(3), 113–128.

Ross, L. E., Steele, L. S., & Epstein, R. (2006). Service use and gaps in services for lesbian and bisexual women during donor insemination, pregnancy, and the postpartum period. *Journal of Obstetrics and Gynecology Canada, 28,* 505–511.

Rosser, B. R. (1999). Homophobia: Description, development, and dynamic of gay bashing. *Journal of Sex Research, 36*(2), 211.

Rossi, A. S. (1978). The biosocial side of parenthood. *Human Nature, 1,* 72–79.

Rothman, S. M. (1978). *Woman's proper place.* New York: Basic Books.

Rowland, D., McMahon, C. G., Abdo, C., Chen, J., Jannini, E., Waldinger, M. D., & Ahn, T. Y. (2010). Disorders of orgasm and ejaculation in men. *Journal of Sexual Medicine, 7*(4 Pt. 2), 1668–1686.

Ruan, F., & Lau, M. P. (2004). China. In R. T. Francoeur & R. J. Noonan (Eds.), *The Continuum international encyclopedia of sexuality* (pp. 182–209). New York/London: Continuum International.

Rudd, J. M., & Herzberger, S. D. (1999). Brother–sister incest, father–daughter incest: A comparison of characteristics and consequences. *Child Abuse and Neglect, 23*(9), 915–928.

Rudolph, K., Caldwell, M. & Conley, C. (2005). Need for approval and children's well-being. *Child Development, 76*(2), 309–323.

Rue, V. M., Coleman, P. K., Rue, J. J., & Reardon, D. C. (2004). Induced abortion and traumatic stress: A preliminary comparison of American and Russian women. *Medical Science Monitor, 10*(10), SR5–SR16.

Ruffman, T., Halberstadt, J., & Murray, J. (2009). Recognition of facial, auditory, and bodily emotions in older adults. *Journals of Gerontology, 64B*(6), 696.

Russell, D. E. H. (1984). *Sexual exploitation: Rape, child sexual abuse, and workplace harassment.* Beverly Hills, CA: Sage.

Russell, D. E. H., & Howell, N. (1983). The prevalence of rape in the United States revisited. *Signs: Journal of Women in Culture and Society,* 688–695.

Russell, S. T., Driscoll, A. K., & Truong, N. (2002). Adolescent same-sex romantic attractions and relationships: Implications for substance use and abuse. *American Journal of Public Health, 92,* 198–202.

Rust, P. C. R. (2000). *Bisexuality in the U.S.* New York: Columbia University Press.

Ryan, C., & Futterman, D. (2001). Social and developmental challenges for lesbian, gay, bisexual youth. *SIECUS Report, 29*(4), 5–18.

Ryan, C., Huebner, D., Diaz, R. M., & Sanchez, J. (2009). Family rejection as a predictor of negative health outcomes in white and Latino lesbian, gay, and bisexual young adults. *Pediatrics, 123*(1), 346–352.

Sable, M., Danis, F., Mauzy, D., & Gallagher, S. (2006). Barriers to reporting sexual assault for women and men: Perspectives of college students. *Journal of American College Health, 55,* 157–162.

Saewyc, E. M., Bearinger, L. H., Heinz, P. A., Blum, R. W., & Resnick, M. (1998). Gender differences in health and risk behaviors among bisexual and homosexual adolescents. *Journal of Adolescent Health, 23*(2), 181–188.

Salter, D., McMillan, D., Richards, M., Talbot, T., Hodges, J., Bentovim, A., ... Skuse, D. (2003). Development of sexually abusive behavior in sexually victimized males. *Lancet, 361*(9356), 471–476.

Salzmann, Z. (2007). *Language, culture, and society* (4th ed.). Boulder, CO: Westview Press.

Samter, W., & Burleson, B. R. (2005). The role of communication in same-sex friendships: A comparison among African Americans, Asian Americans, and European Americans. *Communication Quarterly, 53,* 265–284.

Sánchez, F., & Vilain, E. (2010). Genes and brain sex differences. *Progress in Brain Research, 186,* 65–76.

Sánchez, J. M., Milam, M. R., Tomlinson, T. M., & Beardslee, M. A. (2008). Cardiac troponin I elevation after orogenital sex during pregnancy. *Obstetrics and Gynecology, 111,* 487–489.

Sandnabba, N., Santilla, P., Alison, L., & Nordling, N. (2002). Demographics, sexual behavior, family background and abuse experiences of practitioners of sadomasochistic sex: A review of recent research. *Sexual and Relationship Therapy, 17,* 39–55.

Sandnabba, N. K., & Ahlberg, C. (1999). Parents' attitudes and expectations about children's cross-gender behavior. *Sex Roles, 40*(3–4), 249–263.

Santen, R. J. (1995). The testis. In P. Felig, J. D. Baxter, & L. A. Frolman, (Eds.), *Endocrinology and metabolism* (3rd ed.). New York: McGraw-Hill.

Santilla, P., Sandnabba, N., & Nordling, N. (2000). Retrospective perceptions of family interaction in childhood as correlates of current sexual adaptation among sadomasochistic males. *Journal of Psychology and Human Sexuality, 12,* 69–87.

Sartorius, A., Ruf, M., Kief, C., & Demirakca, T. (2008). Abnormal amygdala activation profile in pedophilia. *European Archives of Psychiatry and Clinical Neuroscience, 258,* 271–279.

Saslow, B., Boetes, C., Burke, W., Harms, S., Leach, M., Lehman, C., ... American Cancer Society Breast Cancer Advisory Group. (2007). American Cancer Society guidelines for breast screening with MRI as an adjunct to mammography. *CA Cancer Journal for Clinicians, 57,* 75–89.

Sato, S. M., Schulz, K. M., Sisk, C. L., & Wood, R. I. (2008). Adolescents and androgens, receptors and rewards. *Hormones and Behavior 53*(5), 647–658.

Saulny, S. (2010, January 30). Black? White? Asian? More young Americans choose all of the above. *New York Times.* Retrieved January 30, 2011, from http://www.nytimes.com/2011/01/30/us/30mixed.html?src=twrhp

Sauter, D., Eisner, F., Ekman, P., & Scott, S. (2010). Cross-cultural recognition of basic emotions through nonverbal emotional vocalizations. *Proceedings of the National Academy of Sciences of the United States of America, 107*(6), 2408.

Savaya, R., & Cohen, O. (2003). Divorce among Moslem Arabs living in Israel: Comparison for reasons before and after the actualization of the marriage. *Journal of Family Issues, 24*(3), 338–351.

Savic, I., Garcia-Falgueras, A., & Swaab, D. (2010). Sexual differentiation of the human brain in relation to gender identity and sexual orientation. *Progress in Brain Research, 186,* 41–62.

Savic, I., & Lindström, P. (2008, June 16). PET and MRI show differences in cerebral asymmetry and functional connectivity between homo- and heterosexual subjects. *Proceedings of the National Academy of Sciences.* Retrieved October 3, 2008, from http://www.pnas.org/cgi/content/abstract/0801566105v1

Savin-Williams, R. C., & Diamond, L. M. (2000). Sexual identity trajectories among sexual minority youths: Gender comparisons. *Archives of Sexual Behavior, 29,* 607–627.

Savin-Williams, R. C., & Dube, E. M. (1998). Parental reactions to their child's disclosure of a gay/lesbian identity. *Family Relations, 47,* 7–13.

Sayal, K., Heron, J., Golding, J., & Emond, A. (2007). Prenatal alcohol exposure and gender differences in childhood mental health problems: A longitudinal population-based study. *Pediatrics, 119,* 426–434.

Scaravelli, G., Vigiliano, V., Mayorga, J. M., Bolli, S., De Luca, R., & D'Aloja, P. (2010). Analysis of oocyte cryopreservation in assisted reproduction: The Italian National Register data from 2005 to 2007. *Reproductive Biomedicine Online, 21*(4), 496–500.

Scarce, M. (1997). *The hidden toll of stigma and shame.* New York: De Capo Press.

Schachter, S., & Singer, J. (1962). Cognitive, social, and physiological determinants of emotional state. *Psychological Review, 69*(5), 379–399.

Schick, V., Herbenick, D., Reece, M., Sanders, S. A., Dodge, B., Middlestadt, S. E., & Fortenberry, J. D. (2010). Sexual behaviors, condom use, and sexual health of Americans over 50: Implications for sexual health promotion for older adults. *Journal of Sexual Medicine, 7*(Suppl. 5), 315–329.

Schiffrin, H., Edelman, A., Falkenstern, M., & Stewart, C. (2010). The associations among computer-mediated communication, relationships, and well-being. *Cyberpsychology, Behavior, and Social Networking, 13*(3), 299–306.

Schneider, F., Habel, U., Kessler, C., Salloum, J. B., & Posse, S. (2000). Gender differences in regional cerebral activity during sadness. *Human Brain Mapping, 9*(4), 226–238.

Schneider, L., Mori, L., Lambert, P., & Wong, A. (2009). The role of gender and ethnicity in perceptions of rape and its aftereffects. *Sex Roles, 60*(5–6), 410–422.

Schneider, M. (1989). Sappho was a right-on adolescent: Growing up lesbian. *Journal of Homosexuality, 17*, 111–130.

Schrodt, P. (2009). Family strength and satisfaction as functions of family communication environments. *Communication Quarterly, 57*(2), 171–186.

Schrodt, P., Ledbetter, A., Jembert, K., Larson, L., Brown, N., & Glonek, K. (2009). Family communication patterns as mediators of communication competence in the parent-child relationship. *Journal of Social and Personal Relationships, 26*(6–7), 853–874.

Schüklenk, U., Stein, E., Kerin, J., & Byne, W. (1997). The ethics of genetic research on sexual orientation. *Hastings Center Report, 27*(4), 6–13.

Schuler, P., Vinci, D., Isosaari, R., Philipp, S., Todorovich, J., Roy, J., & Evans, R. (2008). Body-shape perceptions and body mass index of older African American and European American Women. *Journal of Cross-Cultural Gerontology, 23*(3), 255–264.

Schützwohl, A. (2008). The intentional object of romantic jealousy. *Evolution and Human Behavior, 29*, 92–99.

Schwandt, H., Coresh, J., & Hindin, M. (2010). Marital status, hypertension, coronary heart disease, diabetes, and death among African American women and men: Incidence and prevalence in the atherosclerosis risk in communities study participants. *Journal of Family Issues, 31*(9), 1211–1229.

Schwartz, G., Kim, R., Kolundzija, A., Rieger, G., & Sanders, A. (2010). Biodemographic and physical correlates of sexual orientation in men. *Archives of Sexual Behavior, 39,* 93–109.

Seeber, B., & Barnhart, K. (2006). Suspected ectopic pregnancy. *Obstetrics and Gynecology, 107*(2 pt 1), 399–413.

Segraves, R. T. (2010). Considerations for a better definition of male orgasmic disorder in DSM-V. *Journal of Sexual Medicine, 7*(2 Pt 1), 690–695.

Sehovic, N., & Smith, K. P. (2010). Risk of venous thromboembolism with drospirenone in combined oral contraceptive products. *Annals of Pharmacotherapy, 44*(5), 898–903.

Seidman, S. N. (2007). Androgens and the aging male. *Psychopharmacological Bulletin, 40,* 205–218.

Seidman, S. N., & Rieder, R. O. (1994). A review of sexual behavior in the U.S. *American Journal of Psychiatry, 151,* 330–341.

Seki, K., Matsumoto, D., & Imahori, T. T. (2002). The conceptualization and expression of intimacy in Japan and the United States. *Journal of Cross Cultural Psychology, 33,* 303–319.

Seligman, L., & Hardenburg, S. A. (2000). Assessment and treatment of paraphilias. *Journal of Counseling and Development, 78*(1), 107–113.

Sell, R., Wells, J., & Wypij, D. (1995). The prevalence of homosexual behavior and attraction in the U.S., the U.K., and France: Results of a national population-based sample. *Archives of Sexual Behavior, 24,* 235–249.

Seto, M. C. (2004). Pedophilia and sexual offenses against children. *Annual Review of Sex Research, 15,* 321–362.

Seveso, M., Taverna, G., Giusti, G., Benetti, A., Maugeri, O., Piccinelli, A., & Graziotti, P. (2010). Corporoplasty by plication: Outpatient surgery for the correction of penile cancer. *Archives of Italian Urological Andrology, 82*(3), 164–166.

Sexuality Information and Education Council of the United States. (2004). *Guidelines for comprehensive sexuality education* (3rd ed.). Retrieved September 22, 2005, from http://www.siecus.org/pubs/guidelines/guidelines.pdf

Seymour, A., Murray, M., Sigmon, J., Hook, M., Edmunds, C., Gaboury, M., Coleman, G.,

McLean, V. A., Victims' Assistance Legal Organization. (2000). National Victim Assistance Academy. Retrieved May 22, 2003, from http://www.ojp.usdoj.gov/ovc/assist/nvaa2000/academy/welcome.html

Shafik, A. (1991). Testicular suspension: Effect on testicular function. *Andrologia, 23*(4), 297–301.

Shapiro, S., & Dinger, J. (2010). Risk of venous thromboembolism among users of oral contraceptives: A review of two recently published studies. *Journal of Family Planning and Reproductive Health Care, 36*(1), 33–38.

Sharpsteen, D. J., & Kirkpatrick, L. A. (1997). Romantic jealousy and adult romantic attachment. *Journal of Personality & Social Psychology, 72*(3), 627–640.

Shaver, P., & Hazan, C. (1987). Being lonely, falling in love: Perspectives from attachment theory. *Journal of Social Behavior & Personality, 2*(2, Pt 2), 105–124.

Sheehan, P. (2007). Hyperemesis gravidarum—Assessment and management. *Australian Family Physician, 36,* 698–701.

Sheldon, K. M. (2007). Gender differences in preferences for singles ads that proclaim extrinsic versus intrinsic values. *Sex Roles, 57,* 119–130.

Shelton, J. F., Tancredi, D. J., & Hertz-Picciotto, I. (2010). Independent and dependent contributions of advanced maternal and paternal ages to autism risk. *Autism Research, 3*(1), 30–39.

Shettles, L., & Rorvik, D. (1970). *Your baby's sex: Now you can choose.* New York: Dodd, Mead.

Shibusawa, T. (2009). A commentary on "gender perspectives in cross-cultural couples." *Clinical Social Work Journal, 37,* 230–233.

Shih, G., Turok, D. K., & Parker, W. J. (2011). Vasectomy: The other (better) form of sterilization. *Contraception, 83*(4), 310–315.

Shindel, A., Nelson, C., & Brandes, S. (2008). Urologist practice patterns in the management of premature ejaculation: A nationwide survey. *Journal of Sexual Medicine, 5,* 199–205.

Shoffman, M. (2006, December 11). Italian politicians attack Vatican's "anti-gay" attitude. *Pink News.* Retrieved July 4, 2008, from http://www.pinknews.co.uk/news/view.php?id=3229

Shufaro, Y., & Schenker, J. G. (2010). Cryopreservation of human genetic material. *Annals of New York Academy of Science, 1205,* 220–224.

Shulman, J. L., & Horne, S. G. (2006). Guilty or not? A path model of women's sexual force fantasies. *Journal of Sex Research, 43,* 368–377.

Shulman, L. P. (2010). Gynecological management of premenstrual symptoms. *Current Pain and Headache Reports, 14*(5), 367–375.

Silbert, M. (1998). Compounding factors in the rape of street prostitutes. In A. W. Burgess (Ed.), *Rape and sexual assault II* (pp. 77–90). London: Taylor & Francis.

Silverman, B., & Gross, T. (1997). Use and effectiveness of condoms during anal intercourse. *Sexually Transmitted Diseases, 24,* 11–17.

Silverman, E. K. (2004). Anthropology and circumcision. *Annual Reviews in Anthropology, 33*(1), 419–445.

Silverman, J., Decker, M., McCauley, H., Gupta, J., Miller, E., Raj, A., & Goldberg, A. (2010). Male perpetration of intimate partner violence and involvement in abortions: An abortion-related conflict. *American Journal of Public Health, 1100*(8), 1415–1417.

Simmons, M., & Montague, D. (2008). Penile prosthesis implantation: Past, present, and future. *International Journal of Impotence Research, 20,* 437–444.

Simsir, A., Thorner, K., Waisman, J., & Cangiarella, J. (2001). Endometriosis in abdominal scars. *American Surgeon, 67*(10), 984–987.

Singh, M., Porter, C., & Griffiths, S. (2008). First trimester medical termination of pregnancy: The Nottingham experience. *Journal of Obstetrics and Gynecology, 28,* 315–316.

Slevin, K. F. (2010). "If I had lots of money ... I'd have a body makeover": Managing the aging body. *Social Forces, 88*(3), 1003–1020.

Smith, D. K., Taylor, A., Kilmarx, P. H., Sullivan, P., Warner, L., Kamb, M., ... Mastro, T. D. (2010). Male circumcision in the United States for the prevention of HIV infection and other adverse health outcomes: Report from a CDC consultation. *Public Health Report, 25*(Suppl. 1), 72–82.

Smith, G. D., & Travis, L. (2011). Getting to know human papillomavirus (HPV) and the HPV vaccines. *Journal of the American Osteopathic Association, 111*(3 Suppl. 2), S29–S34.

Smith, K. T. (1971). Homophobia: A tentative personality profile. *Psychological Reports, 29,* 1091–1094.

Smith, M. E. (2005). Female sexual assault: The impact on the male significant other. *Issues in the Mental Health Nursing, 26*(2), 149–167.

Sobsey, D. (1994). *Violence and abuse in the lives of people with disabilities.* Baltimore, MD: Paul H. Brookes.

Society for the Advancement of Sexual Health. (2008). *Public service announcement: Sexual addiction.* Retrieved October 2, 2008, from http://www.sash.net/

Song, A., & Halpern-Felsher, B. (2011). Predictive relationship between adolescent oral and vaginal sex: Results from a prospective, longitudinal study. *Archives of Pediatrics & Adolescent Medicine, 165*(3), 243–249.

Sontag, S. (1979). The double-standard of aging. In J. H. Williams (Ed.), *Psychology of women: Selected readings* (pp. 462–478). New York: W.W. Norton Publishers.

Soper, D. E. (2010). Pelvic inflammatory disease. *Obstetrics and Gynecology, 116*(2 Pt. 1), 419–428.

Sorenson, S., & Brown, V. (1990). Interpersonal violence and crisis intervention on the college campus. *New Directions for Student Services, 49,* 57–66.

Sprecher, S. (2002). Sexual satisfaction in premarital relationships: Associations with satisfaction, love, commitment, and stability. *Journal of Sex Research, 39*(3), 190–196.

Sprecher, S., & Hendrick, S. (2004). Self-disclosure in intimate relationships: Associations with individual and relationship characteristics over time. *Journal of Social and Clinical Psychology, 23*(6), 857–877.

Sprecher, S., & Regan, P. (1996). College virgins: How men and women perceive their sexual status. *Journal of Sex Research, 33*(1), 3–16.

Sprecher, S., & Regan, P. (2002). Liking some things (in some people) more than others: Partner preferences in romantic relationships and friendships. *Journal of Social & Personal Relationships, 19*(4), 463–481.

St Pierre, M., & Senn, C. (2010). External barriers to help-seeking encountered by Canadian gay and lesbian victims of intimate partner abuse: An application of the barriers model. *Violence and Victims, 25*(4), 536–551.

Stacey, D. (2008). No more periods: The safety of continuous birth control. Retrieved March 18, 2008, from http://contraception.about.com/od/prescriptionoptions/p/MissingPeriods.htm

Stark, R. (1996). *The rise of Christianity.* Princeton, NJ: Princeton University Press.

Starkman, N., & Rajani, N. (2002). The case for comprehensive sex education. *AIDS Patient Care and STDs, 16*(7), 313–318.

Steen, S., & Schwartz, P. (1995). Communication, gender, and power: Homosexual couples as a case study. In M. A. Fitzpatrick & A. L. Vangelisti (Eds.), *Explaining family interactions* (pp. 310–343). Thousand Oaks, CA: Sage.

Steiger, H., Richardson, J., Schmitz, N., Israel, M., Bruce, K. R., & Gauvin, L. (2010). Trait-defined eating-disorder subtypes and history of childhood abuse. *International Journal of Eating Disorders, 43*(5), 428–432.

Stein, J. H., & Reiser, L. W. (1994). A study of white, middle-class adolescent boys' responses to 'semenarche.' *Journal of Youth and Adolescence, 23*(3), 373–384.

Stein, R. (2008, May 20). A debunking on teenagers and "technical virginity;" researchers find that oral sex isn't commonplace among young people who avoid intercourse. *The Washington Post.* Retrieved May 29, 2008, from http://www.guttmacher.org/media/nr/nr_euroteens.html

Steiner, A. Z., D'Aloisio, A. A., DeRoo, L. A., Sandler, D. P., & Baird, D. D. (2010). Association of intrauterine and early-life exposures with age at menopause in the Sister Study. *American Journal of Epidemiology, 172*(2), 140–148.

Stephenson, J. M., Imrie, J., Davis, M. M., Mercer, C., Black, S., Copas, A. J., ... Williams, I. G. (2003). Is use of antiretroviral therapy among homosexual men associated with increased risk of transmission of HIV infection? *Sexually Transmitted Diseases, 79*(1), 7–10.

Sternberg, R. J. (1987). Liking versus loving: A comparative evaluation of theories. *Psychological Bulletin, 102*(3), 331–345.

Sternberg, R. J. (1998). *Cupid's arrow: The course of love through time.* New Haven, CT: Yale University Press.

Sternberg, R. J. (1999). *Love is a story.* New York: Oxford University Press.

Stevenson, B., & Isen, A. (2010). Who's getting married? Education and marriage today and in the past. A briefing paper prepared for the Council on Contemporary Families, January 26, 2010. Retrieved January 29, 2011, from http://www.contemporaryfamilies.org/images/stories/homepage/orange_border/ccf012510.pdf

Stevenson, B., & Wolfers, J. (2007). Marriage and divorce: Changes and their driving forces. *Journal of Economic Perspectives, 21*(2), 27–52.

Stevenson, B., & Wolfers, J. (2008). Marriage and the market. Cato Institute. Retrieved January 29, 2011, from http://bpp.wharton.upenn.edu/betseys/papers/Policy%20Papers/Cato%20Unbound.pdf

Stewart, F. H., Ellertson, C., & Cates, W. (2004). Abortion. In R. A. Hatcher, J. Trussell, A. L. Nelson, W. Cates, Jr., F. H. Stewart, & D. Kowal (Eds.), *Contraceptive technology* (18th rev. ed., pp. 673–700). New York: Ardent Media.

Stewart, H. (2005). Señoritas and princesses: The quinceañera as a context for female development. *Dissertation Abstracts, 65*(7-A), 2770, #0419–4209.

Stoller, R. J. (1991). The term perversion. In G. I. Fogel & W. A. Myers (Eds.), *Perversions and near-perversions in clinical practice: New psychoanalytic perspectives* (pp. 36–58). New Haven, CT: Yale University Press.

Stoller, R. J., & Herdt, G. H. (1985). Theories of origins of male homosexuality. *Archives of General Psychiatry, 42,* 399–404.

Storgaard, L., Bonde, J. P., Ernst, E., Spano, M., Andersen, C. Y., Frydenberg, M., & Olsen, J. (2003). Does smoking during pregnancy affect sons' sperm counts? *Epidemiology, 14*(3), 278–286.

Storm, L. (2011). Nurturing touch helps mothers with postpartum depression and their infants. Interview with Deb Discenza. *Neonatal Network, 30*(1), 71–72.

Storms, M. D. (1980). Theories of sexual orientation. *Journal of Personality and Social Psychology, 38,* 783–792.

Storms, M. D. (1981). A theory of erotic orientation development. *Psychological Review, 88,* 340–353.

Strandberg, K., Peterson, M., Schaefers, M., Case, L., Pack, M., Chase, D., & Schlievert, P. (2009). Reduction in staphylococcus aureus growth and exotoxin production and in vaginal interleukin 8 levels due to glycerol monolaurate in tampons. *Clinics in Infectious Diseases, 49*(11), 1718–1717.

Strasburger, V. C., & The Council on Communications and Media. (2010). Sexuality, contraception, and the media. *Pediatrics, 126,* 576–582.

Strauss, L., Gamble, S., Parker, W., Cook, D., Zane, S., & Hamdan, S. (2006). Abortion surveillance—United States, 2003. *Morbidity and Mortality Weekly Report Surveillance Summaries, 55*(11), 1–32.

Strauss, L. T., Herndon, J., Chang, J., Parker, W., Bowens, S., Zane, S., & Berg, C. J. (2004, November 26). Abortion surveillance—United States, 2001. *MMWR Surveillance Summary, 53,* 1–32.

Strine, T. W., Chapman, D. P., & Ahluwalia, I. B. (2005). Menstrual-related problems and psychological distress among women in the United States. *Journal of Women's Health, 14*(4), 316–323.

Struckman-Johnson, C., & Struckman-Johnson, D. (1994). Men pressured and forced into sexual experience. *Archives of Sexual Behavior, 23,* 93–115.

Struckman-Johnson, C., & Struckman-Johnson, D. (2002). Sexual coercion reported by women in three midwestern prisons. *Journal of Sex Research, 39*(3), 217–227.

Stuebe, A. M., Willett, W. C., Xue, F., & Michels, K. B. (2009). Lactation and incidence of premenopausal breast cancer. *Archives of Internal Medicine, 169*(15), 1364–1371.

Stumpe, J., & Davey, M. (2009, May 31). Abortion doctor shot to death in Kansas church. *New York Times.* Retrieved March 14, 2011, from http://www.nytimes.com/2009/06/01/us/01tiller.html

Sullivan, P. S., Drake, A. J., & Sanchez, T. H. (2007). Prevalence of treatment optimism-related risk behavior and associated factors among men who have sex with men in 11 states, 2000–2001. *AIDS Behavior, 11*(1), 123–129.

Svoboda, E. (2011). Breaking up in hard to do. *Psychology Today, 44*(1), 64.

Swaab, D. F. (2004). Sexual differentiation of the human brain: Relevance for gender identity, transsexualism, and sexual orientation. *Gynecological Endocrinology, 19*(6), 201–312.

Swaab, D. F., & Hofman, M. A. (1990). An enlarged suprachiasmatic nucleus in homosexual men. *Brain Research, 537,* 141–148.

Swanson, J. M., Dibble, S., & Chapman, L. (1999). Effects of psychoeducational interventions on sexual health risks and psychosocial adaptation in young adults with genital herpes. *Journal of Advanced Nursing, 29*(4), 840–851.

Taft, C., Resick, P., Watkins, L., & Panuzio, J. (2009). An investigation of posttraumatic stress disorder and depressive symptomatology among female victims of interpersonal trauma. *Journal of Family Violence, 24*(6), 407–416.

Tan, D. H., Kaul, R., Raboud, J. M., & Walmsley, S. L. (2011). No impact of oral tenofovir disoproxil fumarate on herpes simplex virus shedding in HIV-infected adults. *AIDS, 25*(2), 207–210.

Tannen, D. (1990). *You just don't understand: Women and men in conversation.* New York: Ballantine Books.

Tannen, D., Kendall, S., & Gordon, C. (2007). *Family talk: Discourse and identity in four American families.* New York: Oxford University Press.

Tay, J. I., Moore, J., & Walker, J. J. (2000). Ectopic pregnancy. *British Medical Journal, 320*(7239), 916–920.

Taylor, H. E. (2000). Meeting the needs of lesbian and gay young adults. *The Clearing House, 73*(4), 221.

Teitelman, A. (2004). Adolescent girls' perspectives of family interactions related to menarche and sexual health. *Qualitative Health Research, 14*(9), 1292–1308.

Terao, T., & Nakamura, J. (2000). Exhibitionism and low-dose trazodone treatment. *Human Psychopharmacology: Clinical & Experimental, 15*(5), 347–349.

Tewksbury, R. (2007). Effects of sexual assaults on men: Physical, mental, and sexual consequences. *International Journal of Men's Health, 6,* 22–36.

Thomas, S. L., & Ellertson, C. (2000). Nuisance or natural and healthy: Should monthly menstruation be optional for women? *Lancet, 355,* 922–924.

Thompson, K. M. (2009). Sibling incest: A model for group practice with adult female victims of brother-sister incest. *Journal of Family Violence, 24,* 531–537.

Thomson, R., Finau, S., Finau, E., Ahokovi, L., & Tameifuna, S. (2007). Circumcision of Pacific boys: Tradition at the cutting edge. *Pacific Health Dialogue, 13,* 115–122.

Thomson, R., & Murachver, T. (2001). Predicting gender from electronic discourse. *British Journal of Social Psychology, 40*(2), 193–208.

Thorp, J. M., Hartmann, K. E., & Shadigian, E. (2003). Long-term physical and psychological health consequences of induced abortion: Review of the evidence. *Obstetrical and Gynecological Survey, 58*(1), 67–79.

Thorup, J., McLachlan, R., Cortes, D., Nation, T. R., Balic, A., Southwell, B. R., & Hutson, J. (2010). What is new in cryptorchidism and hypospadias—A critical review on the testicular dysgenesis hypothesis. *Pediatric Surgery, 45*(10), 2074–2086.

Tiefer, L. (1991). Historical, scientific, clinical, and feminist criticisms of "the human sexual response cycle" model. *Annual Review of Sex Research, 2,* 1–23.

Tiefer, L. (1996). The medicalization of sexuality: Conceptual, normative, and professional issues. *Annual Review of Sex Research, 7,* 252–282.

Tiefer, L. (2000). A new view of women's sexual problems. *Electronic Journal of Human Sexuality,* (3), 15. Retrieved May 24, 2005, from http://www.ejhs.org/volume3/newview.htm

Tiefer, L. (2001). A new view of women's sexual problems: Why new? Why now? *Journal of Sex Research, 38*(2), 89–96.

Tiefer, L. (2002). Beyond the medical model of women's sexual problems: A campaign to resist the promotion of "female sexual dysfunction." *Sexual & Relationship Therapy, 17*(2), 127–135.

Tirabassi, R. S., Ace, C. I., Levchenko, T., Torchilin, V. P., Selin, L. K., Nie, S., Gu … Yang, K. (2011). A mucosal vaccination approach for herpes simplex virus type 2. *Vaccine, 29*(5), 1090–1098.

Tjaden, P., & Thoennes, N. (2000). *Extent, nature, and consequences of intimate partner violence: Findings from the National Violence Against Women Survey.* Washington, DC: National Institute of Justice and the Centers for Disease Control and Prevention.

Tobian, A. A., Gray, R. H., & Quinn, T. C. (2010). Male circumcision for the prevention of acquisition and transmission of sexually transmitted infections: The case for neonatal circumcision. *Archives of Pediatric Adolescent Medicine, 164*(1), 78–84.

Tokushige, N., Markham, R., Crossett, B., Ah, S., Nelaturi, V., Khan, A., & Fraser, I. (2011). Discovery of a novel biomarker in the urine in women with endometriosis. *Fertility and Sterility, 95*(1), 46–49.

Tomassilli, J., Golub, S., Bimbi, D., & Parsons, J. (2009). Behind closed doors: An exploration of kinky sexual behaviors in urban lesbian and bisexual women. *Journal of Sex Research, 46*(5), 438–445.

Toppari, J., Virtanen, H. E., Main, K. M., & Skakkebaek, N. E. (2010). Cryptorchidism and hypospadias as a sign of testicular dysgenesis syndrome (TDS): Environmental connection. *Birth Defects Research, 88*(10), 910–919.

Toto-Morn, M., & Sprecher, S. (2003). A cross-cultural comparison of mate preferences among university students: The United States vs. the People's Republic of China. *Journal of Comparative Family Studies, 34*(2), 151–170.

Tovar, J., Bazaldua, O., Vargas, L., & Reile, E. (2008). Human papillomavirus, cervical cancer, and the vaccines. *Postgraduate Medicine, 120,* 79–84.

Tramel, J. (2011, April 5). Cowboy to stand trial for rape charges. *McClatchy-Tribune Business News.* Retrieved April 13, 2011, from http://www.tulsaworld.com/news/article.aspx?no=subj&articleid=20110405_93_B5_CUTLIN644366&

Treas, J., & Giesen, D. (2000). Sexual infidelity among married and cohabiting Americans. *Journal of Marriage and Family, 62*(1), 48–61.

Trends in HIV/AIDS Diagnoses. (2005, November 18). Trends in HIV/AIDS Diagnoses—33 states, 2001–2004. *Morbidity and Mortality Weekly Report, 54,* 1149–1153.

Trenholm, C., Devaney, B., Fortson, K., Quay, L., Wheeler, J., & Clark, M. (2007). Impact of four Title V, Section 510 Abstinence Education Programs. Princeton, NJ: Mathematic Policy Research. Retrieved from http://www.mathematica-mpr.com/publications/PDFs/impactabstinence.pdf

Troiden, R. R. (1989). The formation of homosexual identities. In G. Herdt (Ed.), *Gay and lesbian youth* (pp. 43–73). New York: Harrington Park Press.

Trotter, E. C., & Alderson, K. G. (2007). University students' definitions of having sex, sexual partner, and virginity loss: The influence of participant gender, sexual experience, and contextual factors. *Canadian Journal of Human Sexuality, 16,* 11–20.

Trudel, G., Villeneuve, L., Preville, M., Boyer, R., & Frechette, V. (2010). Dyadic adjustment, sexuality, and psychological distress in older couples. *Sexual and Relationship Therapy, 25*(3), 306–315.

Truman, J. L., & Rand, M. R. (2010). Criminal victimization, 2009. National crime victimization survey. Bureau of Justice Statistics. Retrieved from http://www.bjs.gov/content/pub/pdf/cv09.pdf

Trussell, J. Guthrie, K. (2011). Choosing a contraceptive: Efficacy, safety, and personal considerations. In R. A. Hatcher, J. Trussell, A. L. Nelson, W. Cates, D. Kowal, M. S. Policar (Eds) *Contraceptive Technology,* 20th Edition. p. 67. Ardent Media, New York, N.Y.

Trussell, J., Schwartz, E. (2011). Emergency contraception. In R. A. Hatcher, J. Trussell, A. L. Nelson, W. Cates, D. Kowal, M. S. Policar (Eds) *Contraceptive Technology,* 20th Edition. pp. 113-145. Ardent Media, New York, N.Y.

Tzeng, O. (1992). Cognitive/comparitive judgment paradigm of love. In O. Tzeng (Ed.), *Theories of love development, maintenance, and dissolution: Octagonal cycle and differential perspectives* (pp. 133–149). New York: Praeger Publishers.

Uji, M., Shono, M., Shikai, N., & Kitamura, T. (2007). Case illustrations of negative sexual experiences among university women in Japan: Victimization disclosure and reactions of the confidant. *International Journal of Offender Therapy and Comparative Criminology, 51,* 227–242.

United National Children's Fund. (2005). *Early marriage: A harmful traditional practice.* Retrieved July 16, 2008, from http://www.unicef.org/publications/files/Early_Marriage_12.lo.pdf

United Nations Educational, Scientific, and Cultural Organization (UNESCO). (2008). Review of sex, relationships, and HIV education in the schools. UNESCO Global Advisory Group. Retrieved January 26, 2011, from http://unesdoc.unesco.org/images/0016/001629/162989e.pdf

Upchurch, D. M., Aneshensel, C. S., Mudgal, J., & McNeely, C. S. (2001). Sociocultural contexts

of time to first sex among Hispanic adolescents. *Journal of Marriage and Family, 63*(4), 1158.

Upchurch, D. M., Levy-Storms, L., Sucoff, C. A., & Aneshensel, C. S. (1998). Gender and ethnic differences in the timing of first sexual intercourse. *Family Planning Perspectives, 30*(3), 121–128.

Urato, A. C., & Norwitz, E. R. (2011). A guide towards pre-pregnancy management of defective implantation and placentation. *Best Practices and Research in Clinical Obstetrics and Gynecology, 25*(3), 367–387.

U.S. Census Bureau. (2007, September 19). Most people make only one trip down the aisle, but first marriages shorter, census bureau reports. Retrieved from http://www.census.gov/Press-Release/www/releases/archives/marital_status_living_arrangements/010624.html

U.S. Department of Justice, Office of Justice Programs. (2002). Rape and sexual assault: Reporting to police and medical attention, 1992–2000. Retrieved from http://www.ojp.usdoj.gov/bjs/pub/pdf/rsarp00.pdf

U.S. Department of Justice. (2006). Hate crime statistics: Incidents and offenses. Retrieved from http://www.fbi.gov/ucr/hc2006/incidents.html

U.S. Preventive Services Task Force (USPSTF). (2005). Screening for ovarian cancer: Recommendation statement. *American Family Physician, 71*(4), 759–763.

Usatine, R. P., & Tinitigan, R. (2010). Nongenital herpes simplex virus. *American Family Physician, 82*(9), 1075–1082.

Valente, S. M. (2005). Sexual abuse of boys. *Journal of Child and Adolescent Psychiatric Nursing, 18*(1), 10–16.

Valenzuela, C. Y. (2008). Prenatal maternal mnemonic effects on the human neuro-psychic sex: A new proposition from fetus-maternal tolerance-rejection. *La Revista Medica de Chile, 136*(12), 1552–1558.

Valenzuela, C. Y. (2010). Sexual orientation, handedness, sex ratio and fetomaternal tolerance-rejection. *Biological Research, 43*(3), 347–356.

Van de Ven, P., Campbell, D., & Kippax, S. (1997). Factors associated with unprotected anal intercourse in gay men's casual partnerships in Sydney, Australia. *AIDS Care, 9*(6), 637–649.

Van den Heuvel, M., van Bragt, A., Alnabawy, A., & Kaptein, M. (2005). Comparison of ethinyl-estradial pharmacokinetics in three hormonal contraceptive formulation: The vaginal ring, the transdermal patch, and an oral contraceptive. *Contraception, 72,* 168–174.

van Teijlingen, E., Reid, J., Shucksmith, J., Harris, F., Philip, K., Imamura, M., ... Penney, G. (2007). Embarrassment as a key emotion in young people talking about sexual health. *Sociological Research, 12*(2). Retrieved April 15, 2011, from http://www.socresonline.org .uk/12/2/van_teijlingen.html

Vanfossen, B. (1996). ITROWs women and expression conference. Institute for Teaching and Research on Women, Towson, MD: Towson University. Retrieved April 15, 2003, from http://www.towson.edu/itrow

Vardi, Y., McMahon, C., Waldinger, M., Rubio-Aurioles, E., & Rabinowitz, D. (2008). Are premature ejaculation symptoms curable? *Journal of Sexual Medicine, 5,* 1546–1551.

Venkatesh, K., Biswas, J., & Kumarasamy, N. (2008). Impact of highly active antiretroviral therapy on ophthalmic manifestations in human immunodeficiency virus/acquired immune deficiency syndrome. *Indian Journal of Ophthalmology, 56*(5), 391–393.

Versfeld, N. J., & Dreschler, W. A. (2002). The relationship between the intelligibility of time-compressed speech and speech-innoise in young and elderly listeners. *Journal of the Acoustical Society of America, 111,* 401–408.

Verweij, K., Shekar, S., Zietsch, B., Eaves, L., Bailey, J., Boomsma, D., & Martin, N. (2008). Genetic and environmental influences on individual differences in attitudes toward homosexuality: An Australian twin study. *Behavior Genetics, 38,* 257–265.

Vestal, C. (2008, May 16). California gay marriage ruling sparks new debate. *Stateline.* Retrieved from http://www.stateline.org/live/ printable/story?contentId=310206

Vigano, P., Parazzini, F., Somigliana, E., & Vercellini, P. (2004). Endometriosis: Epidemiology and aetiological factors. *Best Practice & Research Clinical Obstetrics & Gynaecology, 18*(2), 177–200.

Vincke, J., & van Heeringen, K. (2002). Confidant support and the mental well-being of lesbian and gay young adults: A longitudinal analysis. *Journal of Community and Applied Social Psychology, 12,* 181–193.

Voller, E., & Long, P. (2010). Sexual assault and rape perpetration by college men: The role of the big five personality traits. *Journal of Interpersonal Violence, 25*(3), 457–480.

Vrabel, K., Hoffart, A., Ro, O., Martinsen, E., & Rosenvinge, J. (2010). Co-occurrence of avoidant personality disorder and child sexual abuse predicts poor outcome in long-standing eating disorder. *Journal of Abnormal Psychology, 119*(3), 623–629.

Vukovic, L. (1992, November–December). Cold sores and fever blisters. *Natural Health,* 119–120.

Wacker, J., Parish, S., & Macy, R. (2008). Sexual assault and women with cognitive disabilities: Codifying discrimination in the United States. *Journal of Disability Policy Studies, 19,* 86–95.

Wagner, E. (1991). Campus victims of date rape should consider civil lawsuits as alternatives to criminal charges or colleges' procedures. *The Chronicle of Higher Education,* August 7, B2.

Wald, A., Zeh, J., Selke, S., Warren, T., Ryncarz, A. J., Ashley, R., ... Corey, L. (2000). Reactivation of genital herpes simplex virus type-2 infection in asymptomatic seropositive persons. *New England Journal of Medicine, 342*(12), 844–850.

Waldinger, R., & Schulz, M. (2010). What's love got to do with it? Social functioning, perceived health, and daily happiness in married octogenarians. *Psychology and Aging, 25*(2), 422–431.

Walker, J., Archer, J., & Davies, M. (2005). Effects of rape on men: A descriptive analysis. *Archives of Sexual Behavior, 34*(1), 69–80.

Wallerstein, E. (1980). *Circumcision: An American health fallacy.* New York: Springer.

Walters, J. (2005, January 2). No sex is safe sex for teens in America. Retrieved October 19, 2005, from http://observer.guardian.co.uk/ international/story/0,6903,1382117,00.html

Wampler, S. M., & Llanes, M. (2010). Common scrotal and testicular problems. *Primary Care, 37*(3), 613–626.

Wang, H., & Amato, P. R. (2000). Predictors of divorce adjustment: Stressors, resources, and definitions. *Journal of Marriage and Family, 62*(3), 655–669.

Wang, S. (2007, November 15). Fertility therapies under the microscope. *Wall Street Journal,* p. D1.

Warin, J. (2000). The attainment of self-consistency through gender in young children. *Sex Roles, 41,* 209–232.

Warner, L., Steiner, M. (2011). Male condoms. In R. A. Hatcher, J. Trussell, A. L. Nelson, W. Cates, D. Kowal, M. S. Policar (Eds) *Contraceptive Technology,* 20th Edition. pp. 371-389. Ardent Media, New York, N.Y.

Warren, J., Harvey, S., & Henderson, J. (2010). Do depression and low self-esteem follow abortion among adolescents? Evidence from a national study. *Perspectives on Sexual and Reproductive Health, 42*(4), 230–235.

Watson, C., & Calabretto, H. (2007). Comprehensive review of conventional and non-conventional methods of management of recurrent vulvovaginal candidiasis. *Australian and New Zealand Journal of Obstetrics and Gynaecology, 47*(4), 262–272.

Wattleworth, R. (2011). Human papillomavirus infection and the links to penile and cervical cancer. *Journal of the American Osteopathic Association, 111*(3 Suppl. 2), S3–S10.

Waxman, H. (2004). Abstinence-only education. Retrieved September 17, 2005, from http:// www.democrats.reform.house.gov/ investigations.asp?Issue=Abstinence-Only+Education

Weatherall, A. (2002). *Gender, language, and discourse.* London: Hove Routledge.

Weed, S. E. (2008). Marginally successful results of abstinence-only program erased by dangerous errors in curriculum. *American Journal of Health Behavior, 32,* 60–73.

Wei, E. H. (2000). Teenage fatherhood and pregnancy involvement among urban, adolescent males: Risk factors and consequences. *Dissertation Abstracts International: Section B, 61*(1-B), #0419–4217.

Weinstock, H., Berman, S., & Cates, W. (2004). Sexually transmitted diseases among American youth: Incidence and prevalence estimates, 2000. *Perspectives in Sex and Reproductive Health, 36*(1), 6–10.

Weiss, H. A., Quigley, M. A., & Hayes, R. J. (2000). Male circumcision and risk of HIV infection in sub-Saharan Africa: A systematic review and metaanalysis. *AIDS, 14,* 2361–2370.

Welch, L. (1992). *Complete book of sexual trivia.* New York: Citadel Press.

West, S., D'Aloisio, A., Agans, R., Kalsbeek, W., Borisov, N., & Thorp, J. (2008). Prevalence of low sexual desire and hypoactive sexual desire disorder in a nationally representative sample of U.S. women. *Archives of Internal Medicine, 168,* 1441–1449.

Whitam, F. L., Daskalos, C., Sobolewski, C. G., & Padilla, P. (1999). The emergence of lesbian sexuality and identity cross-culturally. *Archives of Sexual Behavior, 27*(1), 31–57.

White, S. D., & DeBlassie, R. R. (1992). Adolescent sexual behavior. *Adolescence, 27,* 183–191.

Whitmore, S. K., Zhang, X., Taylor, A. W., & Blair, J. M. (In press). Estimated number of infants born to HIV-infected women in the United States and five dependent areas, 2006. *Journal of Acquired Immune Deficiency Syndrome.*

Whittaker, P. G., Merkh, R. D., Henry-Moss, D., & Hock-Long, L. (2010). Withdrawal attitudes and experiences: A qualitative perspective among young urban adults. *Perspectives in Sex and Reproductive Health, 42*(2), 102–109.

Wikan, U. (1977). Man becomes woman: Transsexualism in Oman as a key to gender roles. *Man, 12,* 304–391.

Wilcox, A. J., Weinberg, C. R., & Baird, D. D. (1995). Timing of sexual intercourse in relation to ovulation. Effects on the probability of conception, survival of the pregnancy, and sex of the baby. *New England Journal of Medicine, 333*(23), 1517–1521.

Williams, J. E., & Best, D. L. (1994). Cross-cultural views of women and men. In W. J. Lonner & R. Malpass (Eds.), *Psychology and culture.* Boston: Allyn & Bacon.

Williams, W. L. (1986). *The spirit and the flesh: Sexual diversity in American Indian culture.* Boston: Beacon Press.

Wilson, C. (2005). Recurrent vulvovaginitis candidiasis: An overview of traditional and alternative therapies. *Advanced Nurse Practitioner, 13*(2), 24–29.

Wilson, C. A., & Davies, D. C. (2007). The control of sexual differentiation of the reproductive system and brain. *Reproduction, 133,* 331–359.

Wilson, D., Dalberth, B., & Koo, H. (2010). "We're the heroes!": Fathers' perspectives on their role in protecting their preteenage children from sexual risk. *Perspectives on Sexual and Reproductive Health, 42*(2), 117–124.

Wilson, G. D. (1987). An ethological approach to sexual deviation. In G. D. Wilson (Ed.), *Variant sexuality: Research and theory* (pp. 84–115). Baltimore: Johns Hopkins University Press.

Wind, R. (2008). Perception that teens frequently substitute oral sex for intercourse a myth. [News release]. New York: Alan Guttmacher Institute. Retrieved September 2, 2008, from http://www.guttmacher.org/media/nr/2008/05/20/index.html

Wiseman, J. (2000). *Jay Wiseman's erotic bondage handbook.* Oakland, CA: Greenery Press.

Wolf, N. (1991). *The beauty myth: How images of beauty are used against women.* New York: W. Morris.

Wolitski, R. J., Valdiserri, R. O., Denning, P. H., & Levine, W. C. (2001). Are we headed for a resurgence of the HIV epidemic among men who have sex with men? *American Journal of Public Health, 91*(6), 883–888.

Wong, E. W., & Cheng, C. Y. (2011). Impacts of environmental toxicants on male reproductive dysfunction. *Trends Pharmacological Science, 32*(5), 290–299.

Woo, J., Fine, P., & Goetzl, L. (2005). Abortion disclosure and the association with domestic violence. *Obstetrics & Gynecology, 105*(6), 1329–1334.

Wood, J. (1999). *Gendered lives: Communication, gender, and culture.* Belmont, CA: Wadsworth.

Woolf, L. M. (2002). Gay and lesbian aging. *SIECUS Report, 30*(2), 16–21.

Workowski, K., & Berman, S. (2010). Sexually transmitted disease treatment guidelines, 2010. *Morbidity and Mortality Weekly Report, 59*(RR-12), 1–110.

World Health Organization. (2008). *Eliminating female genital mutilation: An interagency statement.* Retrieved March 22, 2008, from http://data.unaids.org/pub/BaseDocument/2008/20080227_interagencystatement_eliminating_fgm_en.pdf

World Professional Organization for Transgender Health. (2001). The Harry Benjamin International Gender Dysphoria Association's standards of care for gender identity disorders, sixth version. Retrieved April 17, 2011, from http://wpath.org/Documents2/socv6.pdf

Wright, L., Mulick, P., & Kincaid, S. (2006). Fear of and discrimination against bisexuals, homosexuals, and individuals with AIDS. *Journal of Bisexuality, 6,* 71–84.

Wright, S. (2010). Depathologizing consensual sexual sadism, sexual masochism, transvestic fetishism, and fetishism. *Archives of Sexual Behavior, 39*(6), 1229–1230.

Wu, F., Tajar, A., Beynon, J., Pye, S., Phil, M., Silman, A., … Bartfai, G. (2010). Identification of late-onset hypogonadism in middle-aged and elderly men. *New England Journal of Medicine, 363,* 123–135.

Xu, F., Sternberg, M., Kottiri, B., McQuillan, G., Lee, F., Nahmias, A., … Markowitz, L. E. (2006). Trends in herpes simplex virus type 1 and type 2 seroprevalence in the U.S. *Journal of the American Medical Association, 296,* 964–973.

Yamawaki, N. (2007). Differences between Japanese and American college students in giving advice about help seeking to rape victims. *Journal of Social Psychology, 147,* 511–530.

Yamawaki, N., & Tschanz, B. T. (2005). Rape perception differences between Japanese and American college students: On the mediating influence of gender role traditionality. *Sex Roles, 52*(5–6), 379–392.

Yanagimachi, R. (2011). Problems of sperm fertility: A reproductive biologist's view. *Systems in Biological Reproductive Medicine, 57*(1–2), 102–114.

Yassin, A. A., & Saad, F. (2008). Testosterone and sexual dysfunction. *Journal of Andrology,* 29(6), Epub ahead of print. Retrieved October 29, 2008, from http://www.andrologyjournal.org/cgi/content/abstract/29/6/593

Yen, J., Chang, S., Ko, C., Yen, C., Chen, C., Yeh, Y., & Chen, C. (2010). The high-sweet-fat food craving among women with PMDD: Emotional response, implicit attitudes and rewards sensitivity. *Psychoneuroendocrinology, 35*(8), 1203–1212.

Yllo, K., & Finkelhor, D. (1985). Marital rape. In A. W. Burgess (Ed.), *Rape and sexual assault* (pp. 146–158). New York: Garland.

Yoder, V. C., Virden, T. B., & Amin, K. (2005). Internet pornography and loneliness: An association? *Sexual Addiction & Compulsivity, 12*(1), 19–44.

Young, K. S., Griffin-Shelley, E., Cooper, A., O'Mara, J., & Buchanan, J. (2000). Online infidelity. In A. Cooper (Ed.), *Cybersex: The dark side of the force* (pp. 59–74). Philadelphia, PA: Brunner Routledge.

Yun, R. J., & Lachman, M. E. (2006). Perceptions of aging in two cultures: Korean and American views on old age. *Journal of Cross Cultural Gerontology, 21*(1–2), 55–70.

Zacur, H. A., Hedon, B., Mansourt, D., Shangold, G. A., Fisher, A. C., & Creasy, G. W. (2002). Integrated summary of Ortho Evra contraceptive patch adhesion in varied climates and conditions. *Fertility and Sterility, 77* (2 Suppl. 2), 532–535.

Zhao, Y., Montoro, R., Igartua, K., & Thombs, B. D. (2010). Suicidal ideation and attempt among adolescents reporting "unsure" sexual identity or heterosexual identity plus same-sex attraction or behavior: Forgotten groups? *Journal of the American Academy of Child and Adolescent Psychiatry, 49*(2), 104–113.

Zimmer-Gembeck, M. J., & Helfand, M. (2008). Ten years of longitudinal research on U.S. adolescent sexual behavior: Developmental correlates of sexual intercourse, and the importance of age, gender, and ethnic background. *Developmental Review, 28,* 153–224.

Zinaman, M. J., Clegg, E. D., Brown, C. C., O'Connor, J., & Selevan, S. G. (1996). Estimates of human fertility and pregnancy loss. *Journal of Fertility and Sterility, 65*(3), 503–509.

Zolese, G., & Blacker, C. V. R. (1992). The psychological complications of therapeutic abortion. *British Journal of Psychiatry, 160,* 742–749.

Zurbriggen, E. L., & Yost, M. R. (2004). Power, desire, and pleasure in sexual fantasies. *Journal of Sex Research, 41*(3), 288–300.

Name Index

Abaid, L., 124
Abbasi, S., 158
Abbey, A., 532
Abdo, C., 316
Abdullah, R., 227
Abma, J. C., 196, 200, 203
Abouesh, A., 514
AbouZeid, A. A., 157
Abraham, B., 478
Abramson, P. R., 179, 507
Ace, C. I., 469
Acierno, R., 194, 509, 542
Adair, 108, 109
Adair, L. S., 385
Adams, H. E., 326, 338
Adams-Curtis, L. E., 532–533
Adib-Hajbaghery, M., 115
Adimora, A. A., 192, 198
Adjaye, J., 155
Adler, R. B., 38, 46
Afifi, W., 238
Agan, B., 482
Agans, R., 298
Agaoglu, B., 158
Agnello, C., 374
Agnew, J., 529
Agrawal, S., 371
Ah, S., 119
Ahlberg, C., 84
Ahmetoglu, G., 221, 233
Ahn, T. Y., 304–305
Ahokovi, L., 169
Ainsworth, M. D. S., 231
Akbag, M., 231
Akers, A. Y., 193, 200
Alan Guttmacher Institute, 395, 397, 414, 436, 437
Alanis, M. C., 167
Alarid, L. F., 539
Alatas, C., 363
Albers, K., 372
Albert, 343
Albert, B., 194
Albertsen, P. C., 163
Albouy, B., 299
Alderson, K. G., 195
Alexander, M. A., 507
Alexandre, B., 301
Alison, L., 503
Alkhuja, S., 481
Allen, 361
Allen, B. J., 36
Allen, P. L., 256, 454
Allgeier, E., 527

Allison, L., 503
Alnabawy, A., 415
Alonso-Zaldivar, 455
Althaus, F., 196
Althof, S., 304
Althuis, 411
Altman, C., 336
Amador, J., 229, 260
Amar, E., 301
Amato, P., 246, 249
Amato, P. R., 257
American Cancer Society, 124–127, 129, 131, 160–163
American College of Obstetricians and Gynecologists, 119, 374, 379, 382
American Psychiatric Association, 116, 305, 340, 501, 510
American Psychological Association, 335, 340, 506
Ames, M., 319
Amir, M., 528
Amis, D., 375
Amrein, 225
Andersen, C. Y., 371
Andersen, P. A., 235
Anderson, D. A., 49
Anderson, F. D., 112, 113
Anderson, J. G., 113
Anderson, L., 540
Anderson, M., 548
Anderson, P. B., 540
Andersson, L., 360
Andre, E., 43
Andrianne, R., 301
Aneshensel, C. S., 194, 197
Angier, N., 70, 72
Ankum, 372
Antheunis, M., 42
Antypa, E., 157
Apgar, V., 379
Aquinas, T., 10
Aragon, S. R., 332
Aranda, C., 475
Archer, J., 540
Arck, P., 373
Arena, J. M., 241
Arias, R., 421
Ariely, D., 228
Aries, E., 36
Armour, B. S., 548
Armstrong, E., 240
Armstrong, L., 160
Aron, A., 226
Arrigo, B., 529

Arroba, 402, 414
Ashley, R., 468
Asplund, B., 419
Atanackovic, G., 358
Athanasiadis, A., 69
Athanasiou, S., 467
Athenstaedt, U., 34
Austin, E. L., 191, 335
Austin, S., 331
Awadalla, N., 360
Axsom, D., 240
Ayala, M., 114
Azam, S., 101

Back, M., 42
Badgett, L., 334
Bagley, D., 143
Baguley, S., 464
Bailey, A., 323
Bailey, B. P., 43
Bailey, J., 338
Bailey, J. M., 321
Bailey, R. C., 167
Bain, J., 155
Baird, D. D., 111
Bakanic, V., 532
Baker, M., 156
Balaban, B., 363
Balsam, K., 538
Bamdad, T., 471
Bancroft, J., 295, 510
Bane, C., 271
Barbarch, L., 41
Bardeguez, 455
Bardenheuer, K., 413
Barkan, H., 539
Barnden, N., 354, 369, 374
Barnhart, K., 372
Baron, N. S., 43
Barrera, S. L., 111
Barrett, H. M., 546
Barrow, R., 455
Bart, 530
Bartfai, G., 155
Bartholomae, S., 194, 199, 200
Bartholomew, K., 227
Barton, I., 299
Bartz, 420
Basow, S., 529
Bassil, N., 155
Basson, 299
Basson, B., 279
Basson, R., 296
Basu, A., 382

I-1